I0799454

STONES FROM THE INSIDE

RARE AND UNSEEN IMAGES

BILL WYMAN

ACC ART BOOKS

STONES
FROM THE INSIDE
RARE AND UNSEEN IMAGES

ICONICIMAGES
FINE ART ARCHIVES PUBLISHING CREATIVE

CEO
Robin Morgan

Editor
Carrie Kania

Design Director
Stephen Reid

Production
Mariona Vilarós and Adam Powell

www.iconicimages.net

ACC ART BOOKS

Publisher
James Smith

Editors
Andrew Whittaker, Bryn Porter

Design
Craig Holden

Production
Stephen Mackinlay

www.accartbooks.com

To my late uncle Jack Jeffrey:

For giving me his Brownie Box Camera on 1 February 1959,
which inspired me to see the world in a different way.

INTRODUCTION

BILL WYMAN

I recognise that most people know me first and foremost for my music. My friends and family, however, also know me as a keen photographer. It's been a passion of mine for many, many years. And something that I continue to this very day.

I was given my first camera, a Brownie Box Camera, by my uncle Jack Jeffery (my mother's younger brother) on my return from serving my National Service stint in the RAF in Germany. I immediately took to taking pictures in and around my home in South London – concentrating not on family and friends, but on interesting buildings, park gates and monuments – the reason, I know not why.

I joined The Rolling Stones in December 1962. After some success, I was able, a few years later, to purchase my first serious camera – a Nikkormat, together with a 135 Nikon lens – in Paris, France.

From that time on I began to take photos in earnest, both at home and on tour with The Rolling Stones, preferring, for some reason, to photograph subjects when they were not aware of my camera, or were otherwise occupied. I took them mainly to illustrate my daily diaries.

I've continued to take photographs – even to the present day. I've been lucky enough to have met – and in some instances, become close friends with – several photographers over the years. I've been continually inspired by their work, and when the camera was focused on me I always paid close attention, in hopes that I would be able to hone my own photographic art into something a little bit better than just taking 'snaps.'

I have been asked many times over the years, what I might have been if I hadn't been a Rolling Stone for three decades. My reply was always that I would have loved to have been a curator at a museum, running a library or, best of all, taking up photography as a career. As none of these ever happened, I amused myself throughout my travels by taking photographs of the people around me.

I am proud to have had my photos accepted as more than just casual 'snaps'.

Right: Self-portrait – taken in the New Forest, Hampshire, during a picnic with my parents and girlfriend in July 1967.

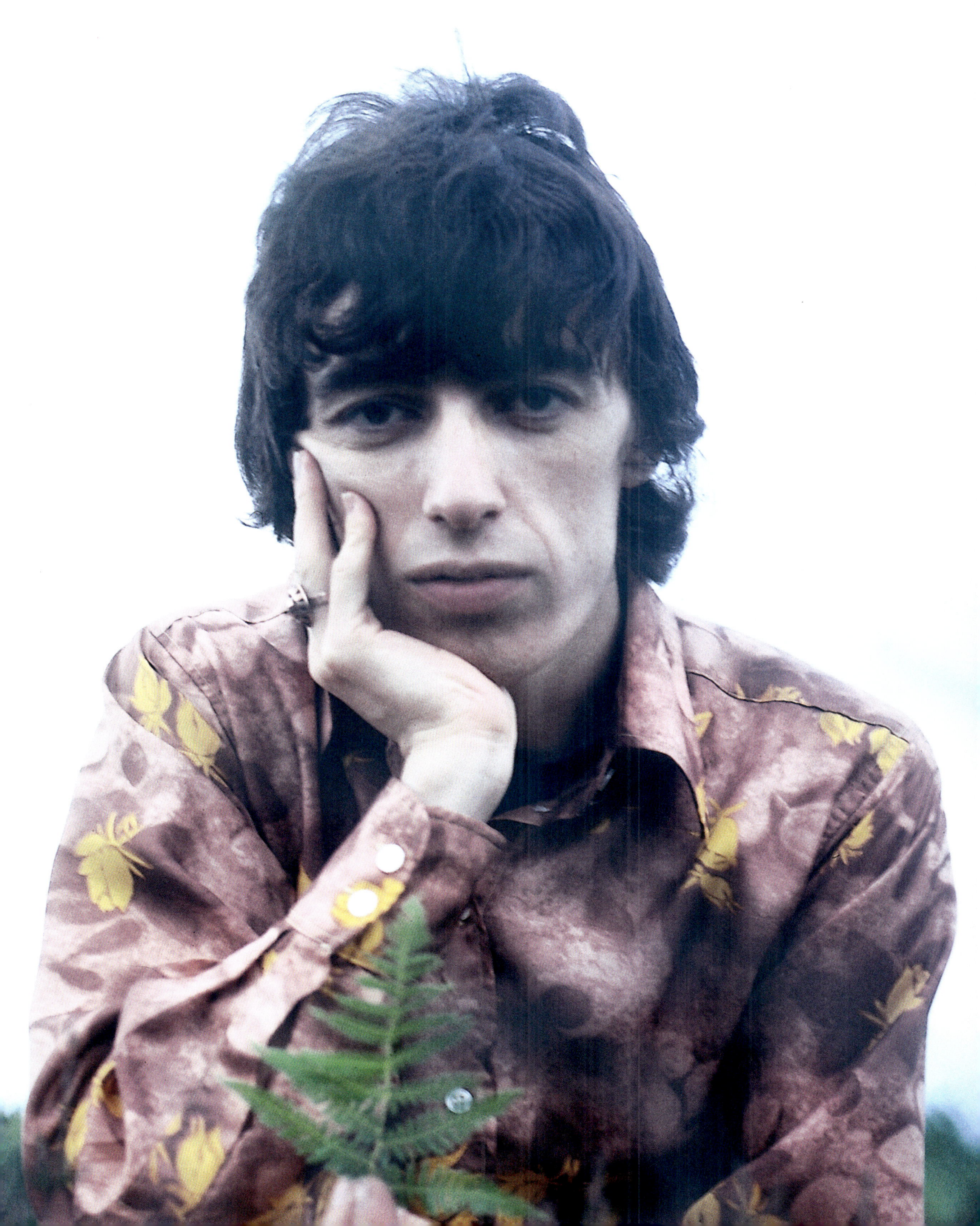

“PHOTOGRAPHY – ALONG WITH MUSIC – HAS BROUGHT ME GREAT JOY OVER THE YEARS. AND I JUST HAPPEN TO HAVE WORKED ALONGSIDE SOME VERY INTERESTING SUBJECTS”

BILL WYMAN

Right: Keith Richards, looking very elegant on the plane from Los Angeles to Sydney, Australia, 14 February 1966, for the commencement of our second tour there with The Searchers.

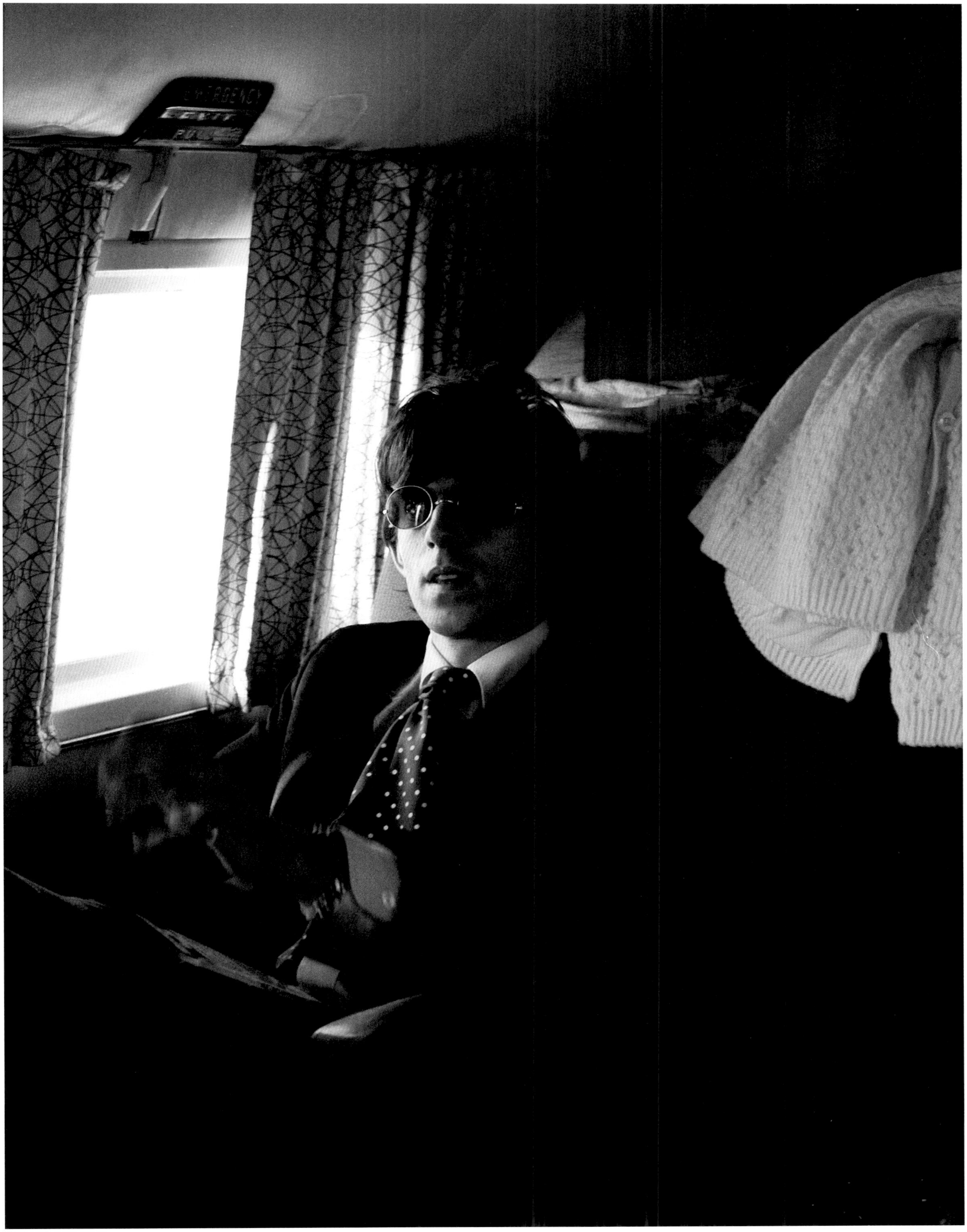

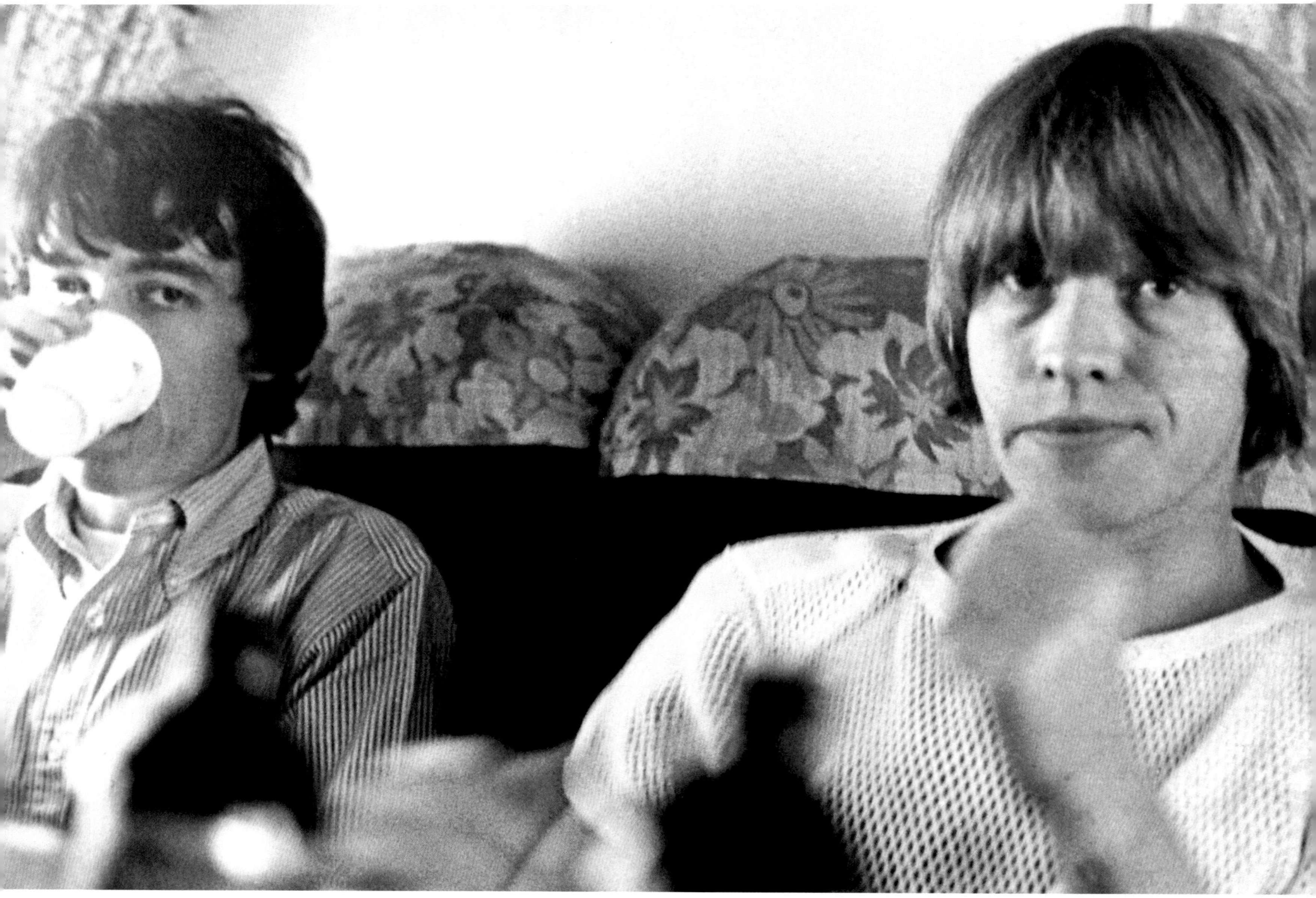

Brian Jones and I, and Brian alone, dressed very summery on an internal flight during the Australian Tour – February 1966.

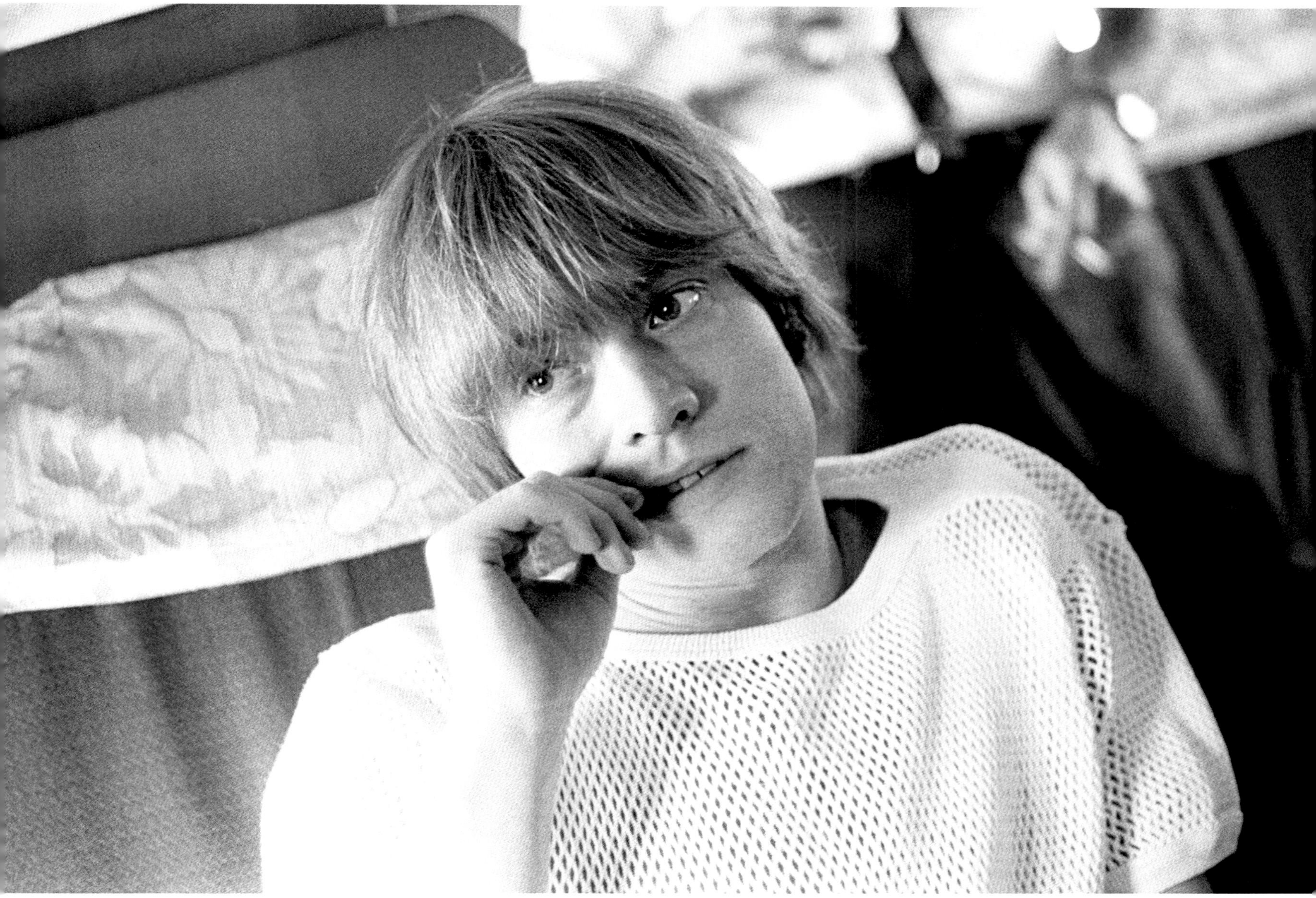

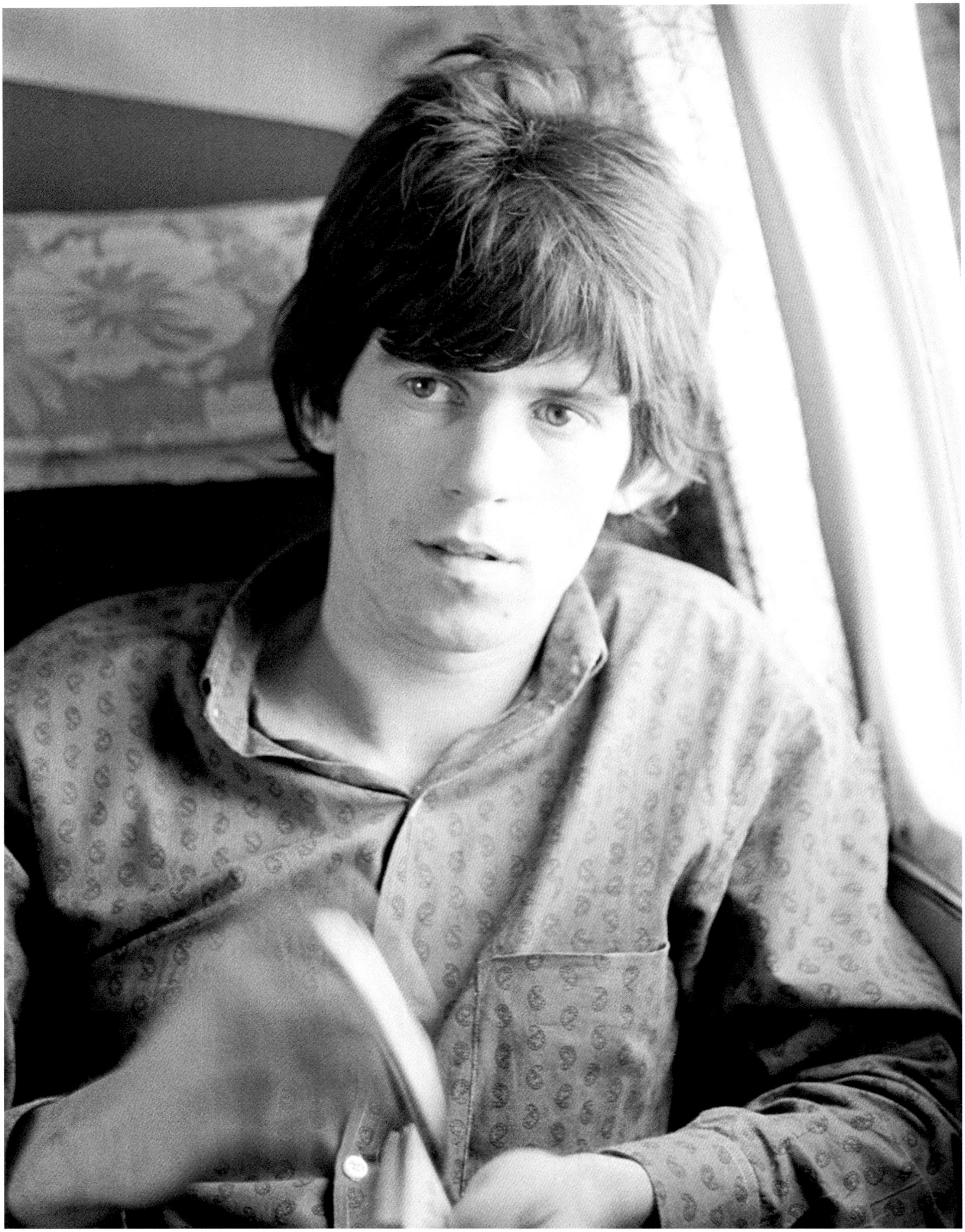

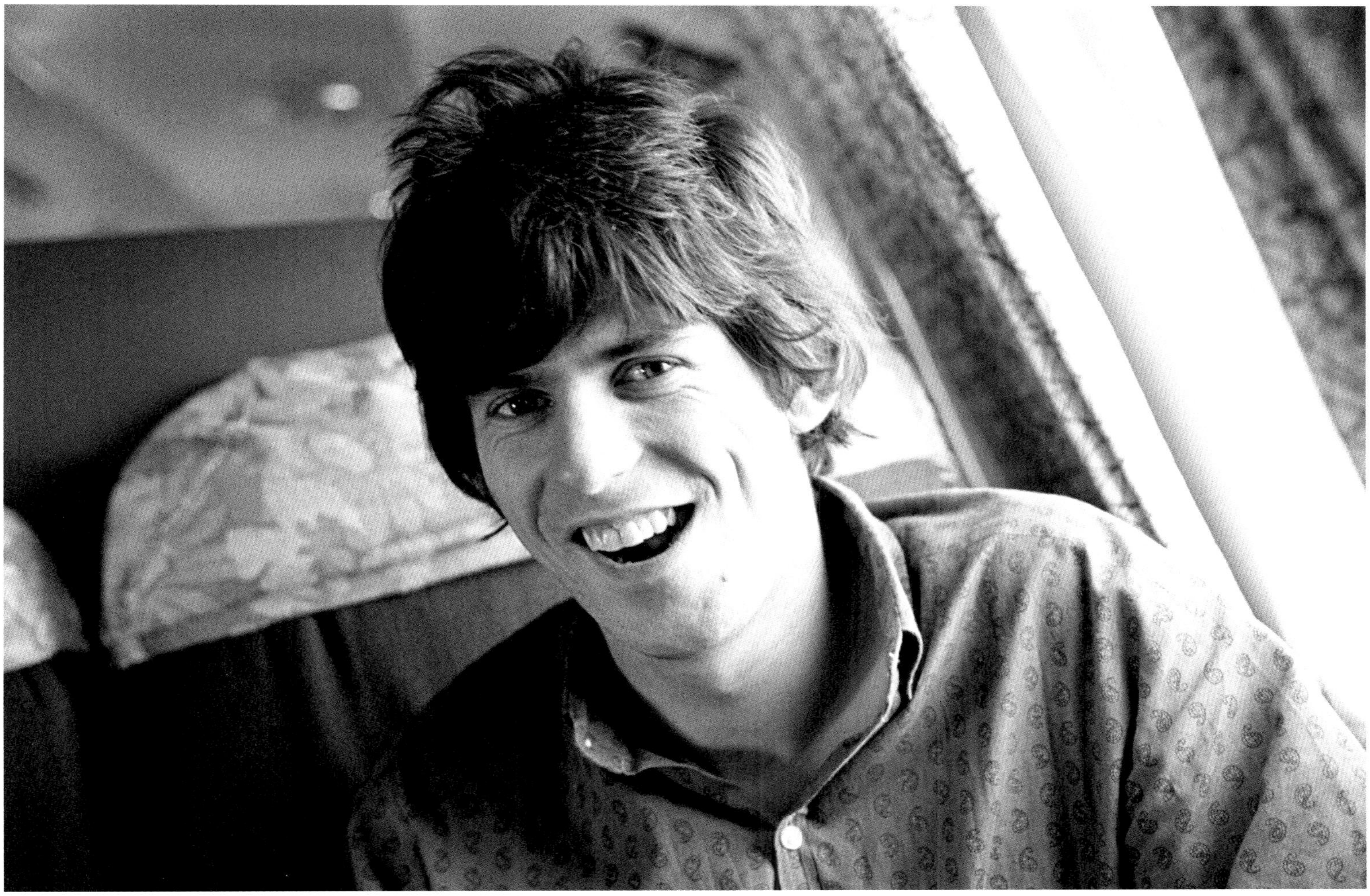

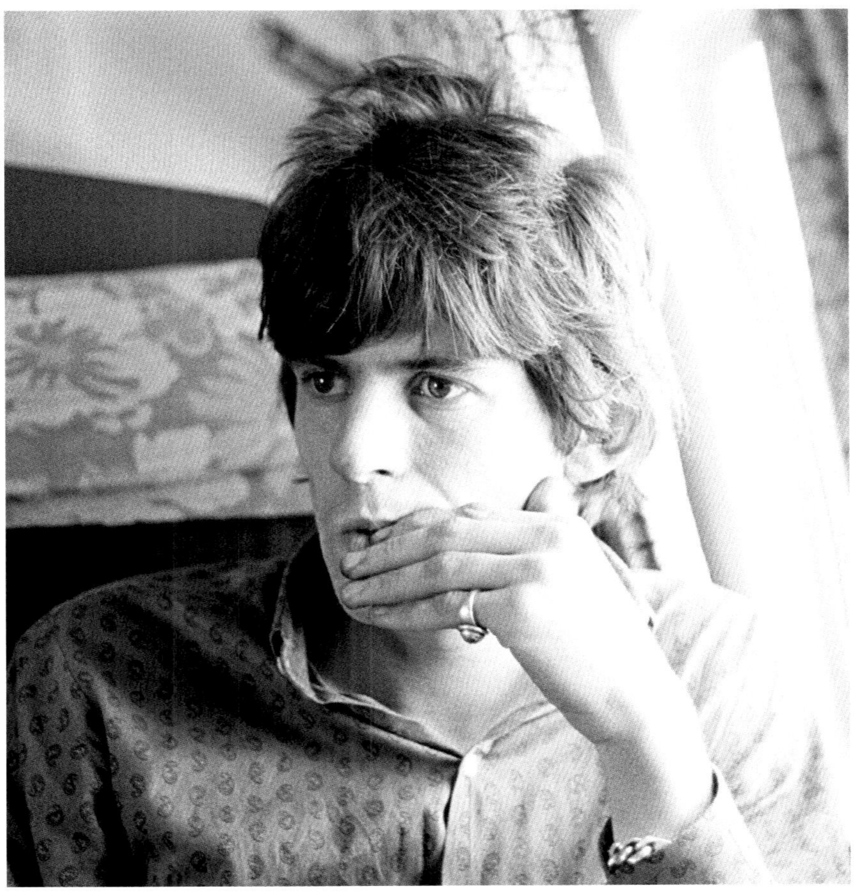

Keith across the aisle, in a summer shirt on an internal flight during the Australian Tour – February 1966.

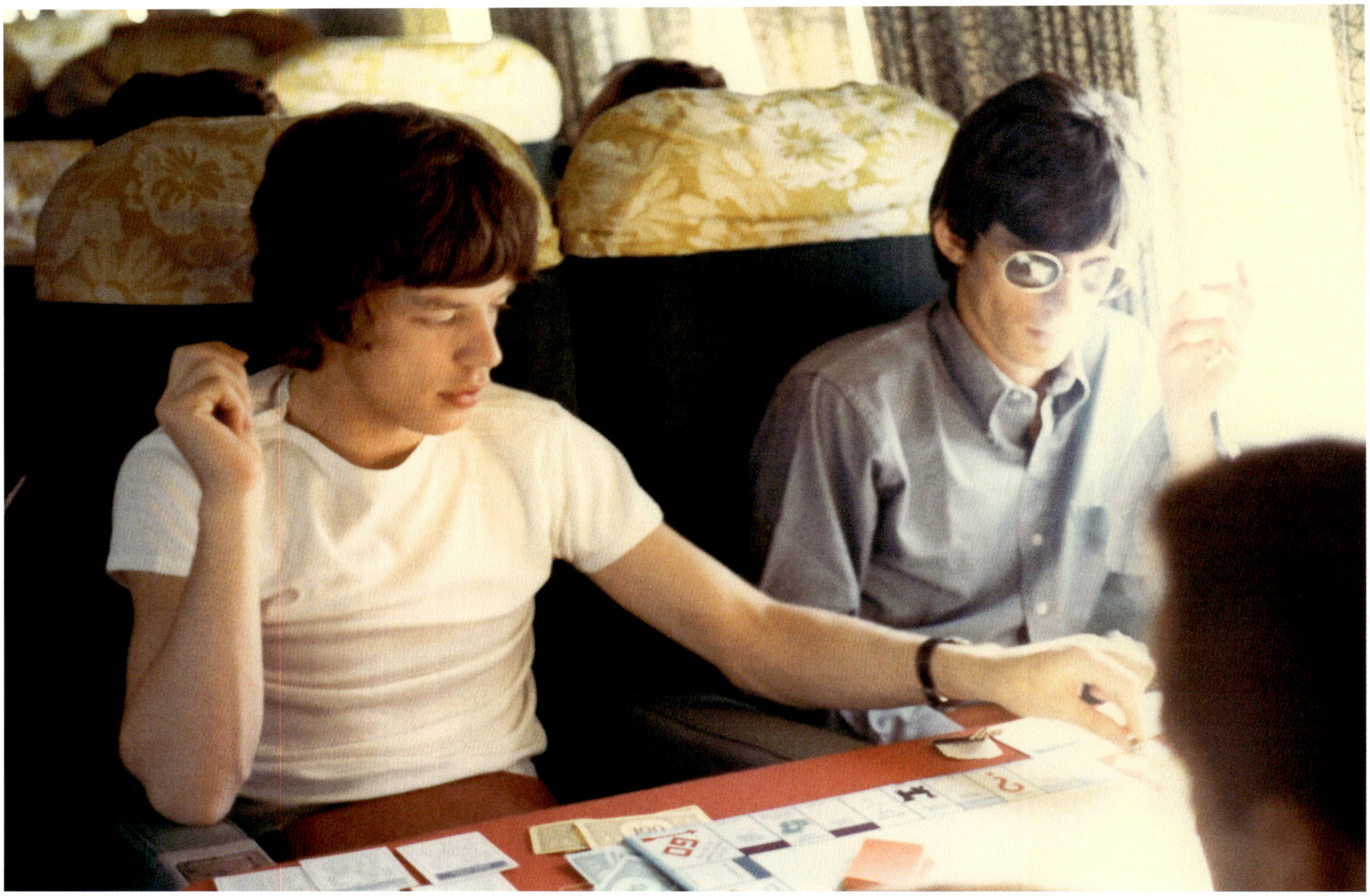

Mick Jagger and Keith playing Monopoly to pass the time during a long internal flight on the Australian Tour – February 1966. **Right:** Charlie Watts looks on, surprised by their antics.

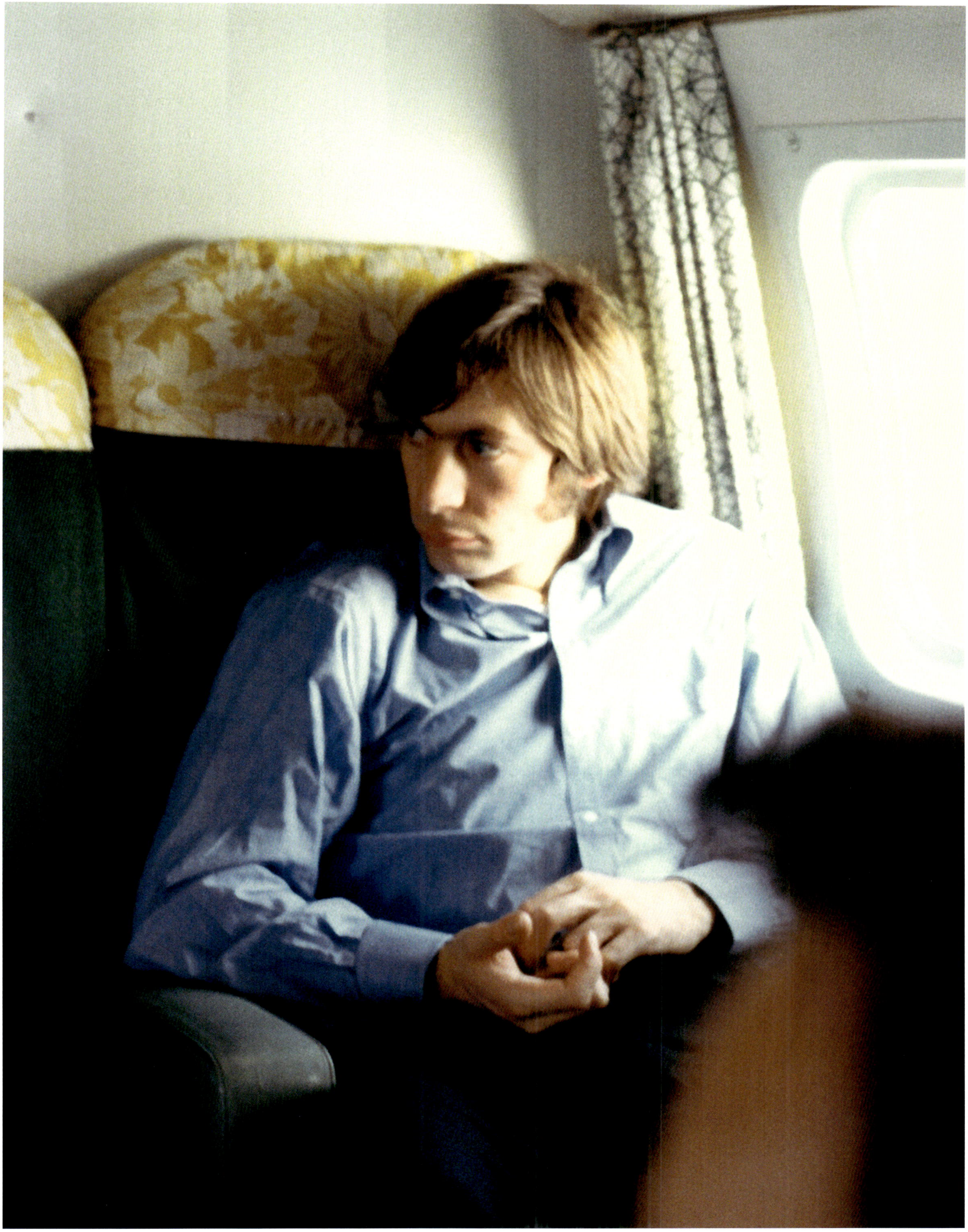

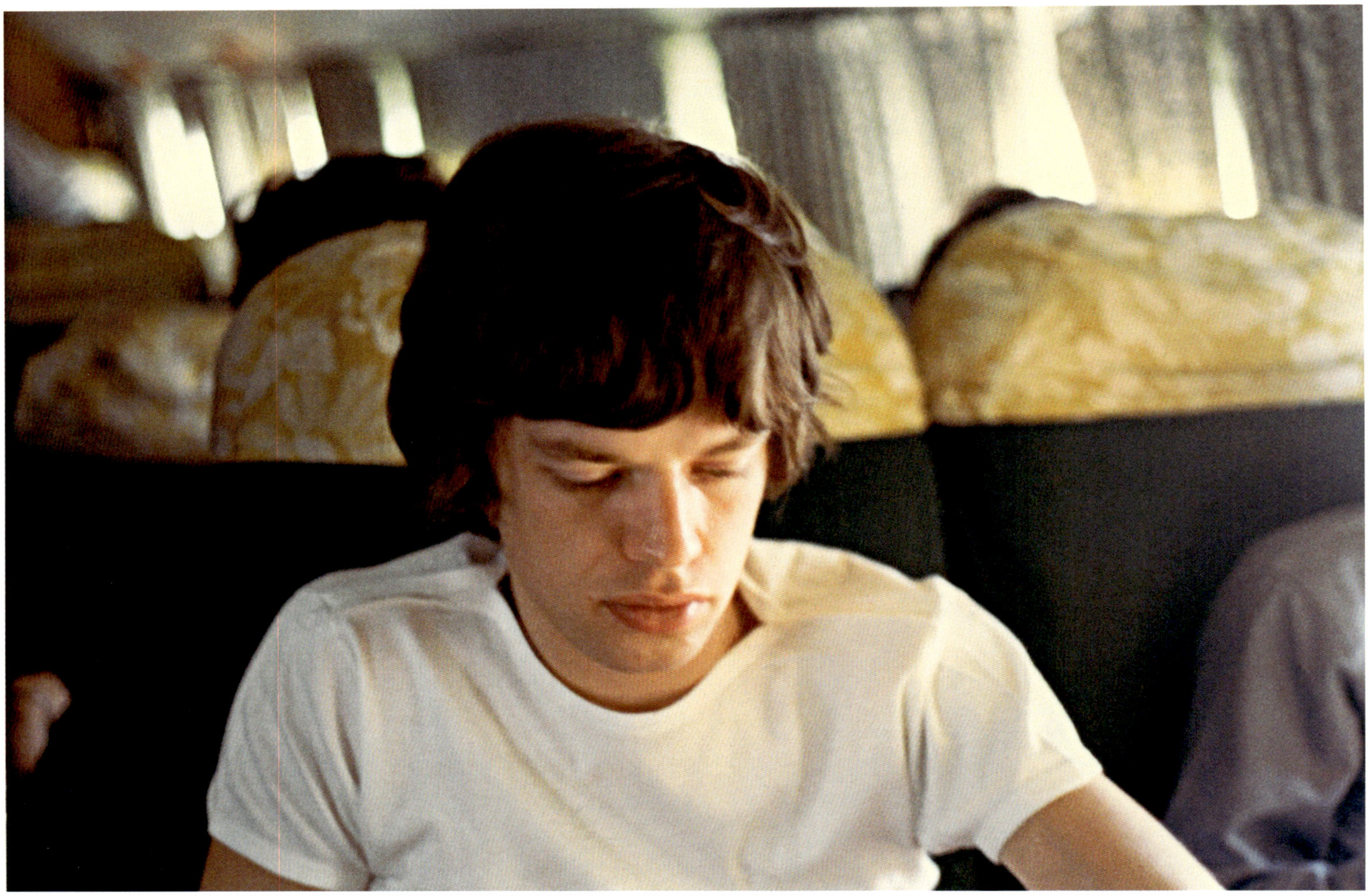

Mick buying a hotel on the Monopoly board, hoping for no turbulence.
Right: Mick in a striped shirt on the plane, and something has tickled him.

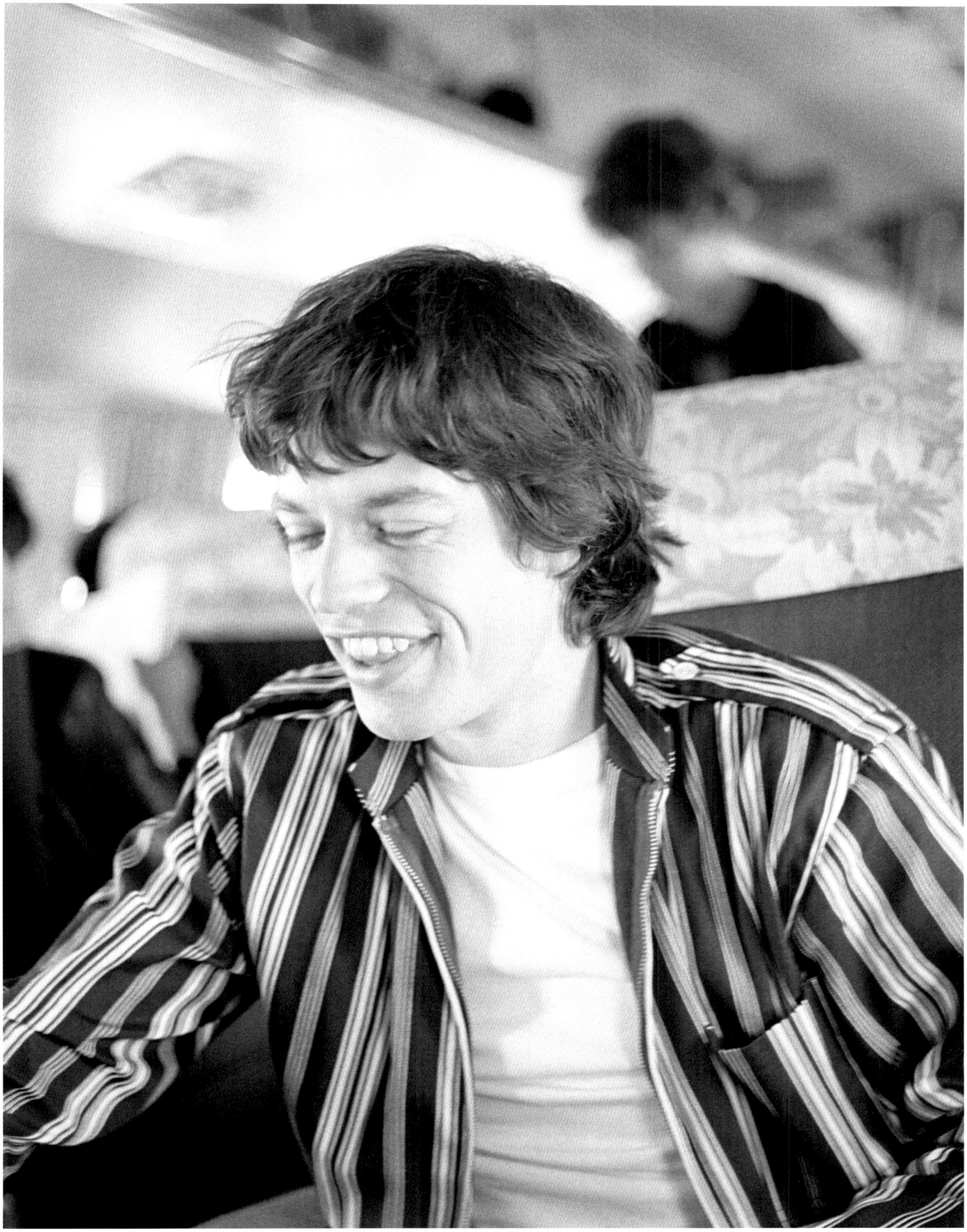

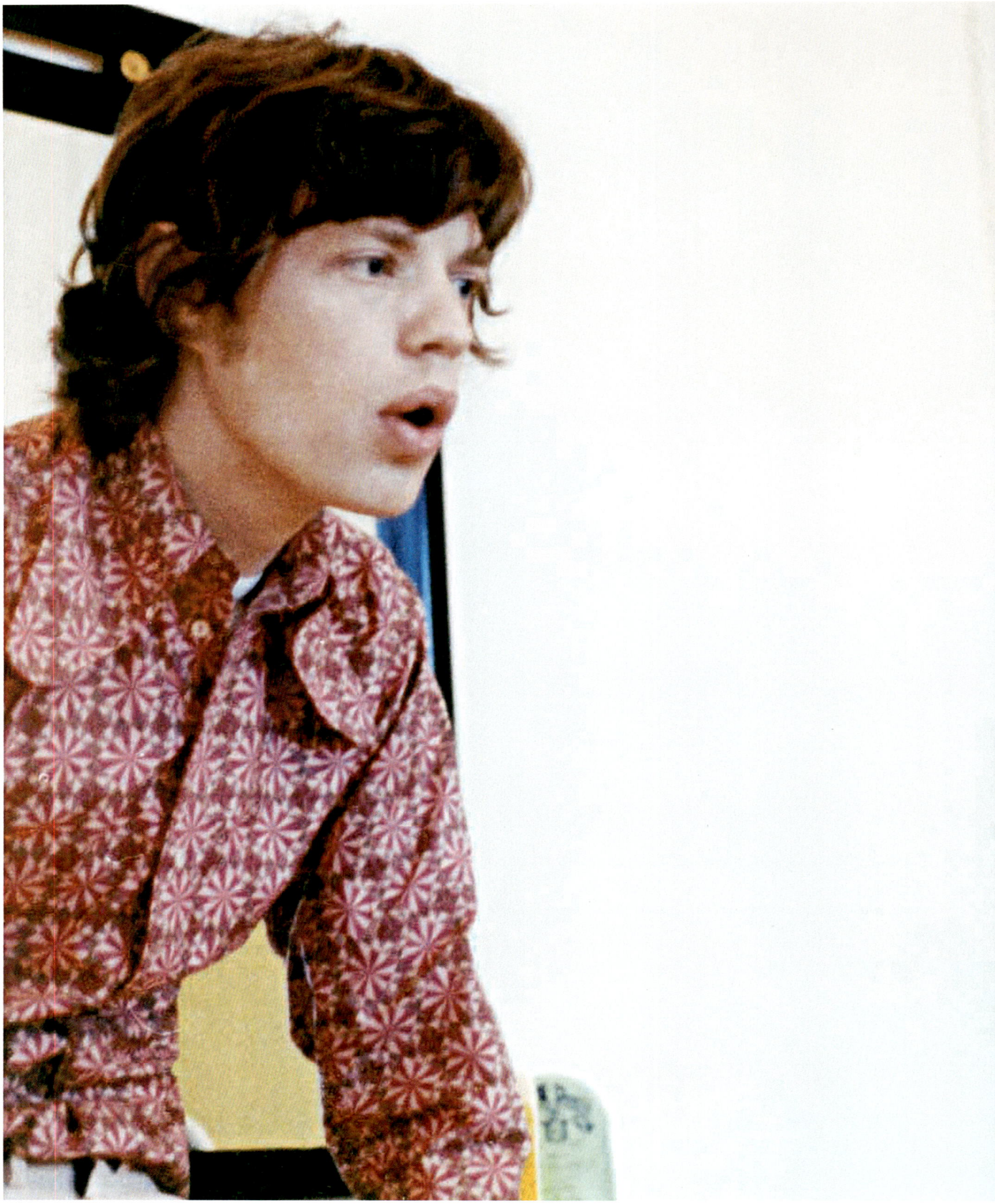

Mick in the dressing room before a show,
with a security cop at the door.

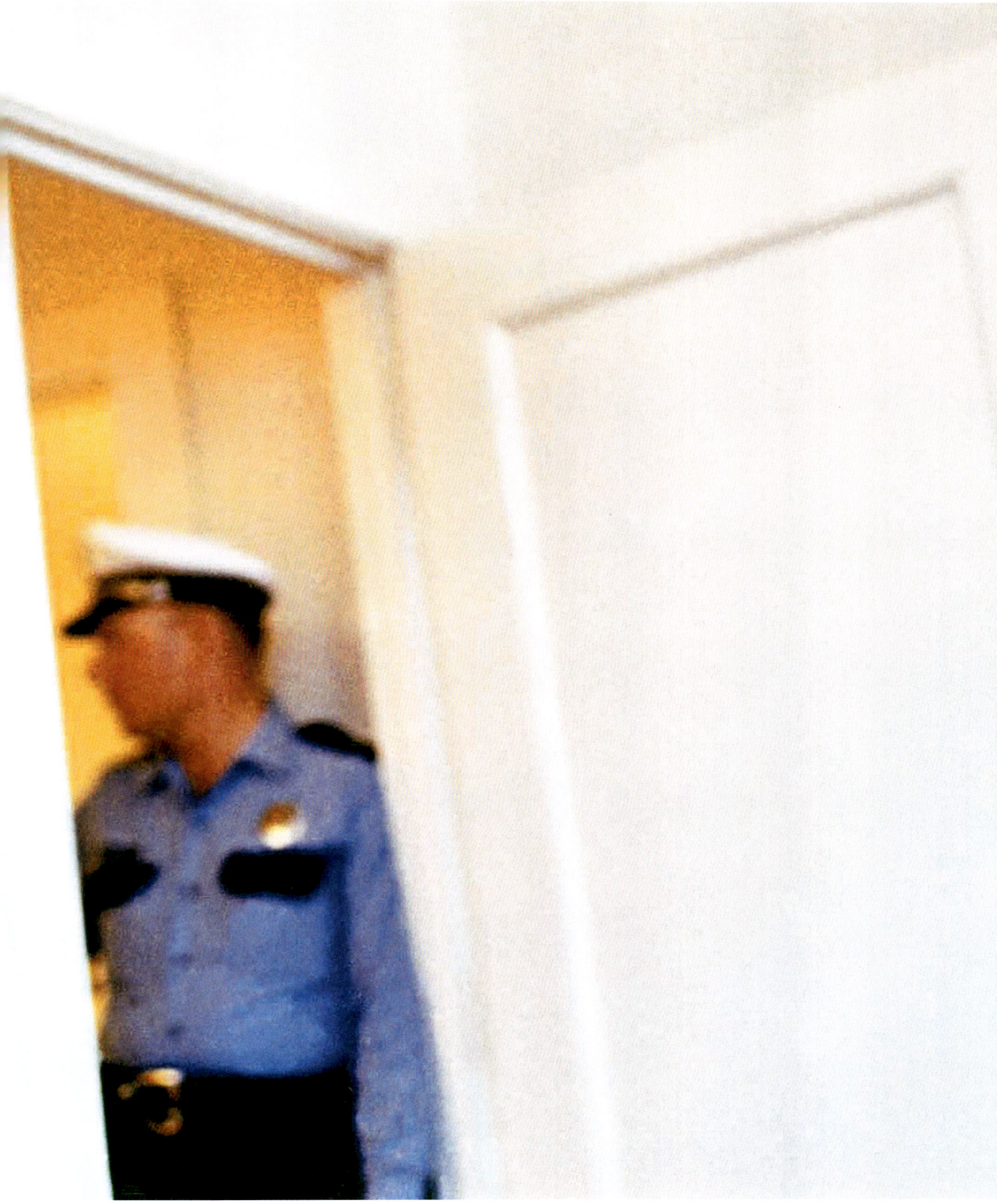

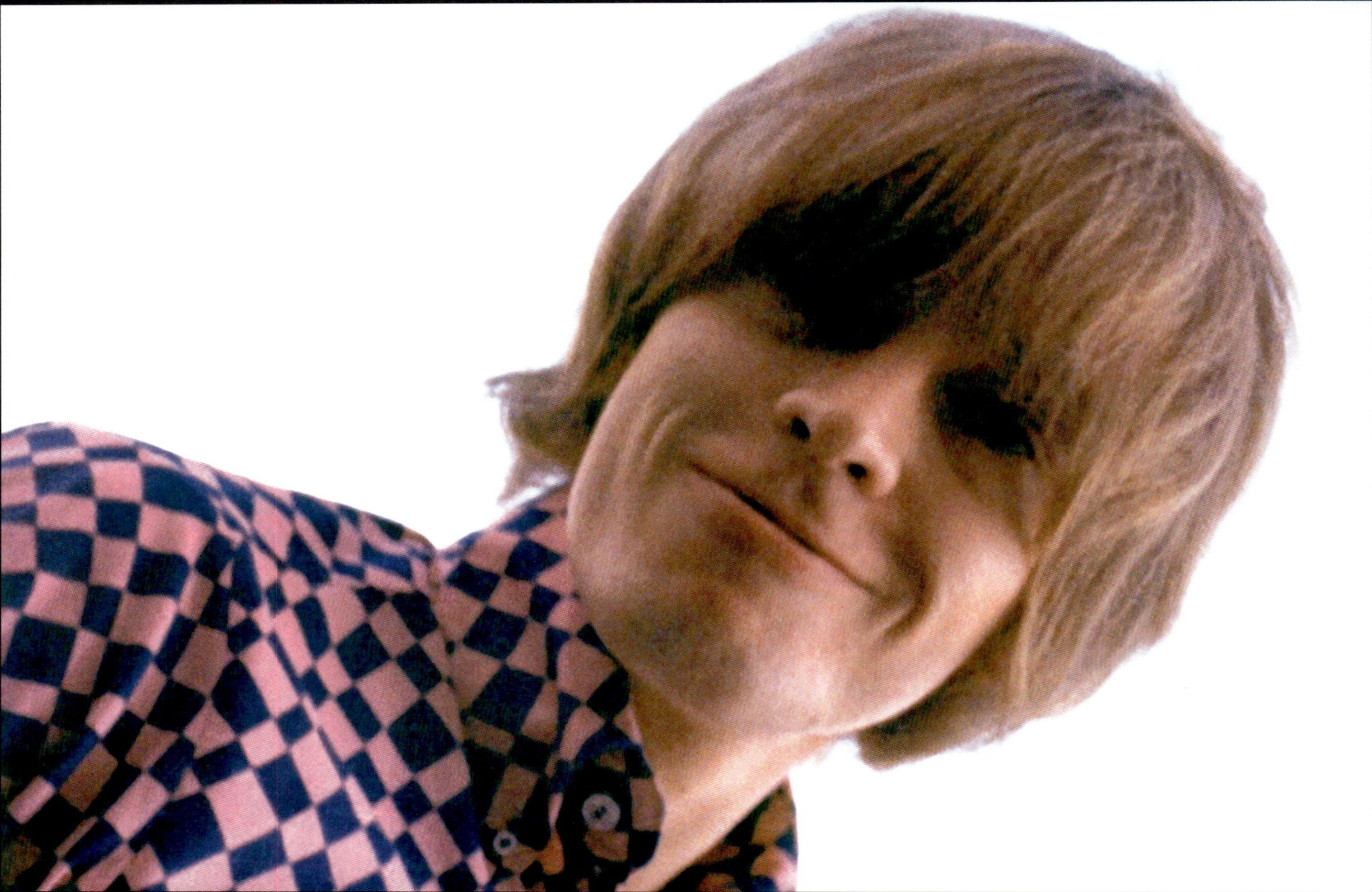

Brian wanting to be in the picture, backstage – February 1966.
Right: Brian looking very dapper at the RCA Studios in Hollywood, Los Angeles, during our recording session there

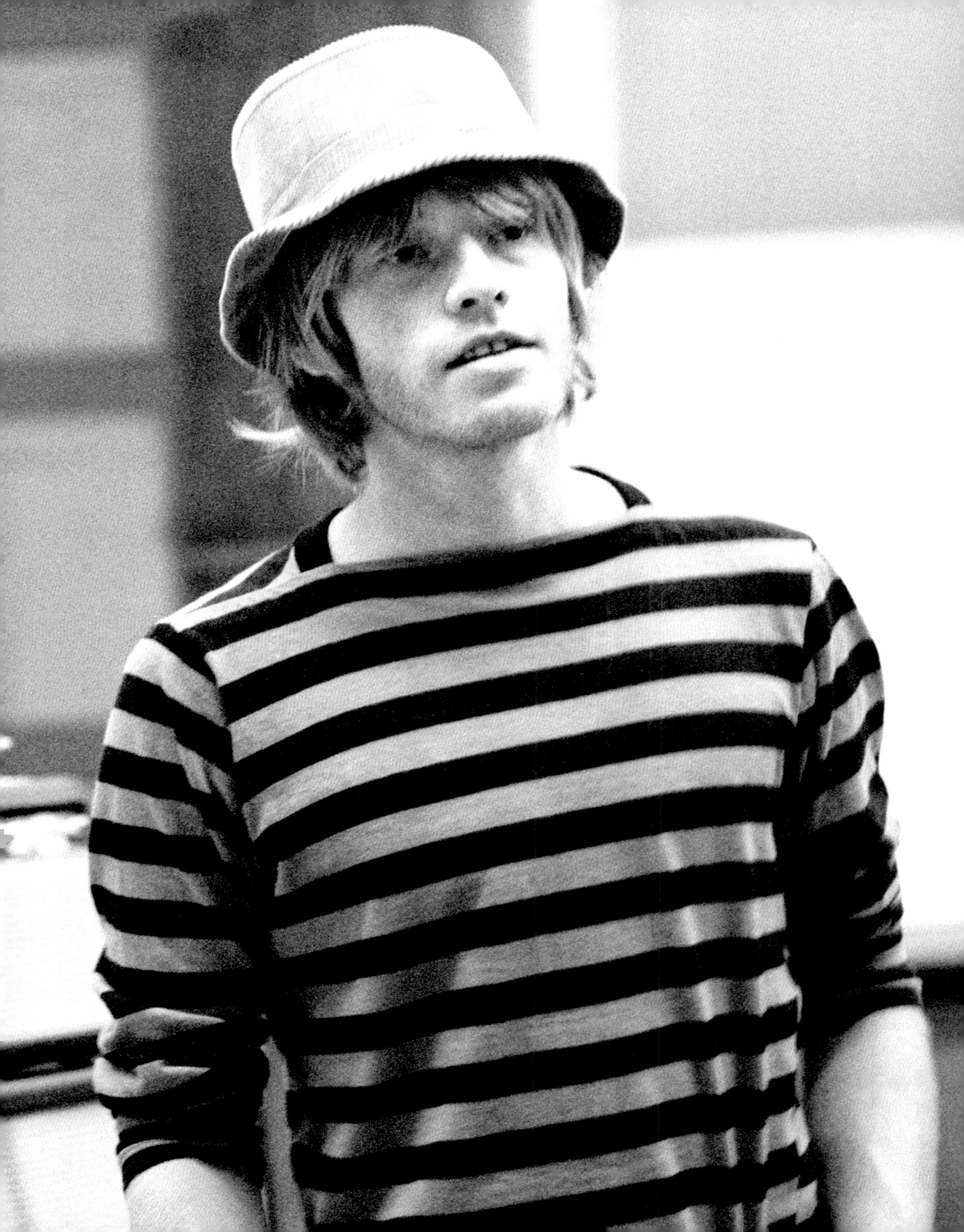

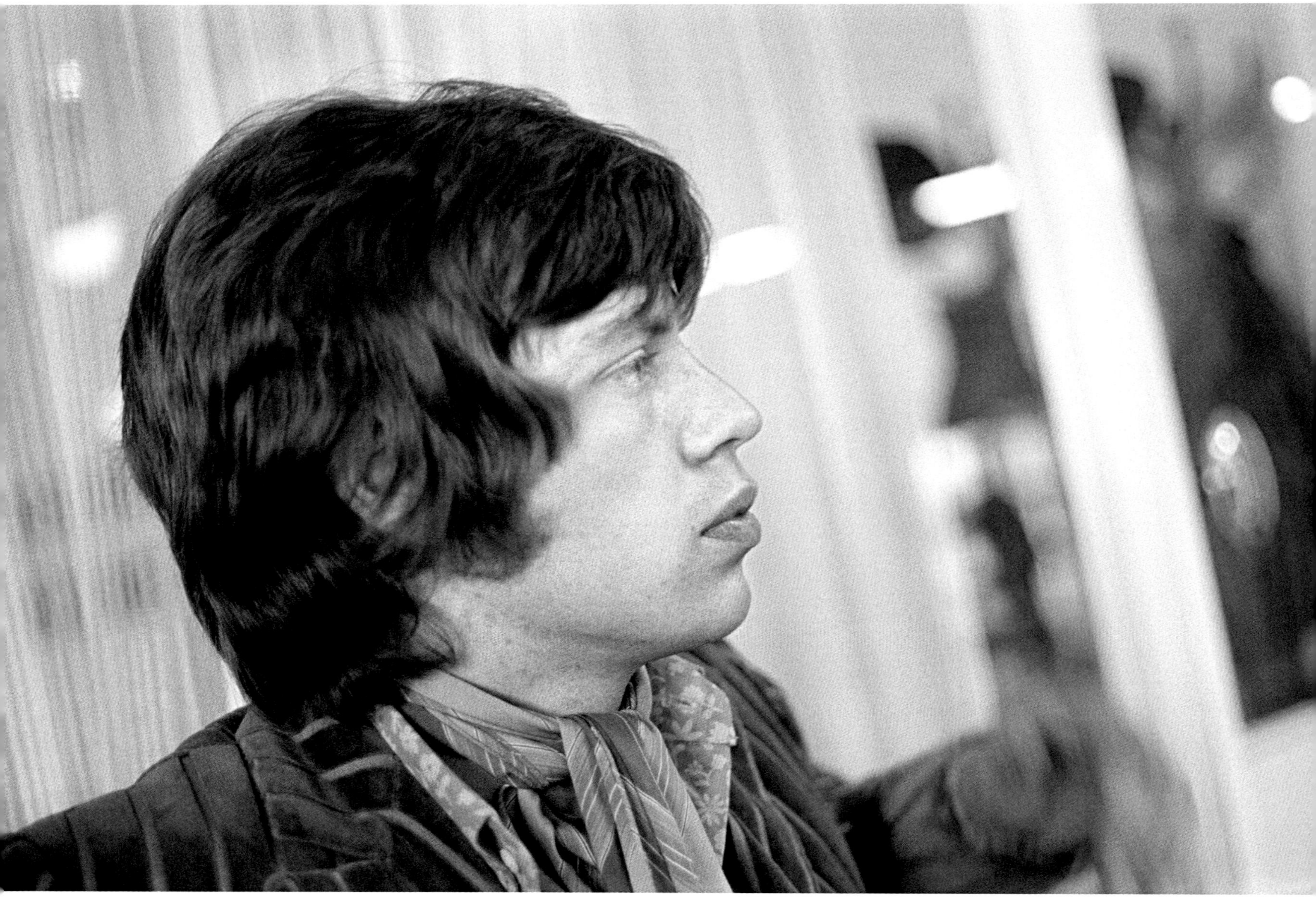

Mick arriving at the studio for our recording session.
Right: Keith laying down a rhythm with his guitar pick in his mouth at the RCA Studios in Hollywood, Los Angeles, – March 1966.

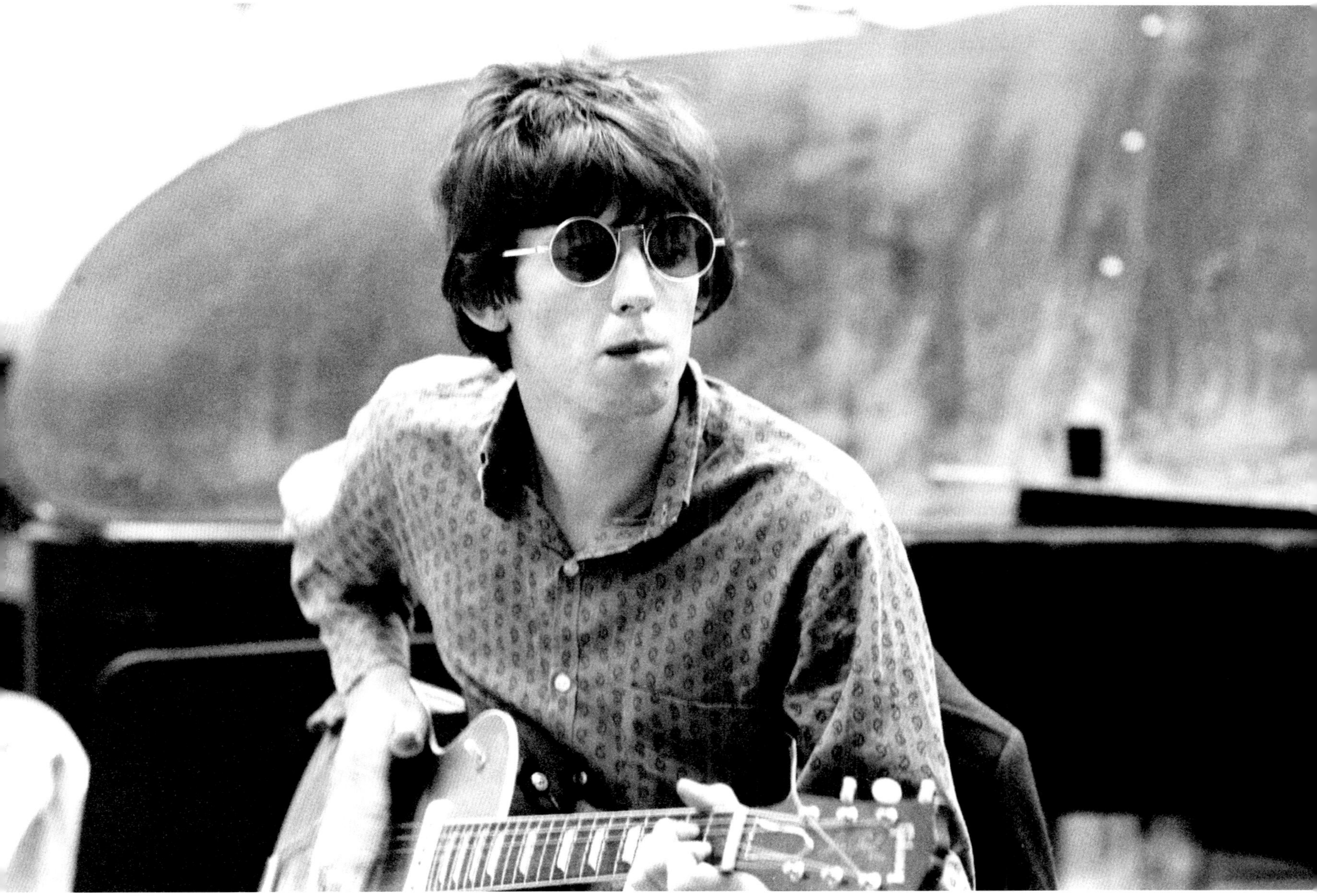

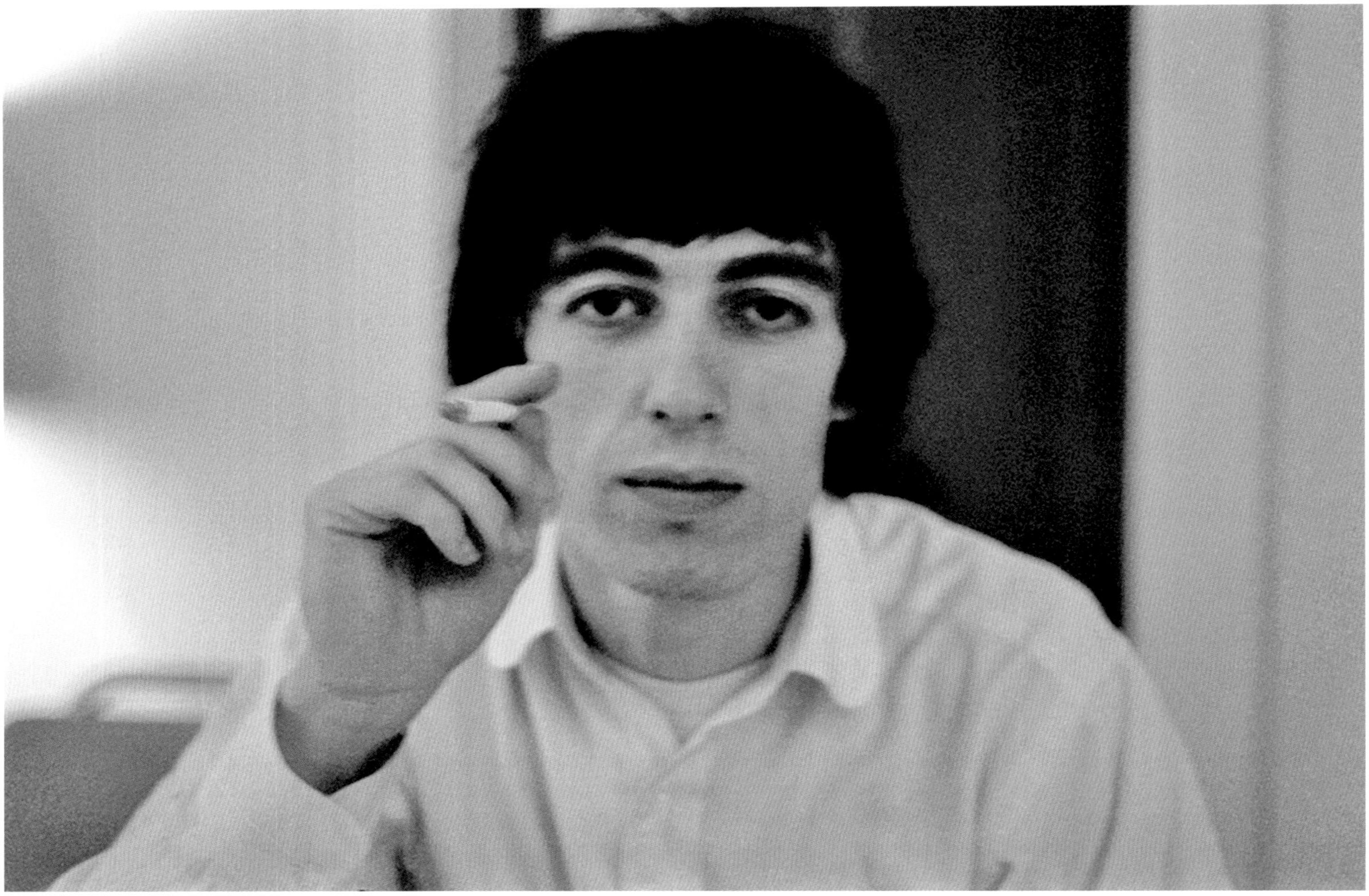

Self-portrait, taken in the RCA studio mirror.
Right: A fine shot of Charlie in the studio, deep in concentration – March 1966.

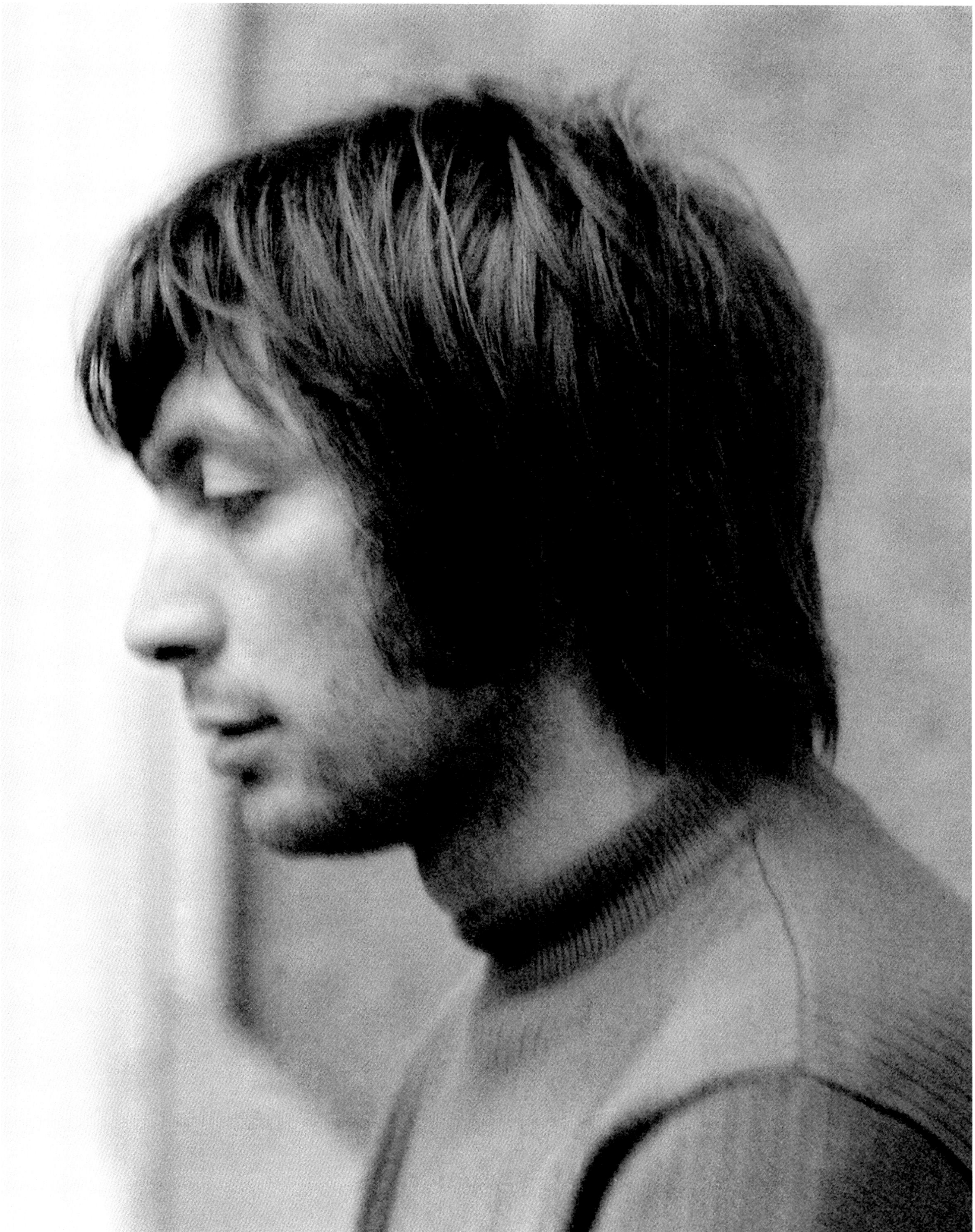

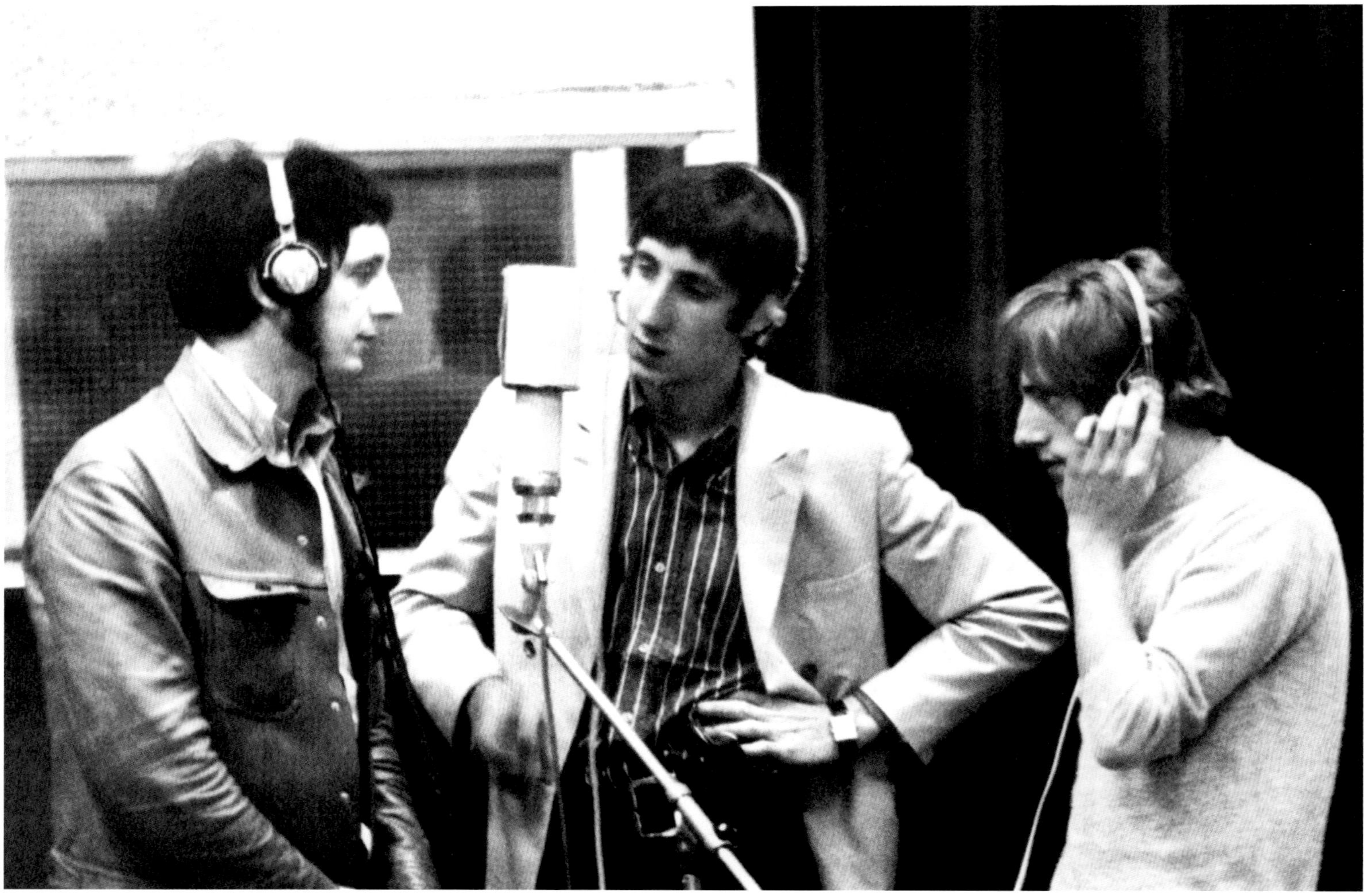

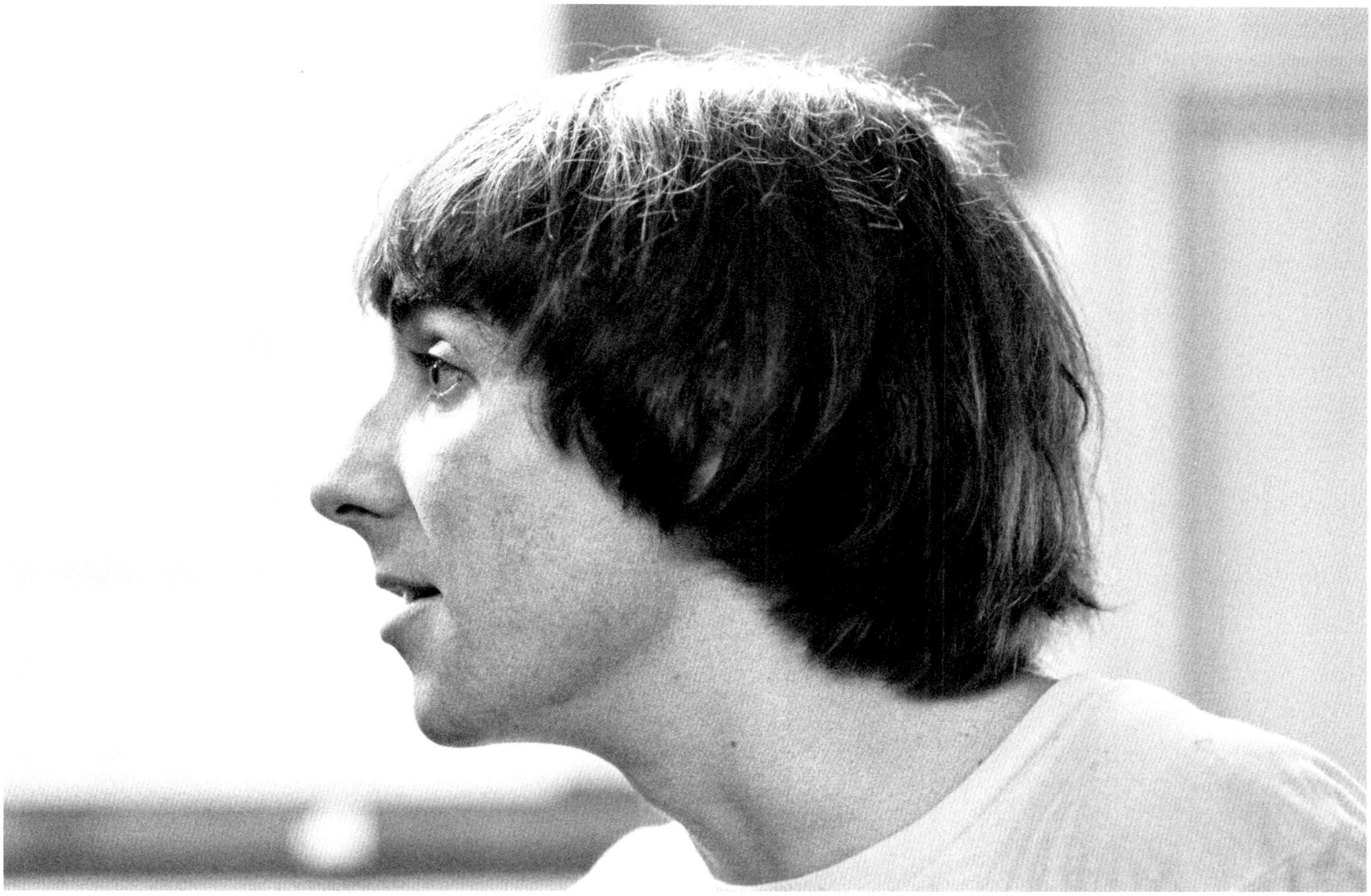

Being great friends with Keith Moon and John Entwhistle, I was invited to their recording session in London in June 1966. I took my camera, and captured these nice shots of the band.

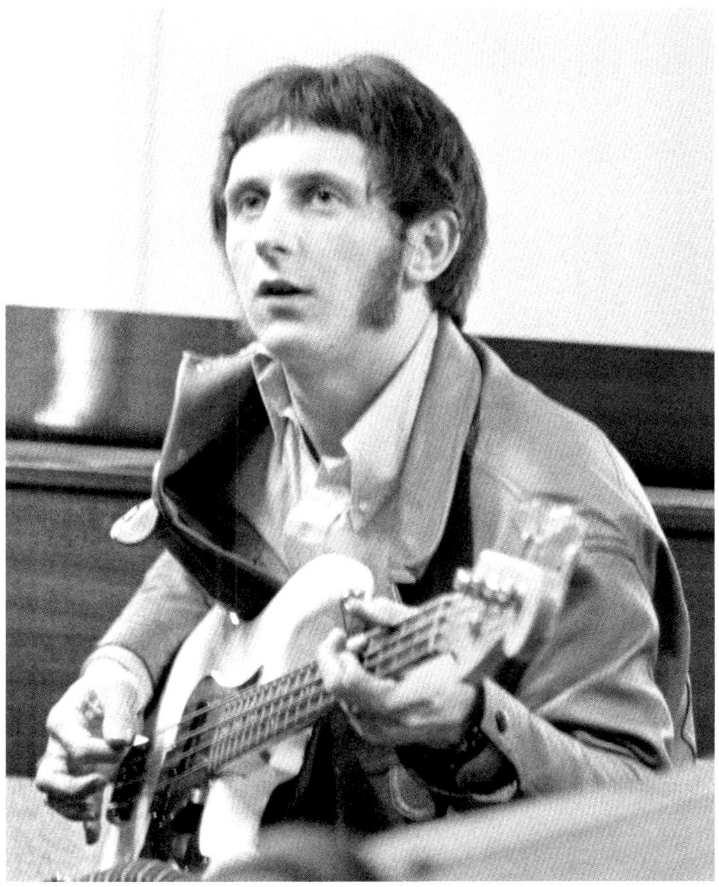

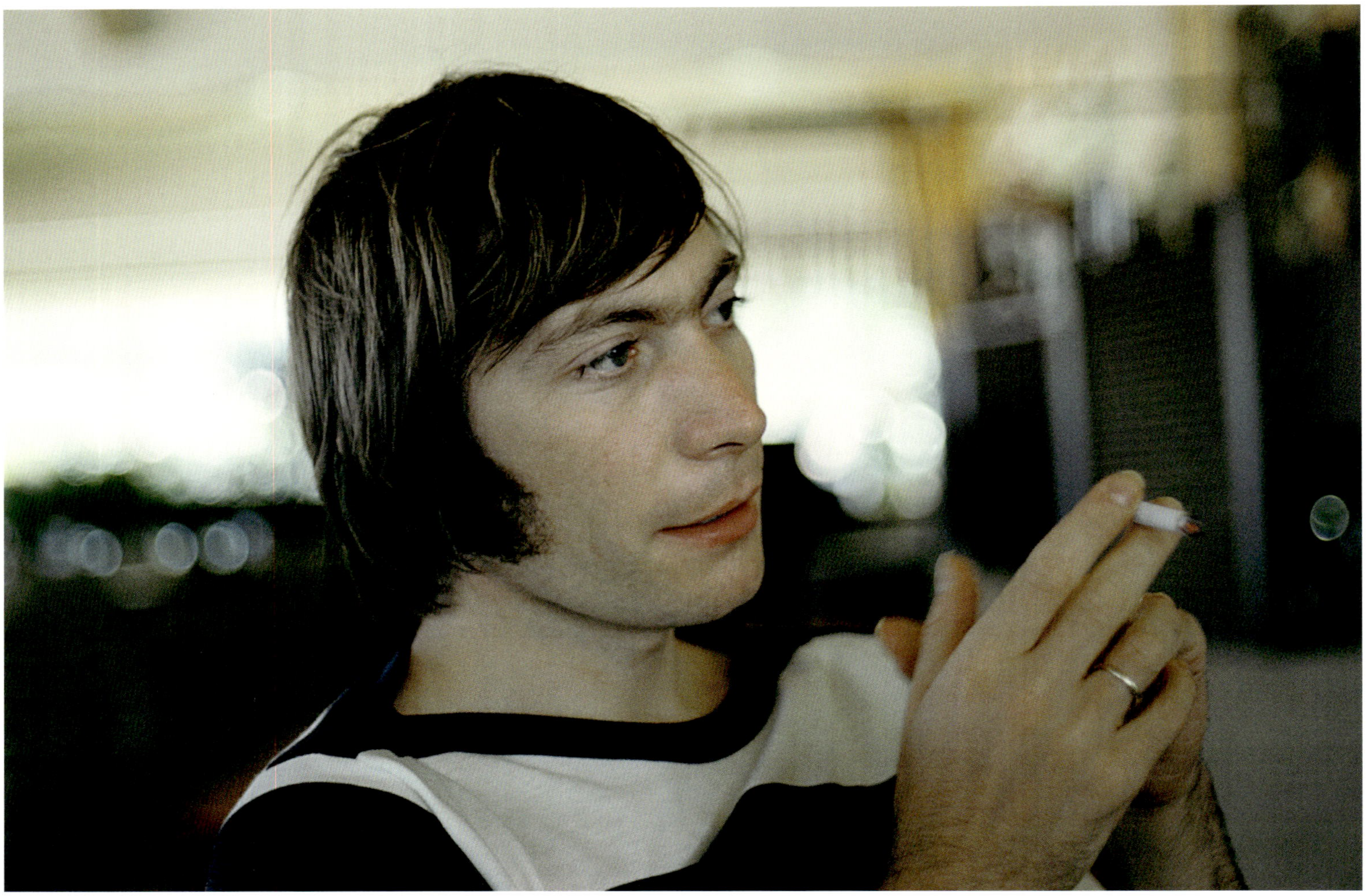

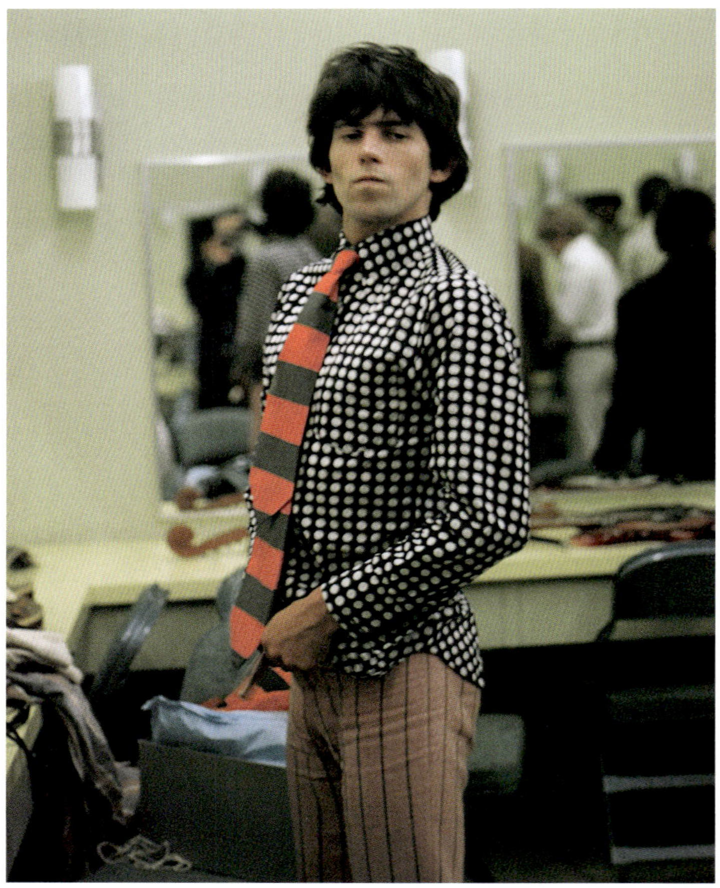

Charlie in our dressing room before a show in San Francisco, watching Keith get ready, and being rather surprised by his bizarre colour scheme – 26 July 1966.

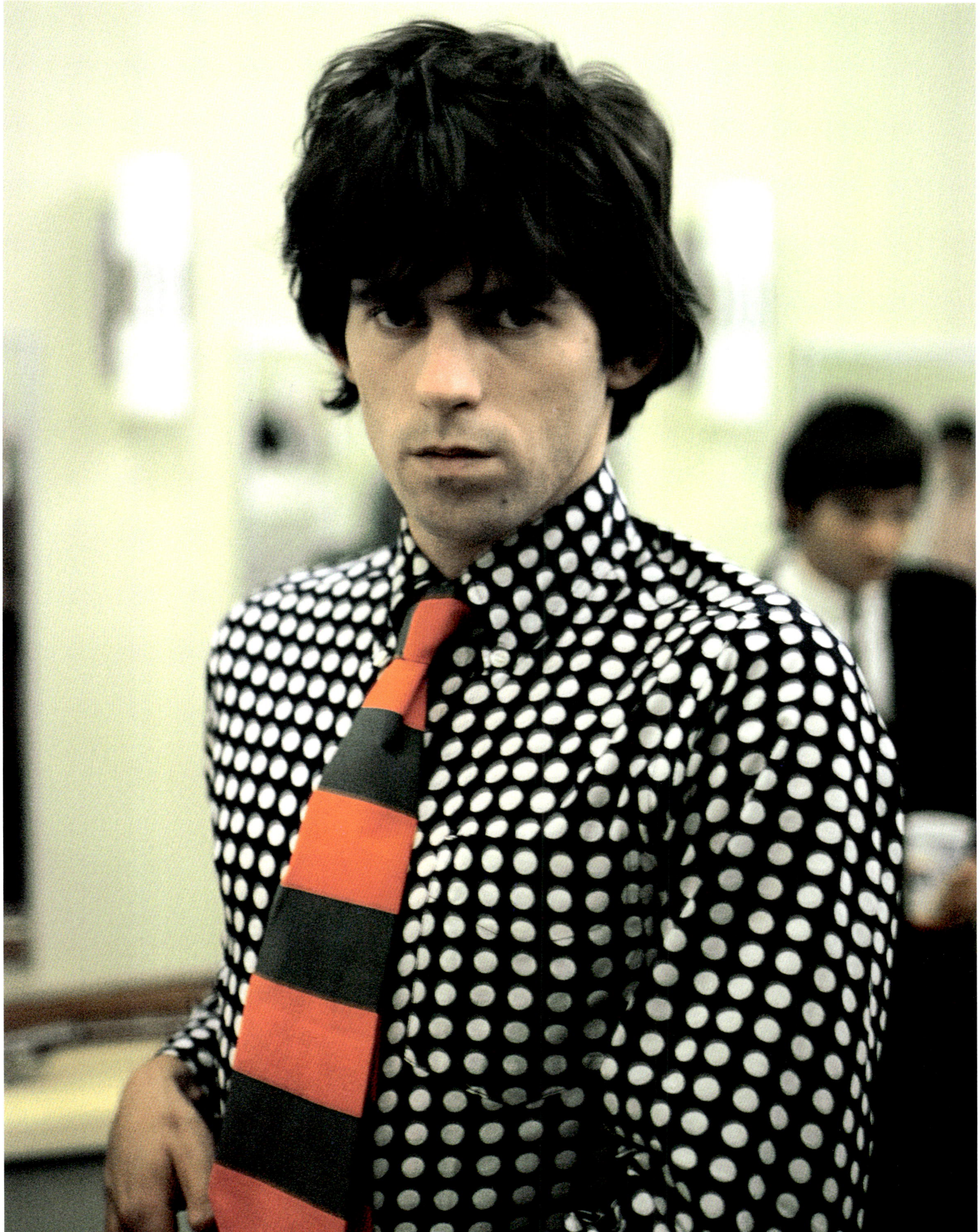

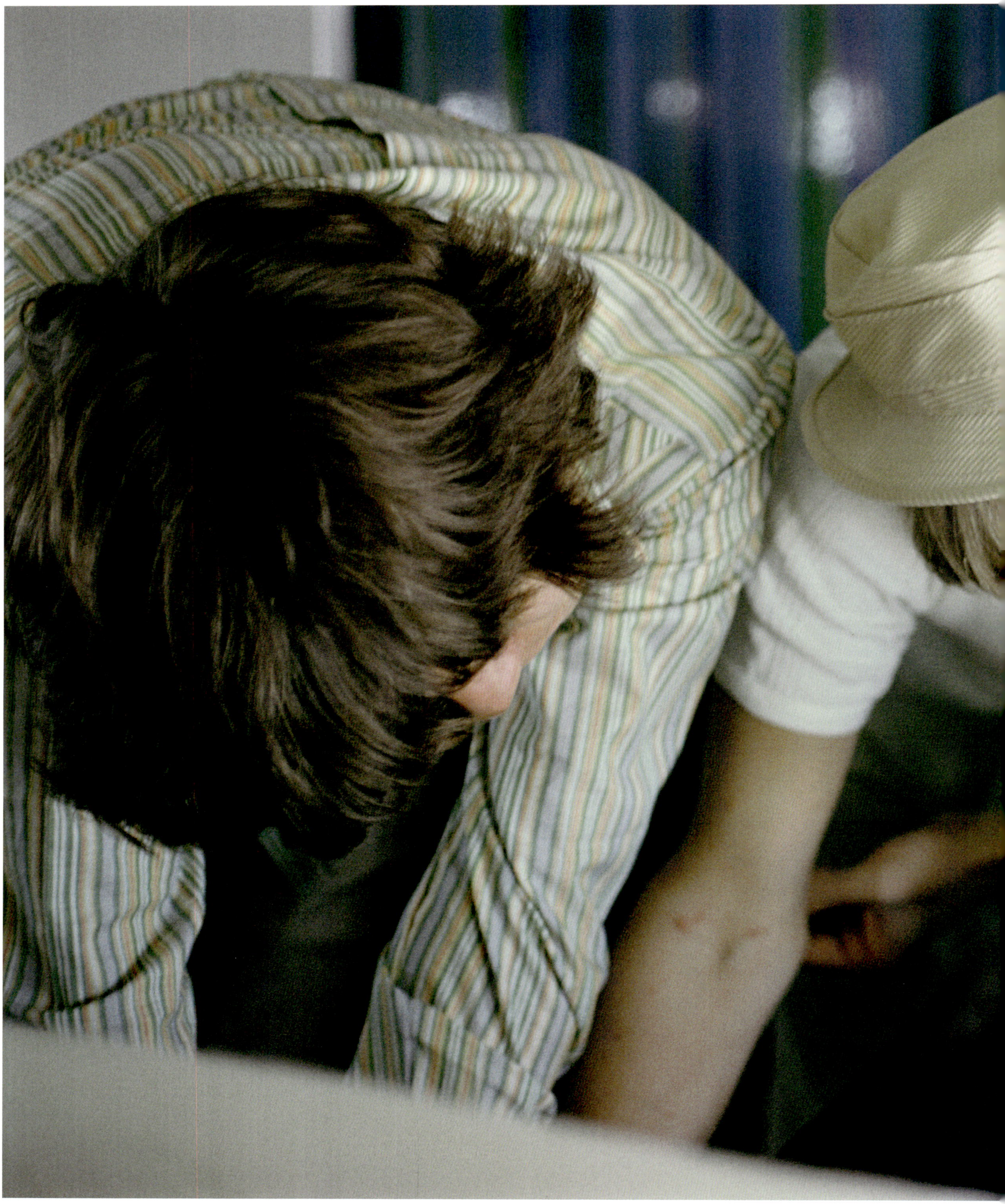

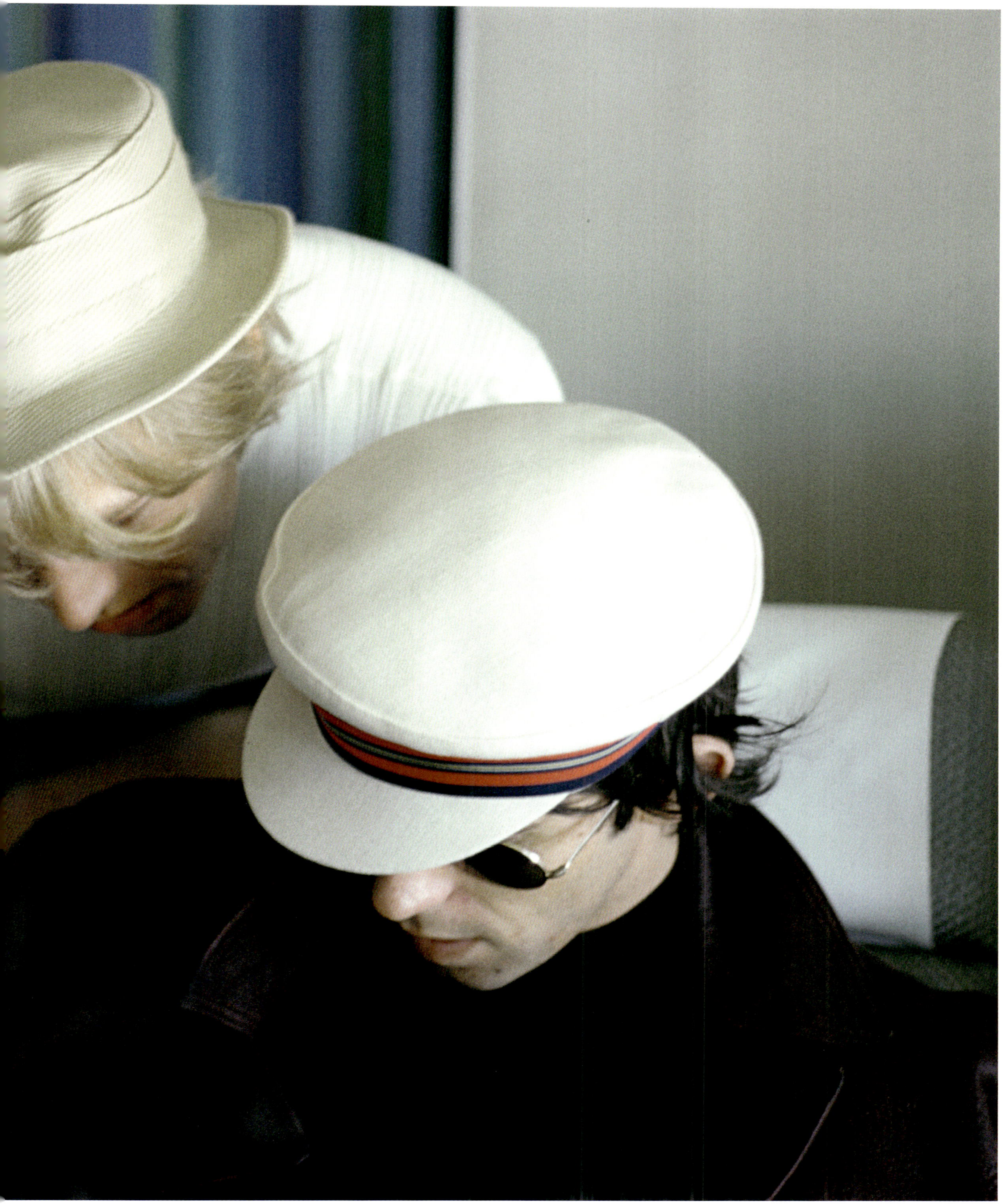

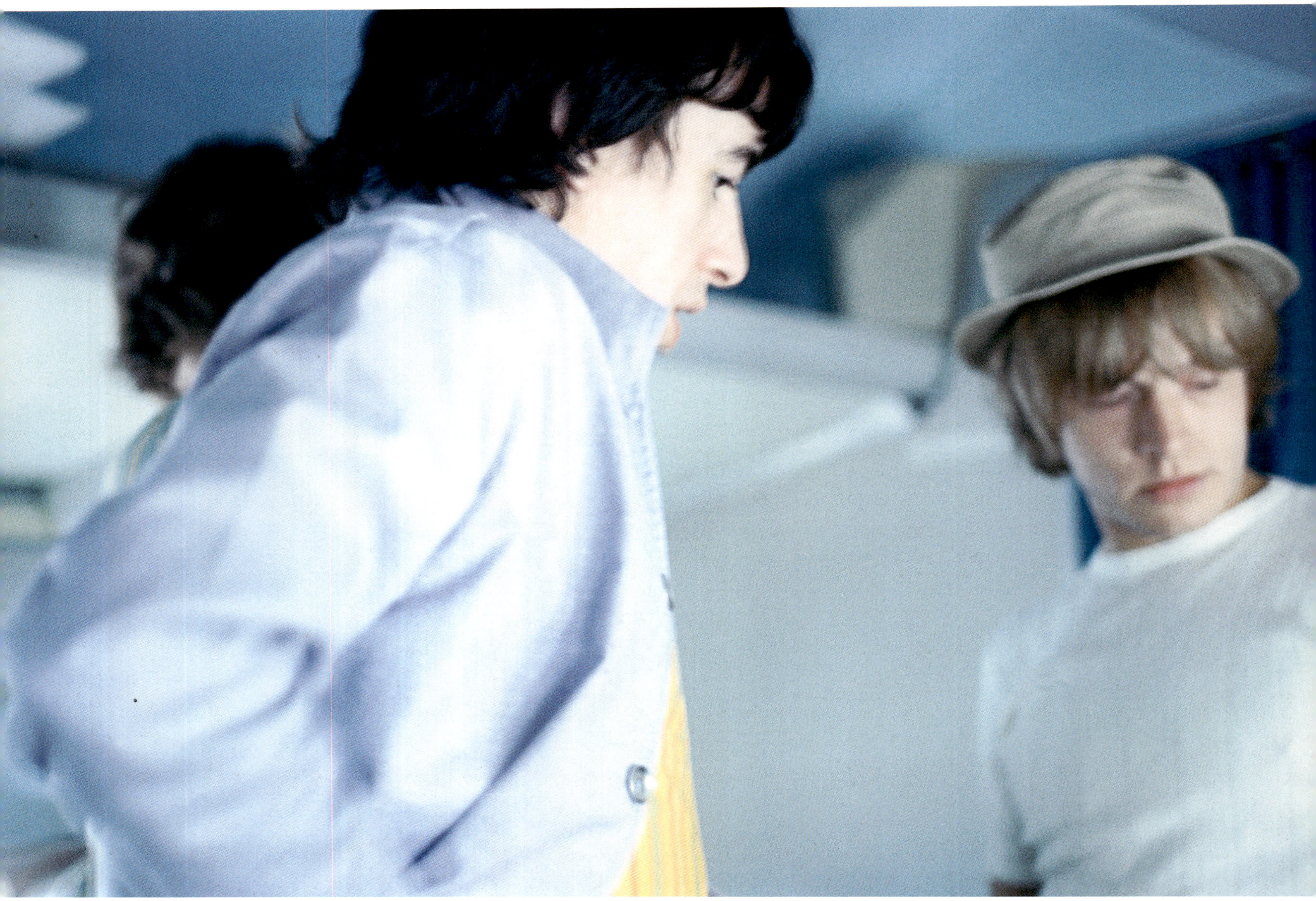

Brian and me changing seats, and Brian now settled, on the flight from Los Angeles to Honolulu, for our show there the next day – 27 July 1966.

Previous pages: Mick and Brian, sharing a magazine moment with Keith during our flight from Los Angeles to Honolulu – 27 July 1966.

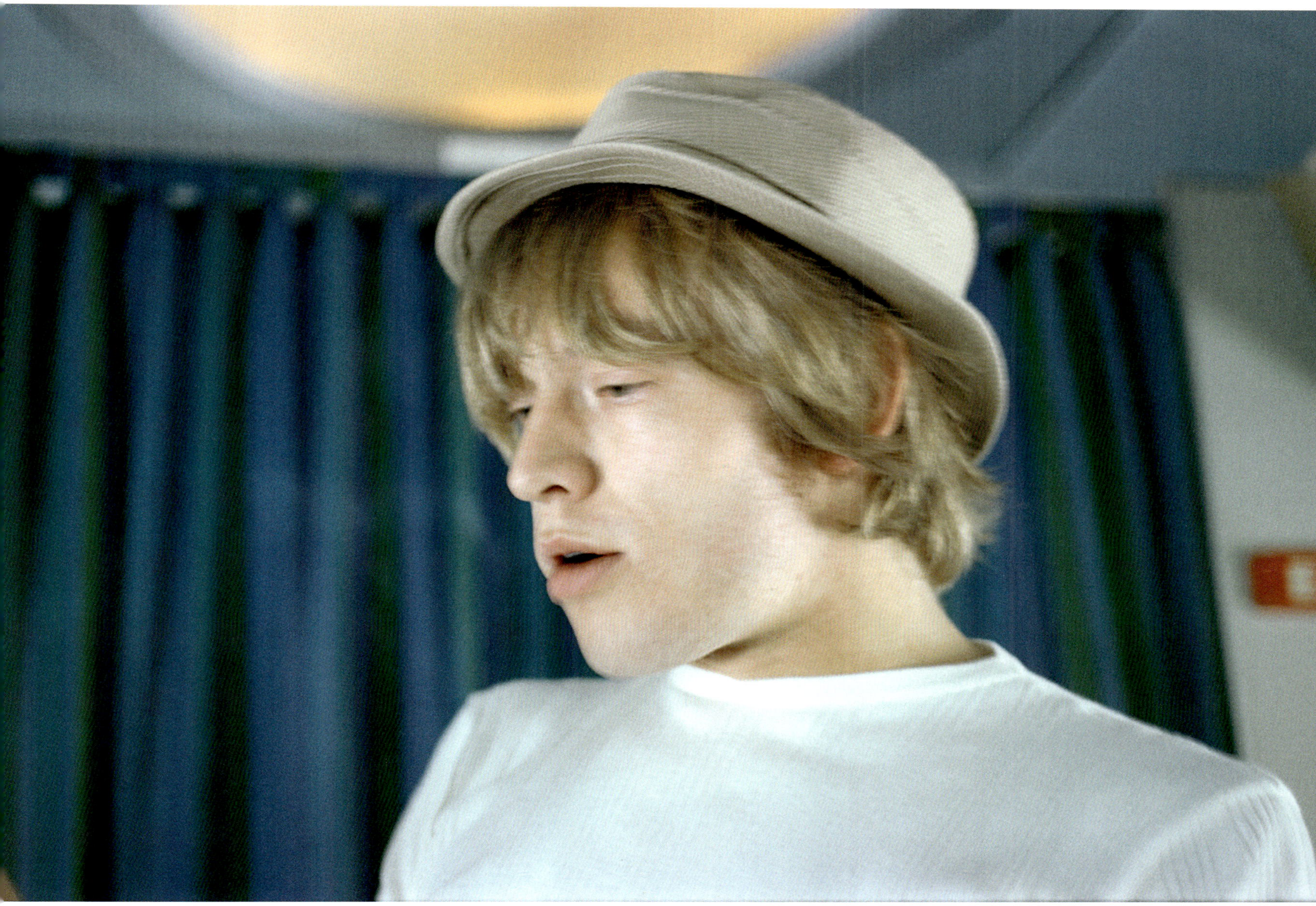

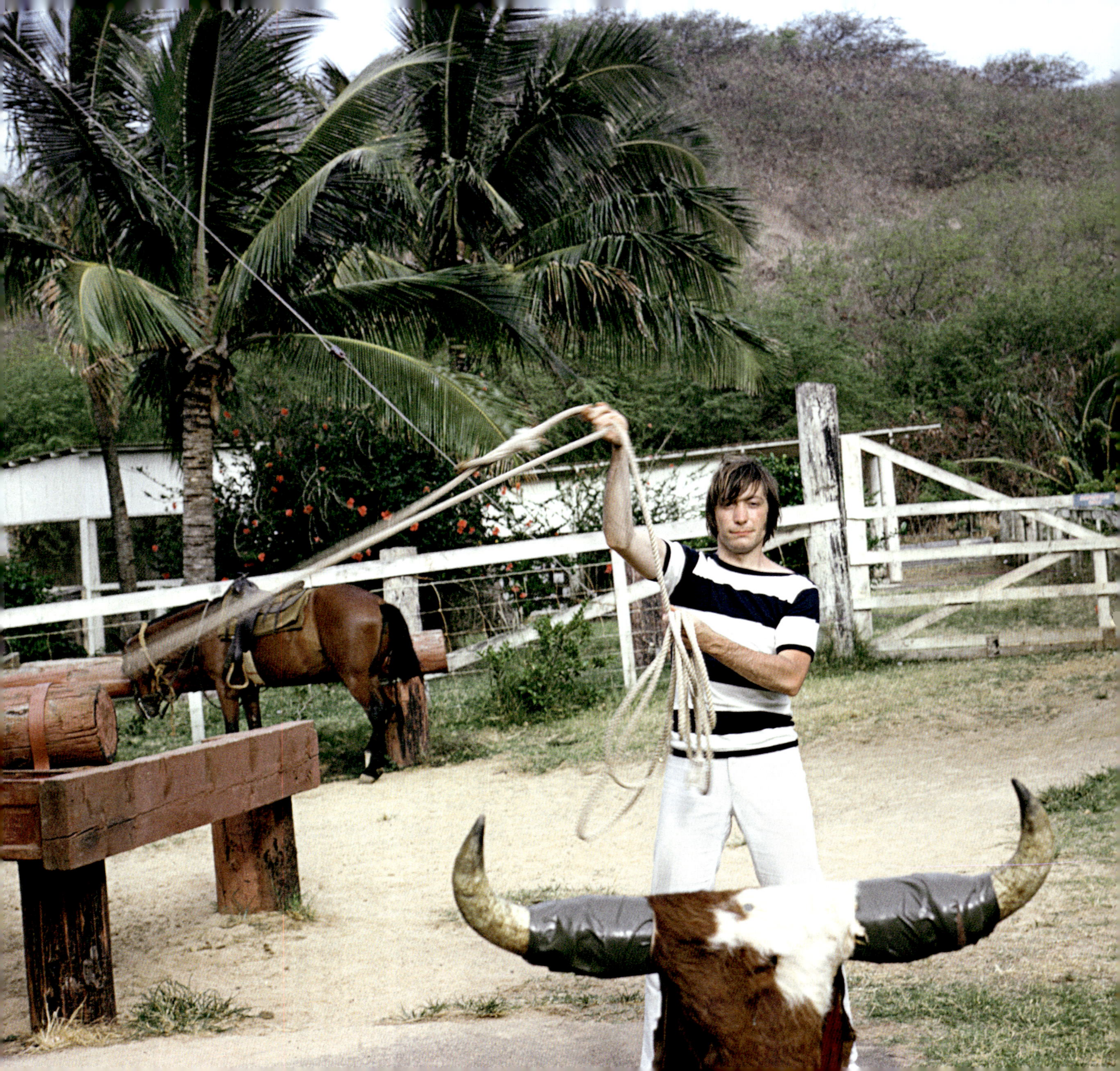

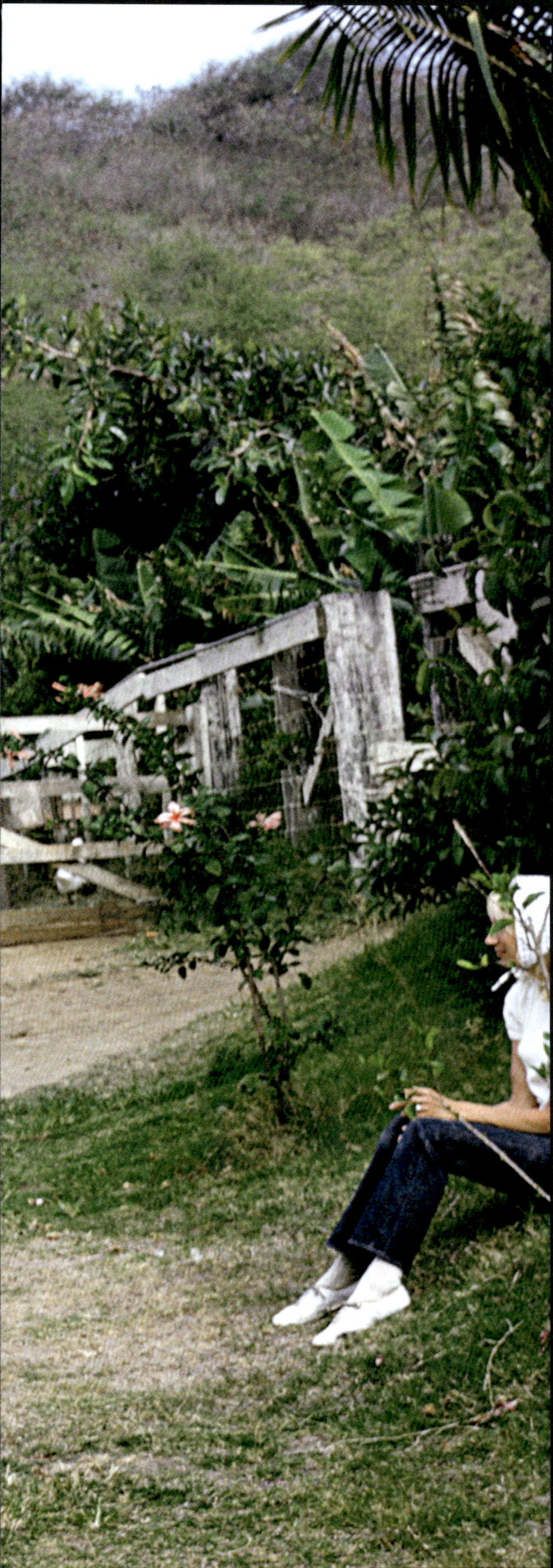

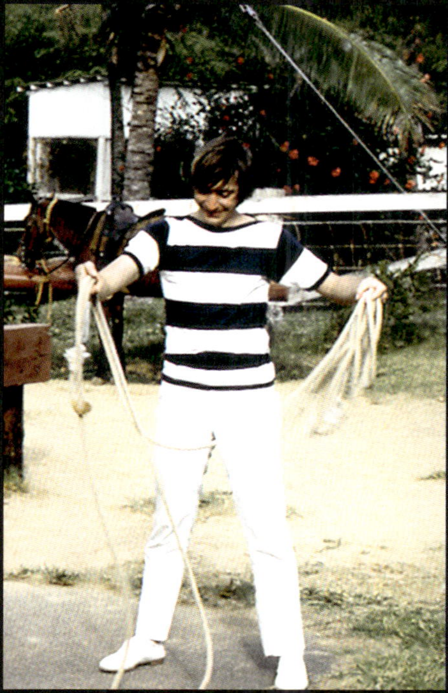

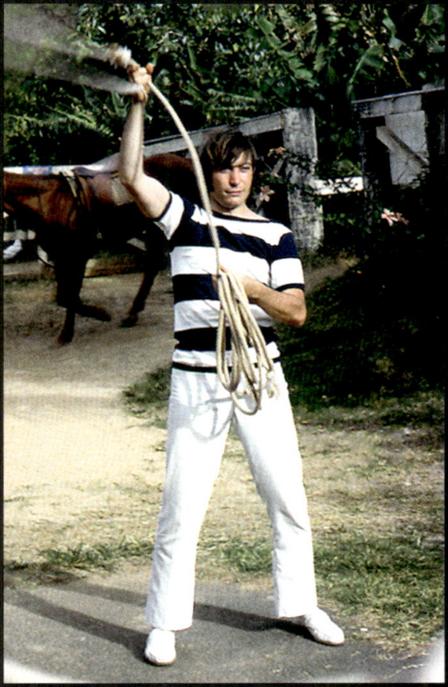

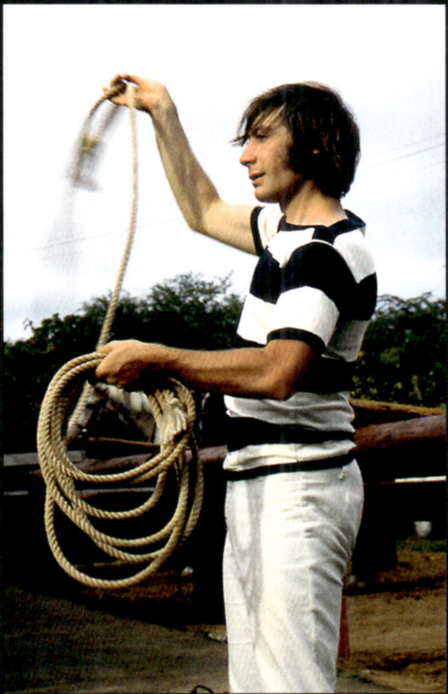

Having decided with Charlie and his wife Shirley, who had joined him here, to go pony-trekking in the Hawaiian hills, I took my camera along and captured these nice shots of Charlie trying his hand with a lasso – 30 July 1966.

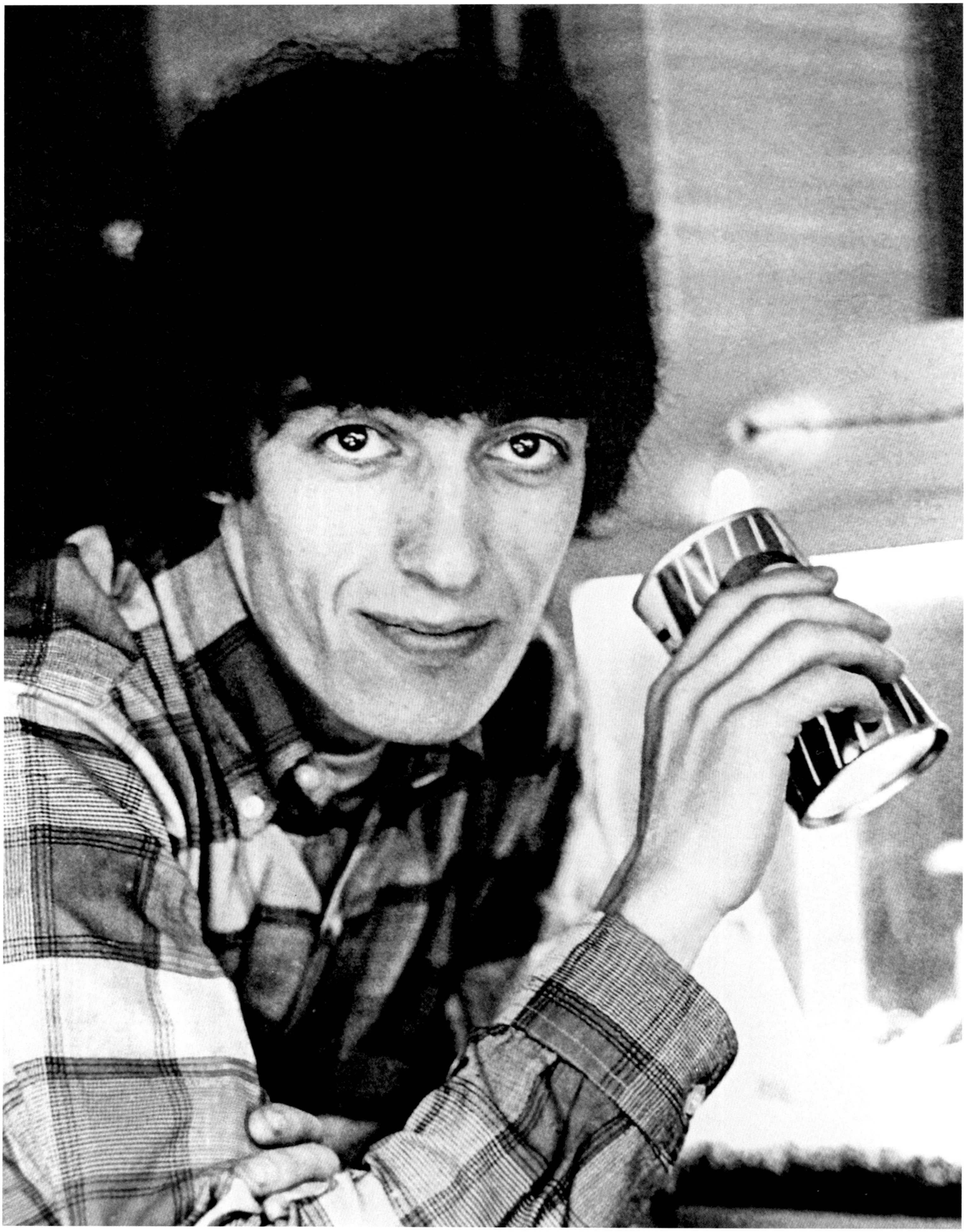

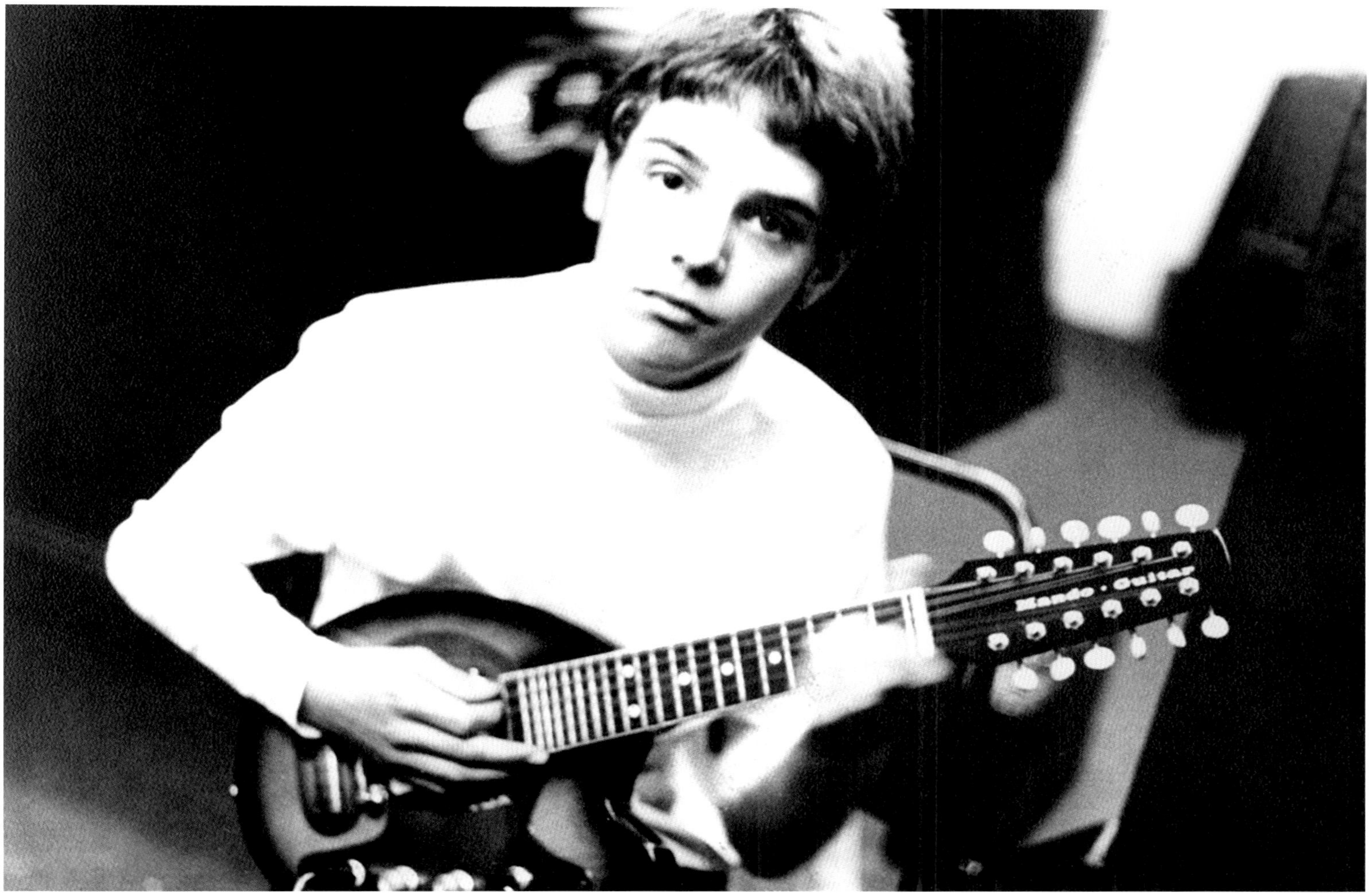

I took the young 16-year-old Peter Frampton into the Pye recording studio in London to record with the band Moon's Train, and captured this shot of him playing my Vox Mando Guitar – 7 September 1966.
Left: Me at our home, The Oaks, on the Keston Park Estate in Keston, Kent – September 1966.

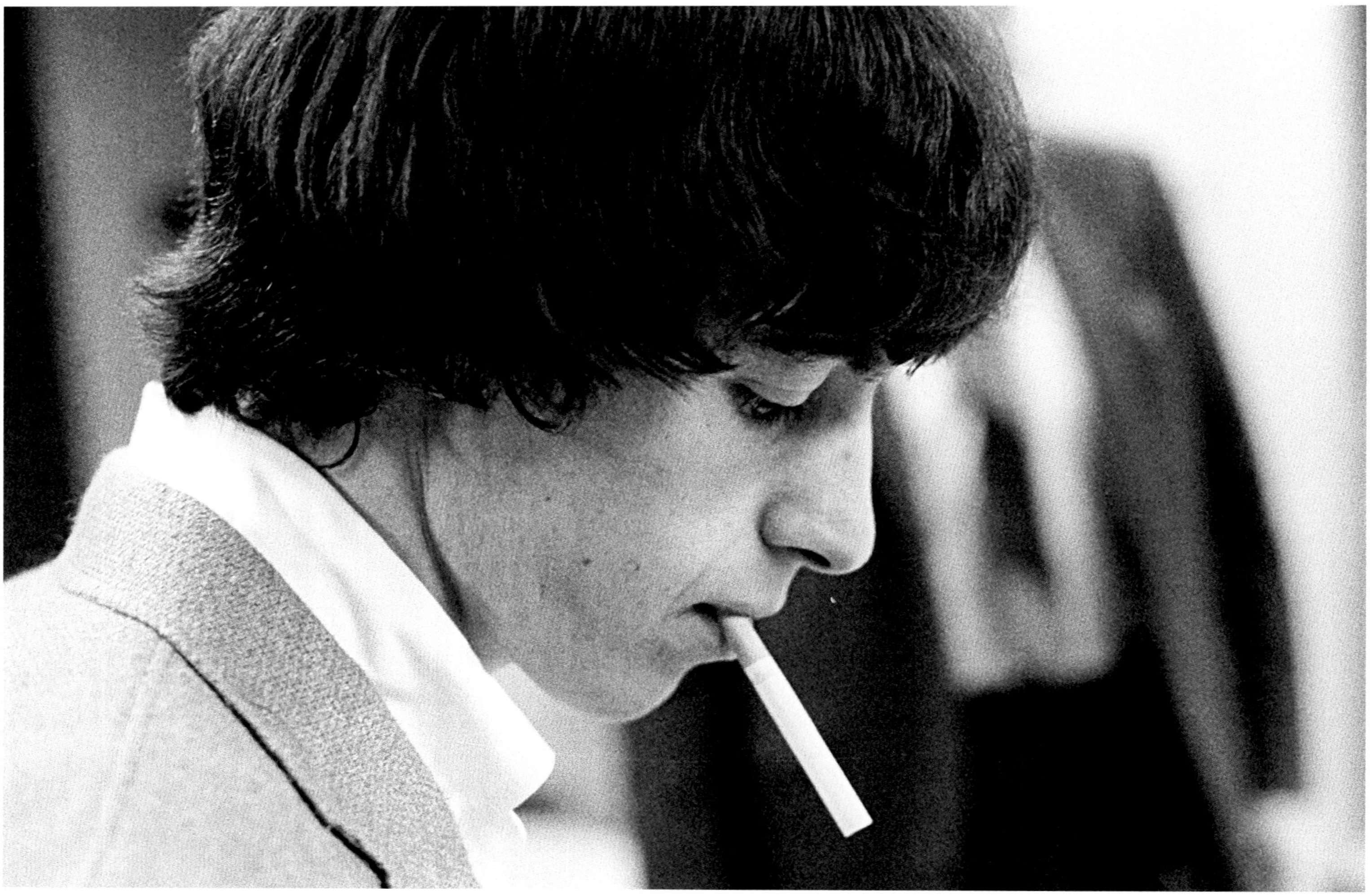

Me in the dressing room with a cigarette.
Right: Keith at the microphone; both photographs taken at Olympic Studios, Barnes – October 1966.
Following pages: Mick tidying vocals on the live recordings from the UK Tour – October 1966. Brian looks on.

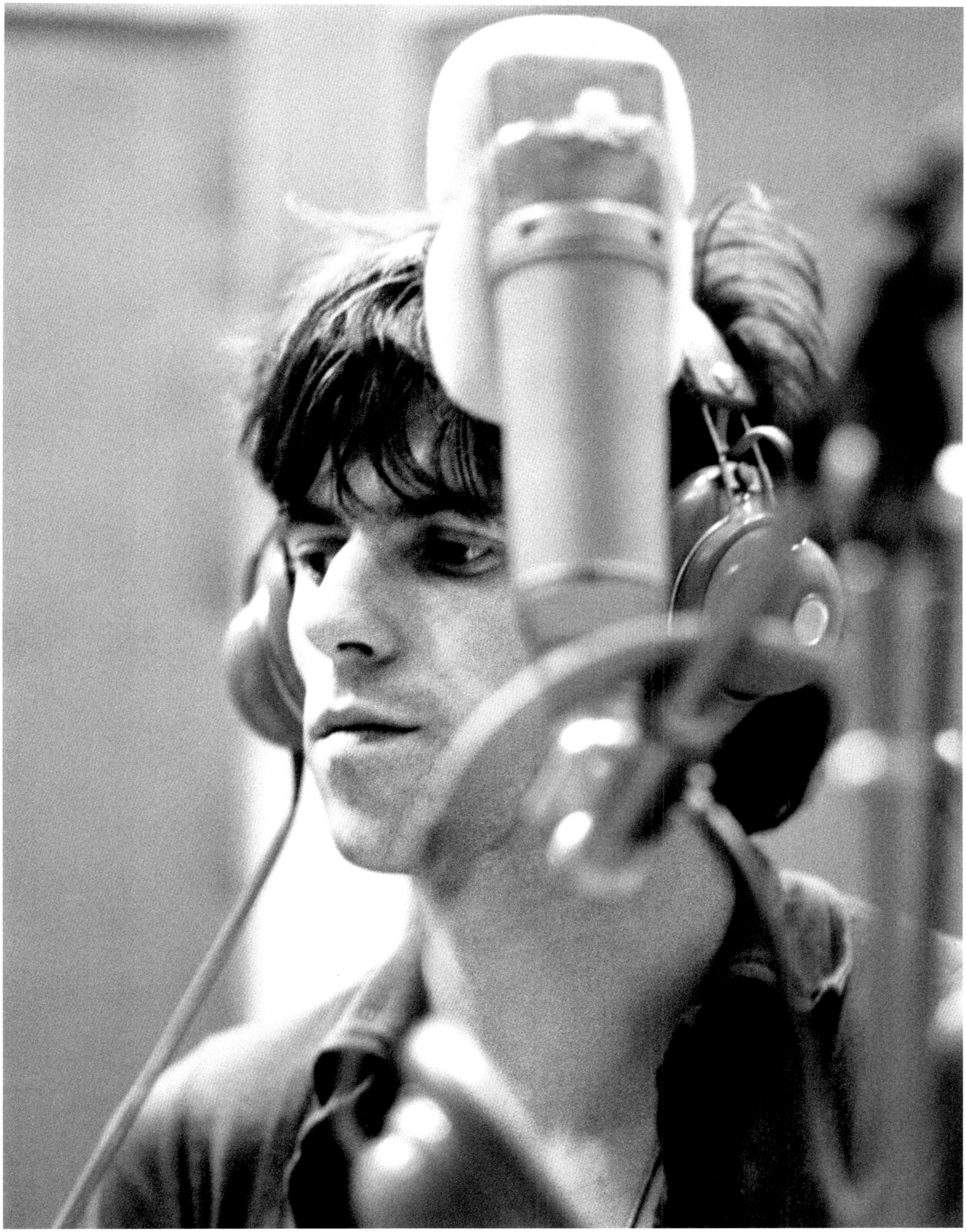

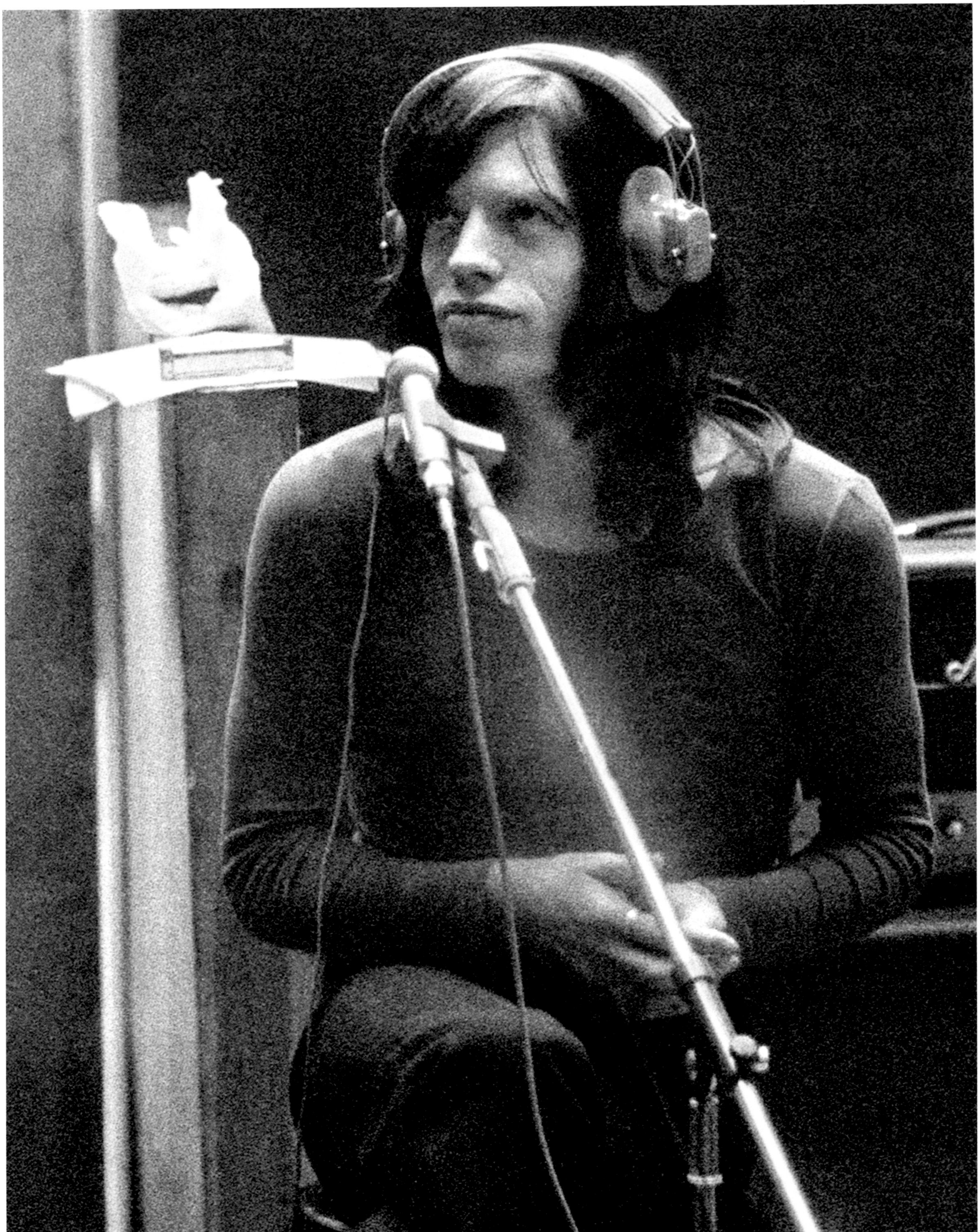

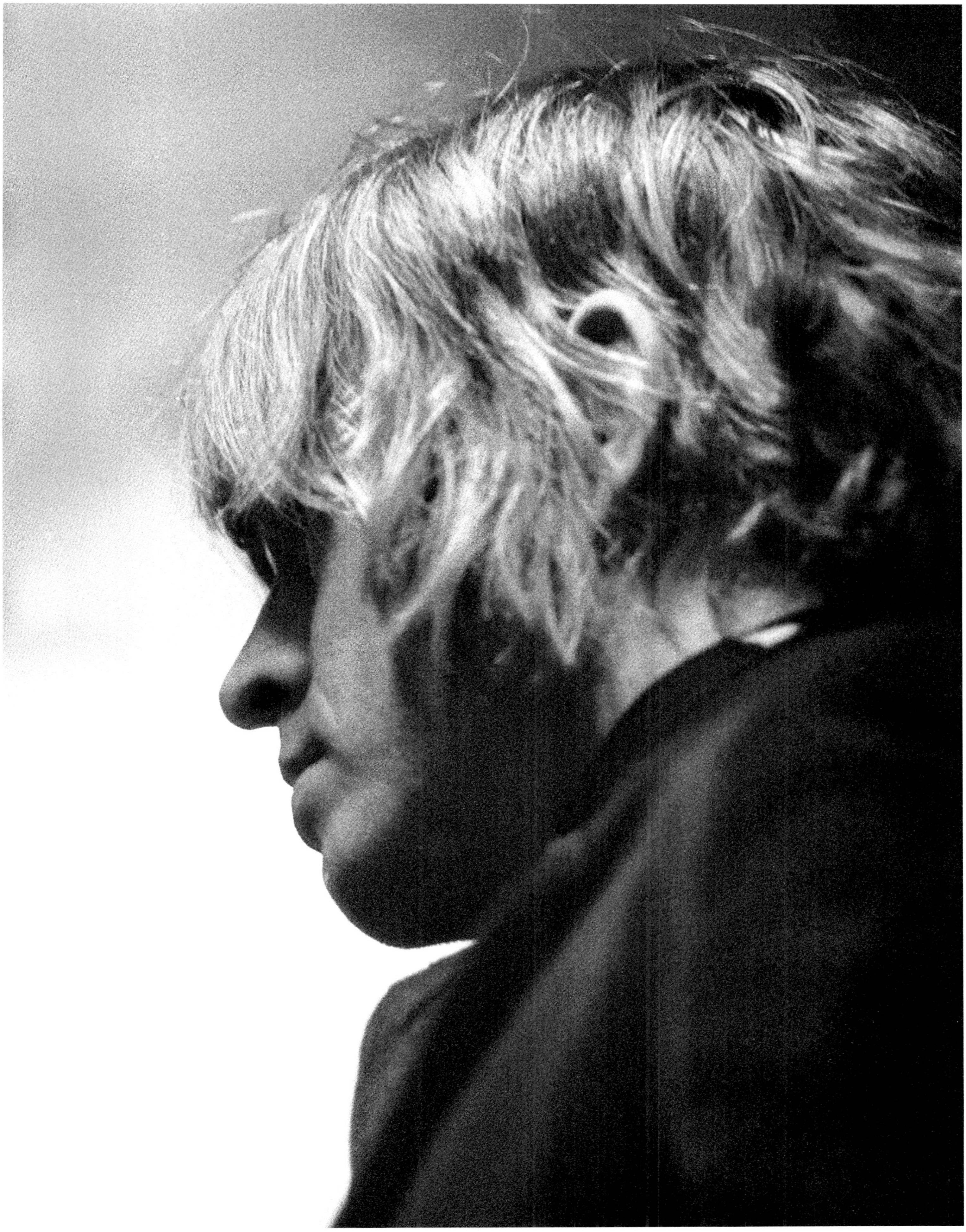

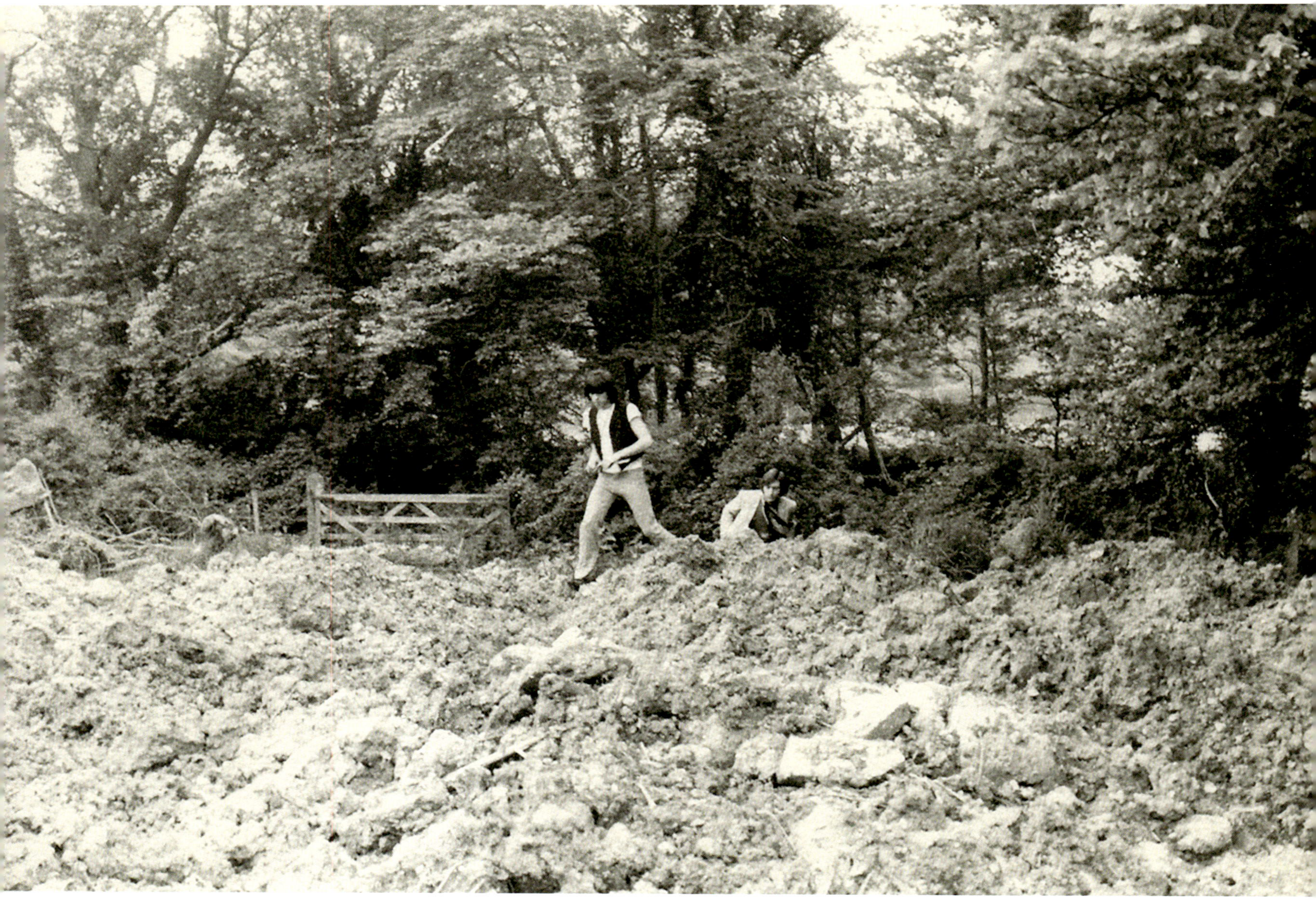

Keith and Charlie returning from a toilet break across a badly ploughed field, during our tour of England in October 1966.

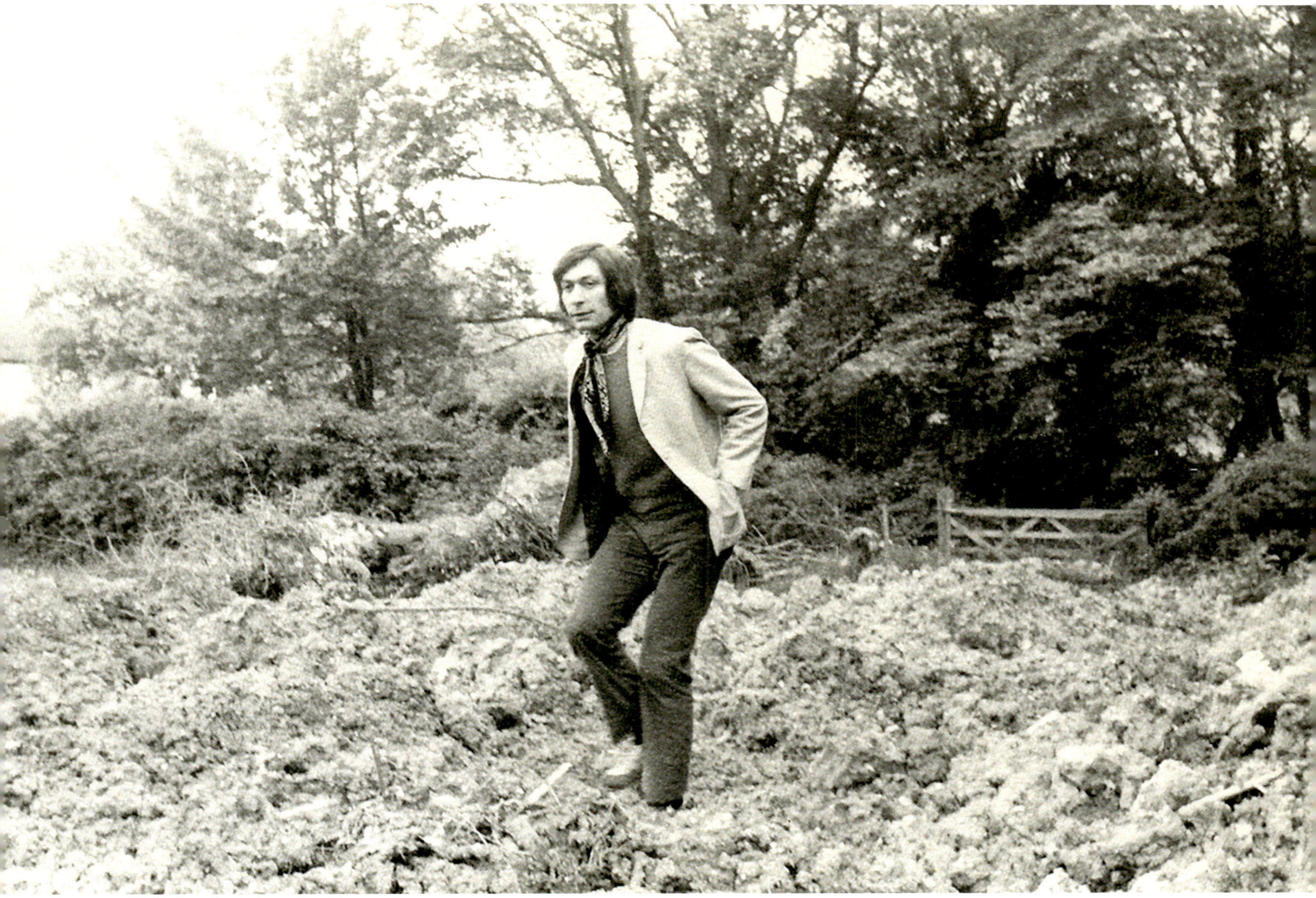

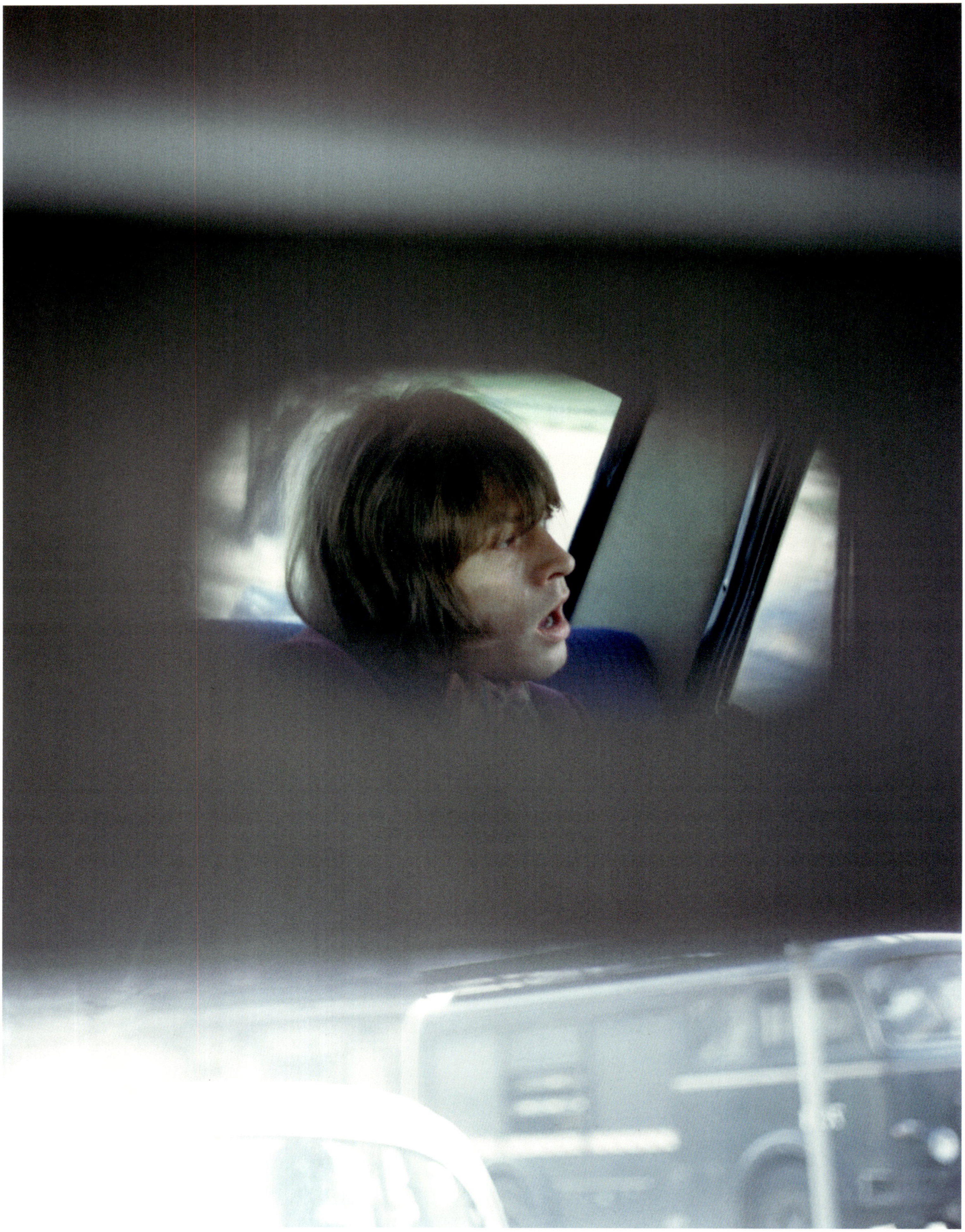

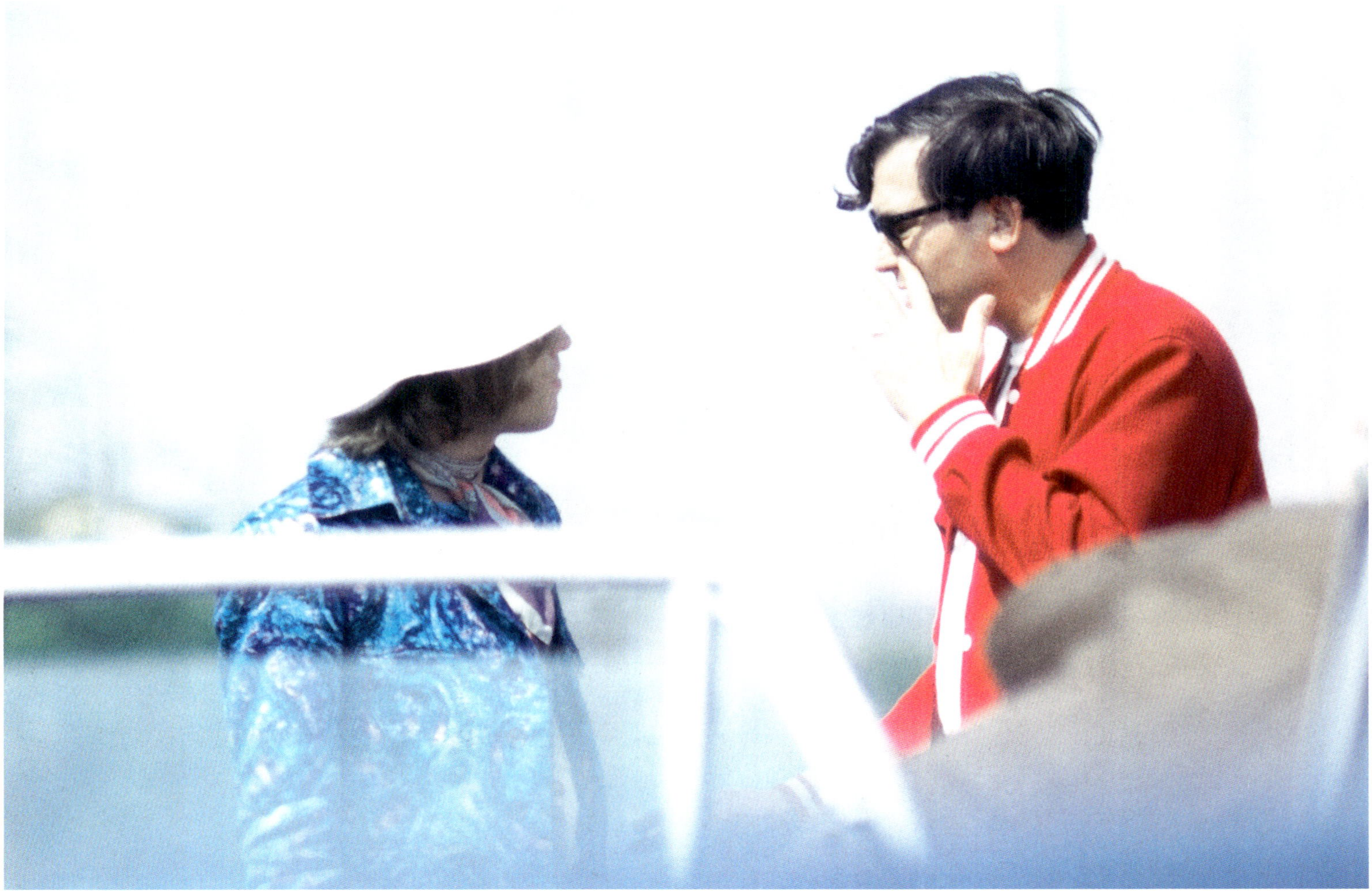

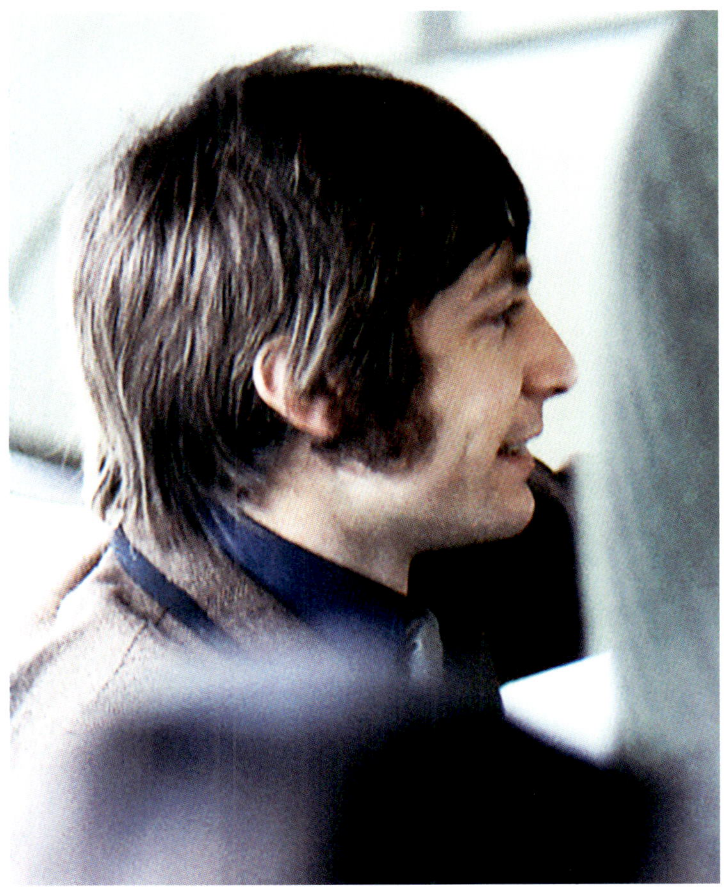

Left: Brian and I were travelling in the back of a chauffeured car on the way to our concert at the Palazzo dello Sport in Milan, Italy, when I saw him in the driver's mirror, and took this very unusual photo – 8 April 1967.
Above: Brian talking with Tom Keylock after a car stop on the way to our concert in Bologna, Italy – 5 April 1967.
Right: Charlie leaving Gothenberg, Sweden, in the airport bus to the plane for our flight to Hamburg, Germany – 28 March 1967.

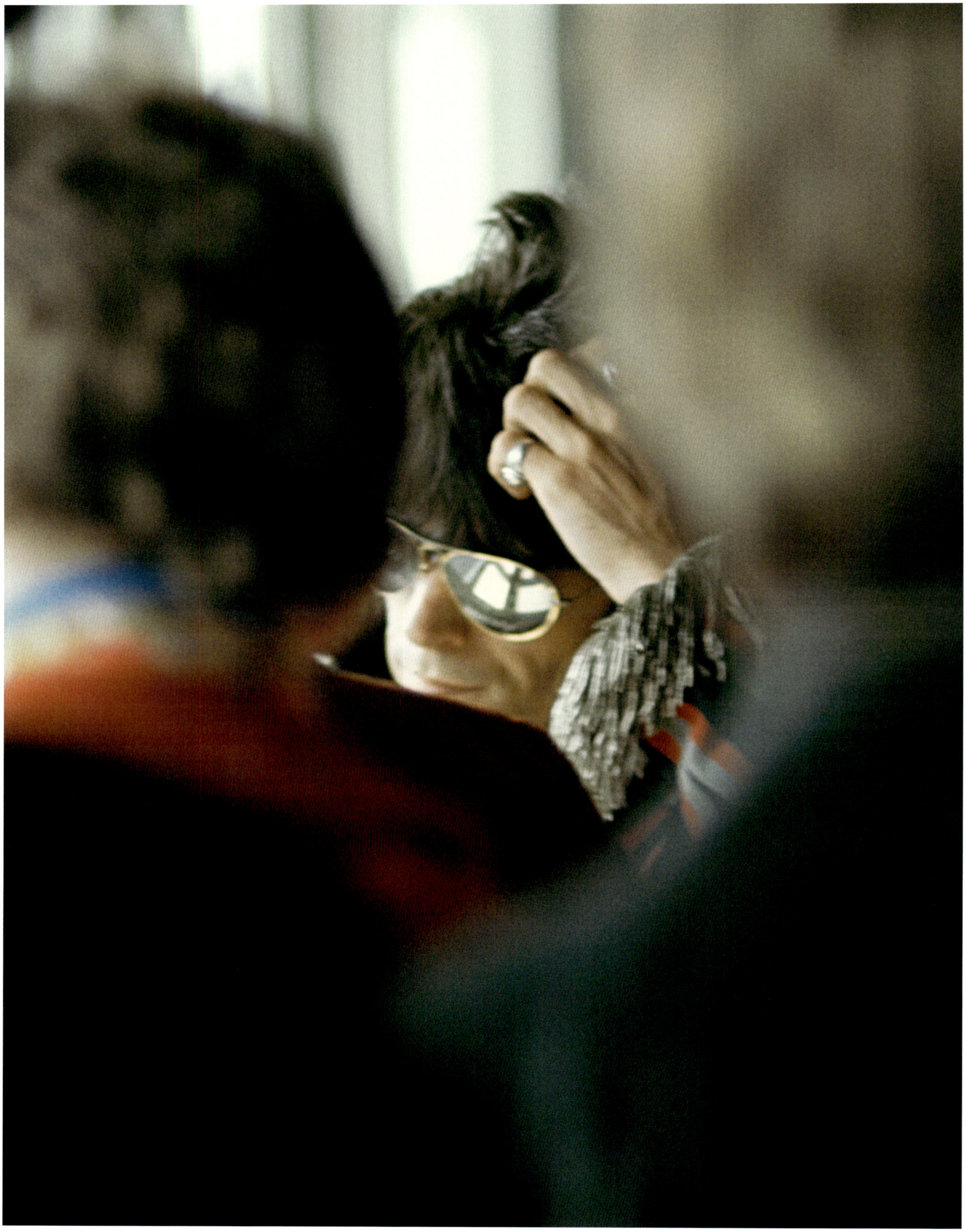

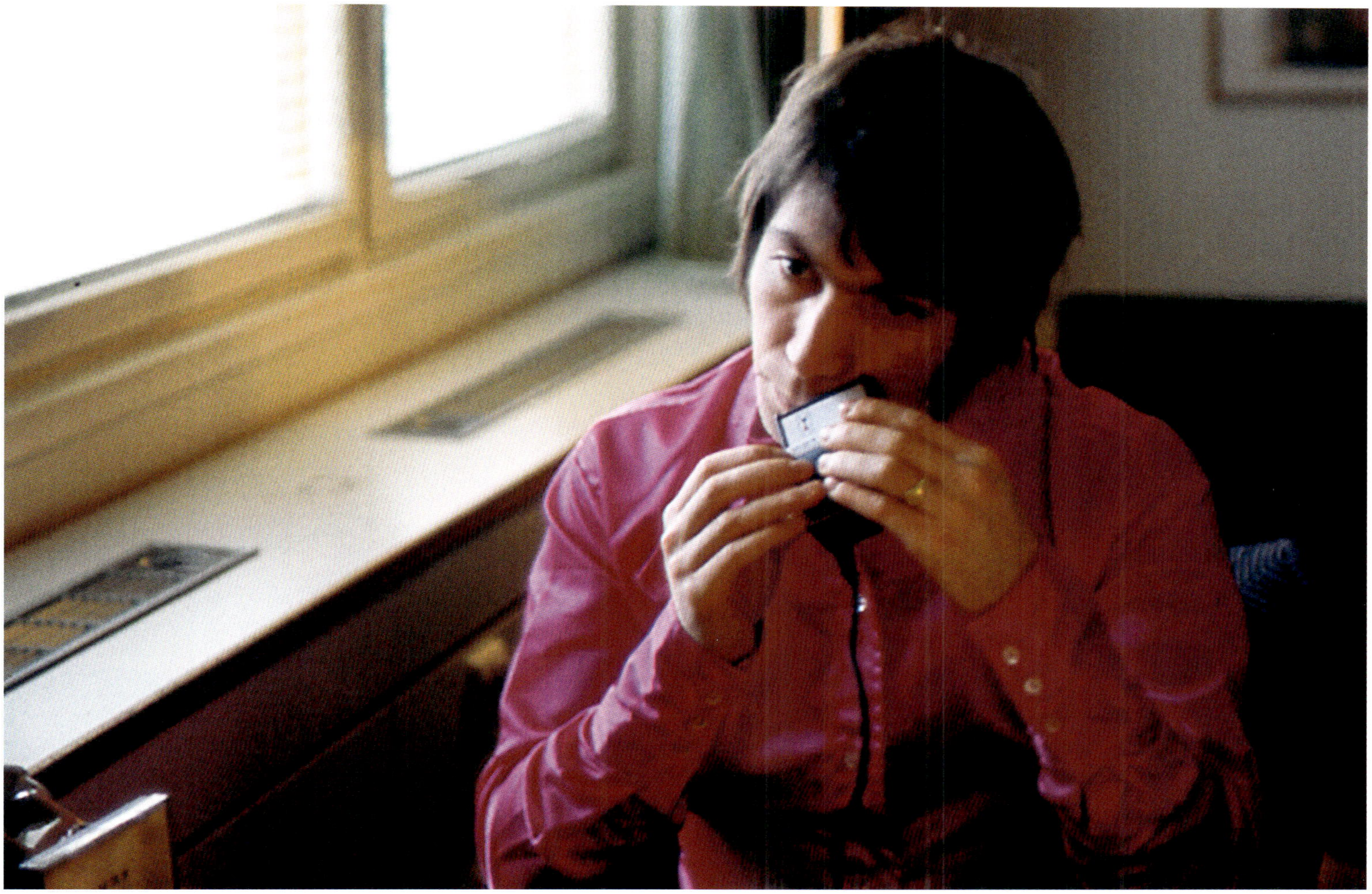

Charlie shaving in the dressing room in Bremen, Germany, gaudily dressed in a bright rose-coloured shirt – 29 March 1967. **Left:** Keith amongst other passengers on the airport bus to board our flight to Hamburg – 28 March 1967.

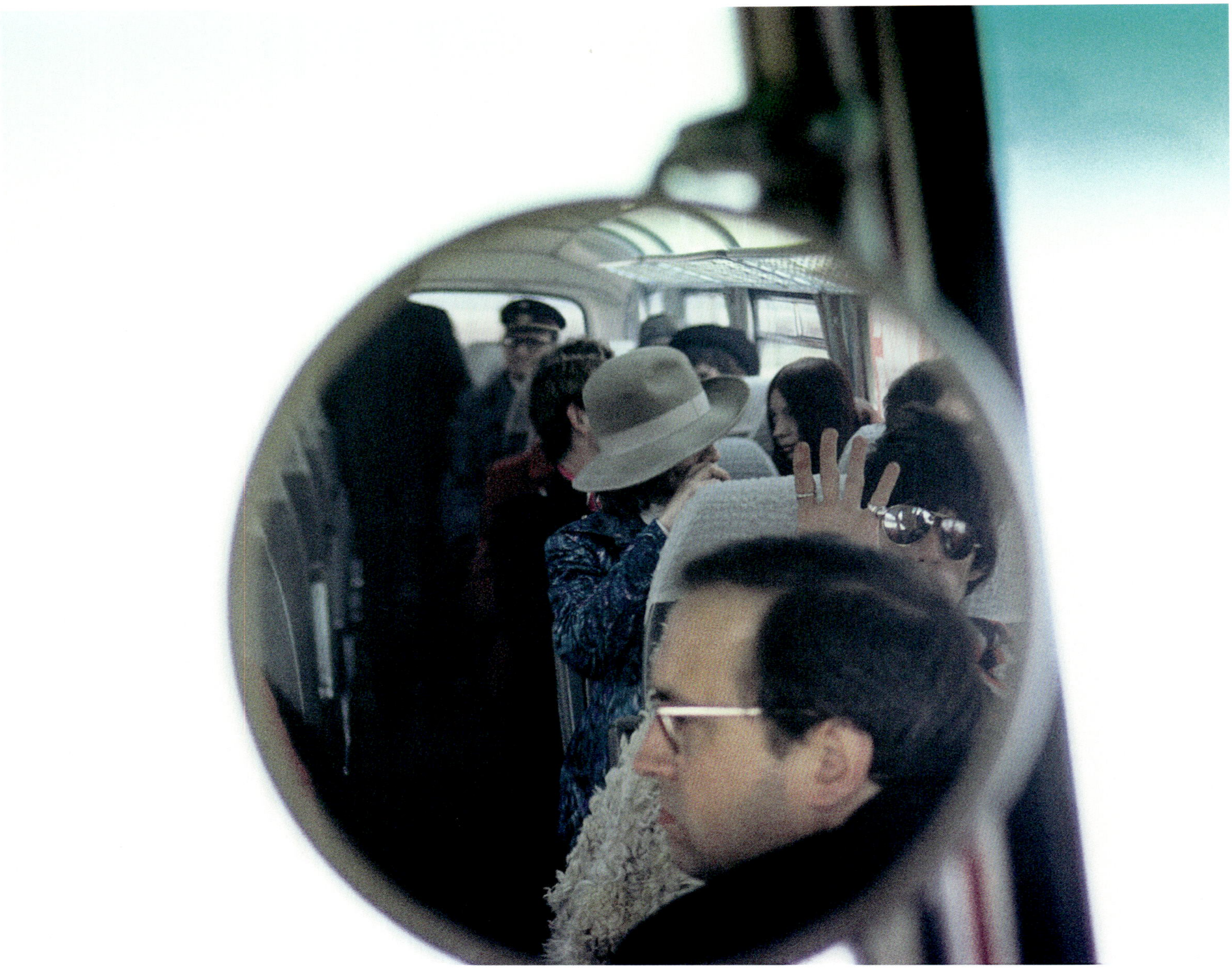

Shot of the Stones and other passengers through the airport bus wing mirror in Vienna, Austria – 2 April 1967.
Right: Mick and Brian amongst other passengers on that same bus.

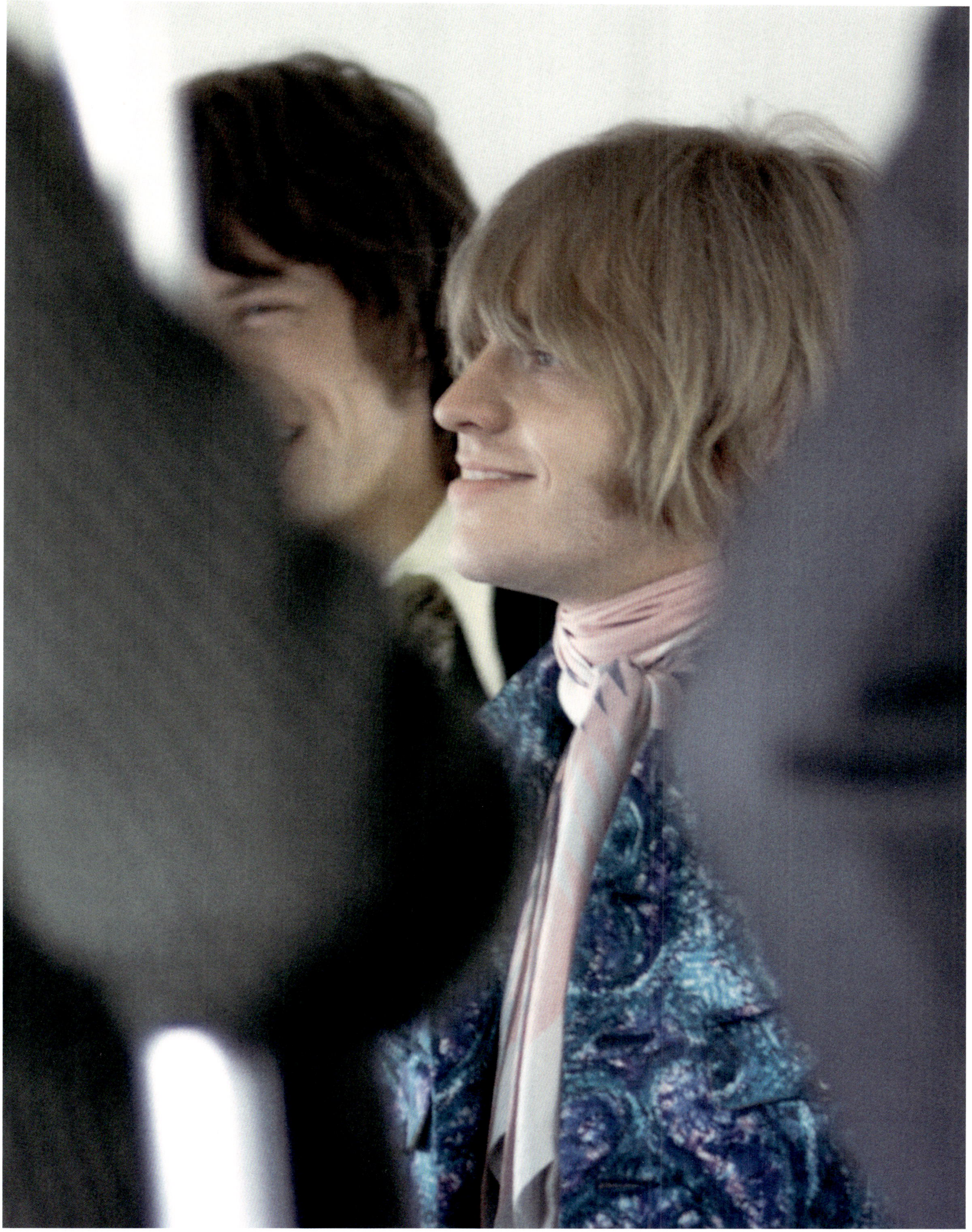

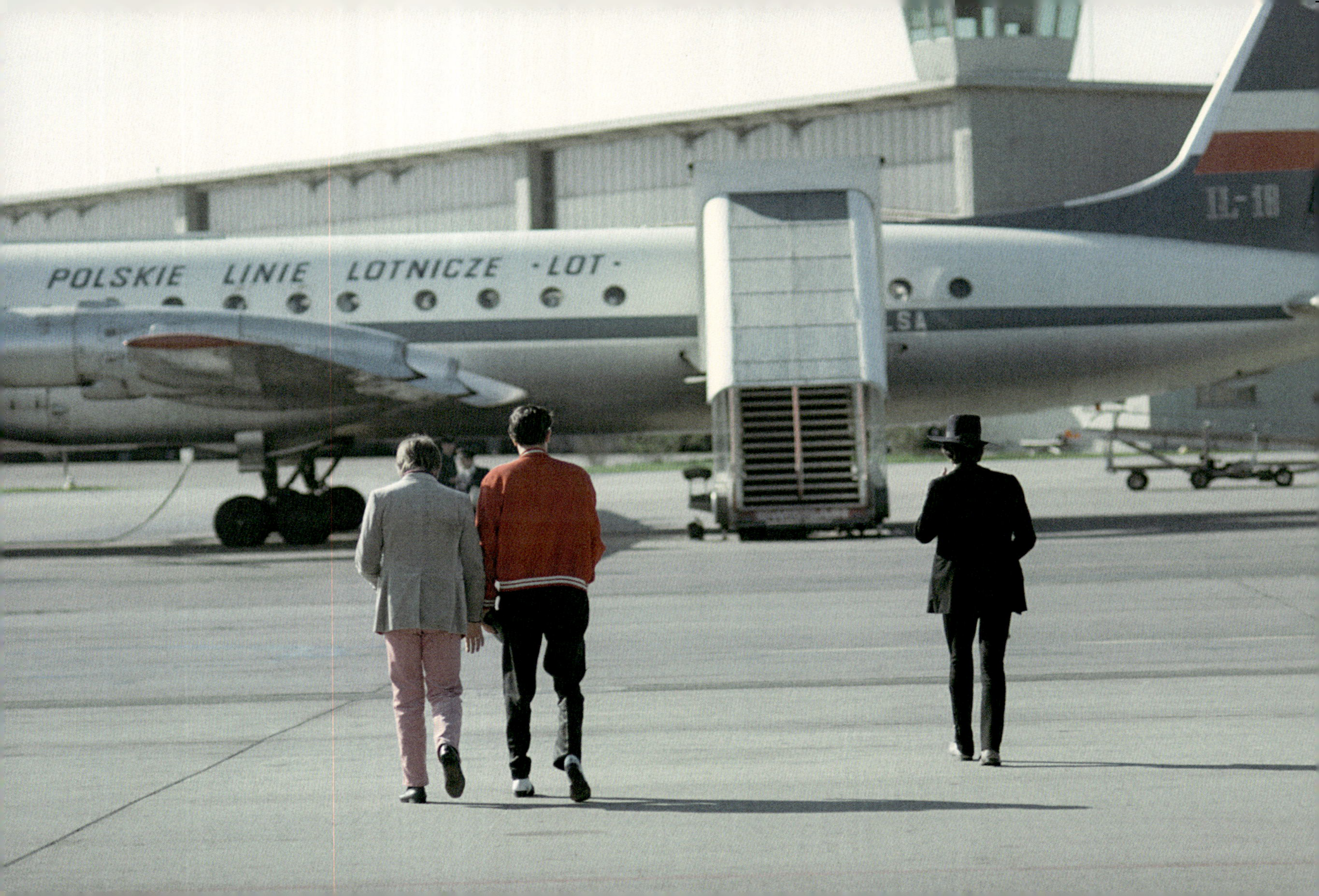
POLSKIE LINIE LOTNICZE -LOT-
IL-18

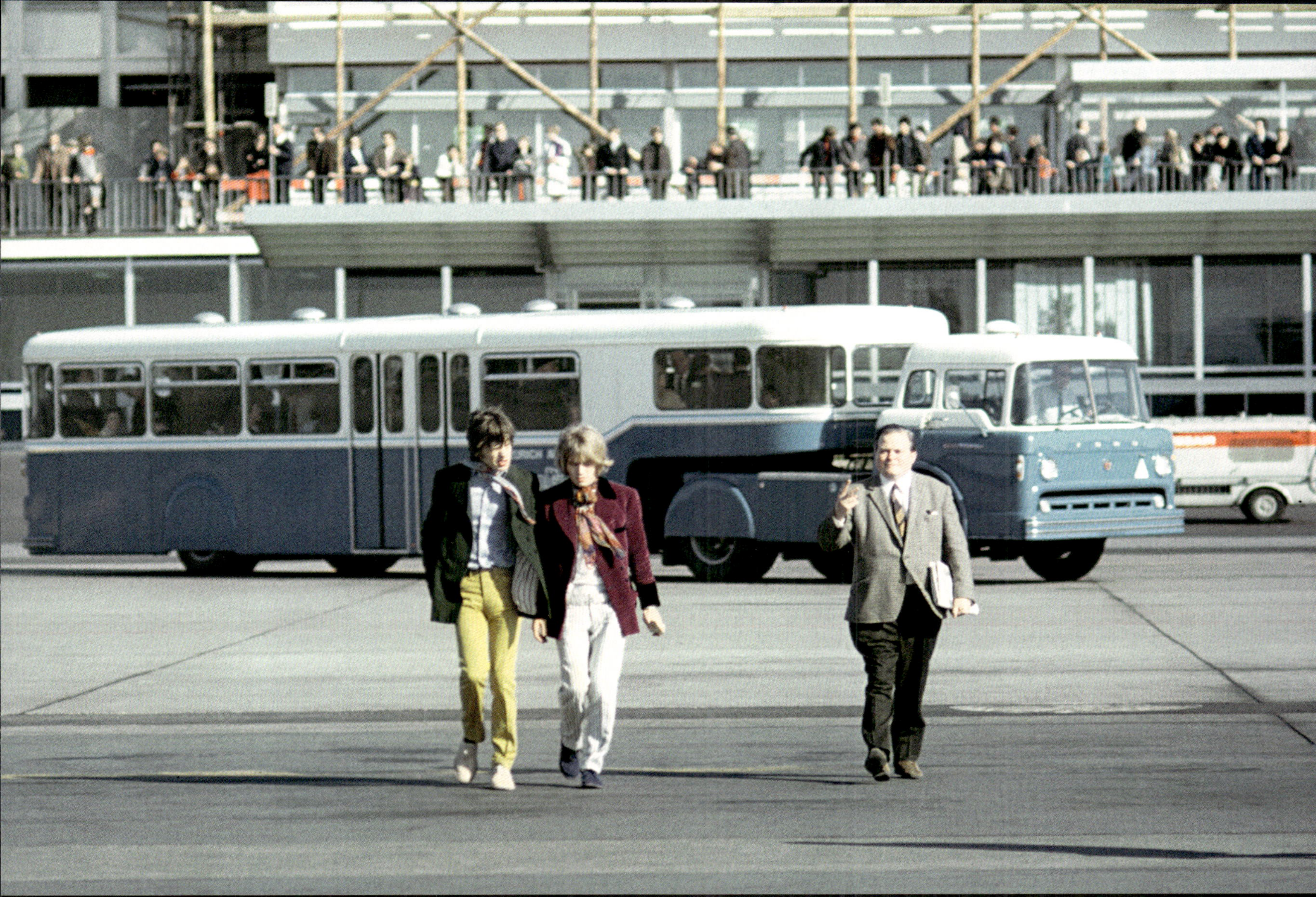

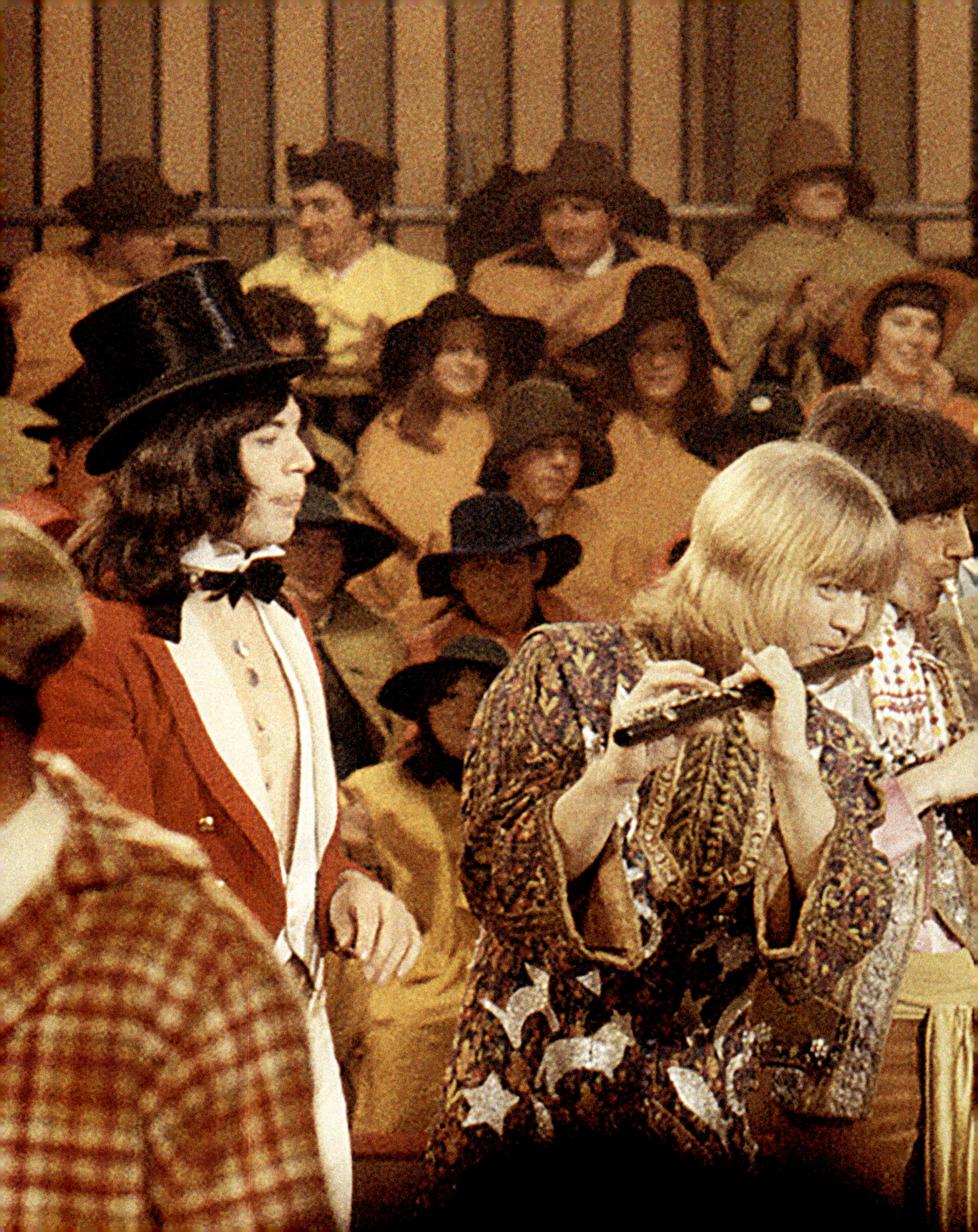

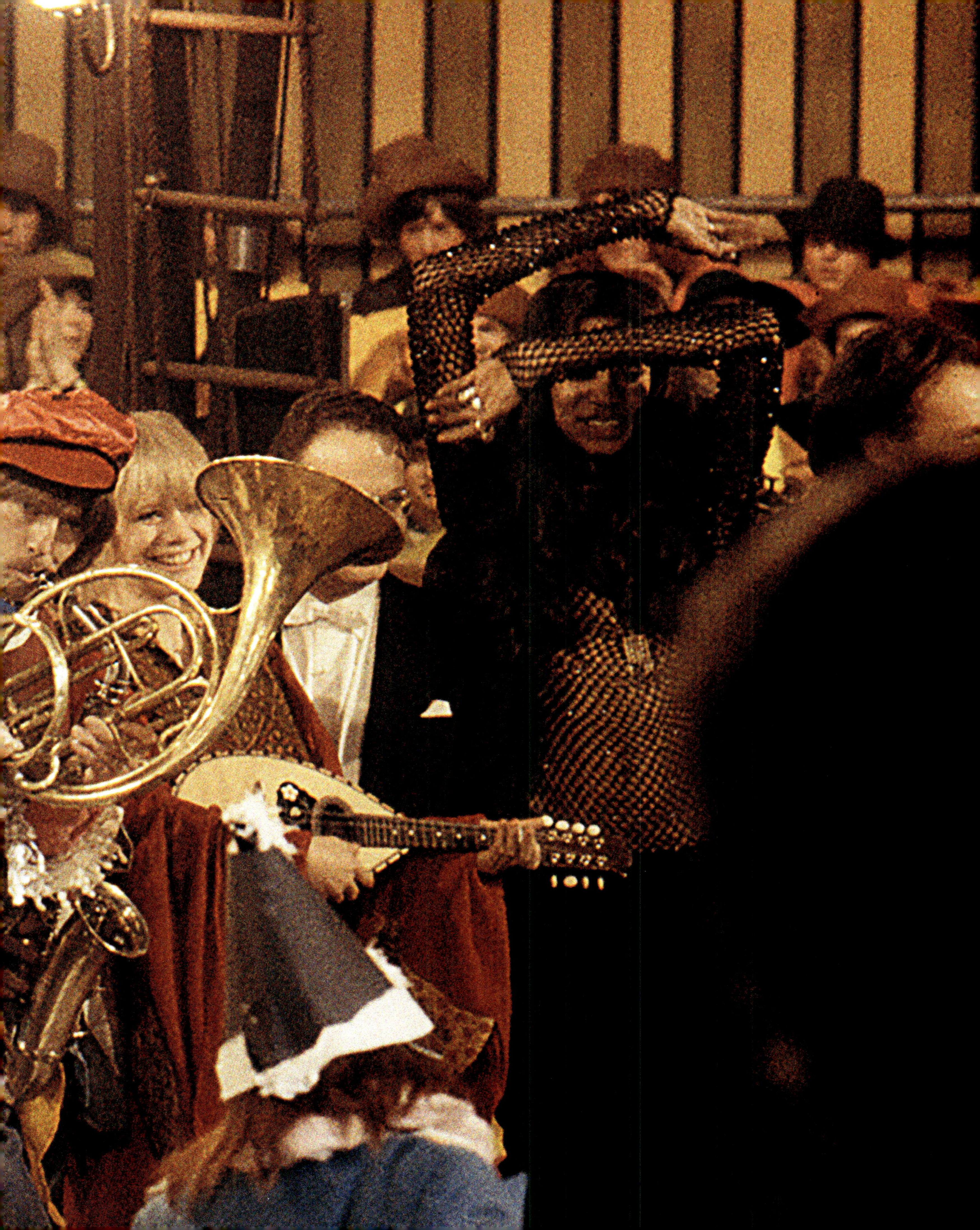

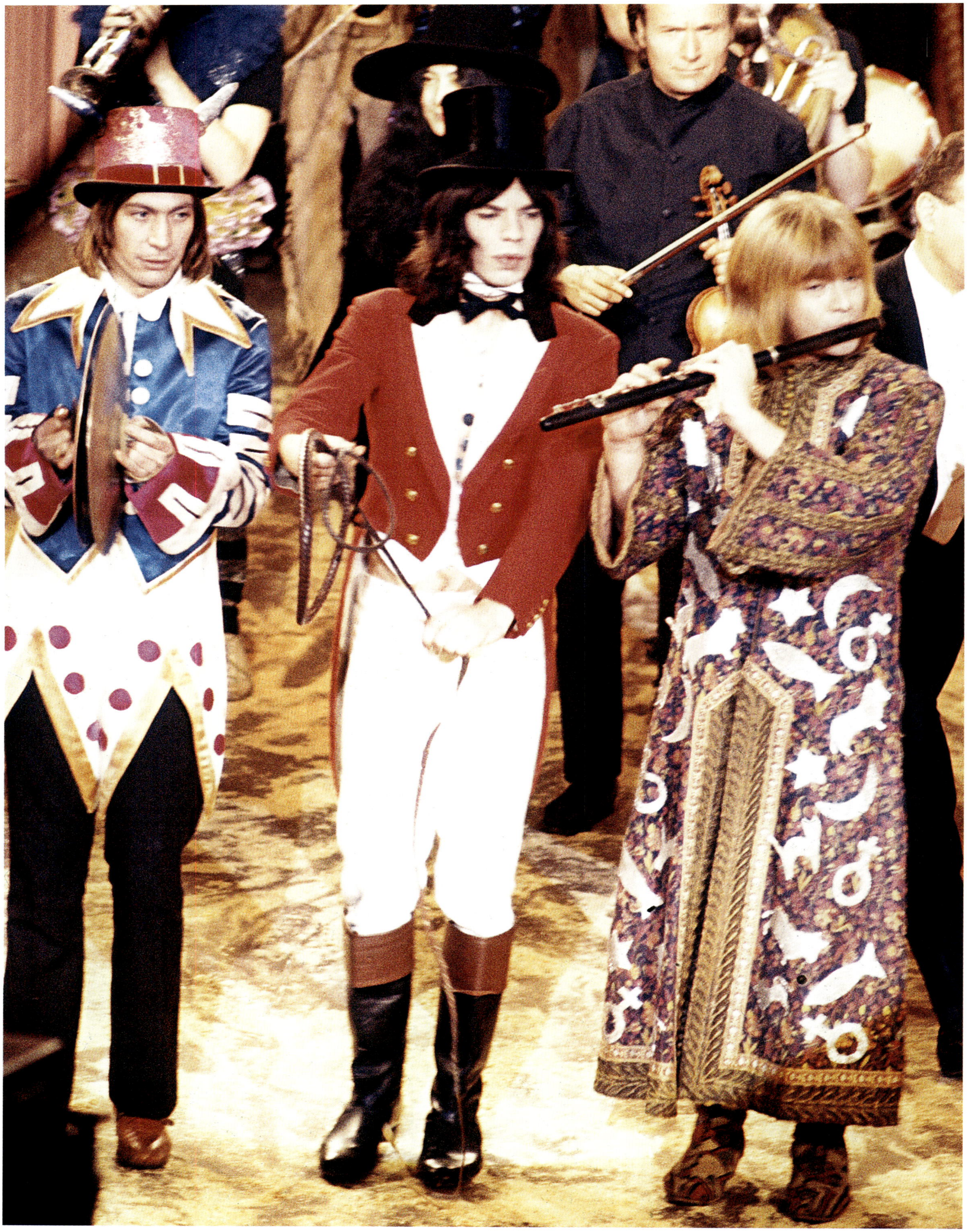

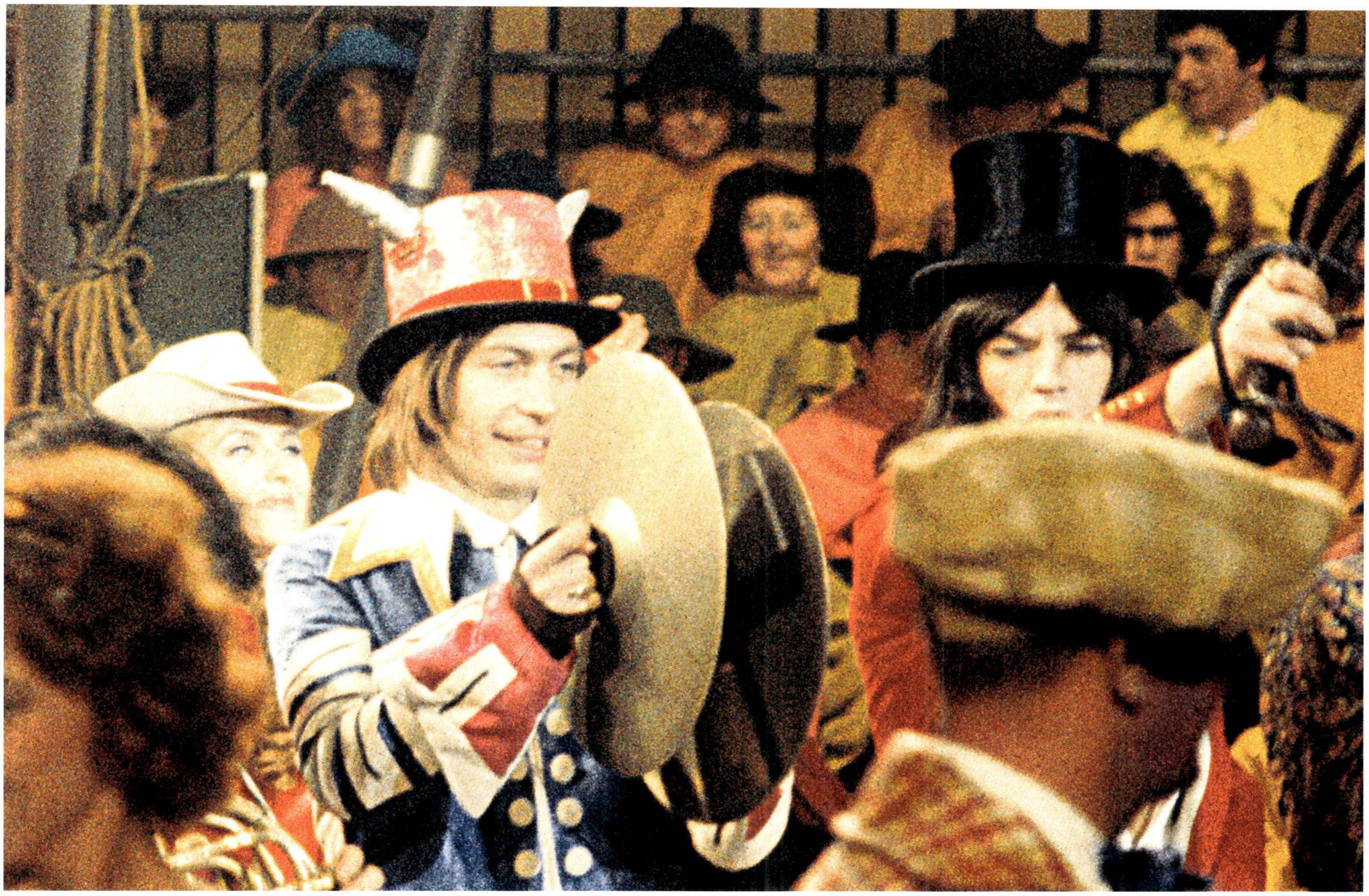

Charlie (with cymbals) and Mick, at the Rock and Roll Circus filming – 10 December 1968.
Left: Charlie, Mick and Brian – as above.
Previous pages: Mick, Brian, me, Eric Clapton, Marianne Faithfull, pianist Julius Katchen, and Donyale Luna – as above.
Following pages: Stones in cloaks (Charlie sitting) – as above.

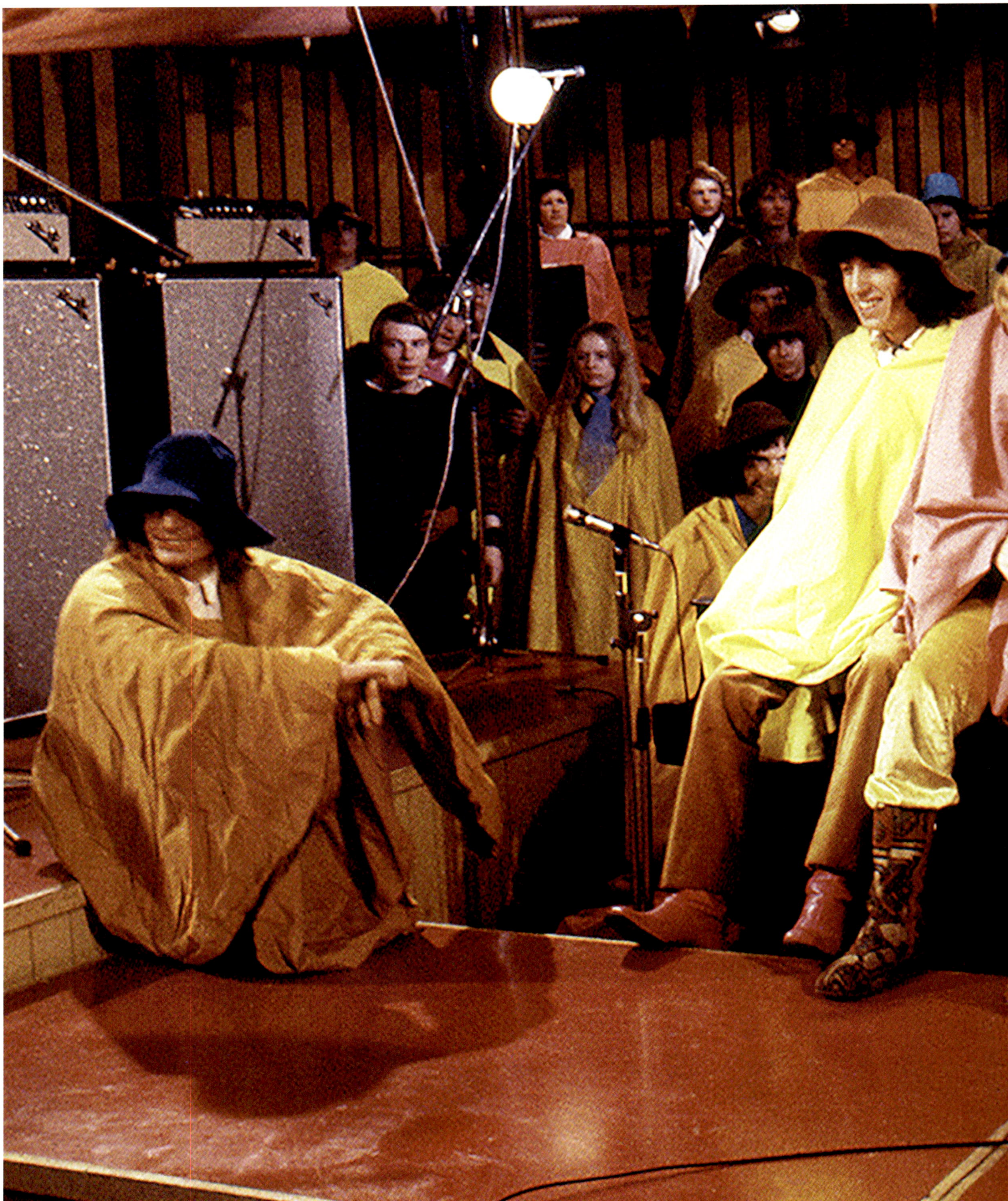

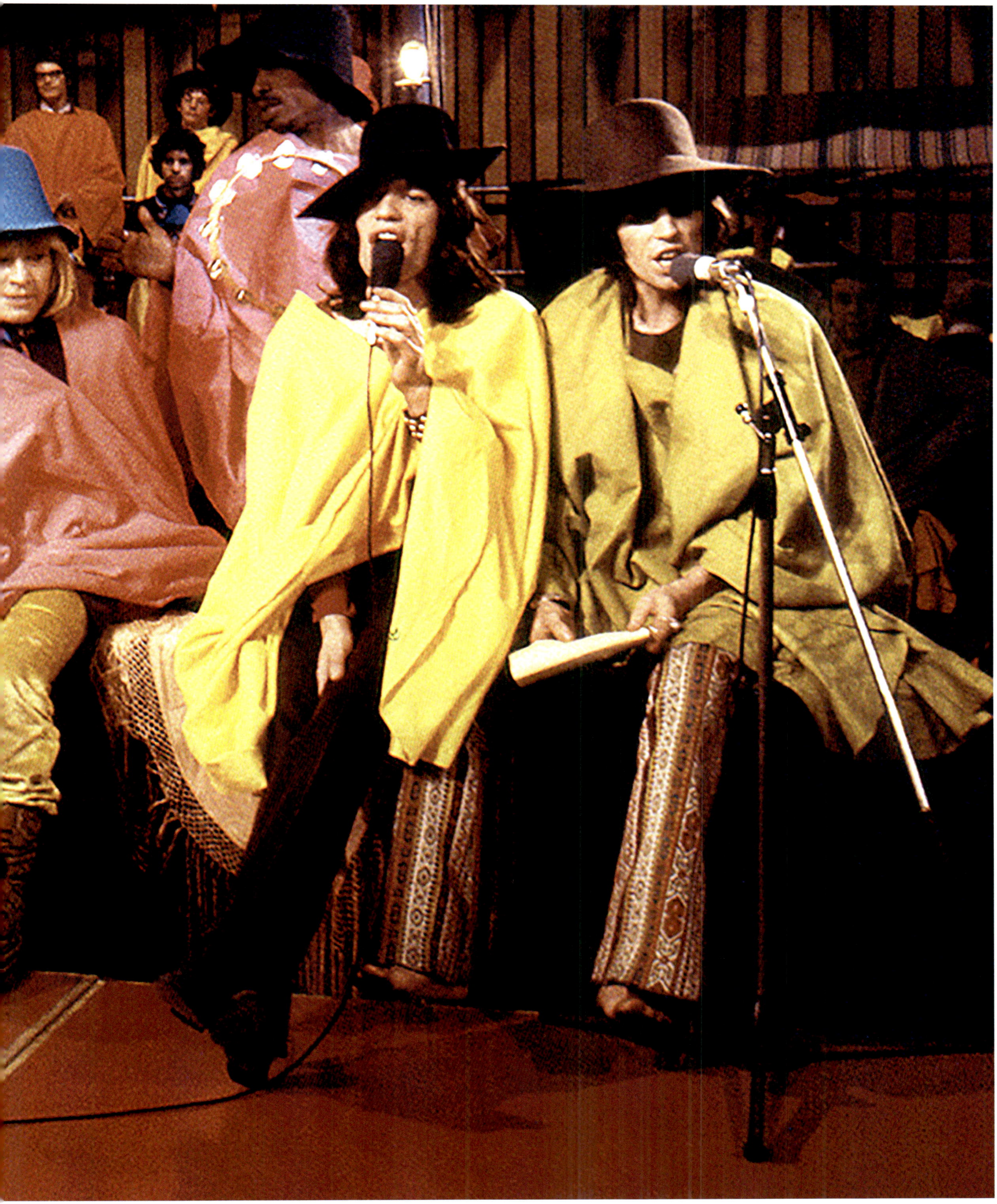

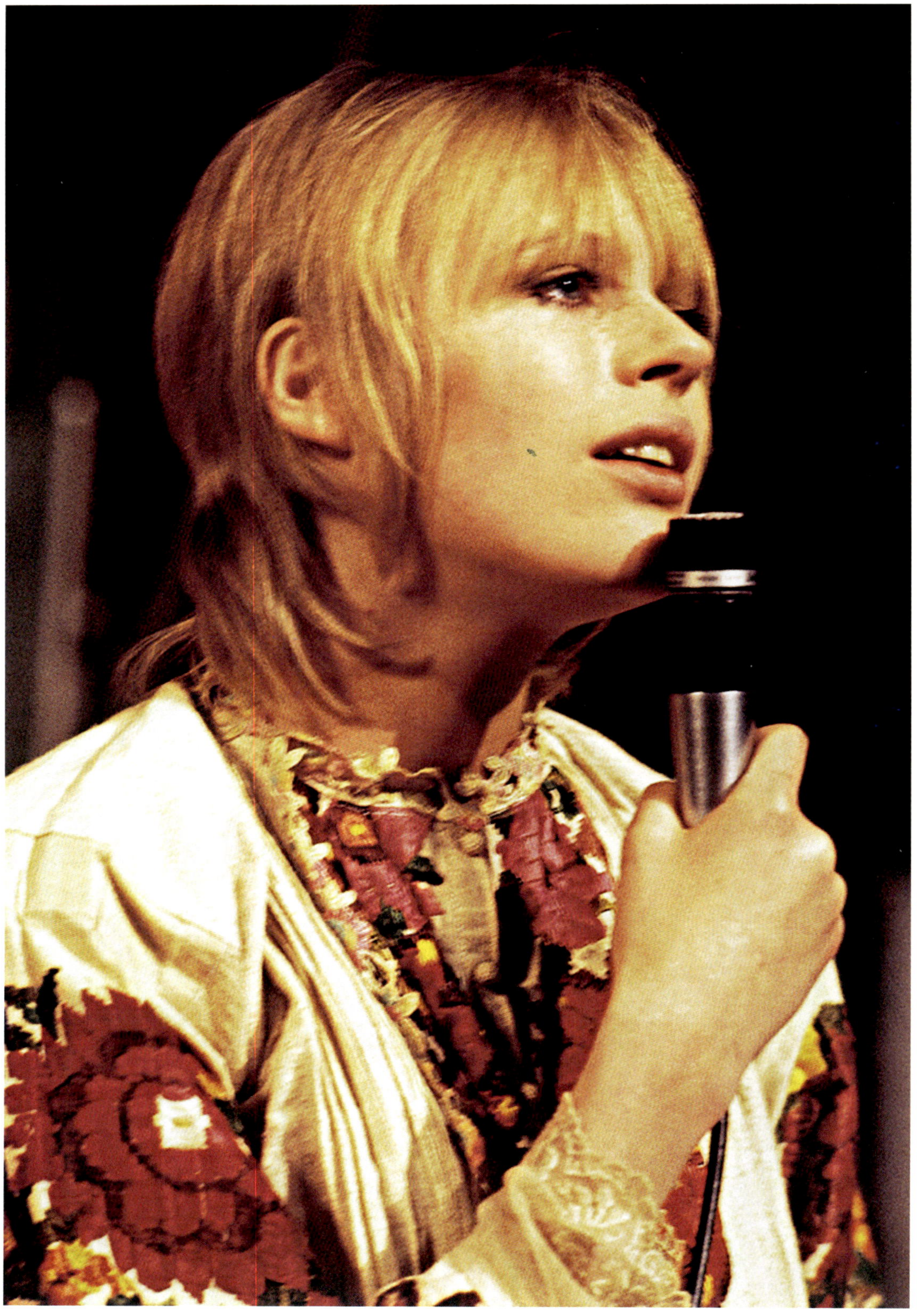

Marianne Faithfull singing at the filming of the Rock and Roll Circus – 10 December 1968.

Right: Marianne singing, in a different outfit – as above.

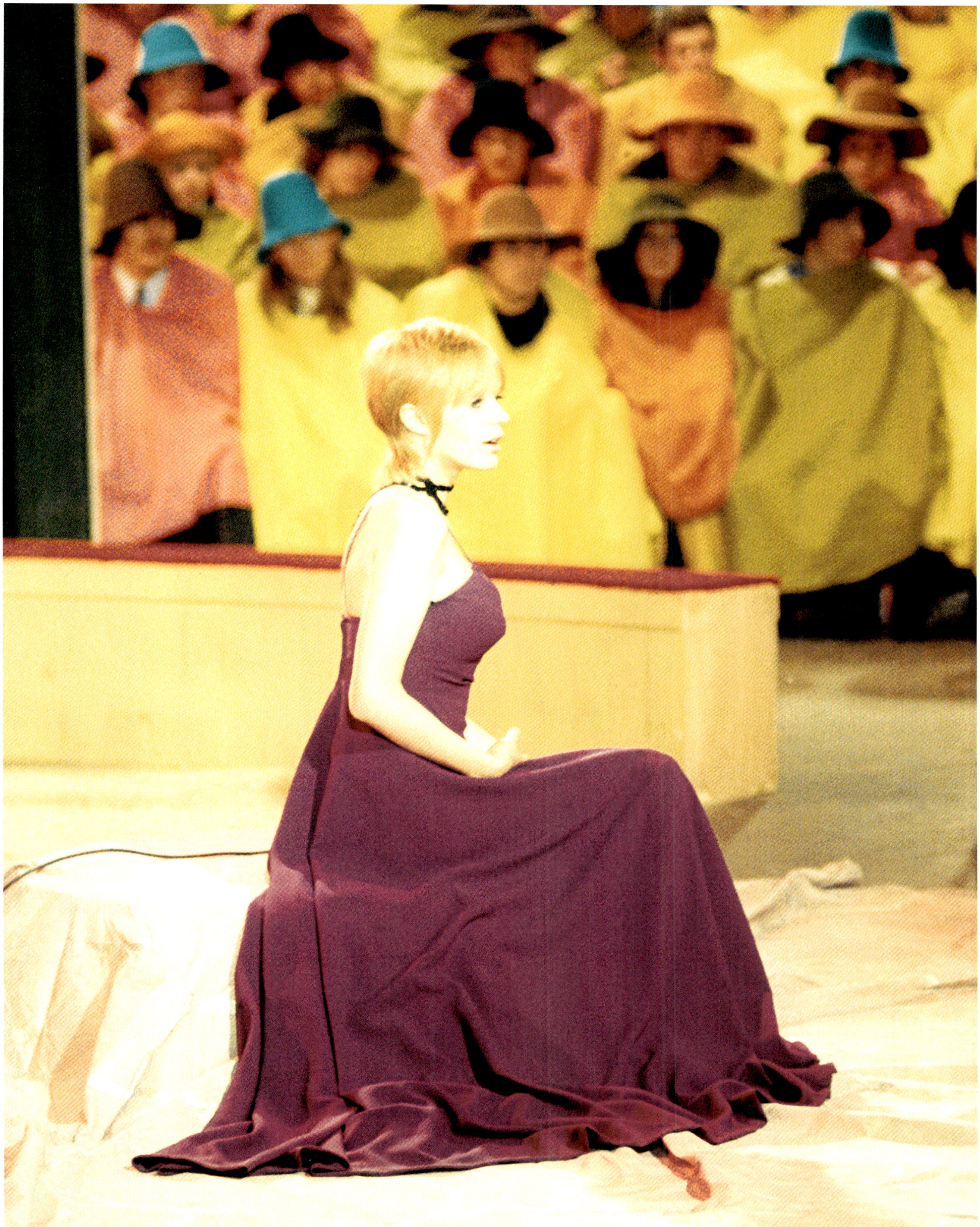

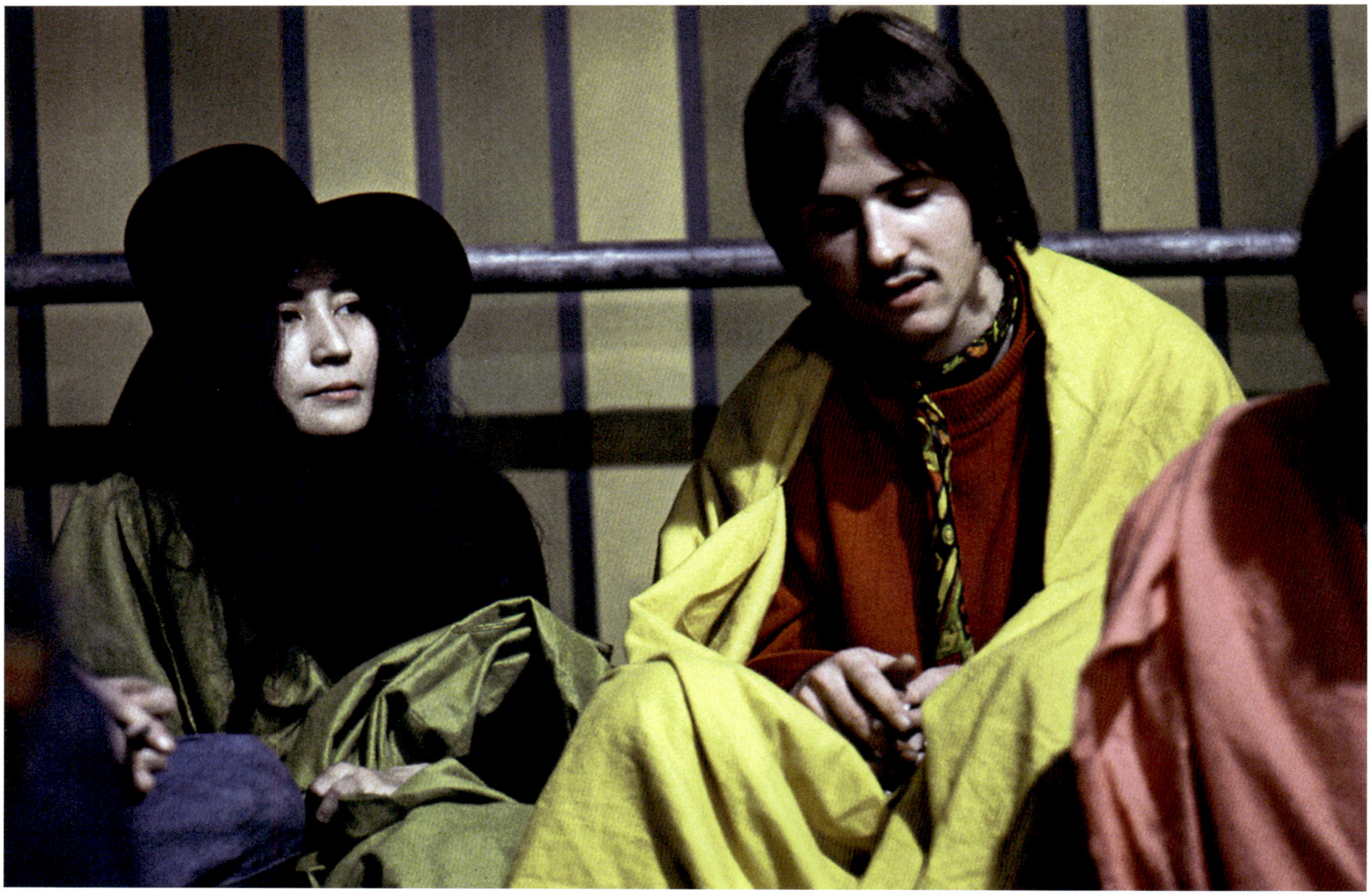

Yoko Ono sitting next to a guest at the filming of the Rock and Roll Circus – 10 December 1968.
Right: John Lennon smoking and contemplating – as above.

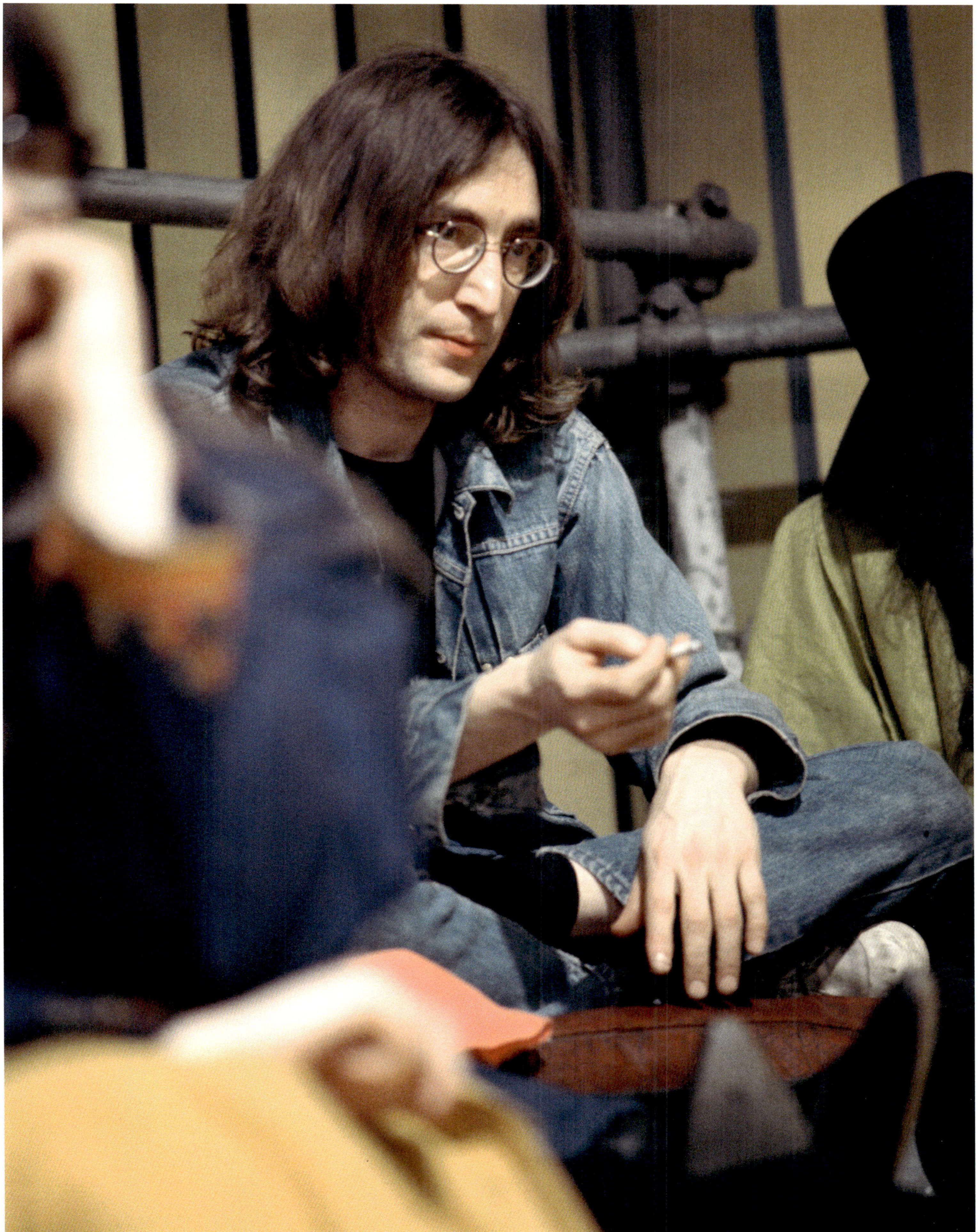

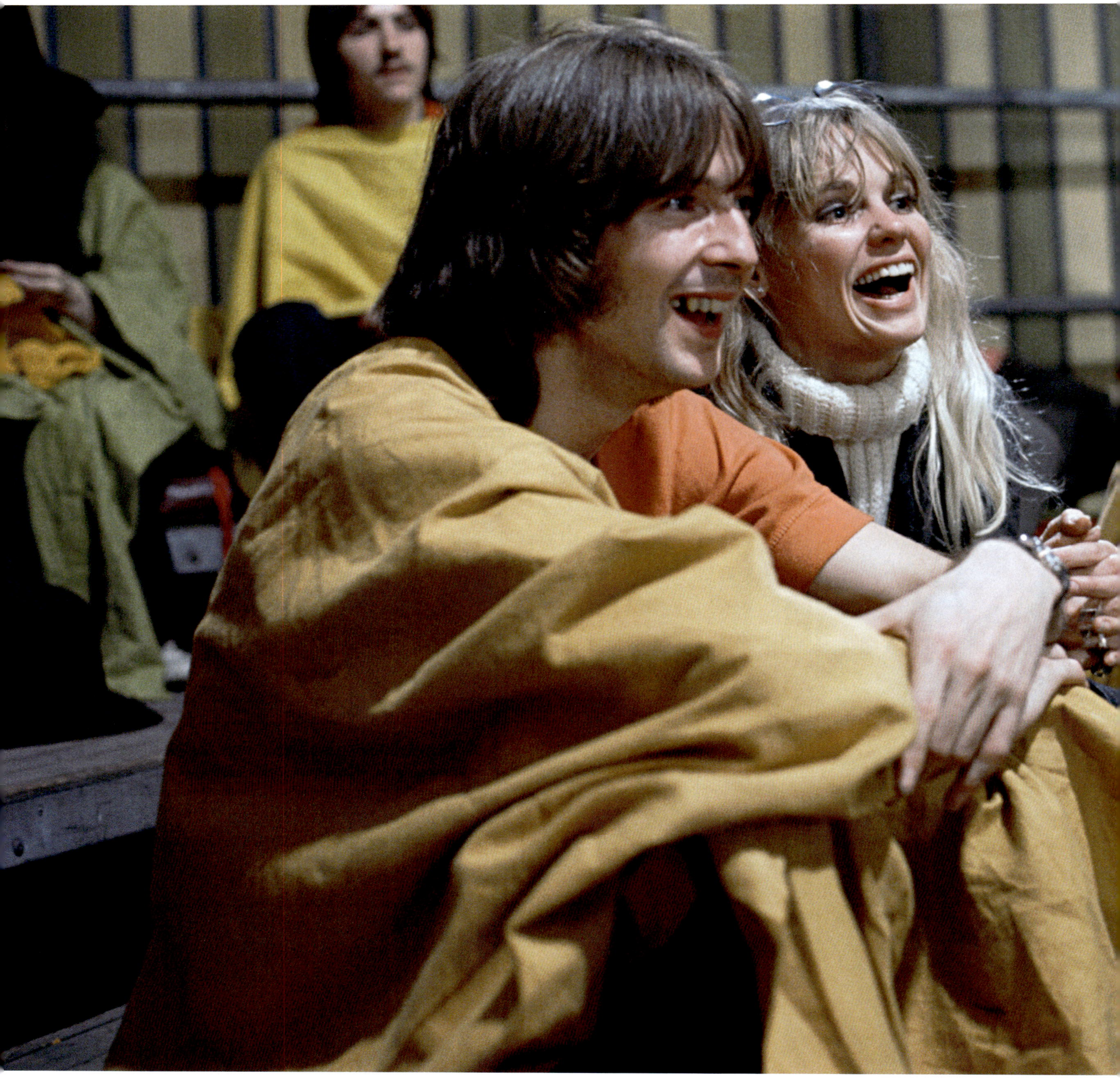

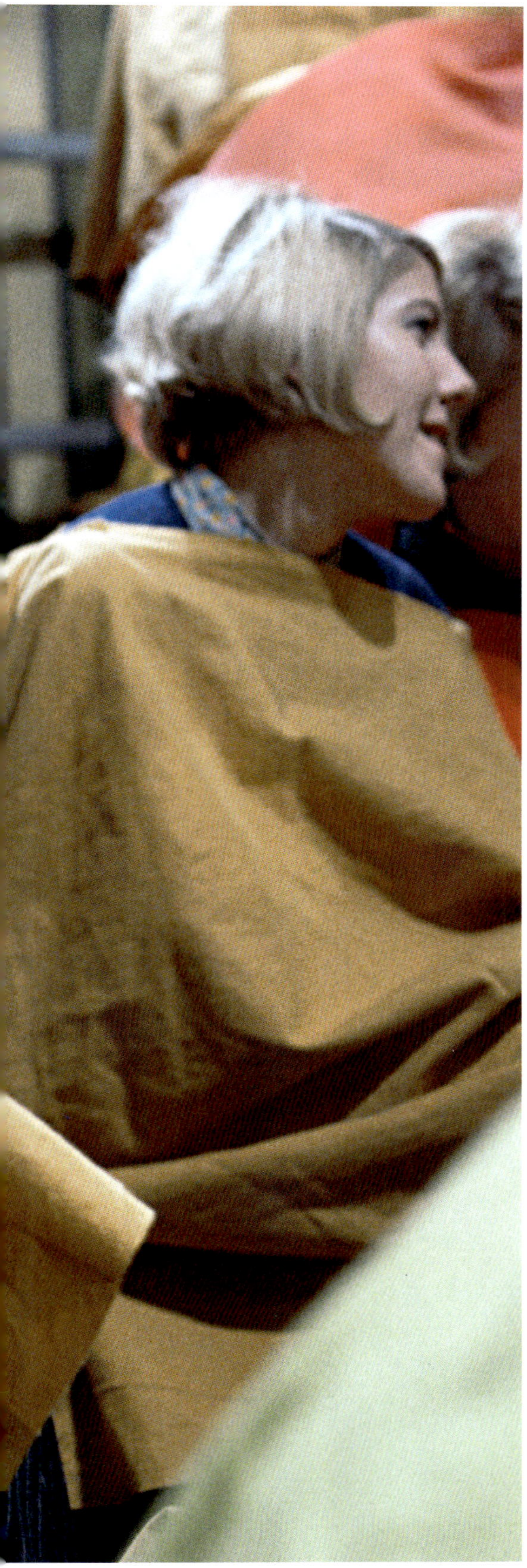

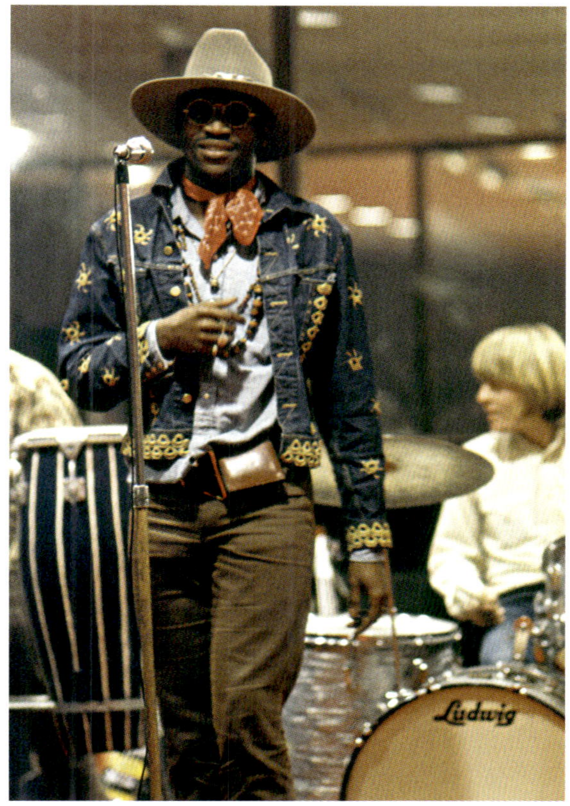

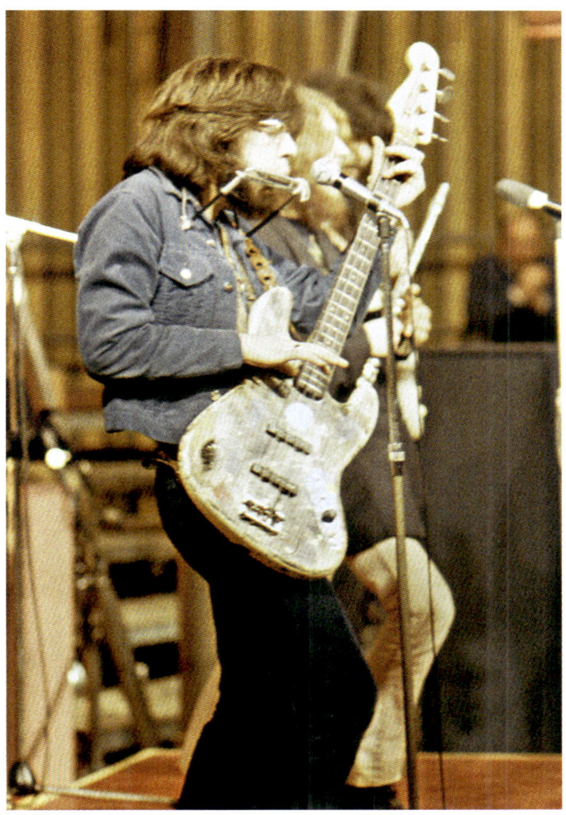

Eric Clapton and his lady seeing the funny side of something at the filming of the Rock and Roll Circus – 10 December 1968.

Left: Jethro Tull Band performing – as above .

Above: Taj Mahal at rehearsals in the Marie Antoinette Room at the Londonderry House Hotel, London, on 9 December 1968 – he was unable to perform at the Circus as the Home Office refused to give him and his band working permits.

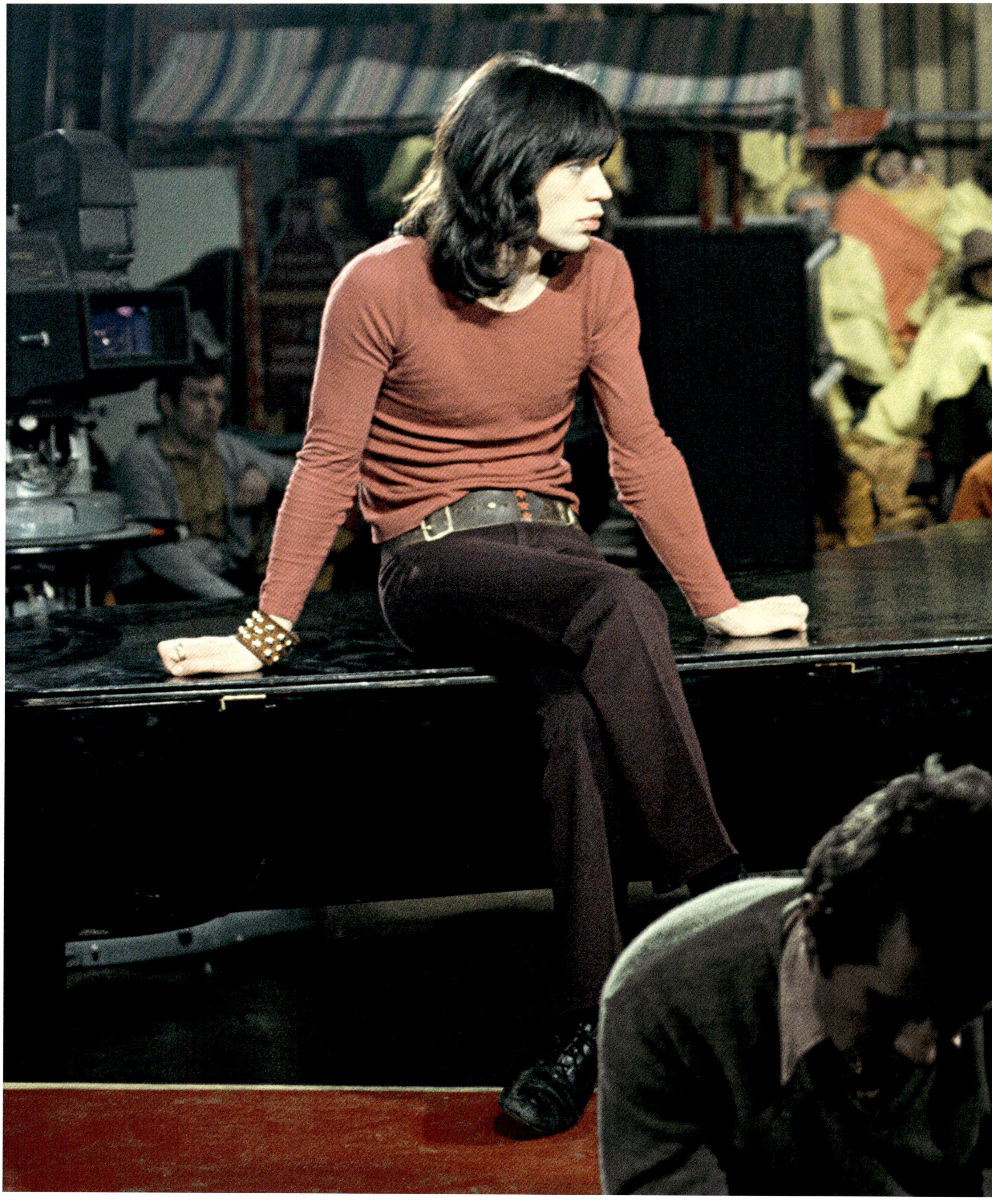

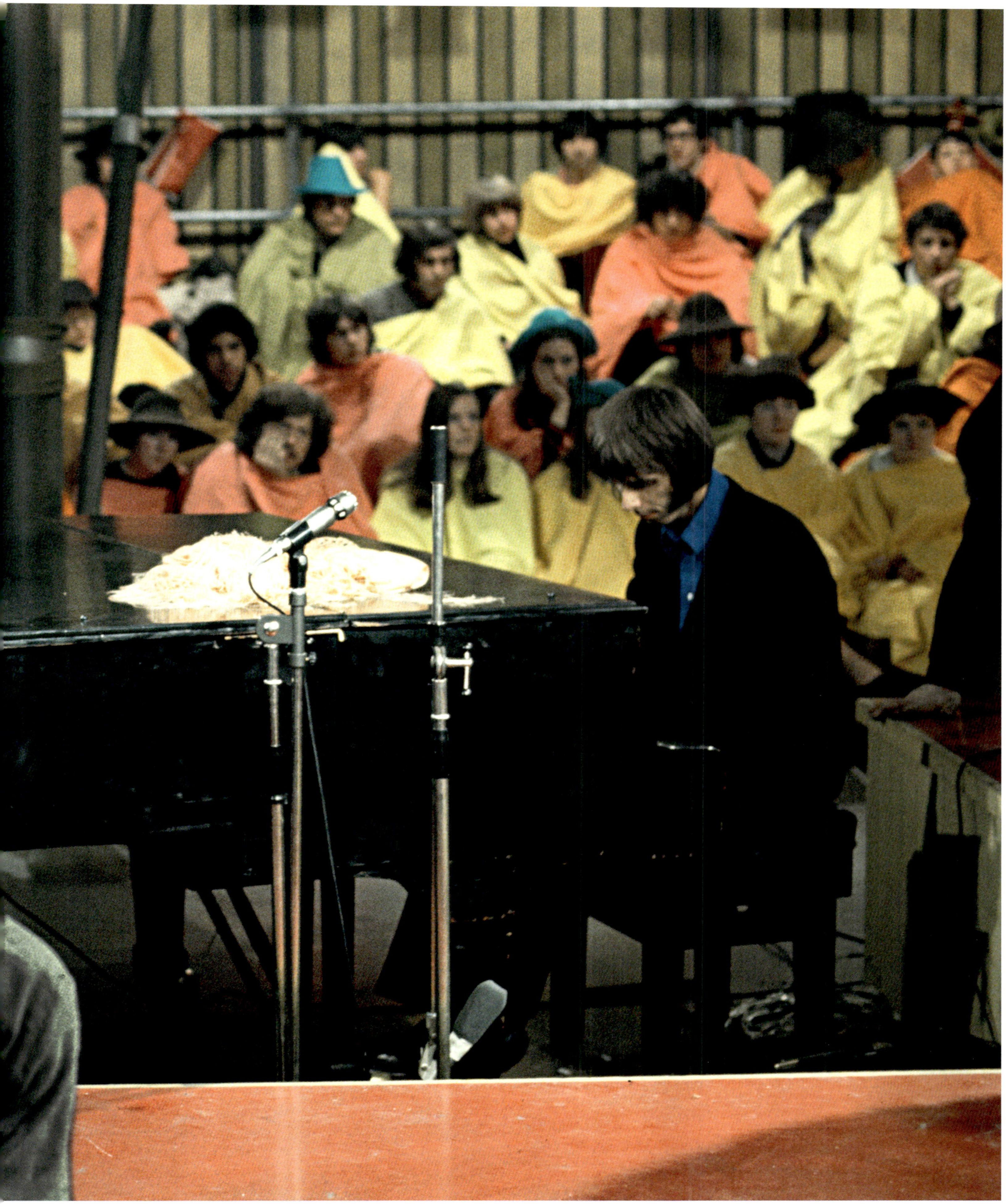

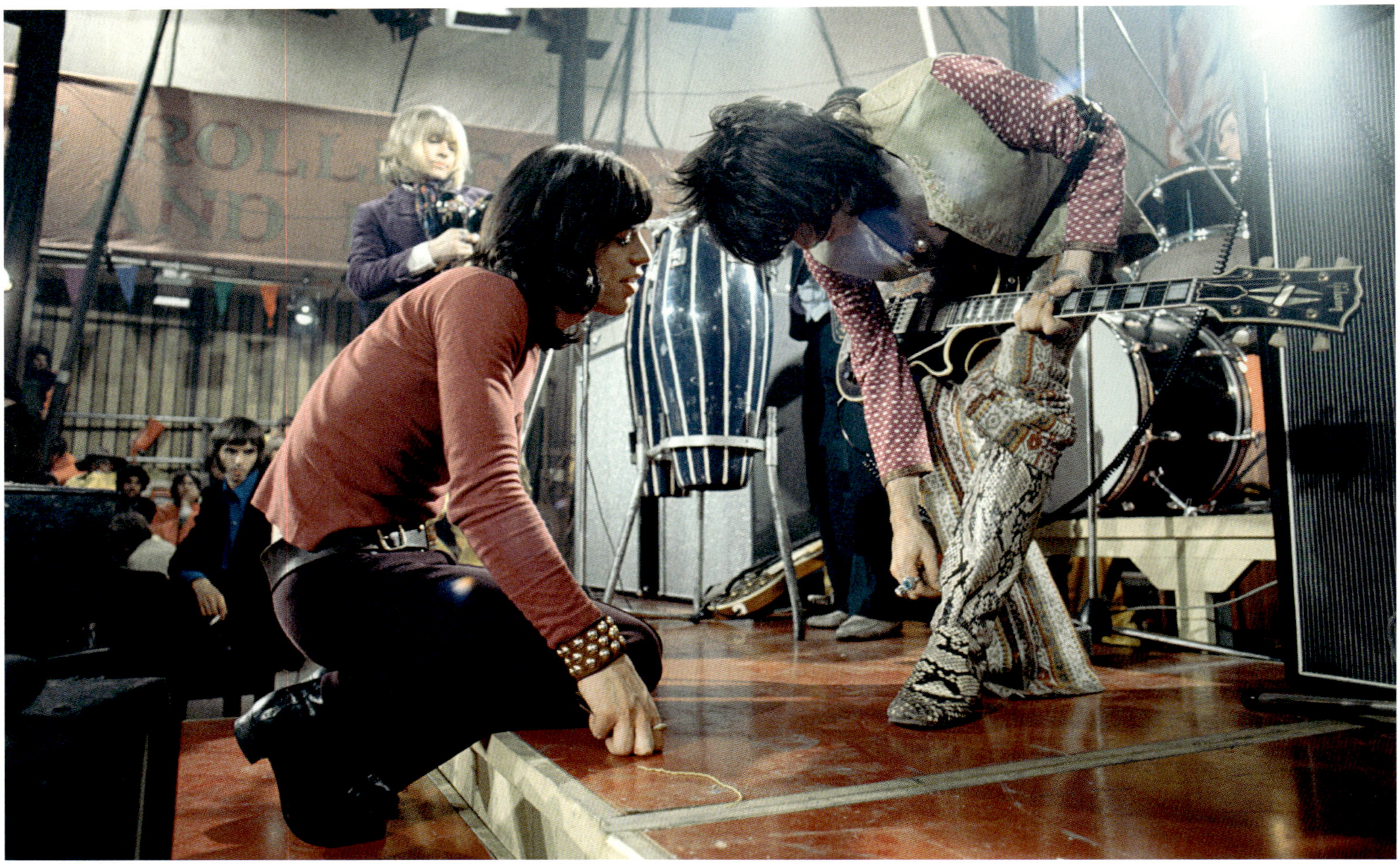

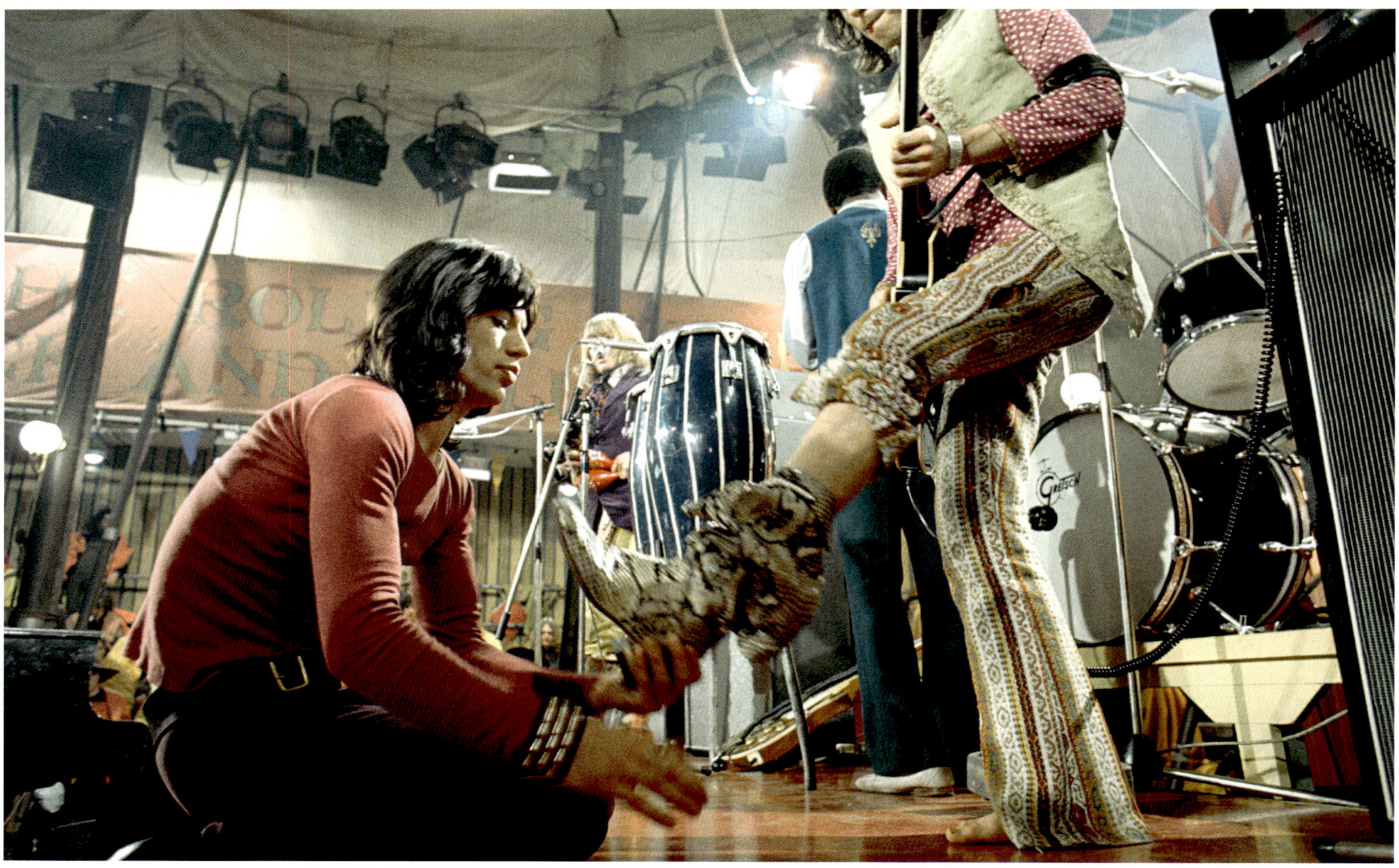

Mick singing with the John Lennon 'Super Group' of Mitch Mitchell (drums), John Lennon and Eric Clapton (guitars), and Keith Richards (bass) on the second day of filming of the Rock and Roll Circus – 11 December 1968.

Left: Two shots of Mick Jagger helping Keith with his snake-skin boots – 'Keith Giving Mick The Boot', as I would always say – as above.

Previous pages: Mick Jagger relaxing between filming, sitting on Nicky Hopkins' piano (seen sitting on the right) – as above.

Following pages: The Stones performing later on the second day when everyone was tired – as above.

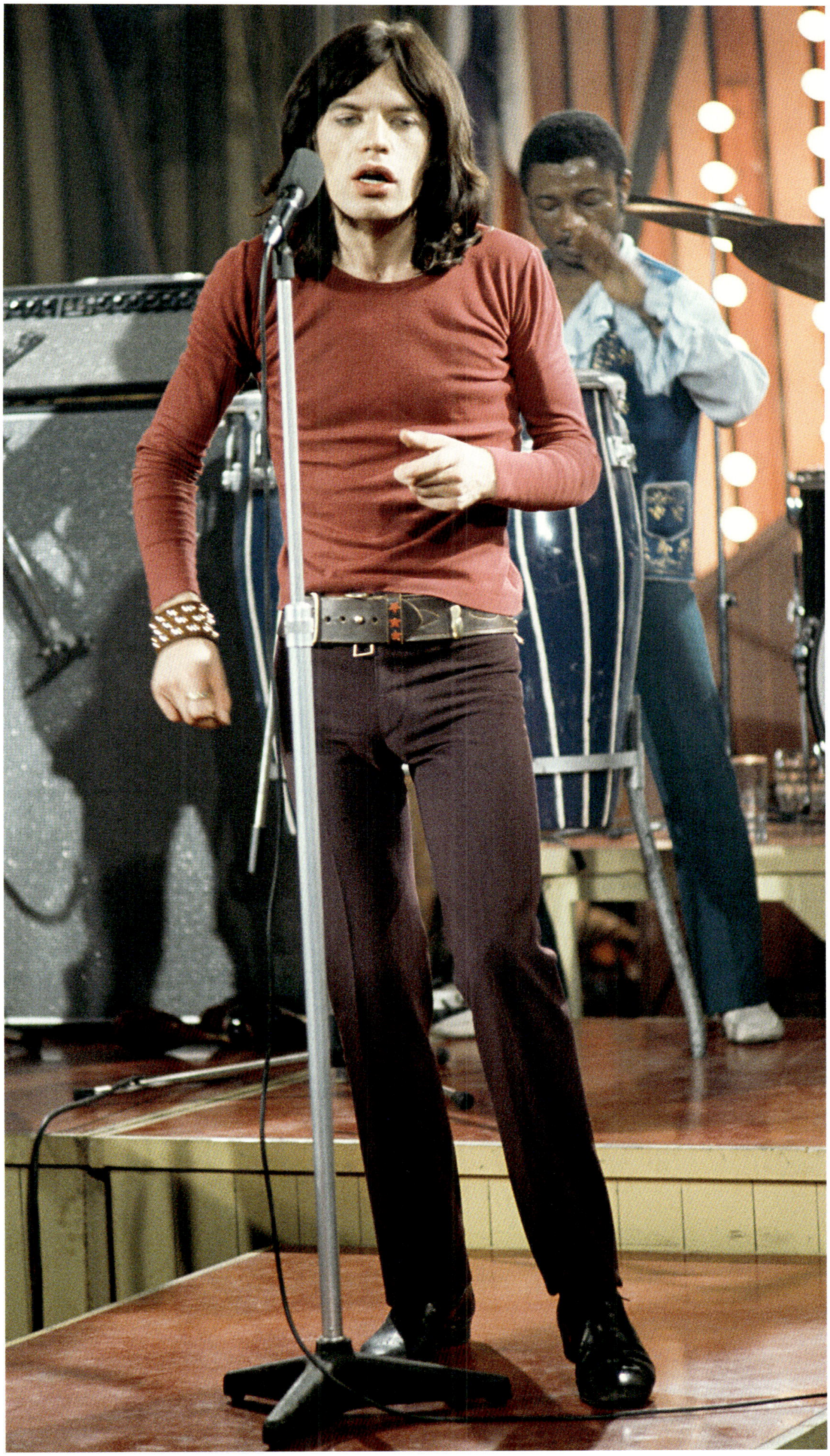

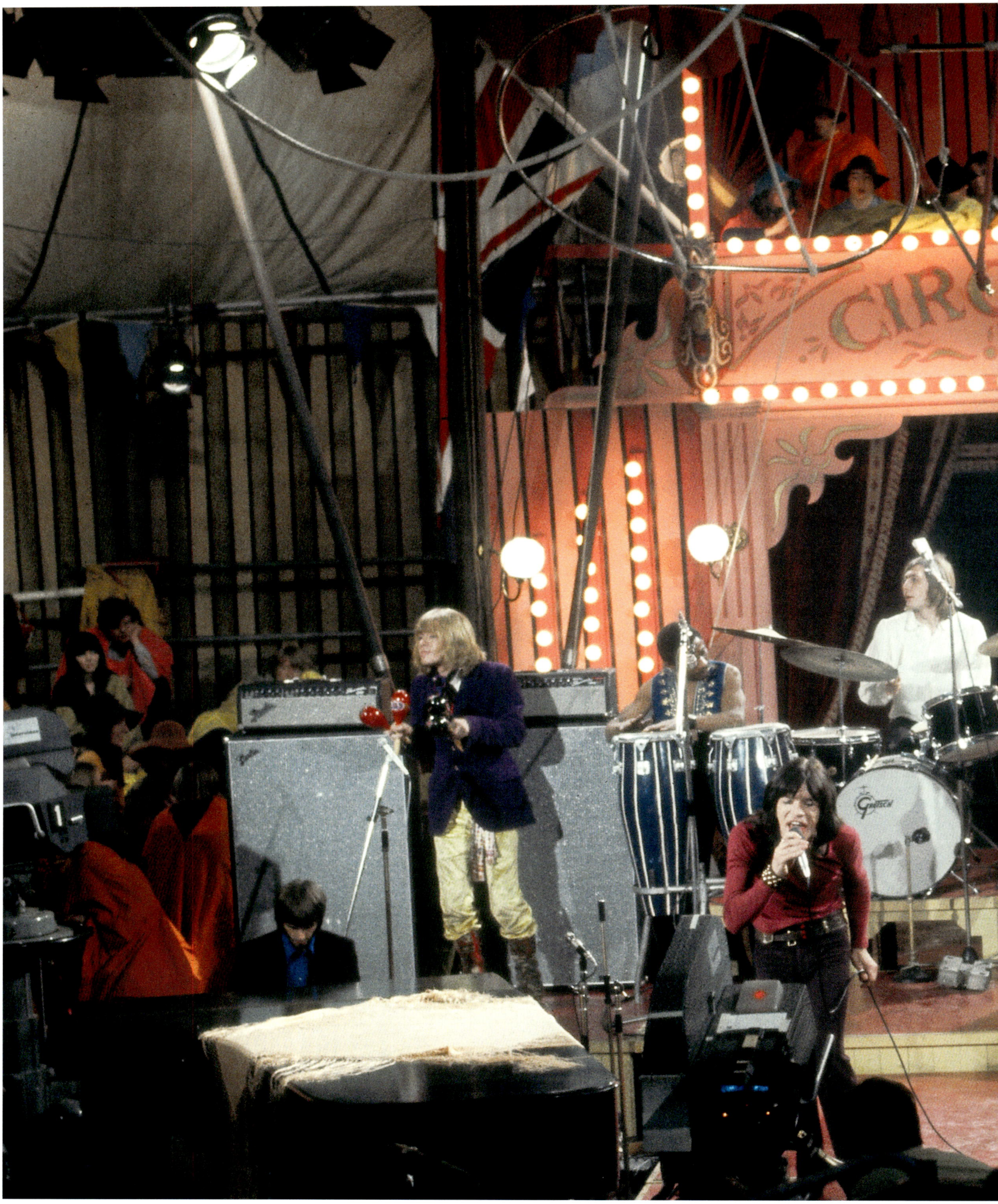

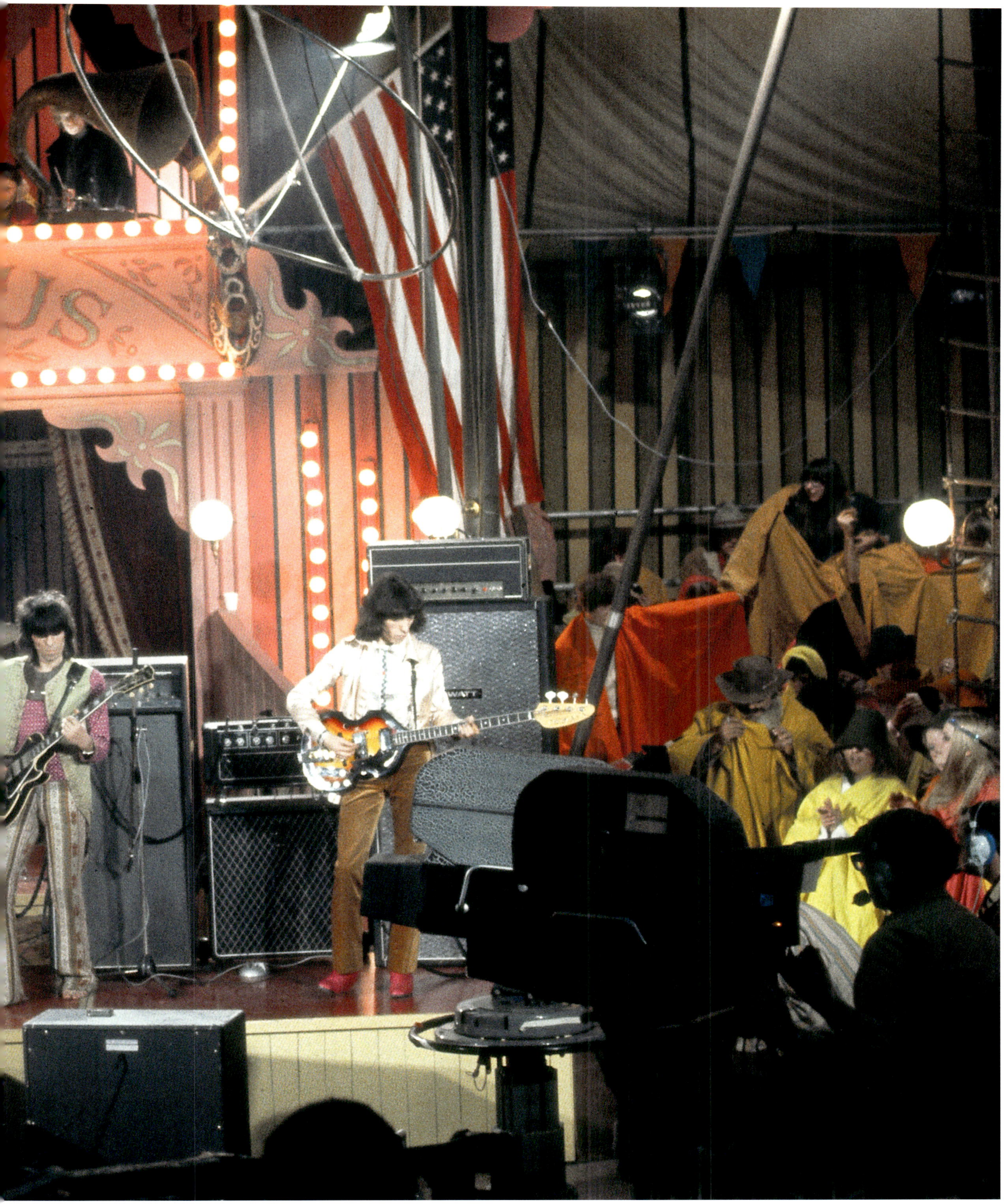

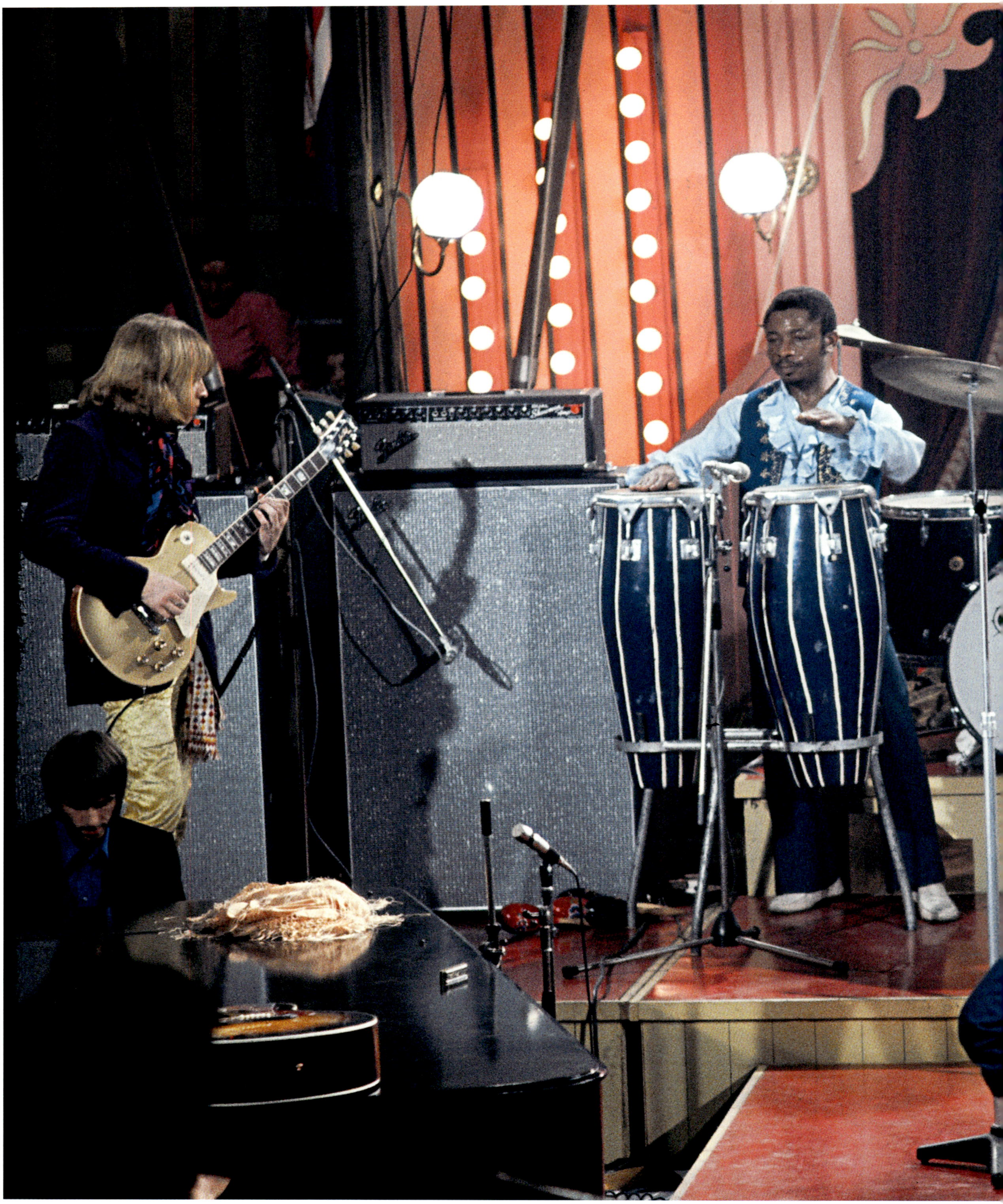

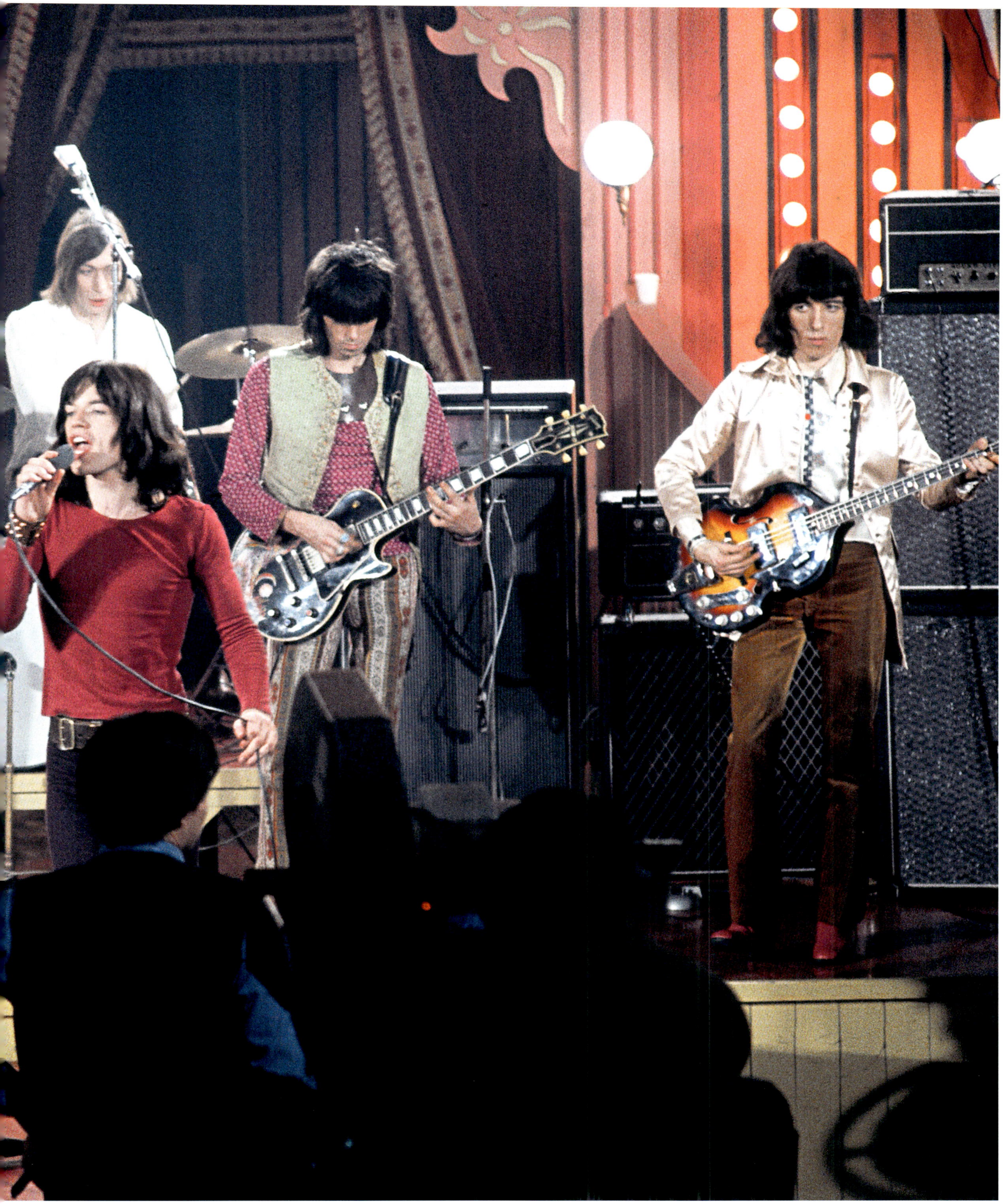

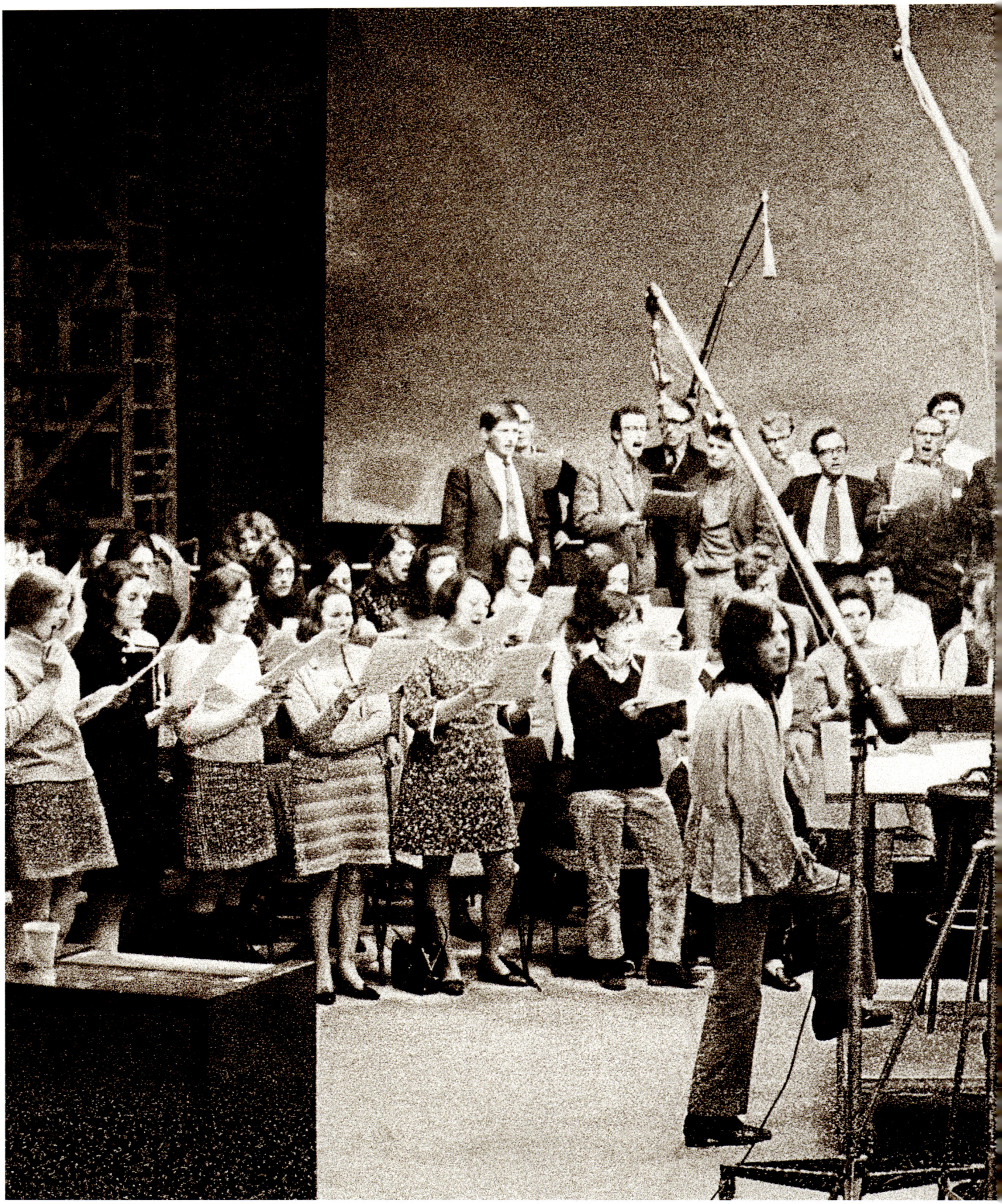

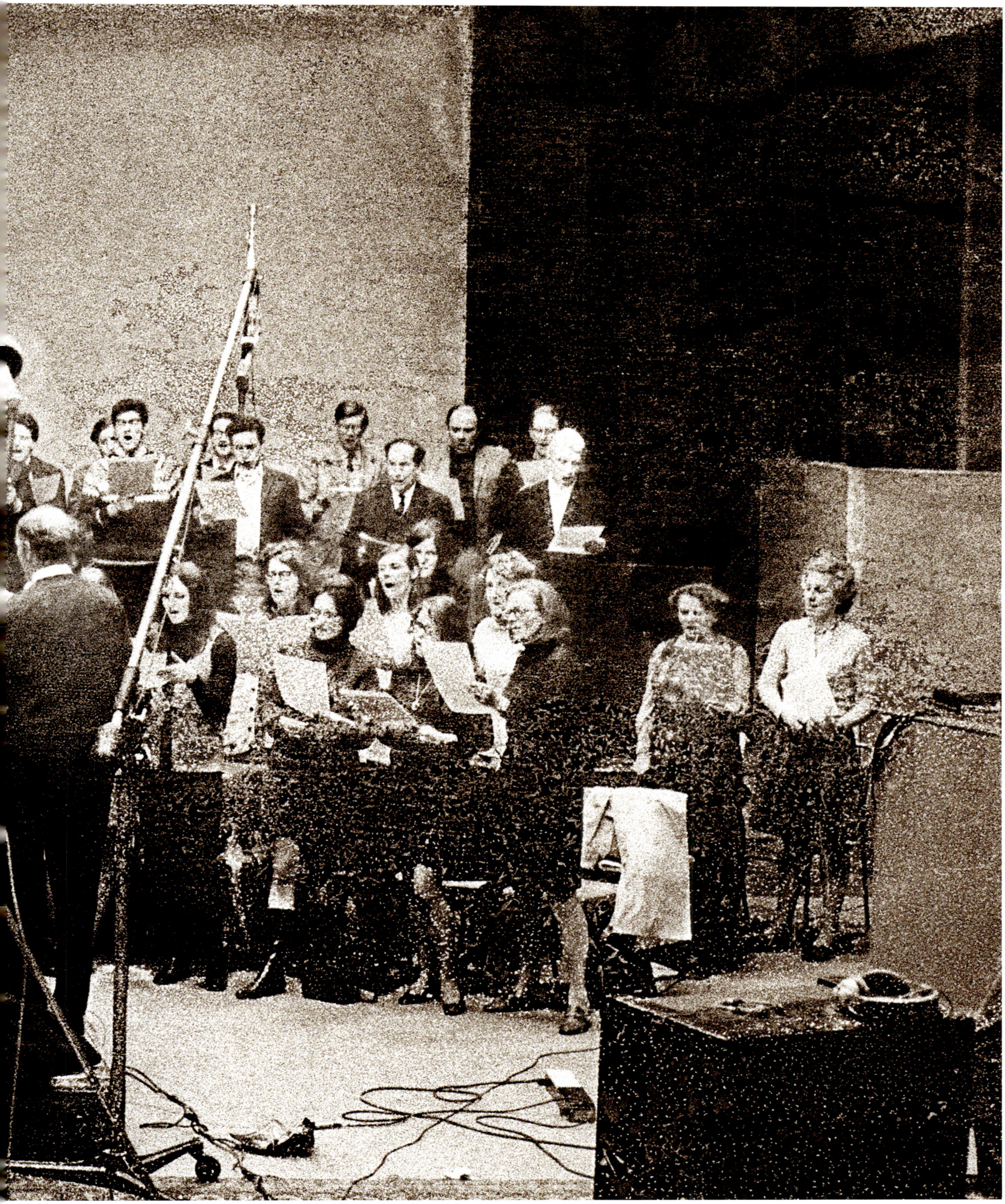

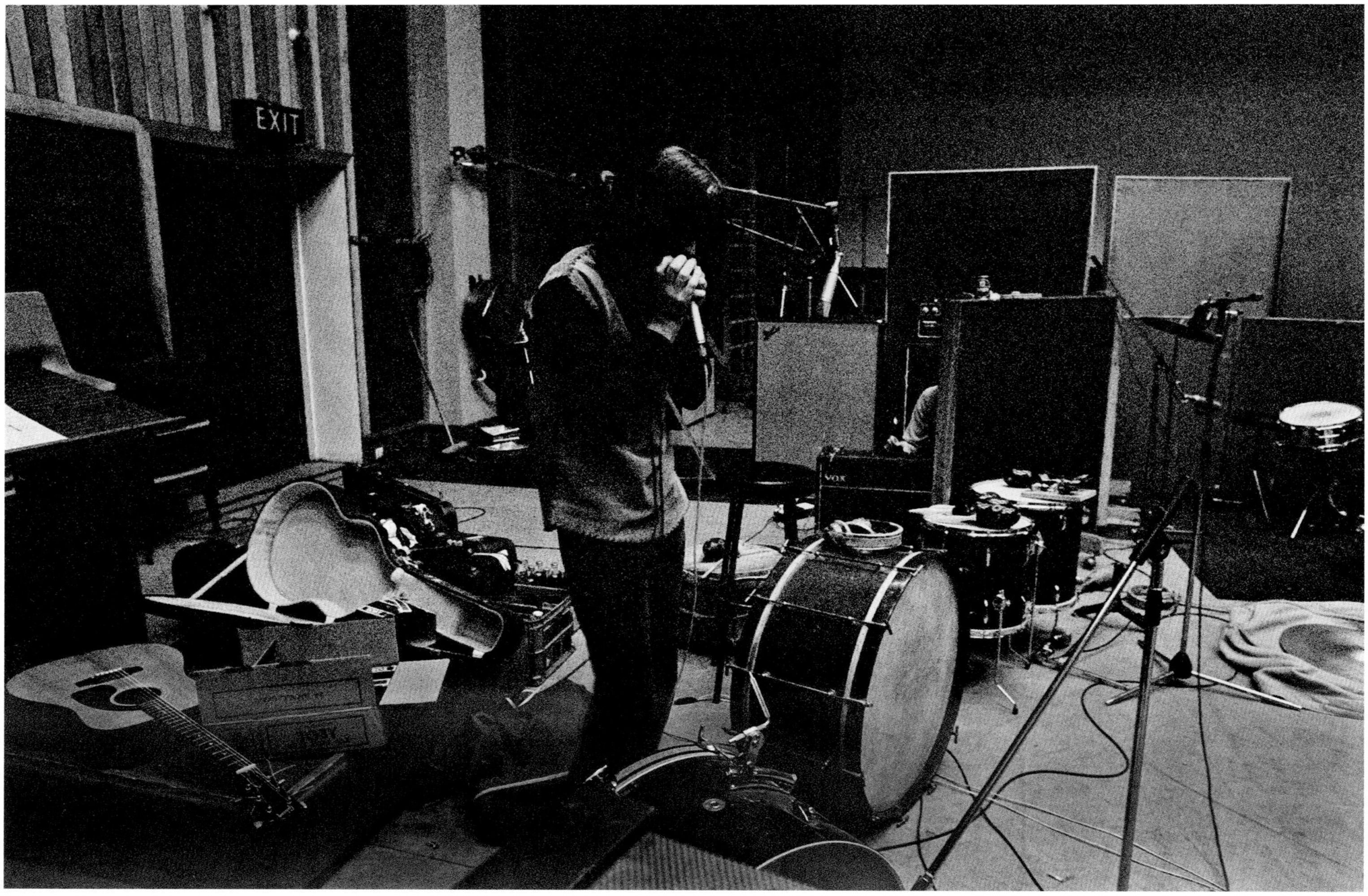

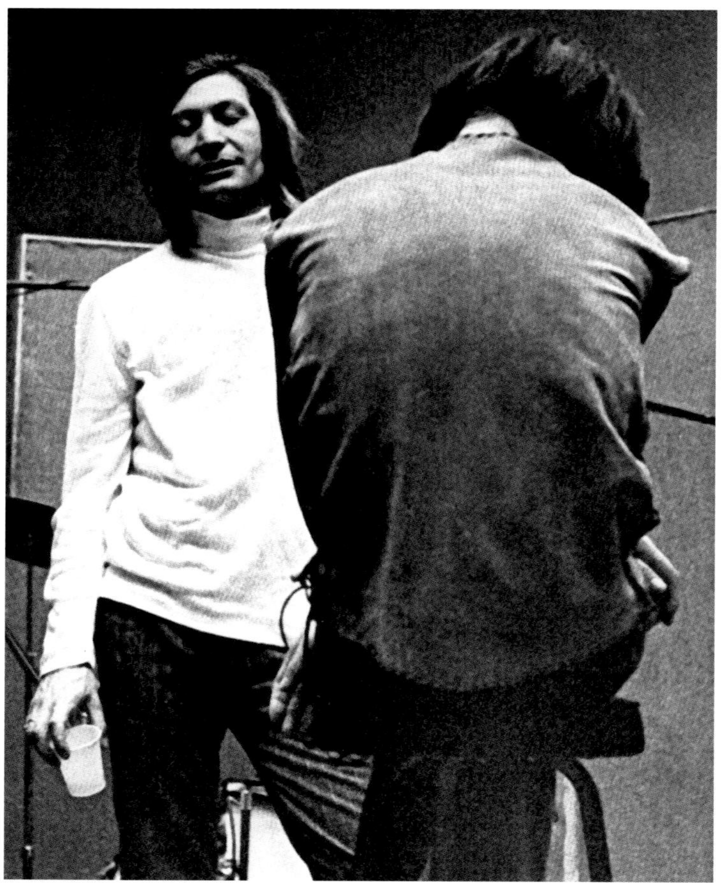

Previous pages: One of only two existing photos of the choir at Olympic Studios, Barnes, singing the introduction to 'You Can't Always Get What You Want' under the direction of Jack Nitzsche (Phil Spector's producer), with Mick helping out – 15 March 1969 .

Above: Mick trying out harmonicas to overdub on the track – as above.

Left: Charlie giving Mick his opinion – as above.

Right: Charlie spinning the drumsticks at Olympic Studios – later that same day.

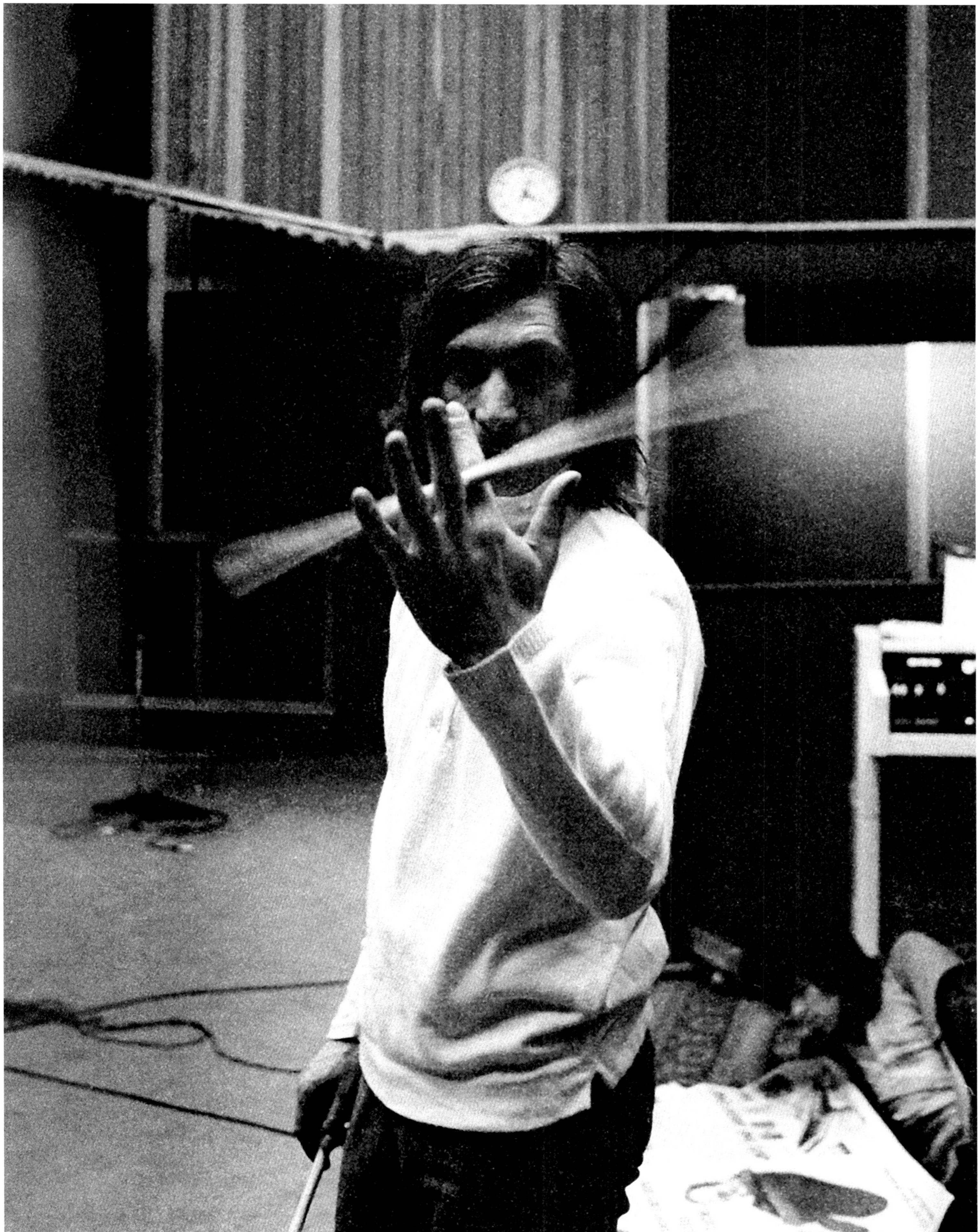

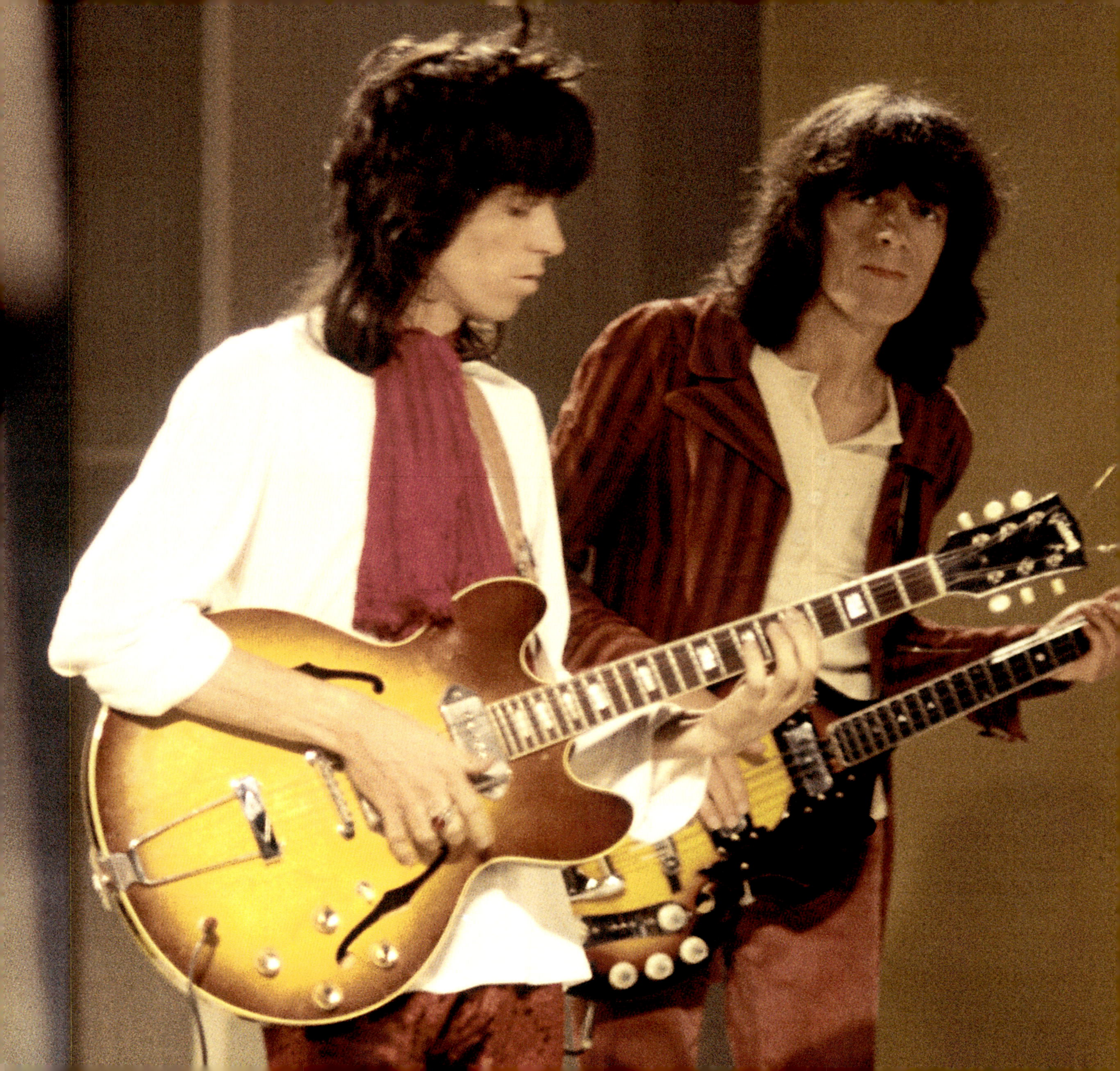

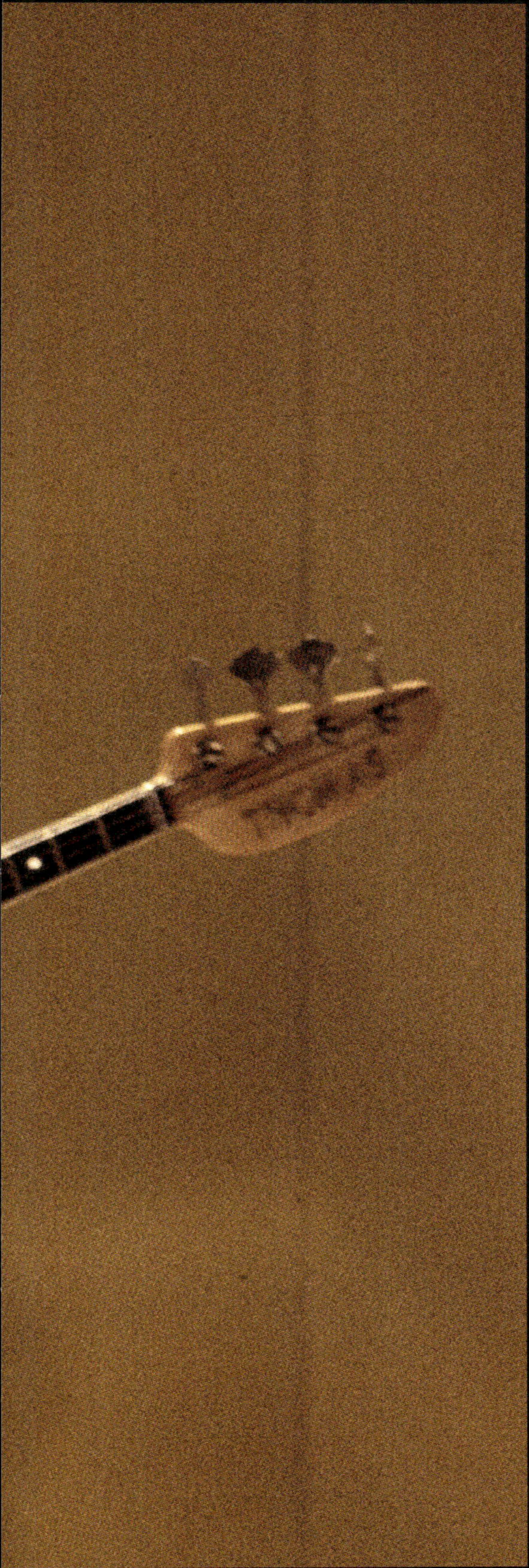

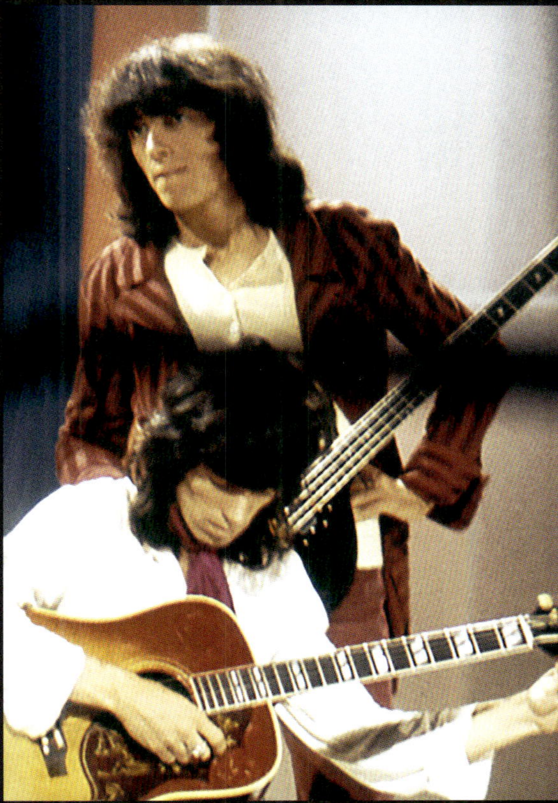

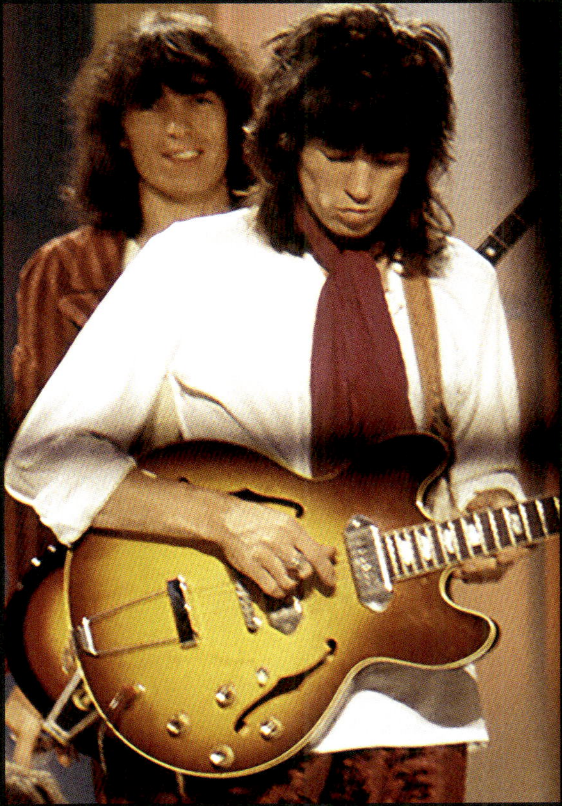

Keith and me performing on *The David Frost Show* – 16 June 1969.
Following pages: The Stones (less Mick Taylor) performing on *The David Frost Show* – 16 June 1969.

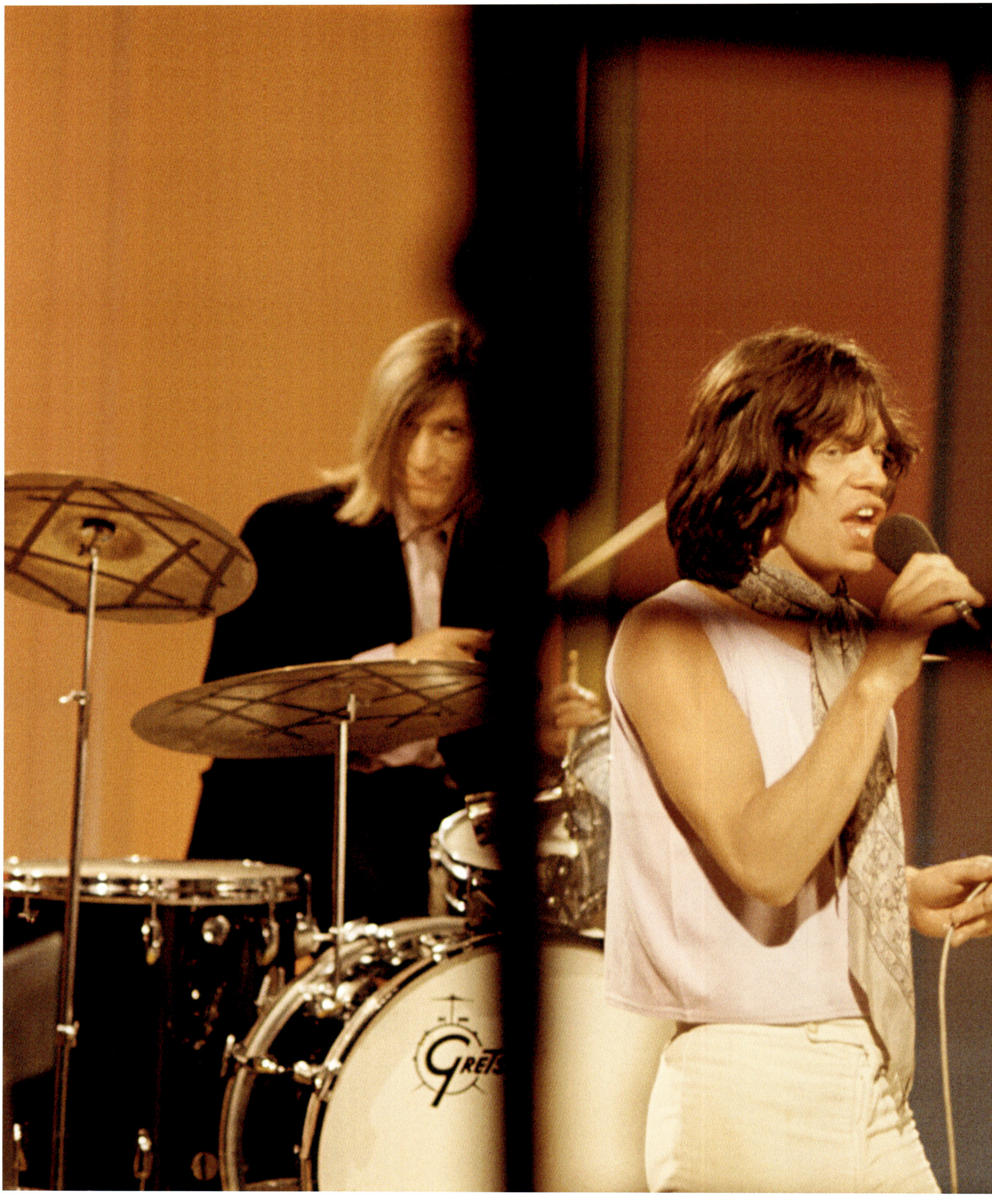

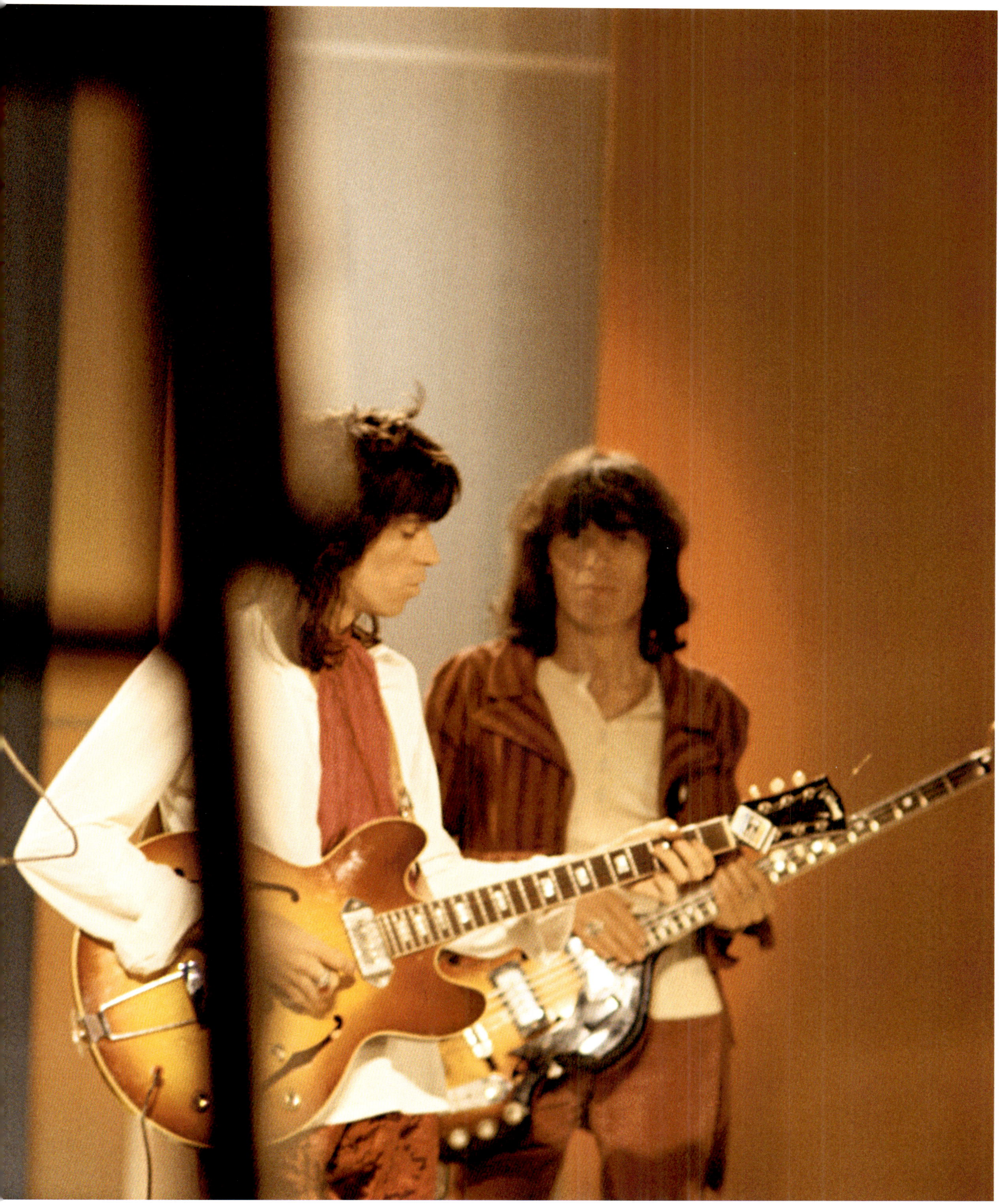

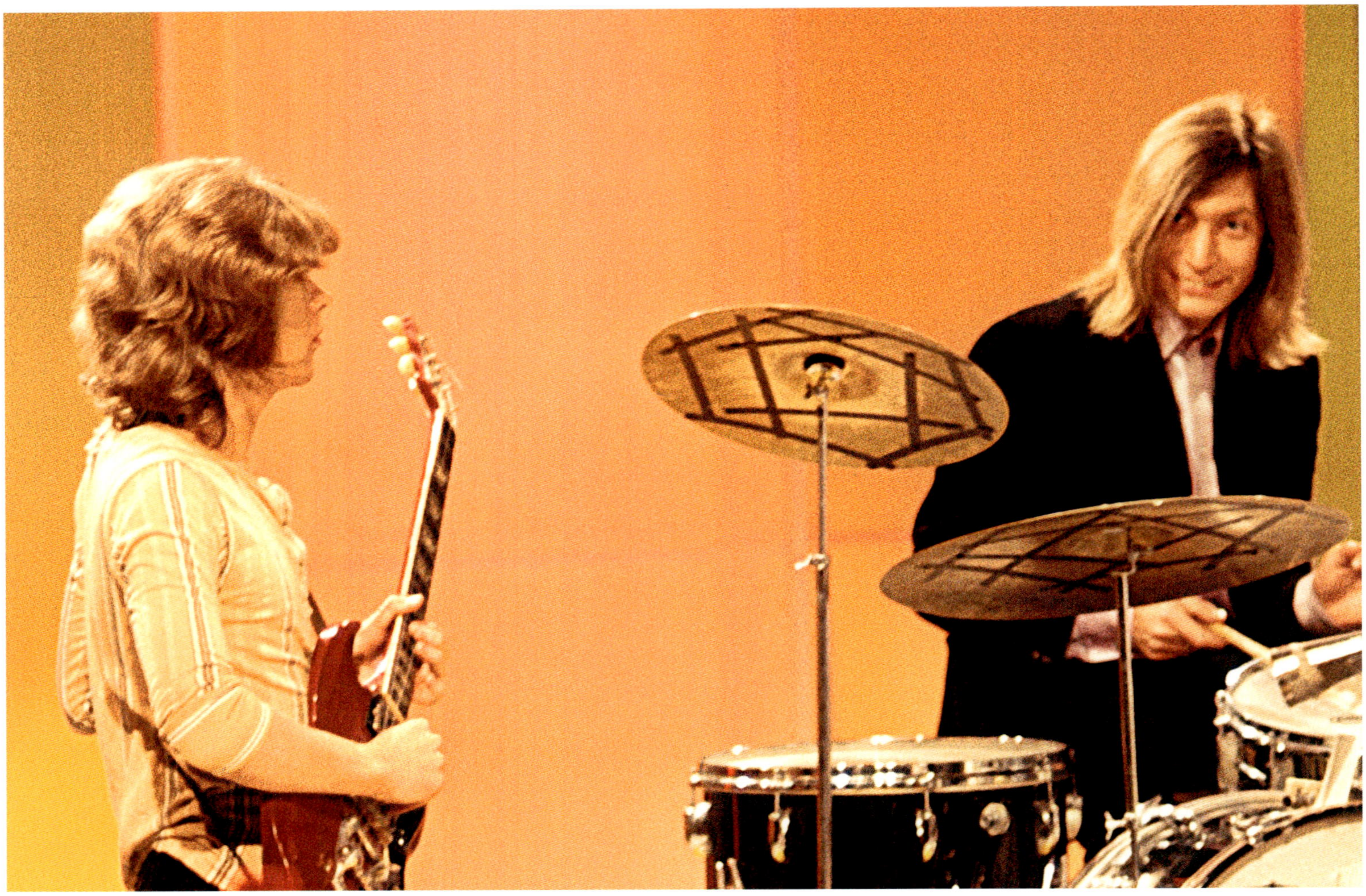

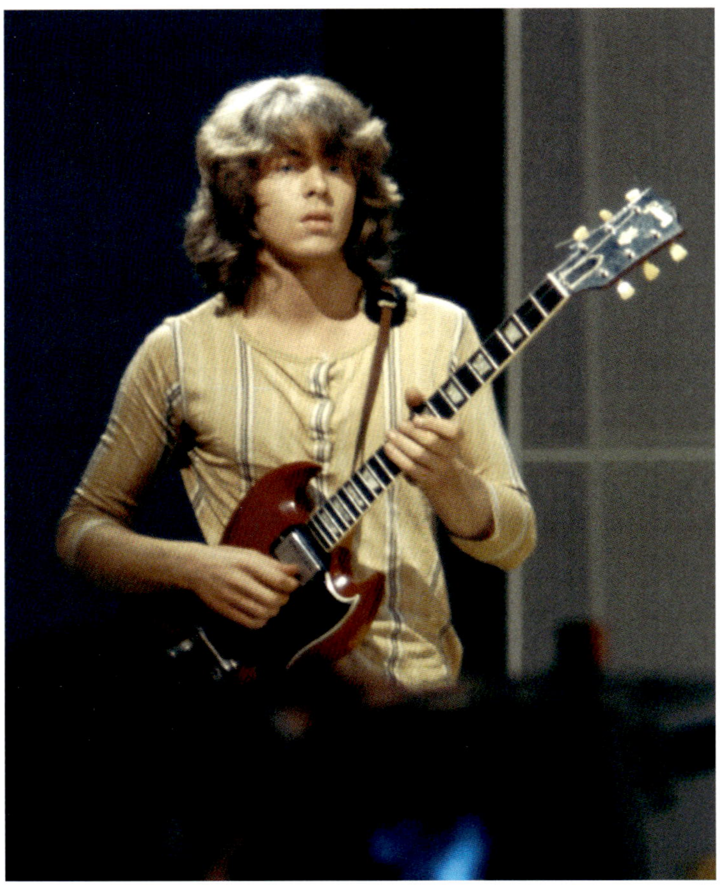

Mick Taylor and Charlie together, and as single shots, on *The David Frost Show* – 16 June 1969.

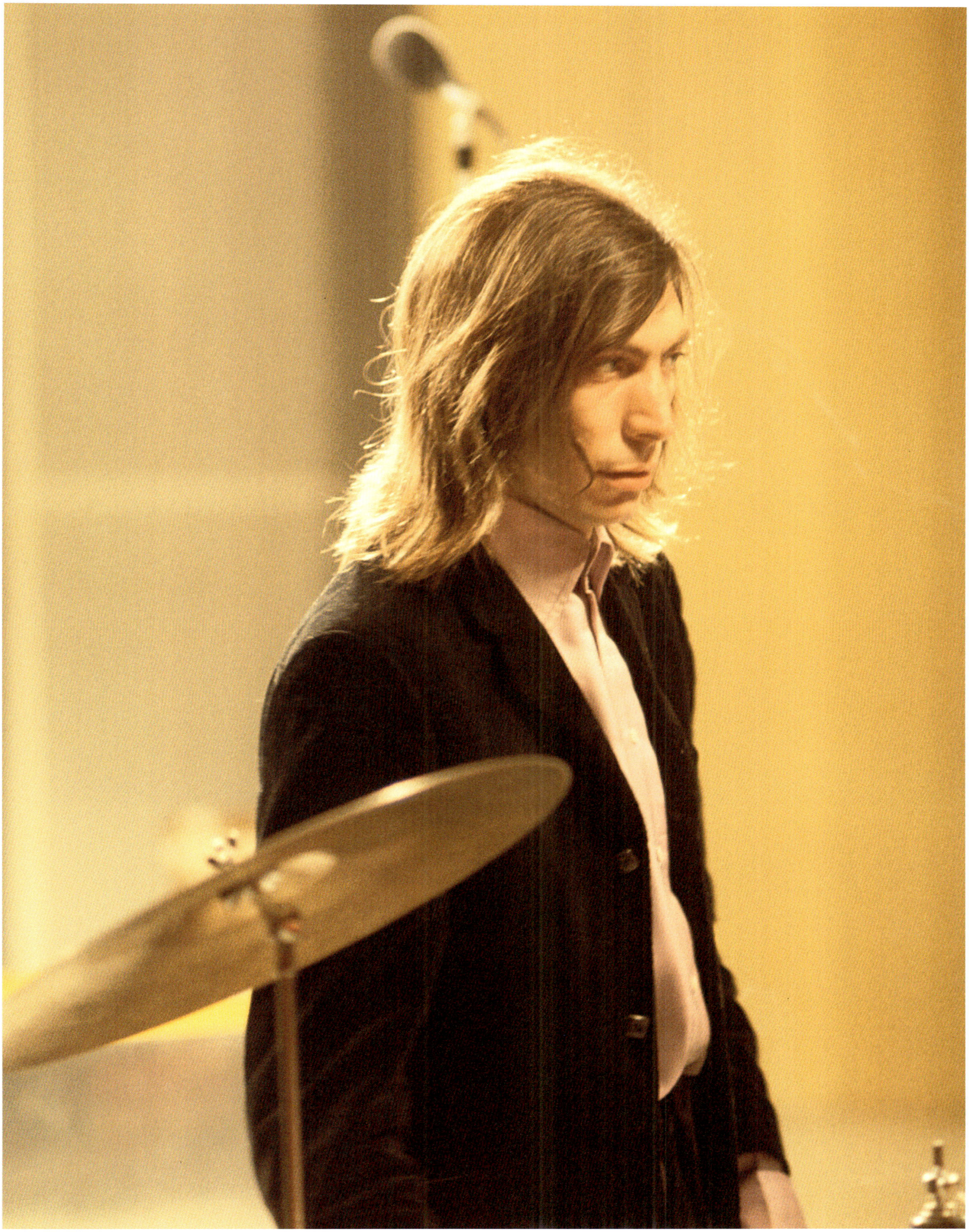

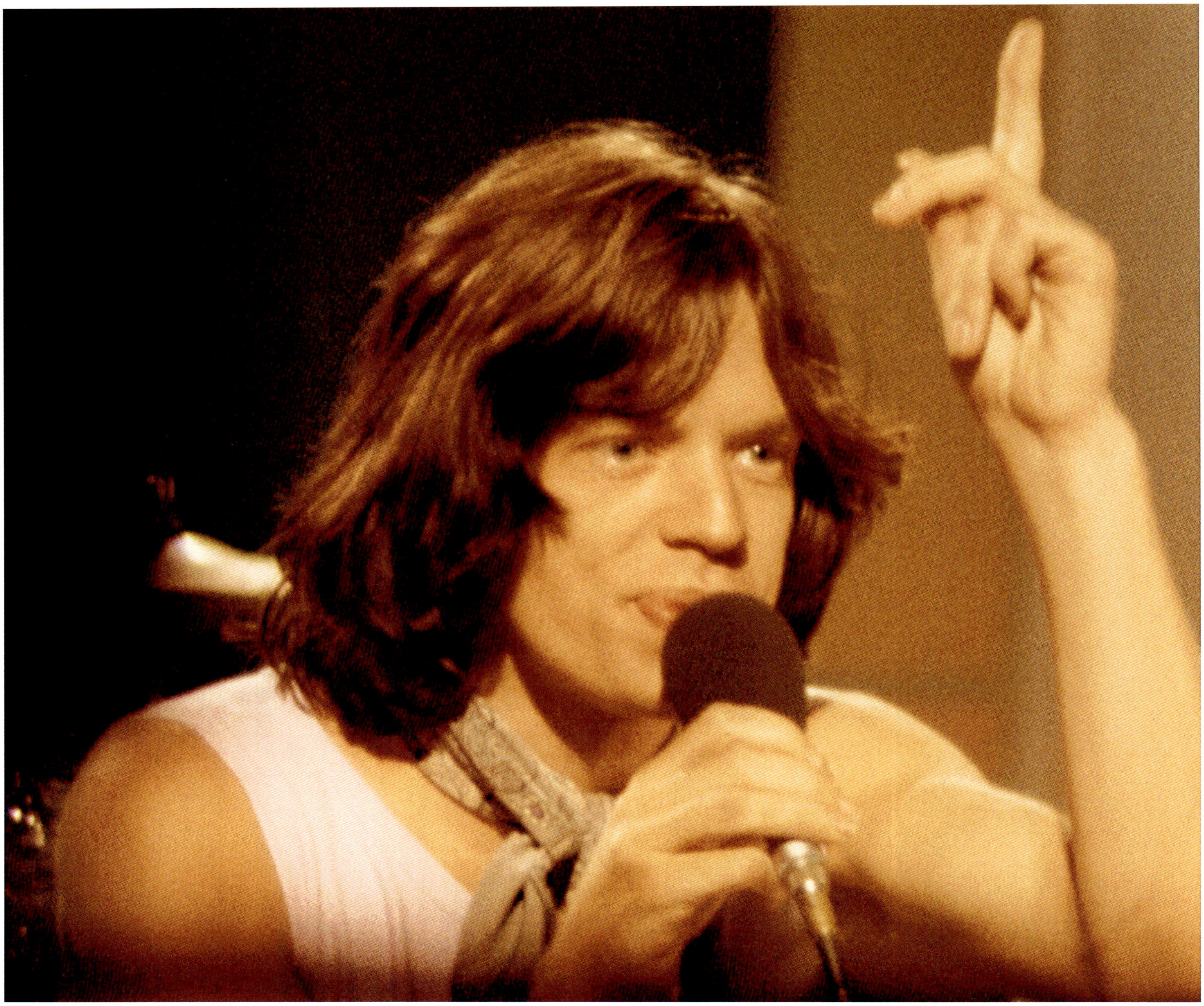

Mick singing on *The David Frost Show* – 16 June 1969.
Right: Mick Taylor at Apple Studios, London – 4 July 1969.
Following pages: Mick alone and with the other Stones at Apple Studios, London – 4 July 1969.

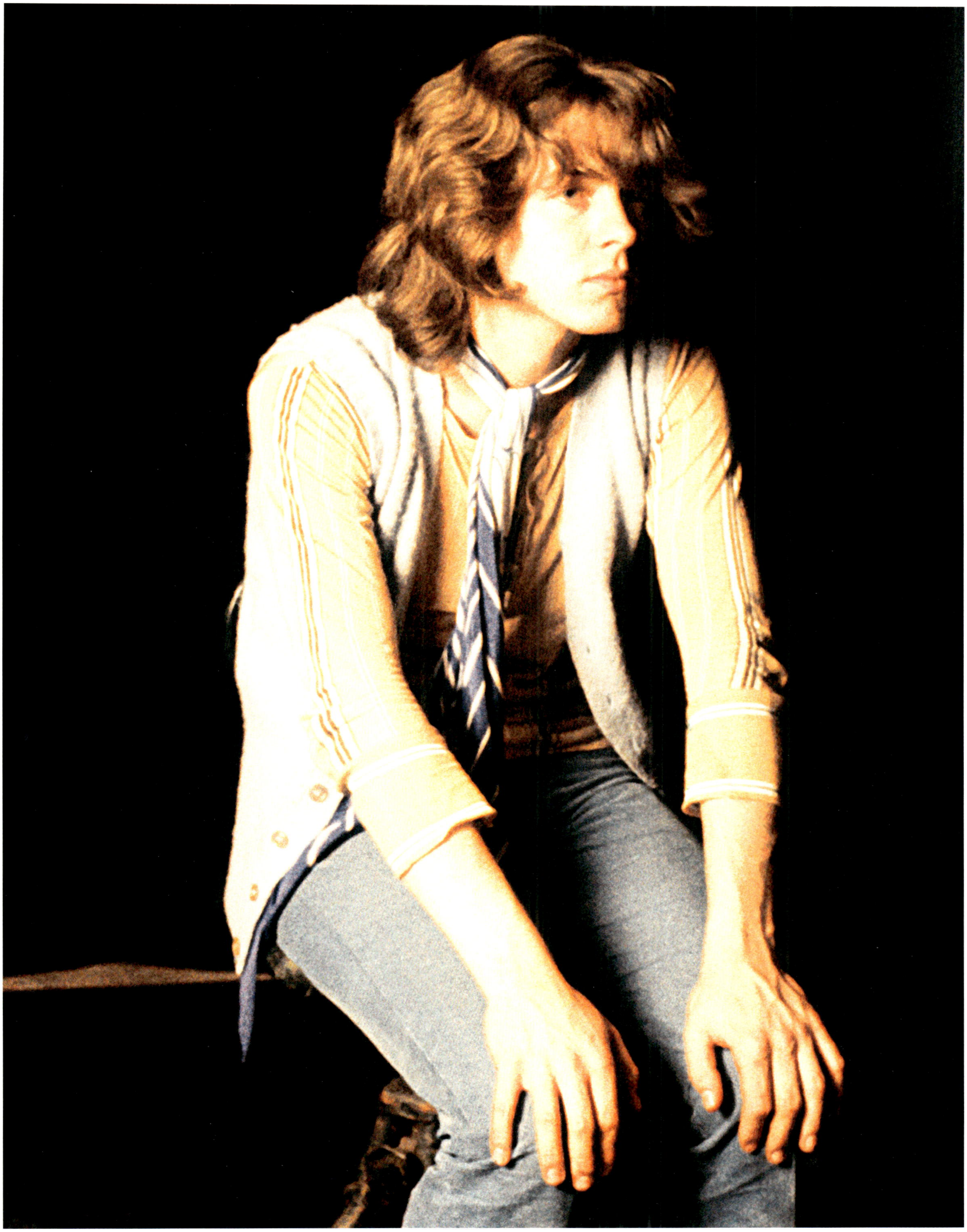

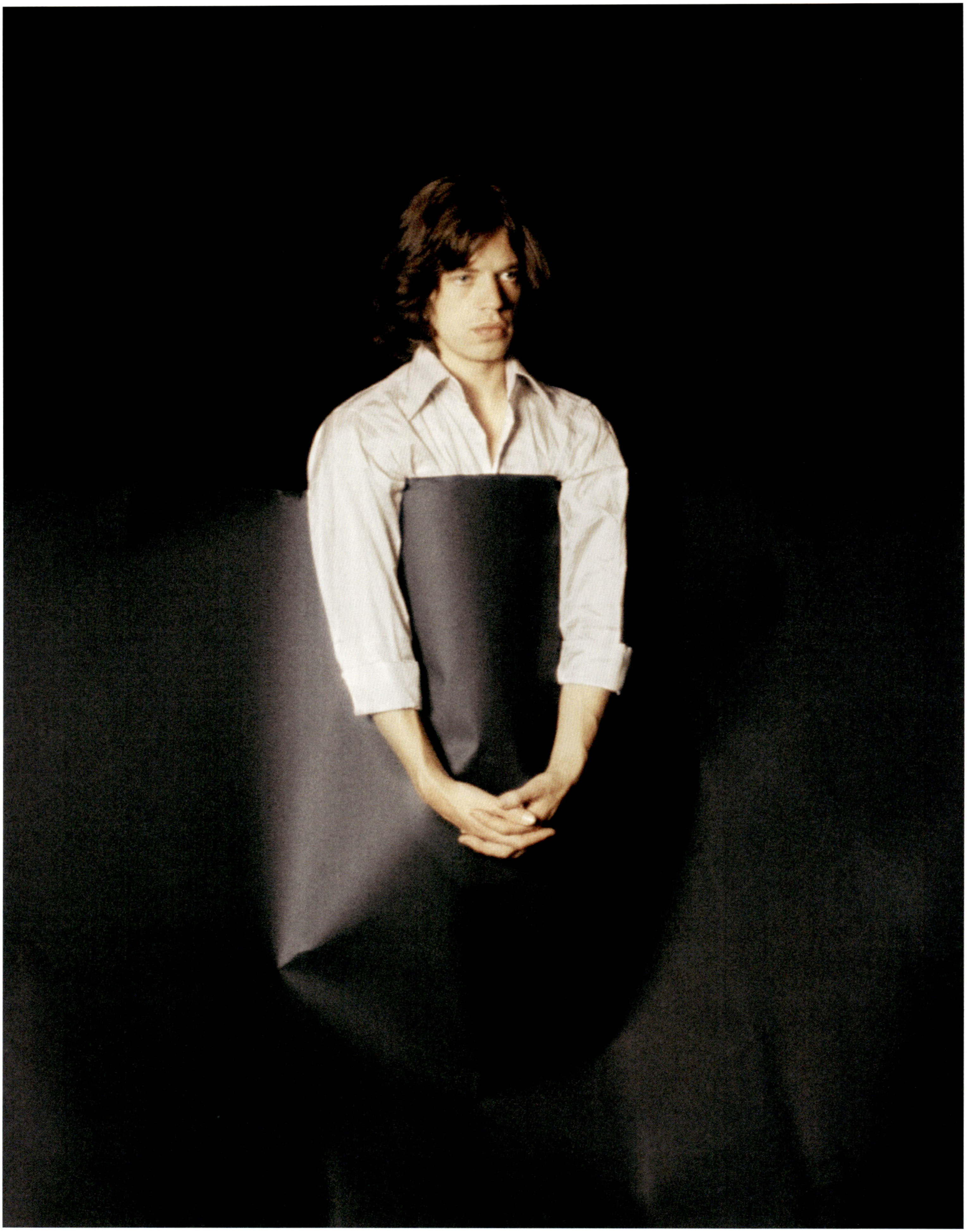

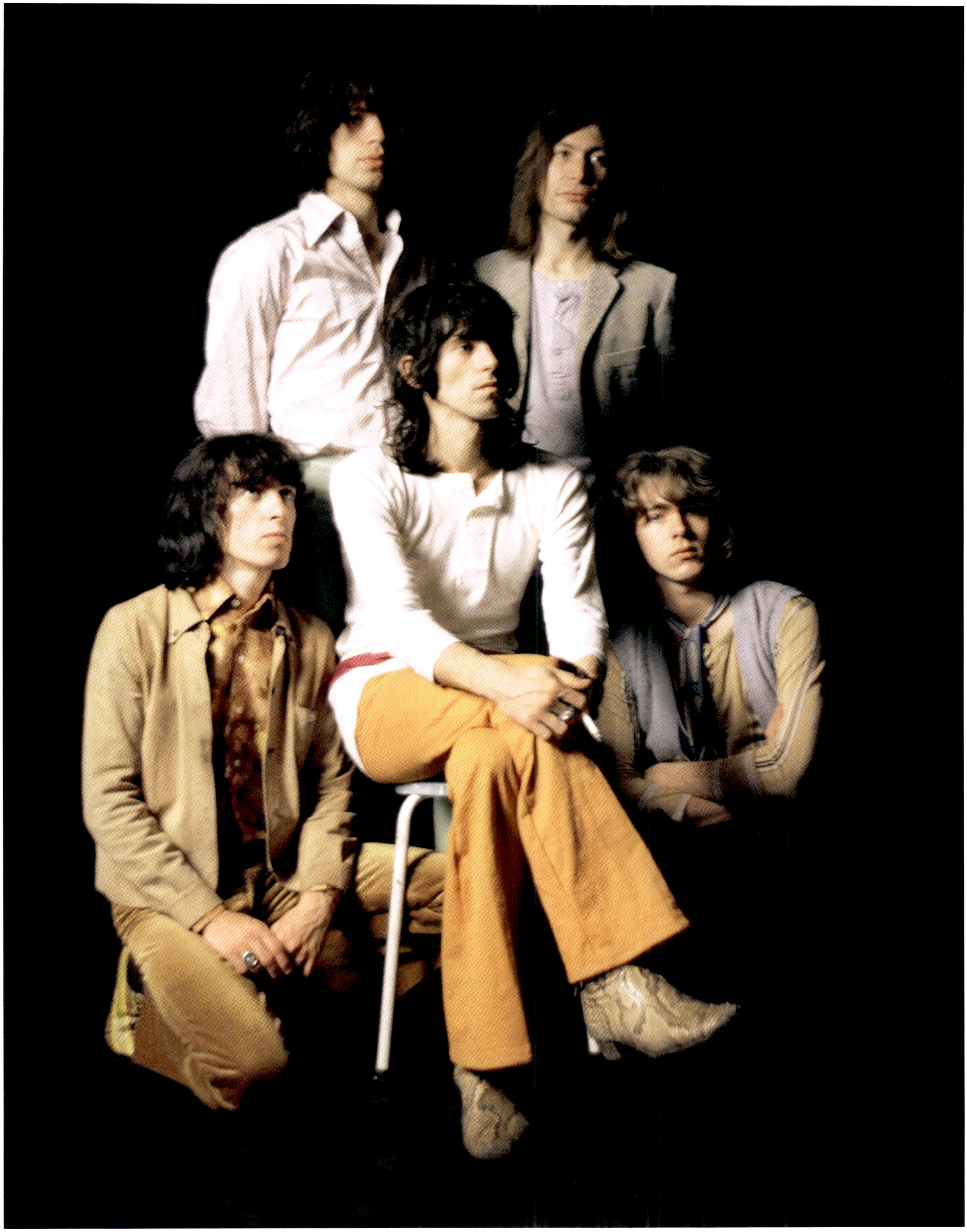

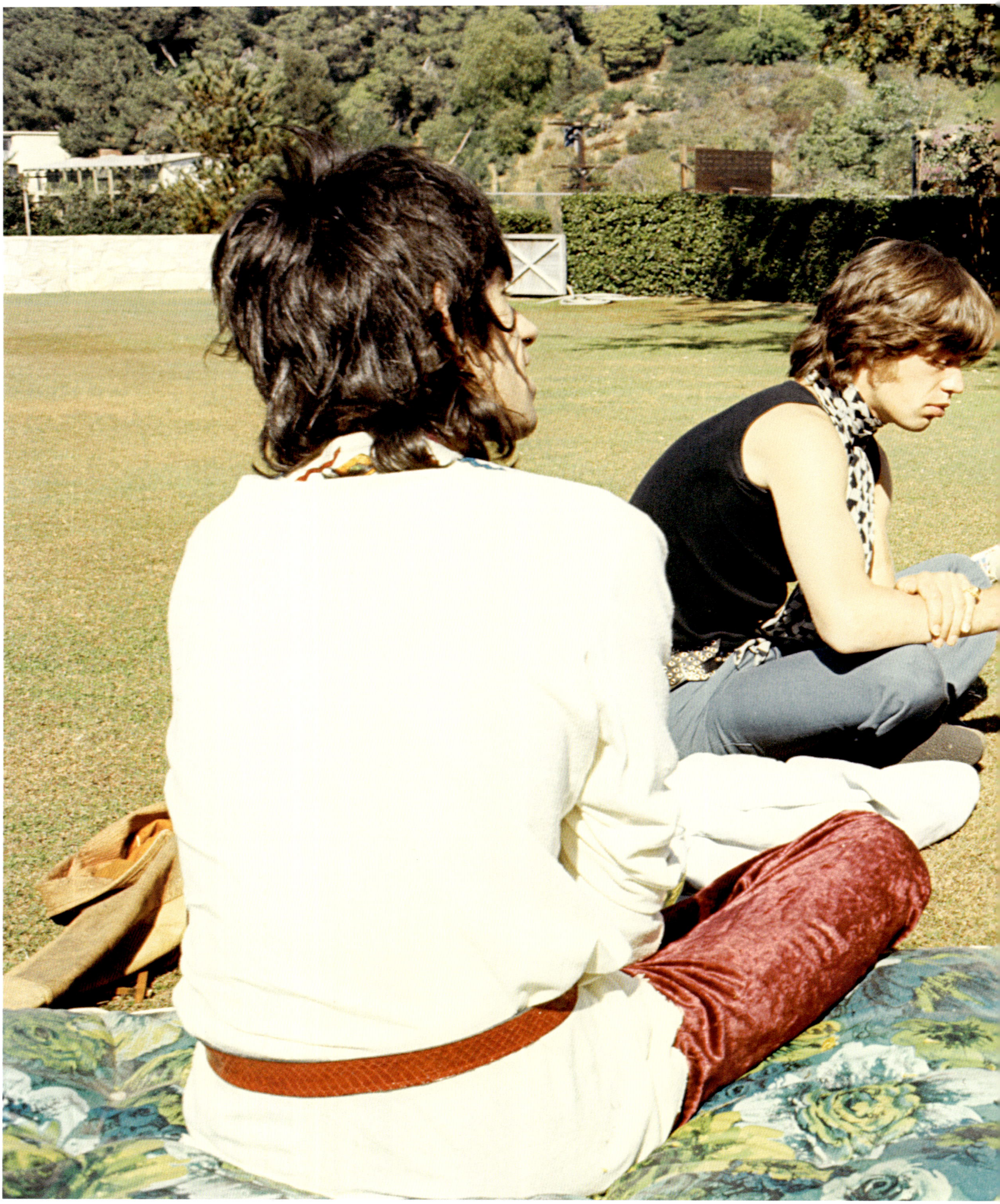

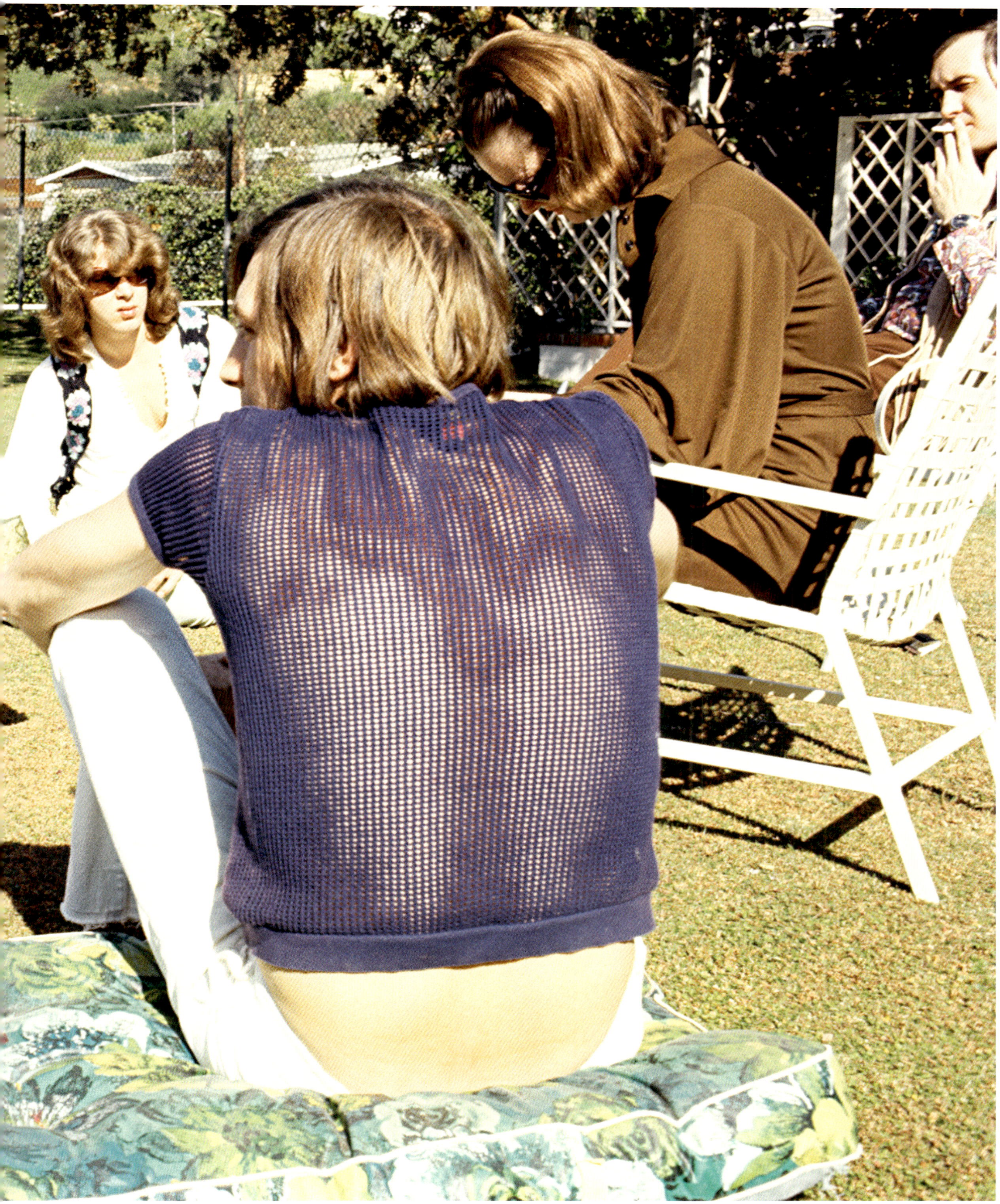

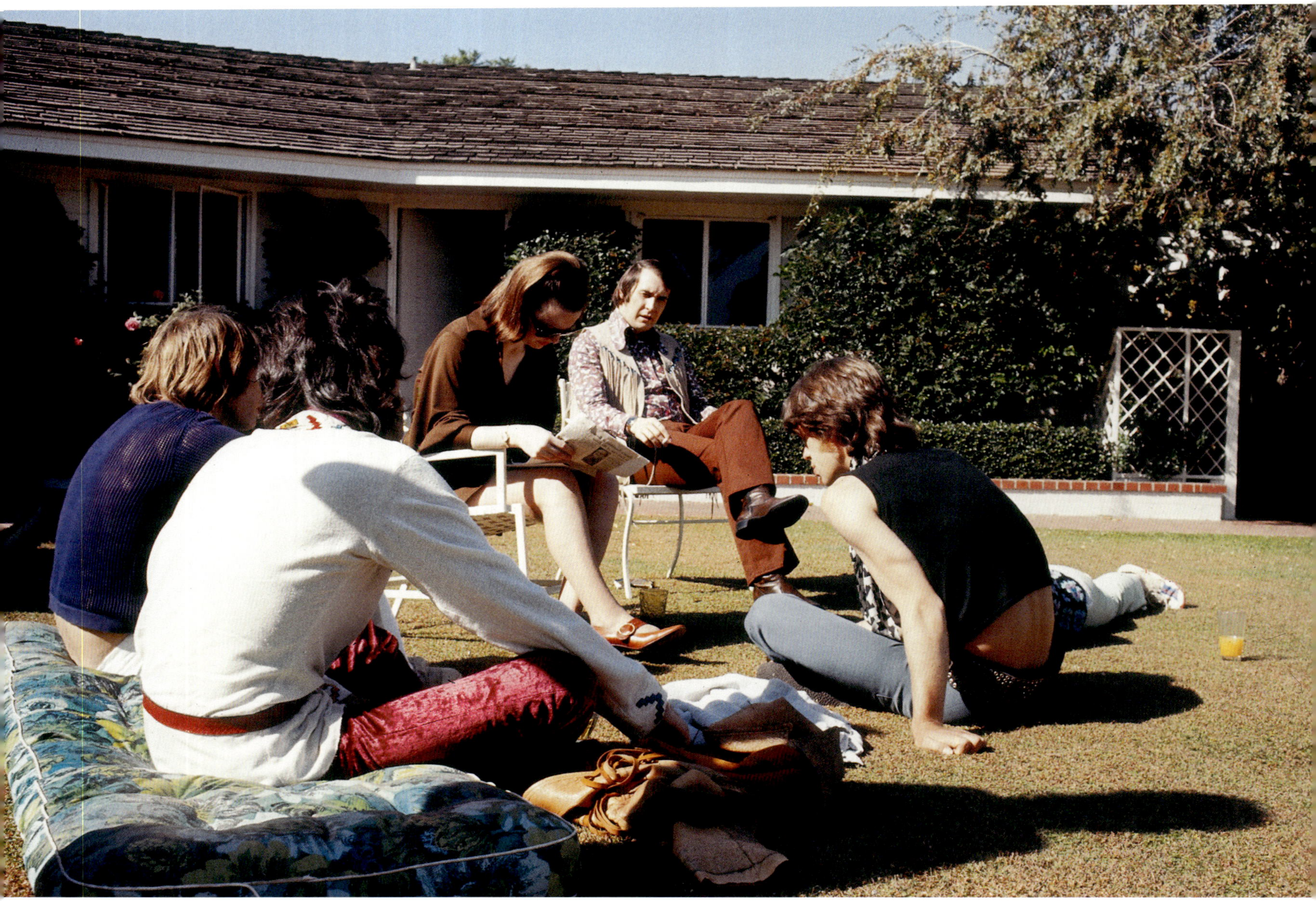

Two shots of the Stones in the grounds of The Dupont House above Los Angeles, doing an interview – 18 October 1969.
Previous pages: Stones in the grounds of The Dupont House doing interviews and photos – as above.
Following pages: Three more shots of the Stones in the grounds of The Dupont House. Plus one of Charlie returning to the fray with his lunch – as above.

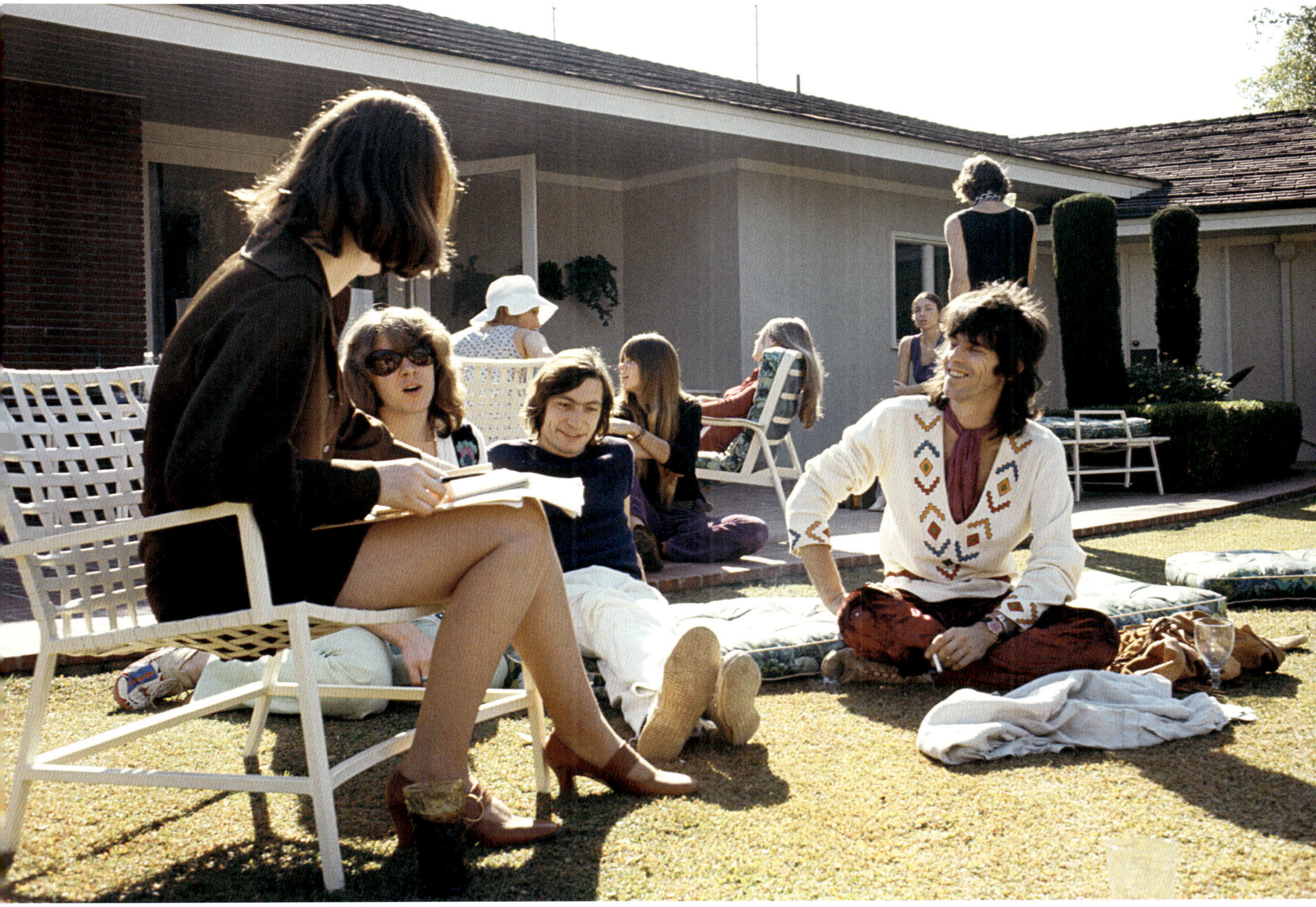

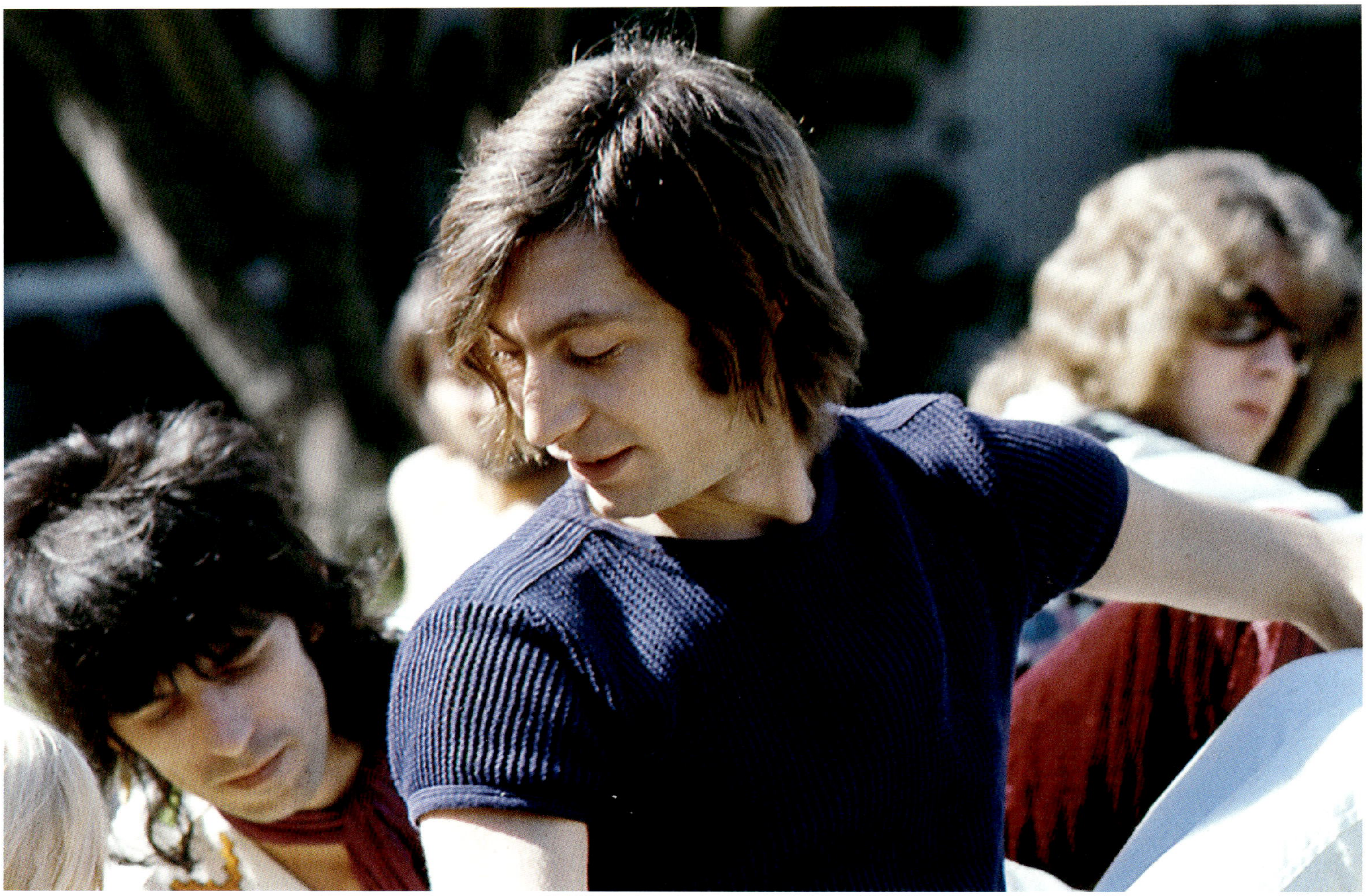

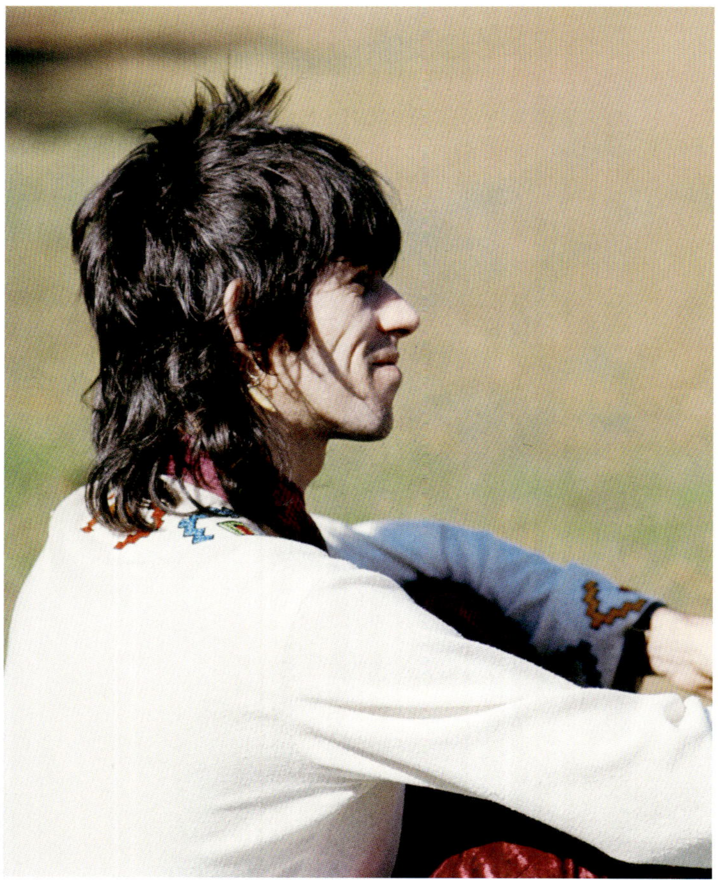

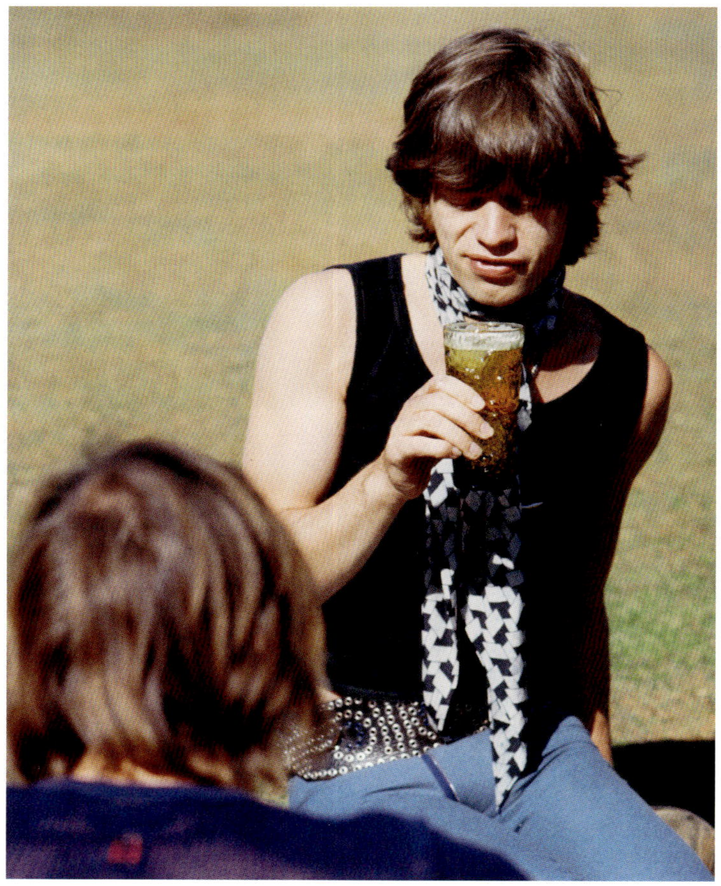

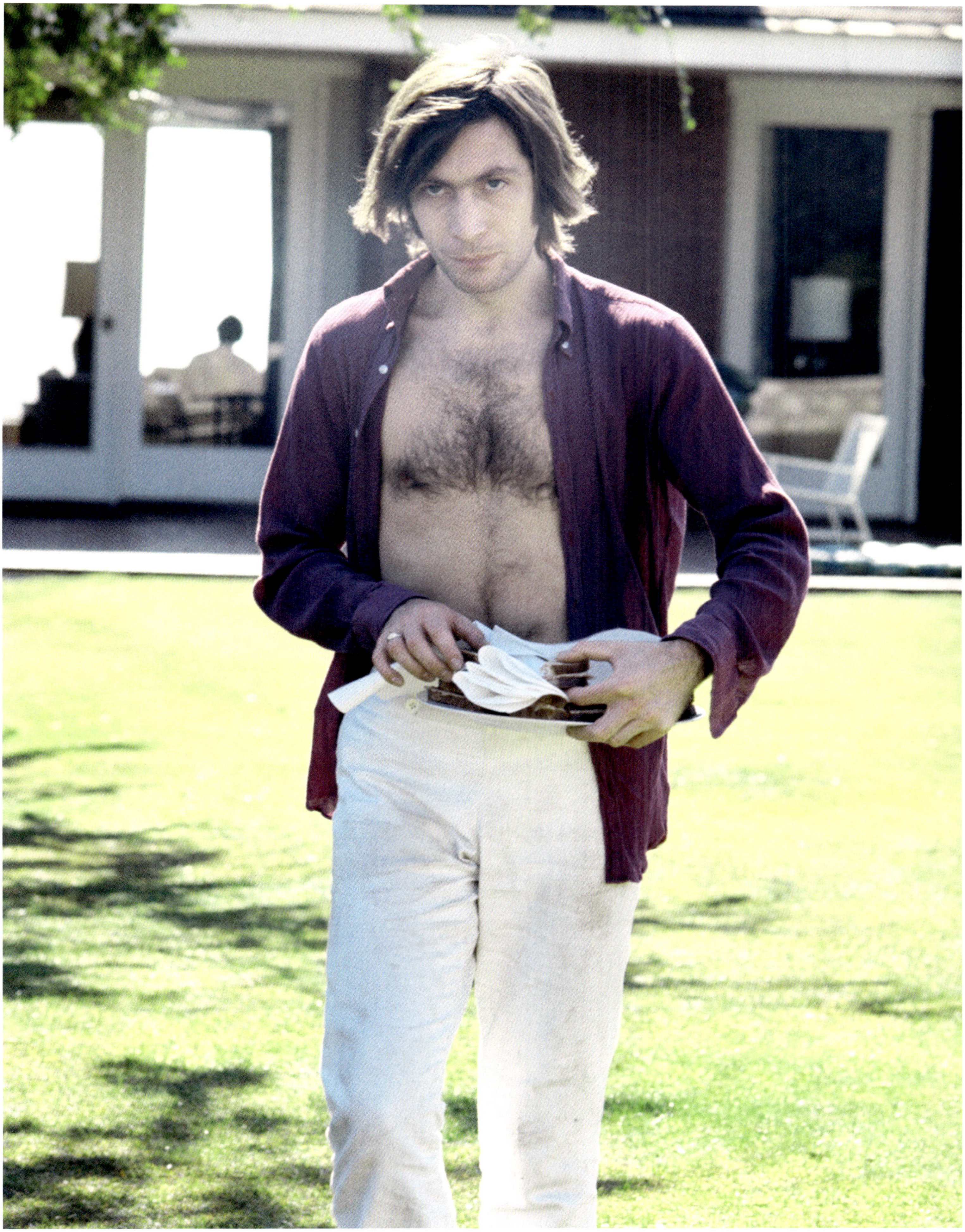

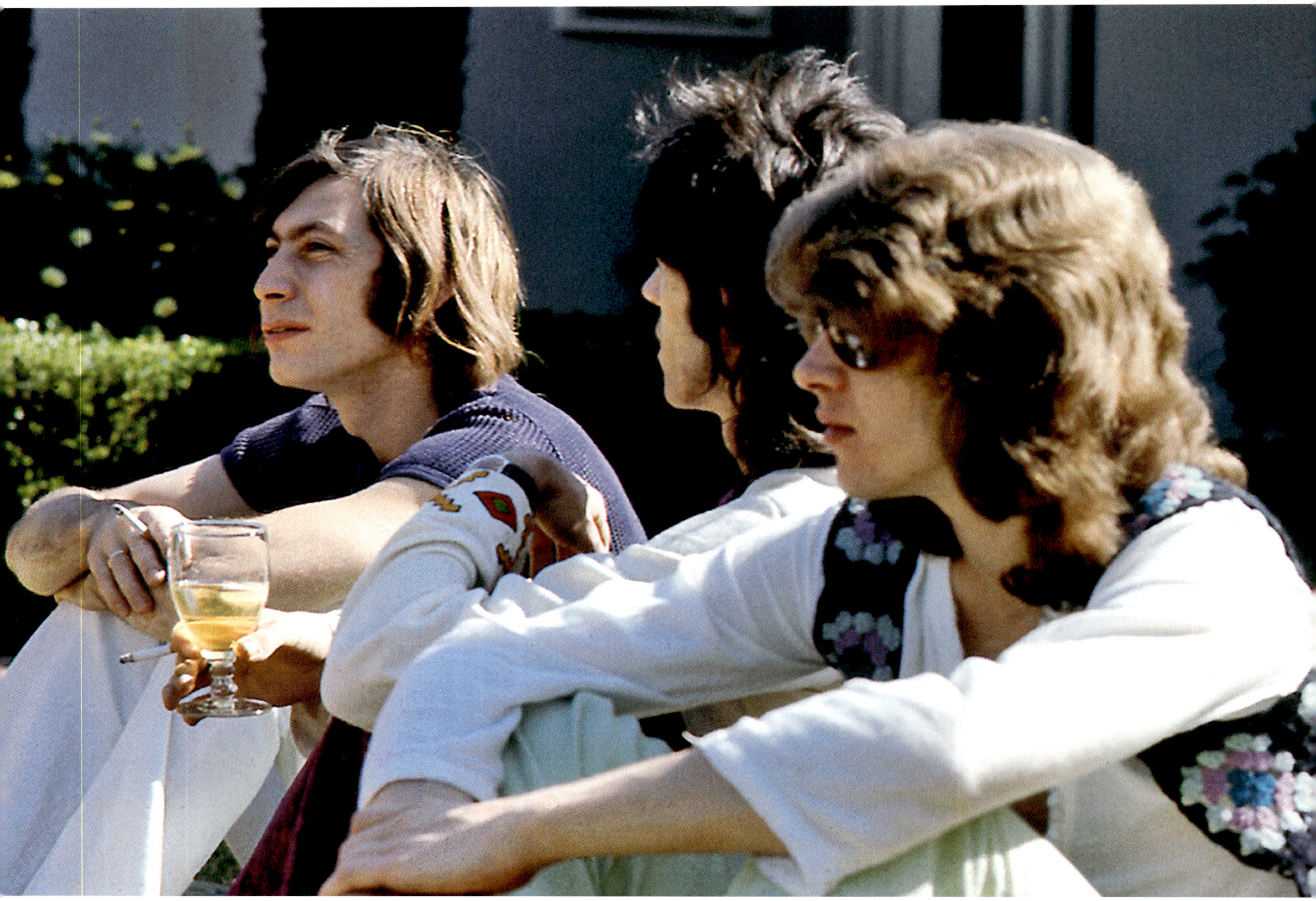

Two more shots of the Stones in the grounds of The Dupont House – 18 October 1969.

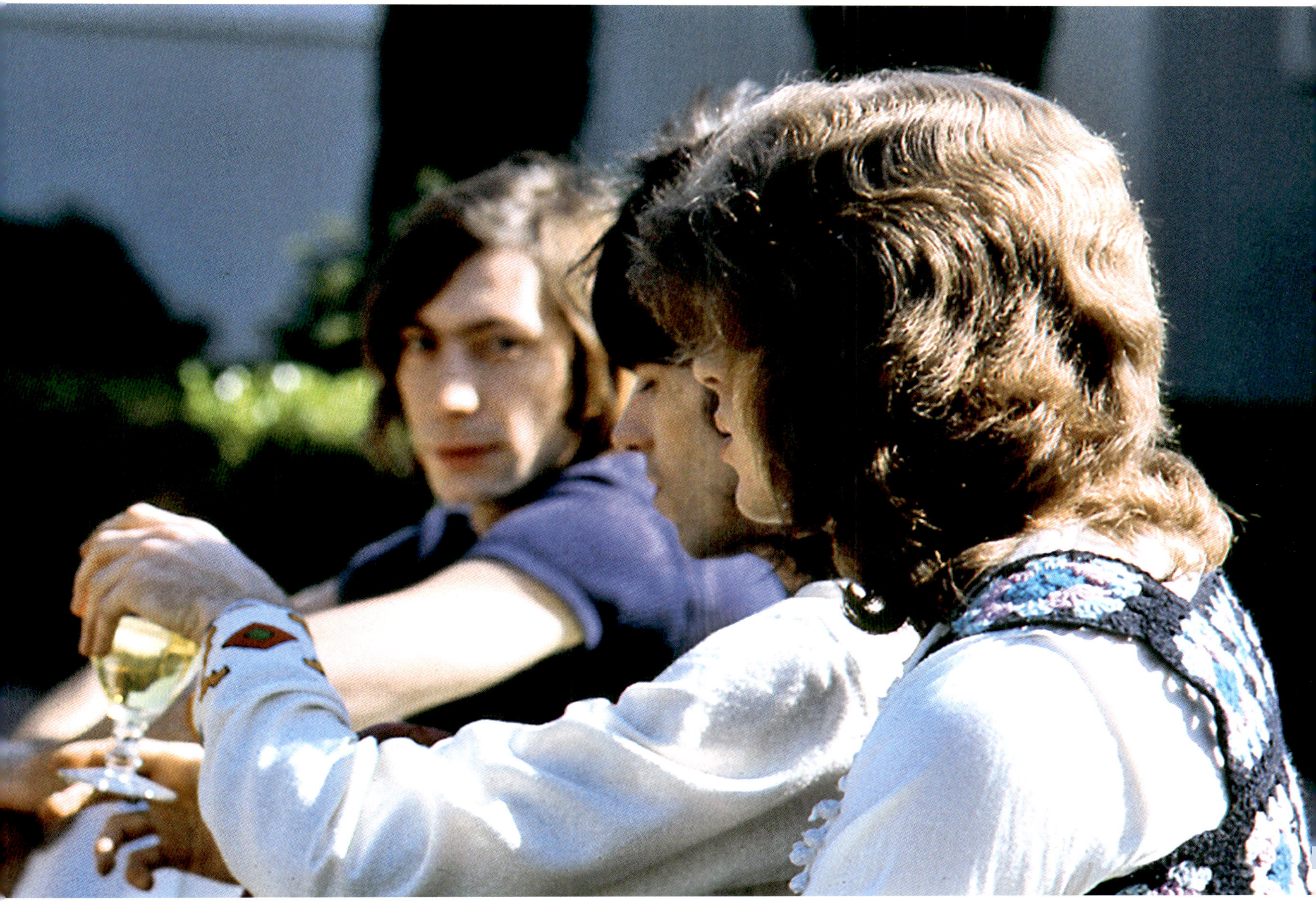

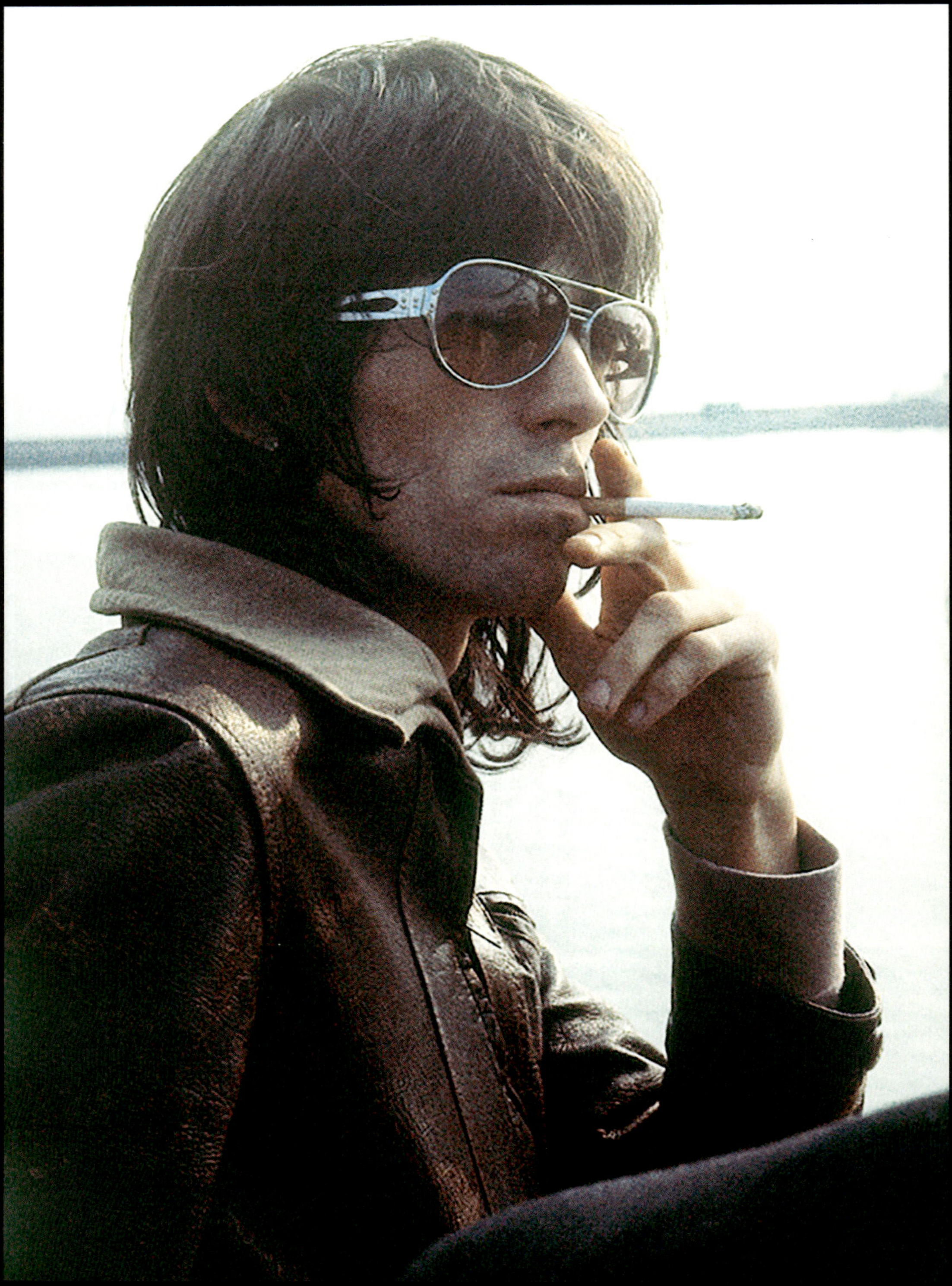

Shot of Keith on the ferry from Helsingør, Denmark, to Helsingborg, Sweden, – 30 August 1970.
Right: Mick deep in thought backstage at the Deutschlandhalle in West Berlin – 16 September 1970.

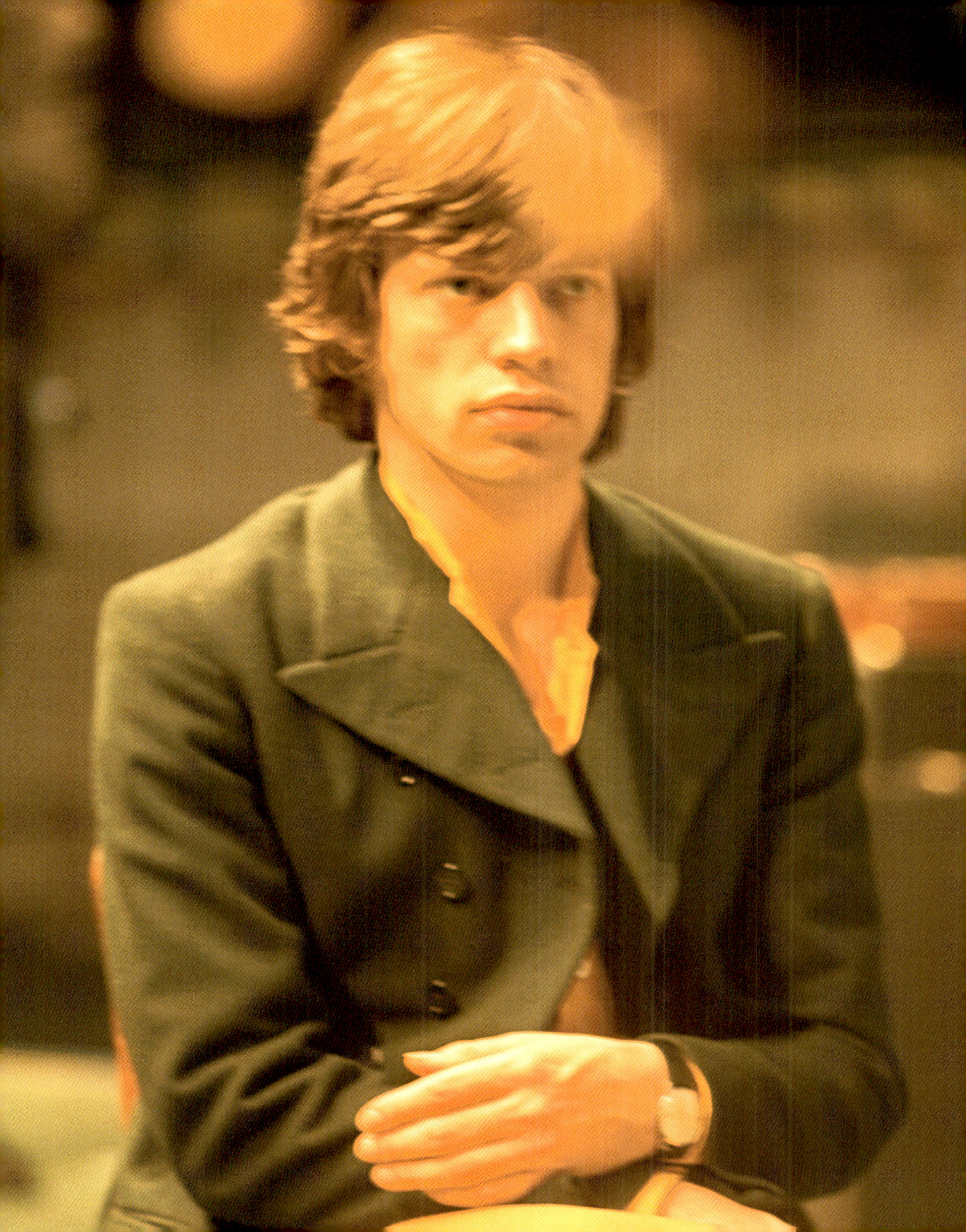

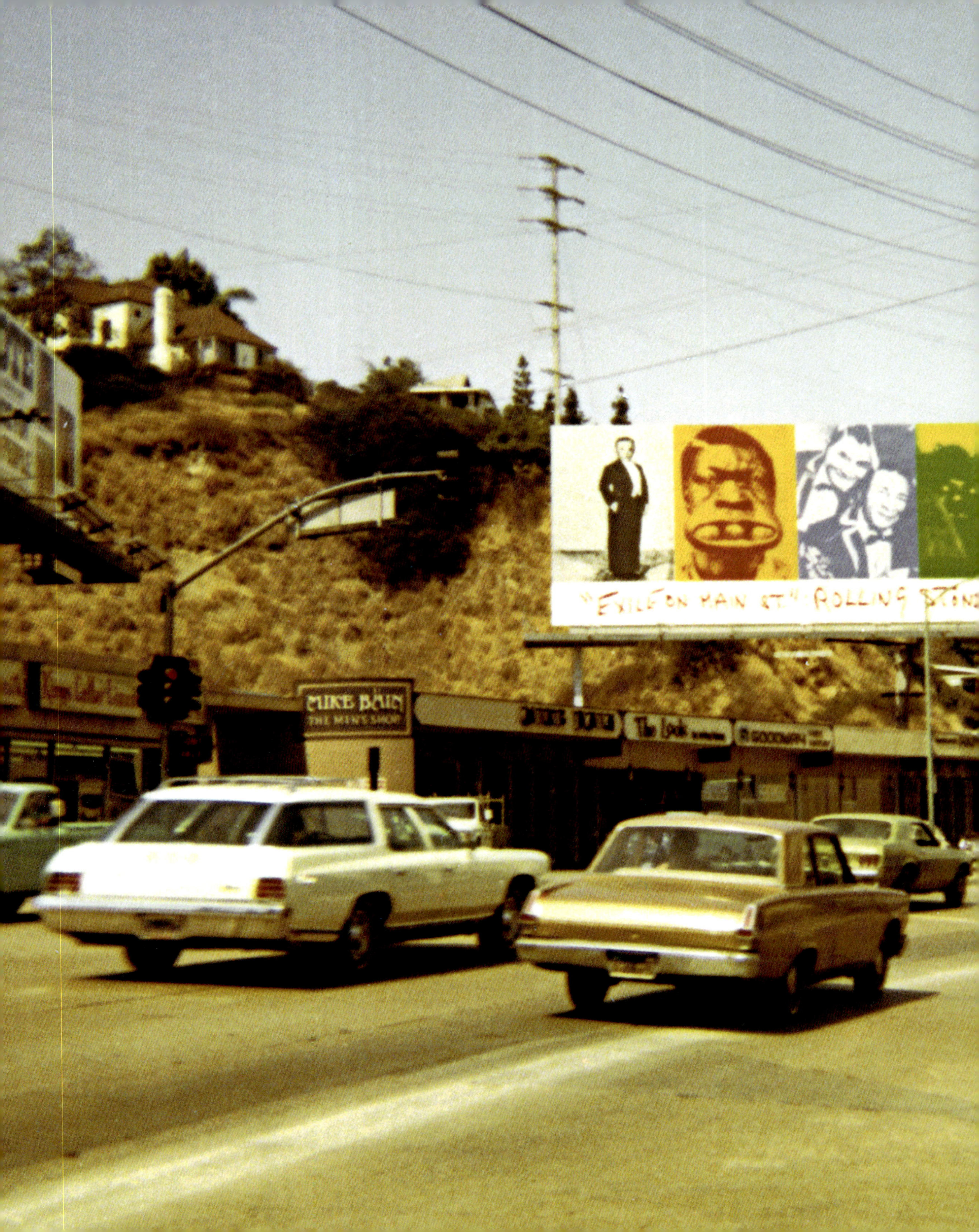
"EXILE ON MAIN ST." ROLLING
MIKE BAIN
THE MEN'S SHOP

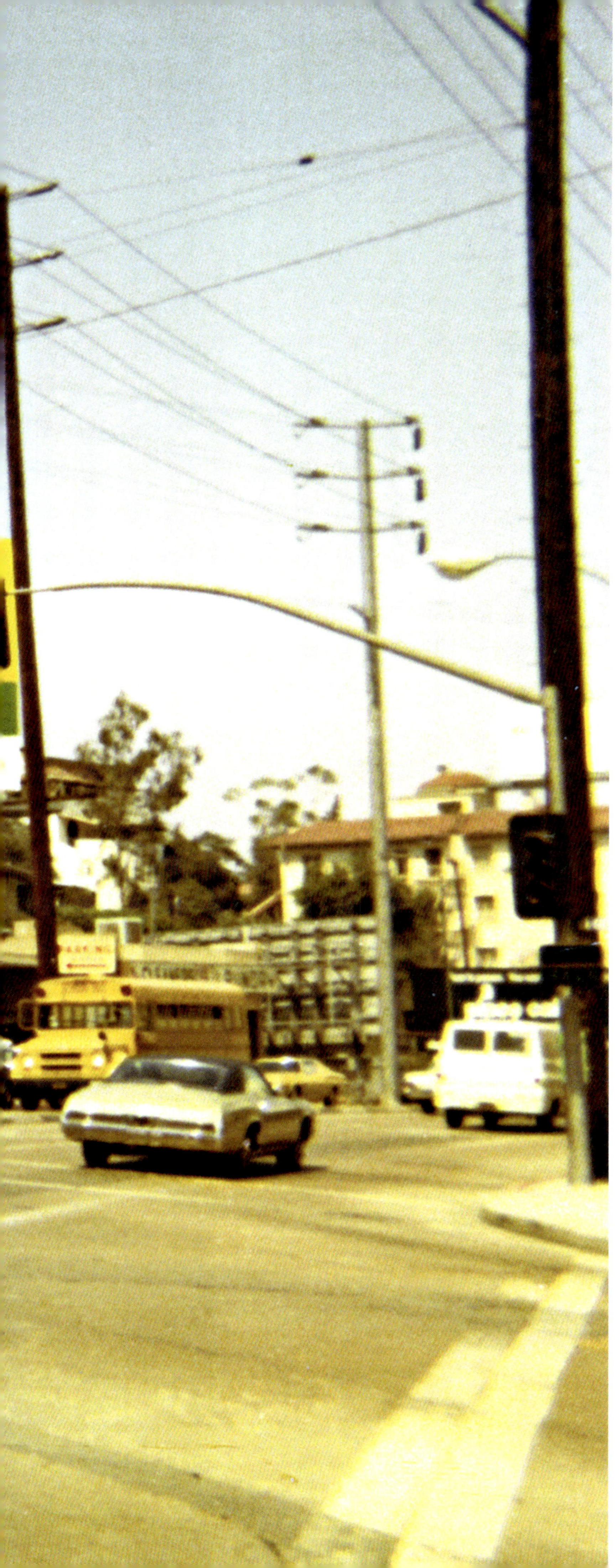

Photo of a Stones billboard advertising our album *Exile On Main Street* that I took from the car – July 1972.

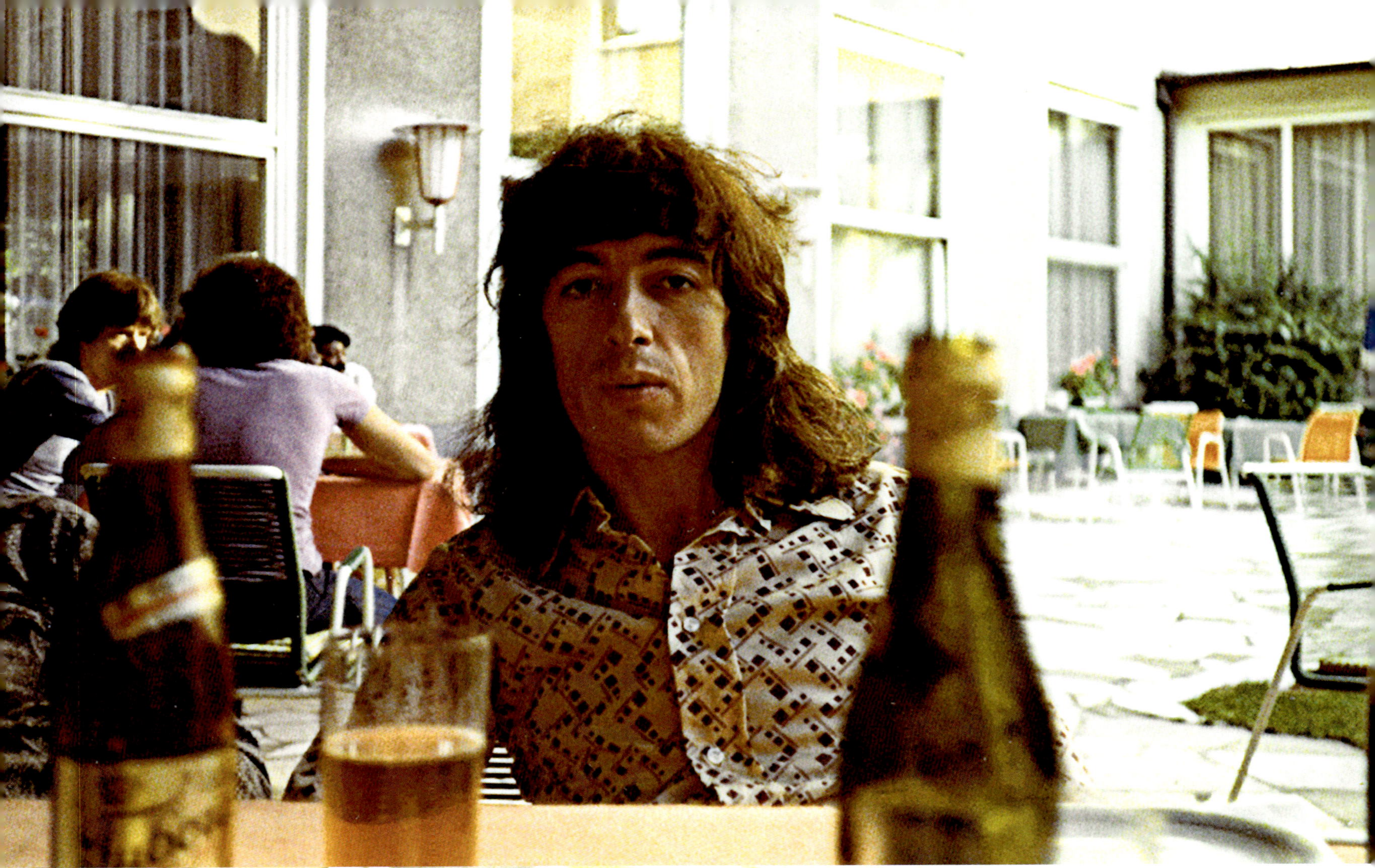

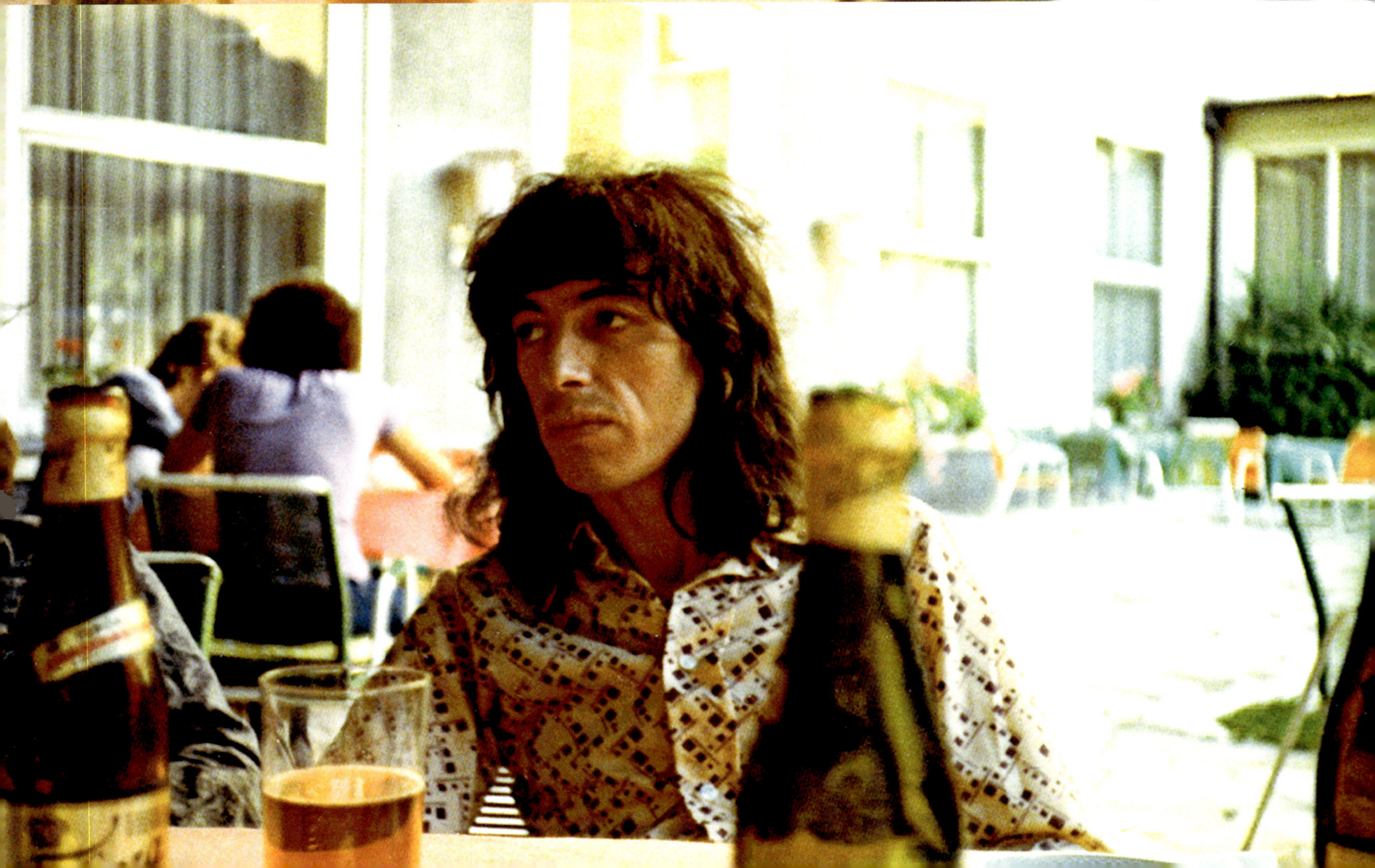

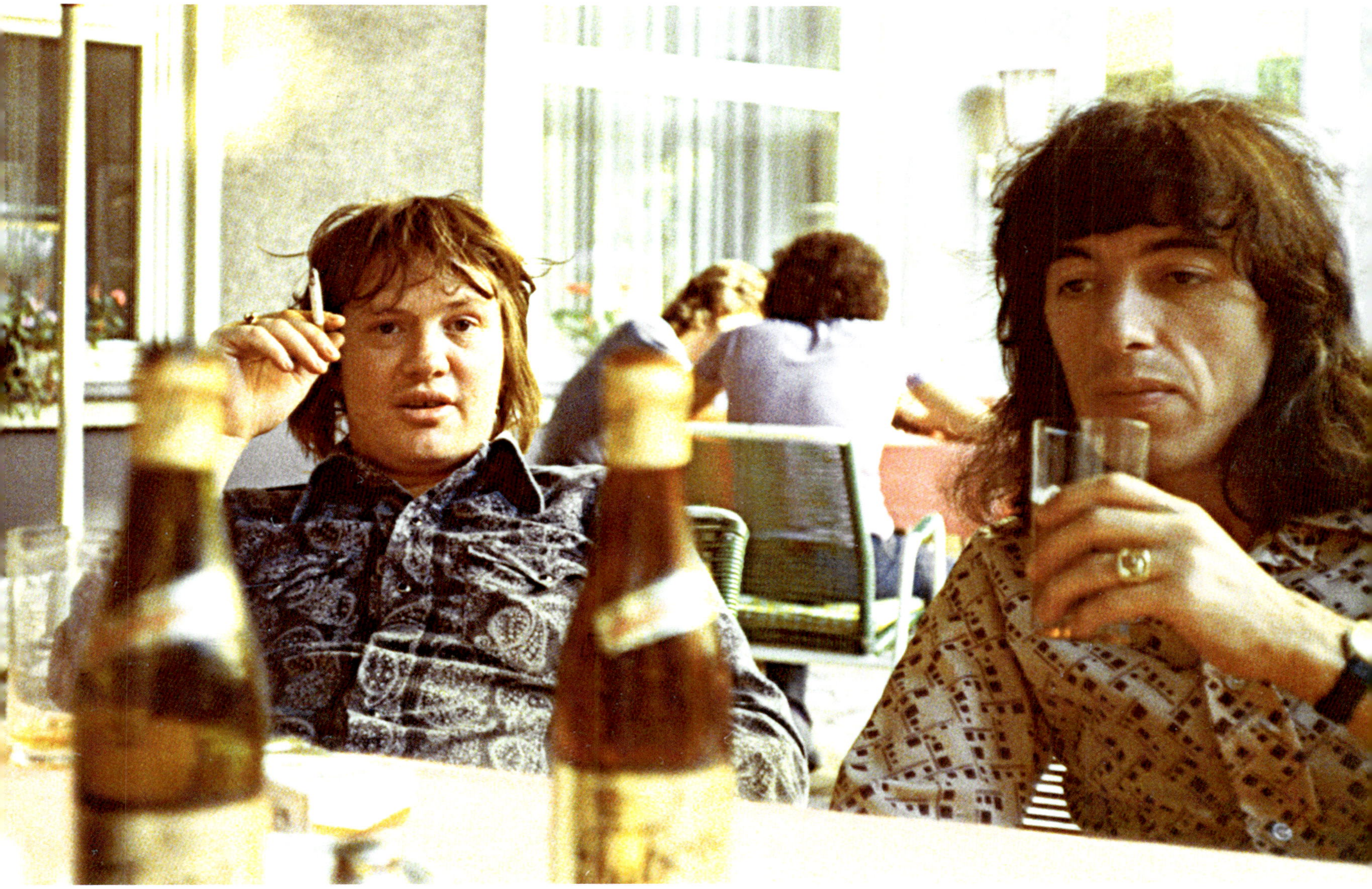

Sitting in the sun with saxophonist Bobby Keys outside the small Mannheimer Hof Hotel in Mannheim, West Germany, before our show at the Eisstadion – 3 September 1973.

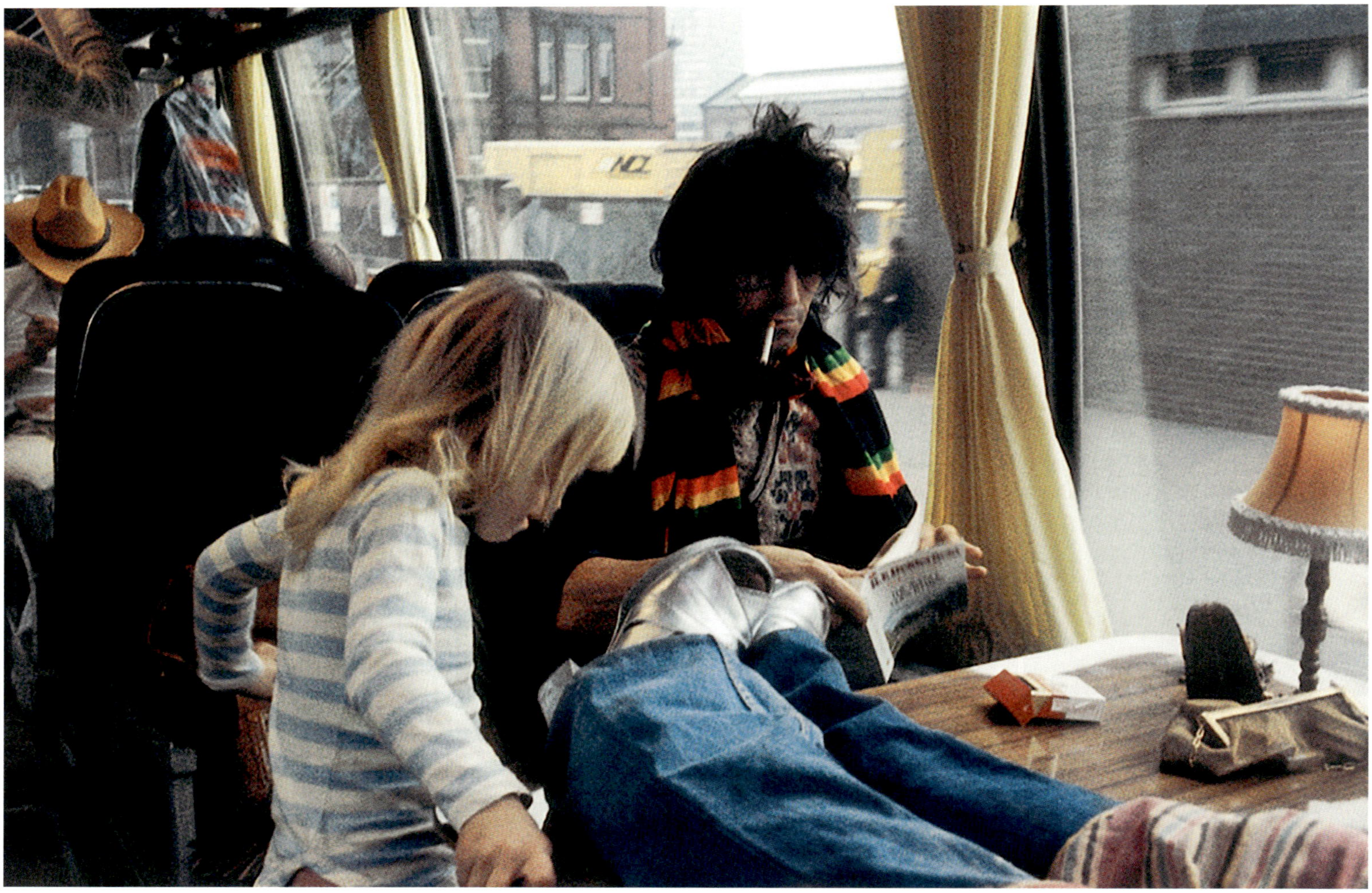

Keith with son Marlon in the coach from Manchester to Newcastle – 13 September 1973.
Right: Charlie wearing a silly wig, with daughter Seraphina and my son Stephen in the background, and Keith sleeping – same bus, same date.

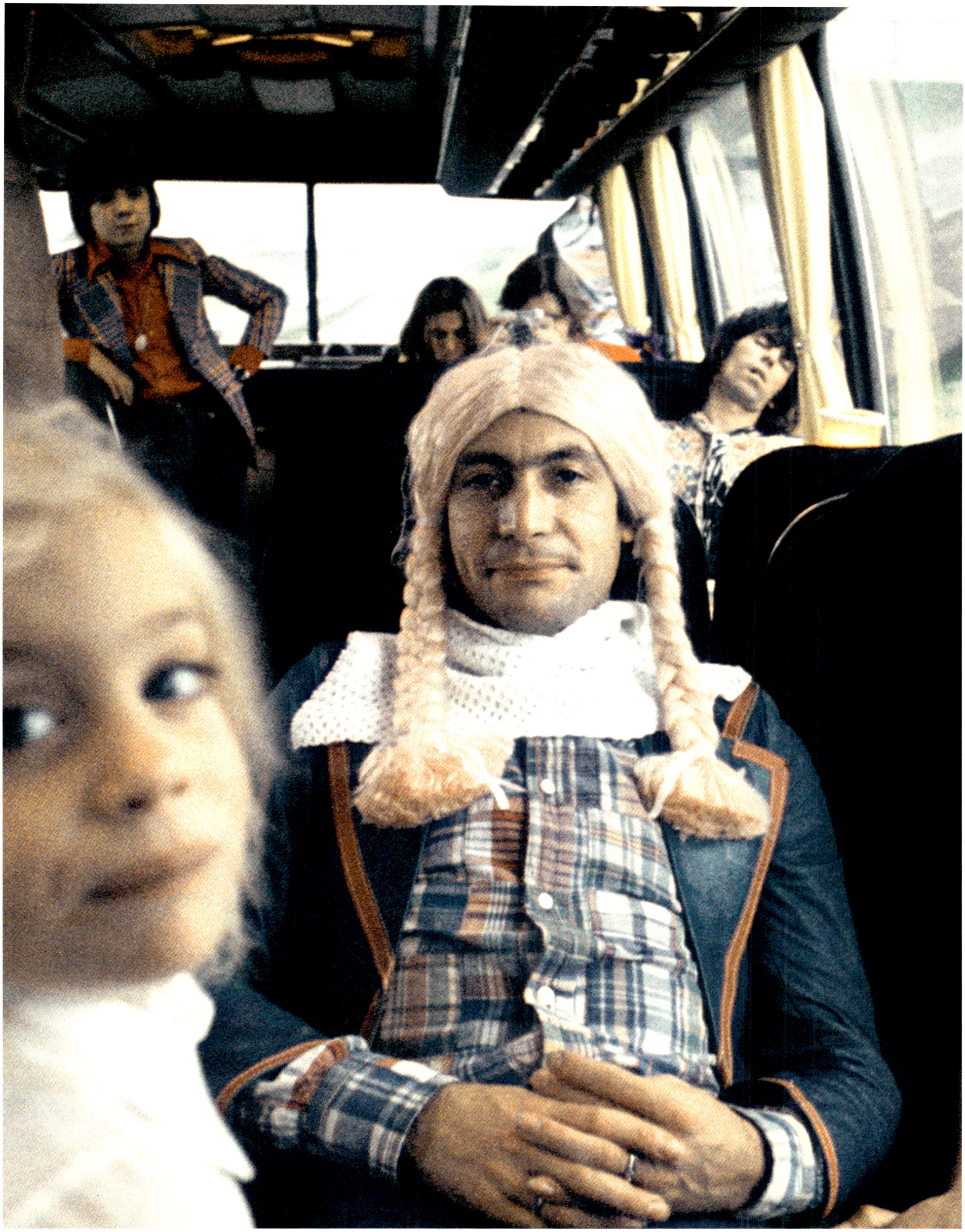

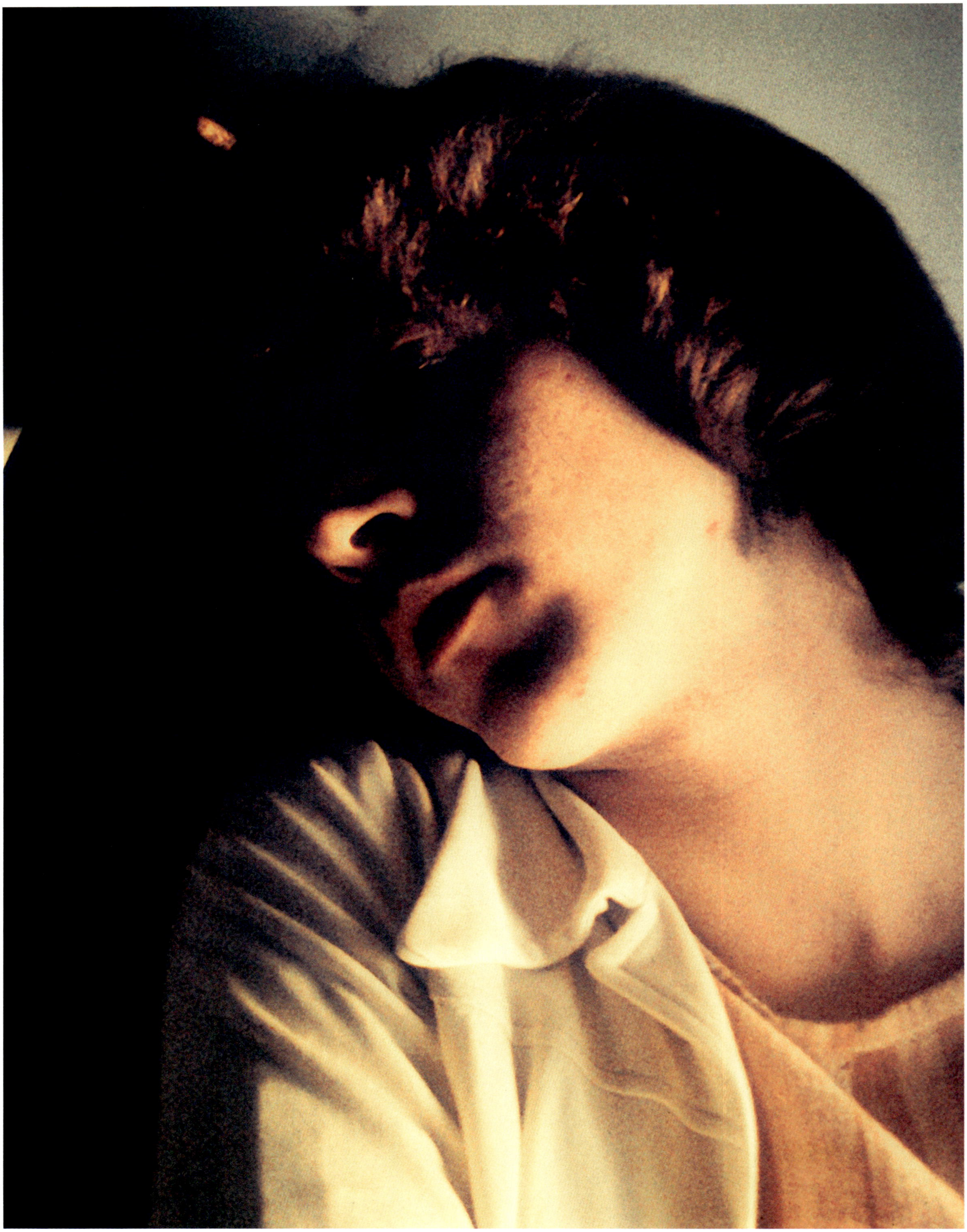

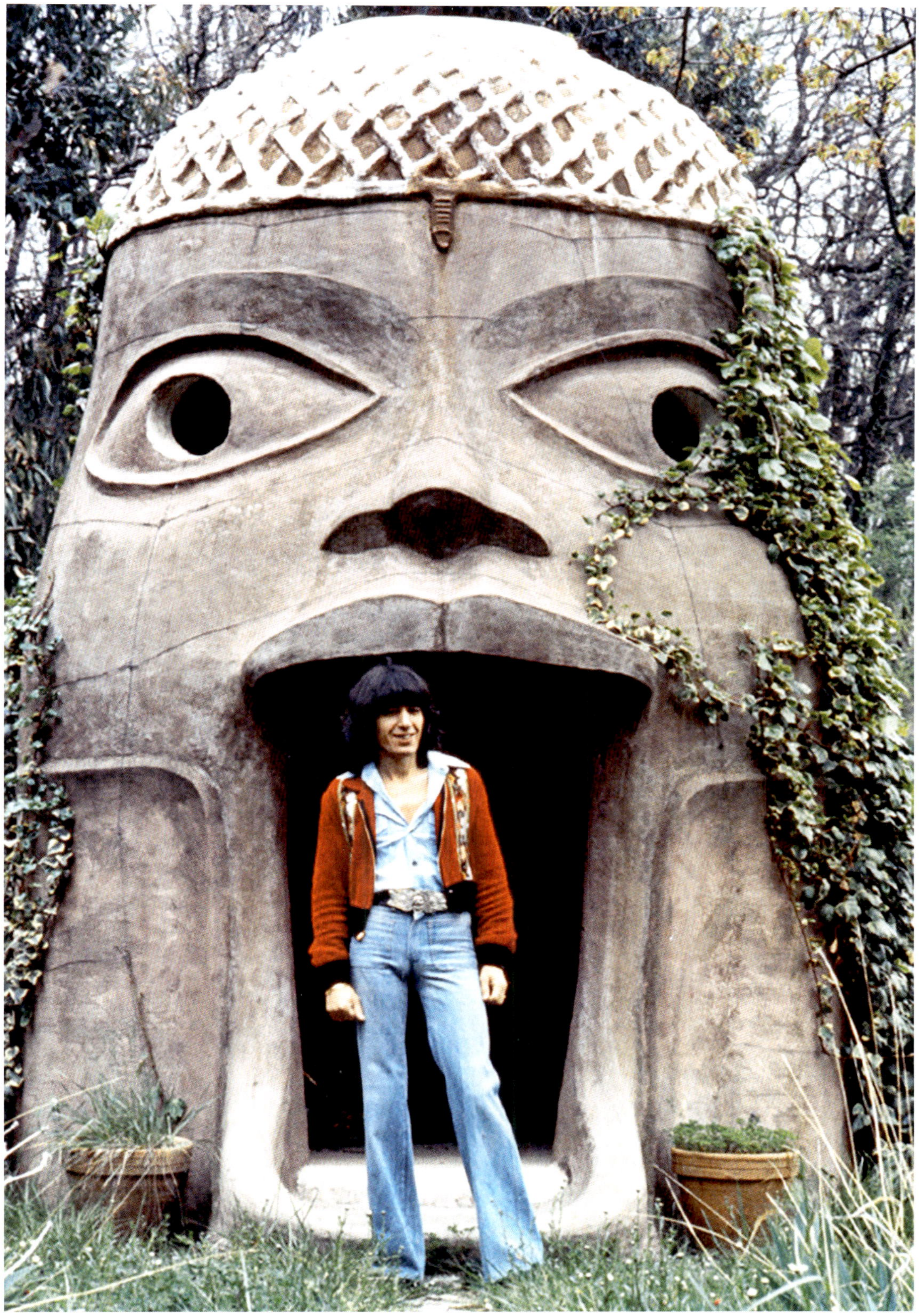

Mick Taylor sleeping on the plane from Gothenburg, Sweden, to Copenhagen, Denmark, after our concert at the Scandinavium Stadium there – 6 October 1973.

Above: Me posing at the mouth entrance of the African head statue in the garden of our house L'Oustaraun in Vence, France – 12 April 1974.

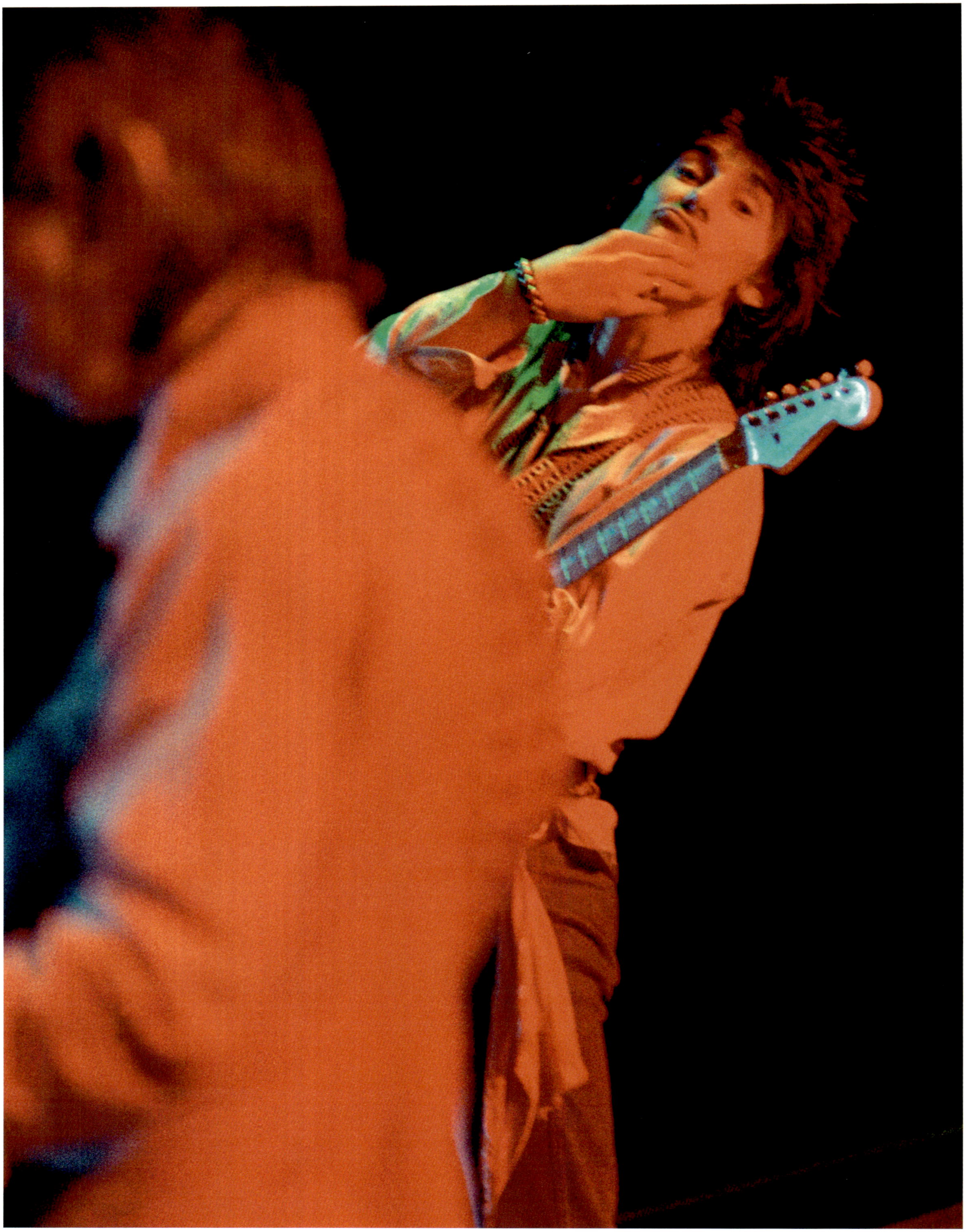

Shots of Ronnie and Charlie, taken with my red filter at rehearsals at Andy Warhol's house in Montauk, Long Island – 12 May 1975.

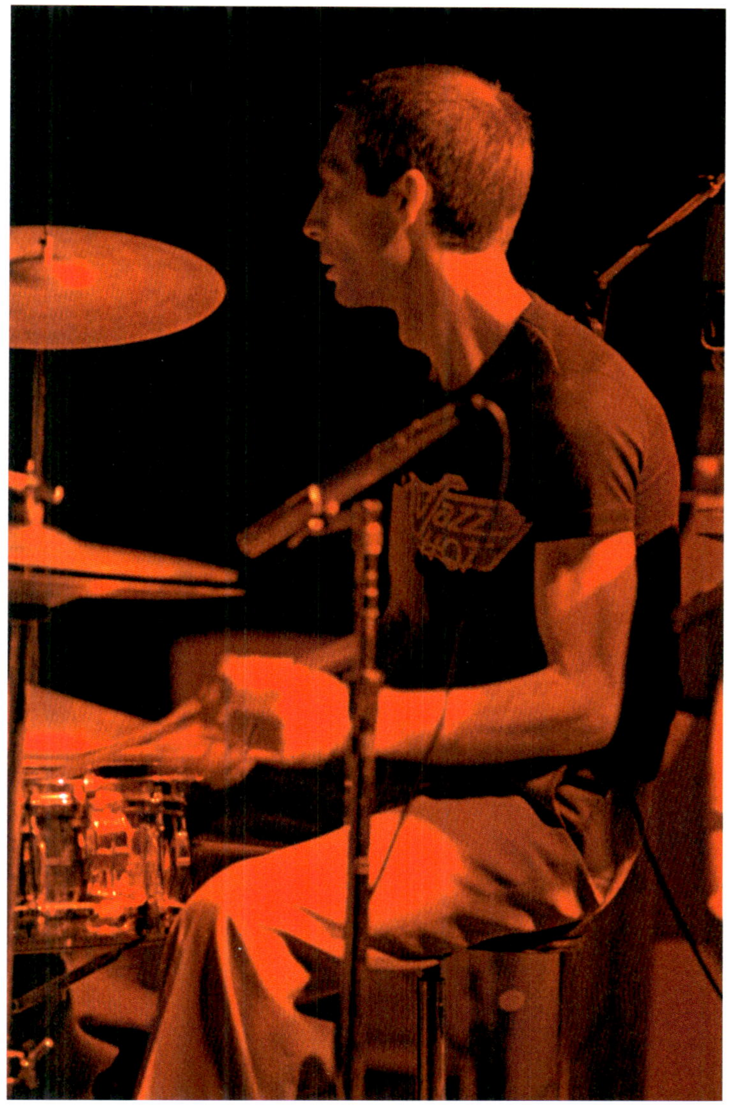

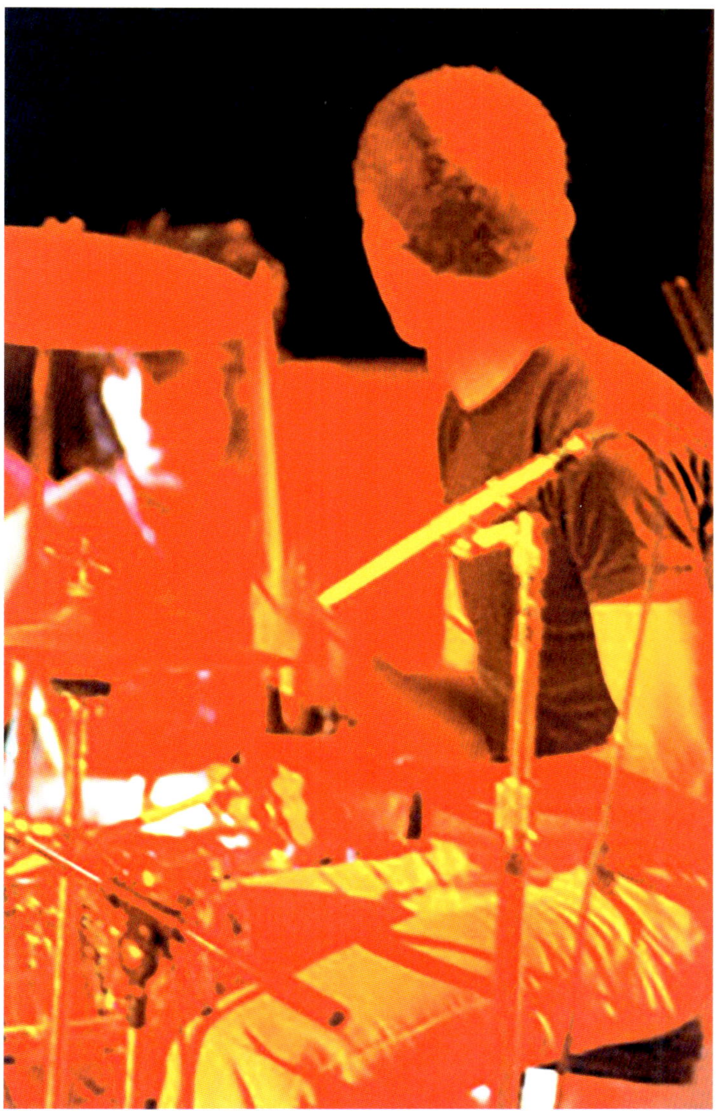

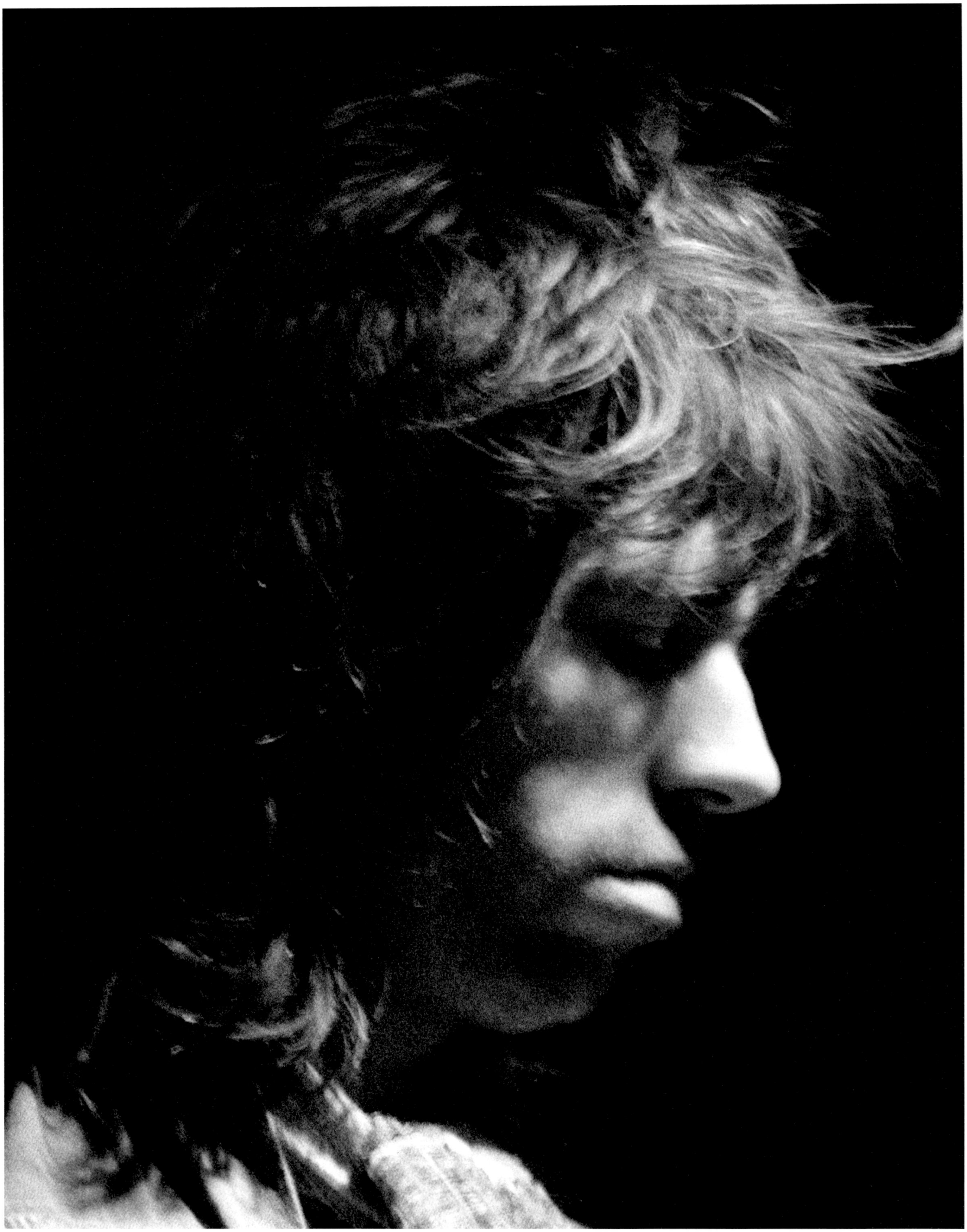

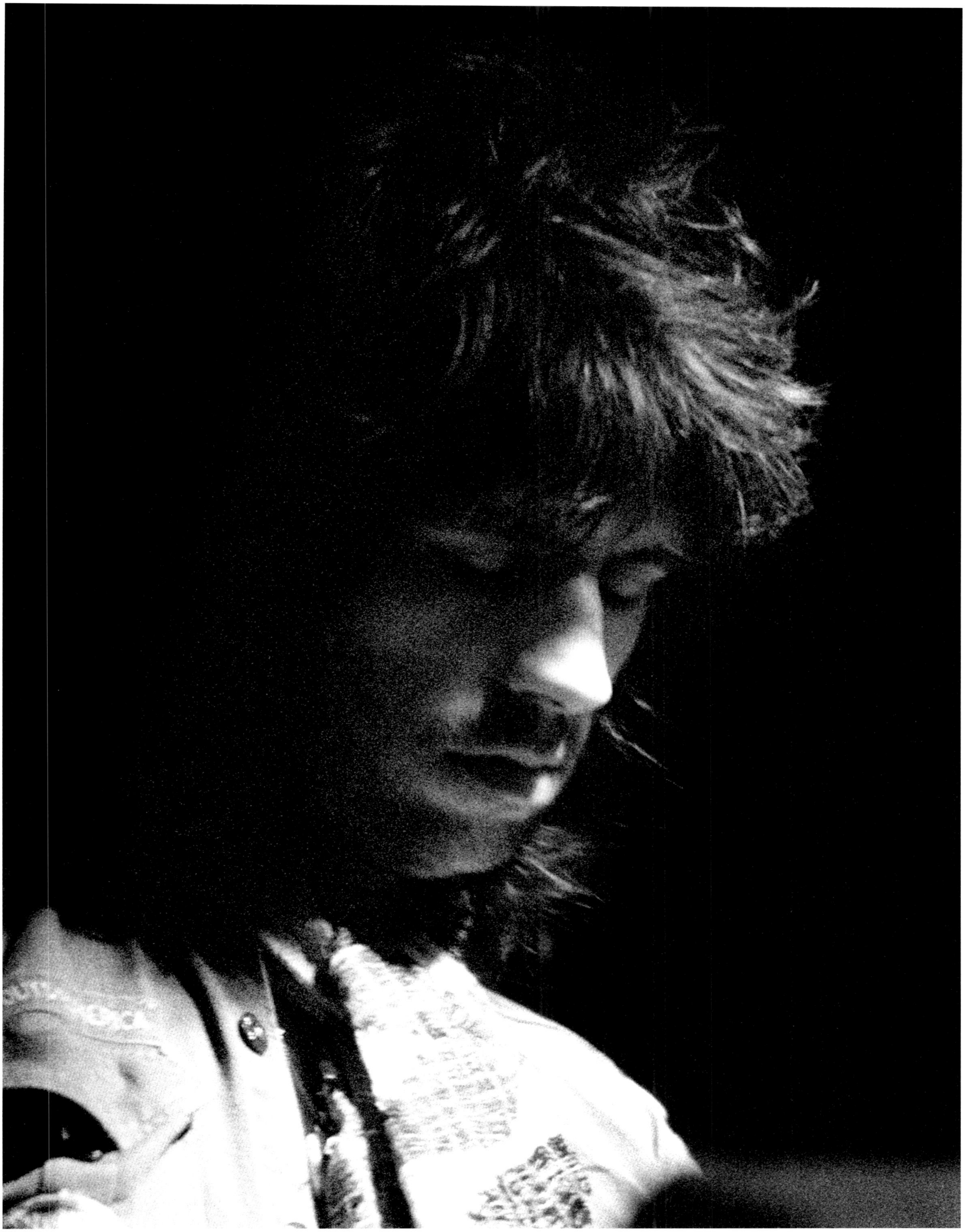

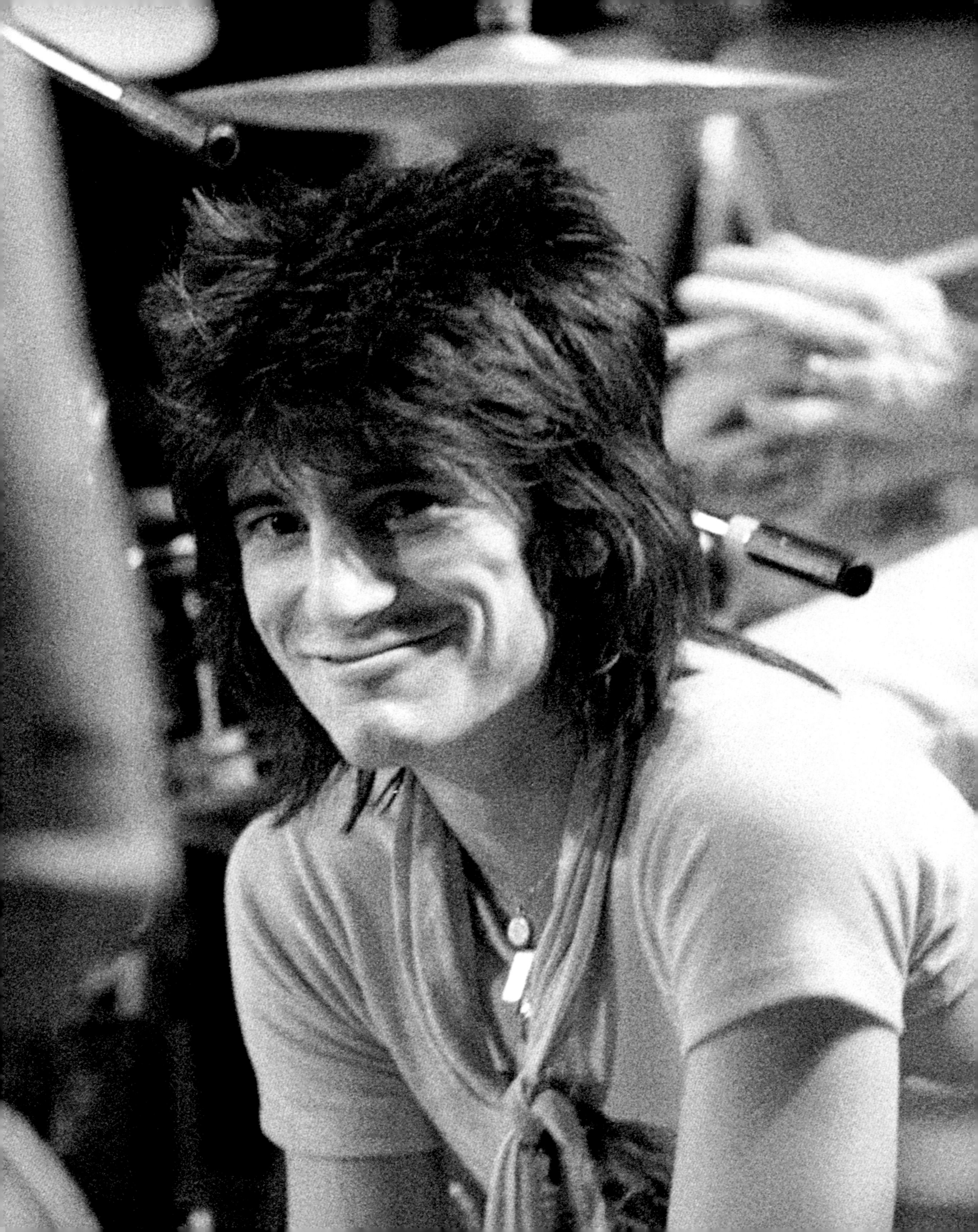

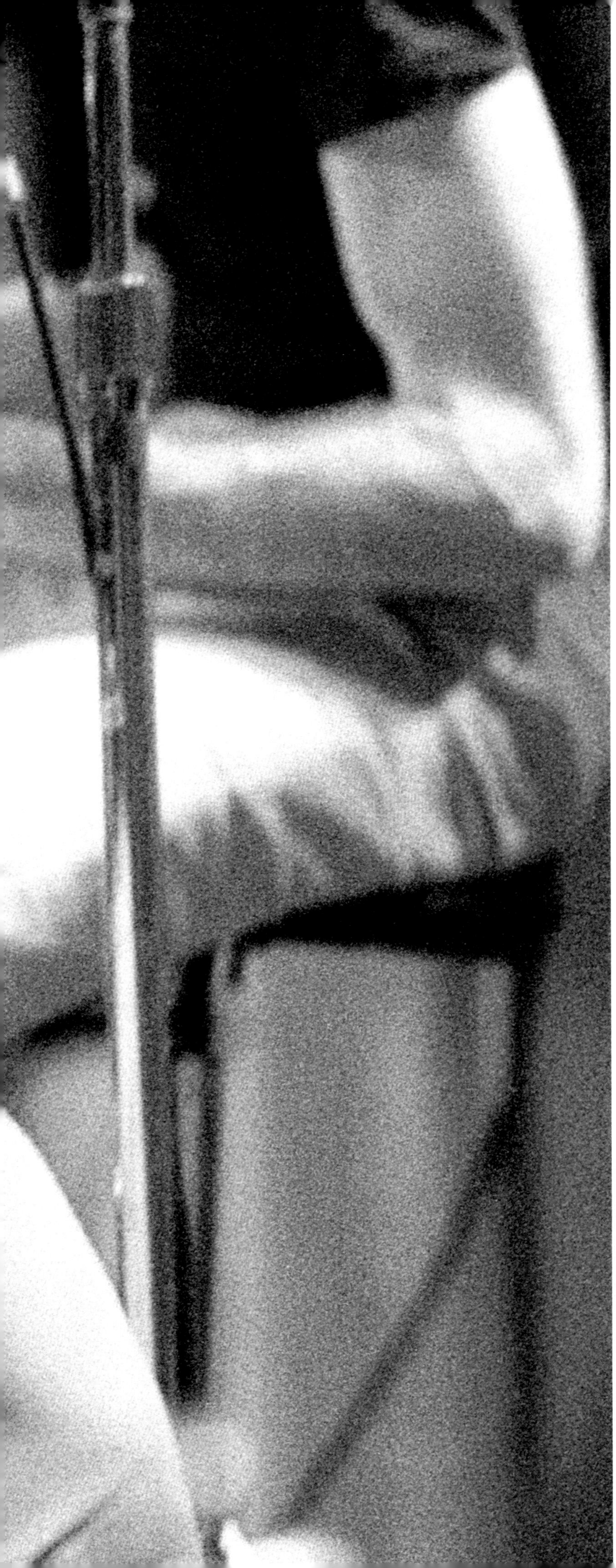

Shot of Ronnie at rehearsals on the new stage setup in a hangar at Newburgh Airport, in New York State – 2[illegible] May 1975.
Previous pages: Two shots of Keith, thinking, in the Musicland recording studio in Munich, West Germany – 25 March 1975.

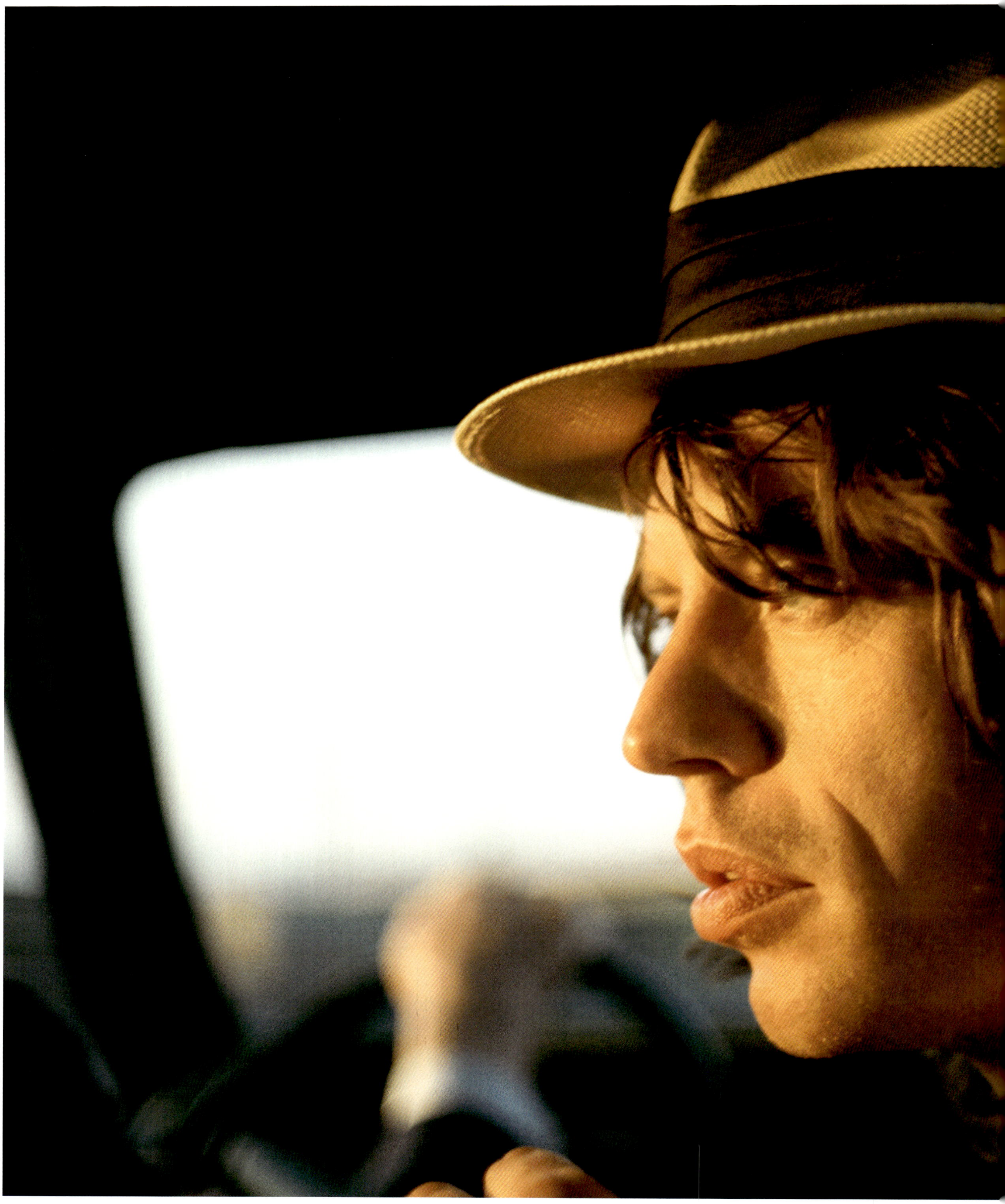

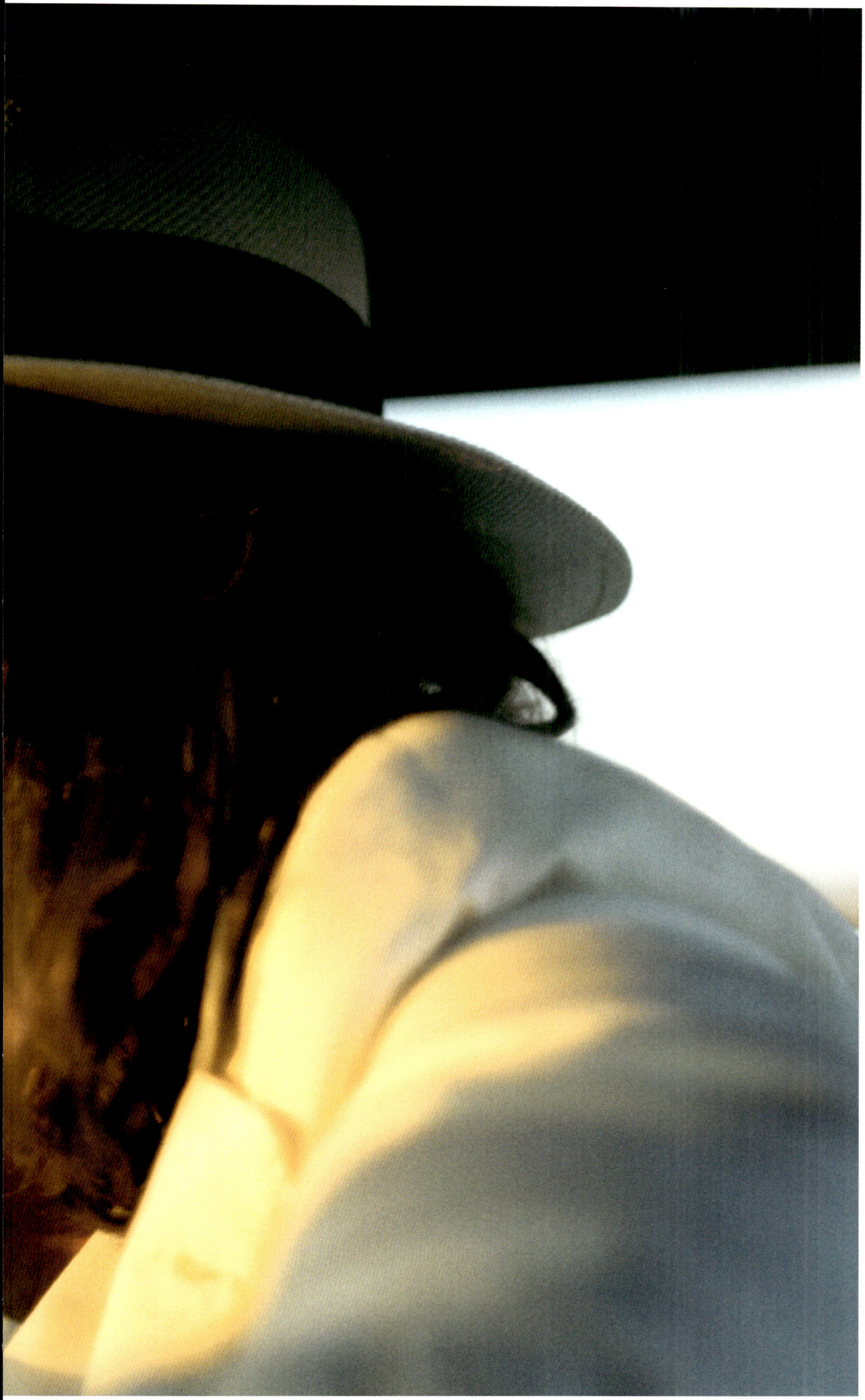

Shot of Mick in the bus on the way to our concert at the Maple Leaf Gardens, Toronto, Canada – 18 June 1975.

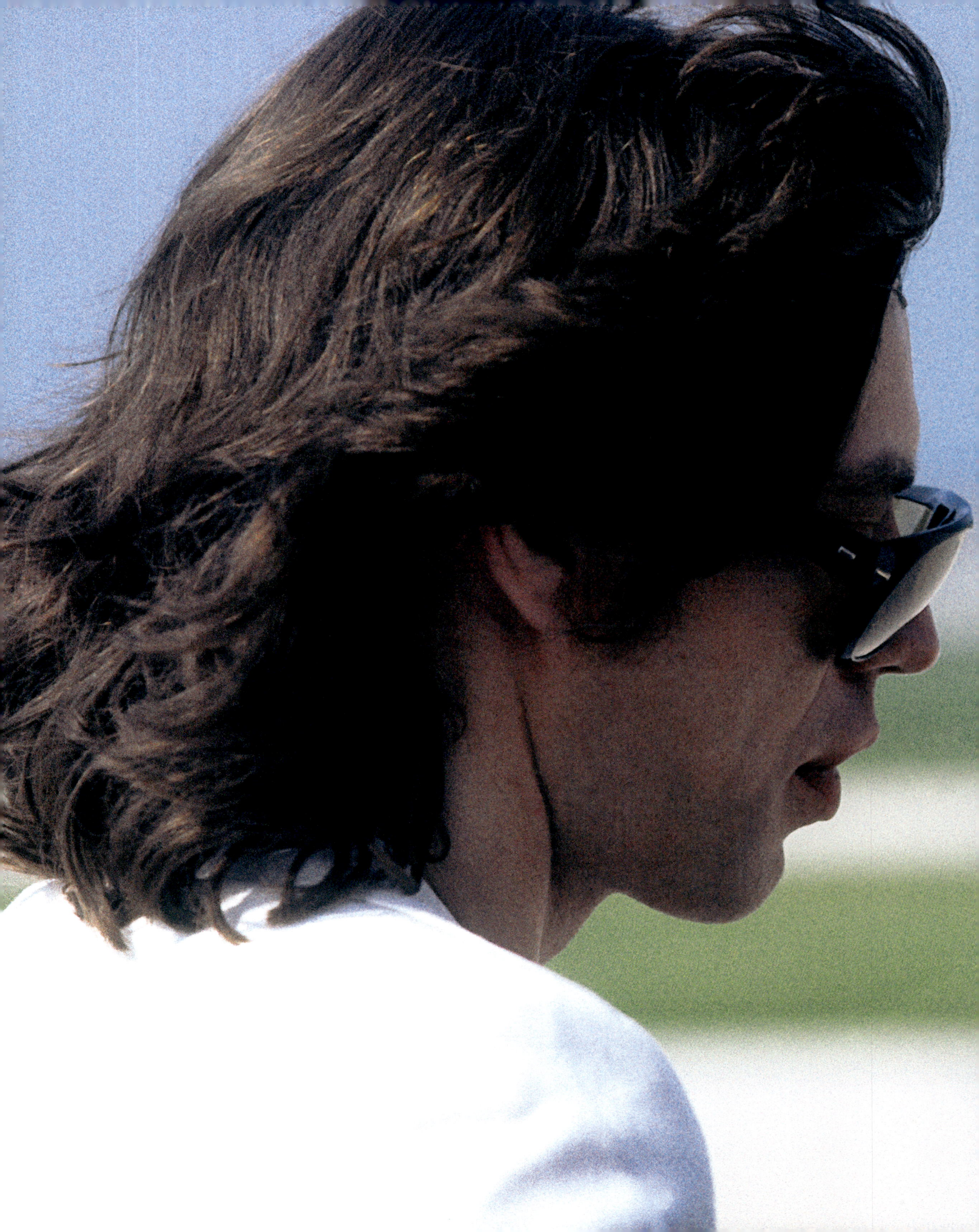

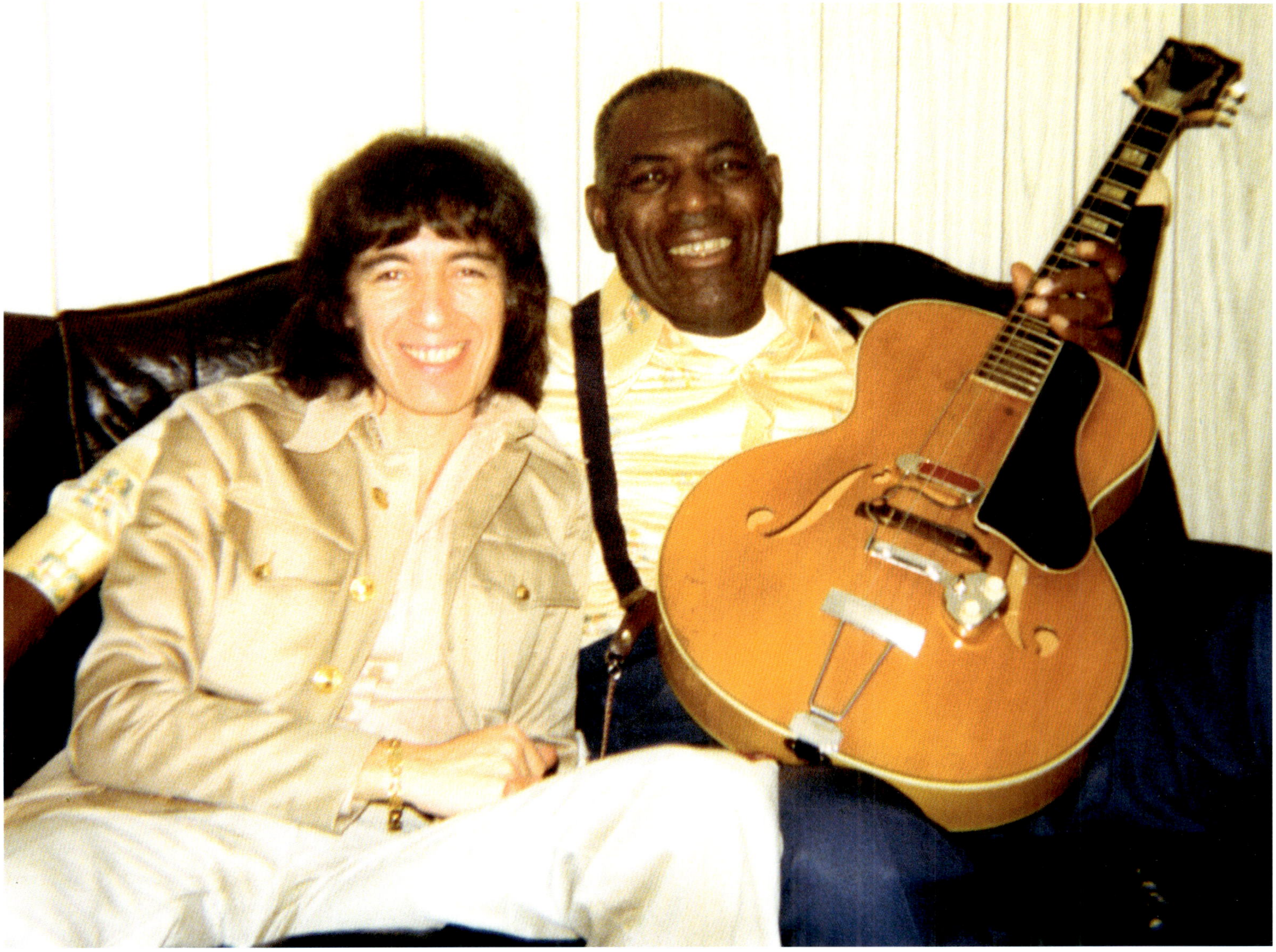

Mick leaving the Starship plane in Saint Paul, Minnesota, after flying from Milwaukee, for our concert at The Civic Centre in Saint Paul – 9 June 1975.

Above: Me with Howlin' Wolf, talking music at his house in Chicago, Illinois, after dinner there with his family – 25 July 1975.

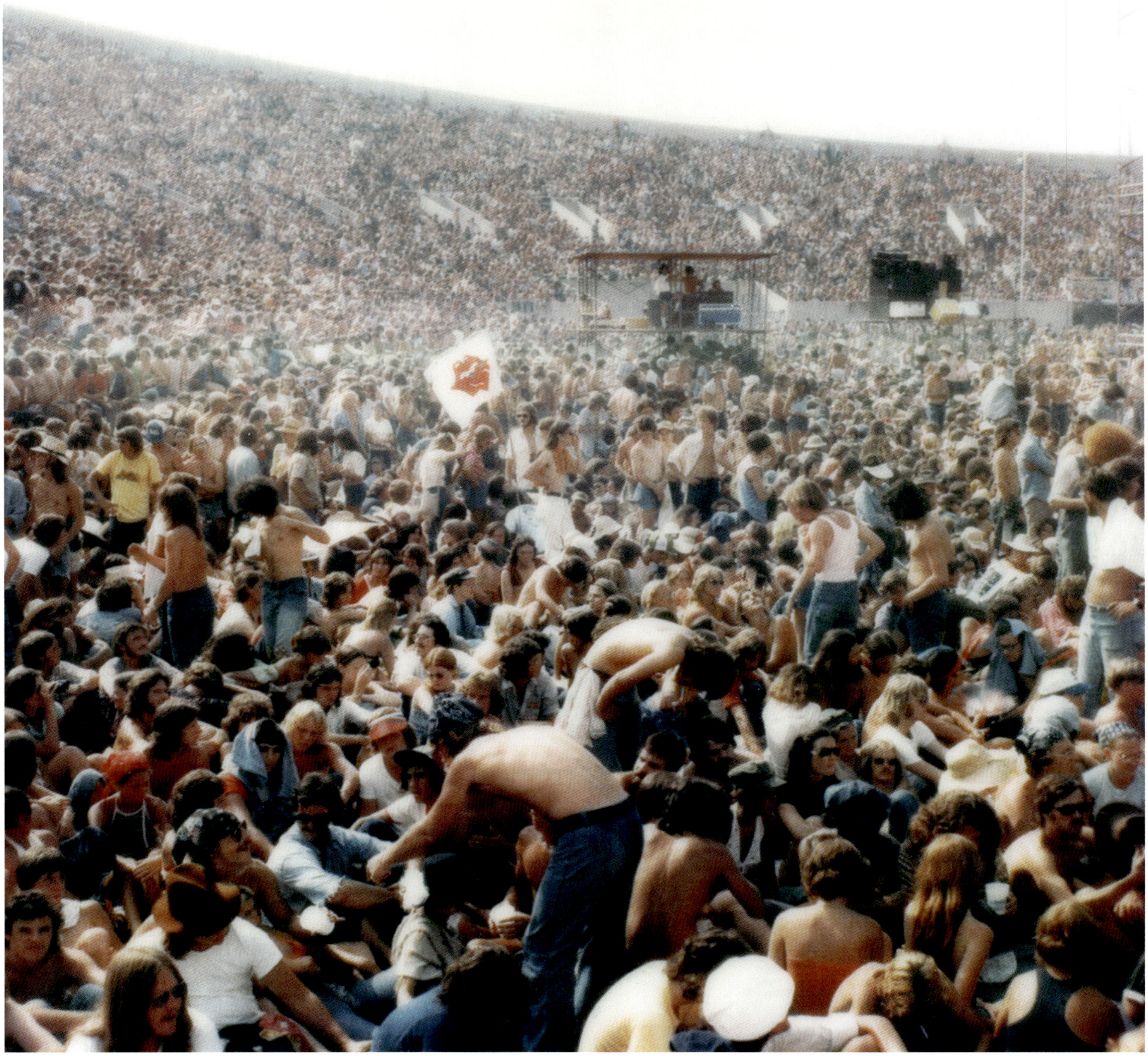

A small section of the crowd at The Cotton Bowl, in Dallas, Texas – 6 July 1975.
Right: Baby elephant 'security' backstage at The Memorial Stadium, in Memphis, Tennessee – 4 July 1975.

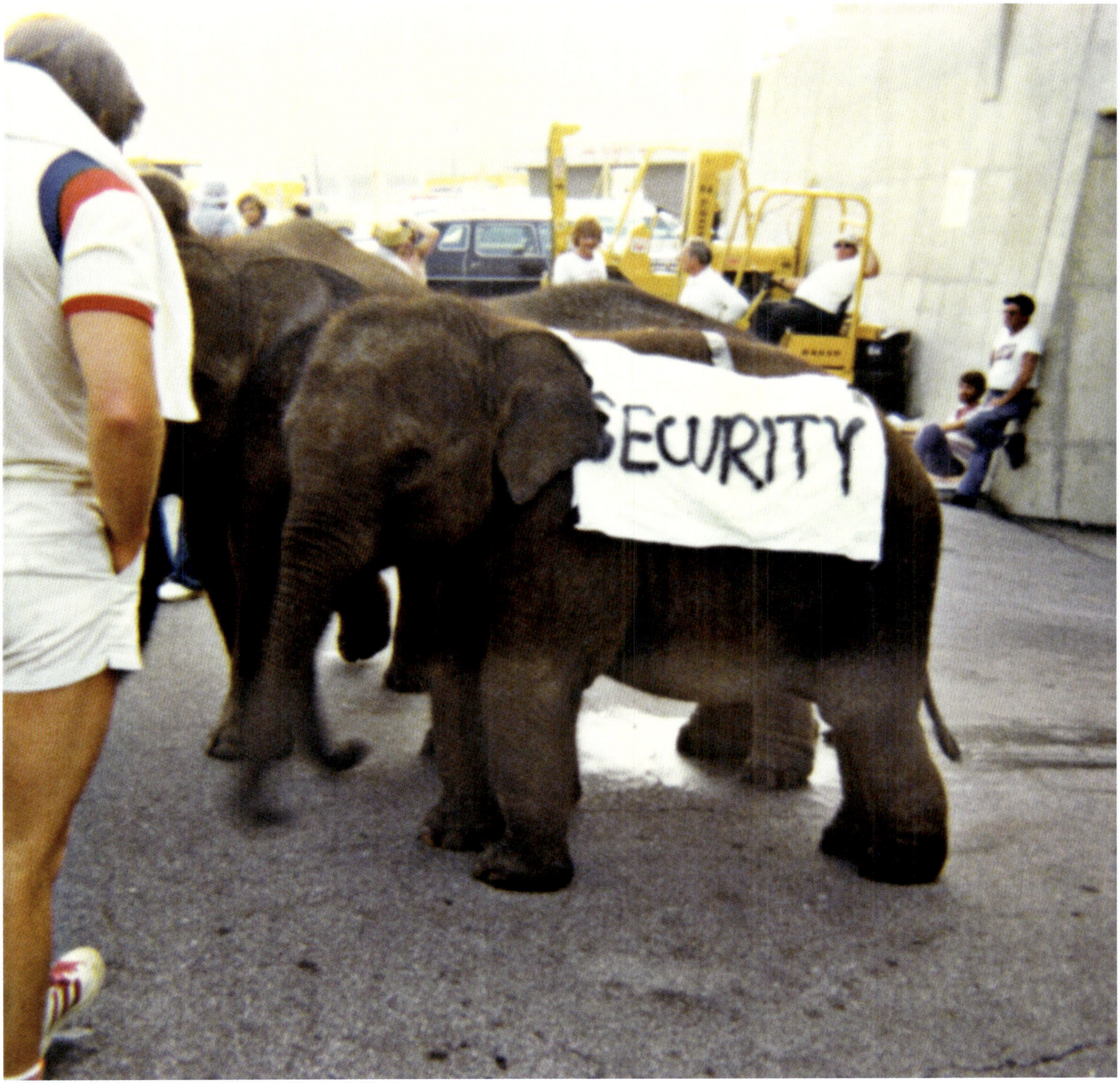
SECURITY

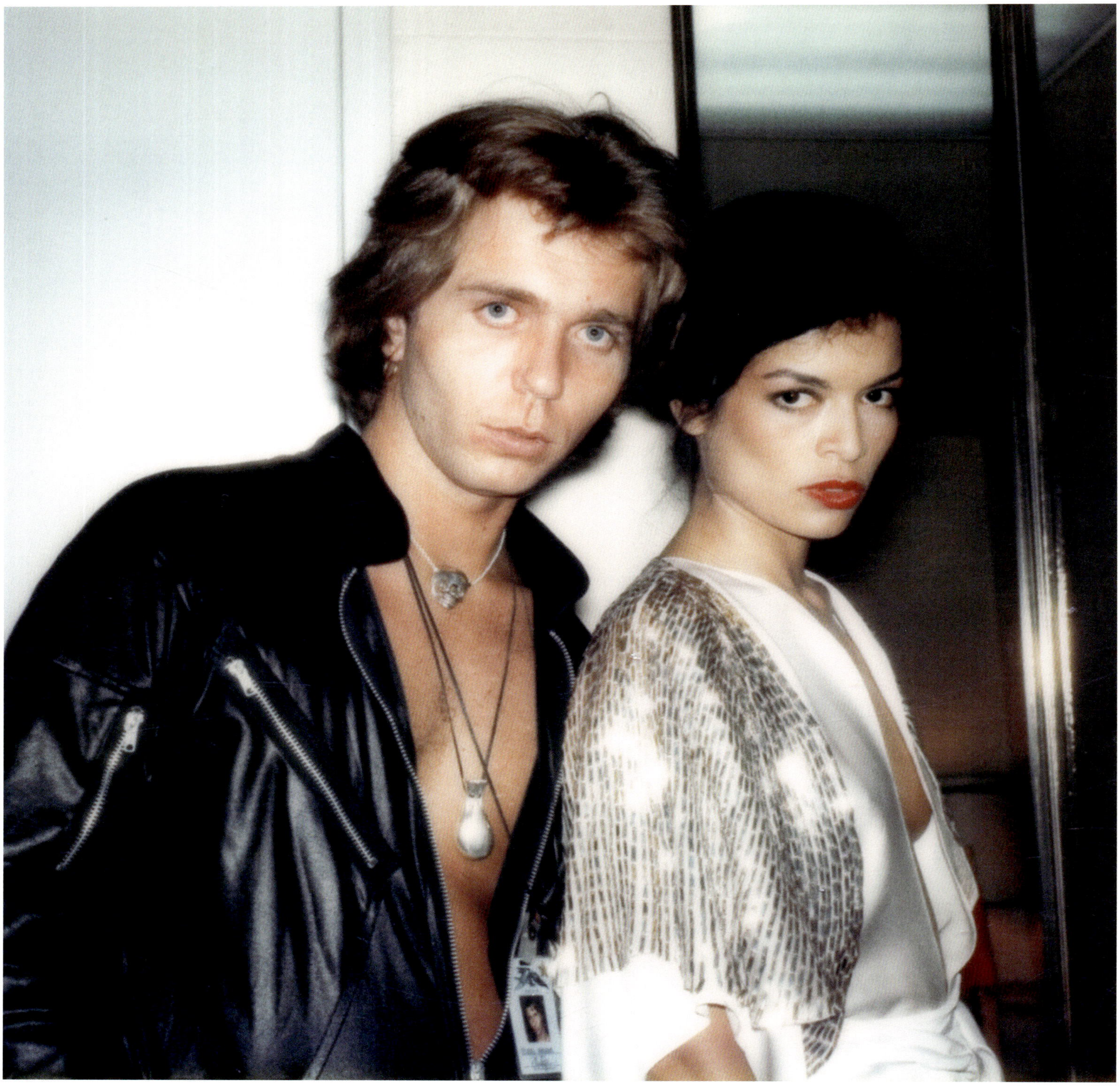

Makeup artist Pierre LaRoche and Bianca Jagger backstage at the Capital Centre in Washington, DC – 1 July 1975.
Right: Charlie wearing a stunning headdress, with wife Shirley backstage at The Cotton Bowl, in Dallas, Texas – 6 August 1975.

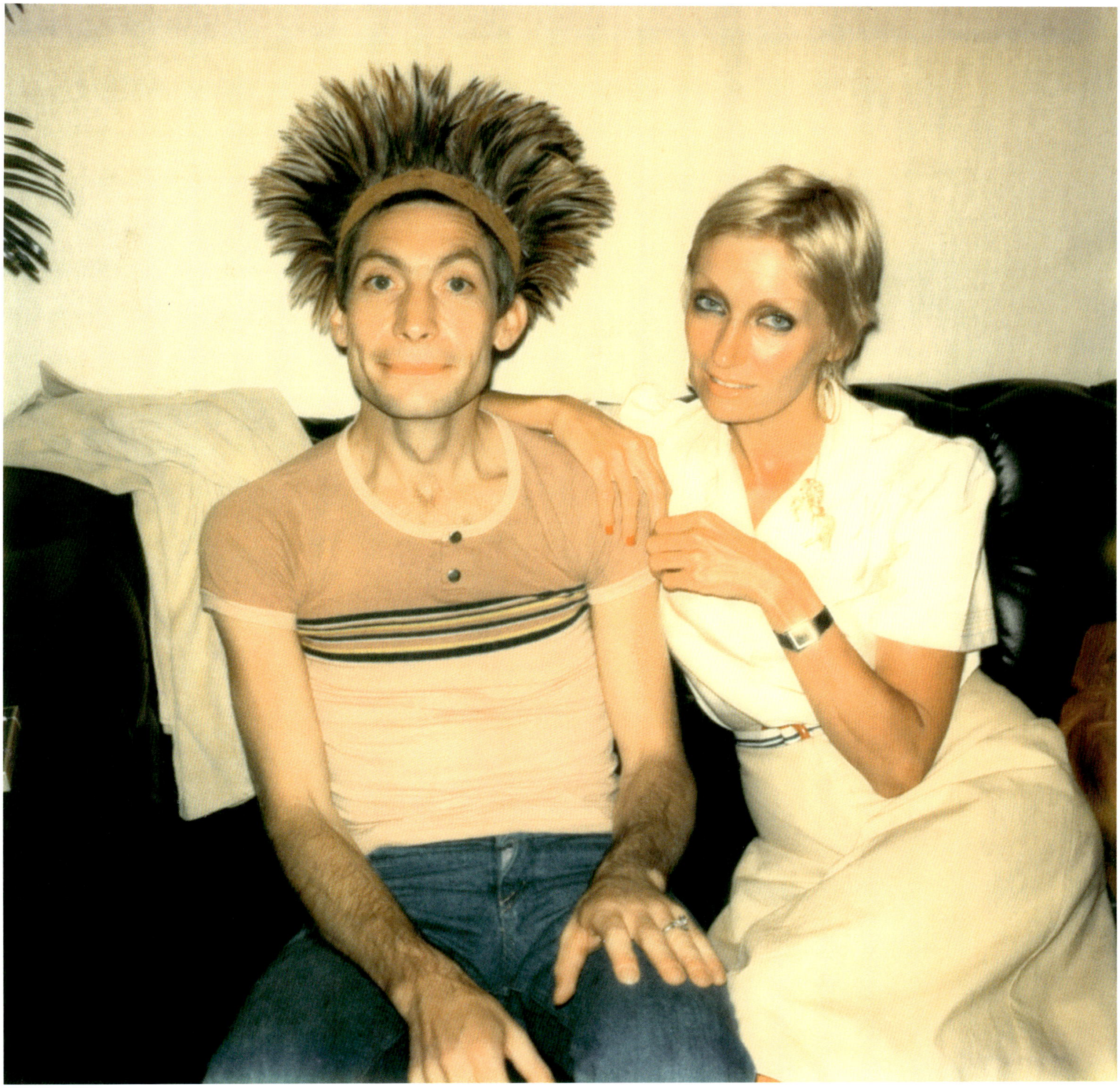

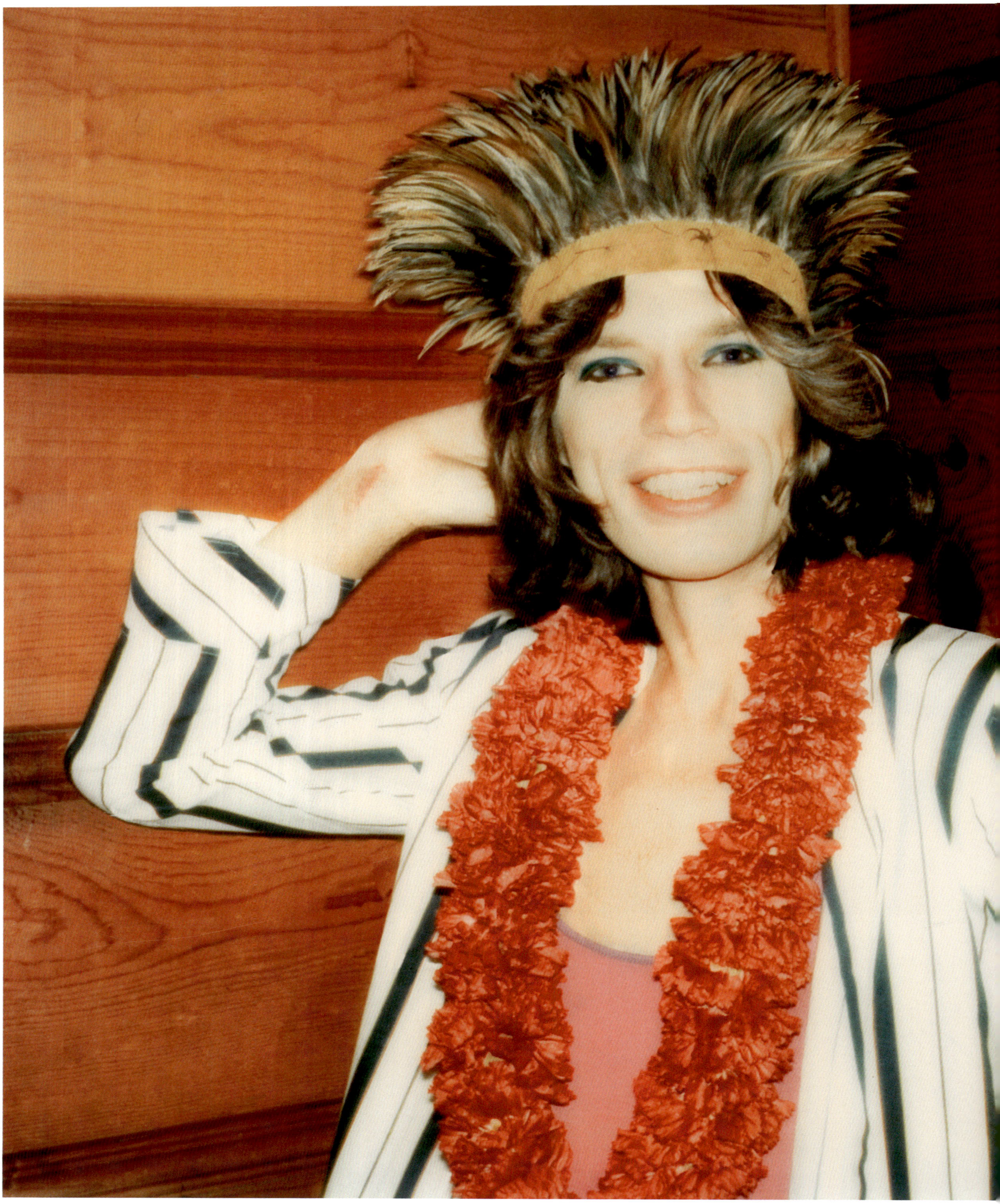

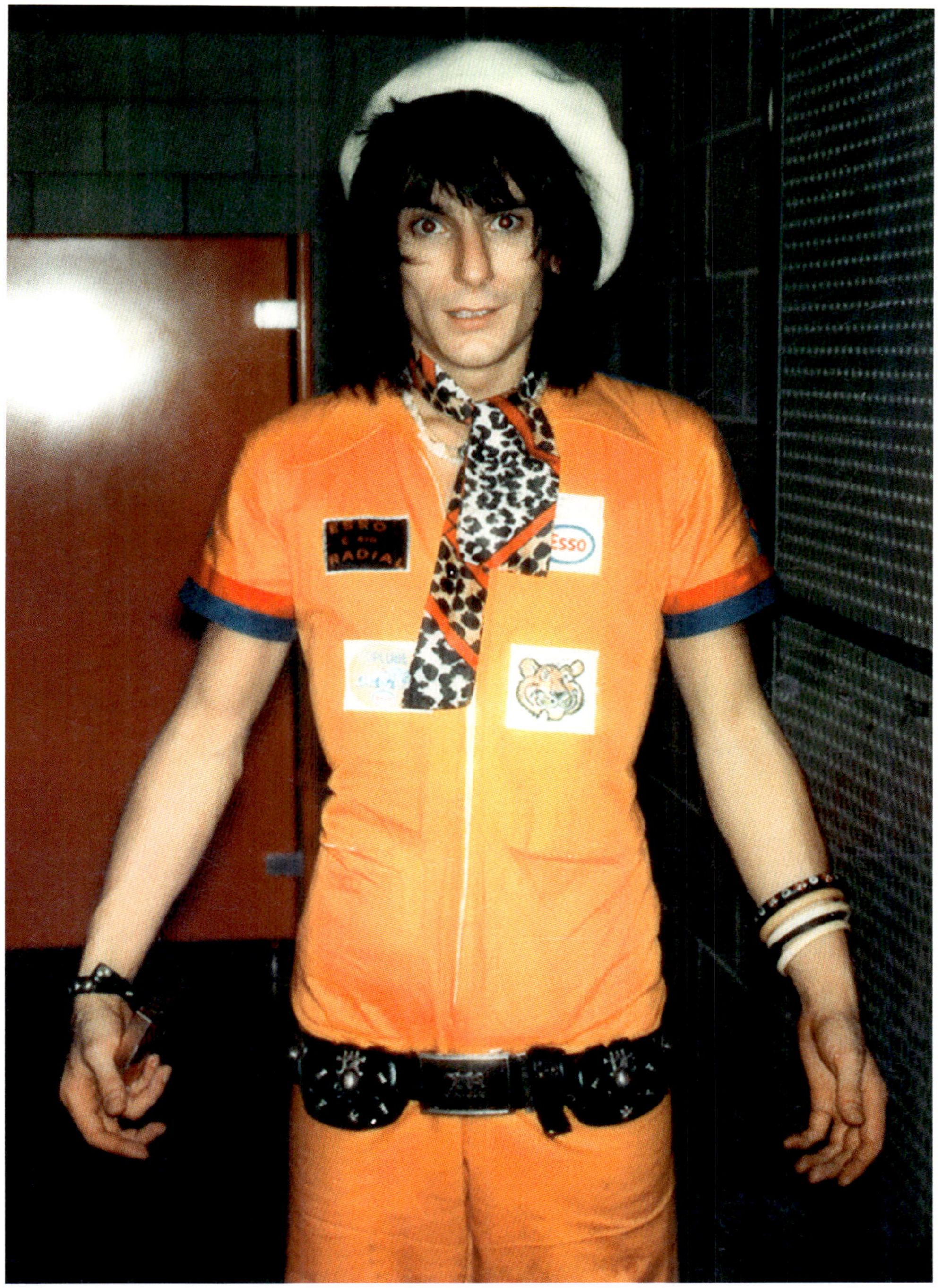

Mick backstage, having borrowed Charlie's headdress at The Cotton Bowl, in Dallas, Texas – 6 August 1975.
Above: Ronnie, trapped by his slipped belt, backstage at The Spectrum, in Philadelphia, Pennsylvania – 29 June 1975.

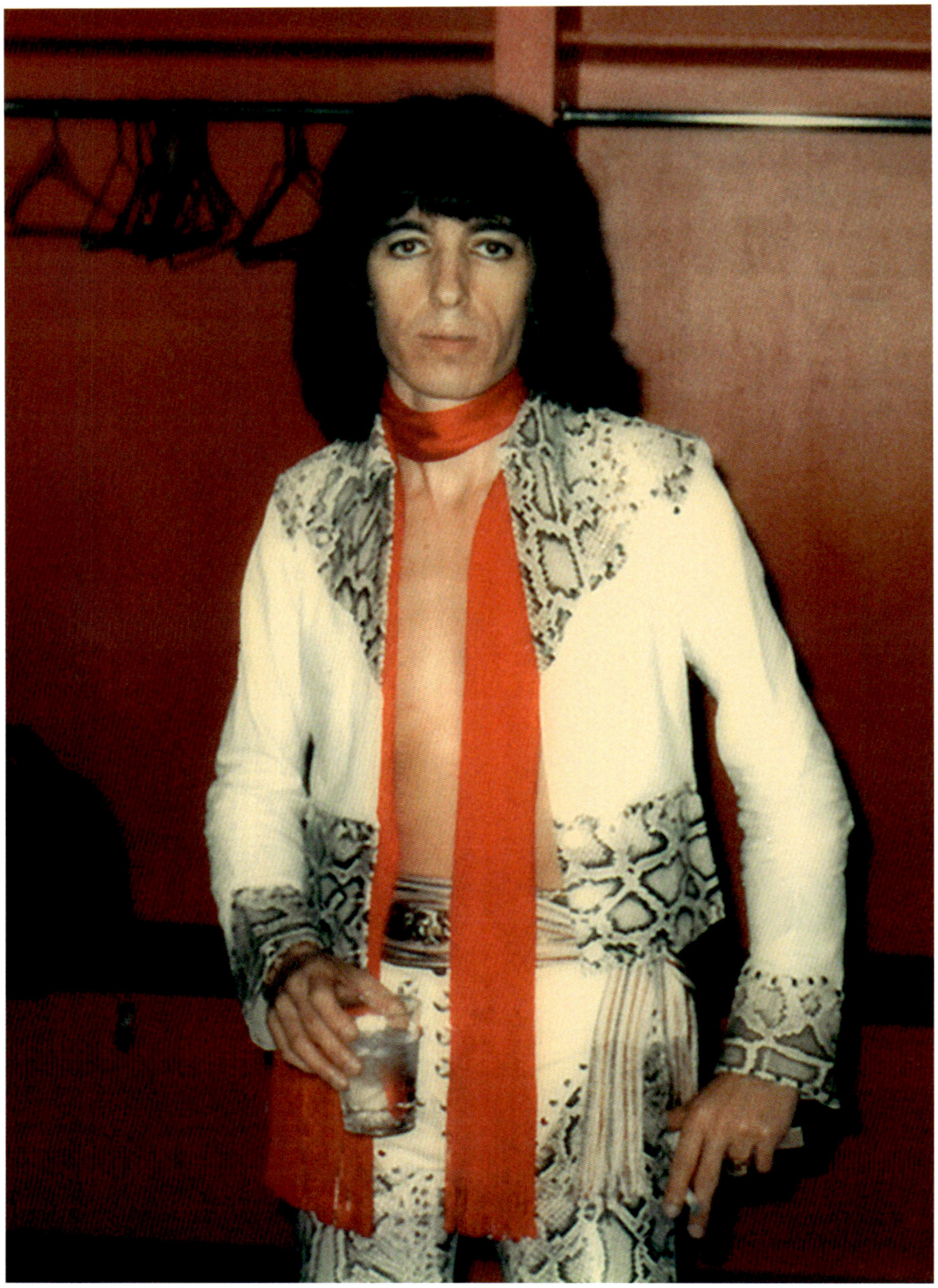

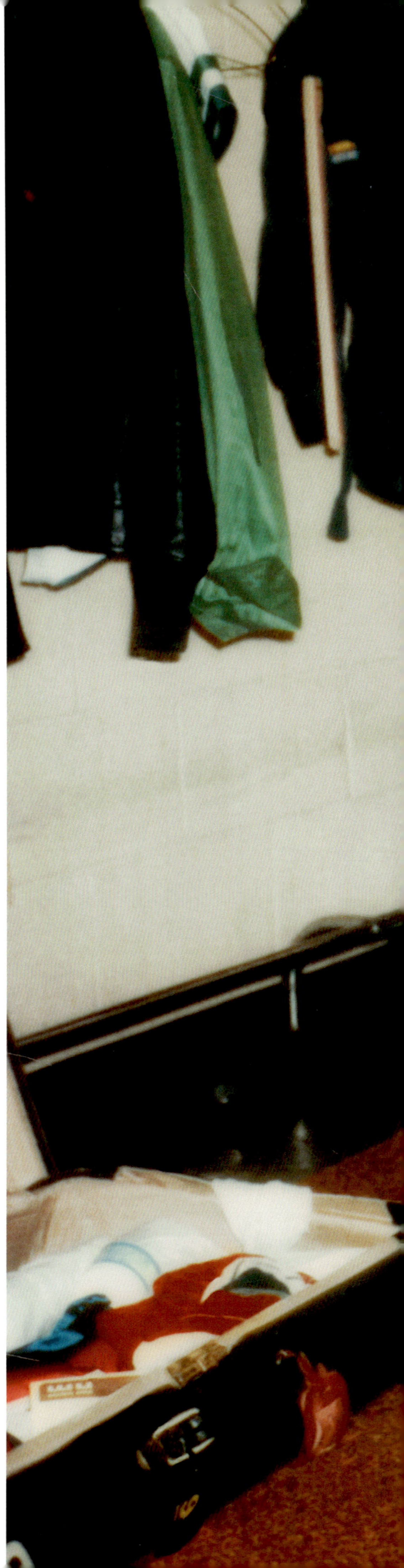

Me wearing my white leather and python outfit backstage at the Rich Stadium, in Buffalo, New York – 8 August 1975.
Right: Mick getting dressed backstage on tour – August 1975.

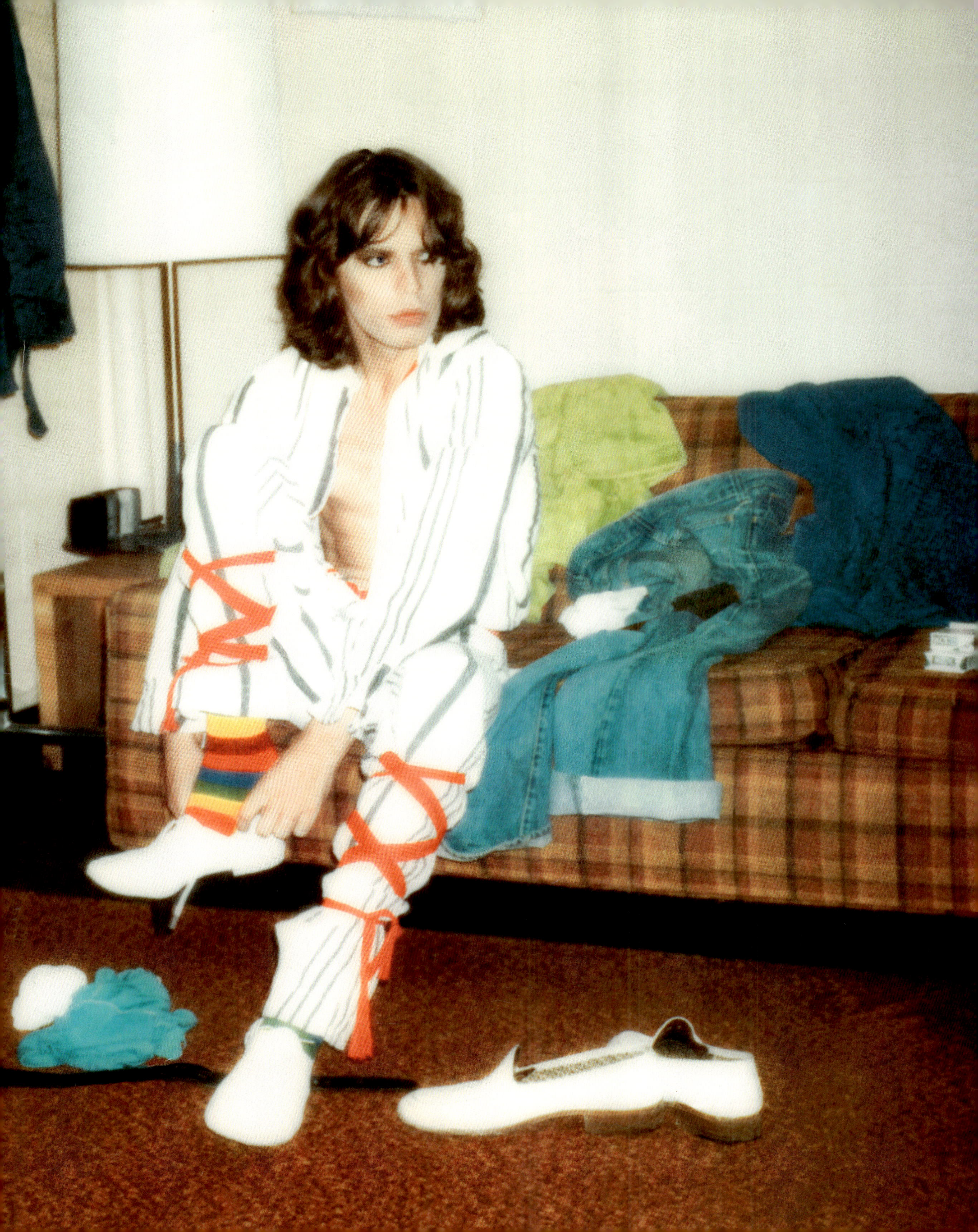

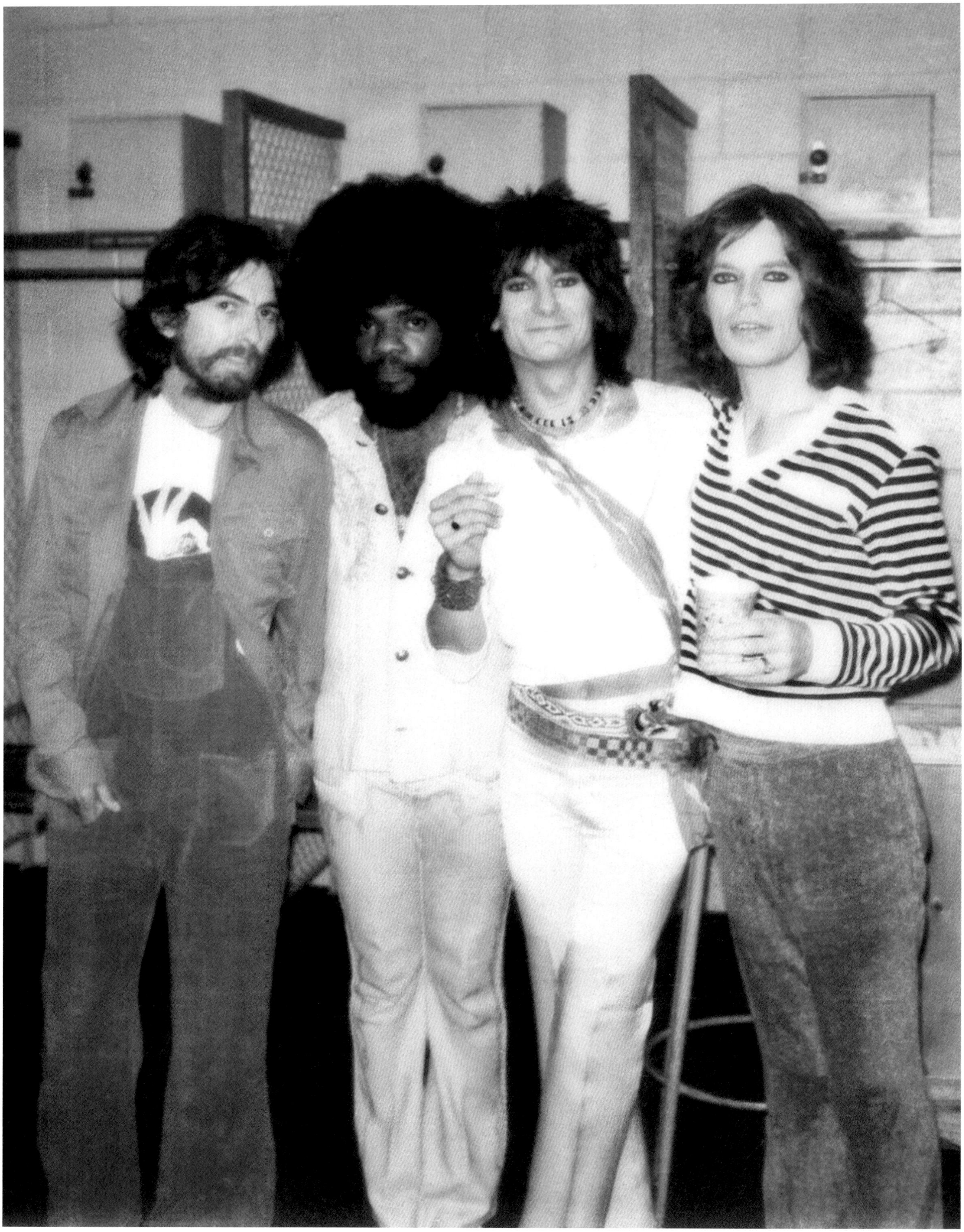

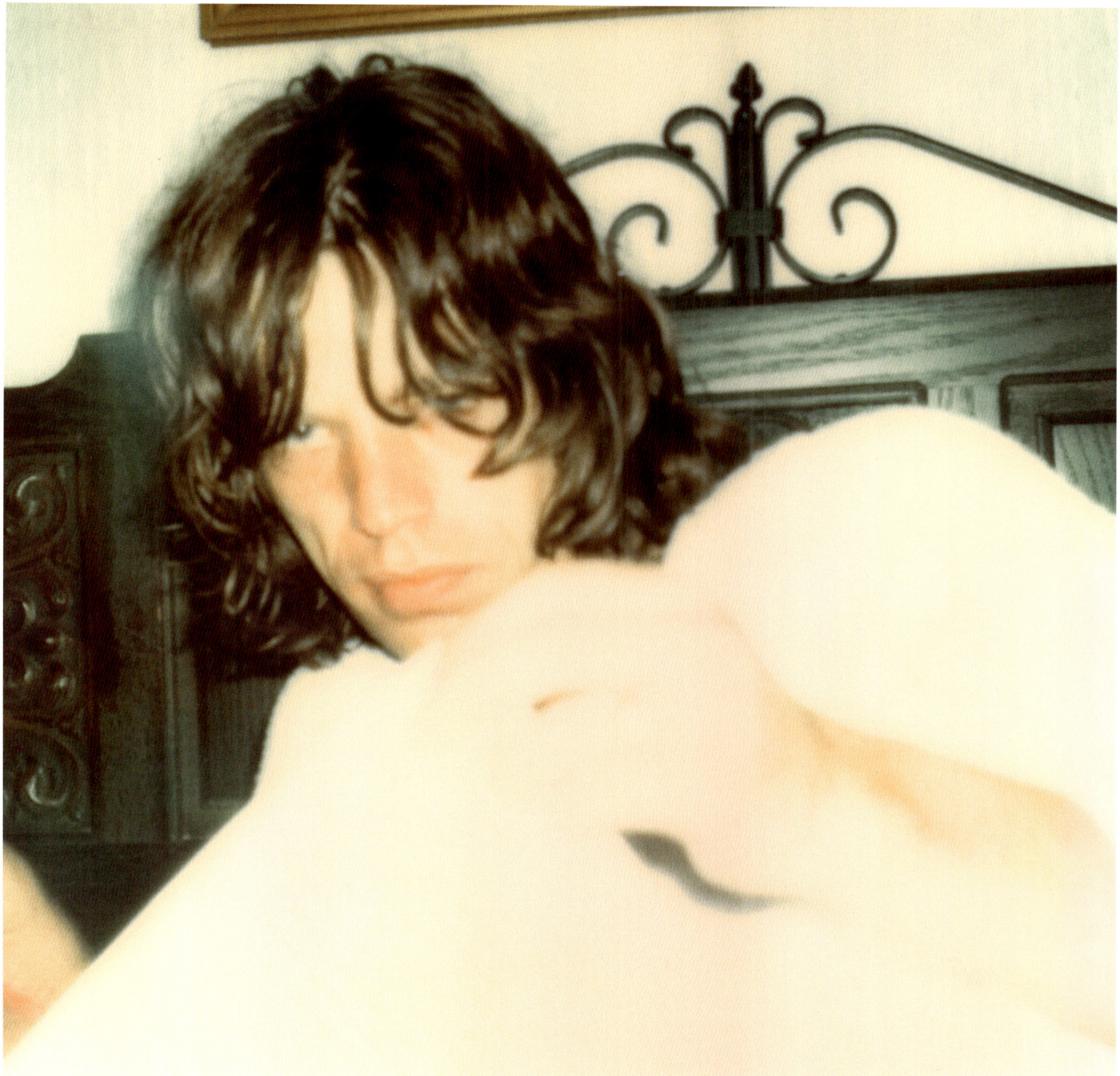

George Harrison, Billy Preston, Ronnie and Mick backstage before our concert at The Forum in Los Angeles – 13 July 1975.
Above: Mick waking up on tour – August 1975.

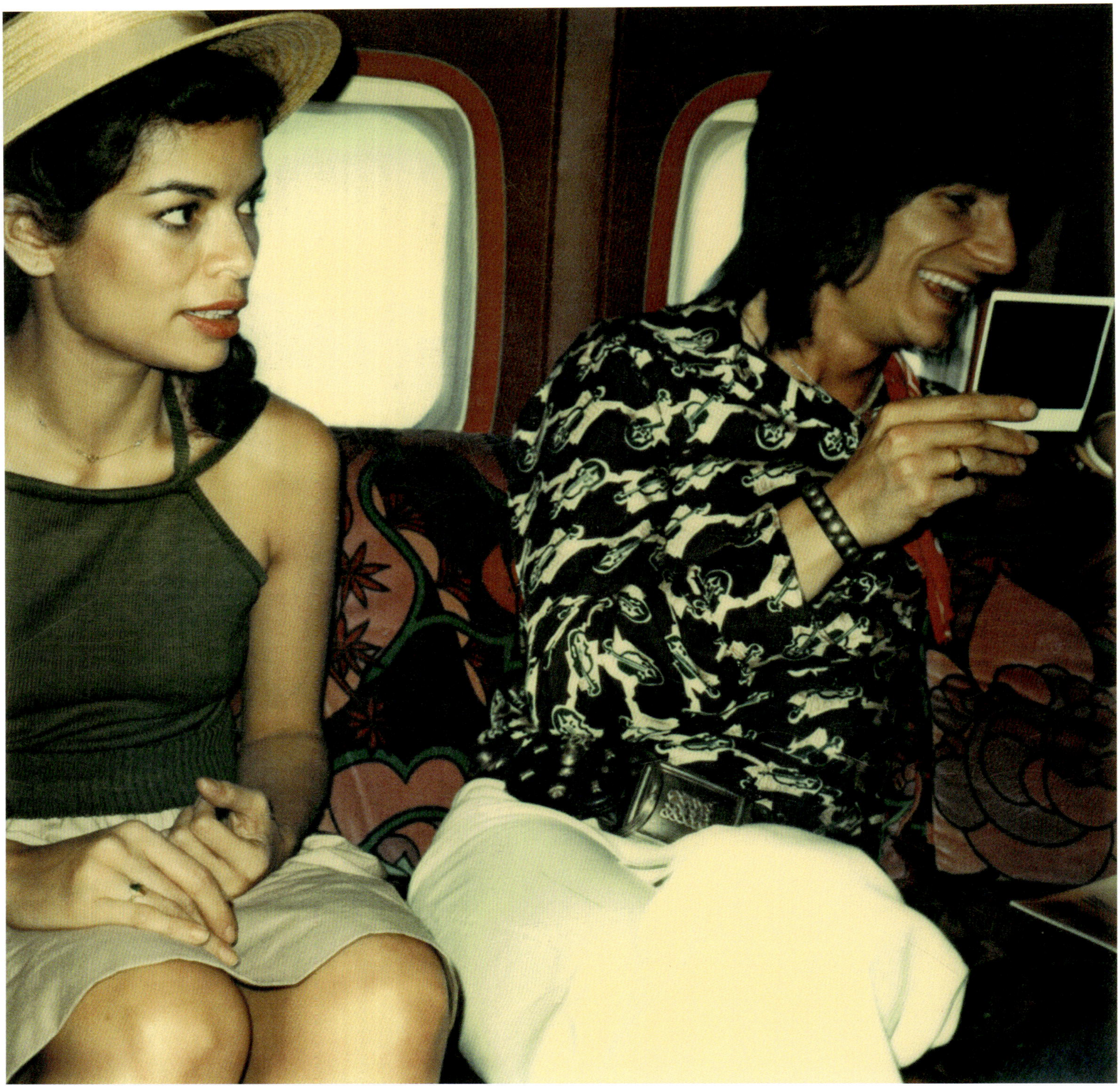

Bianca Jagger and Ronnie on the Starship plane, leaving Buffalo for New York after performing to 80,000 fans – 8 August 1975. **Right**: Steve Stills and I at Gary and Marta Kellgren's house in Los Angeles – 24 August 1975. Dr. John making a phone call at the airport after our flight from New York to Los Angeles – 9 December 1975.

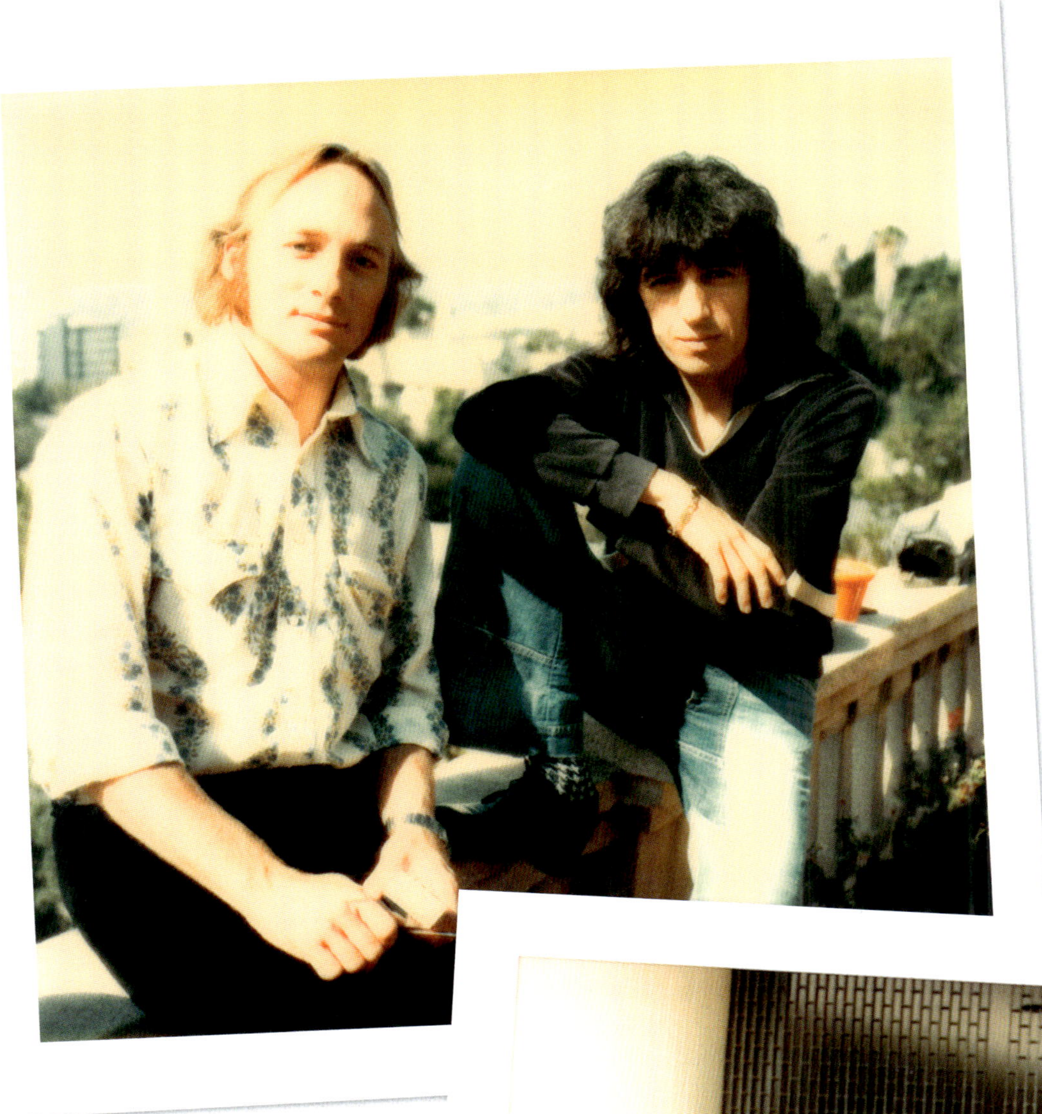

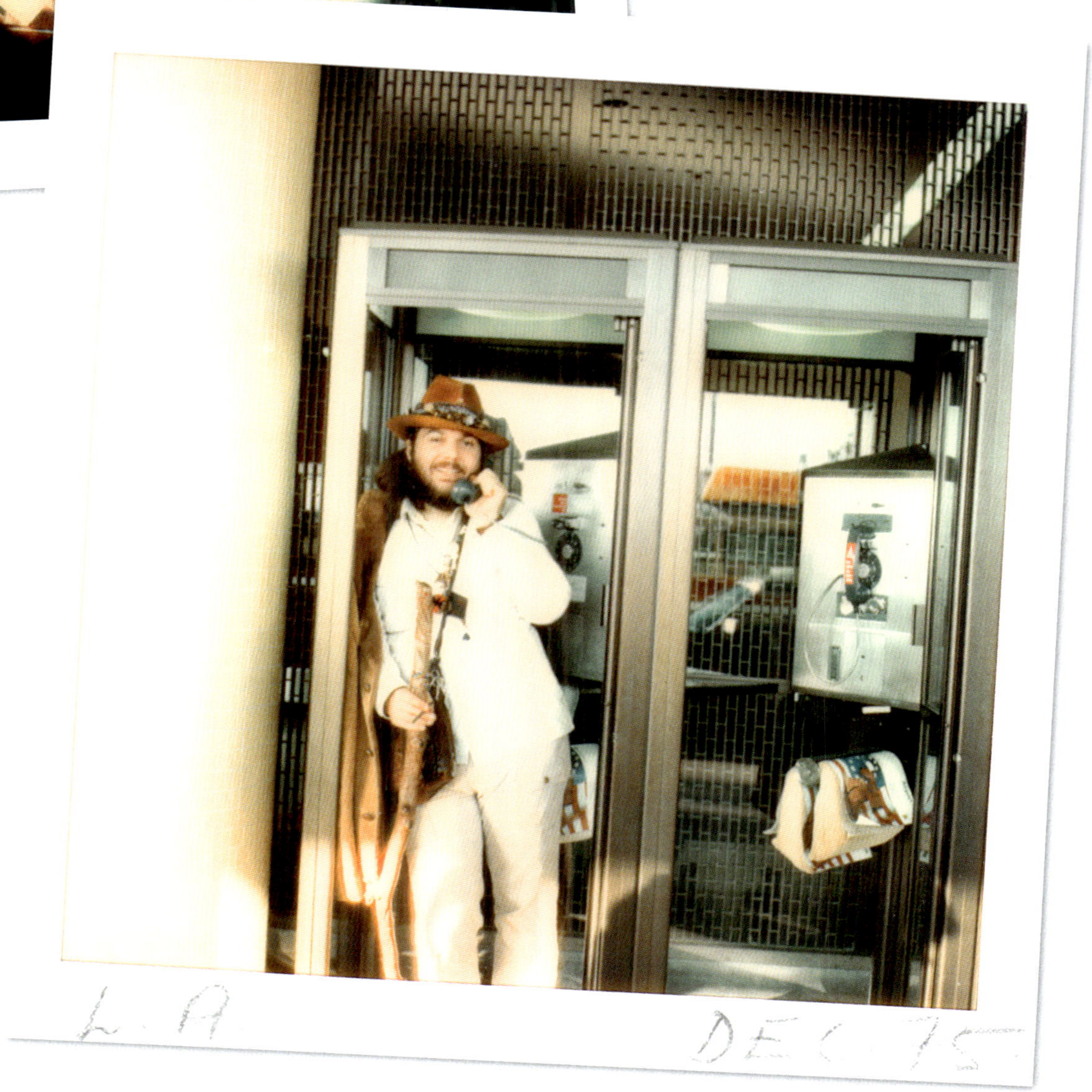
L.A
DEC 75

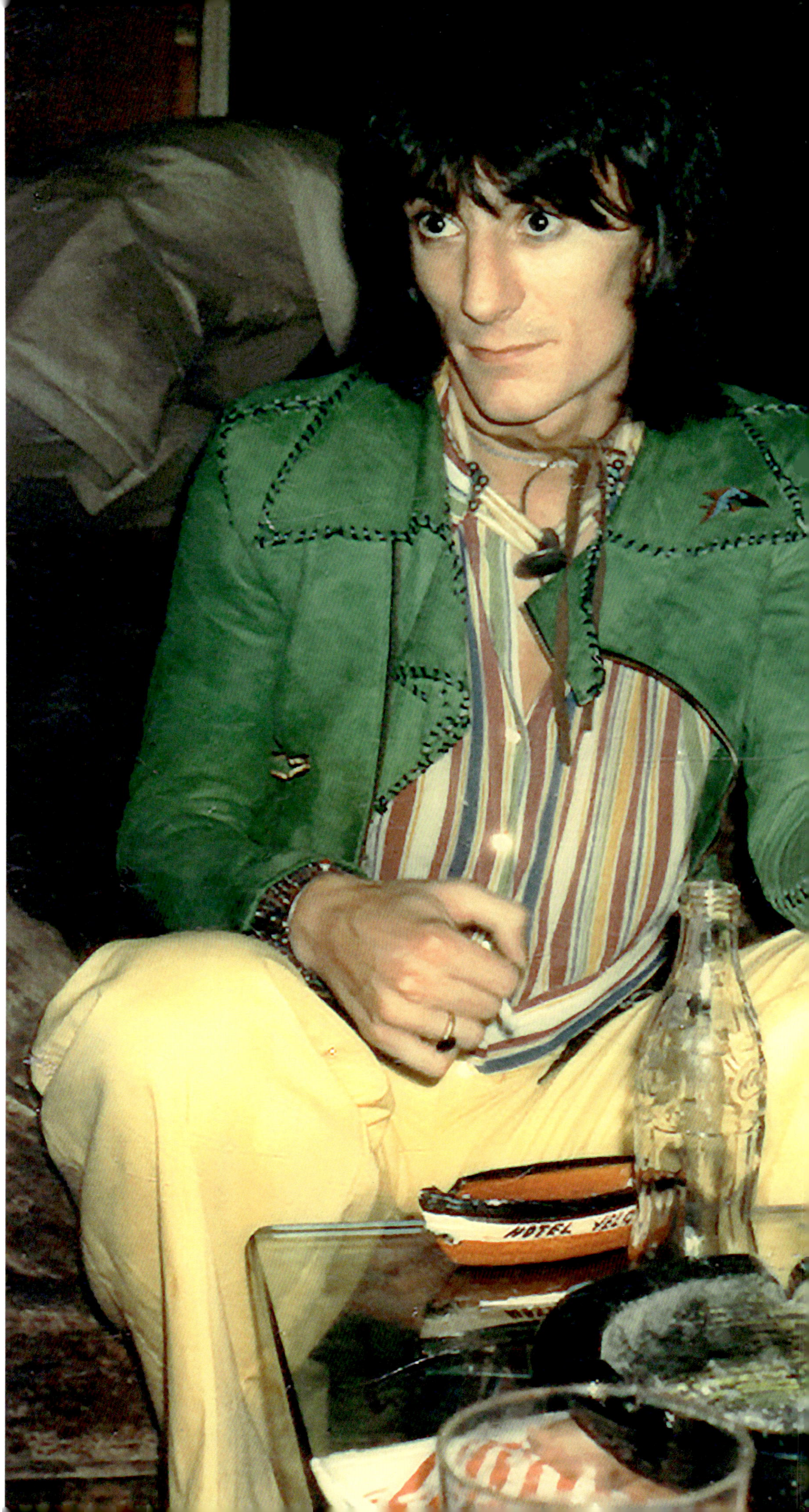

Ronnie and a camera-shy David Bowie at the Kellgren house in Los Angeles – 3 September 1975.

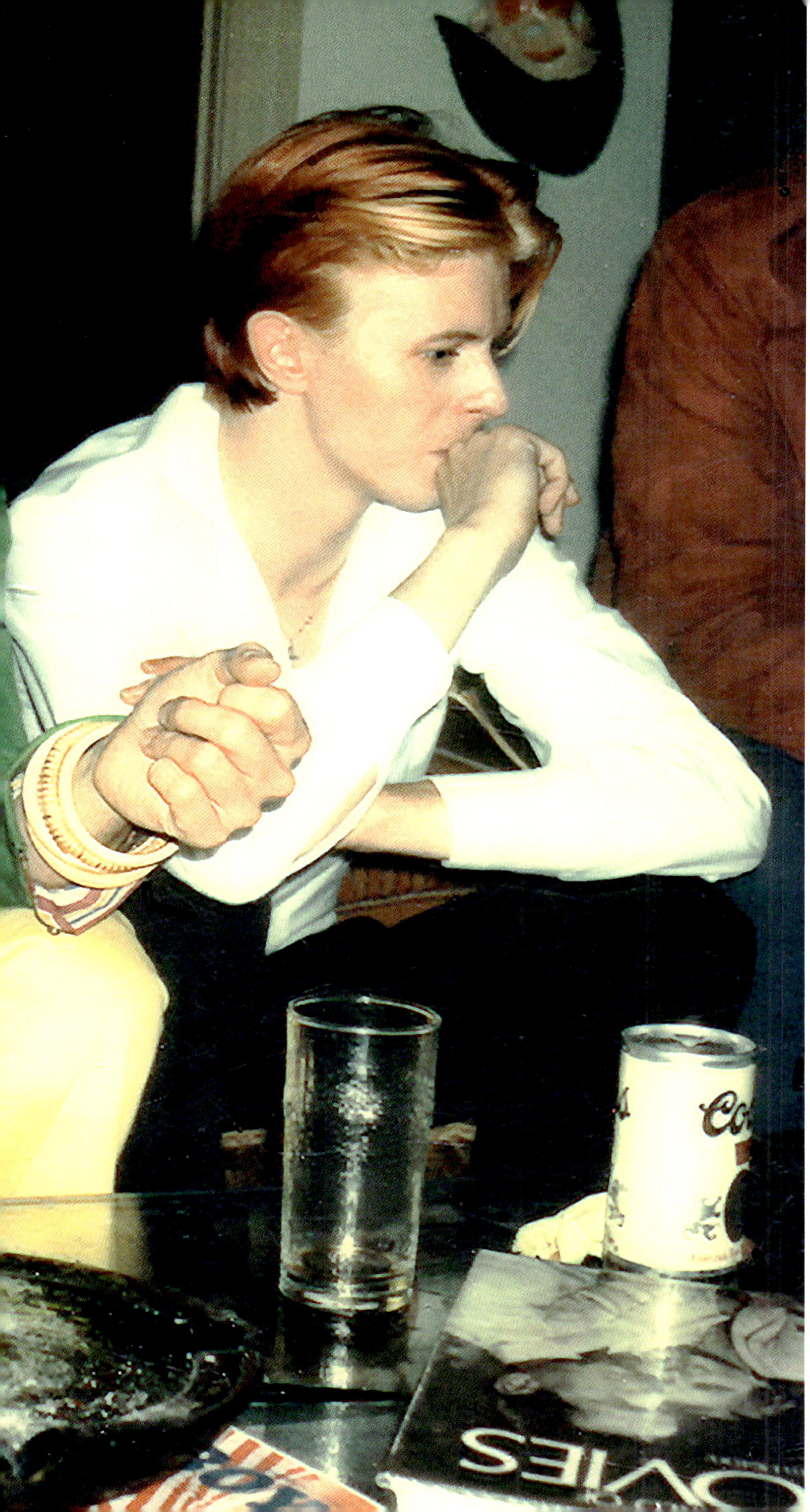

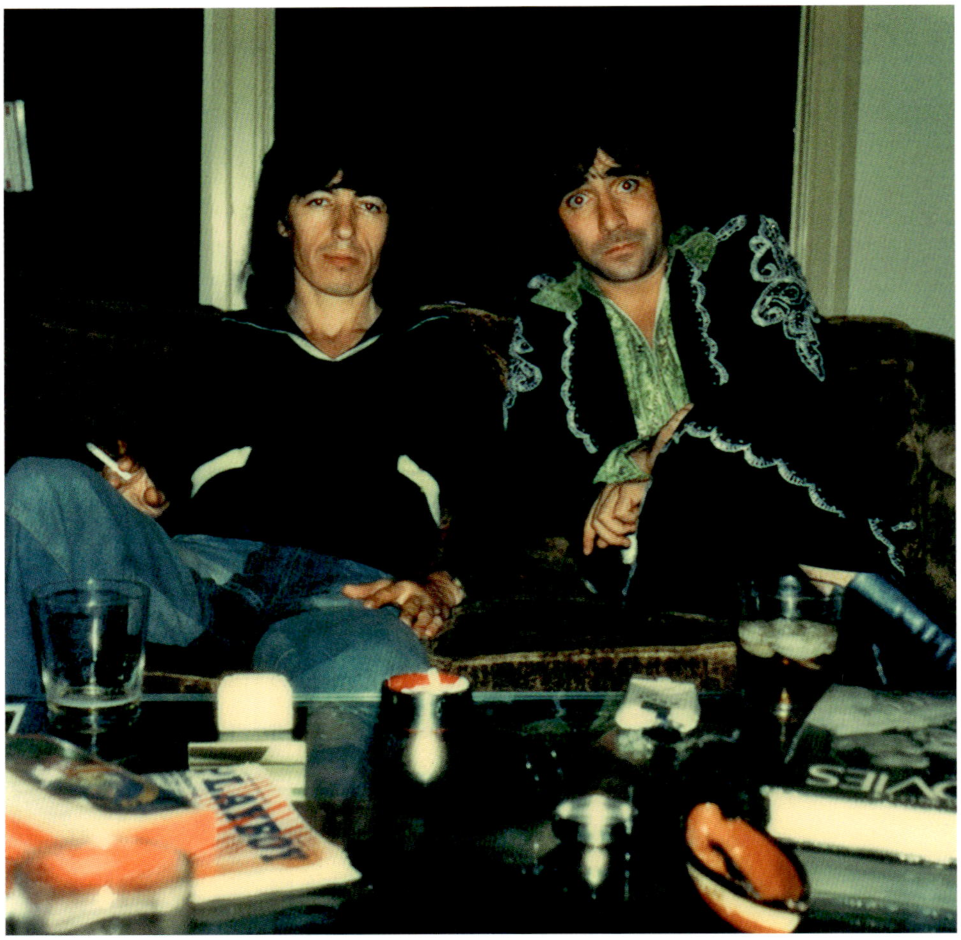

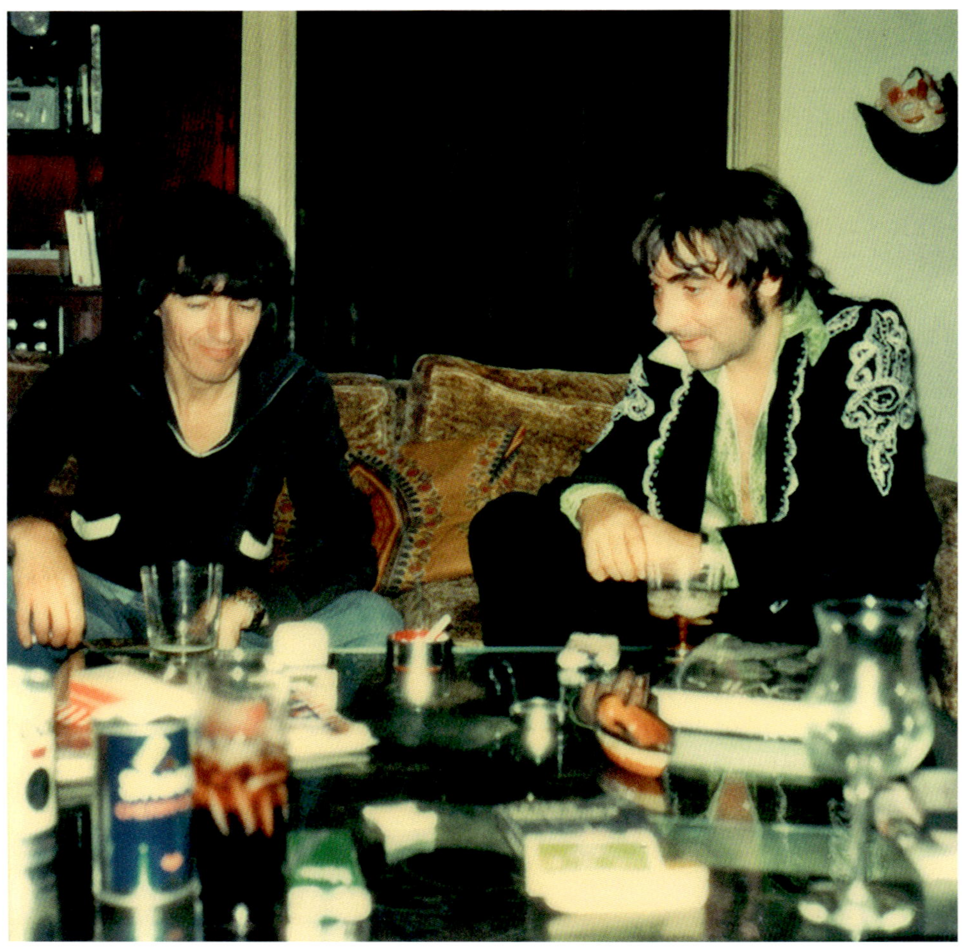

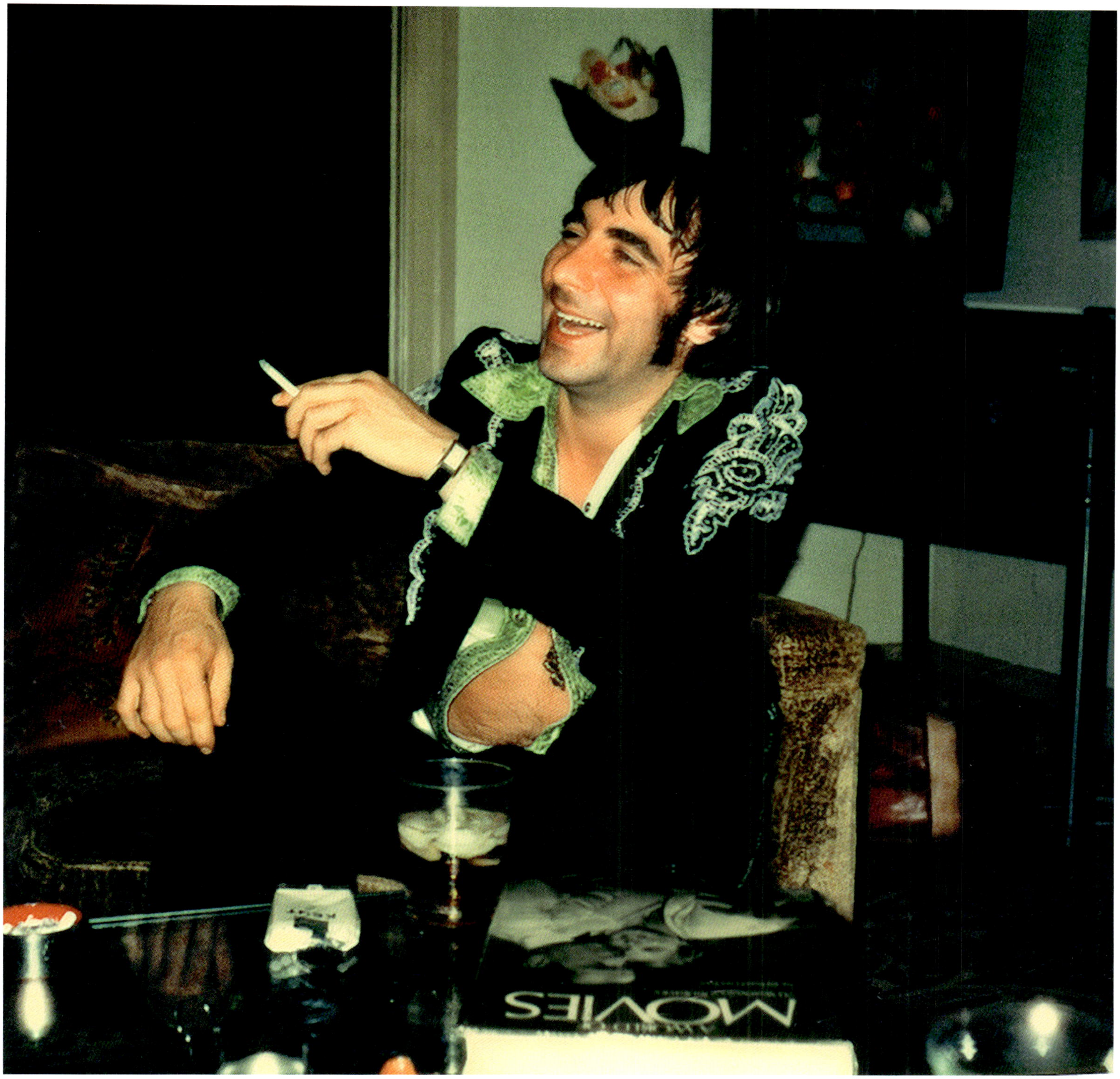

Three shots of me with my great mate Keith Moon at the Kellgren house in Los Angeles – 2 September 1975.

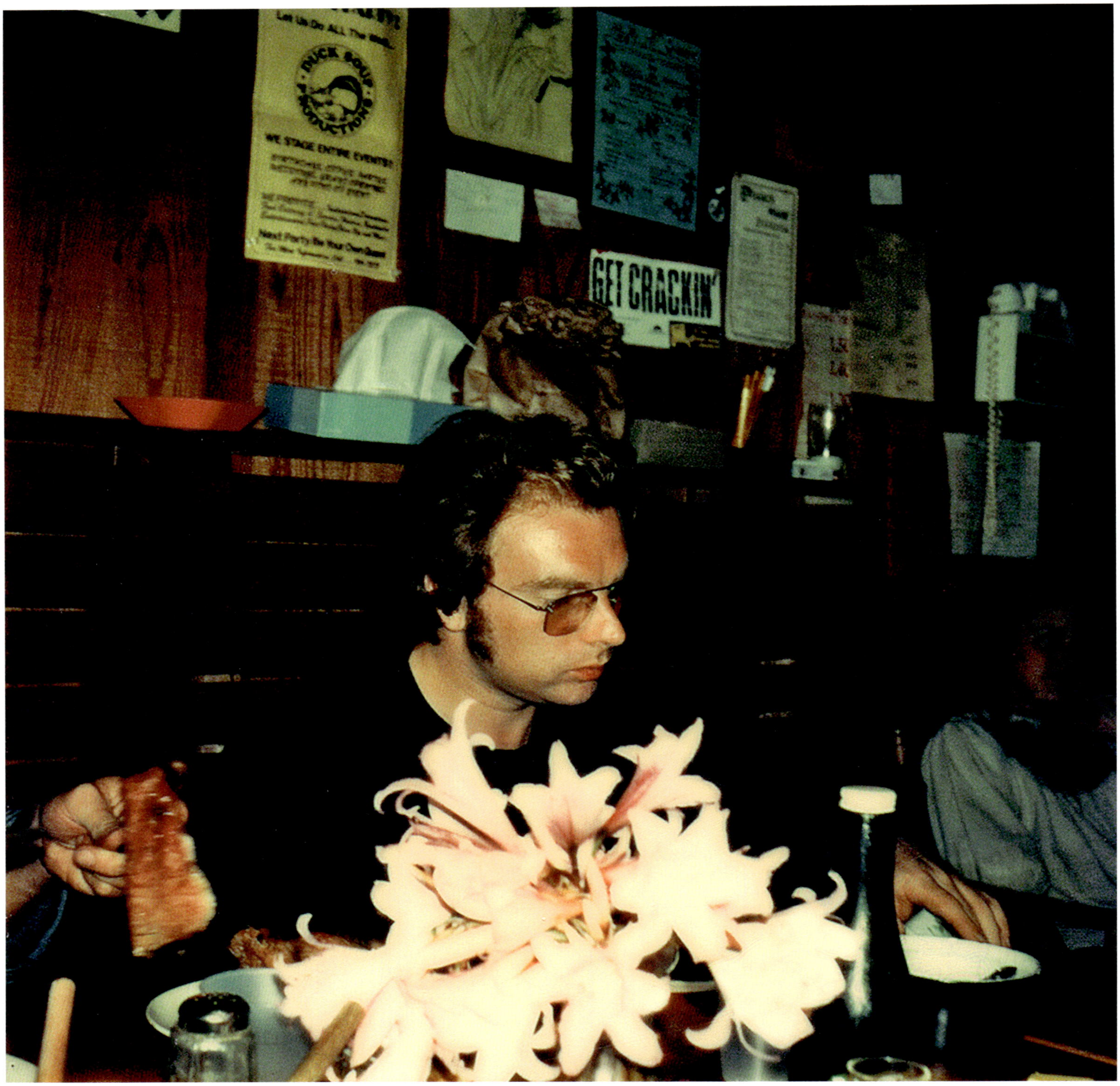

Van Morrison at his home in Sausalito before joining us in the studio there – 27 August 1975.
Right: Me with Bonnie and Ruth Pointer, then me solo at the mic, doing overdubs on my solo album, *Stone Alone*, at The Record Plant in Los Angeles – December 1975.

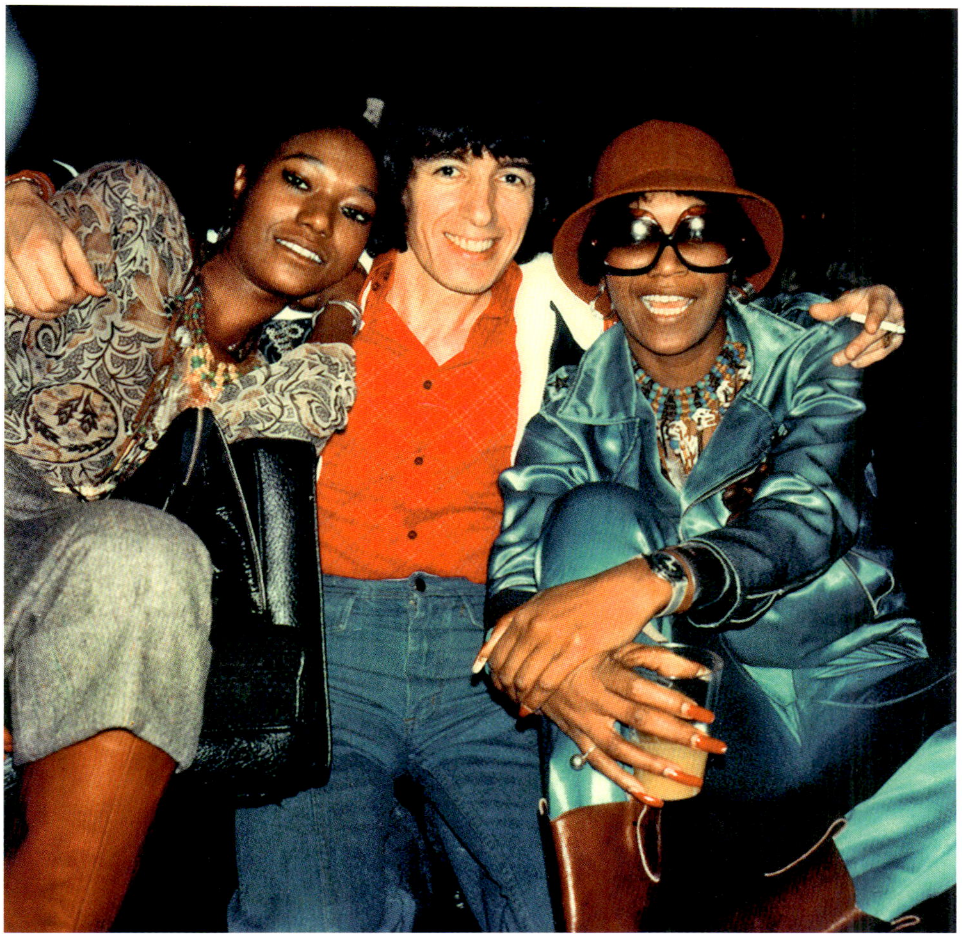

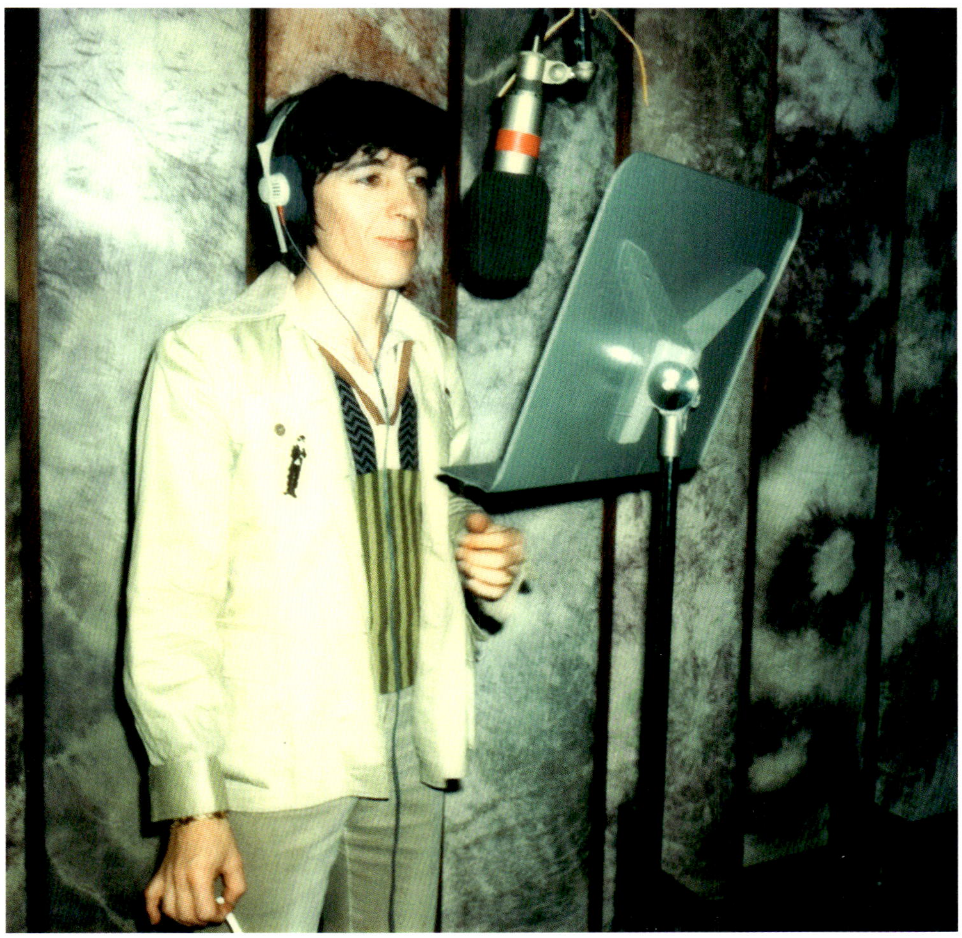

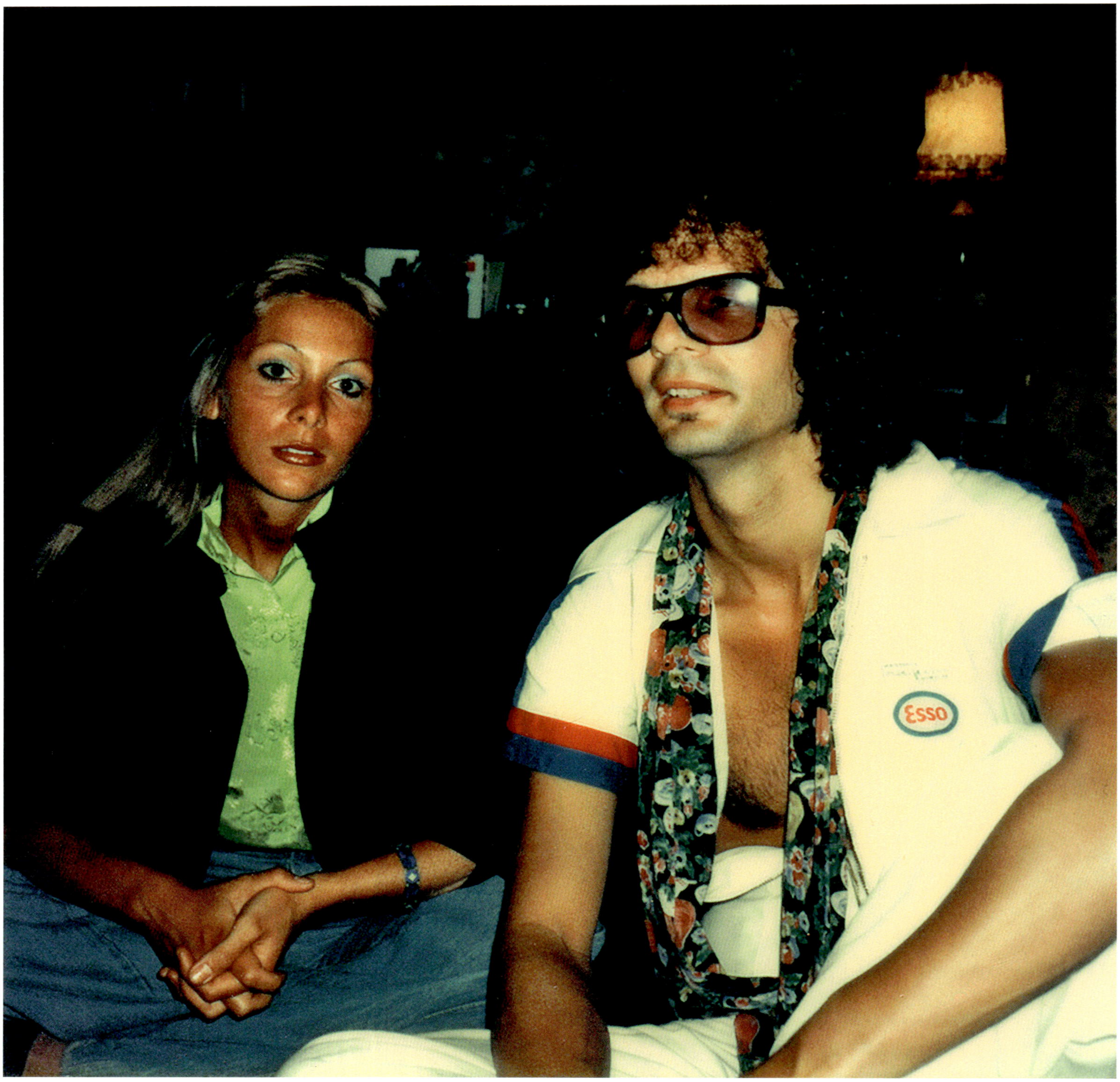

Al Kooper and his lady at the Kellgren house in Los Angeles – 2 September 1975.
Right: Ronnie and David Bowie at the Kellgren house – 4 September 1975.

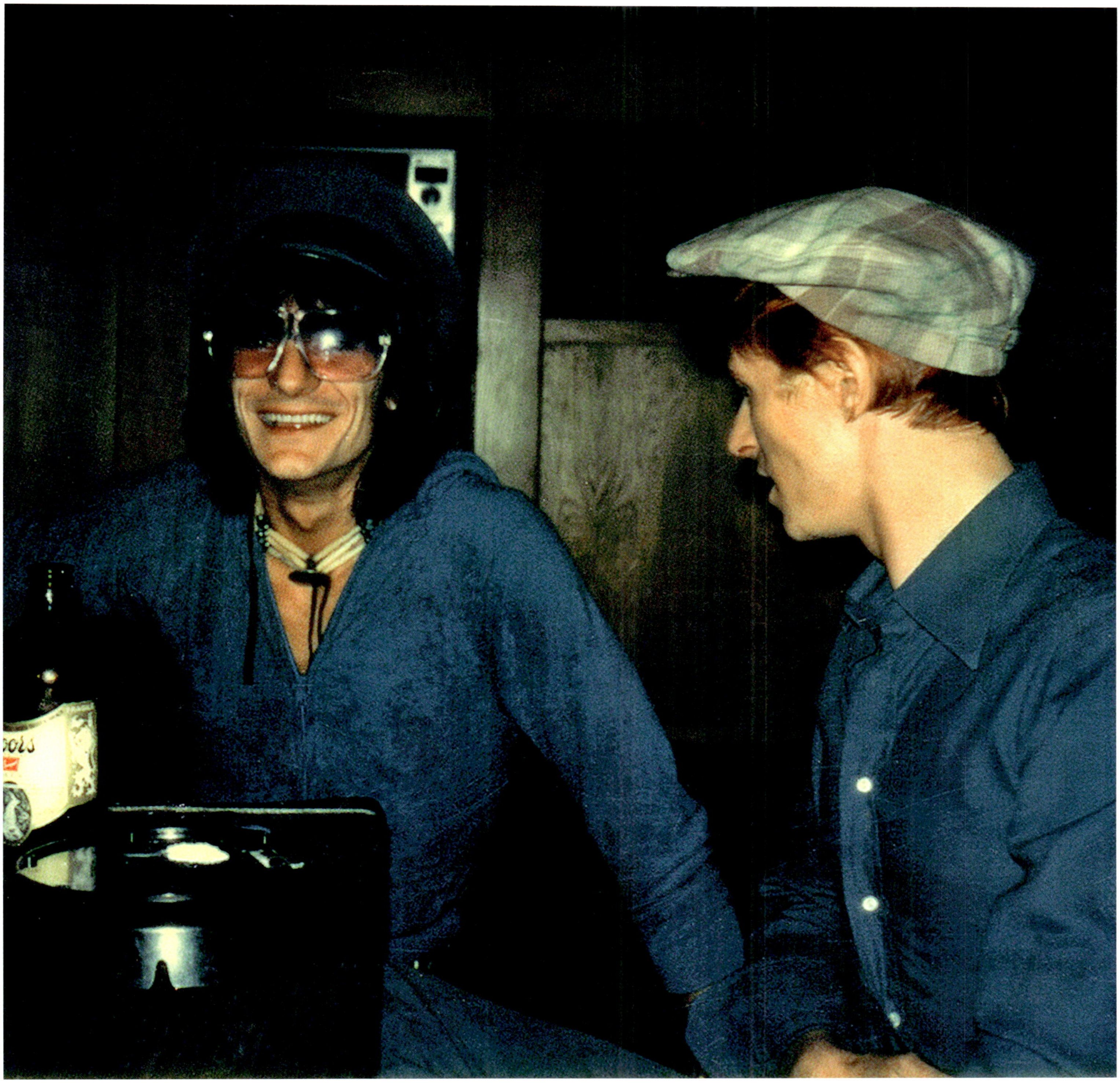

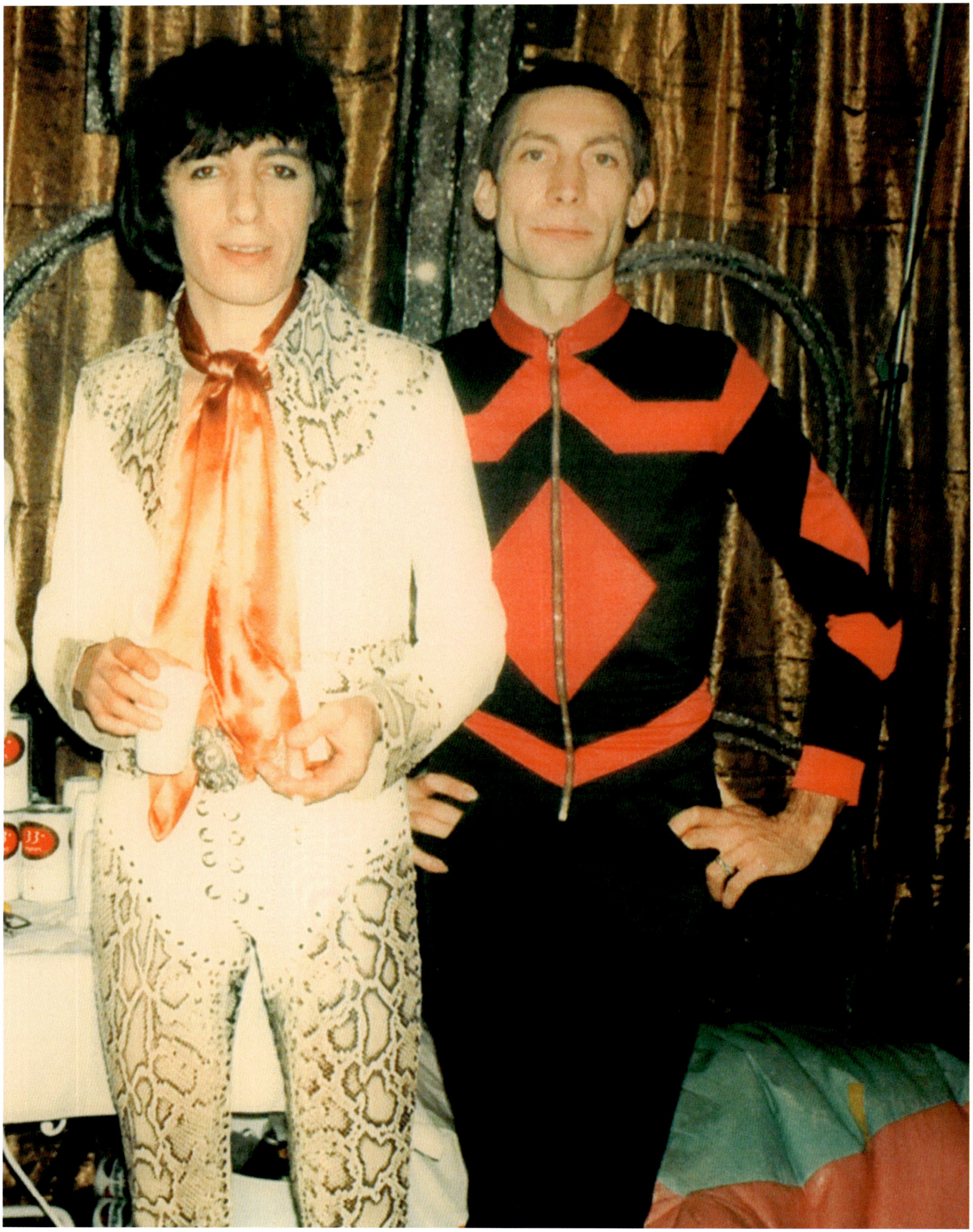

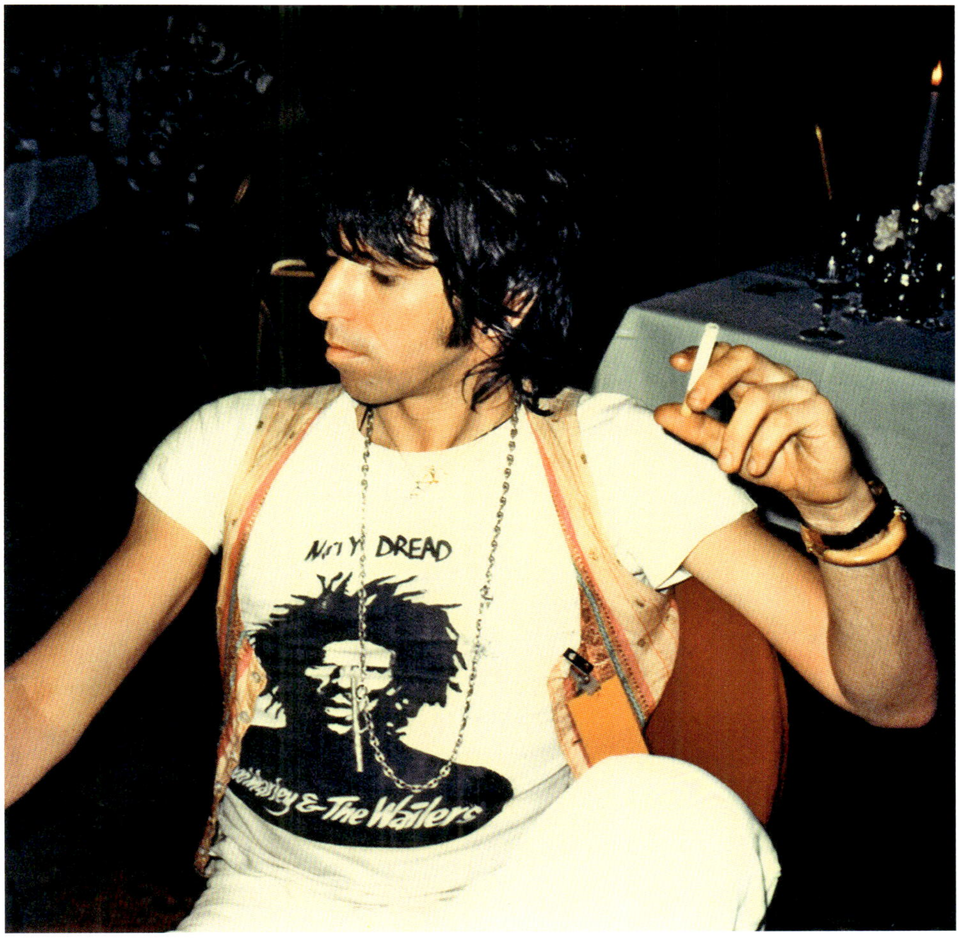

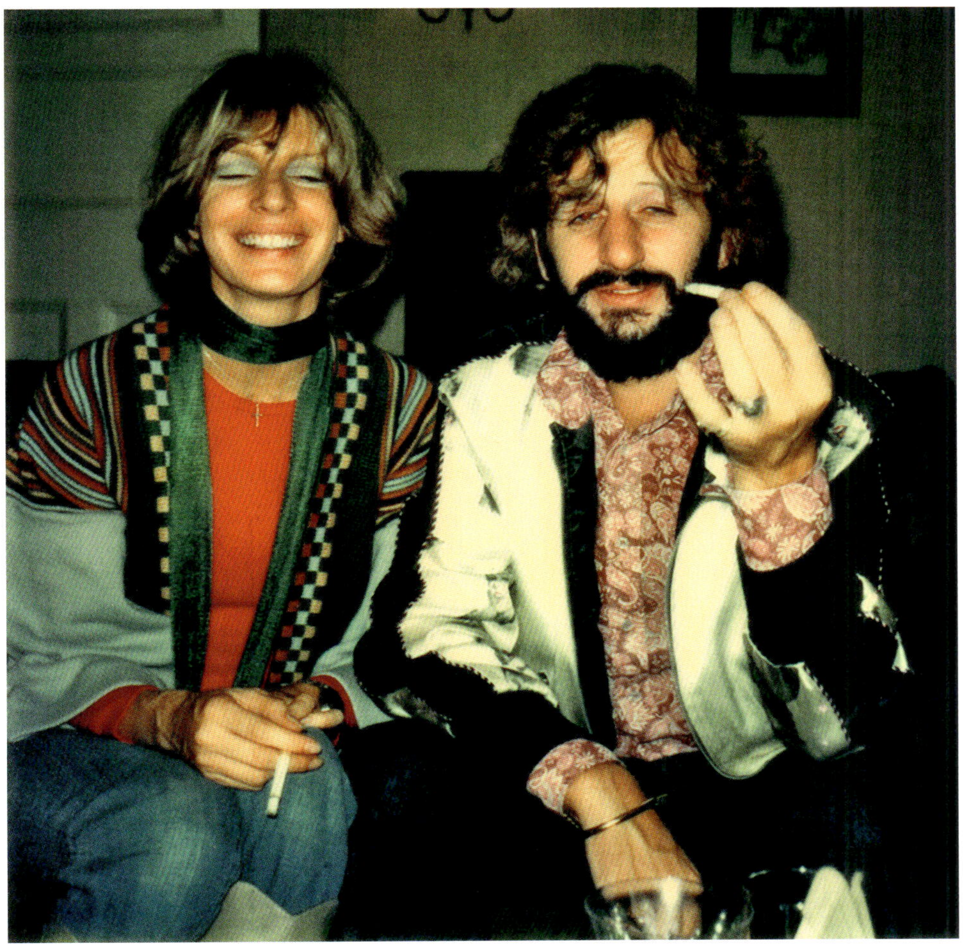

Keith backstage at The Osteenhalle in Kiel, West Germany – 2 May 1976.
Far left: Charlie and I backstage at Aux Abattoirs in Paris – 6 June 1976.
Left: Chris O'Dell and Ringo at Dukes Hotel, London – 10 September 1975.

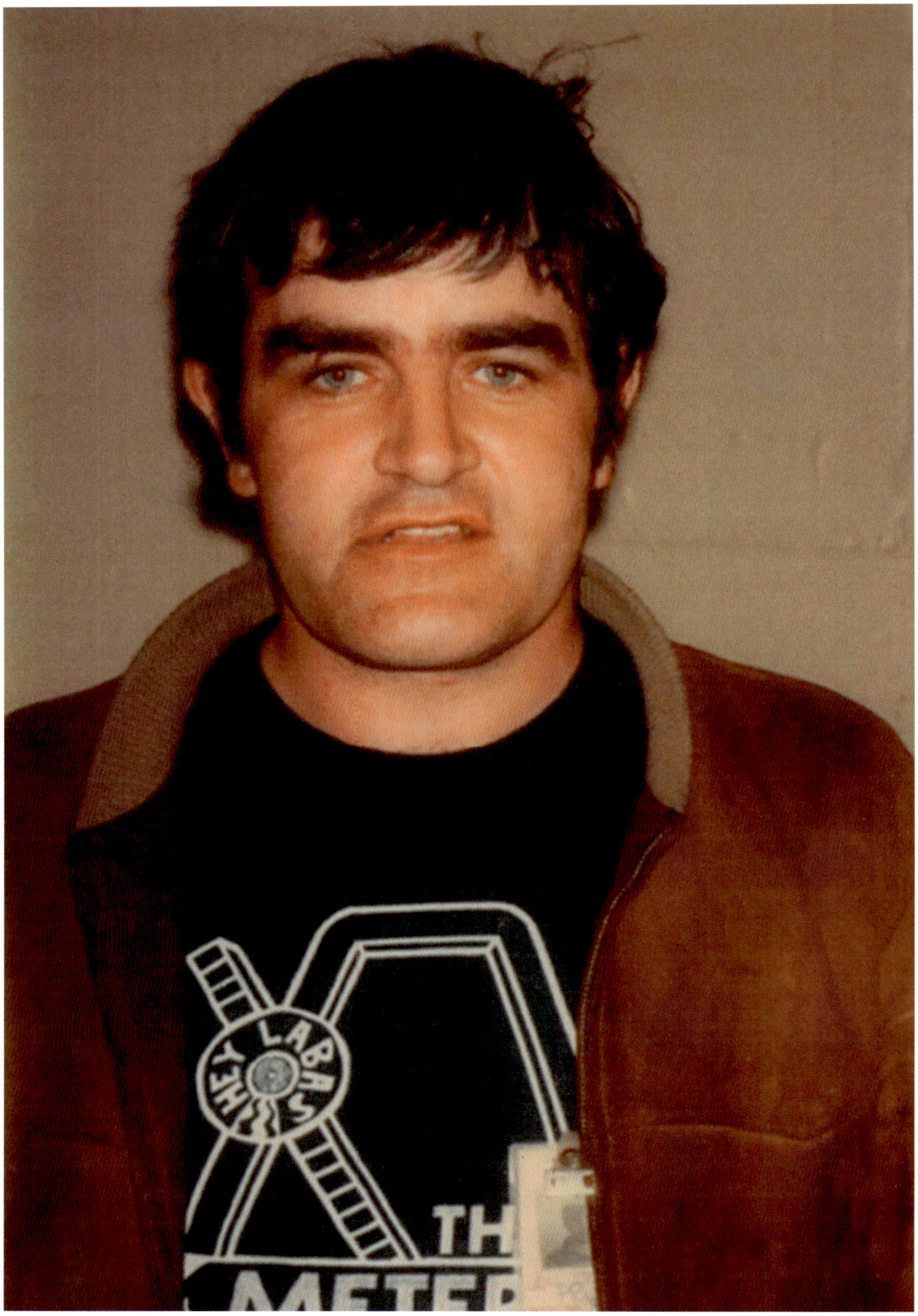

Ian Stewart looking great backstage at The Westfalenhalle in Dortmund, West Germany – 1 June 1976.
Right: Ronnie tuning up backstage at Aux Abattoirs in Paris – 5 June 1976.

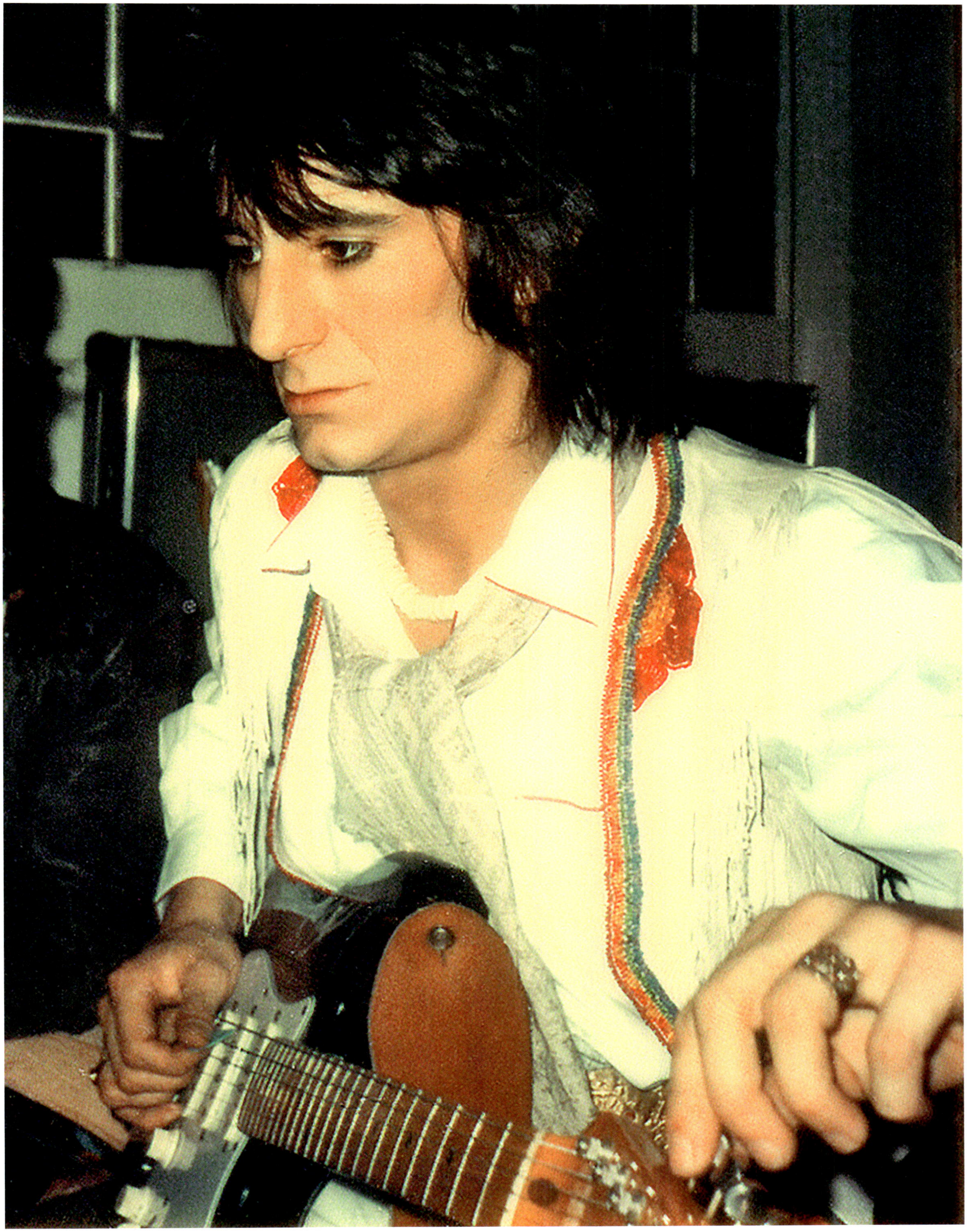

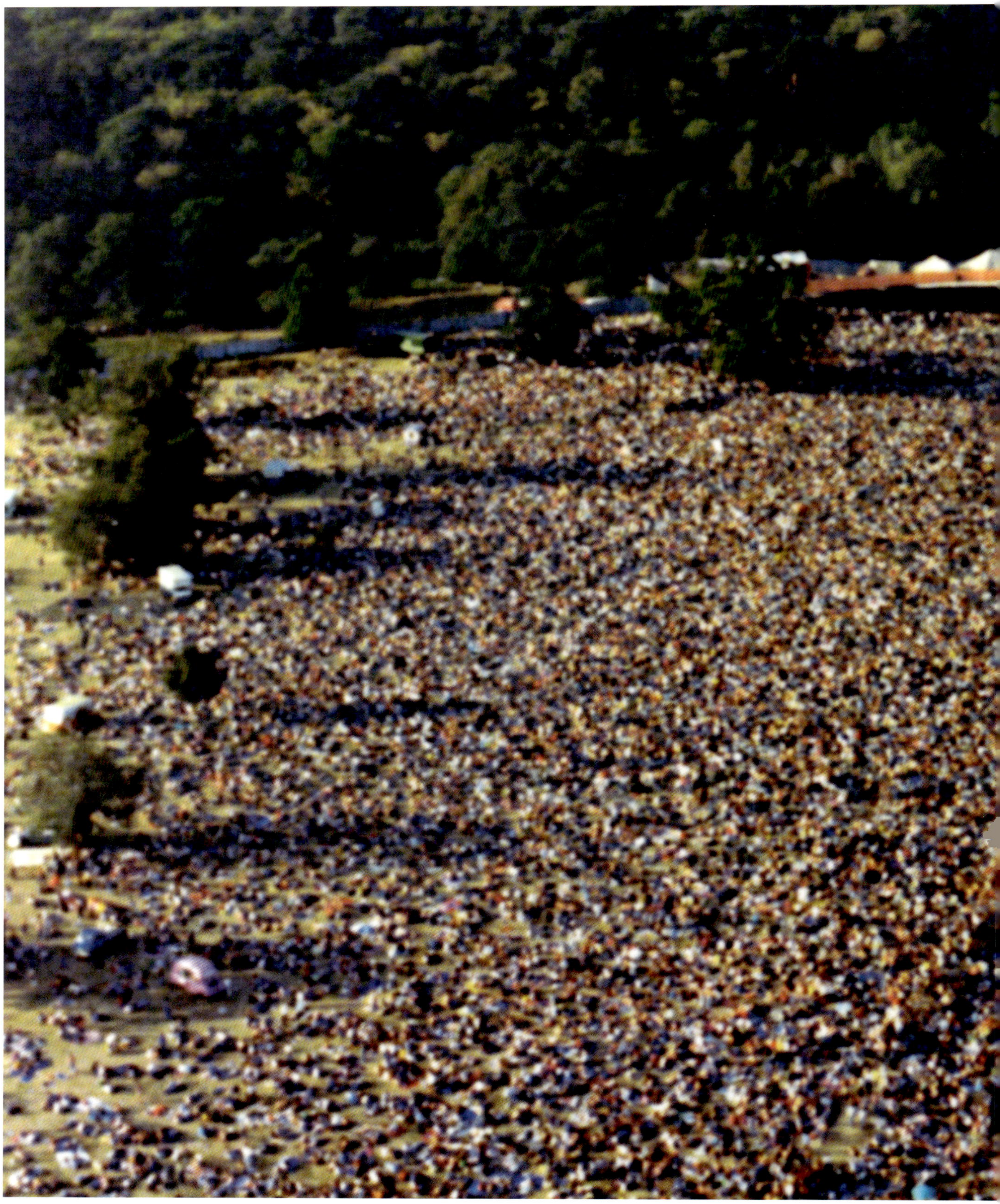

My helicopter shot of the massive audience
at our concert at Knebworth – 21 August 1976.

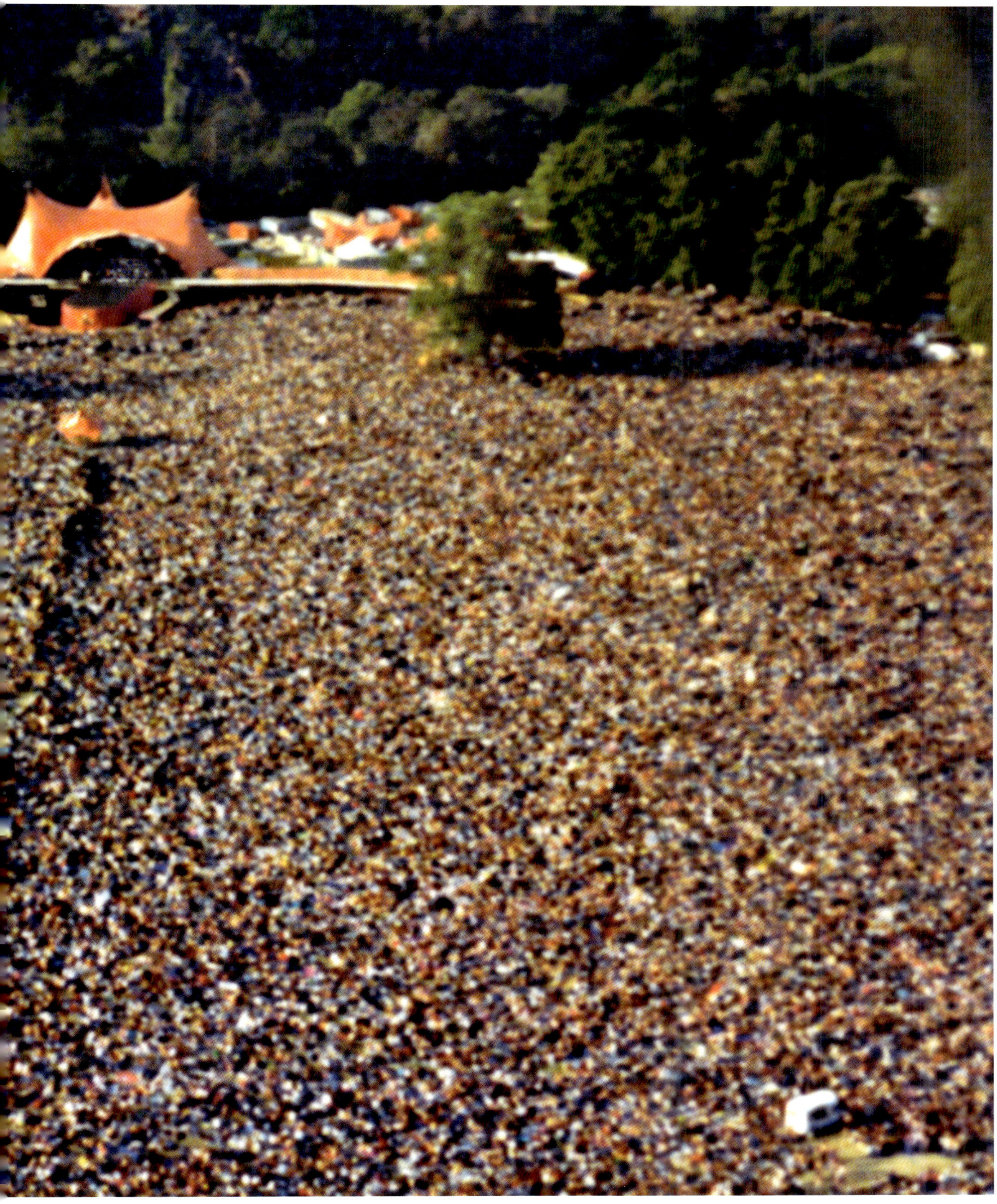

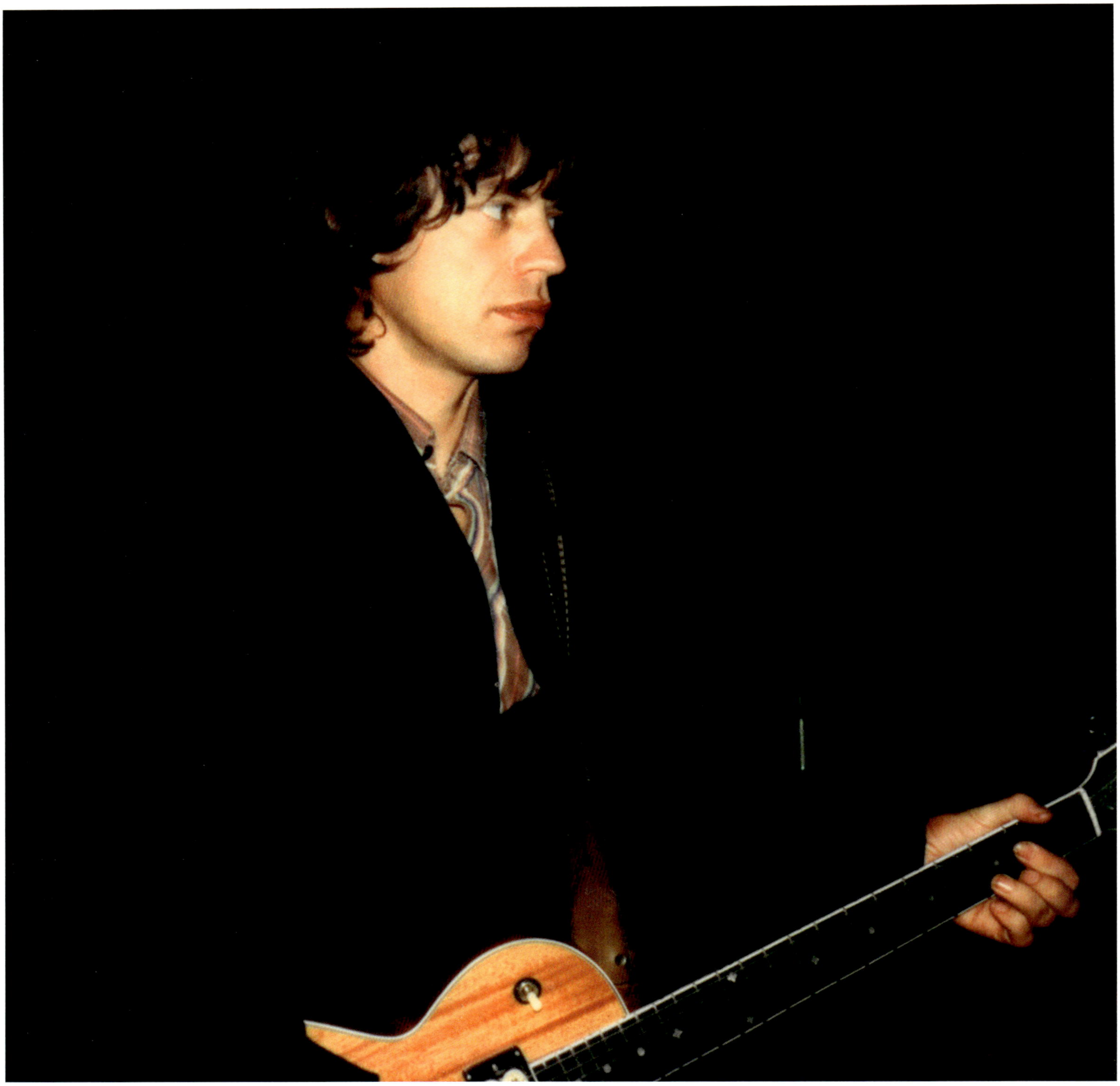

Mick in the Pathé Marconi recording studio in Paris – 22 October 1977.
Above right: Chatting to Harry Nilsson at the Tramp Club in London – 27 January 1977.
Right: Having a drink with Margaret Trudeau backstage at The El Mocambo Club in Toronto, Canada, before our concert there – 5 March 1977.

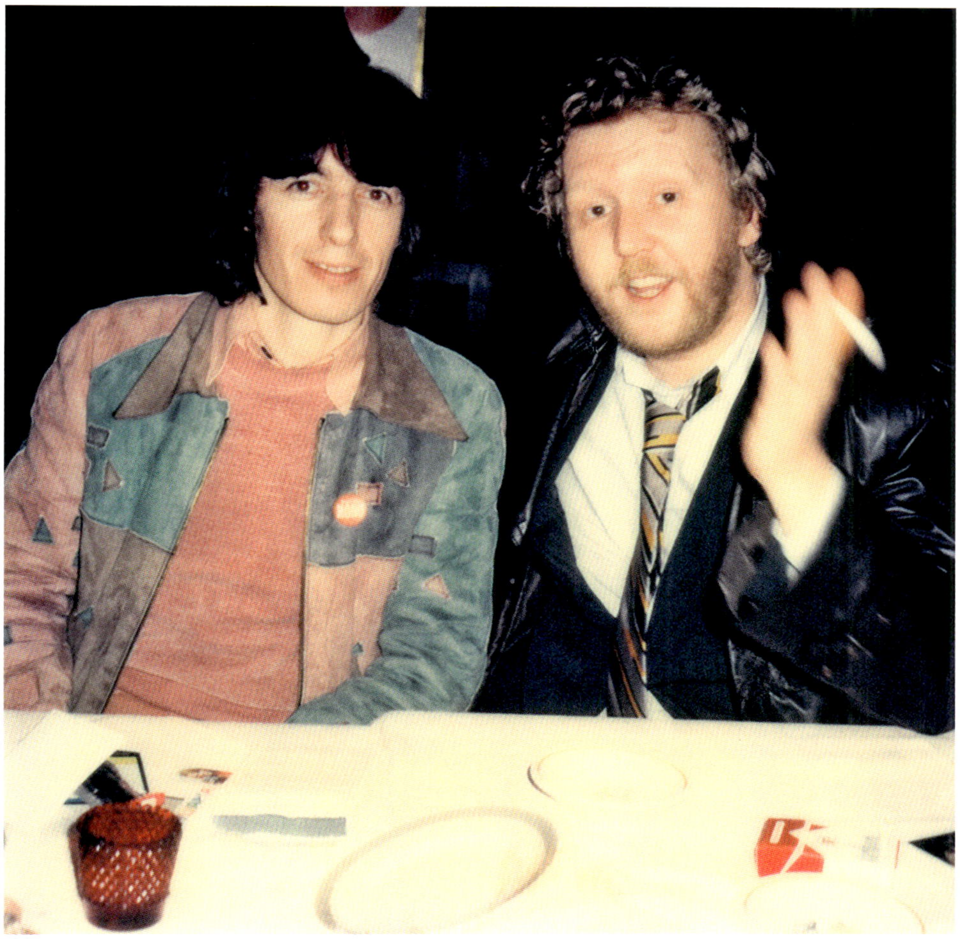

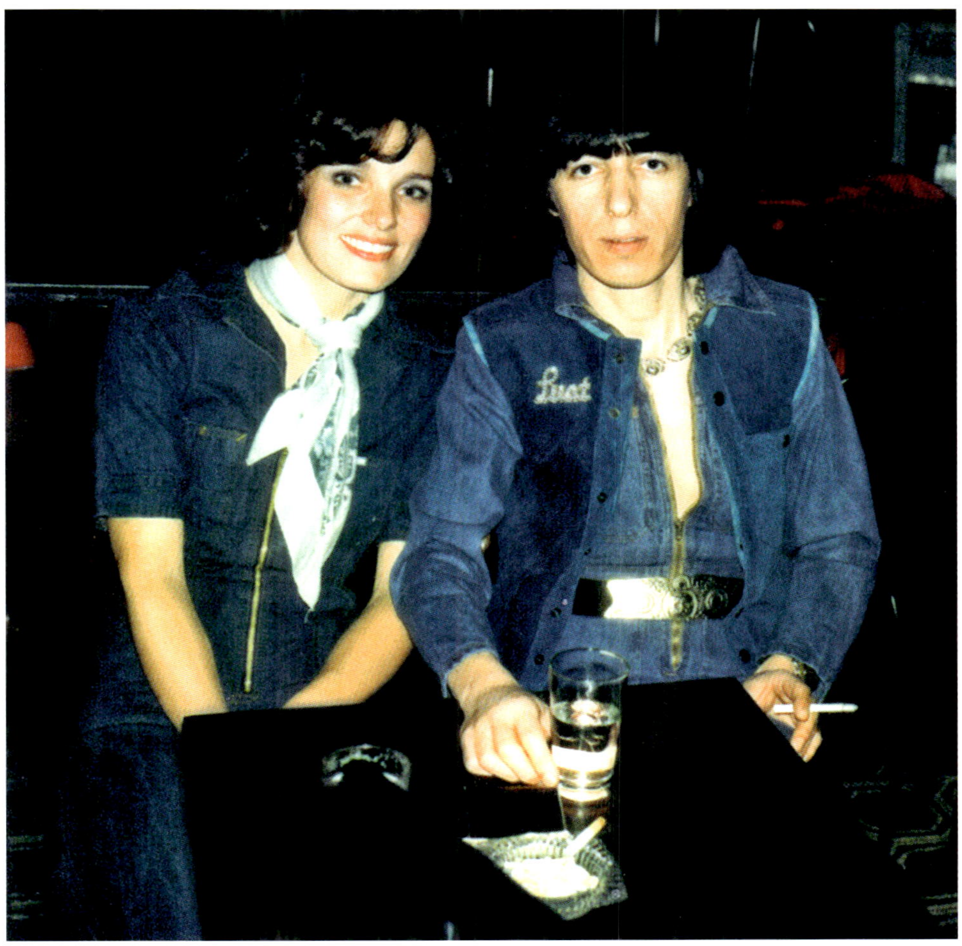

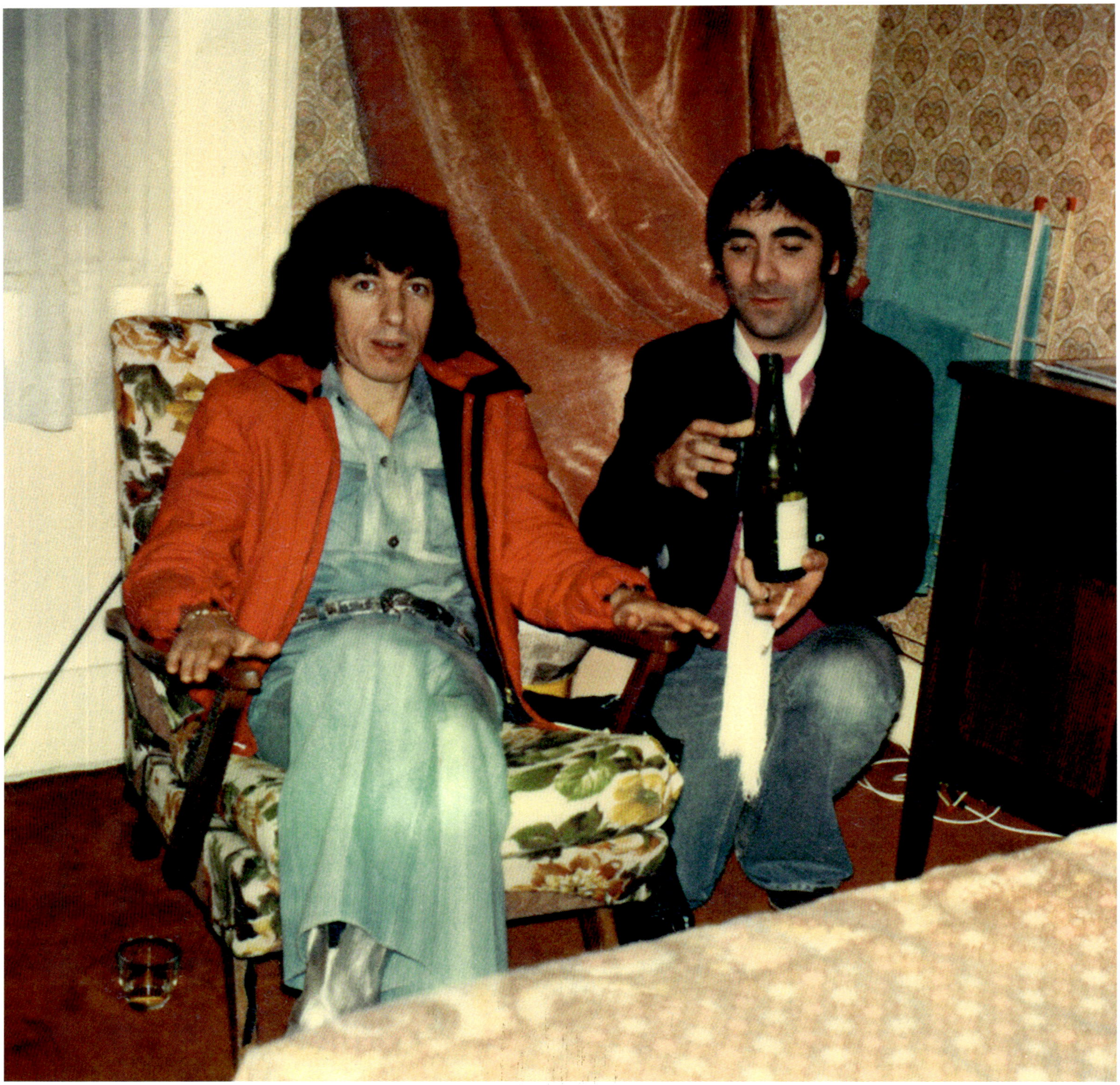

Two shots of Keith Moon: one with me; one with his lady, Annette Walter Lax. Both taken at their mews flat in London – 1 November 1977.

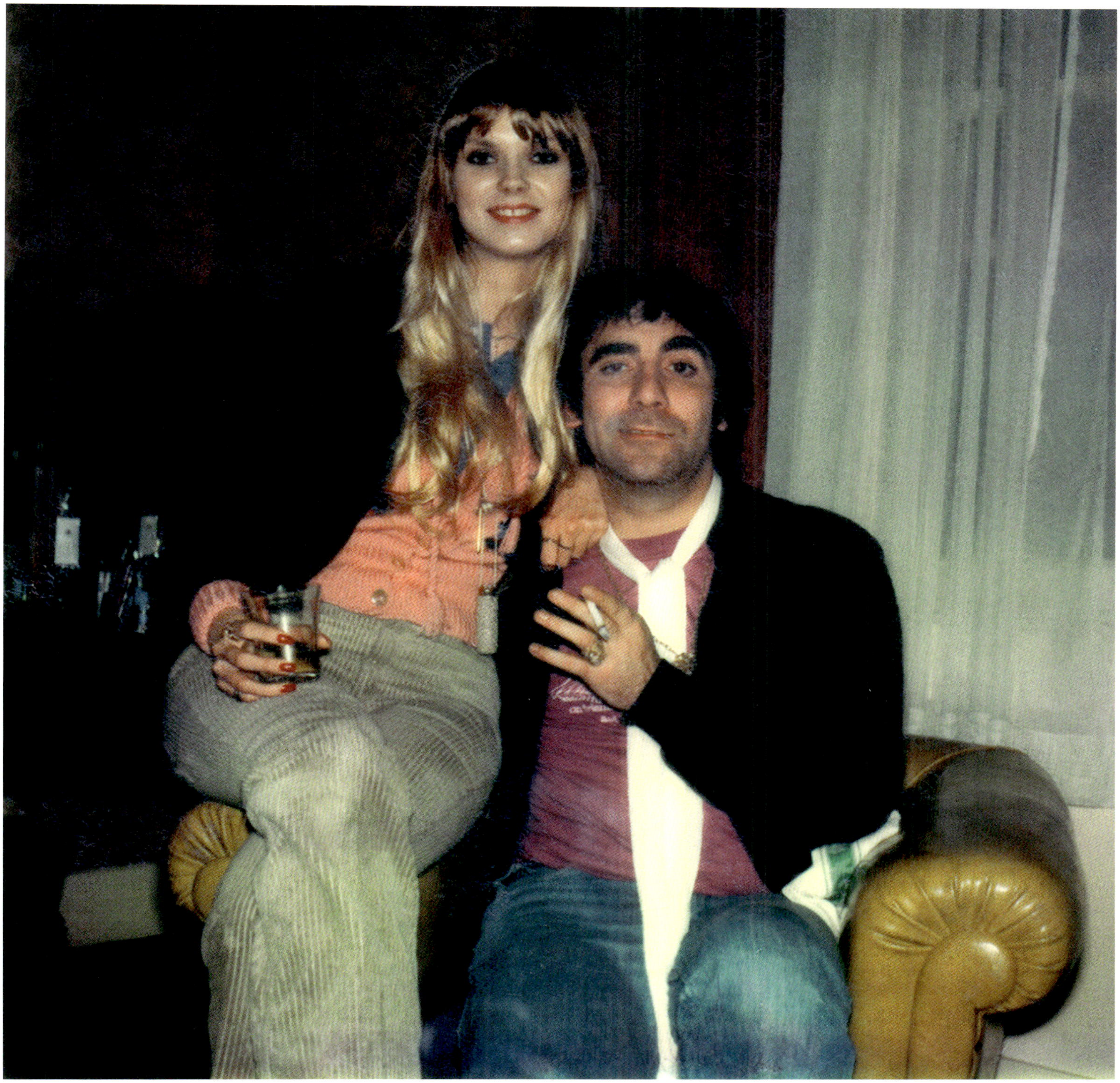

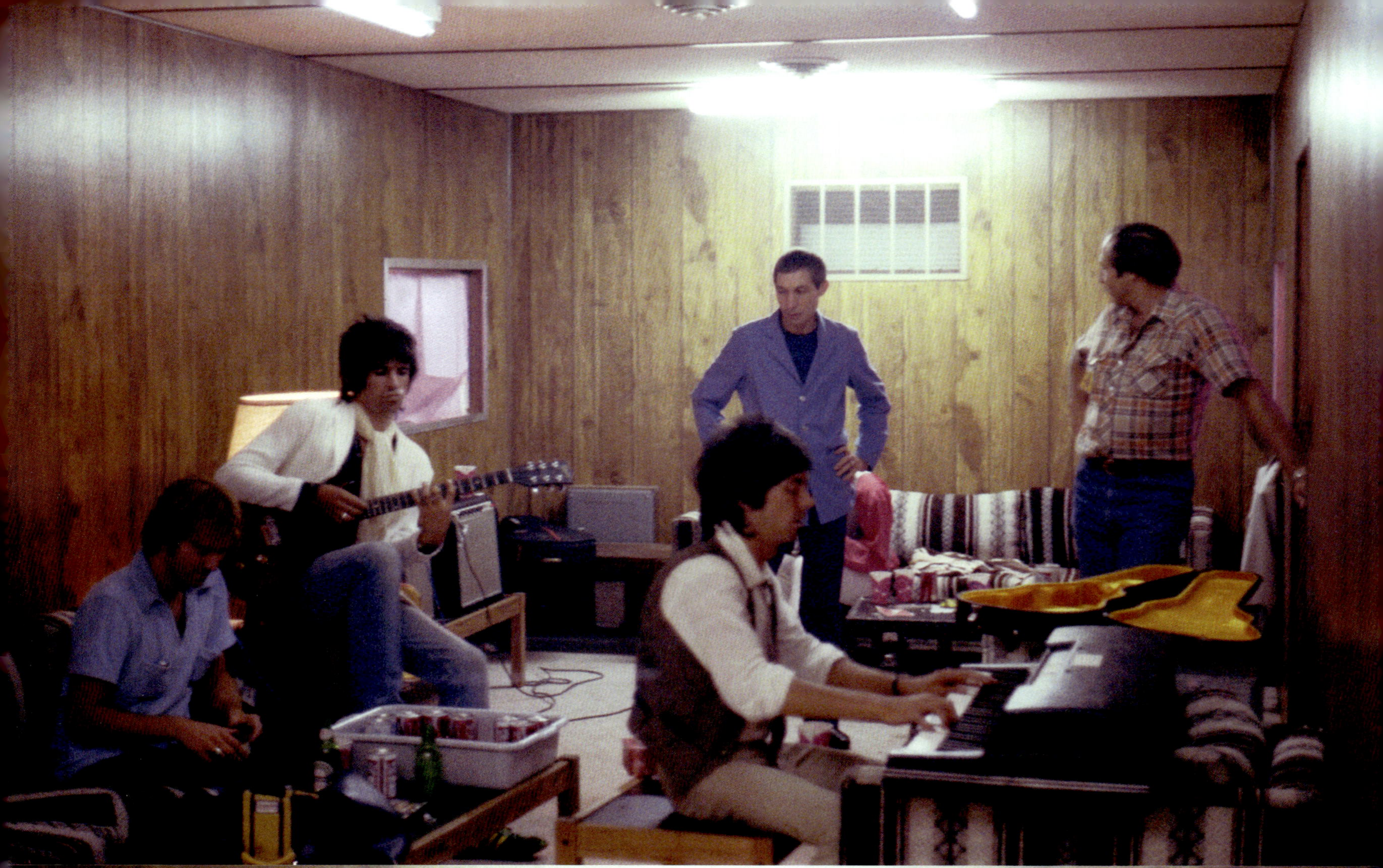

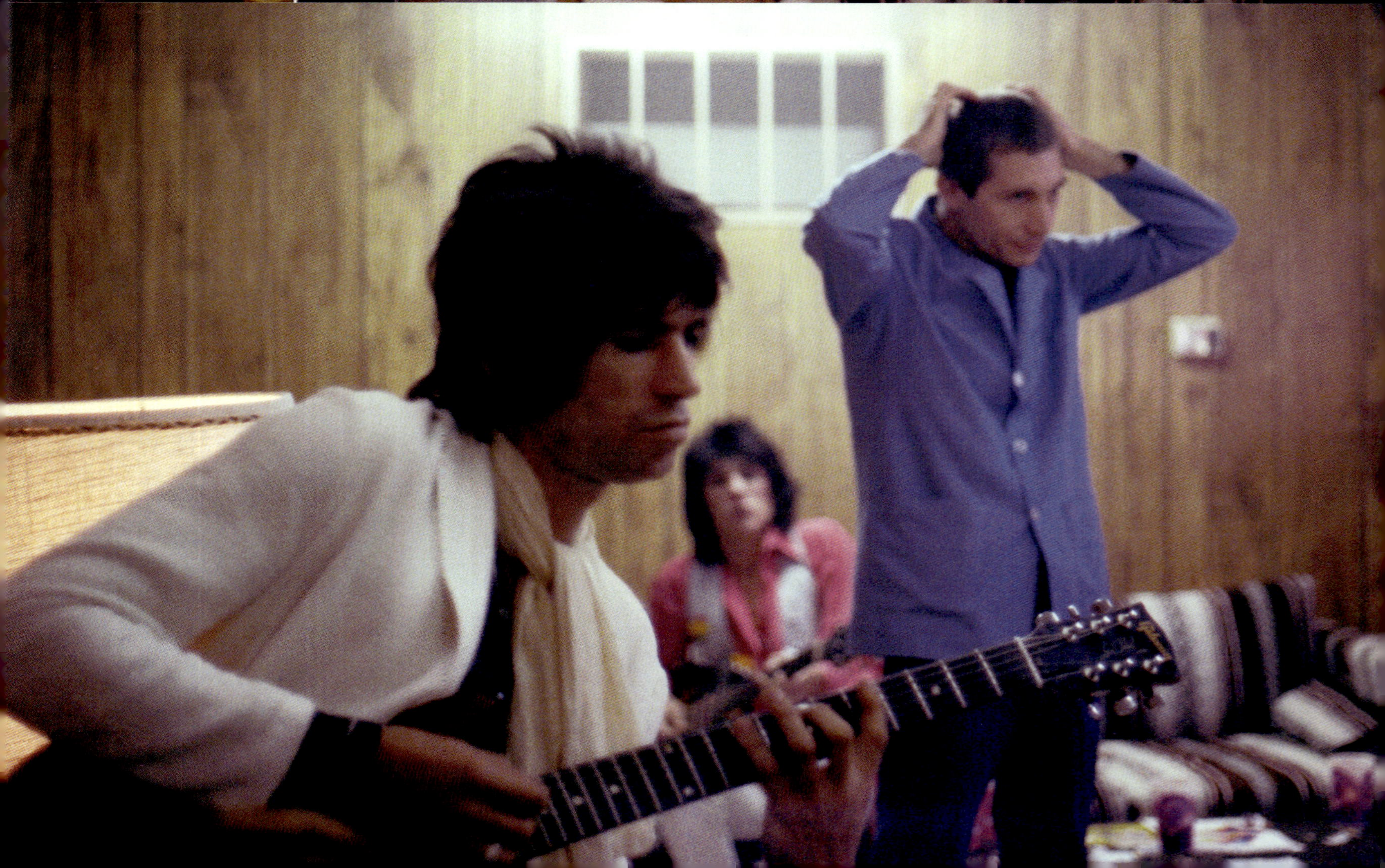

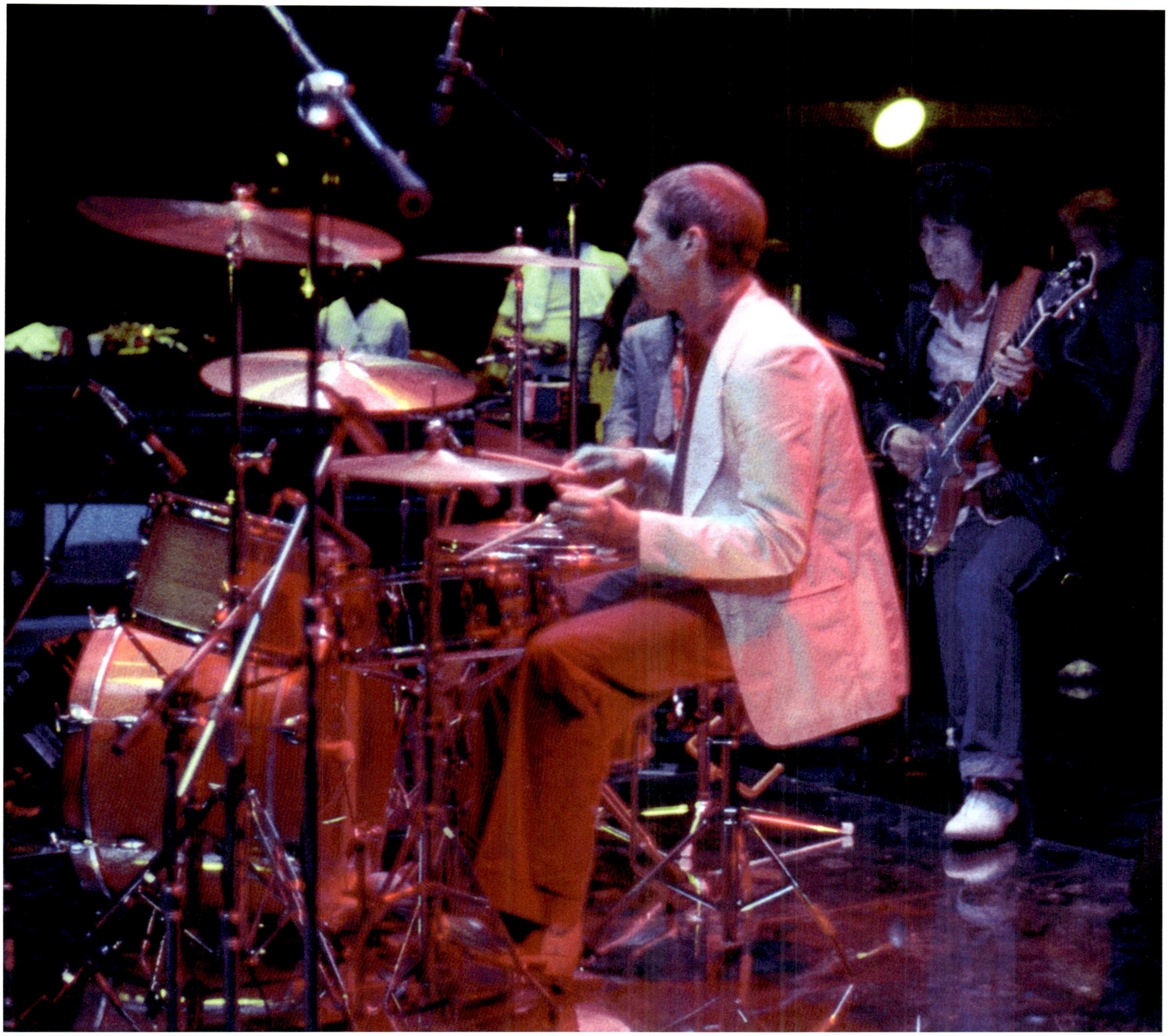

Charlie and Ronnie rehearsing backstage at The Fox Theatre in Atlanta, Georgia – 12 June 1978.

Left: Two shots of the Stones rehearsing backstage – July 1978.

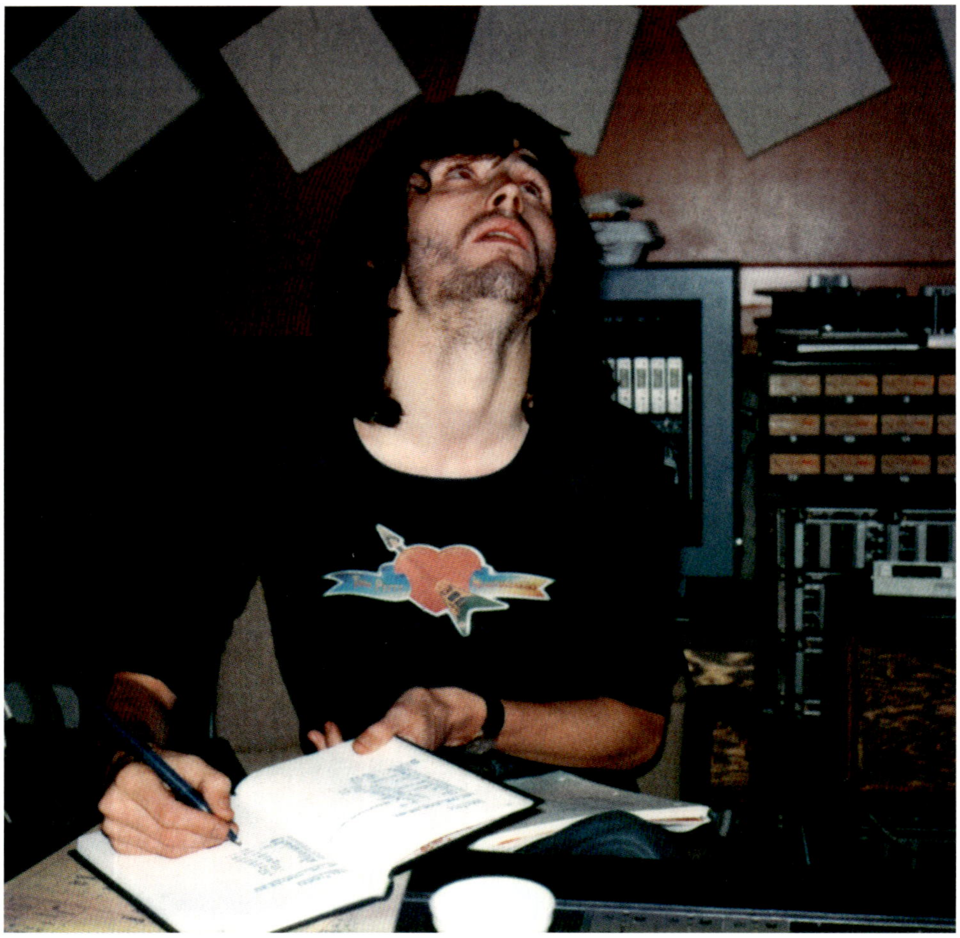

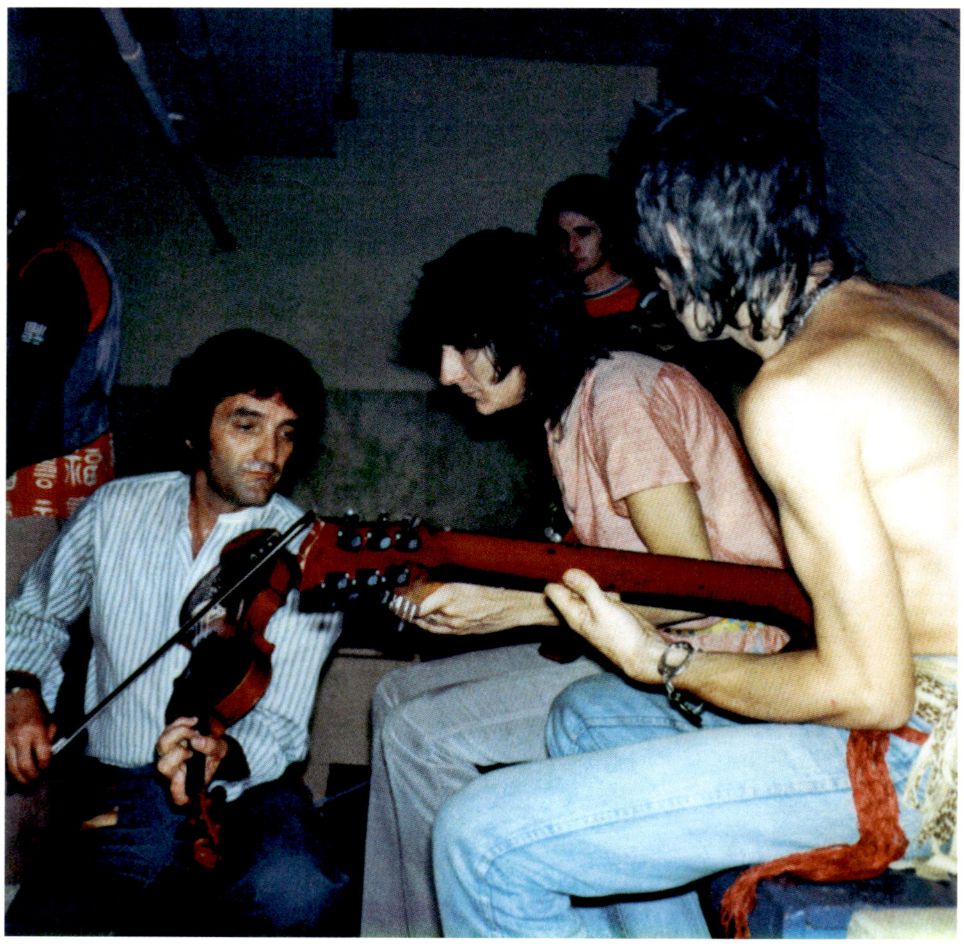

Keith working on ideas at the recording session in Los Angeles – 28 August 1978.
Above right: Ronnie playing his pedal steel at the recording session in Los Angeles – 5 September 1978.
Right and far right: Two shots of Keith and Ronnie running through songs with Doug Kershaw. I'd arranged for him to play with us that night at The Community Center Arena in Tucson, Arizona – 21 July 1978.

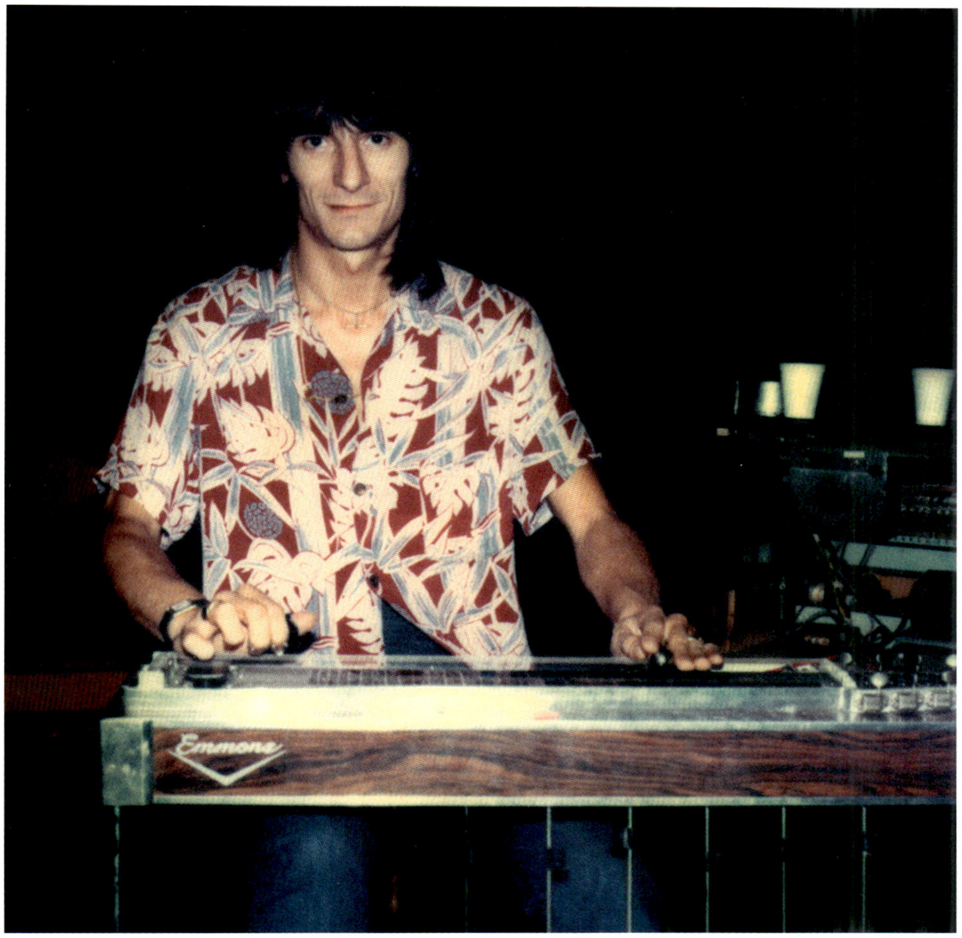
Emmons

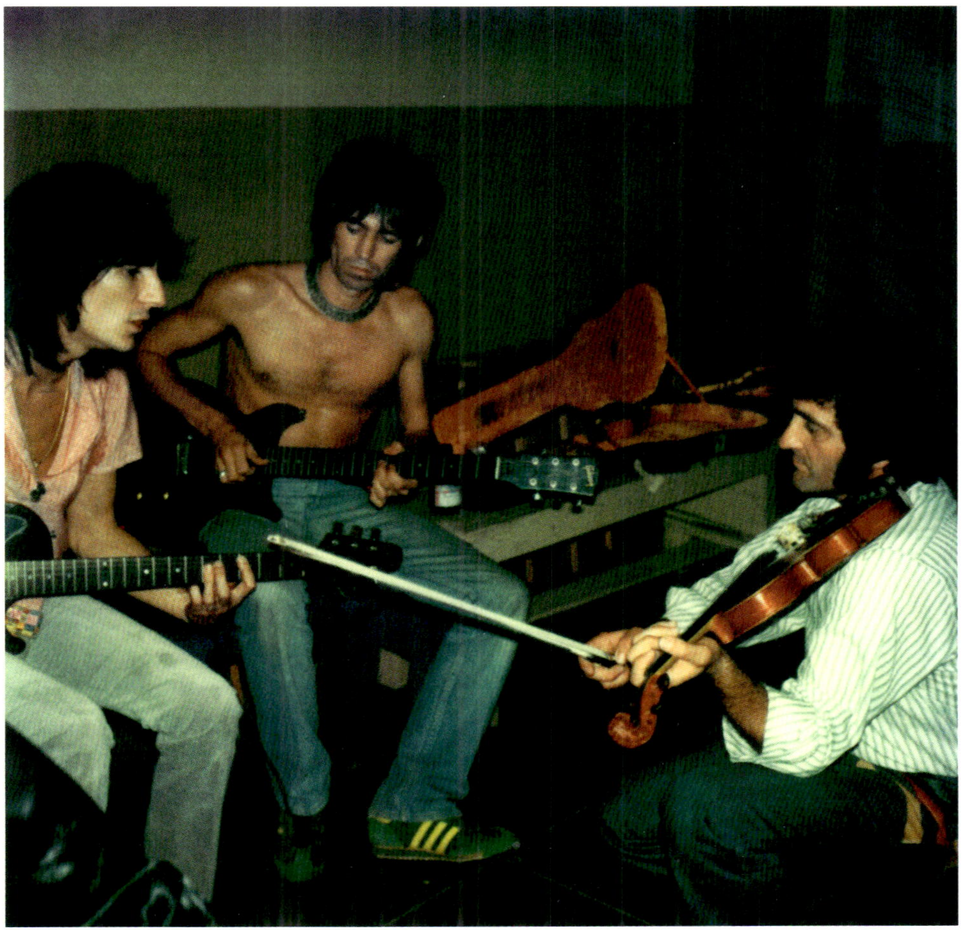

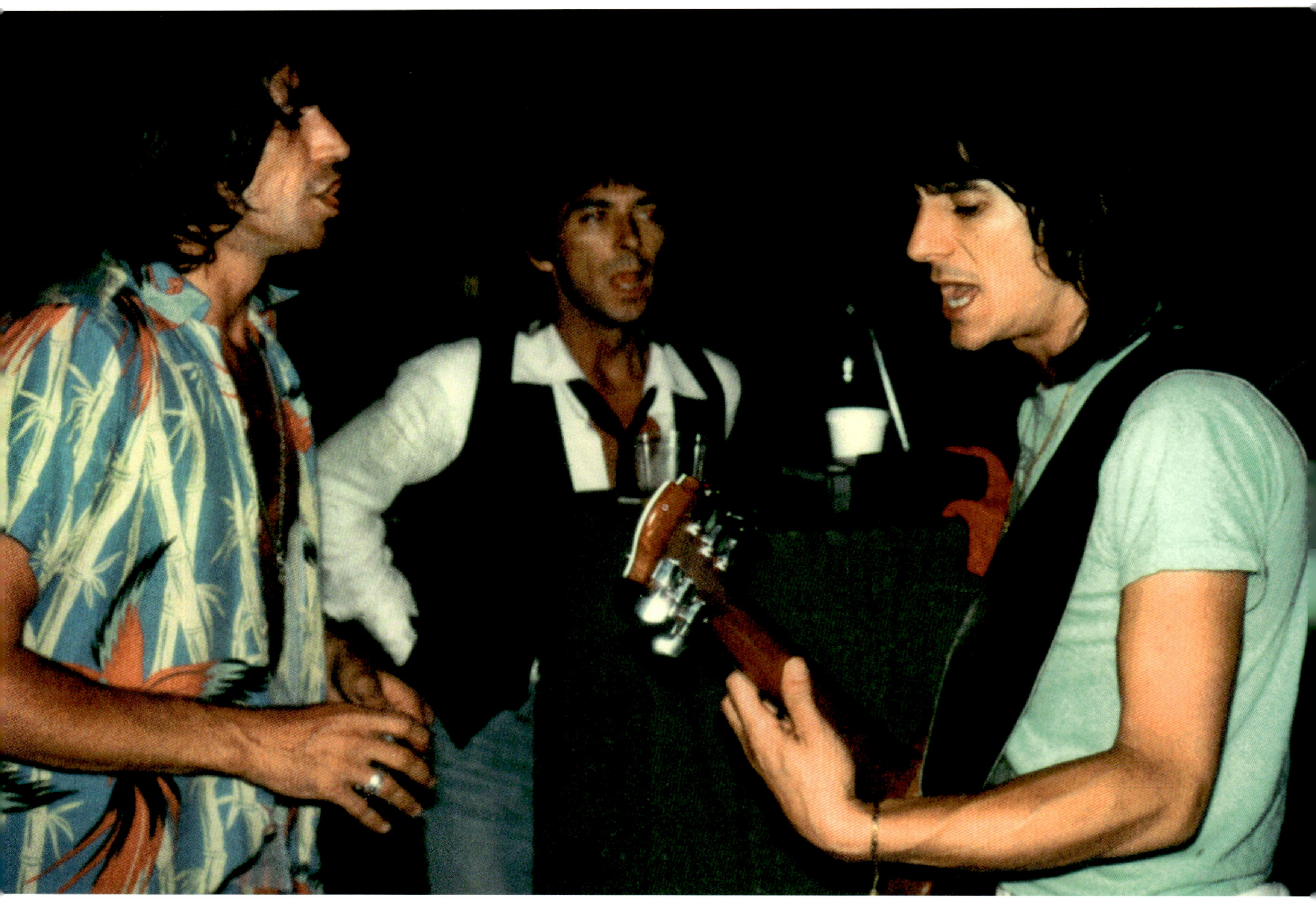

Keith, Ian McLagan and Ronnie working on ideas at the recording session in Los Angeles – 29 August 1978.
Right: Keith crashed out, fast asleep under the piano at the recording session in Los Angeles – 4 September 1978.

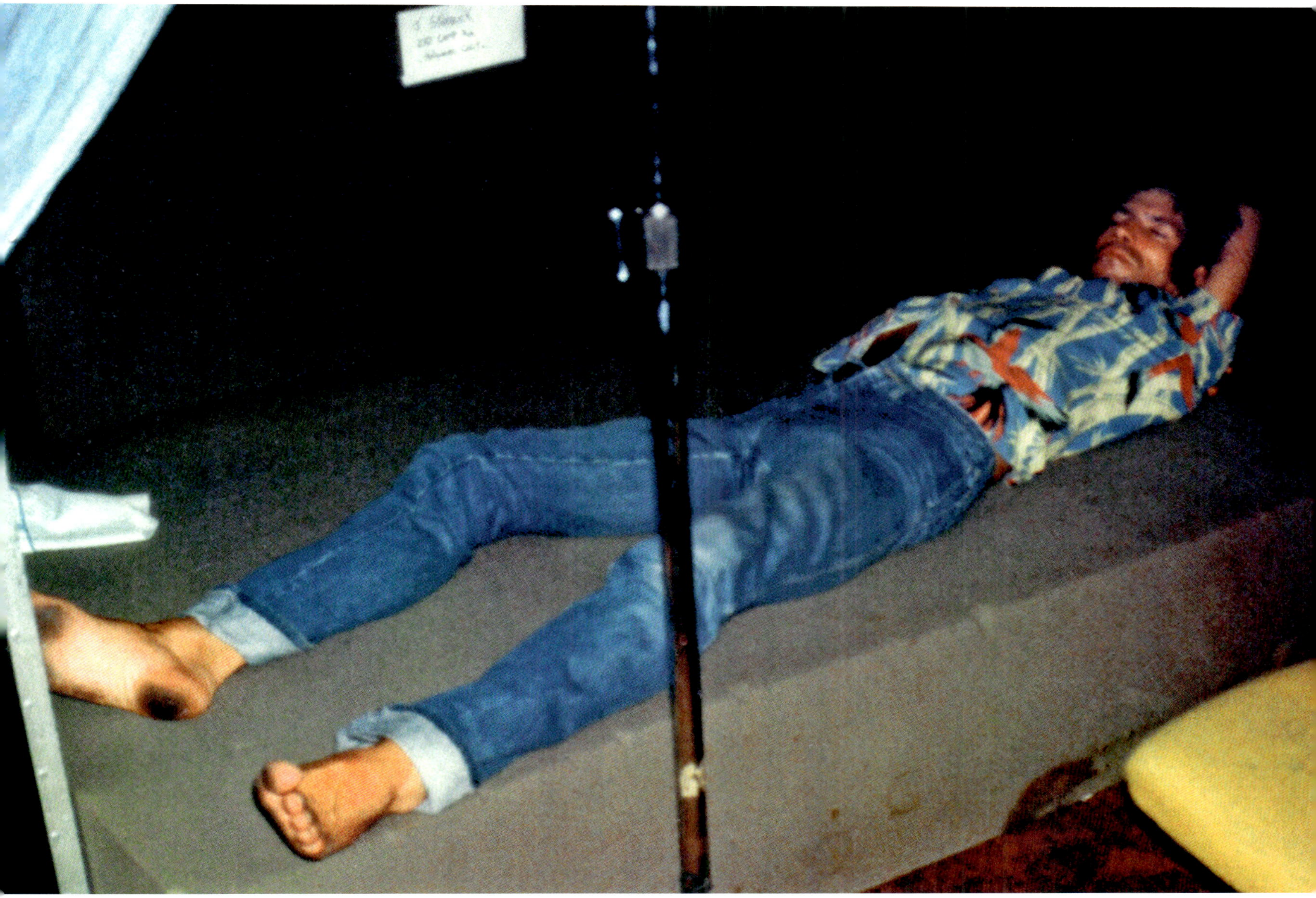

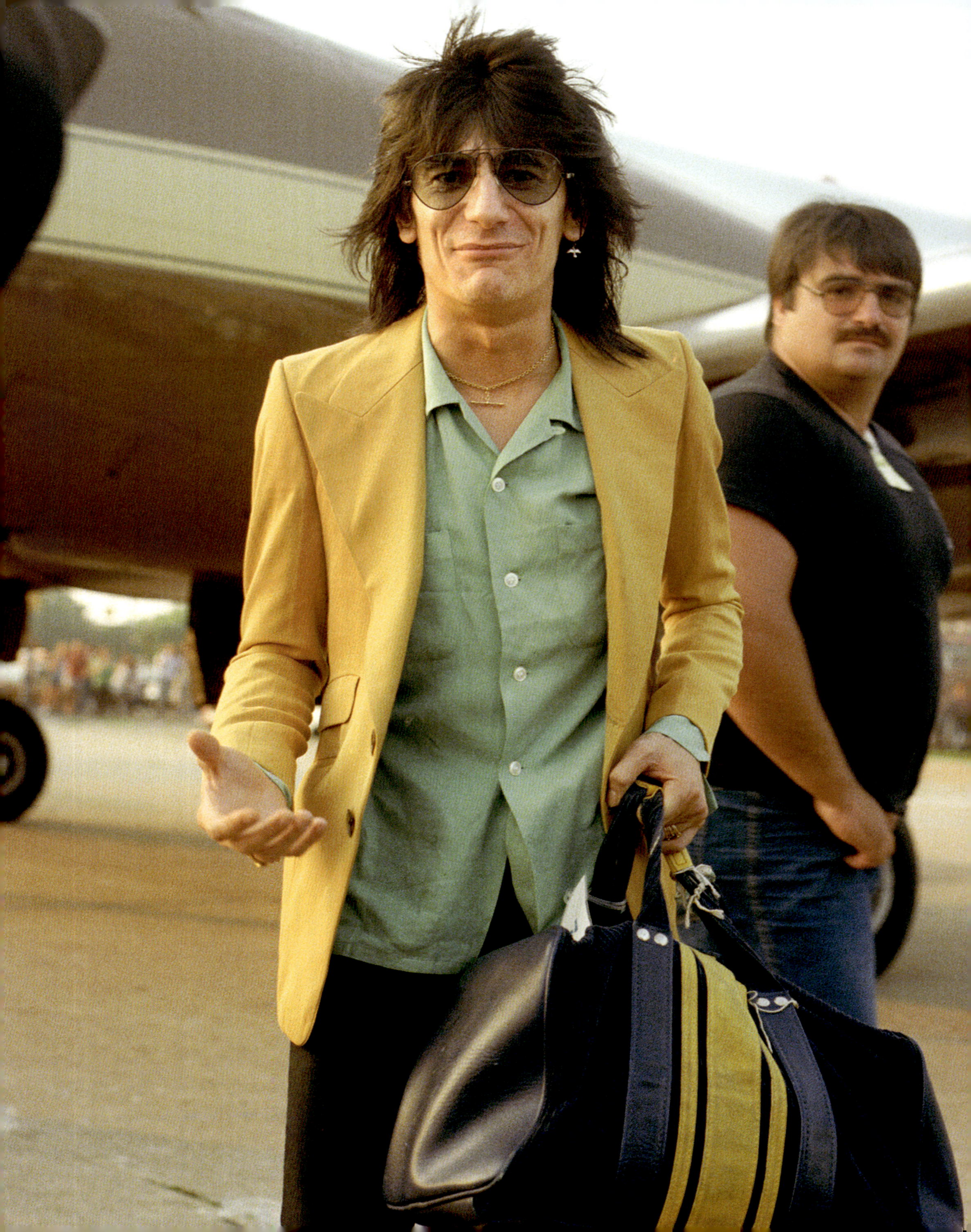

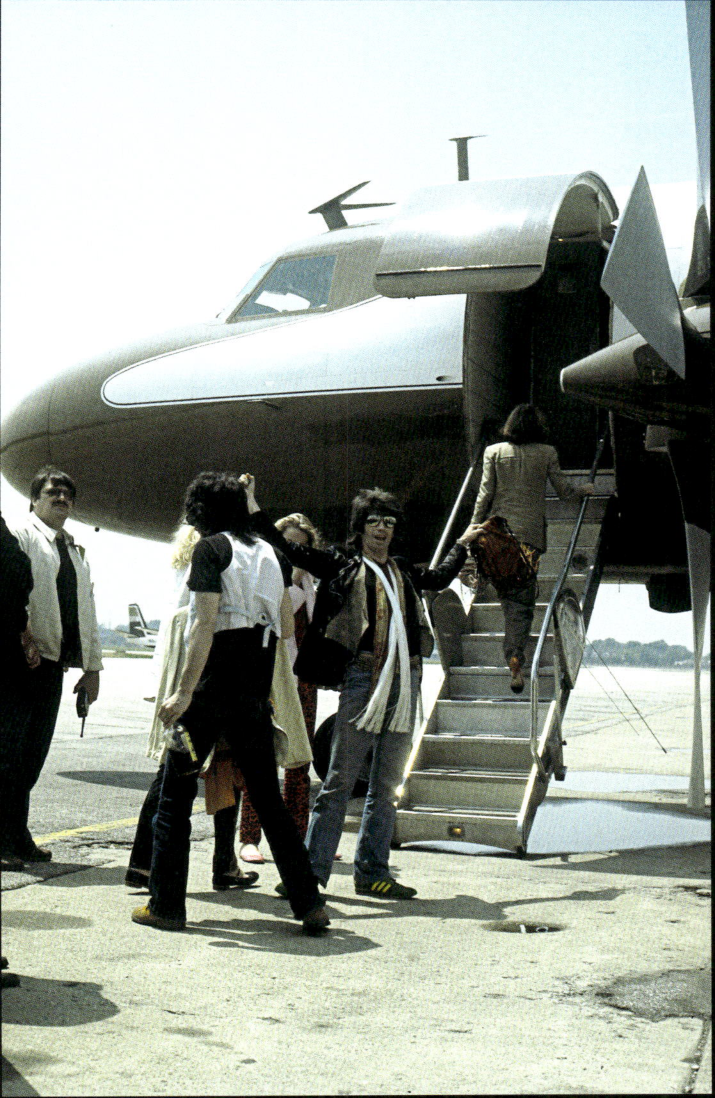

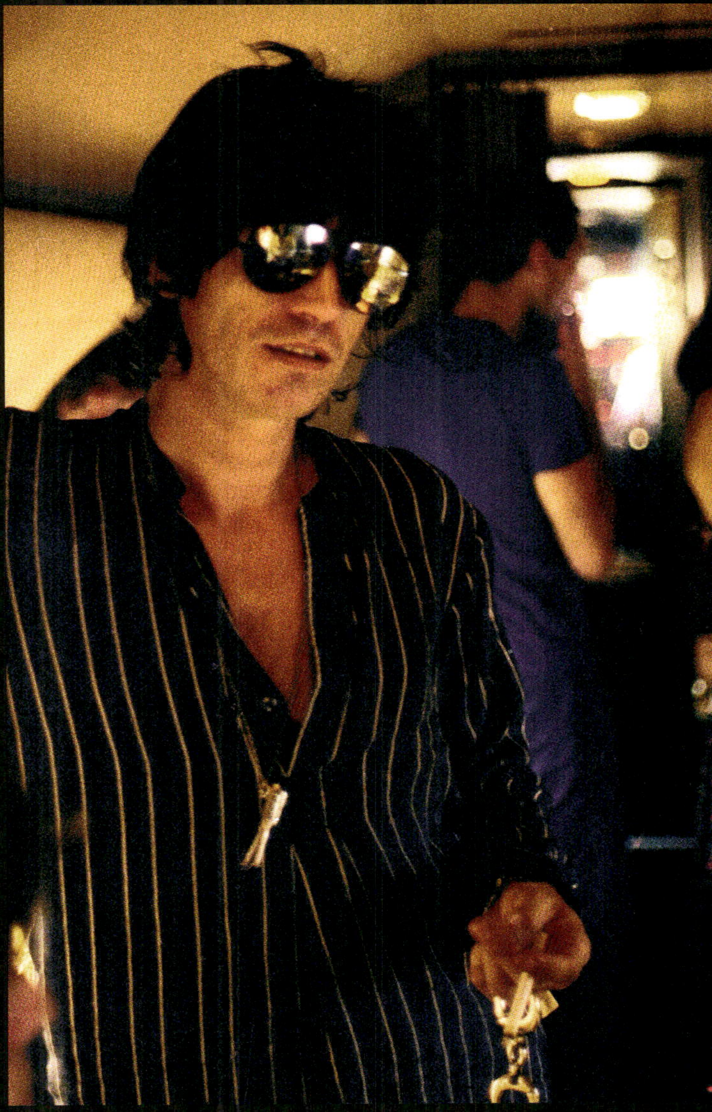

Two shots of the boys preparing to board The Starship in Chicago for the flight to Cleveland, Ohio – 1 July 1978.
Right: Keith on board during the flight from Atlanta to New York – 13 June 1978.

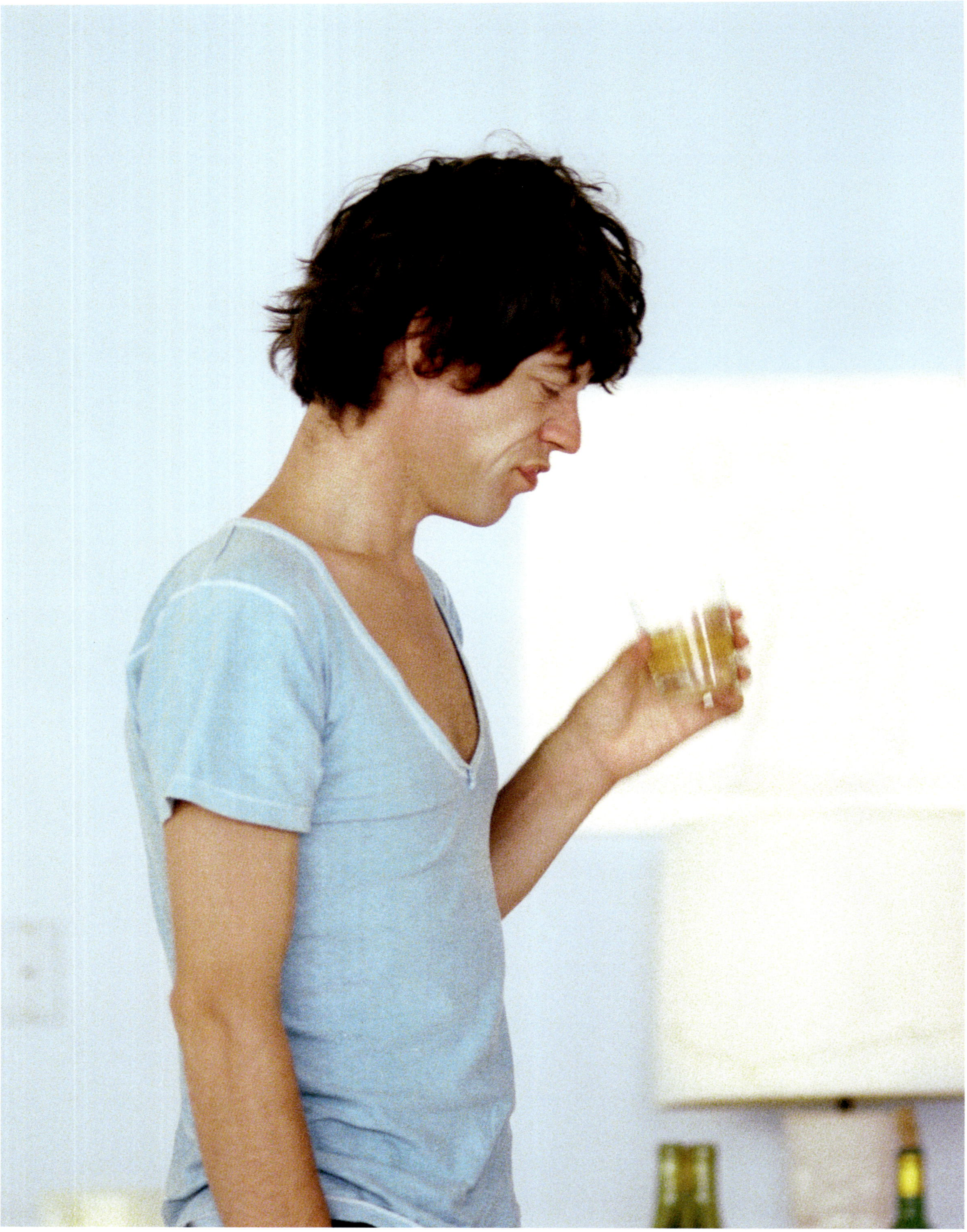

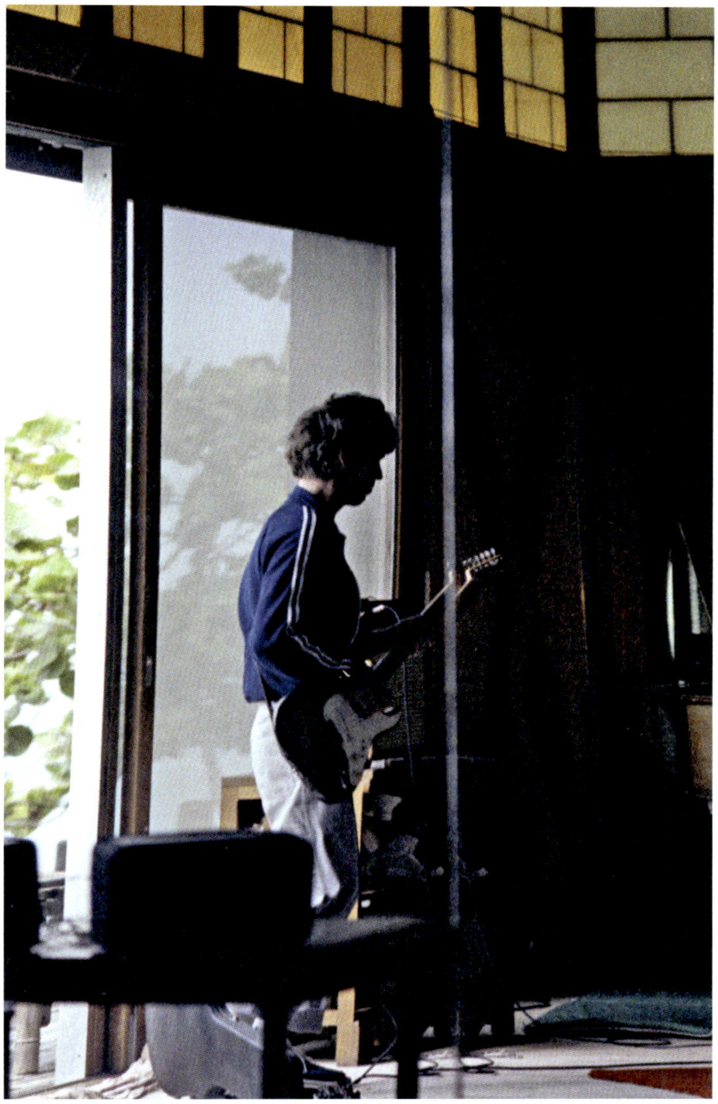

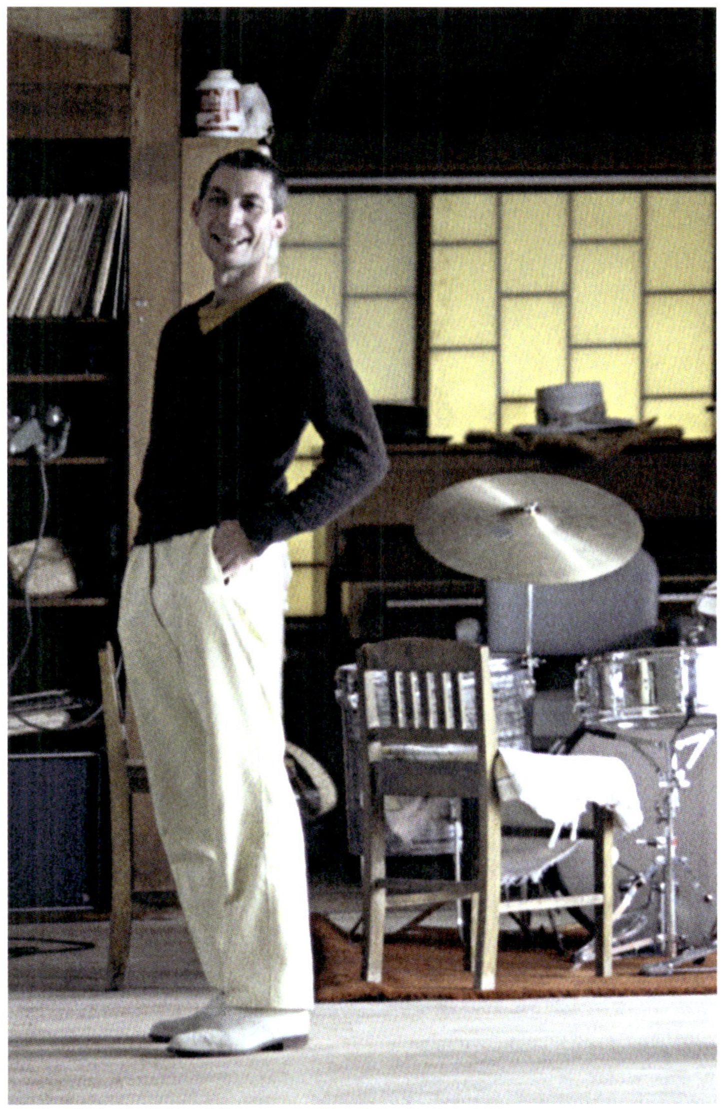

Mick playing guitar, and a happy Charlie smiling at me in the rehearsal room in Nassau in the Bahamas – 22 January 1979.
Left: Mick, not very happy with what he just drank at the communal house in Nassau – 22 January 1979.
Following pages: Charlie quizzical and Ronnie smiling (with camera) at the communal house in Nassau – 31 January 1979.

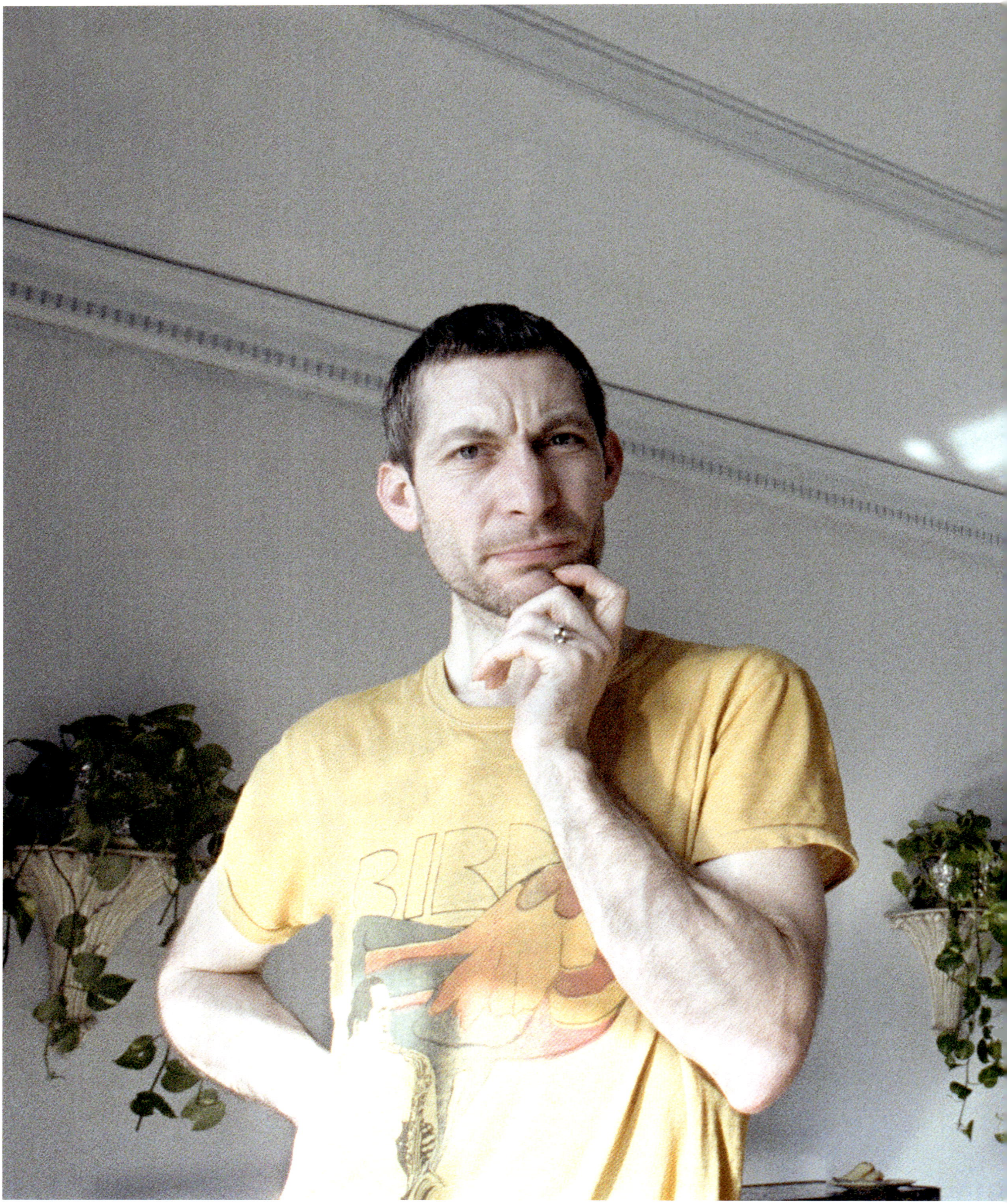

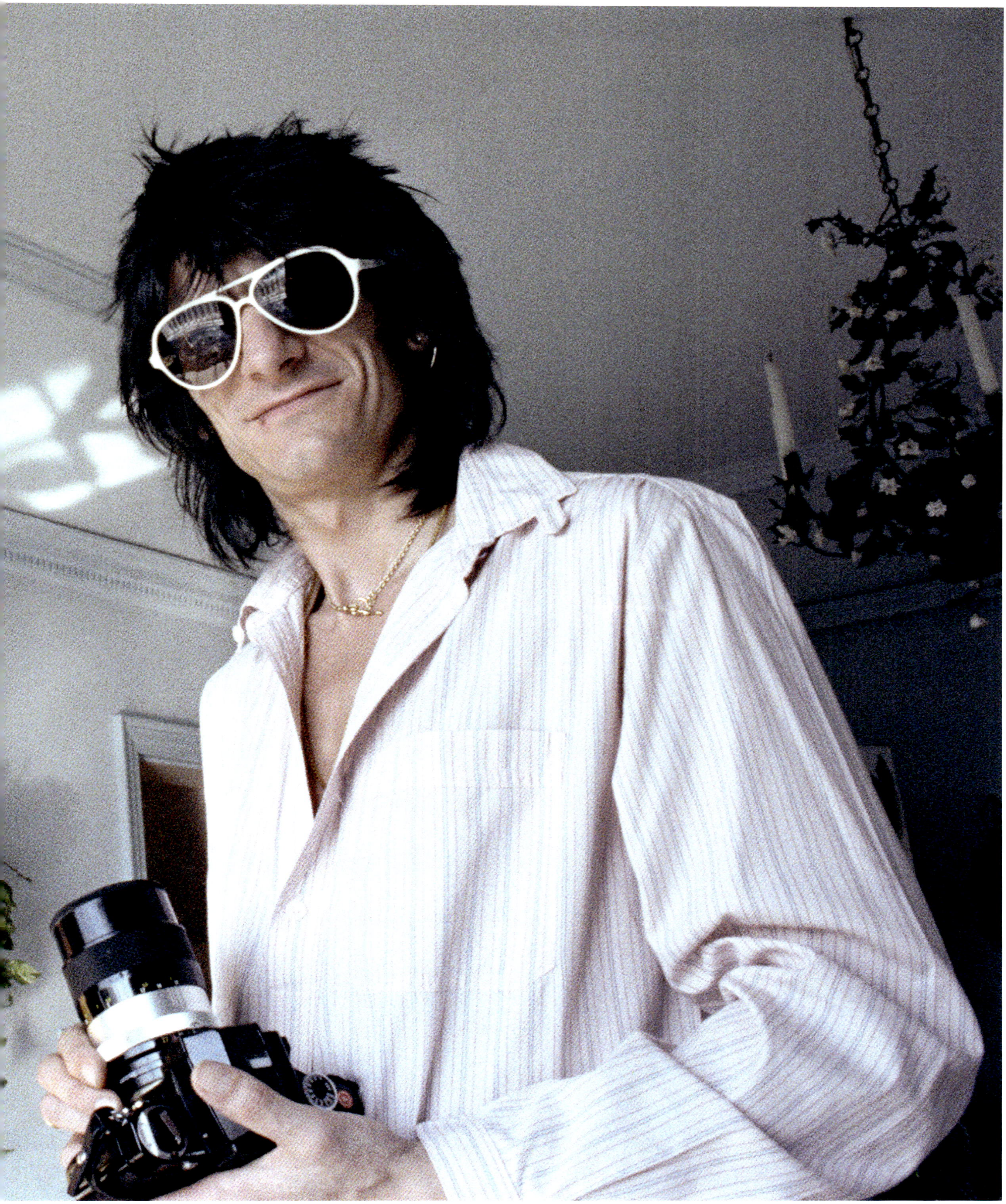

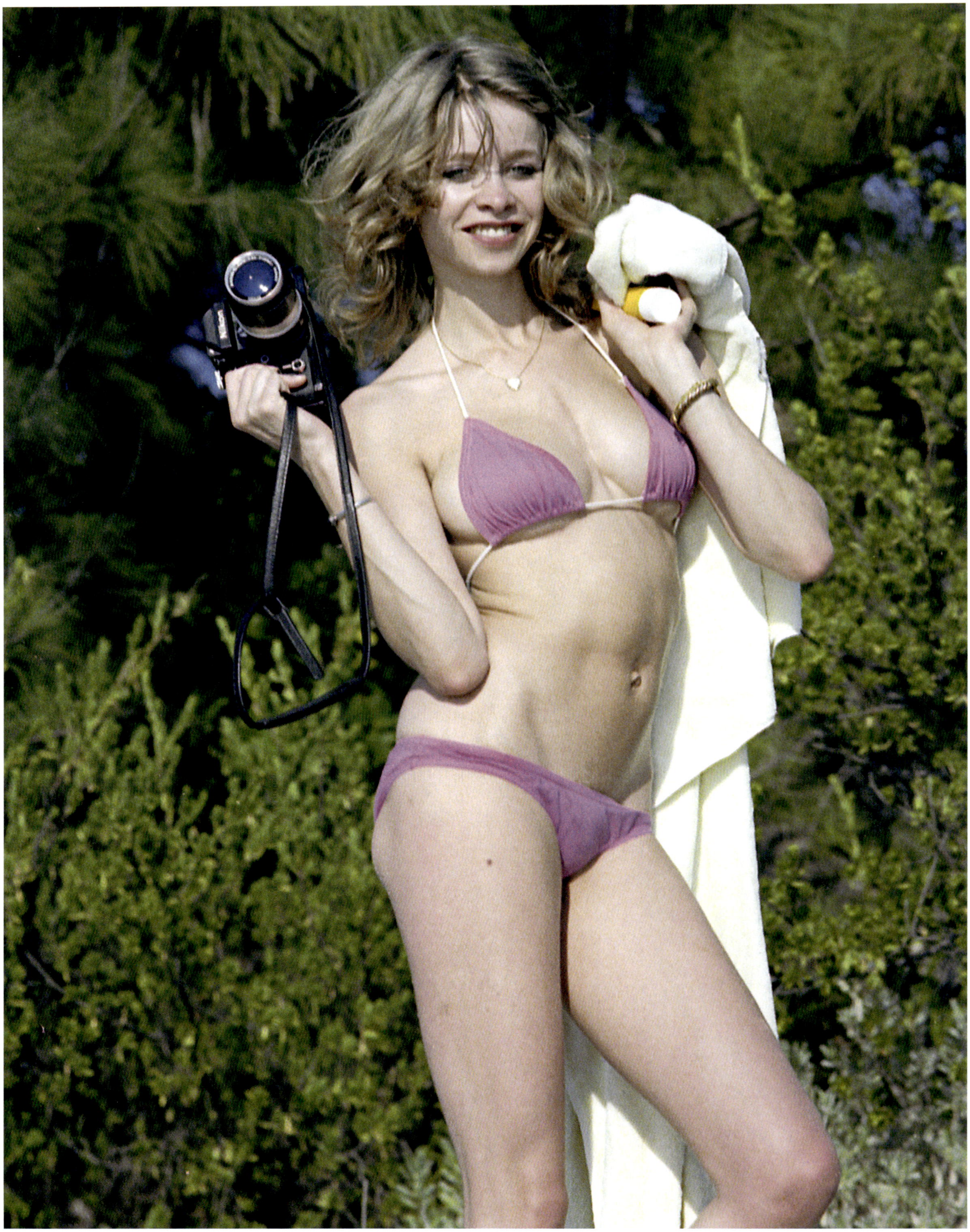

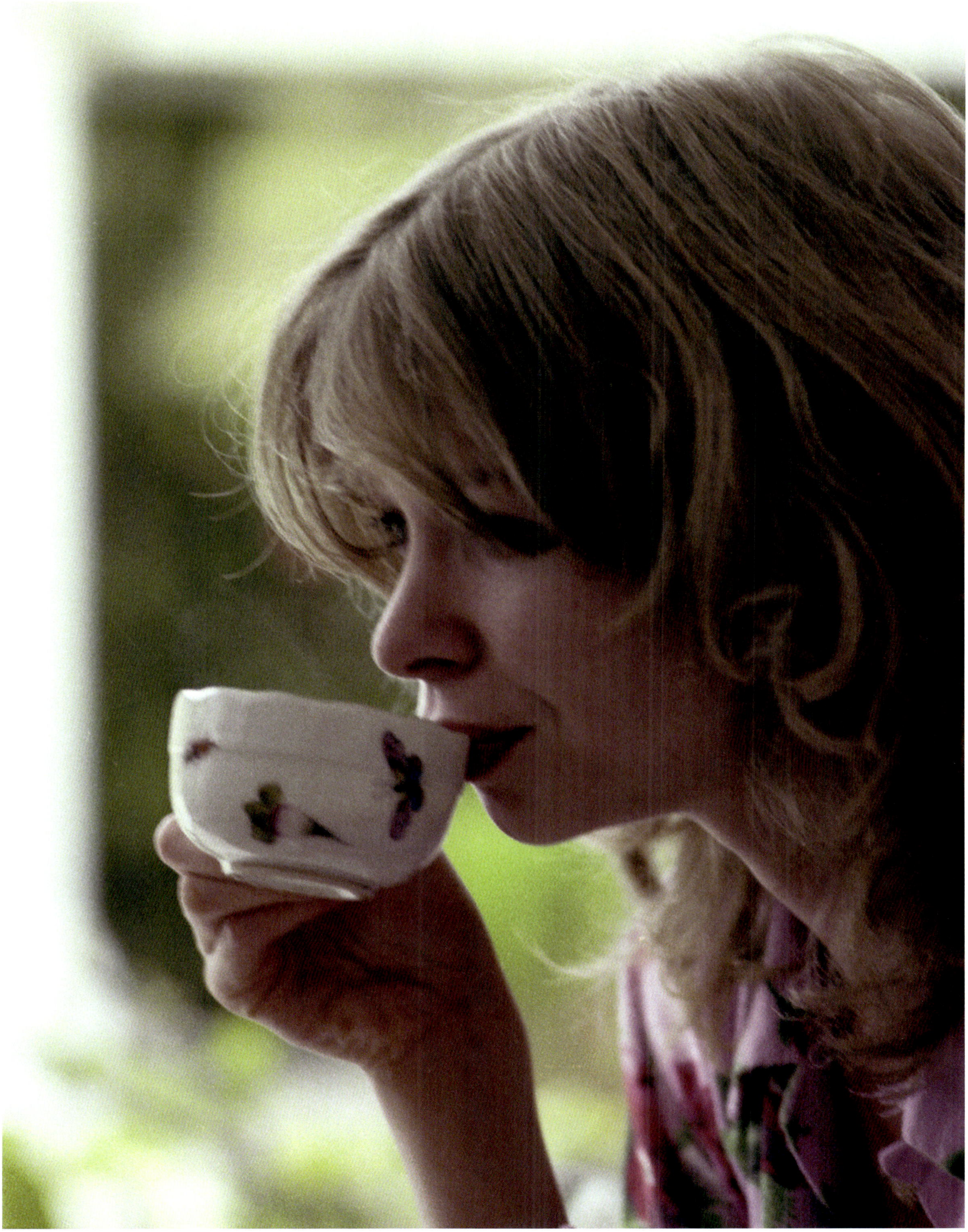

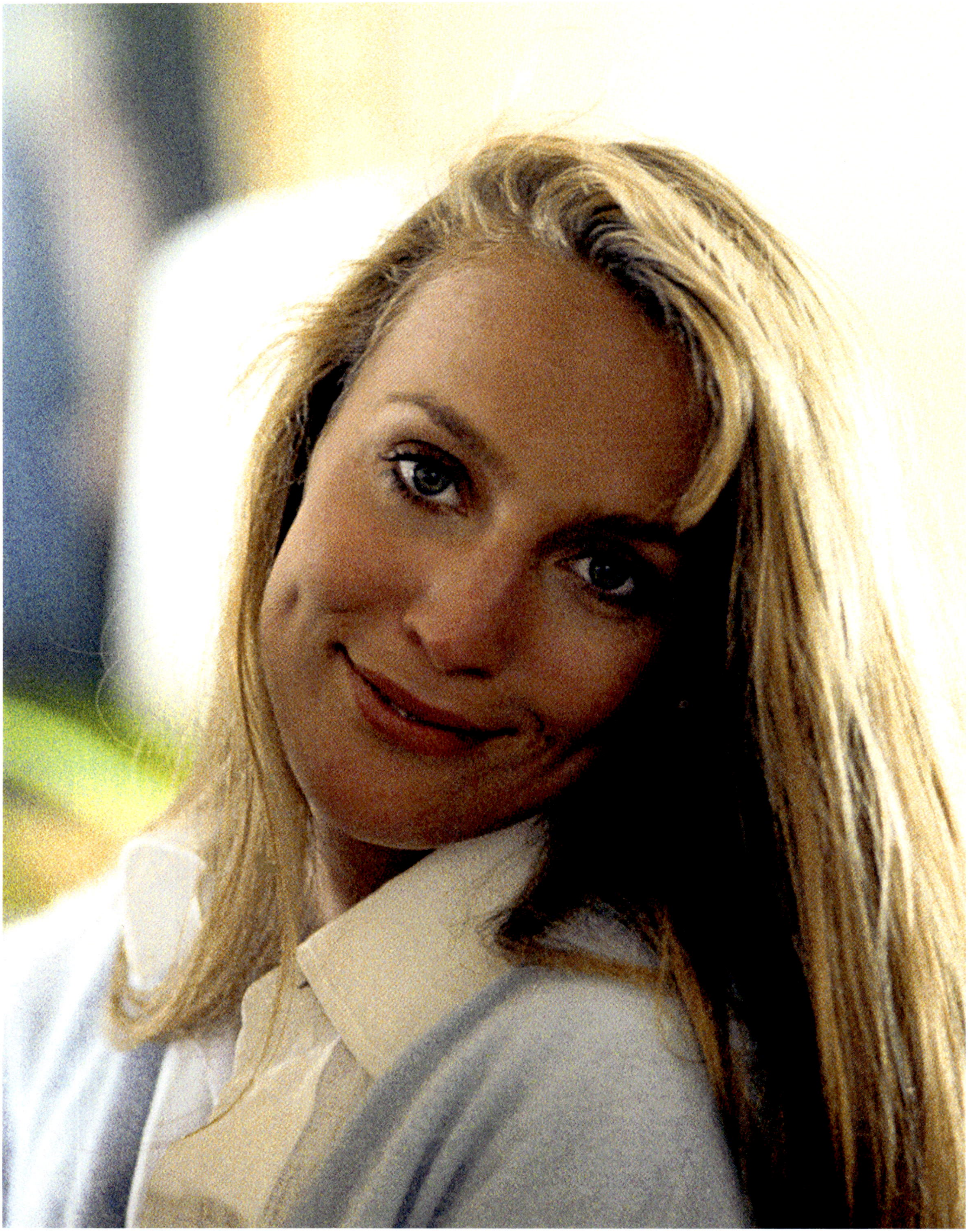

Mick at the microphone in the rehearsal room in Nassau – 29 January 1979.
Left: Jerry Hall making an amusing pose for me at the house in Nassau – 1 February 1979.
Previous pages: Jo Wood posing on the beach in Nassau – 4 February 1979.
Jo enjoying a cup of tea at the communal house in Nassau – 1 February 1979.

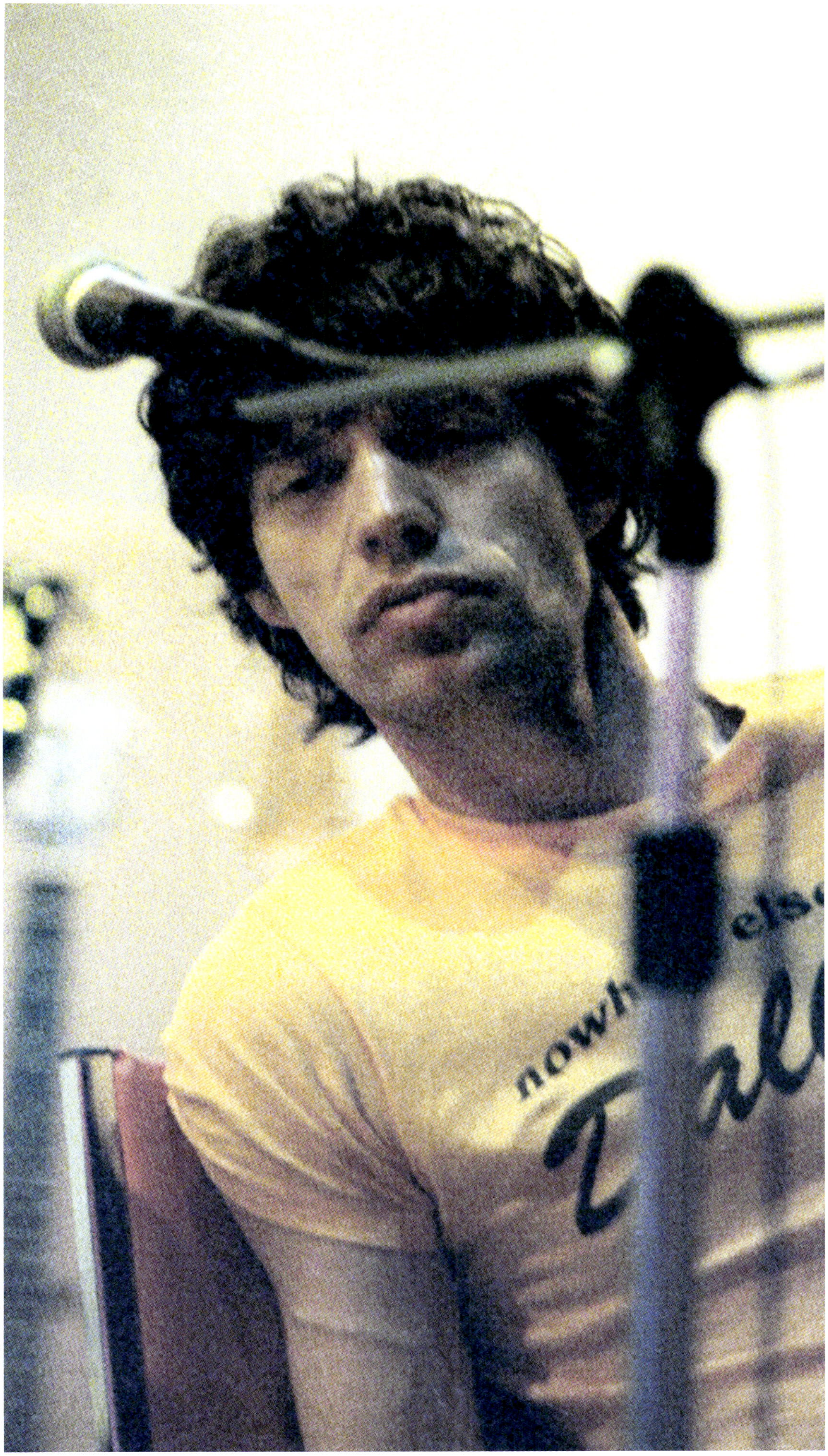

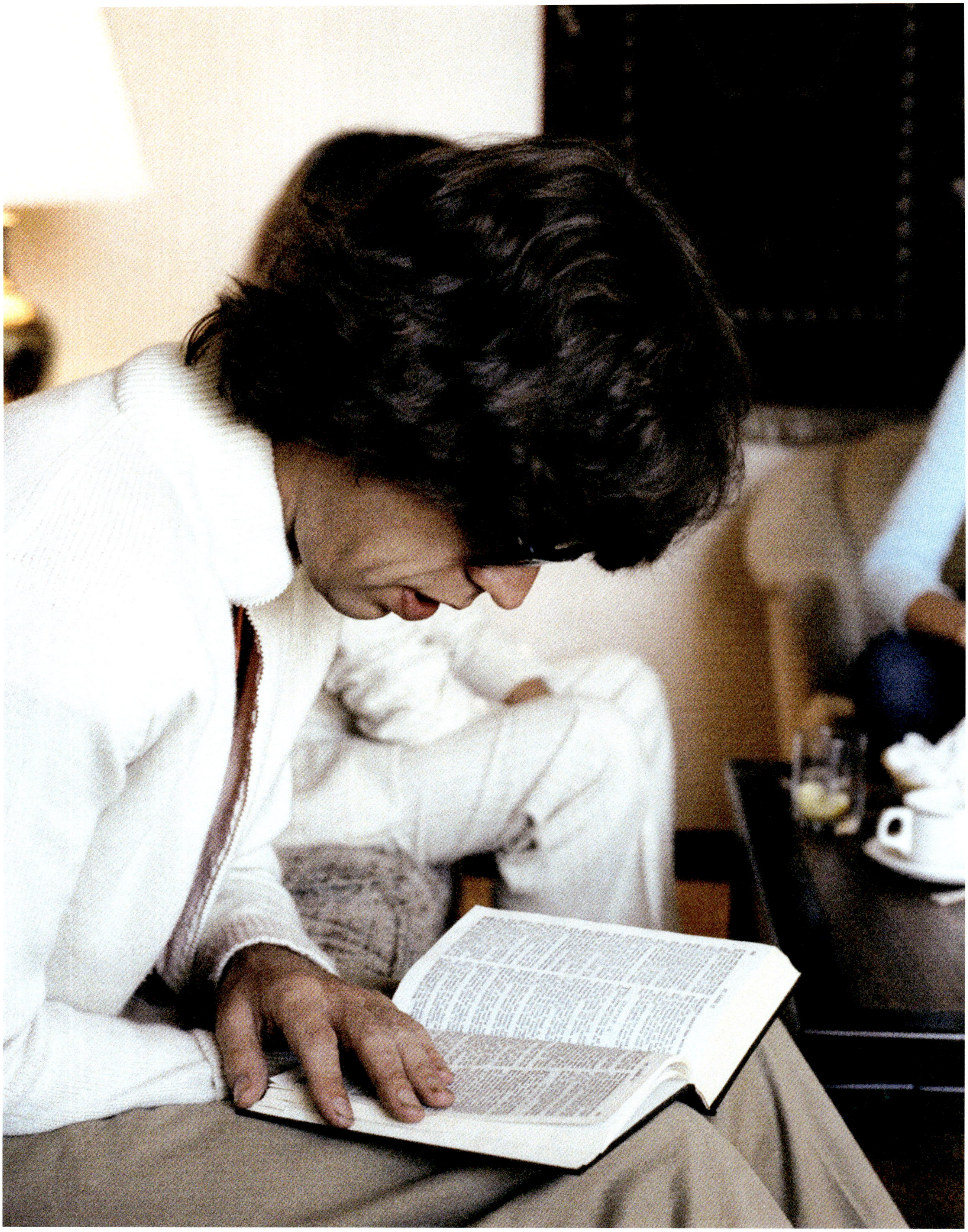

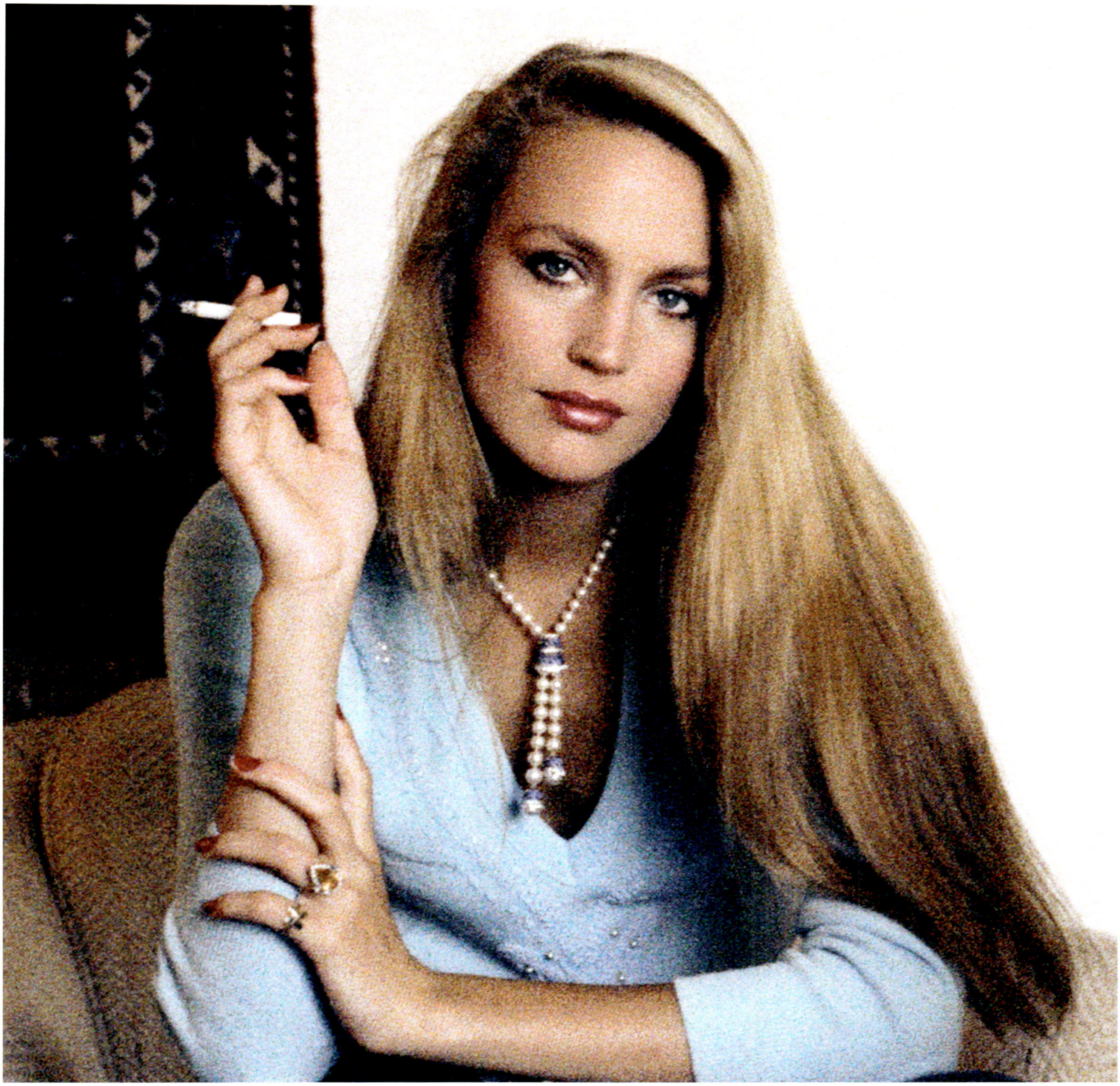

Jerry posing for me across the room – 22 April 1979.
Left: Mick reading the Bible (as W.C. Fields would say, 'looking for loopholes') in the hotel in Toronto, Canada – 22 April 1979.

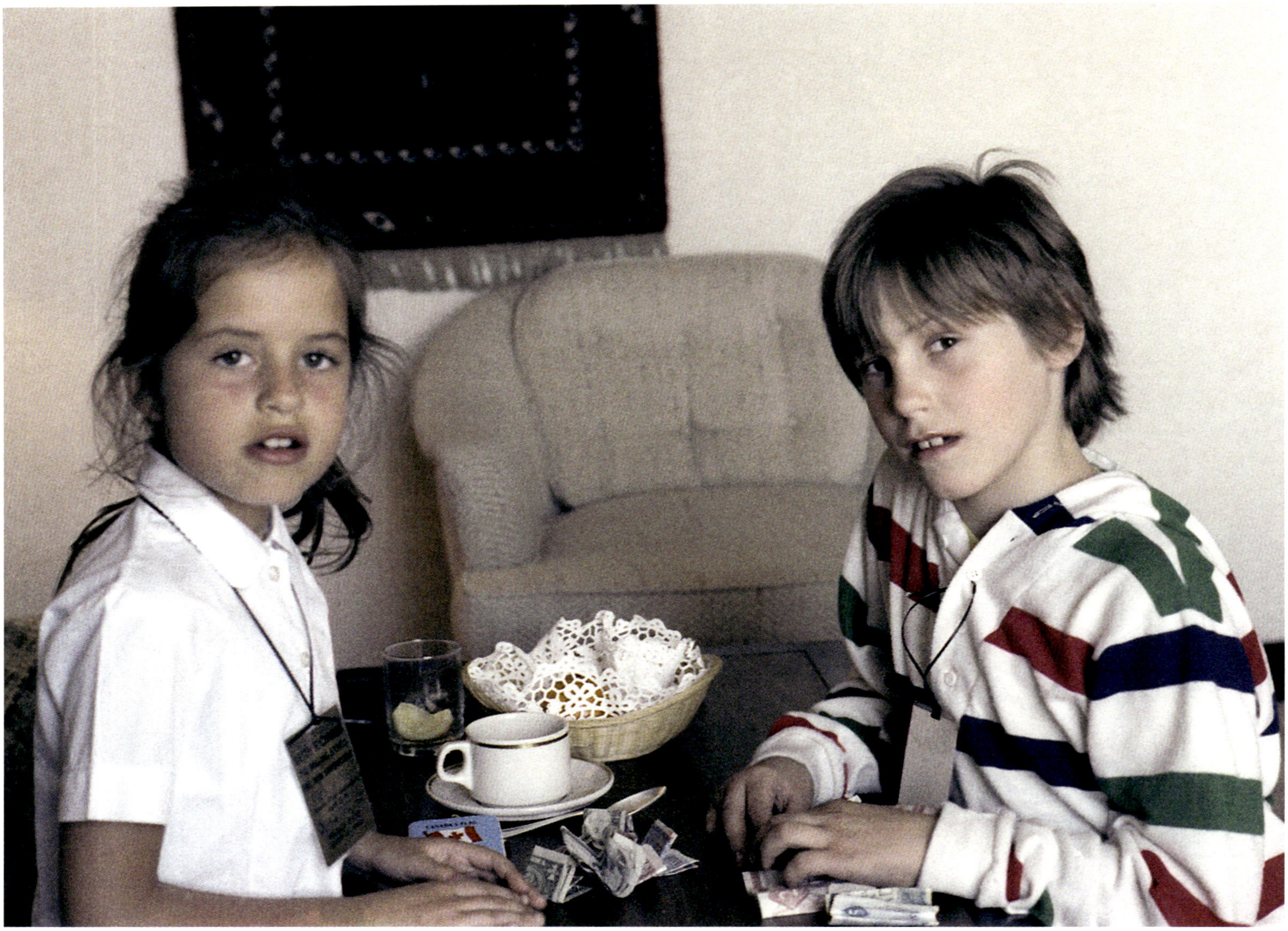

Mick's daughter Jade and Marlon sorting out their money backstage at The Oshawa Civic Auditorium in Ontario, Canada – 22 April 1979.
Right: Jerry in the bus on the way there – 22 April 1979.

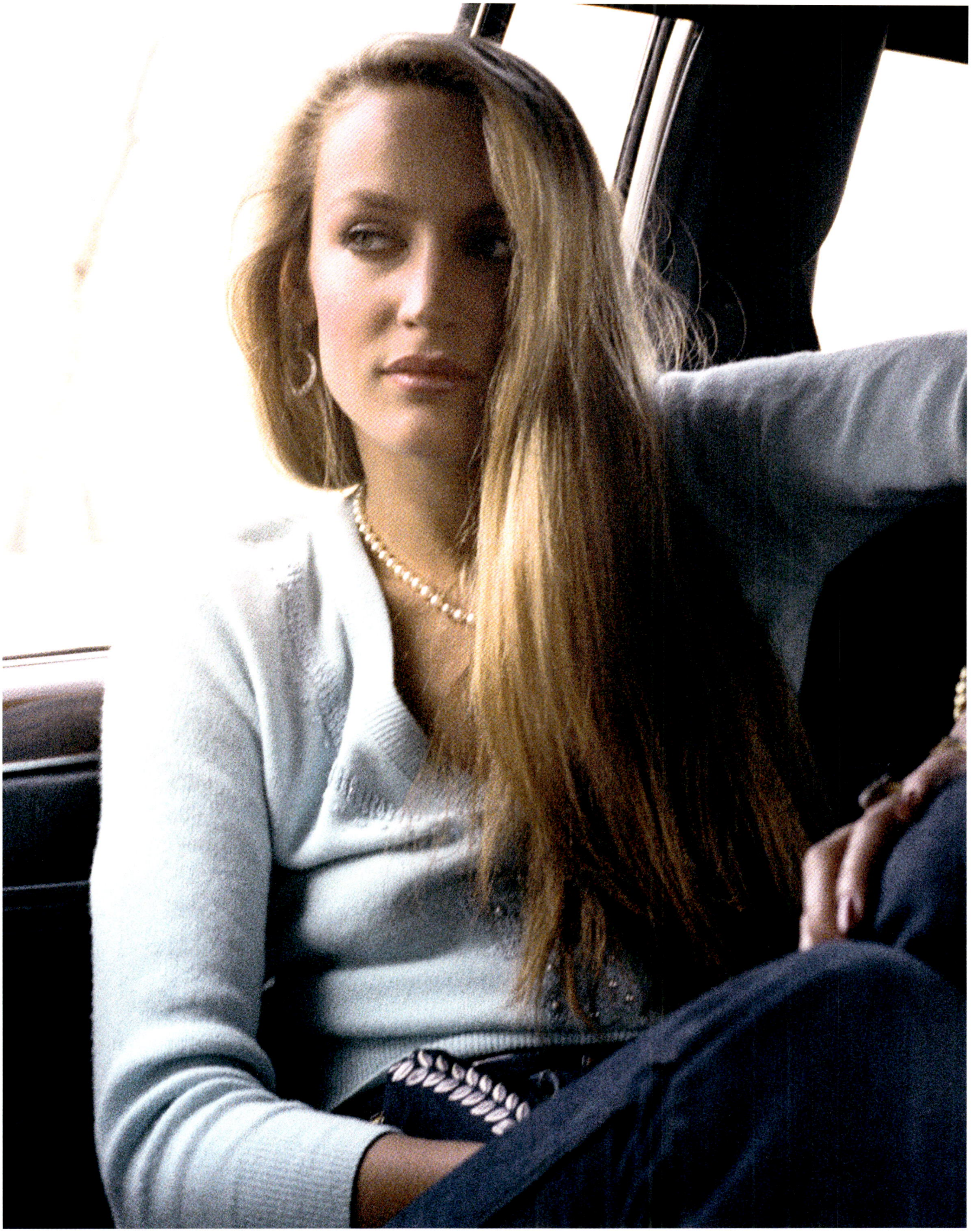

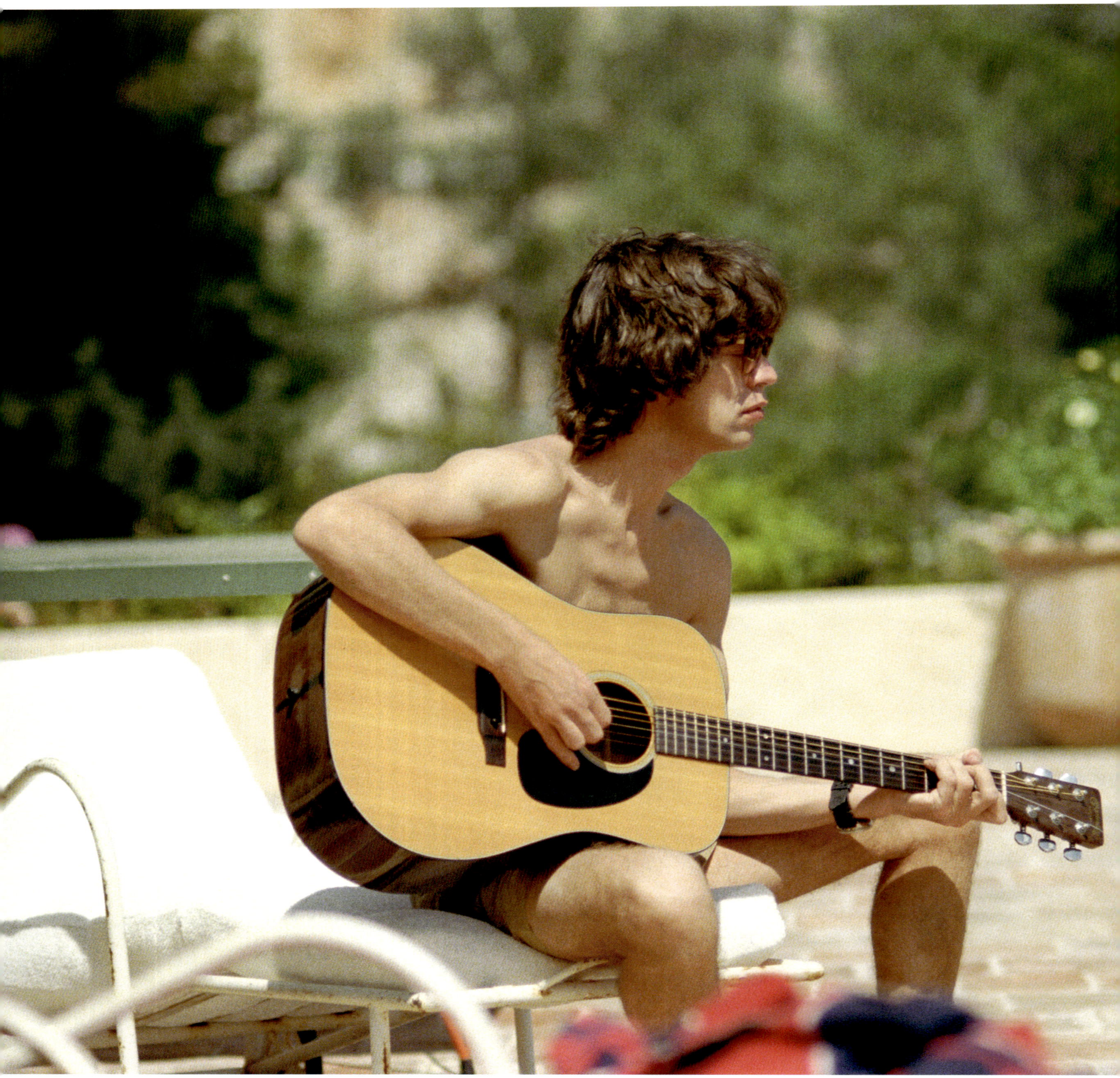

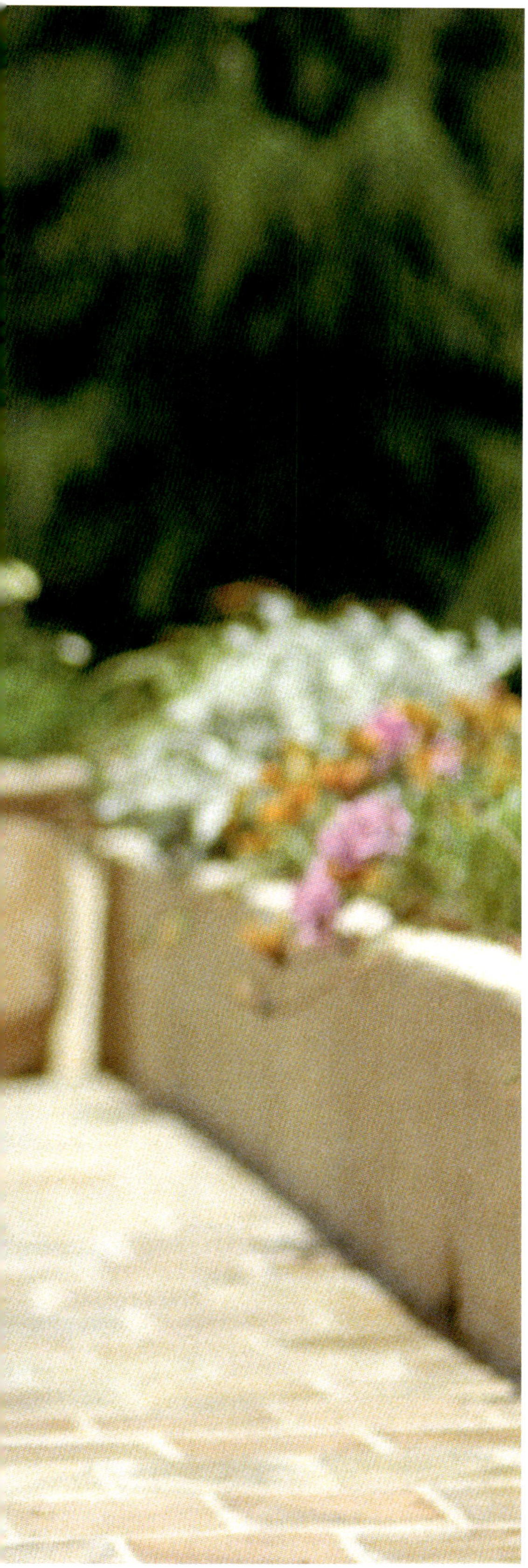

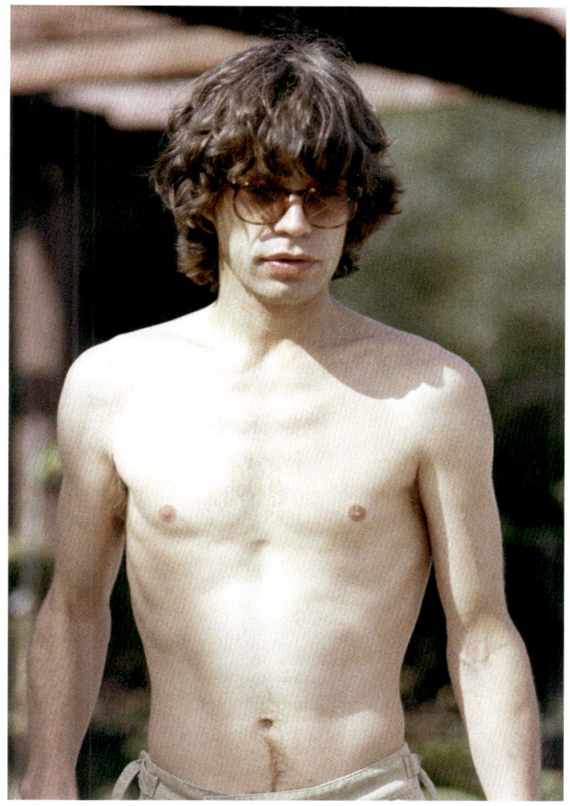

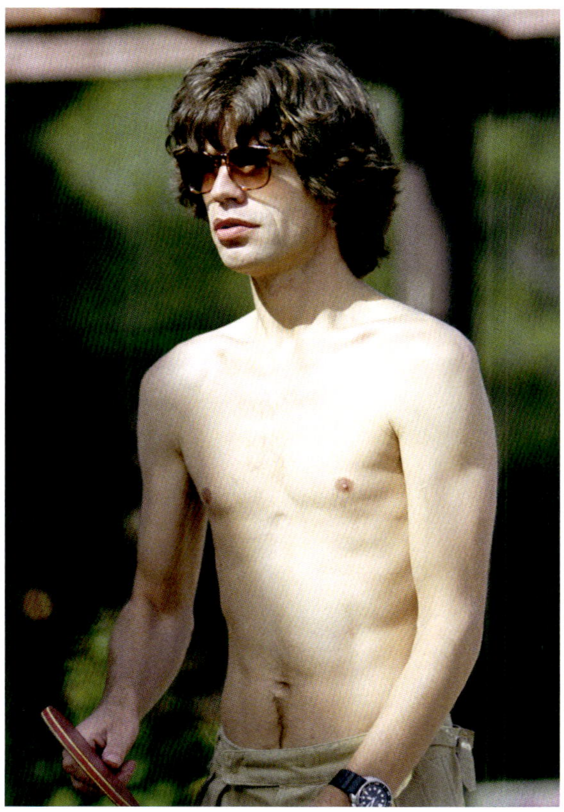

Three shots of Mick on the terrace of my house in Vence, France – 25 May 1979.

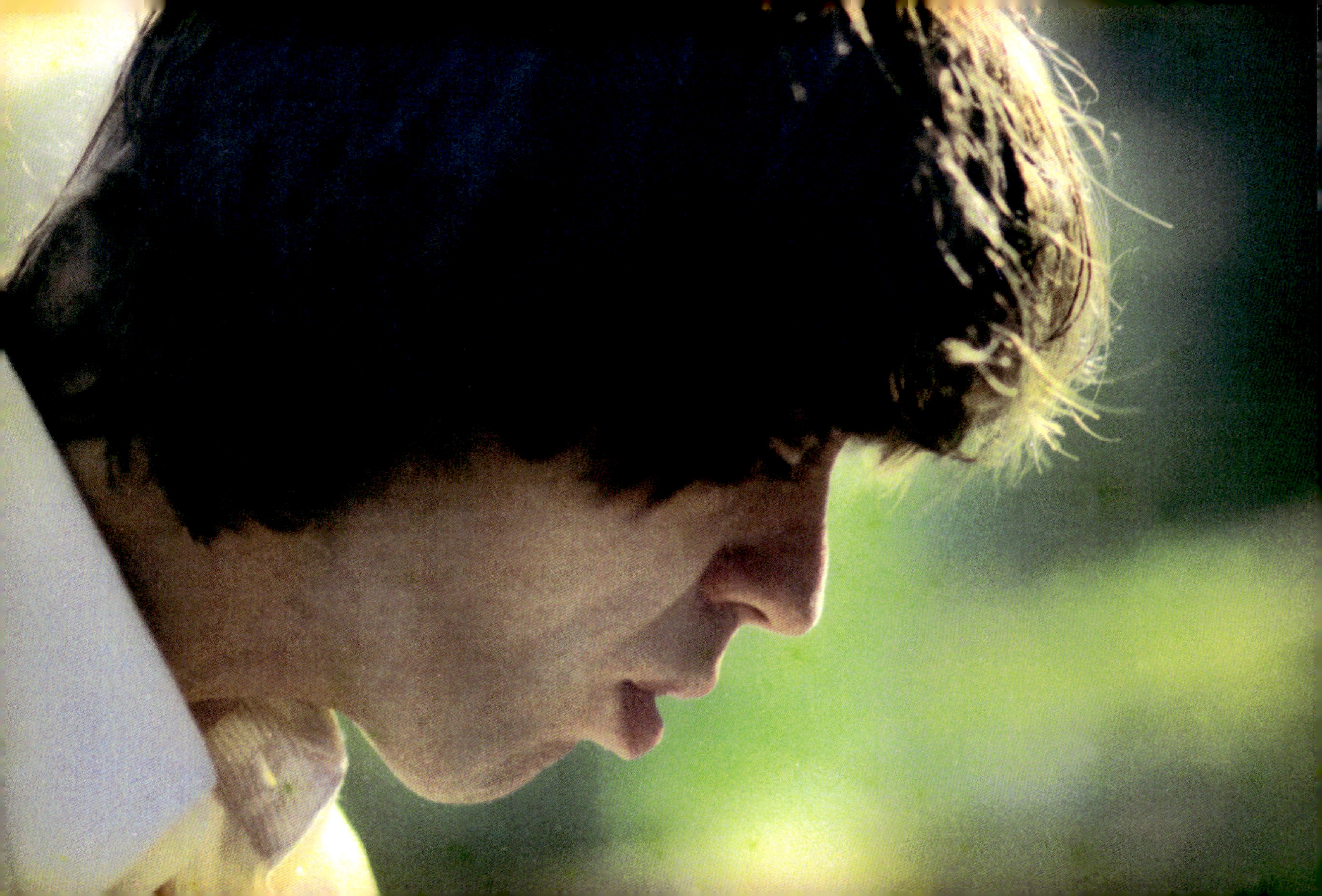

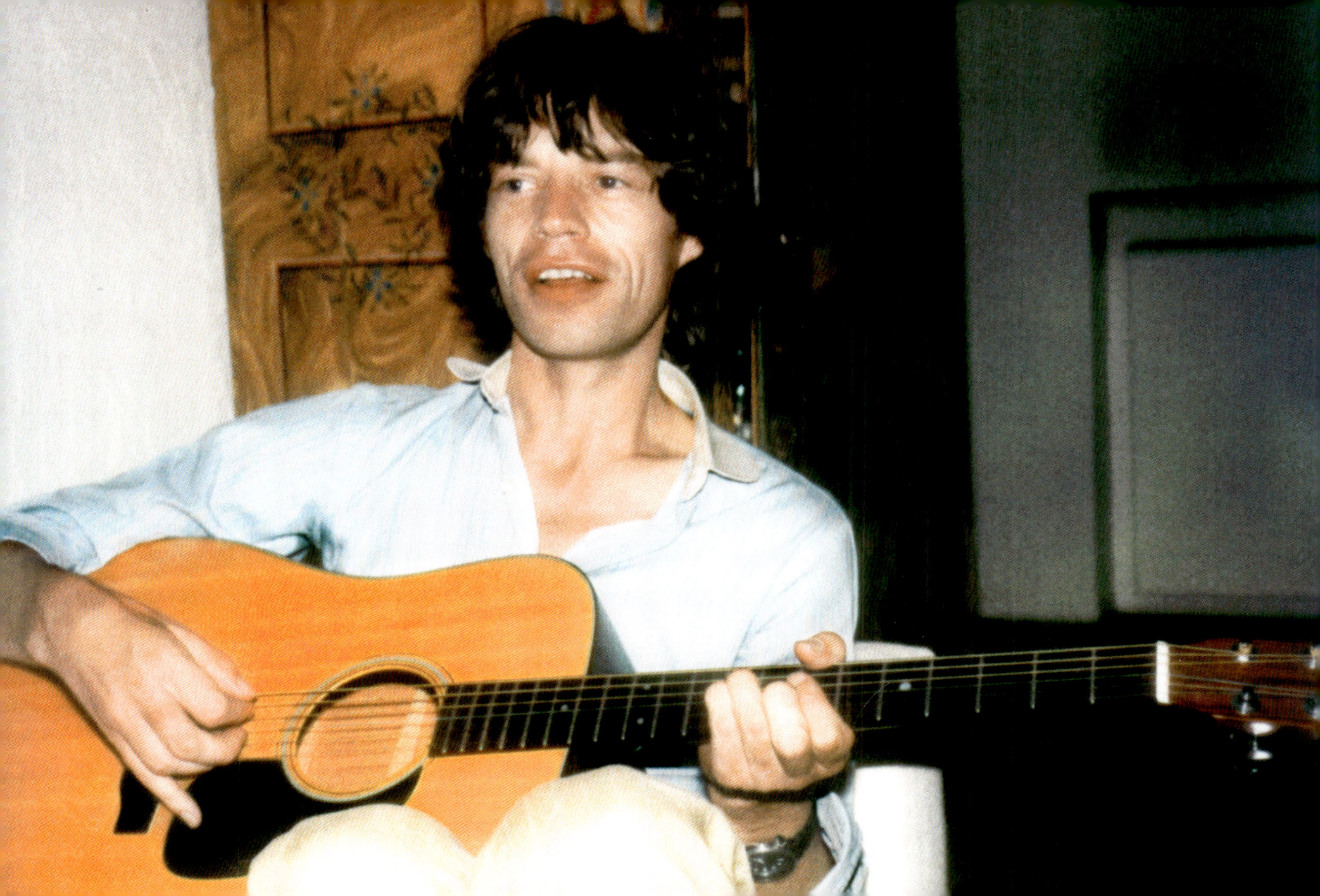

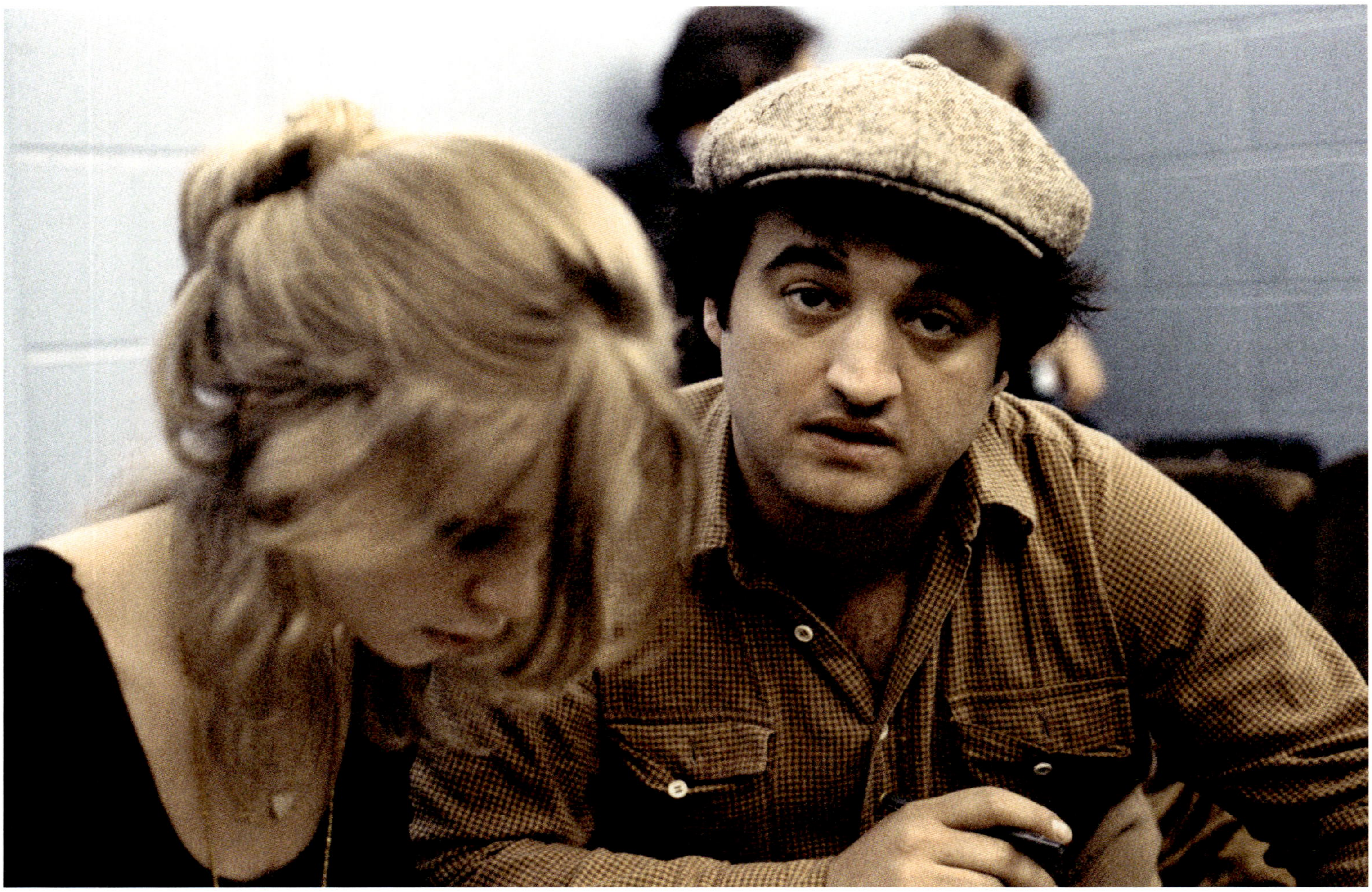

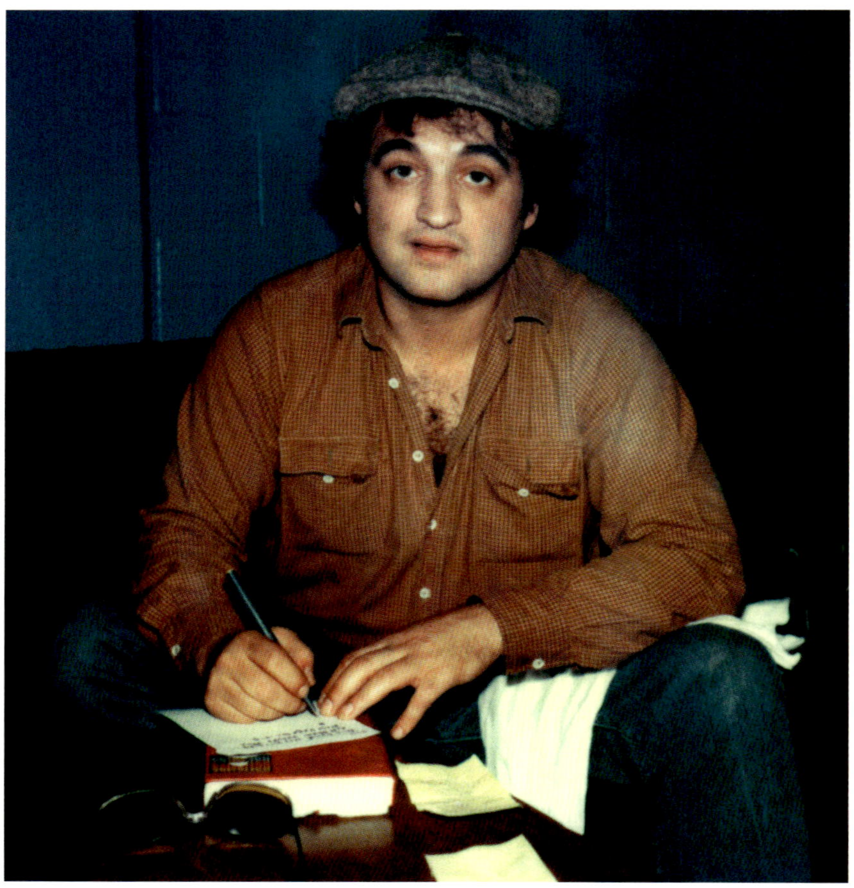

Jo Wood with John Belushi, and John writing a note backstage at The Oshawa Civic Auditorium in Ontario – 22 April 1979. **Right:** Dan Ayckroyd backstage at the *Saturday Night Live* studio in New York – 7 October 1978.

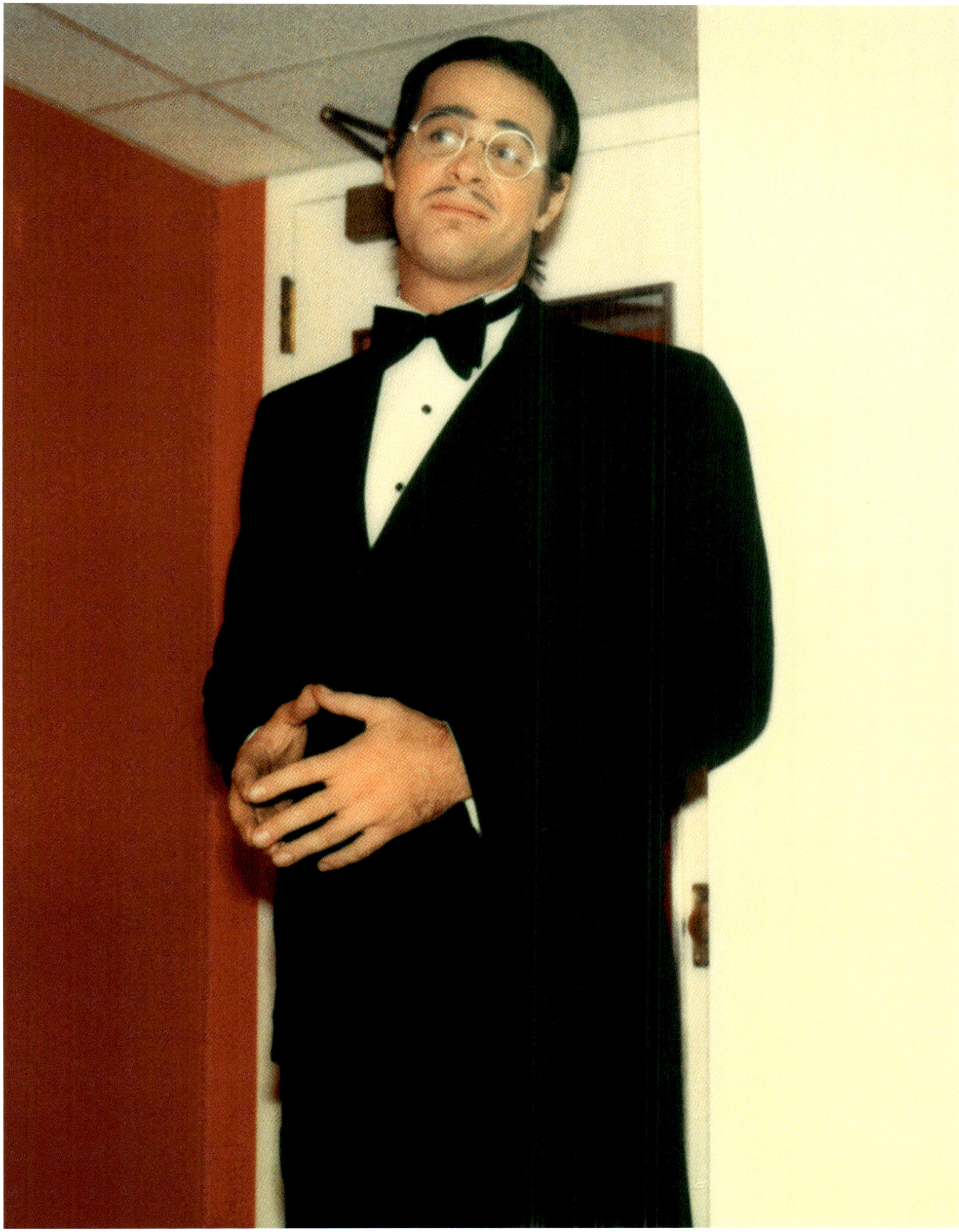

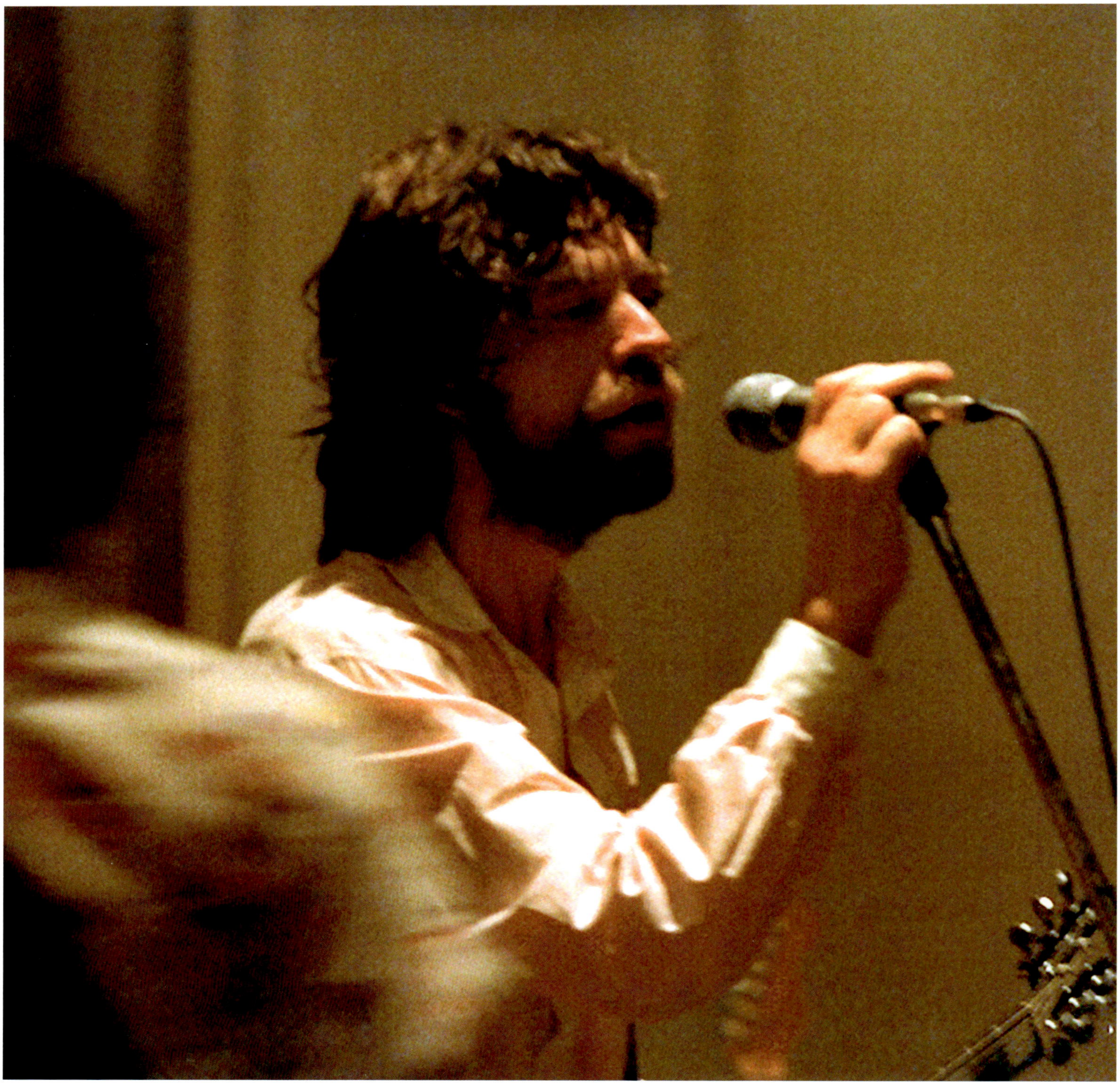

Mick (bearded) with Keith in the Pathé
Marconi recording studio in Paris
– 26 July 1979.

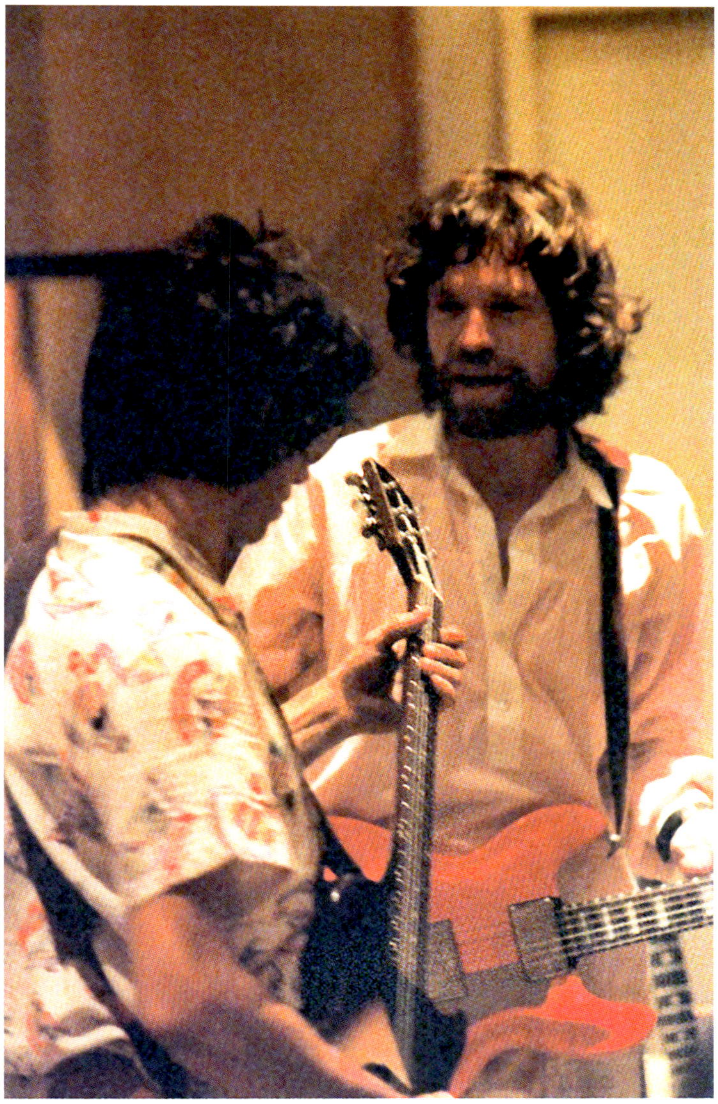

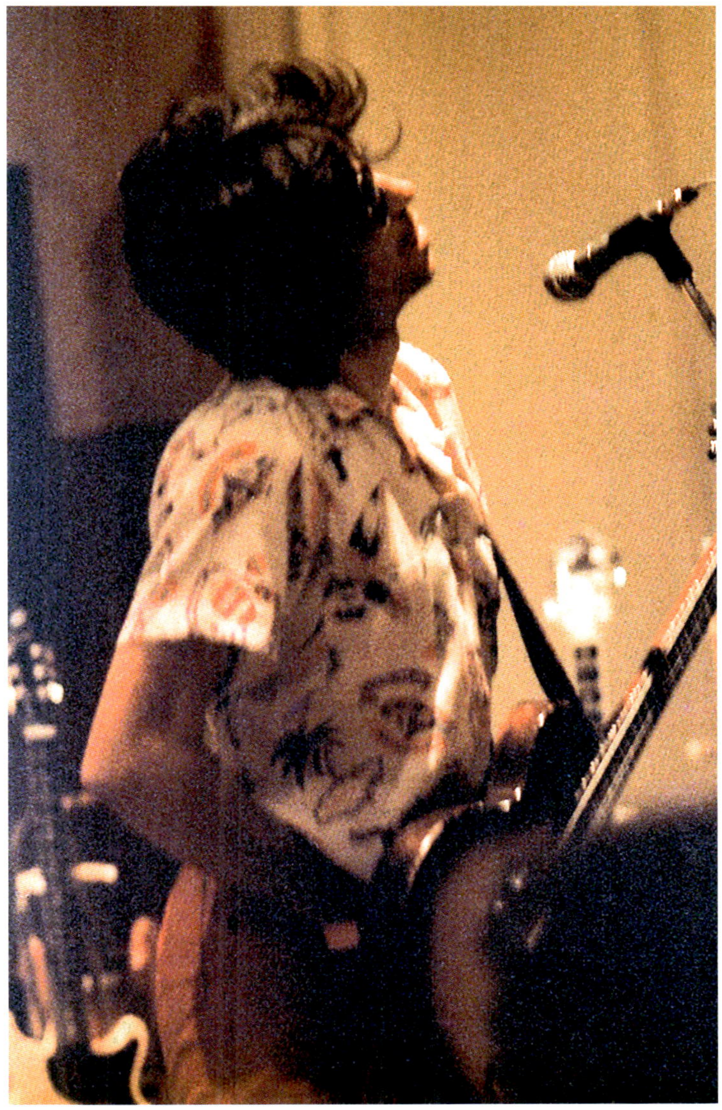

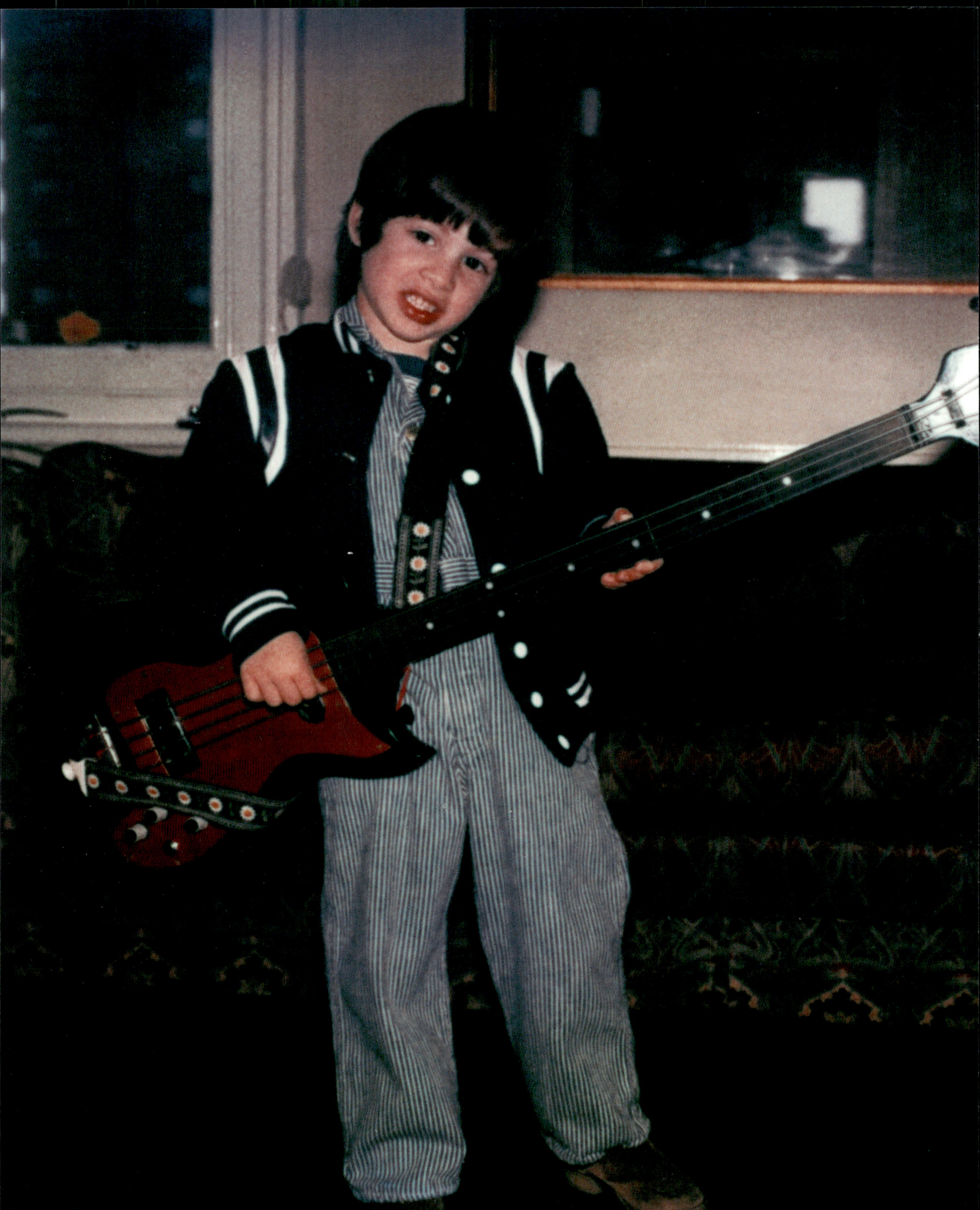

A young Mark Ronson, not yet 5 years old, posing with my home-made bass guitar at the Ronson's house in London – 19 March 1980.

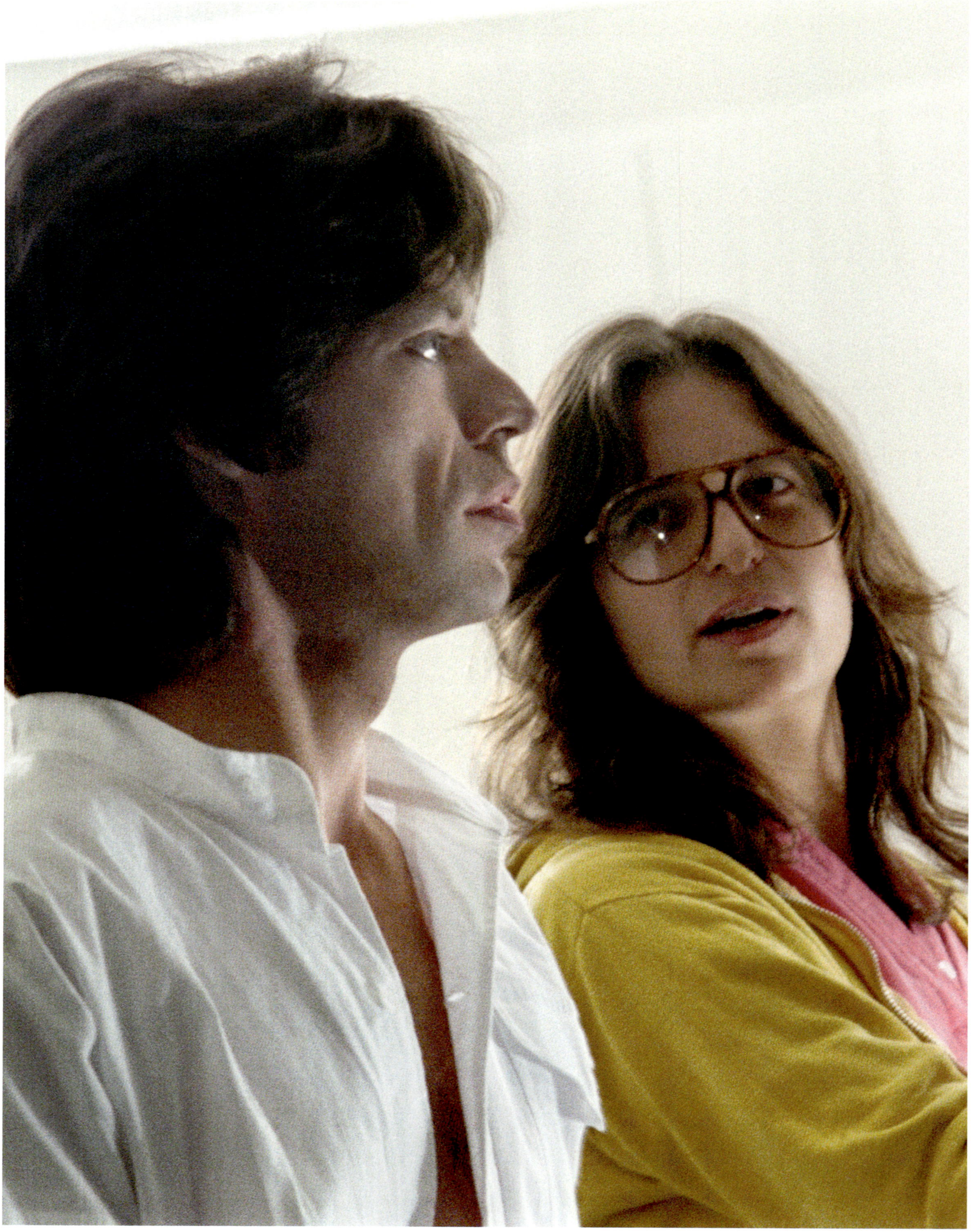

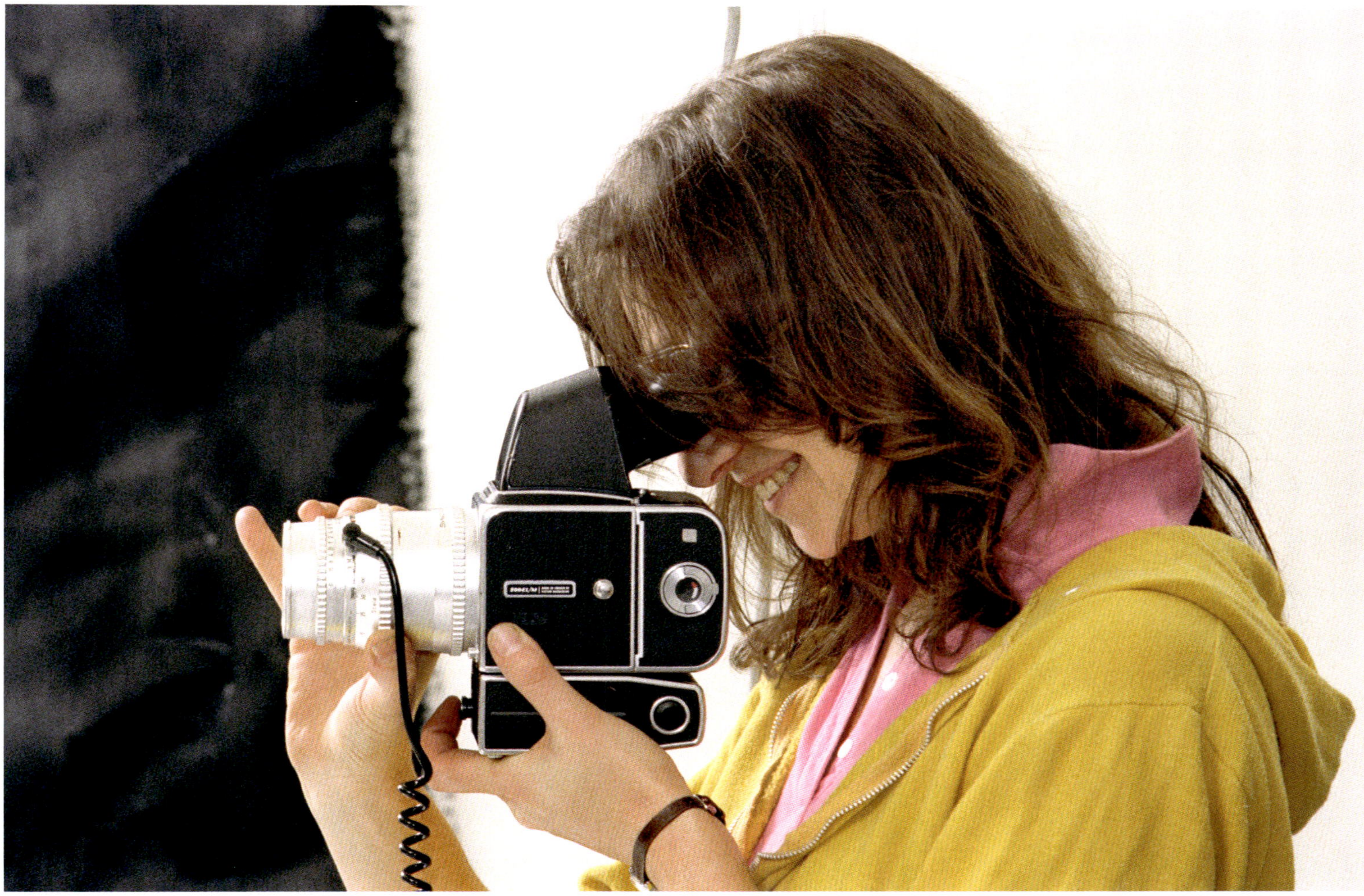

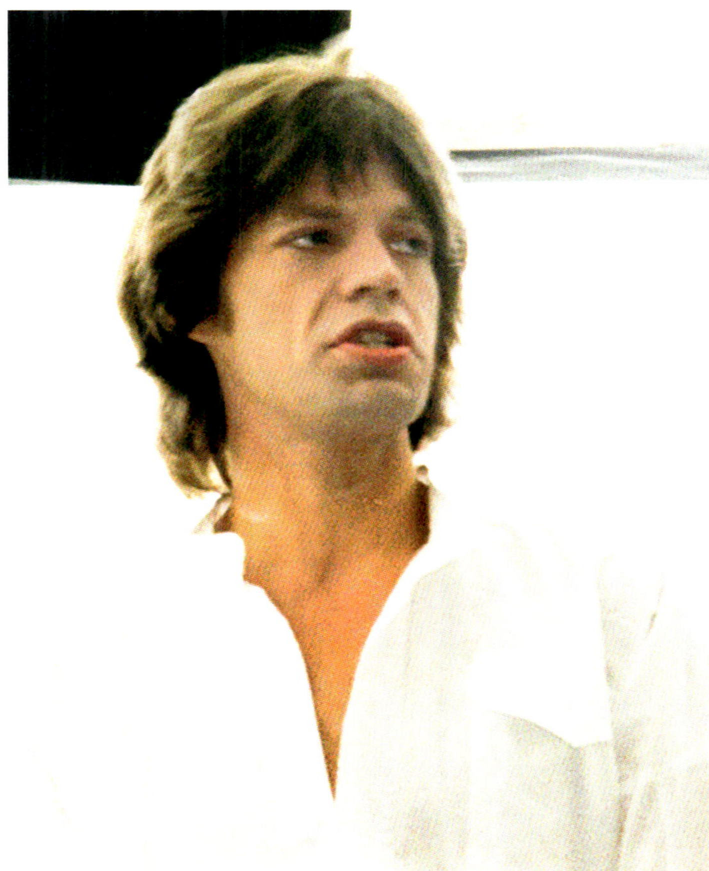

Mick with Annie Leibovitz at the Rolling Stones' photo session at the Abromowitz Studio in New York – 27 March 1980.

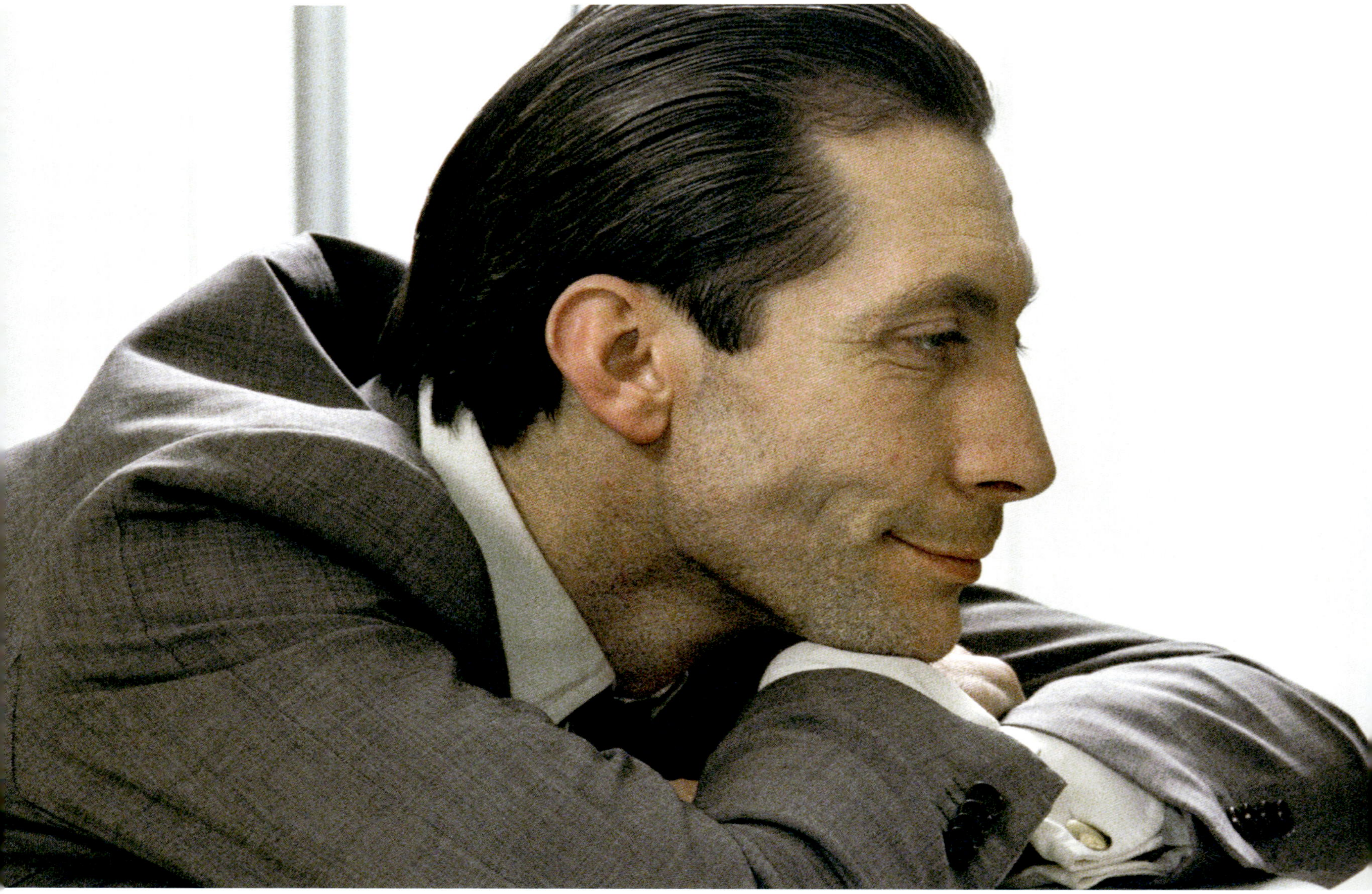

My photos of Charlie ('hurry up and wait')
at the Annie Leibovitz photo session
– 27 March 1980.

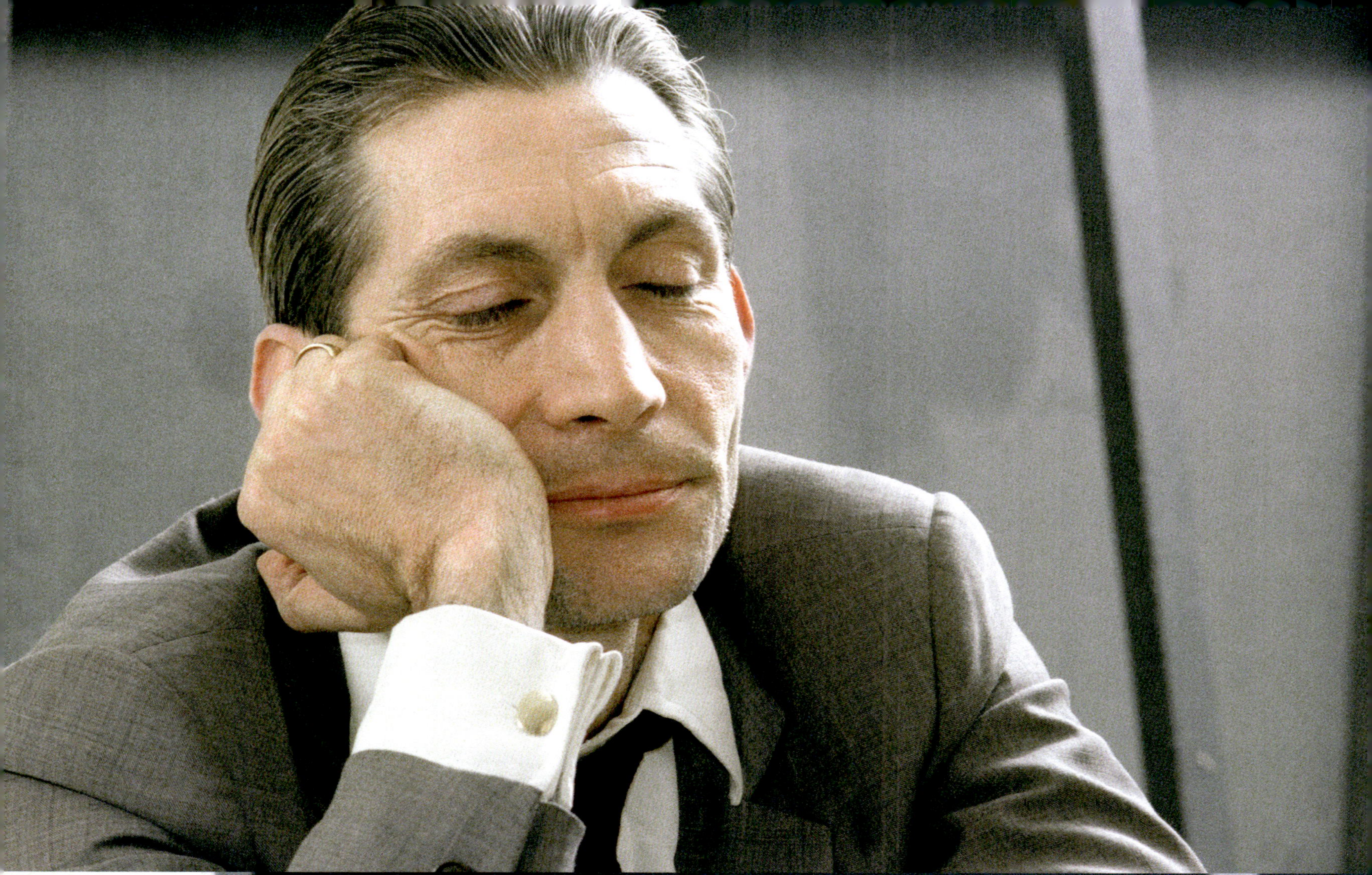

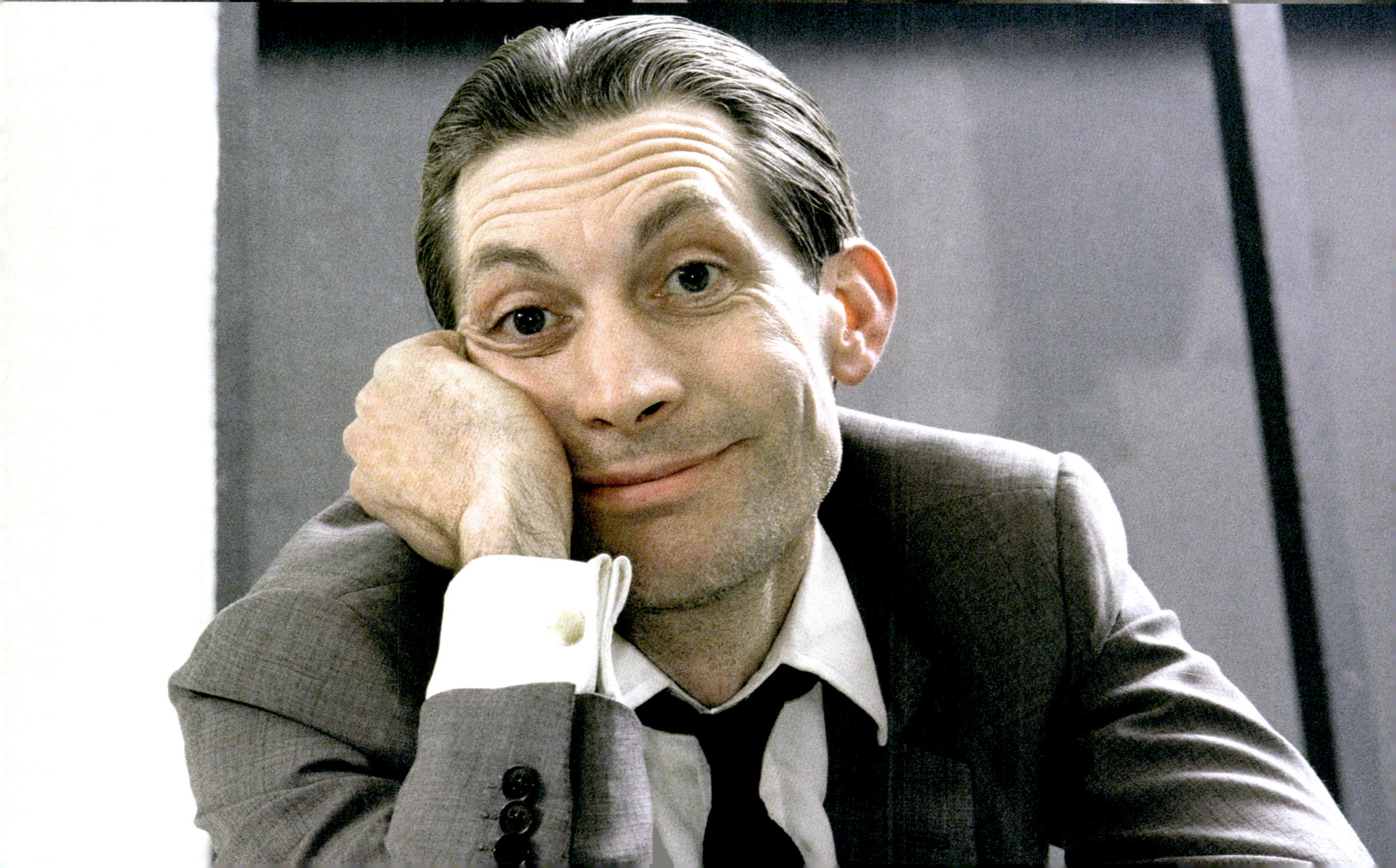

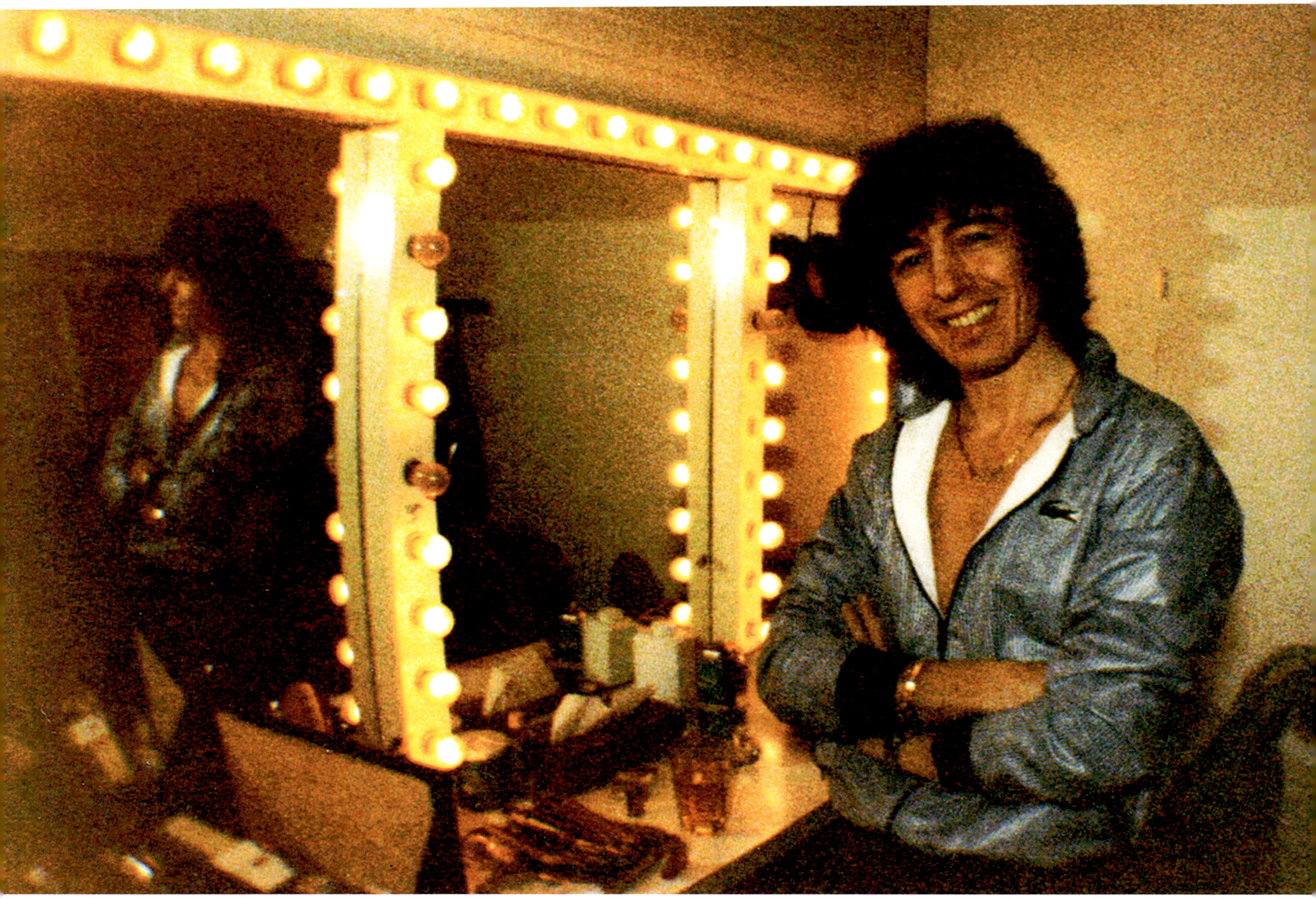

My arty photos of myself and Annie Leibowitz at the above photo session – 27 March 1980.

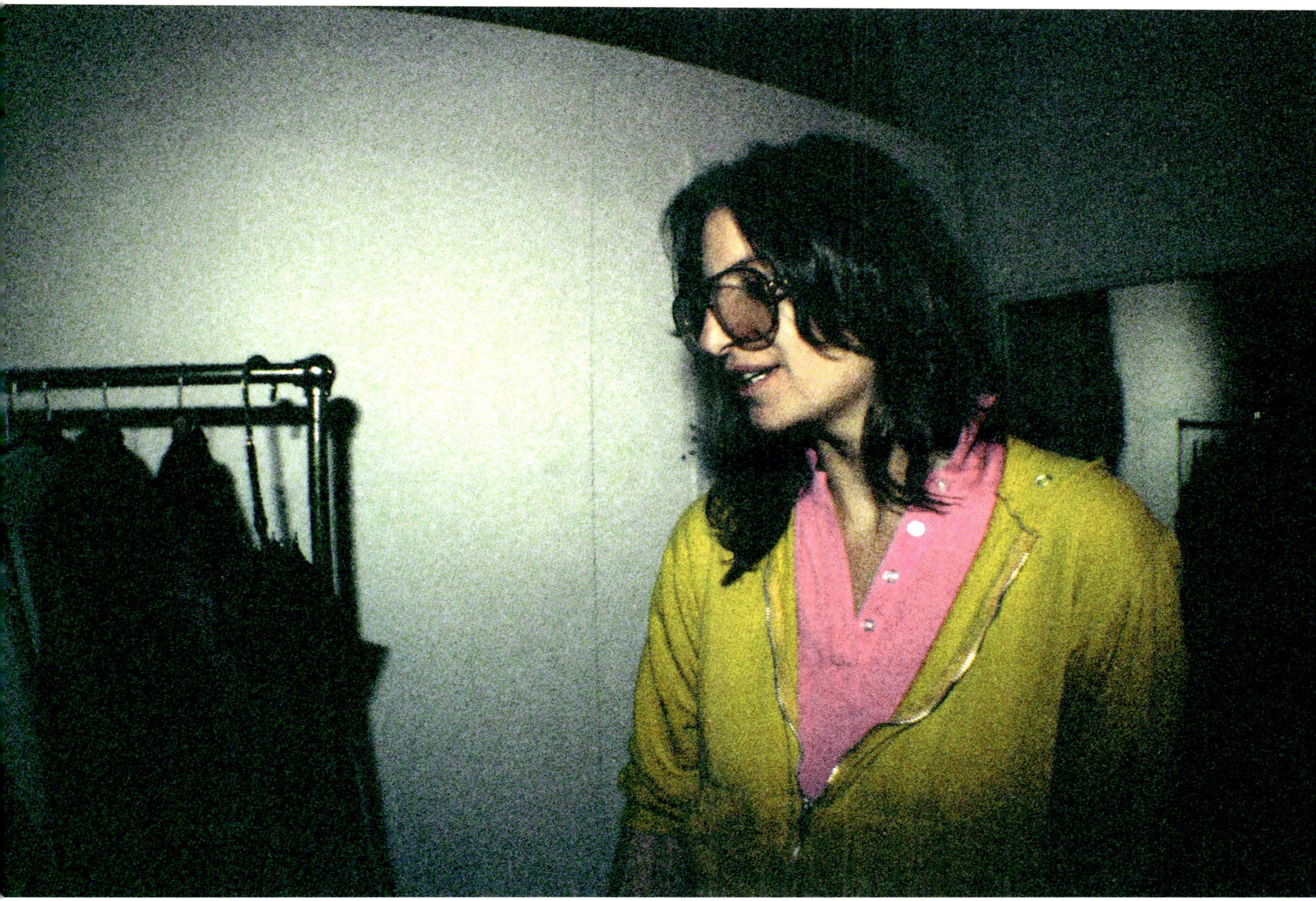

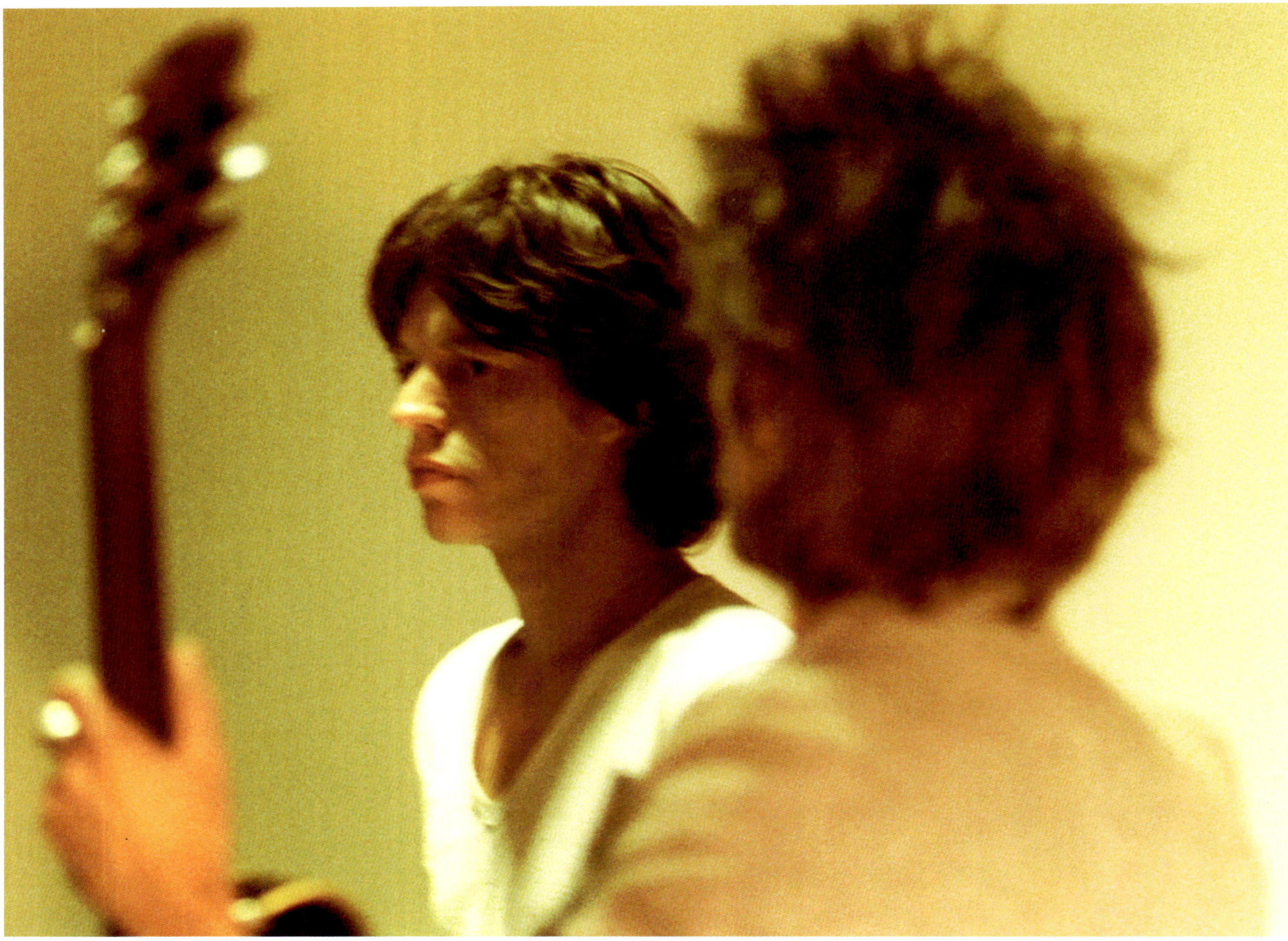

Mick and Keith at the Stones' video shoot at
the Modern Telecommunications studio
the next day – 28 March 1980.

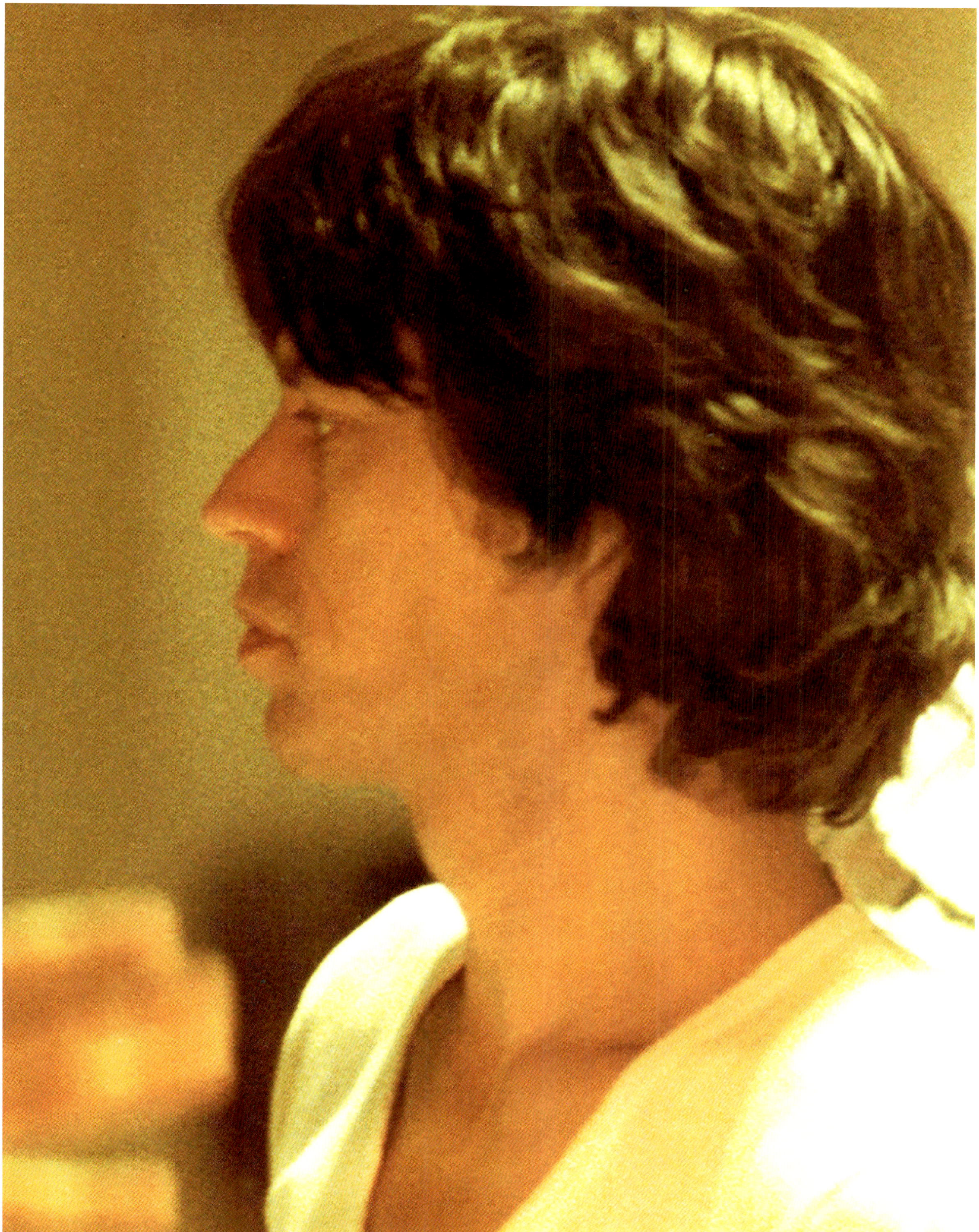

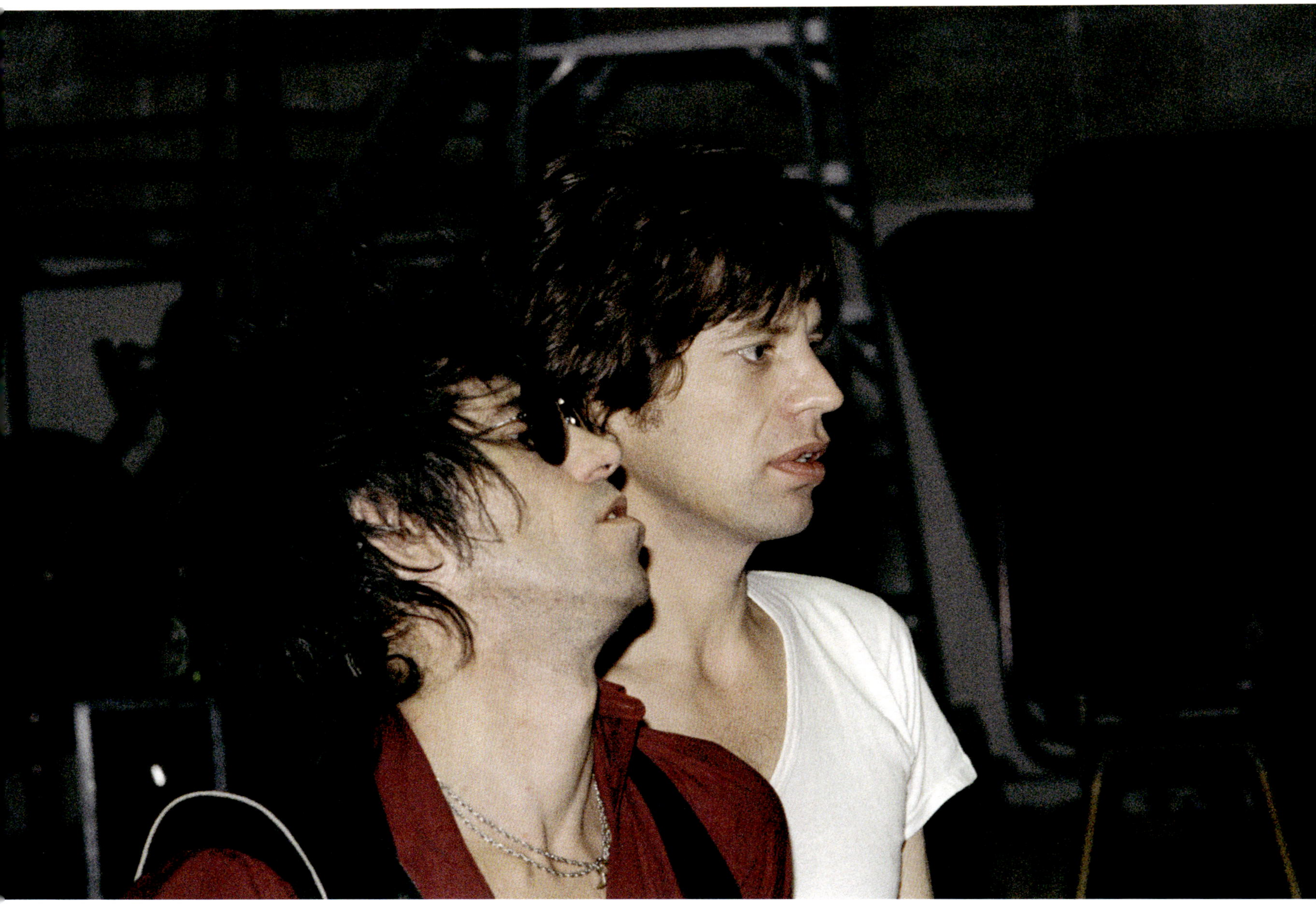

Two more shots of Mick and Keith
at the Stones' video shoot – 28 March 1980.

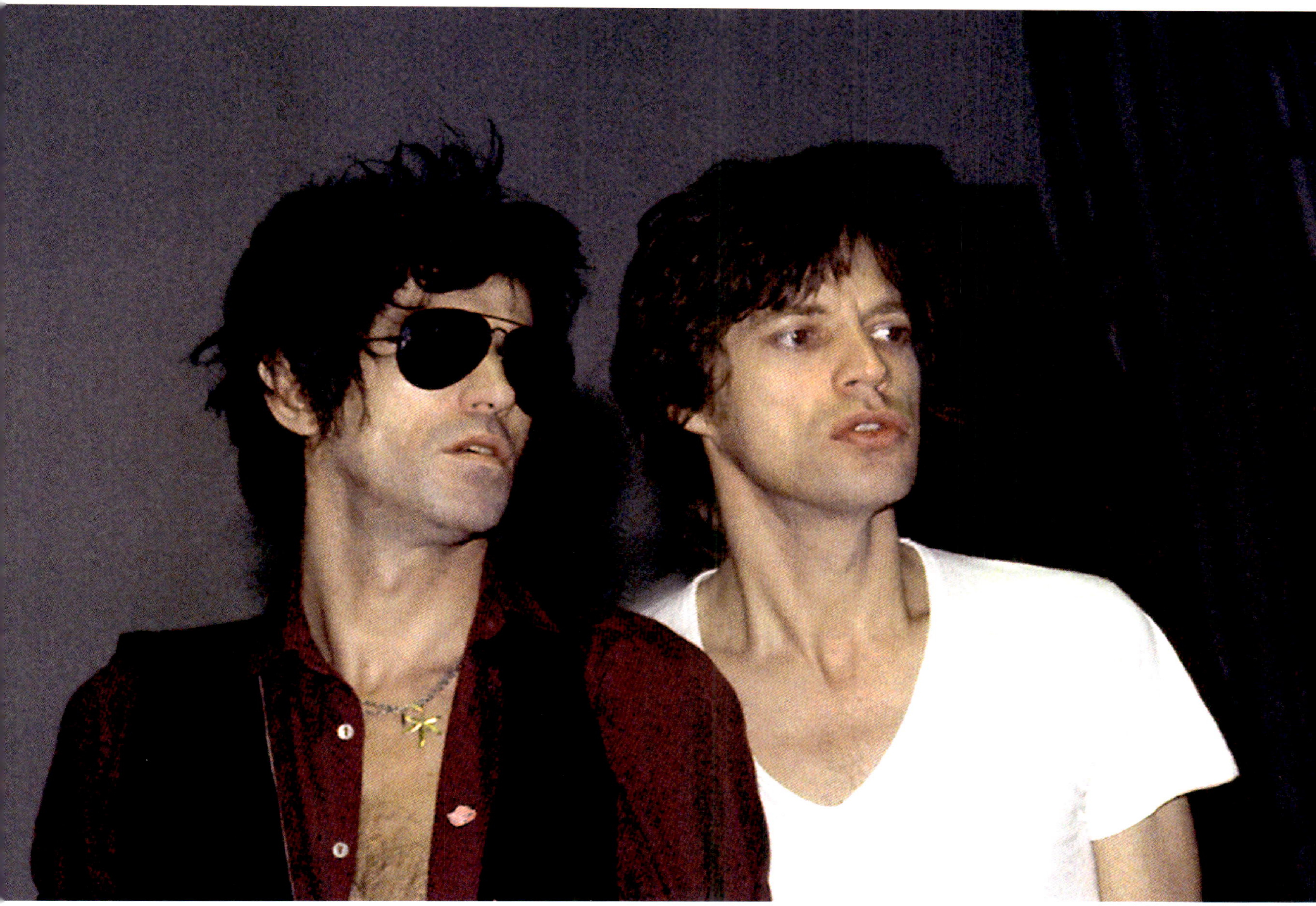

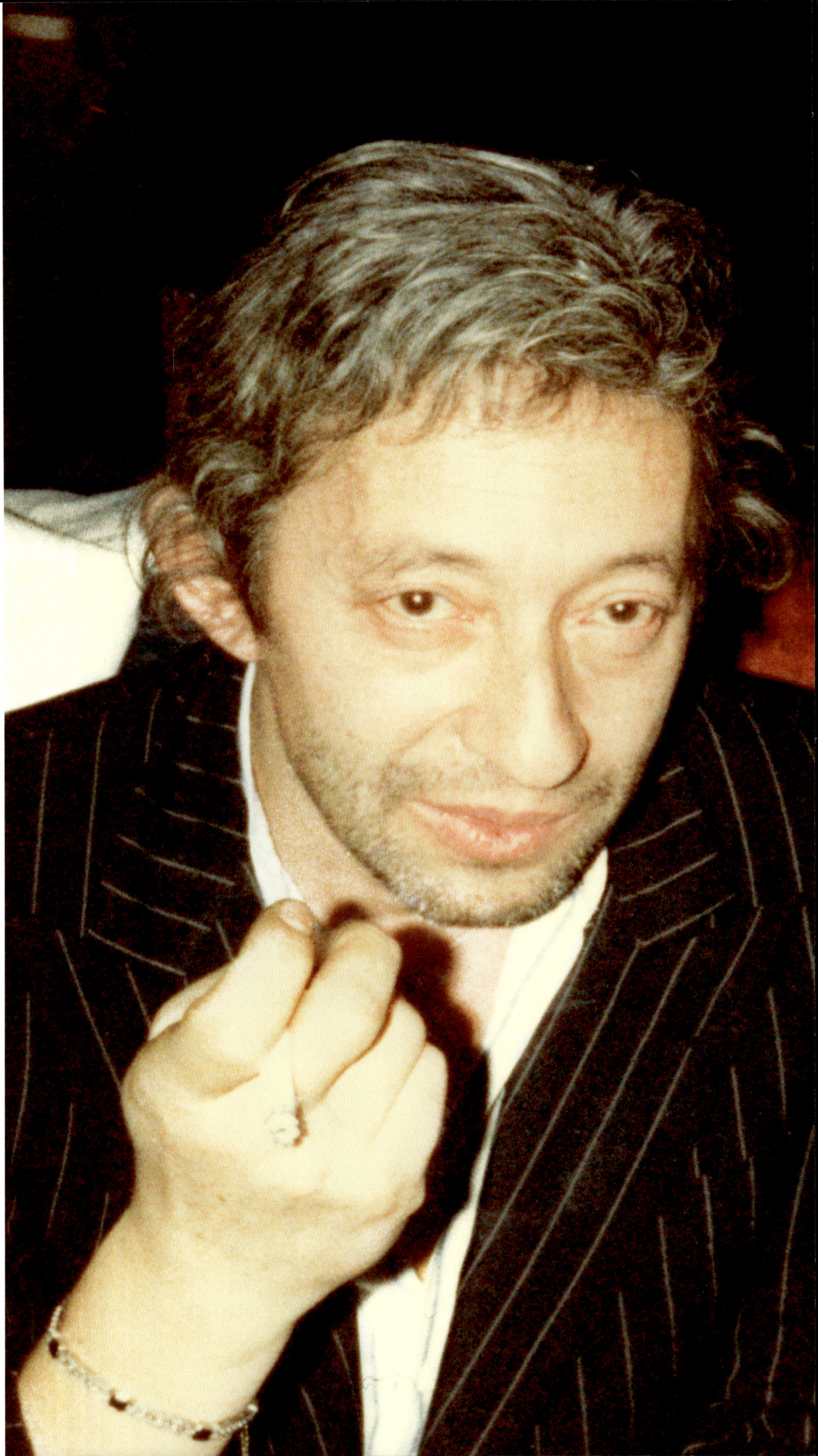

Serge Gainsbourg and I after a late evening and night in the clubs of Paris – 10 April 1981.

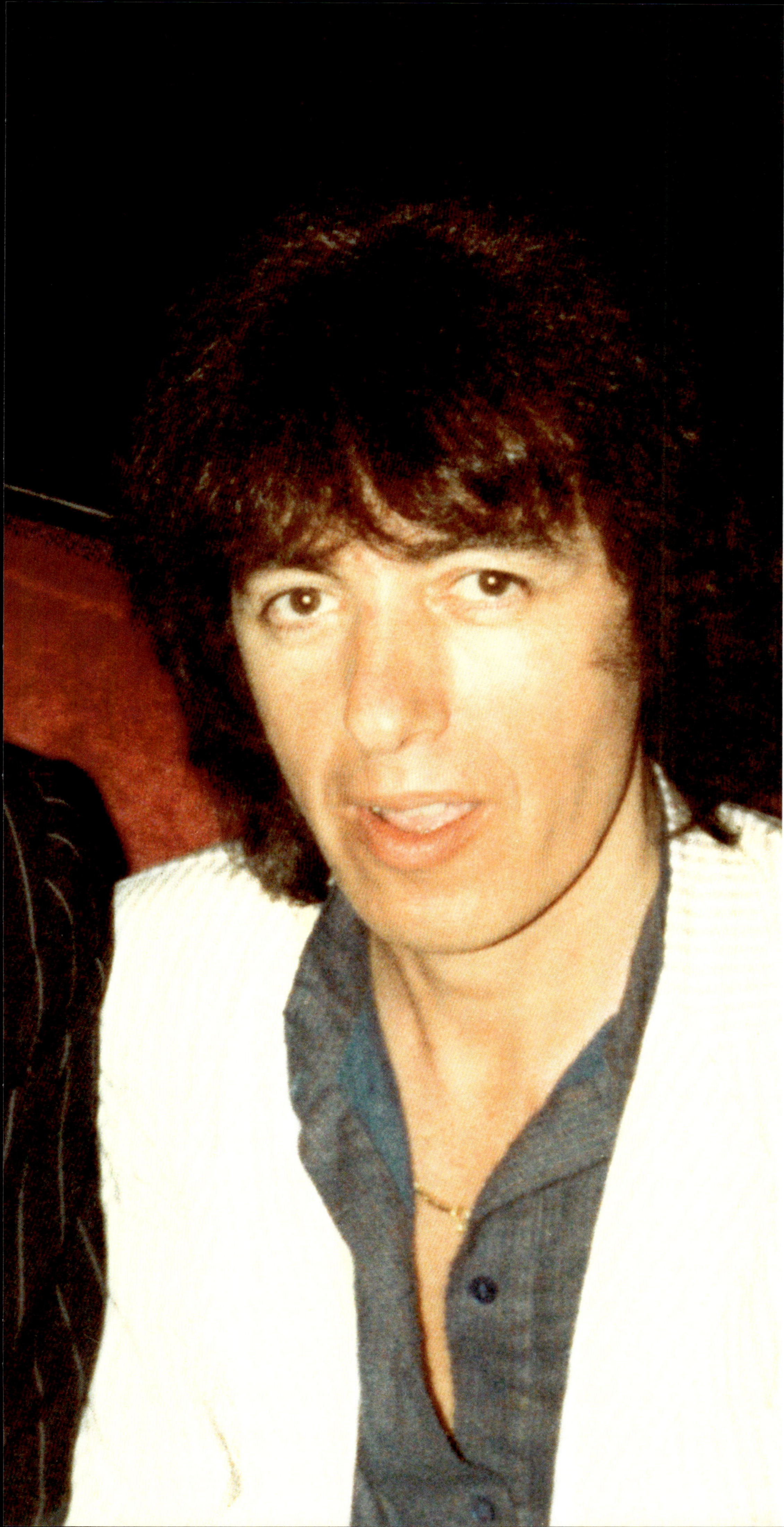

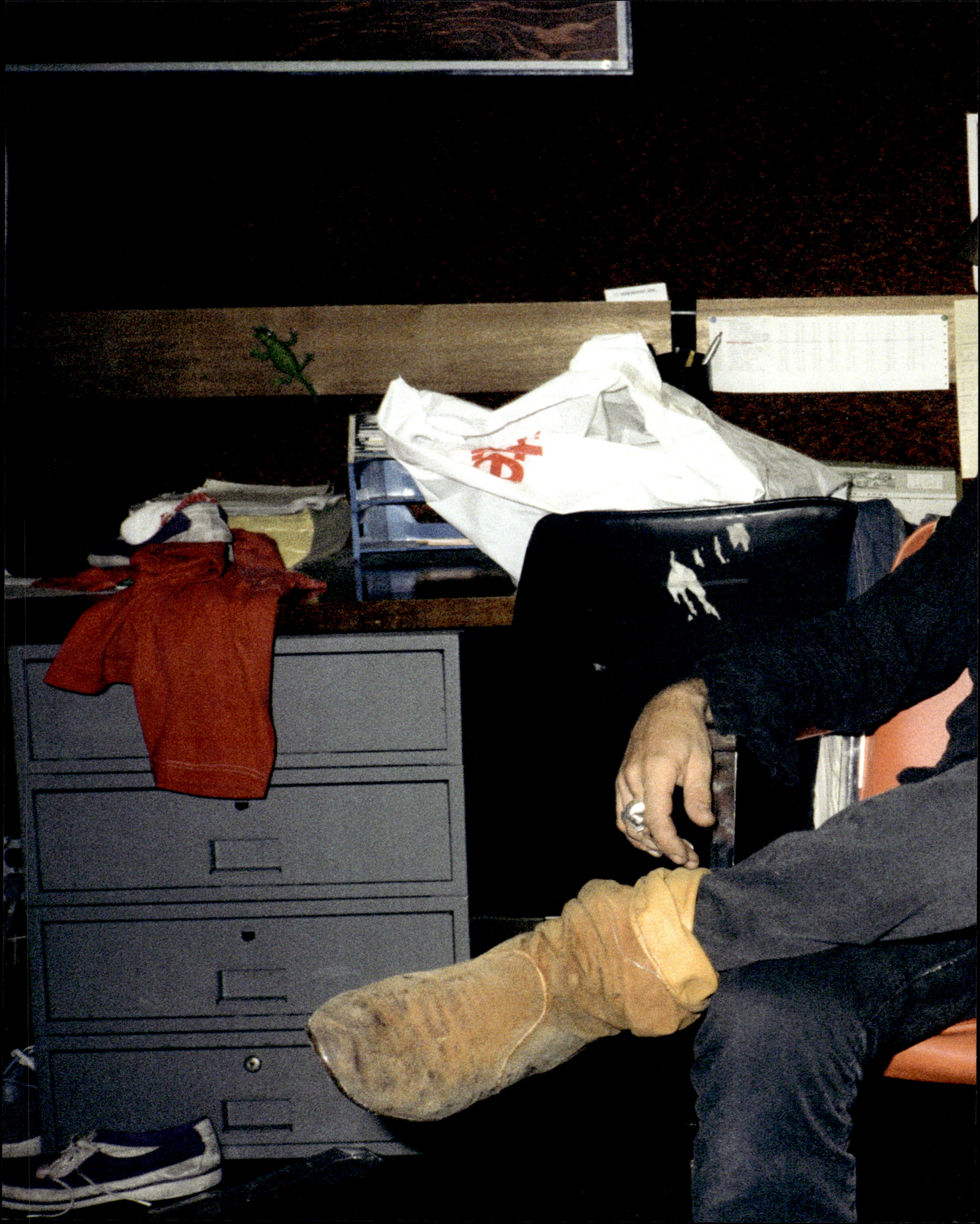

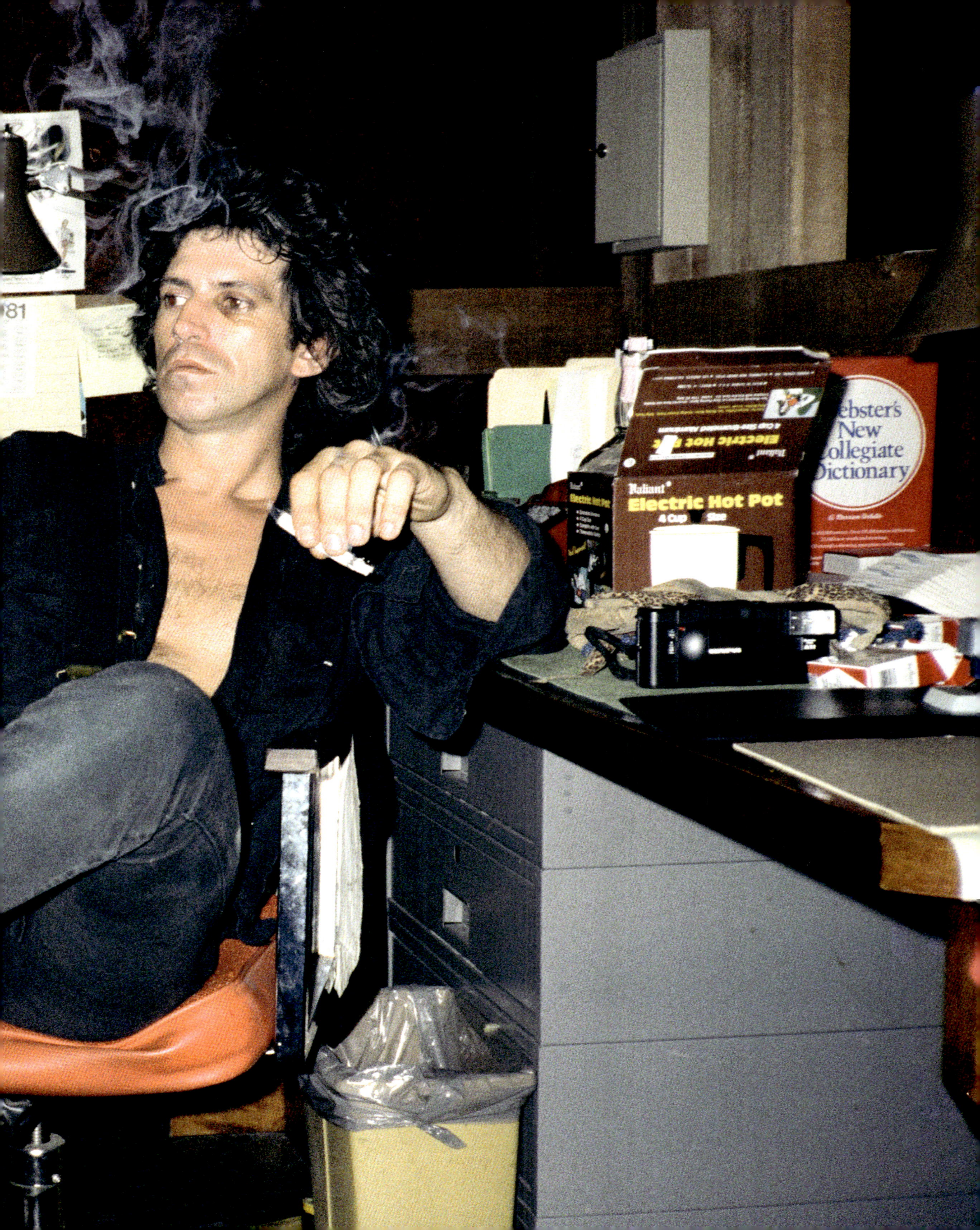
81
Valiant
Electric Hot Pot
4 Cup Size
ebster's
New
ollegiate
Dictionary

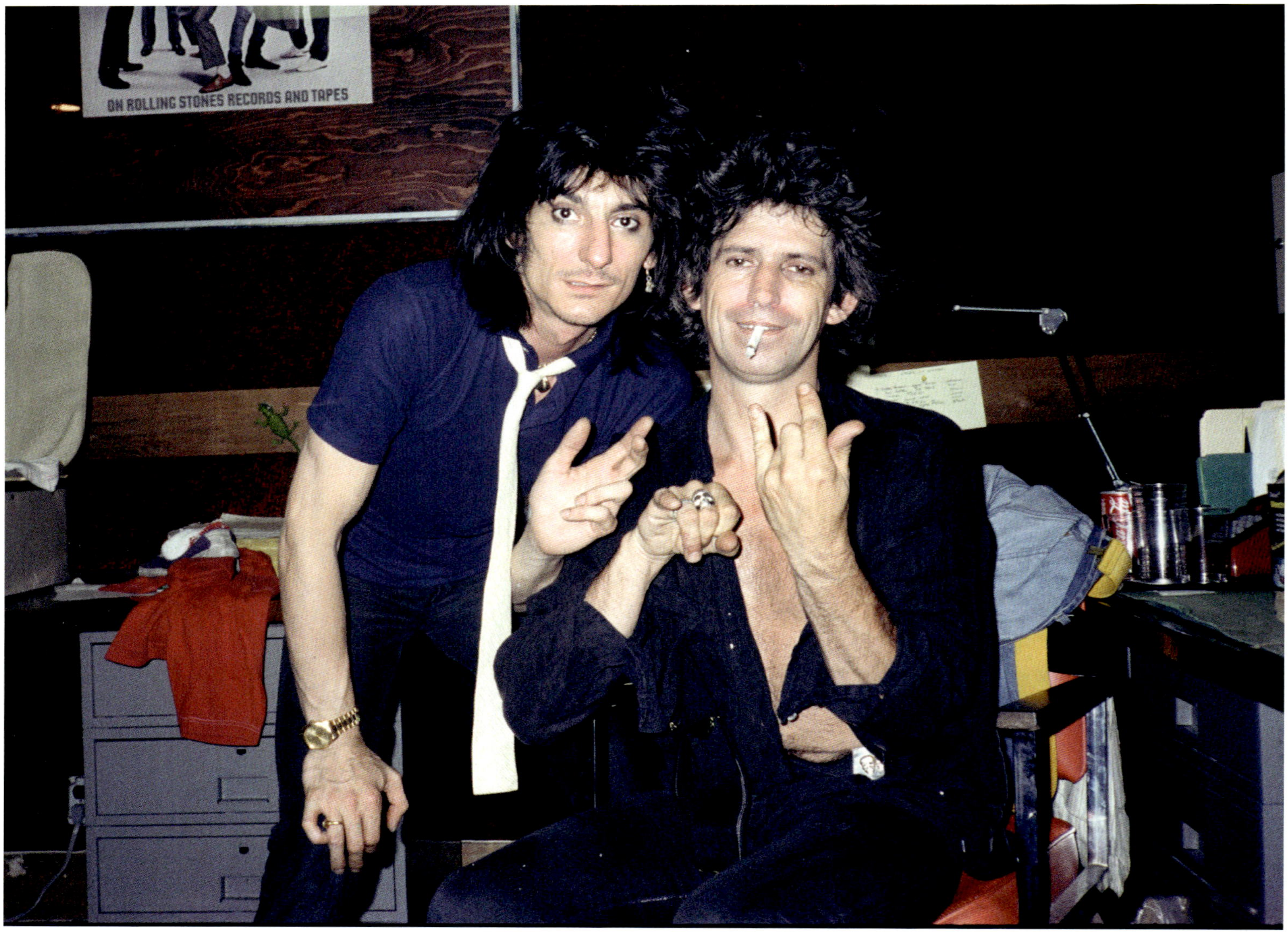

Ronnie and Keith on 29 – 30 June 1981 at the SIR Studio, New York, rehearsing for the promo film shoot.
Previous pages: Keith relaxing in the Rolling Stones' office in New York (with the black eye that Chuck Berry gave him) – 30 June 1981.
Following pages: Keith making a joint at the SIR Studio, New York, while Charlie (crossed arms) watches the performance – 30 June 1981.

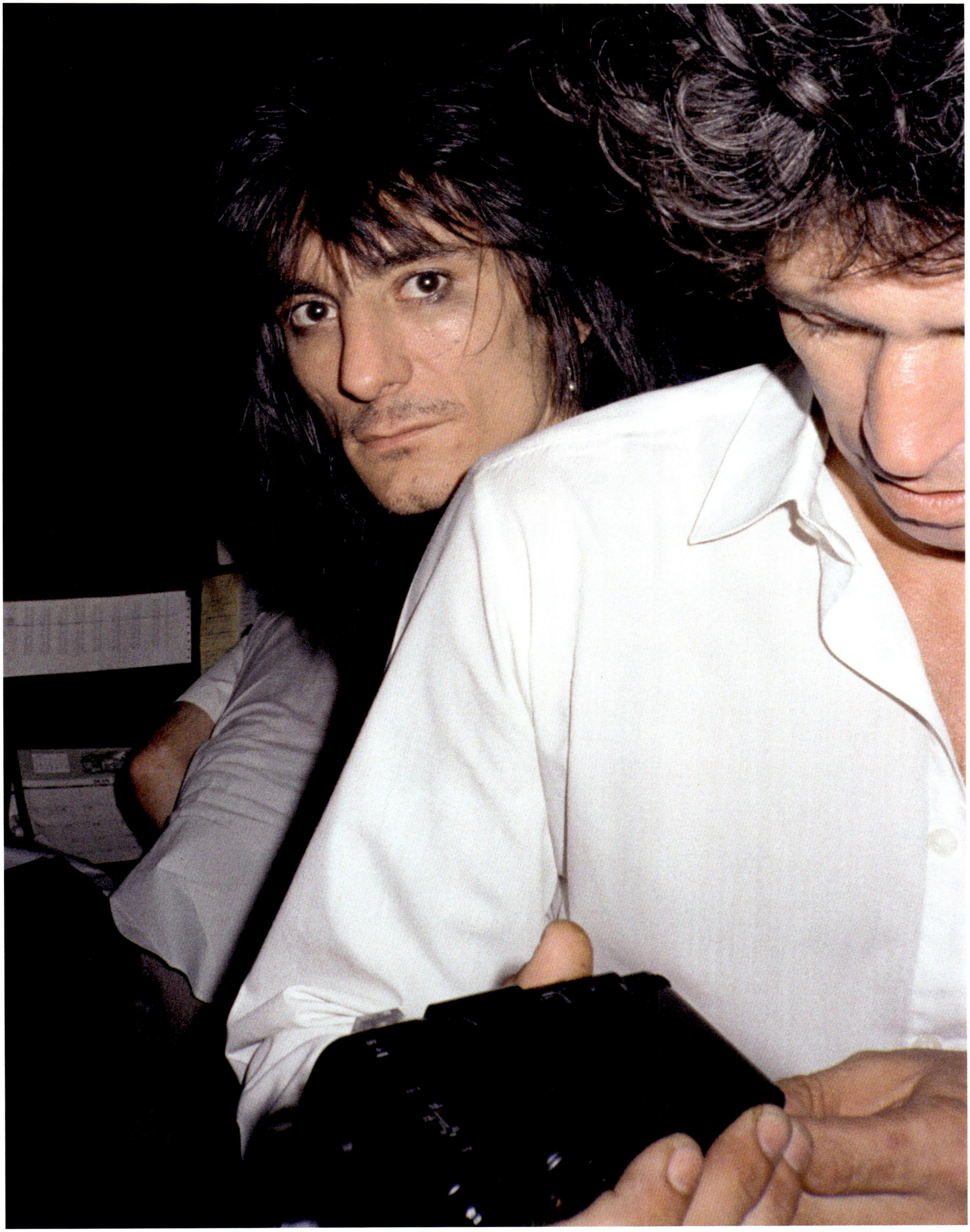

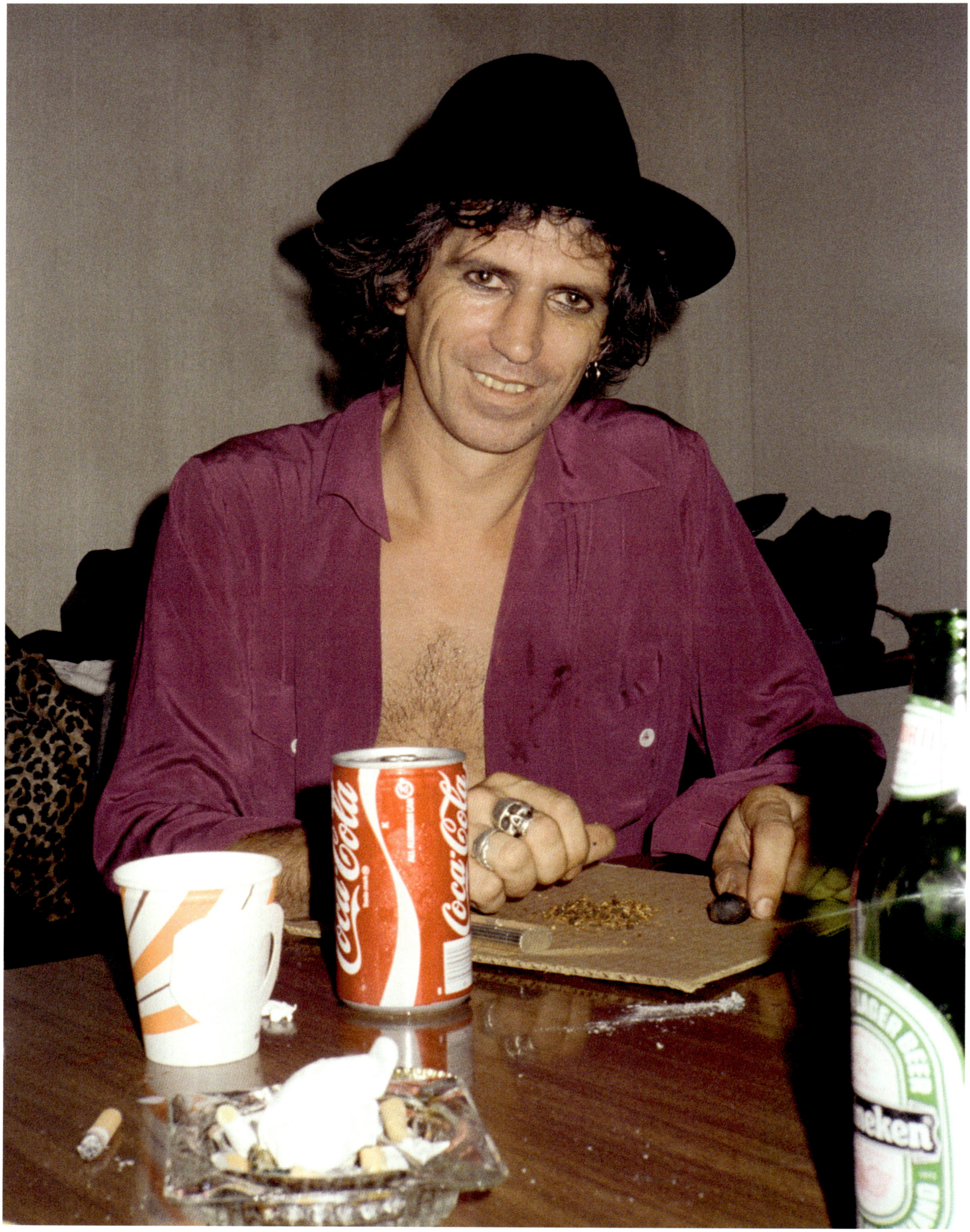
Coca-Cola
Coca-Cola

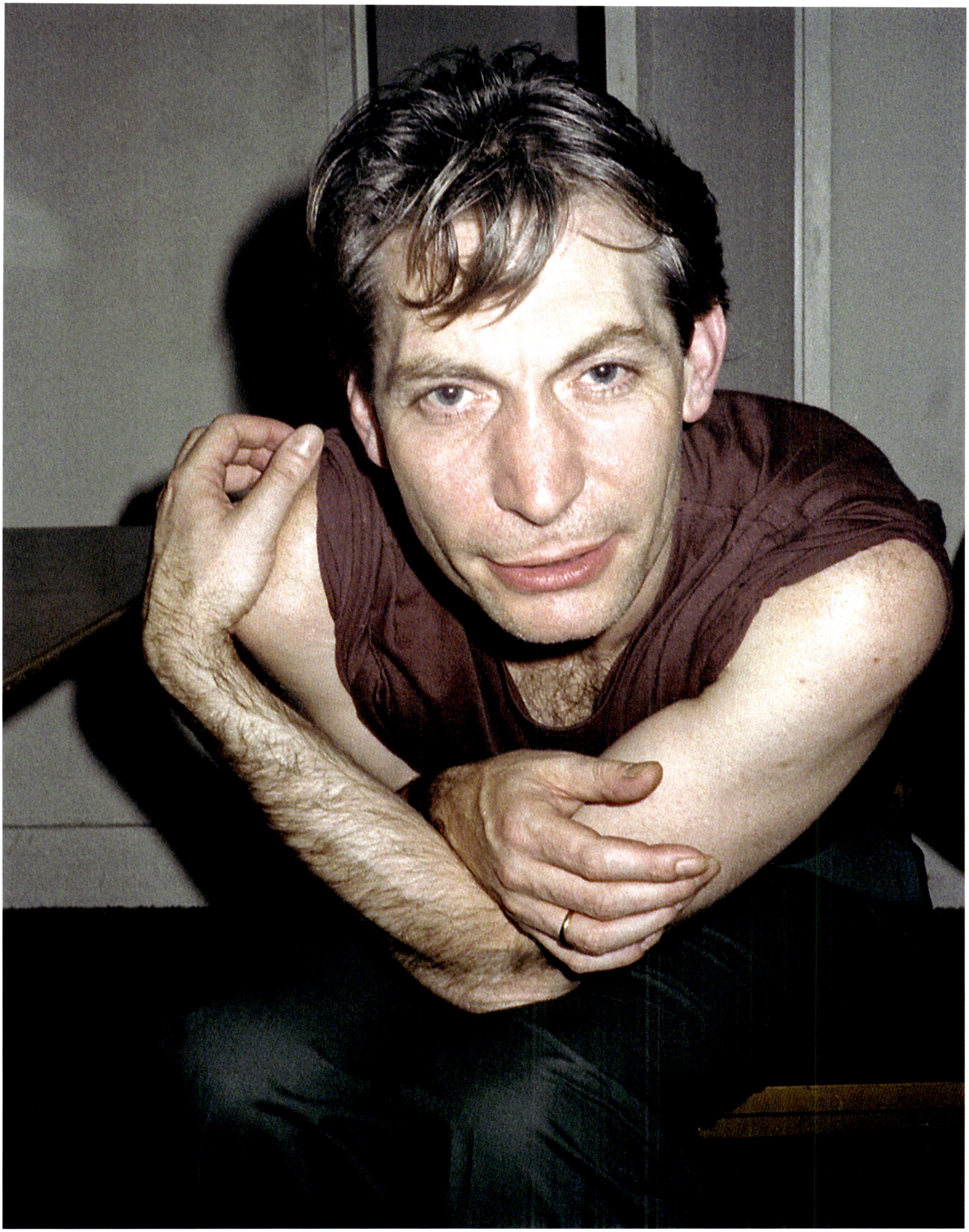

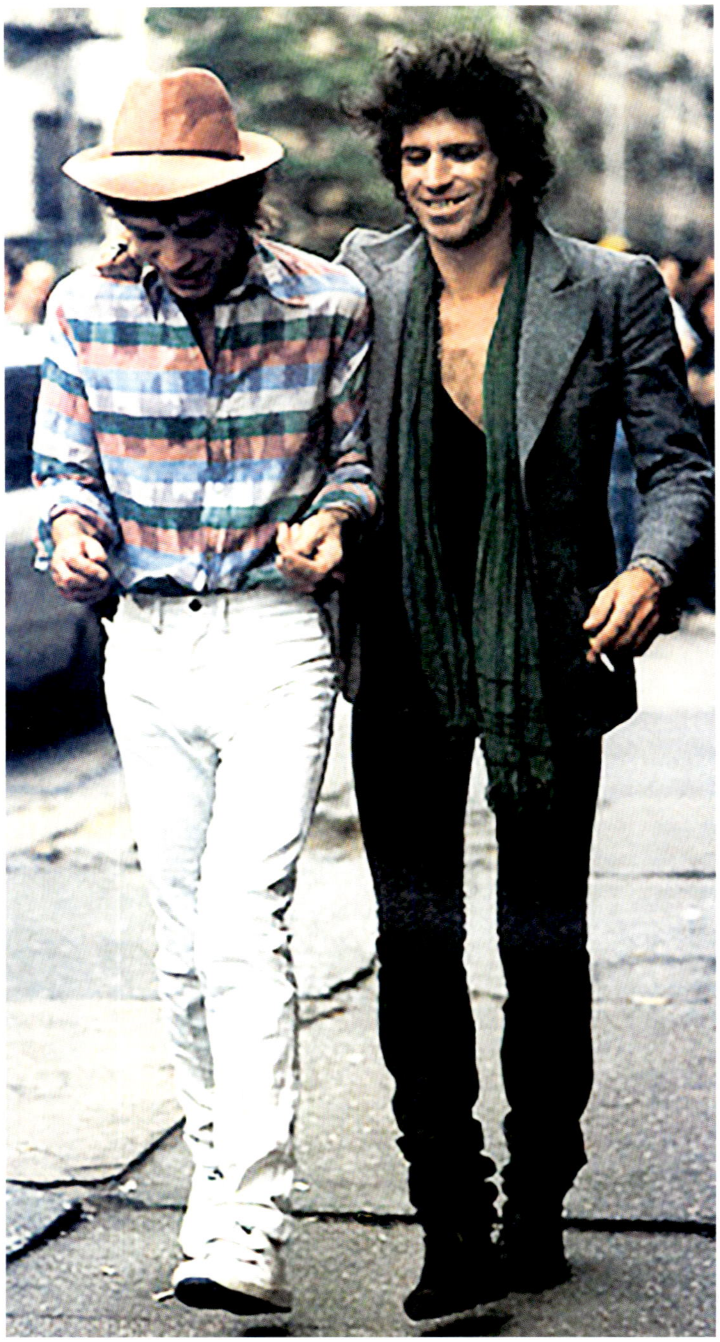

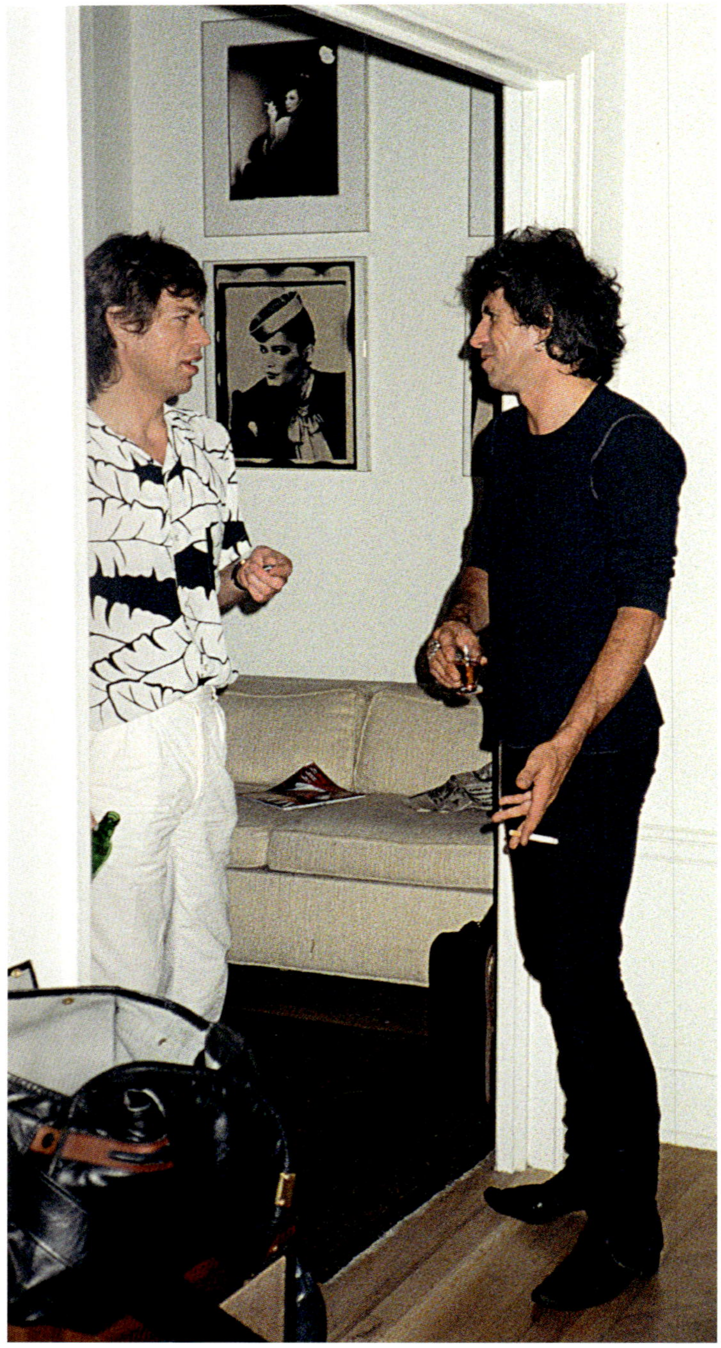

Mick and Keith on the street during the video filming of 'Waiting On A Friend' in New York – 2 July 1981.
Right: Mick and Keith chatting.
Far Right: Ronnie poses on a sofa at the promo video shoot in the New York studio apartment of photographer Arthur Elgort – 3 July 1981.

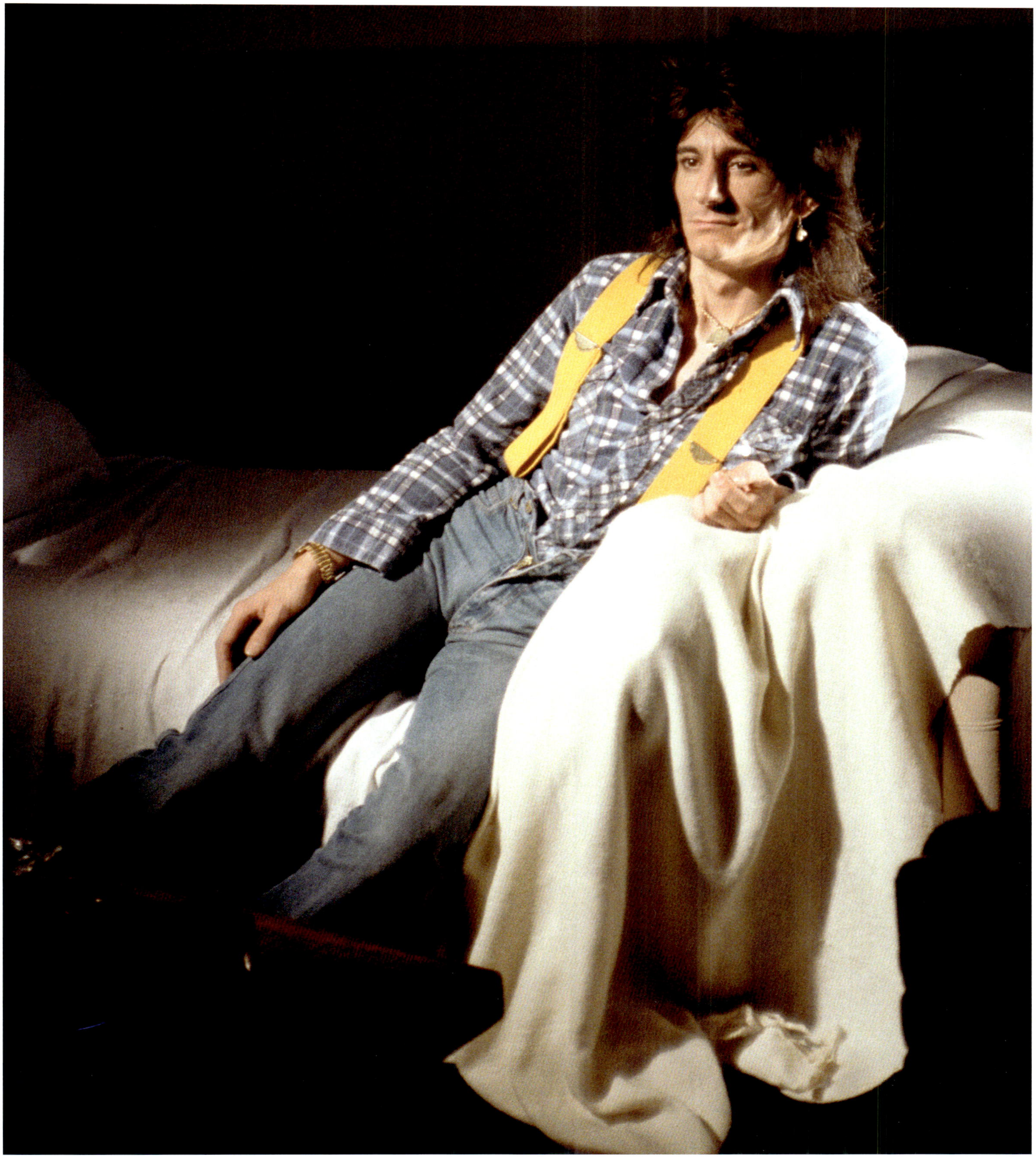

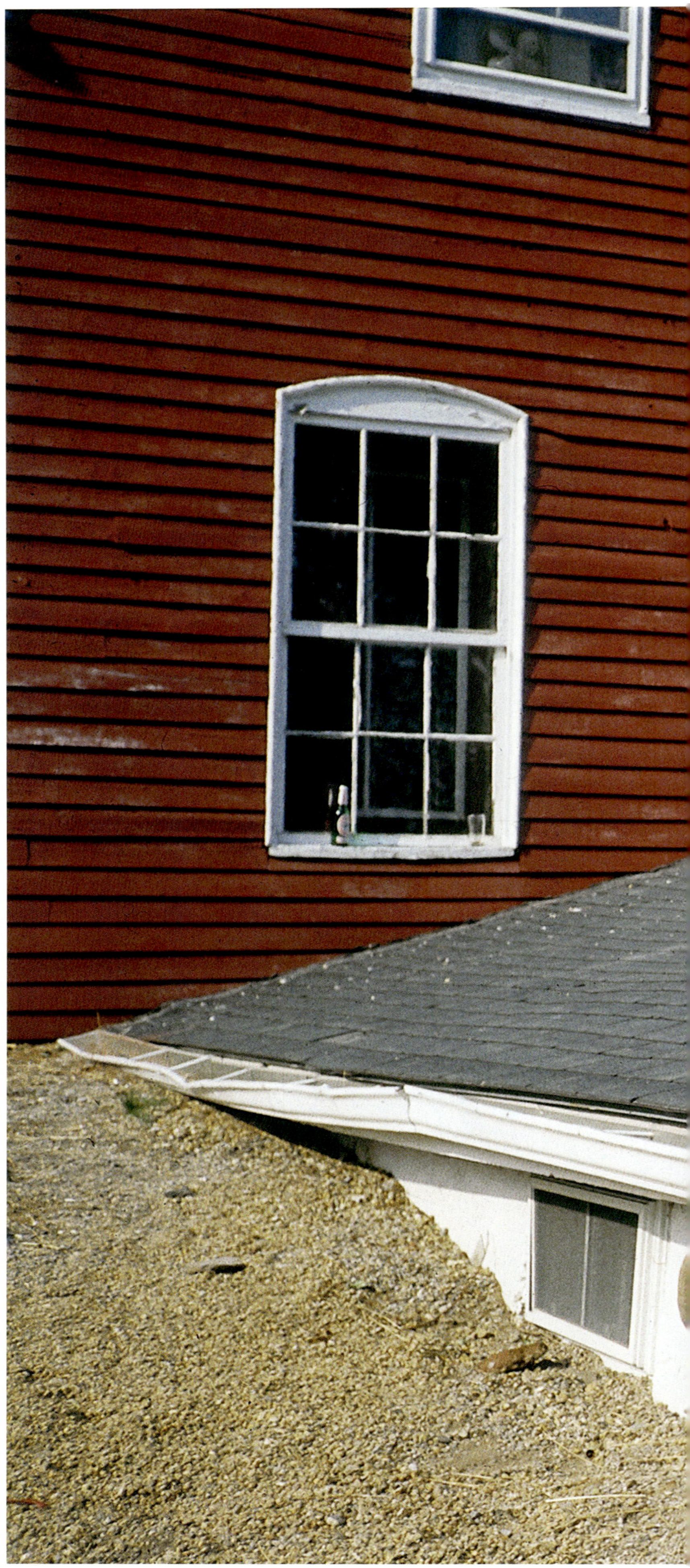

My girlfriend Astrid Lundstrom and Jerry Hall sitting on the low roof at Longview Farm in North Brookfield, Massachusetts, where the Stones were recording – 19 August 1981.

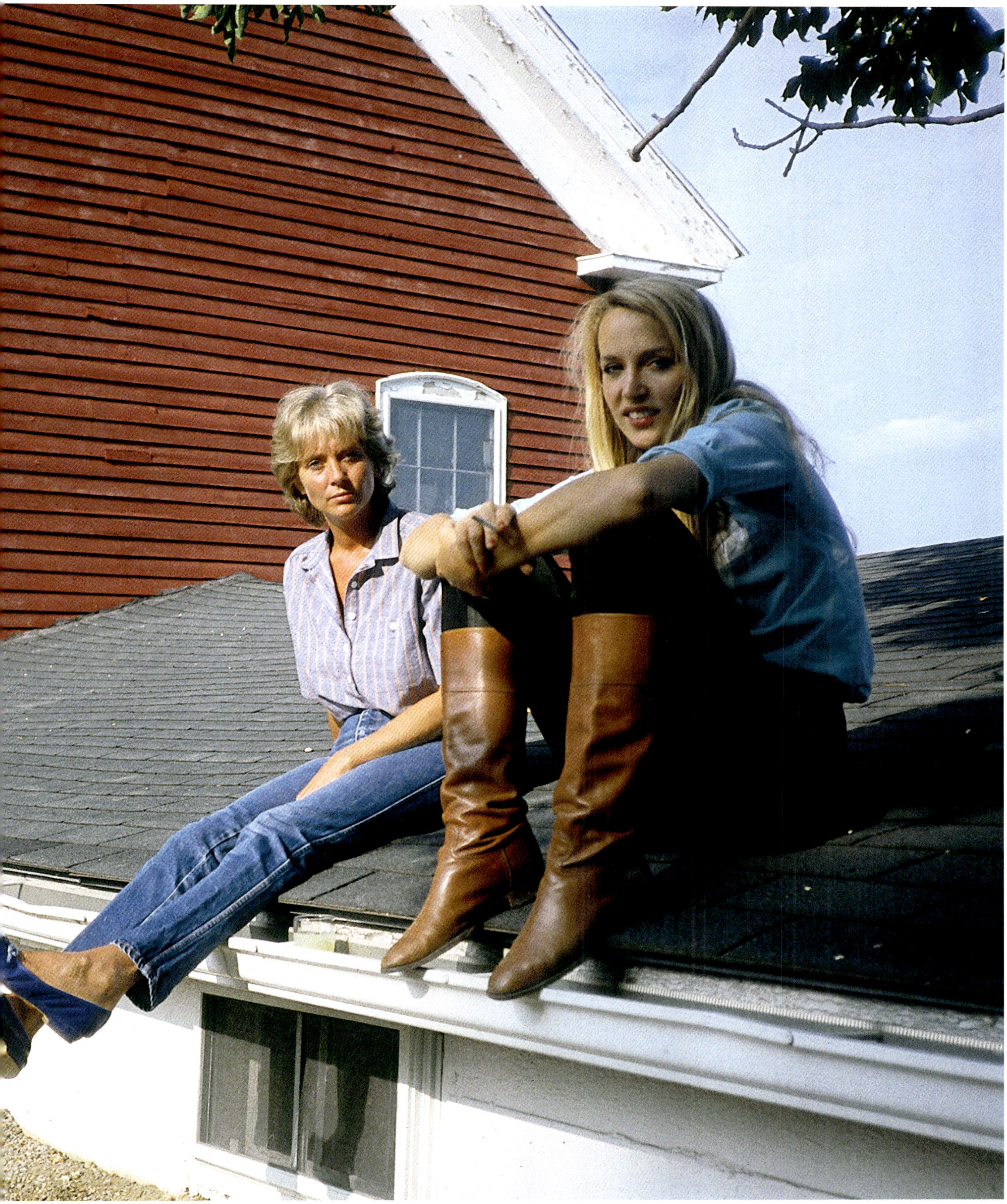

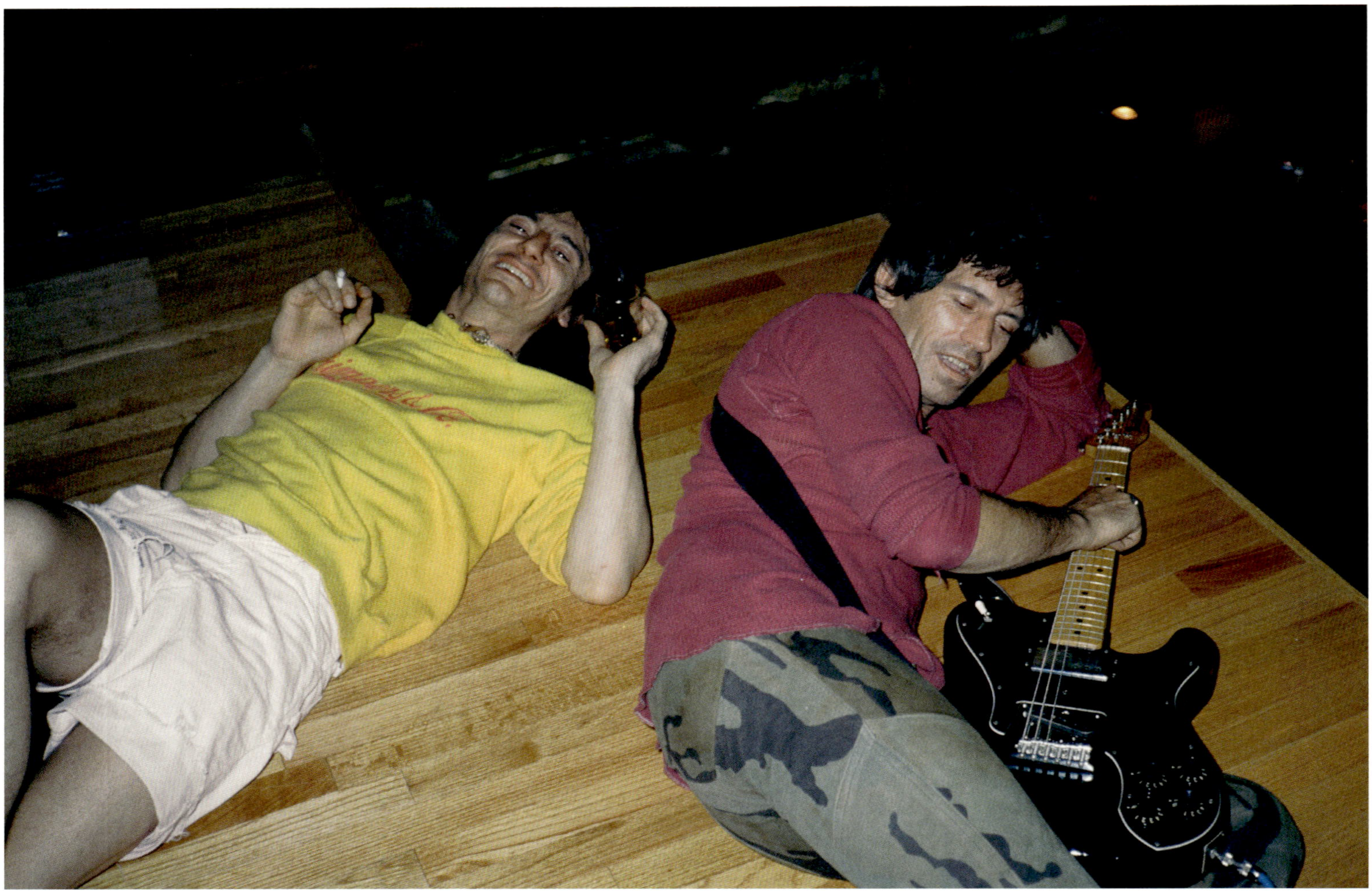

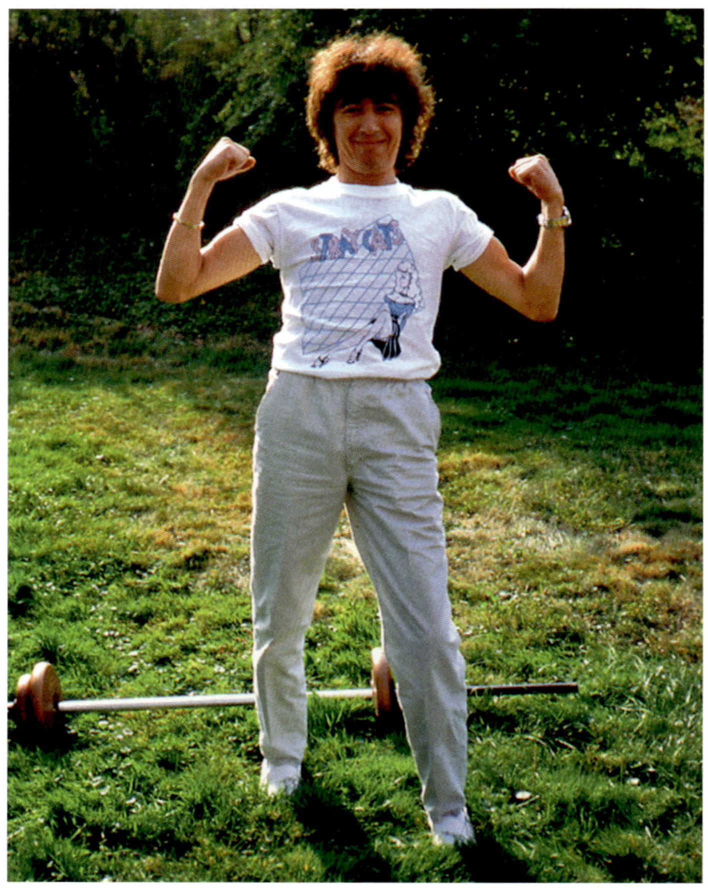

Ronnie and Keith on the studio floor, taking a break from recording, Longview Farm – 24 August 1981.
Far right: Ronnie being silly for me in the studio that same day.
Right: Me, exercising after a two-mile run and a bit of weight lifting – 19 August 1981.

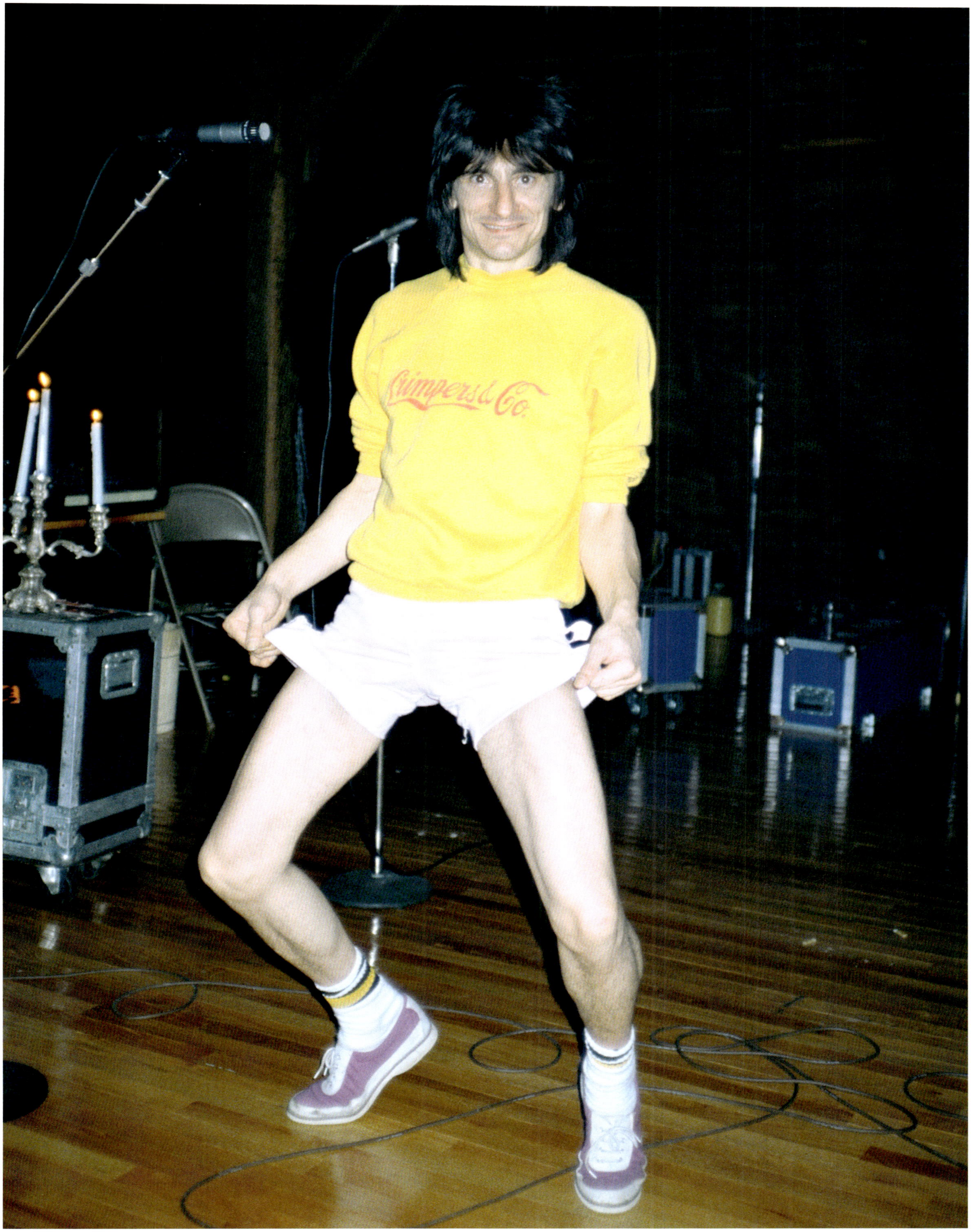

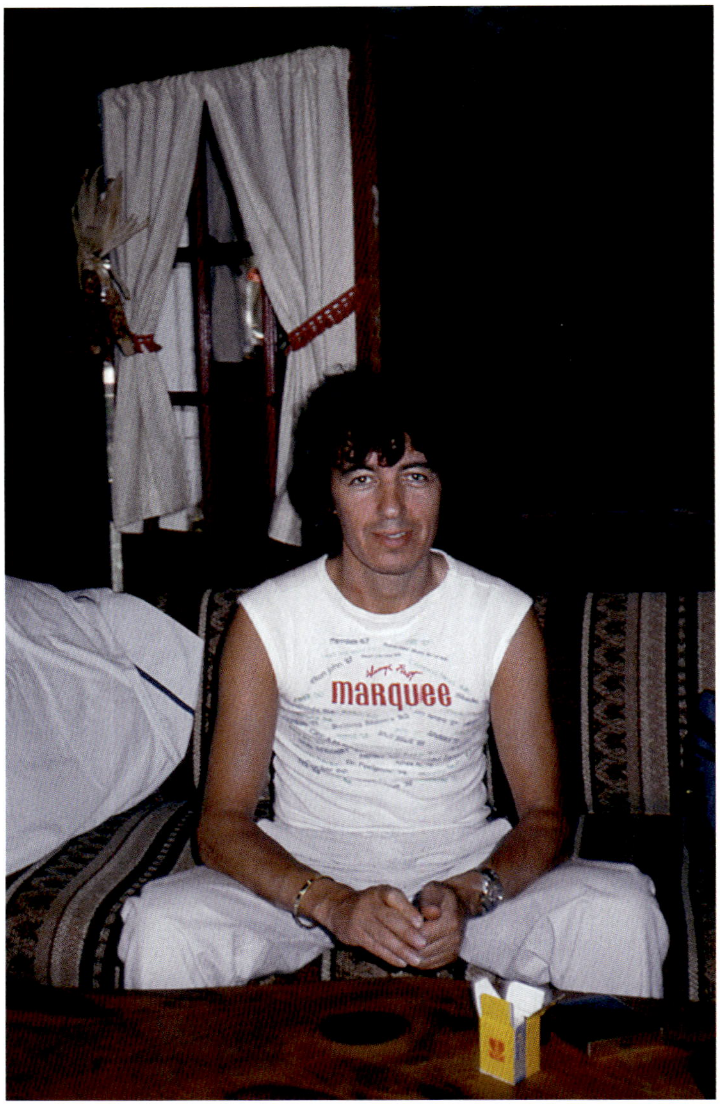

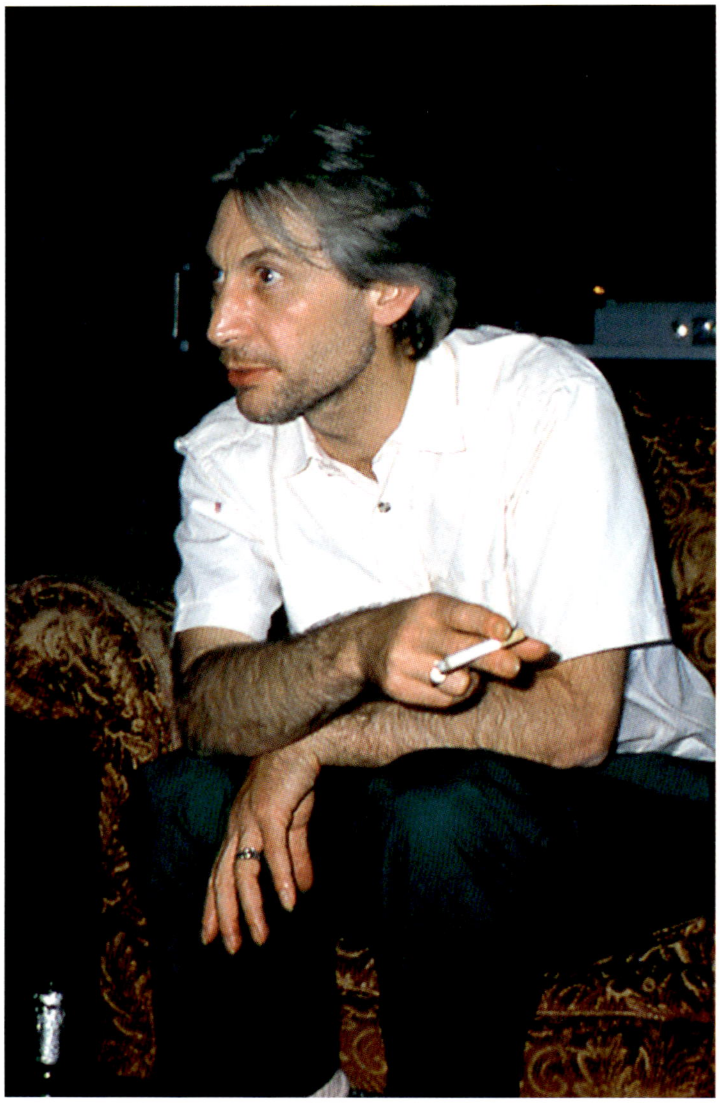

Me sitting in my hotel room – 28 August 1981.
Right: Charlie relaxing in the studio – 18 August 1981.
Far right: Ronnie recording in a happy frame of mind – 25 August 1981.

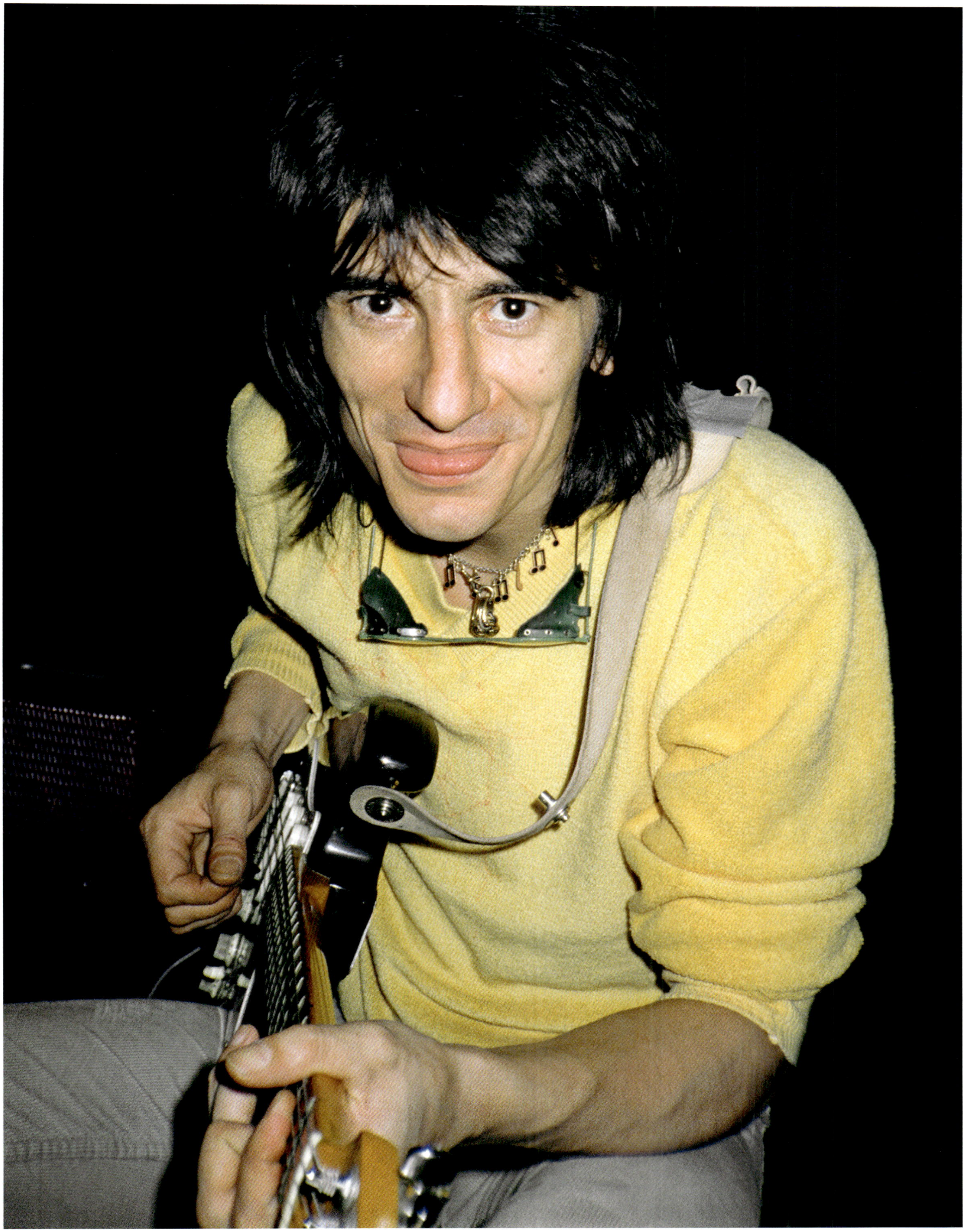

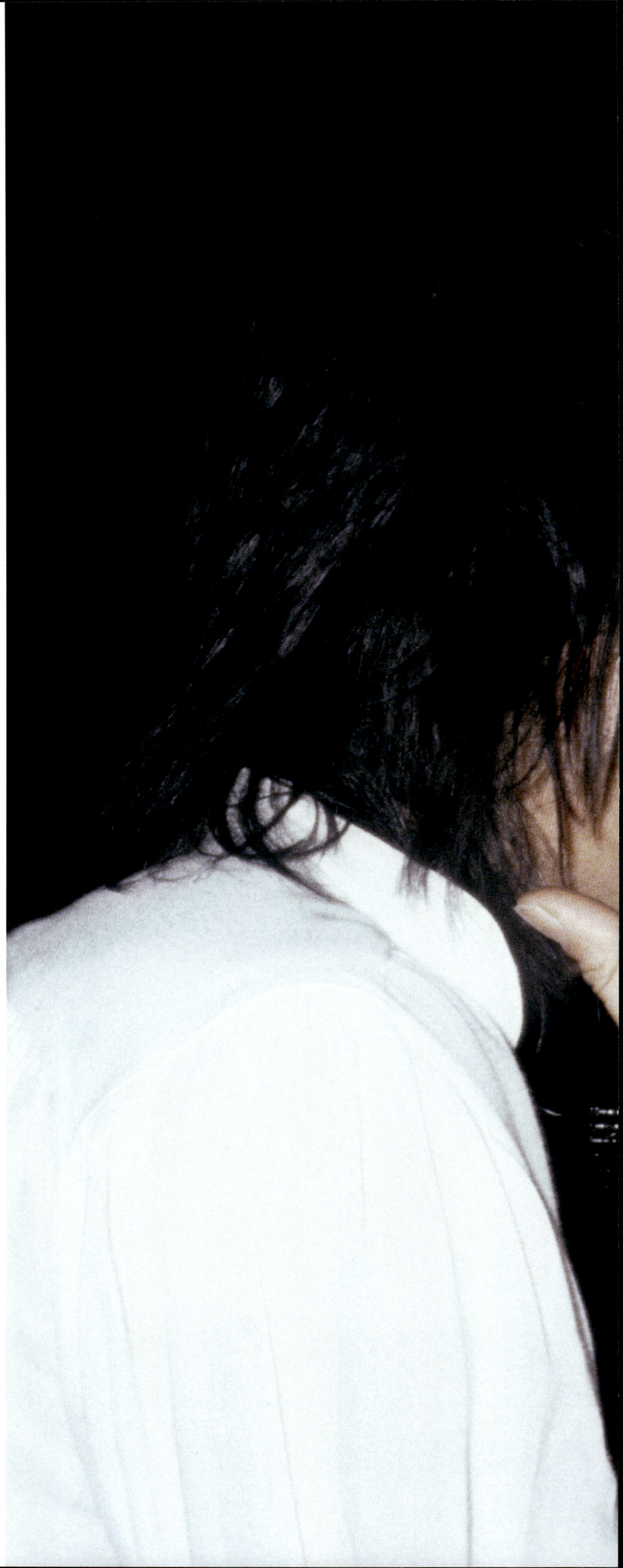

Ronnie and Keith in the studio ('you'll never guess what happened') – 30 August 1981.

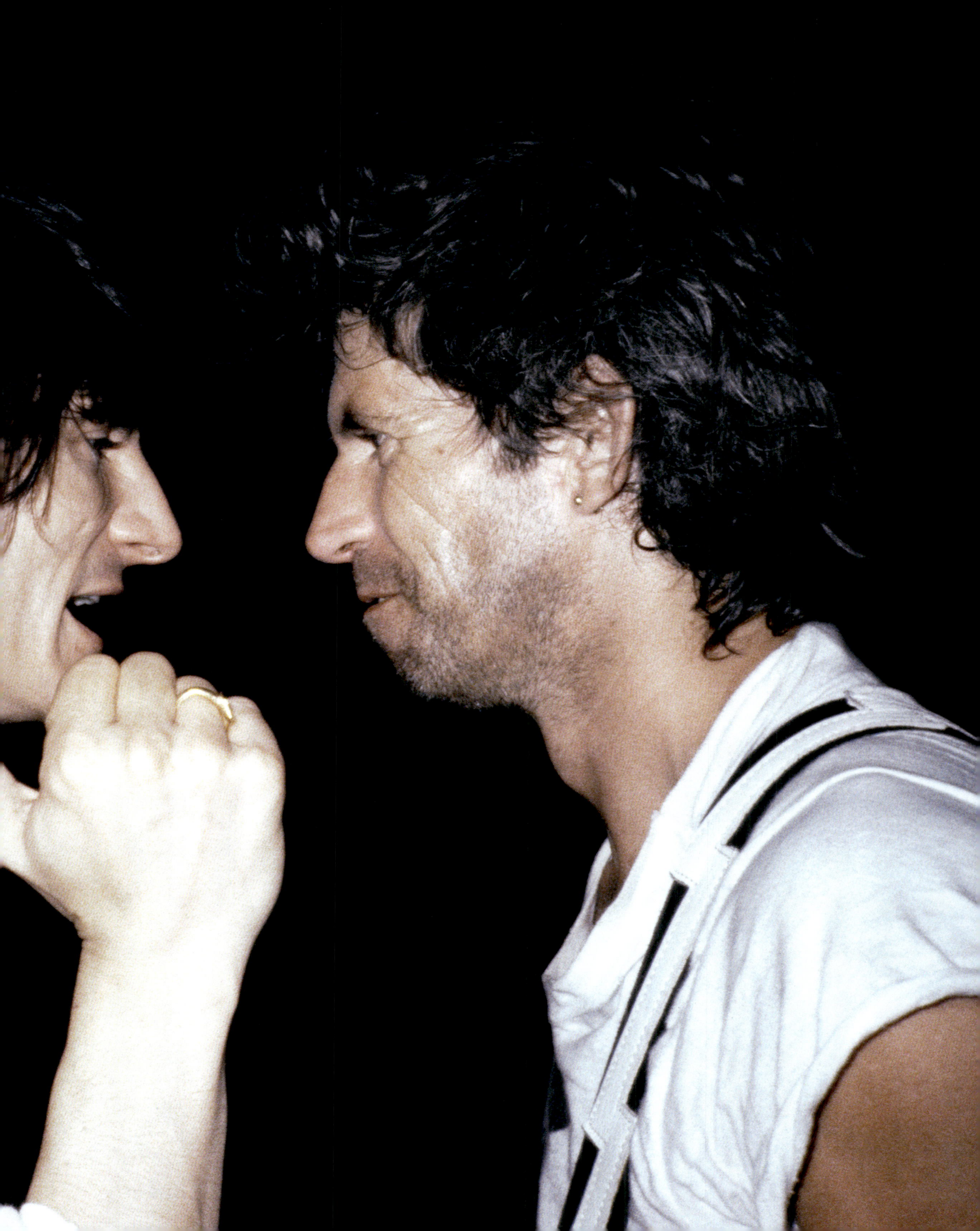

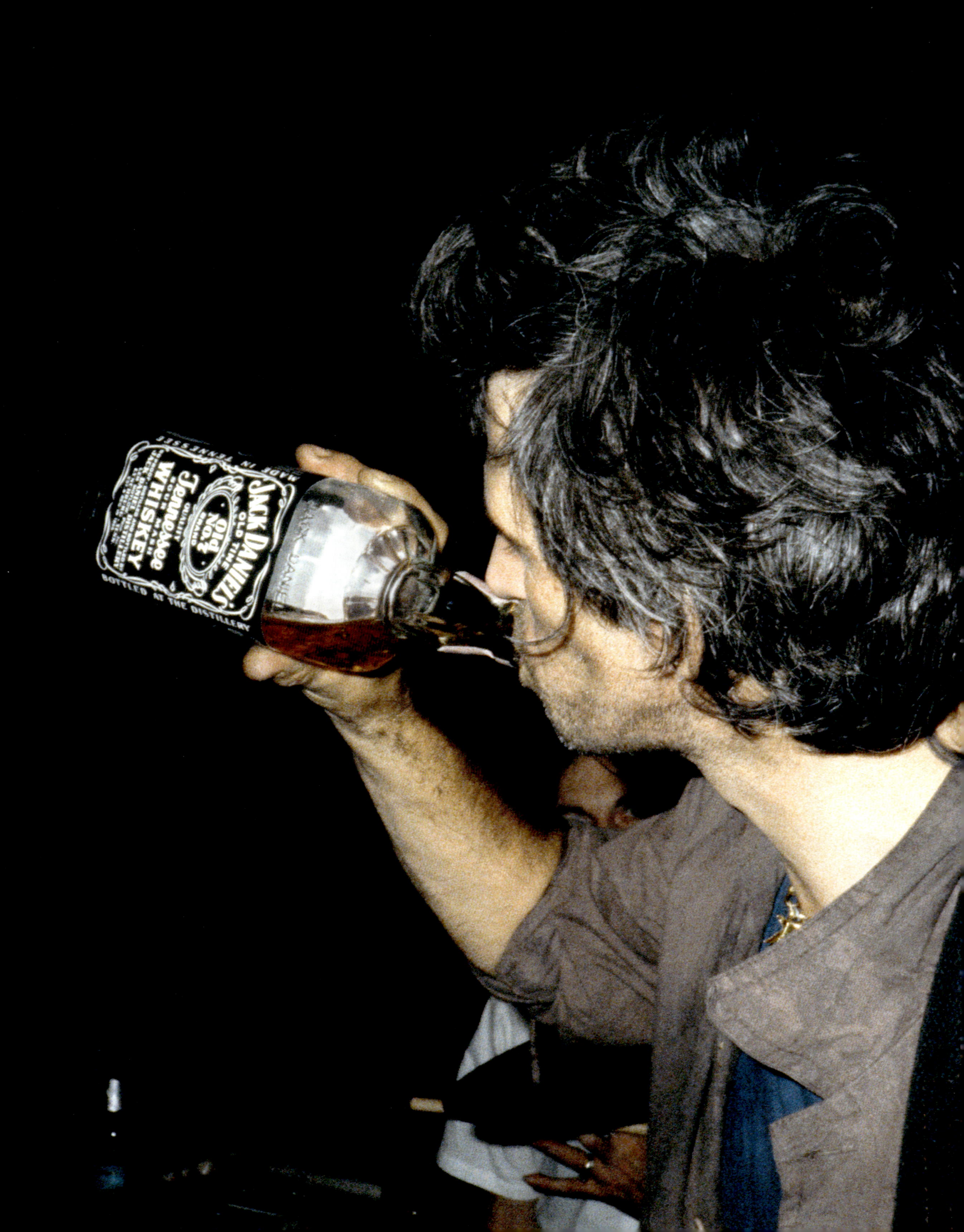
MADE IN TENNESSEE
JACK DANIEL'S
OLD TIME
Old No.7
Tennessee
WHISKEY
BOTTLED AT THE DISTILLERY

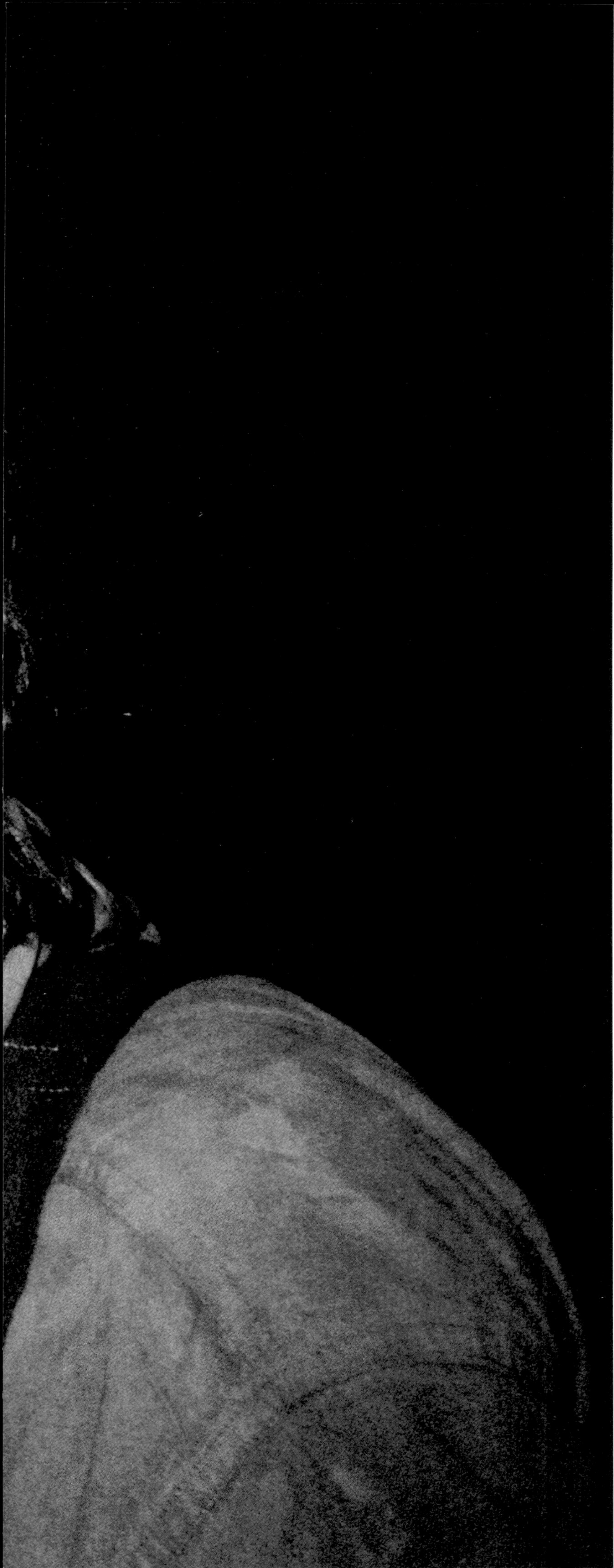

Keith with his favourite Jack Daniels in the studio – 6 September 1981.

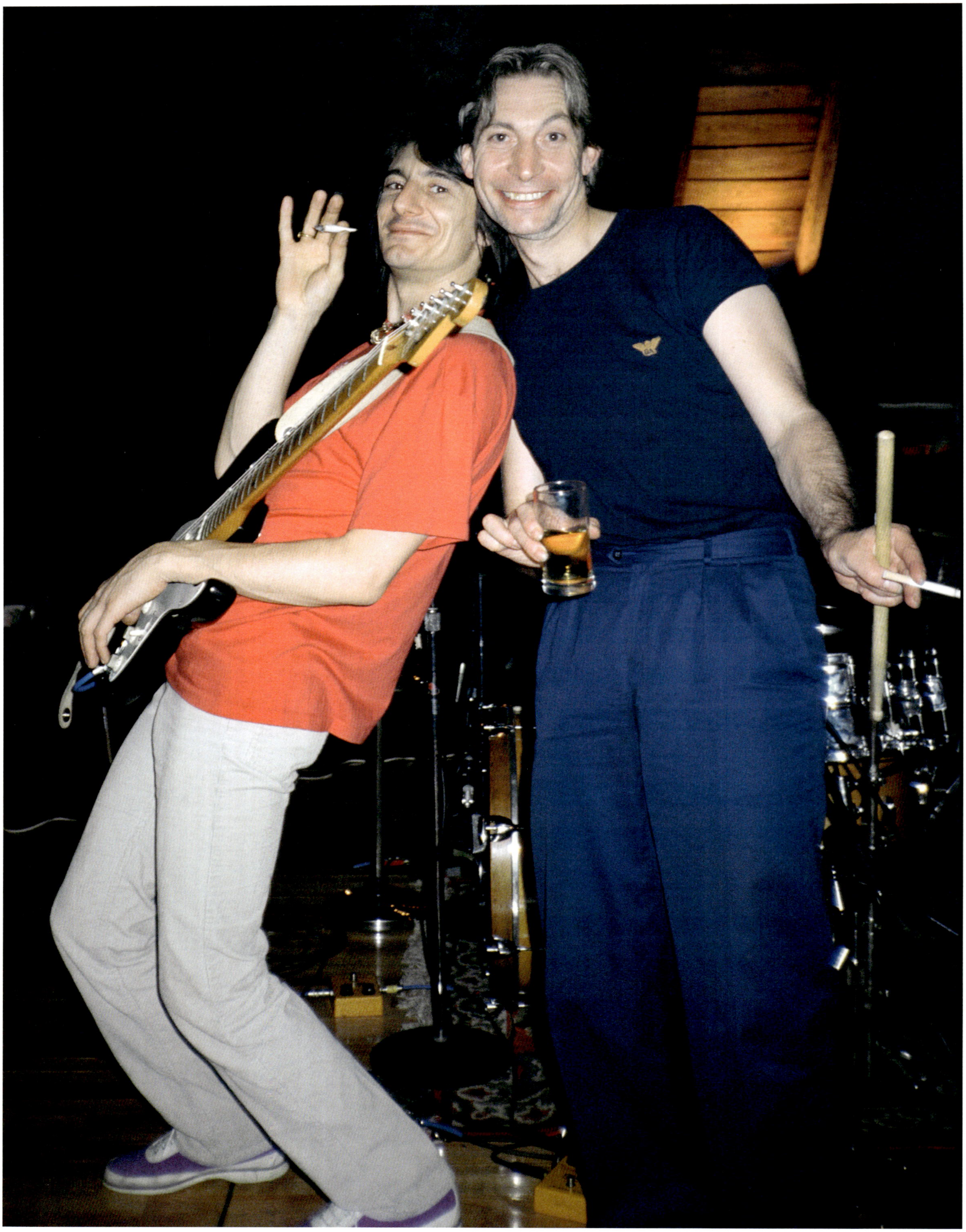

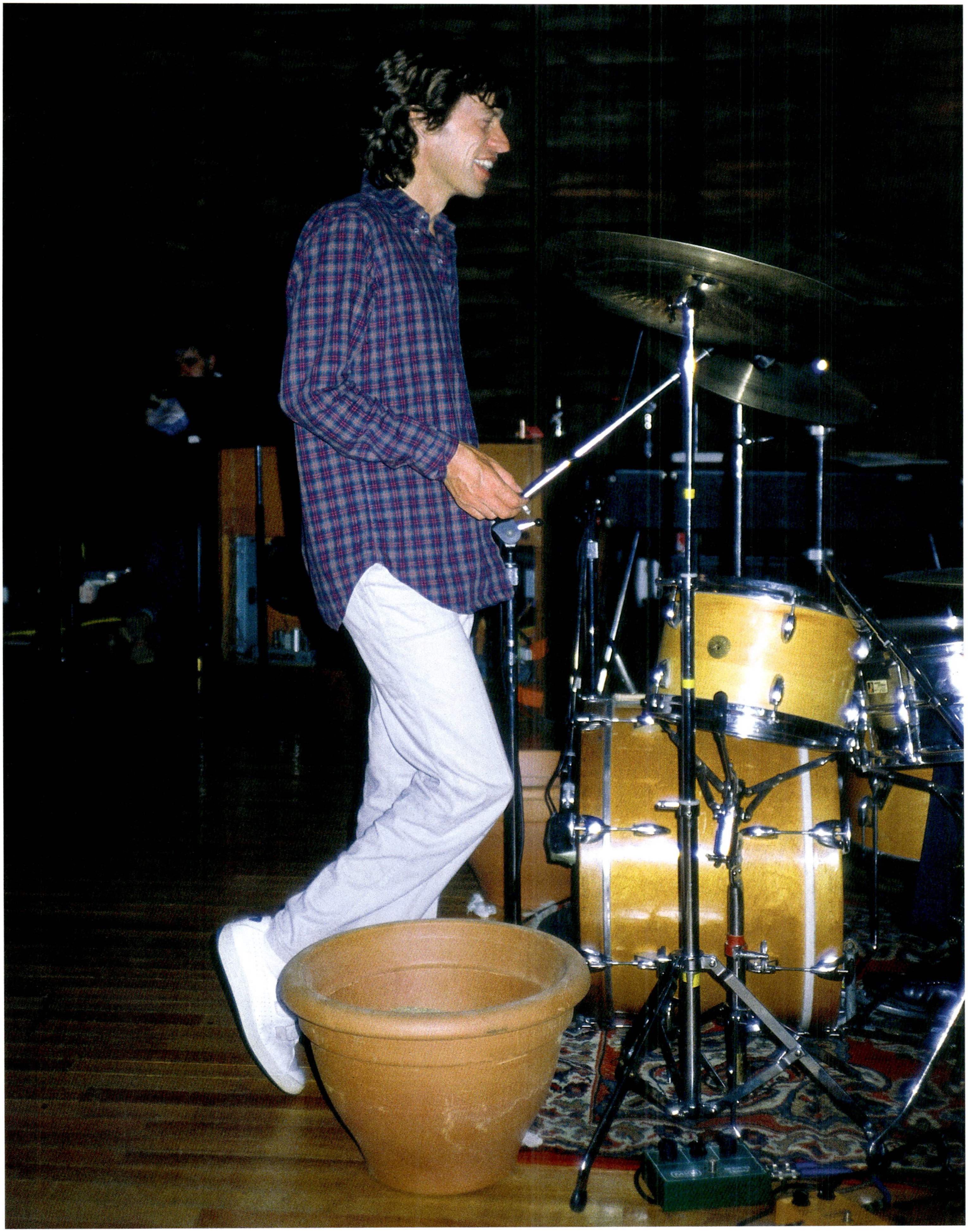

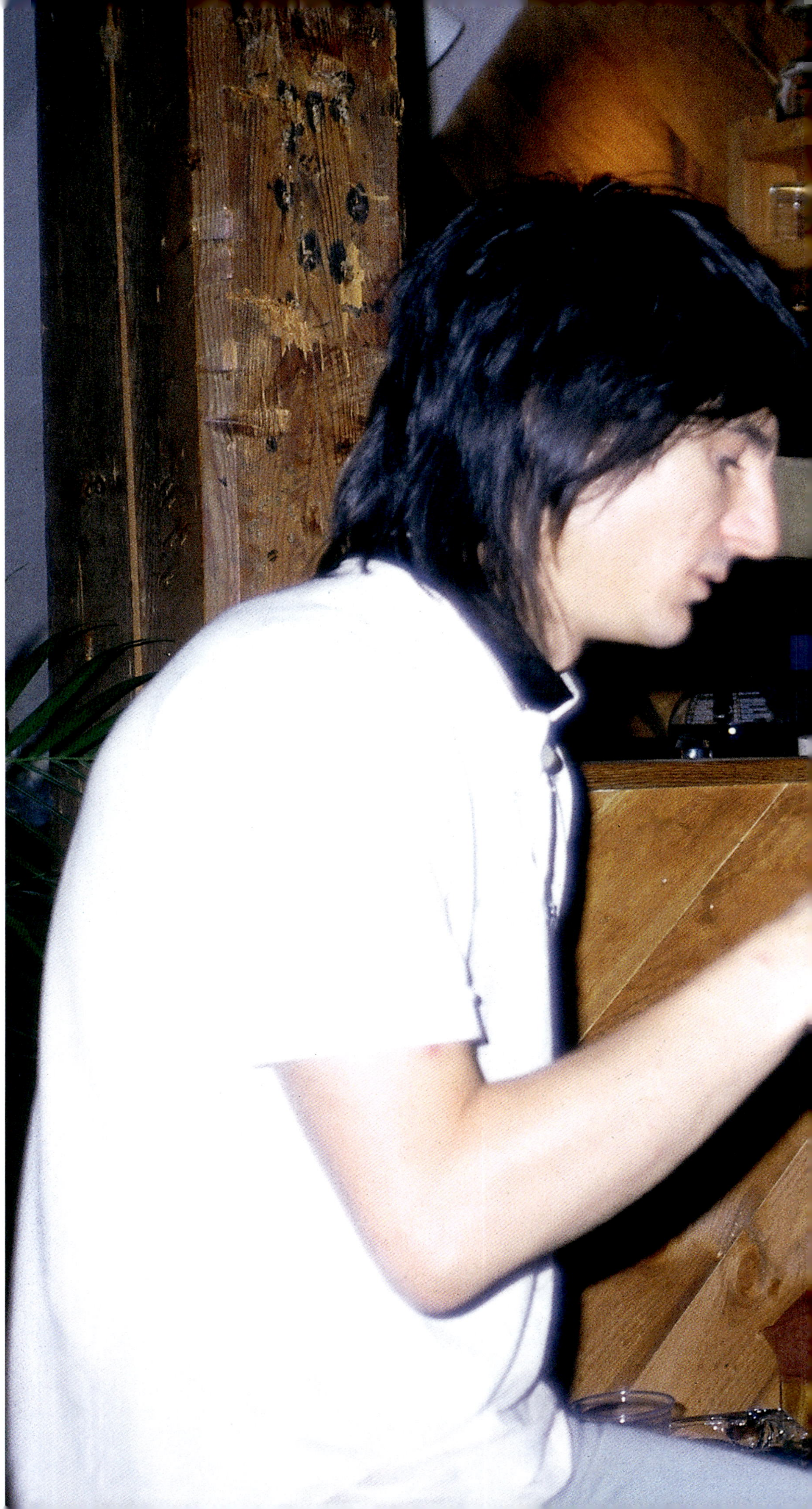

Ronnie and Keith taking a break in the studio – 6 September 1981.
Previous pages: Ronnie and Charlie 'hamming it up' for me in the studio – 28 August 1981. Mick chatting to an unseen Charie at the drums in the studio – 23 September 1981.
Following pages: Keith ('I could have been a bare-fist fighter') with Mick and Ronnie in the studio – 7 September 1981.

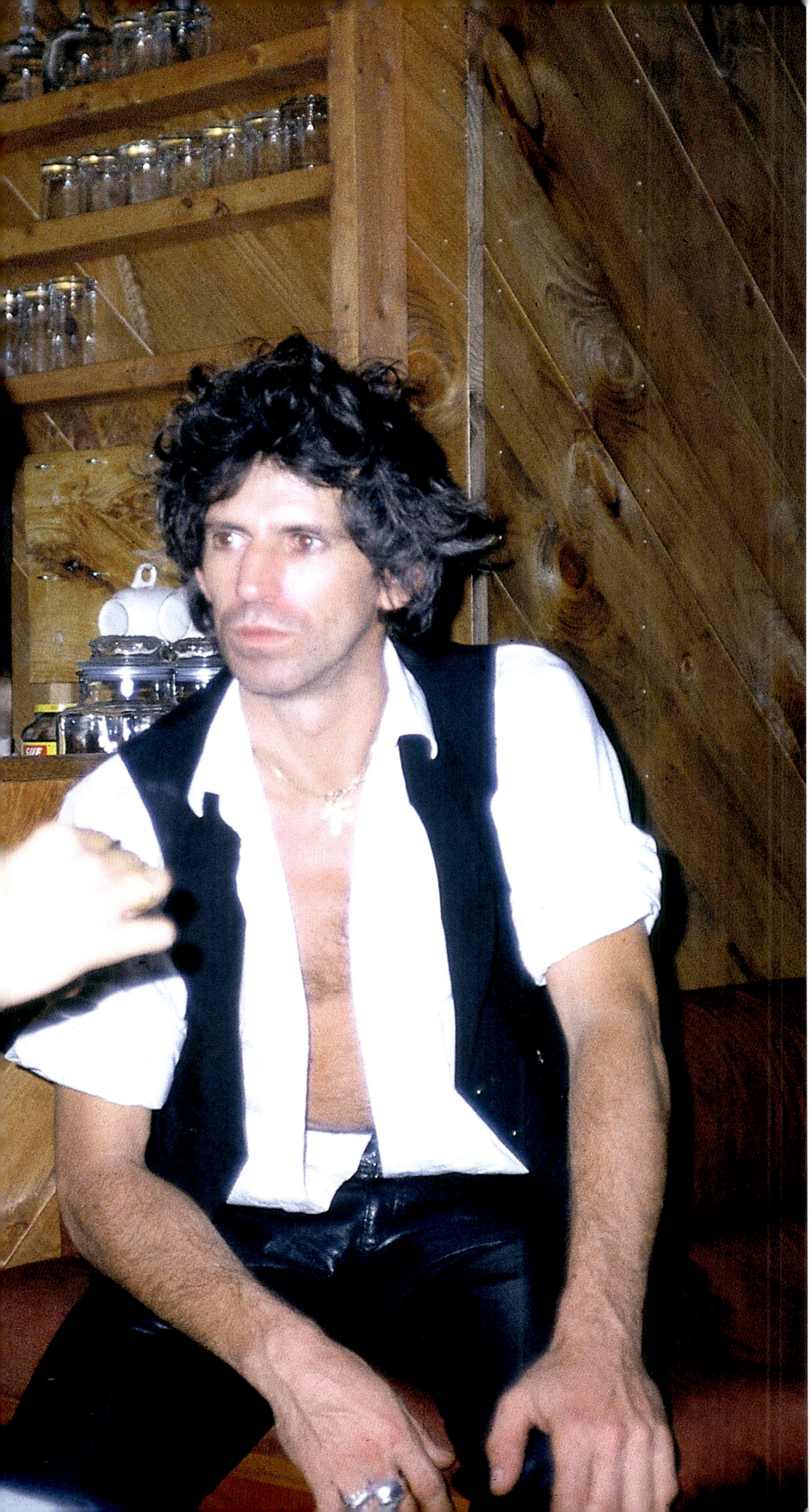

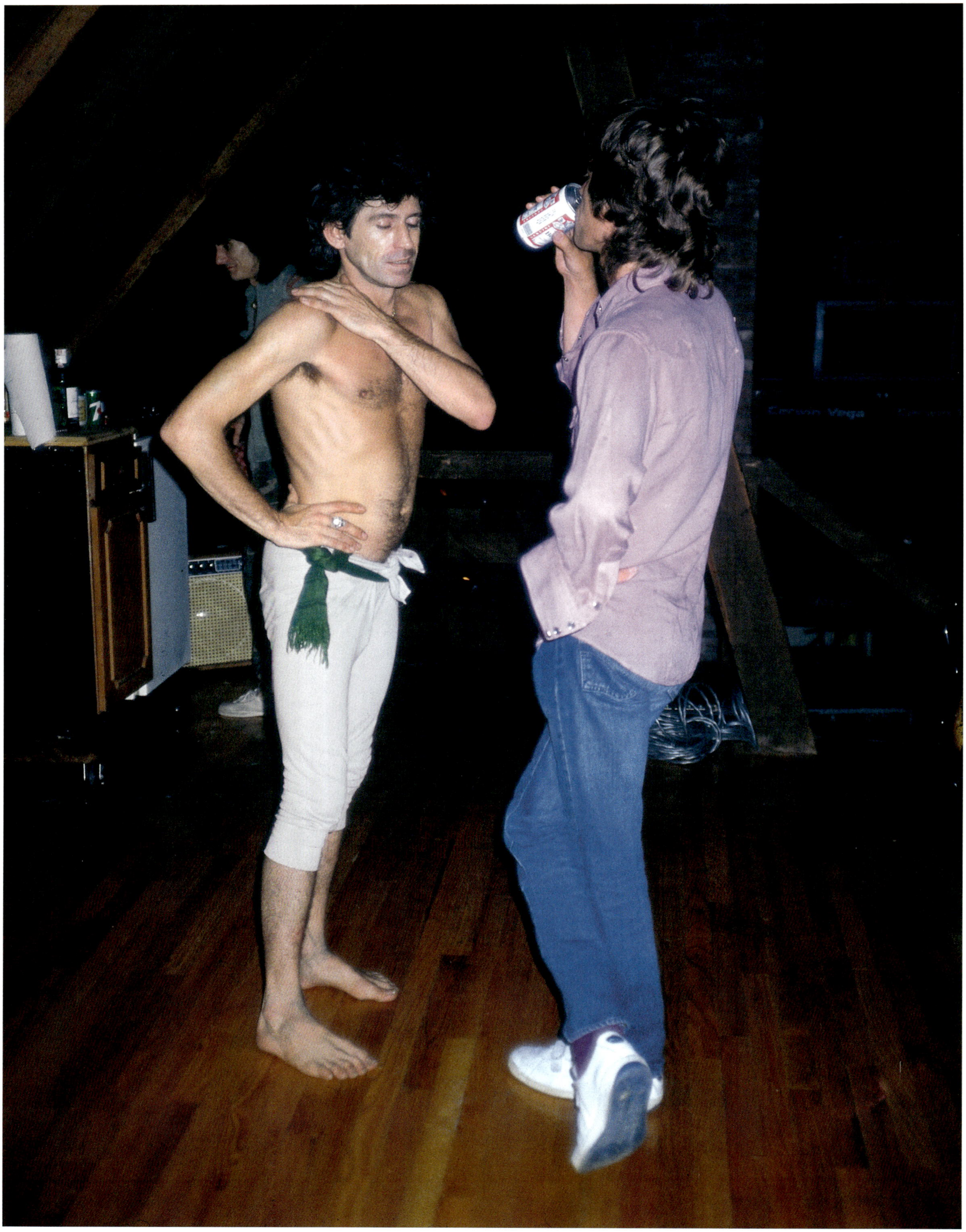

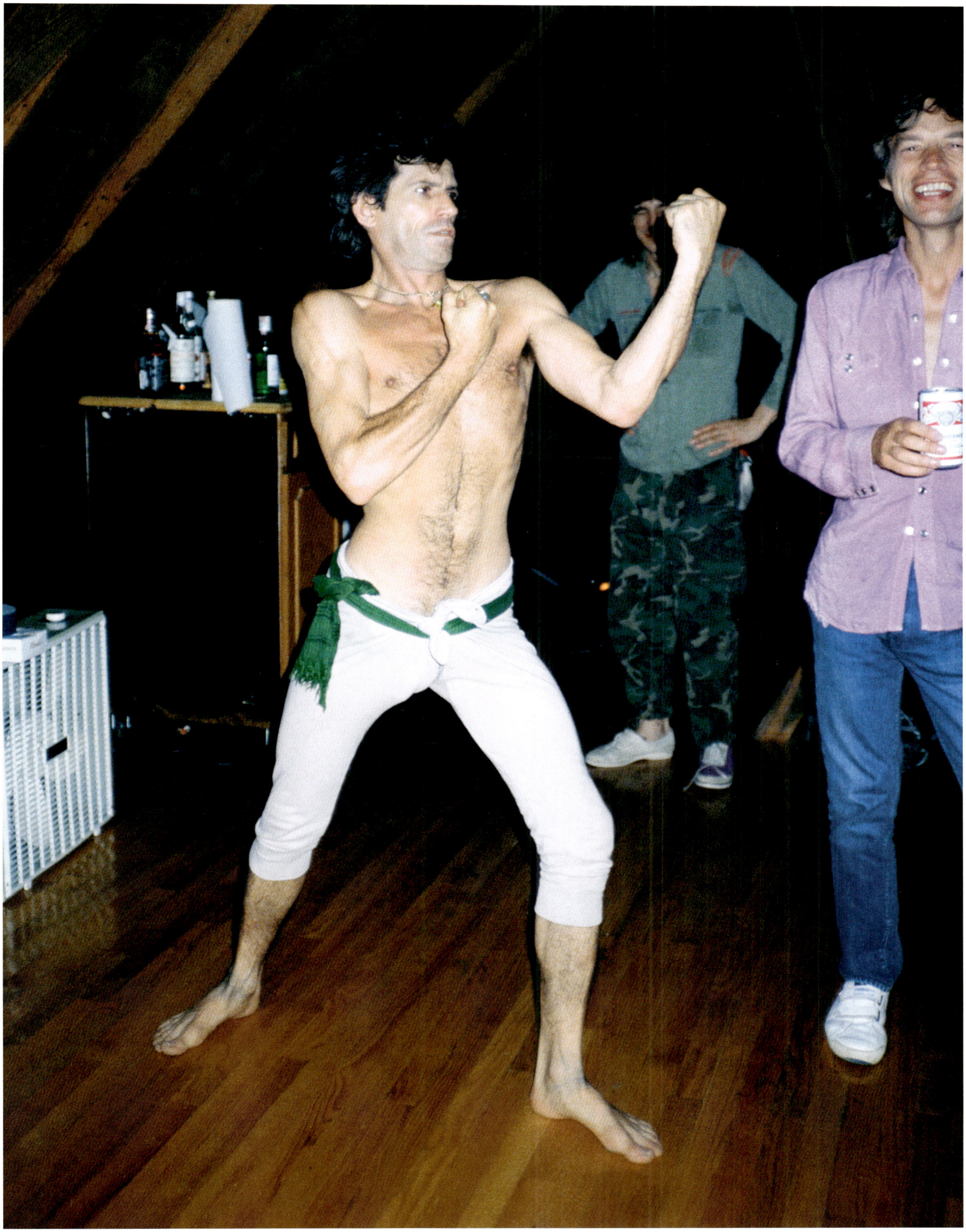

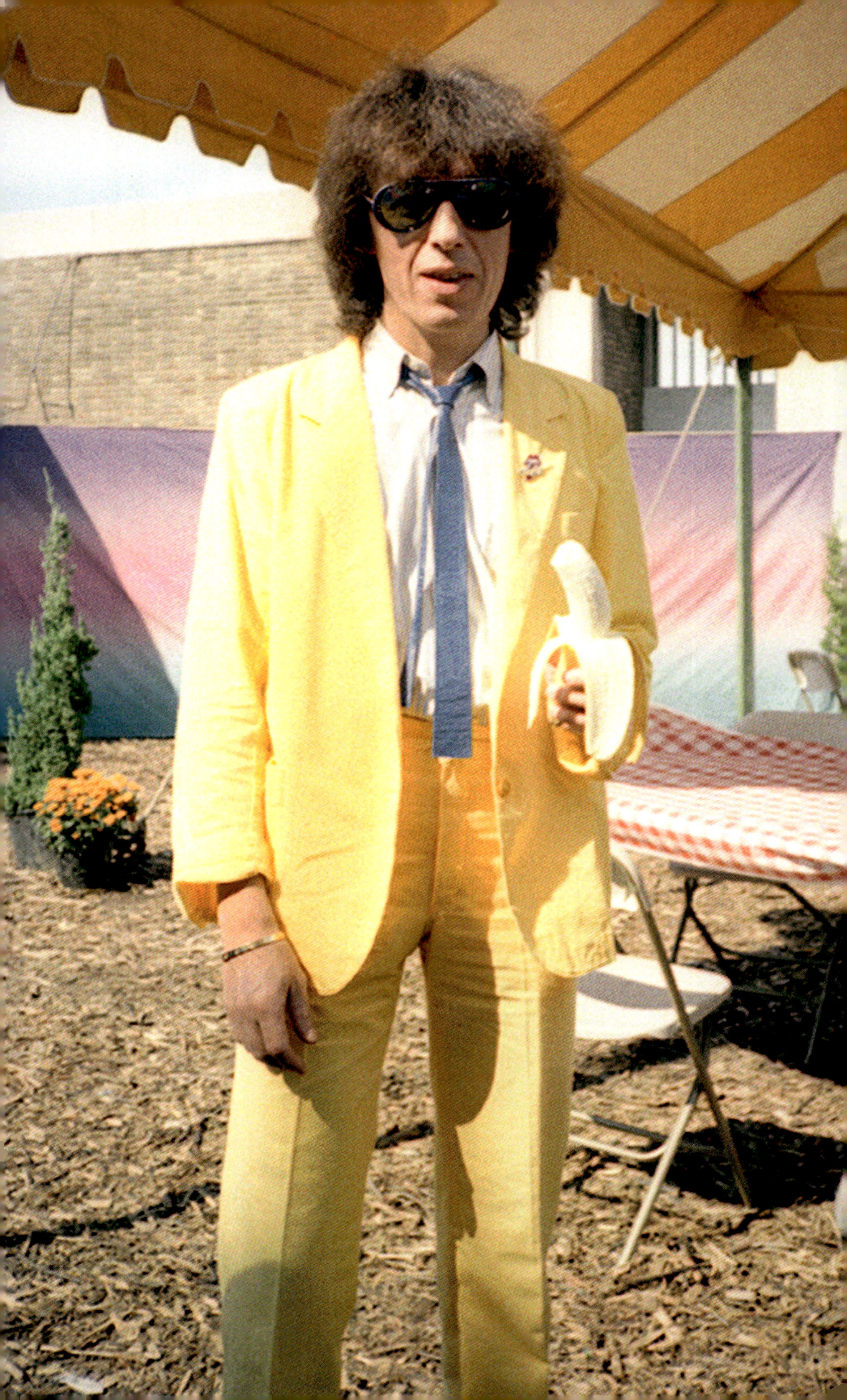

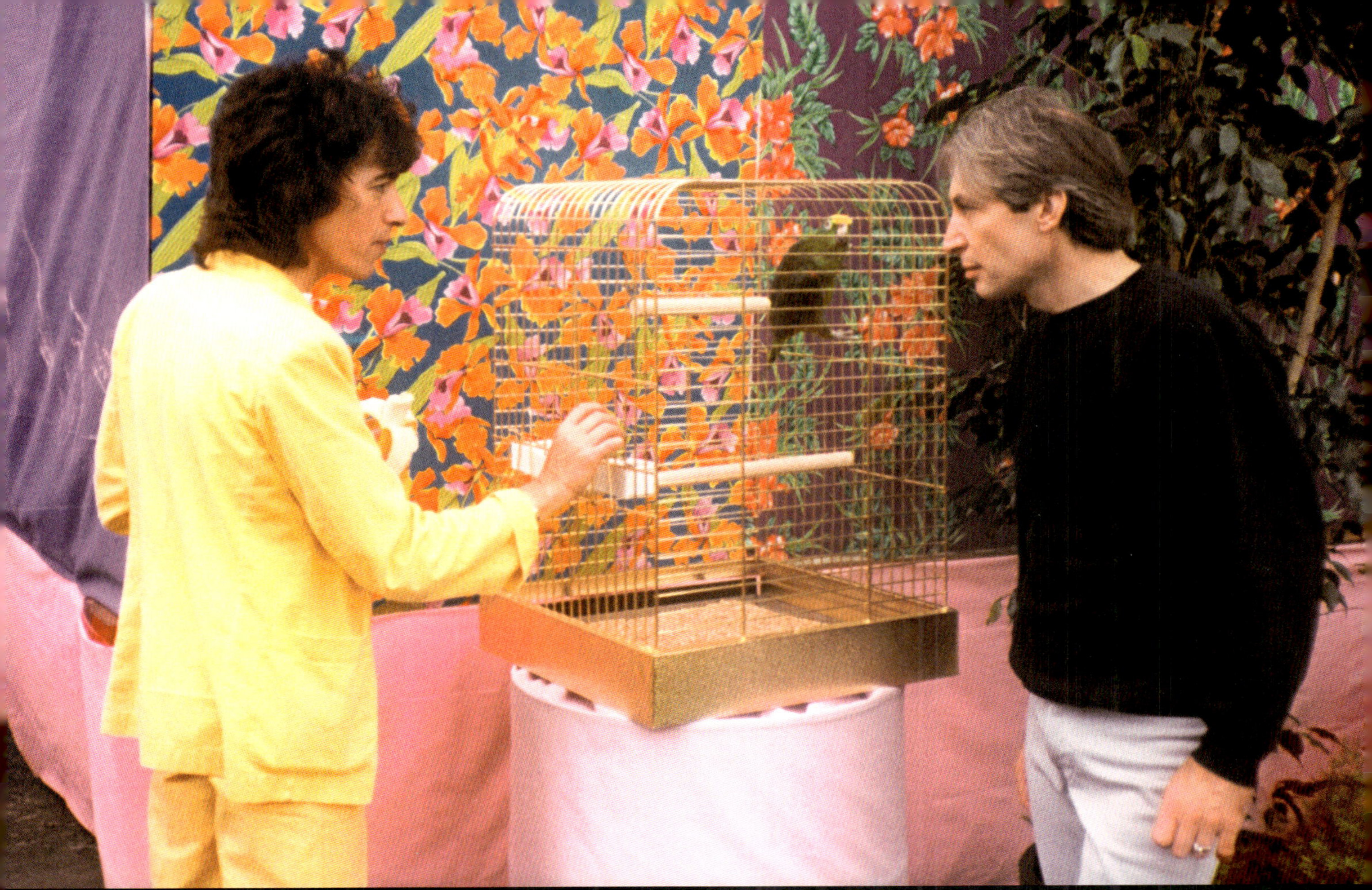

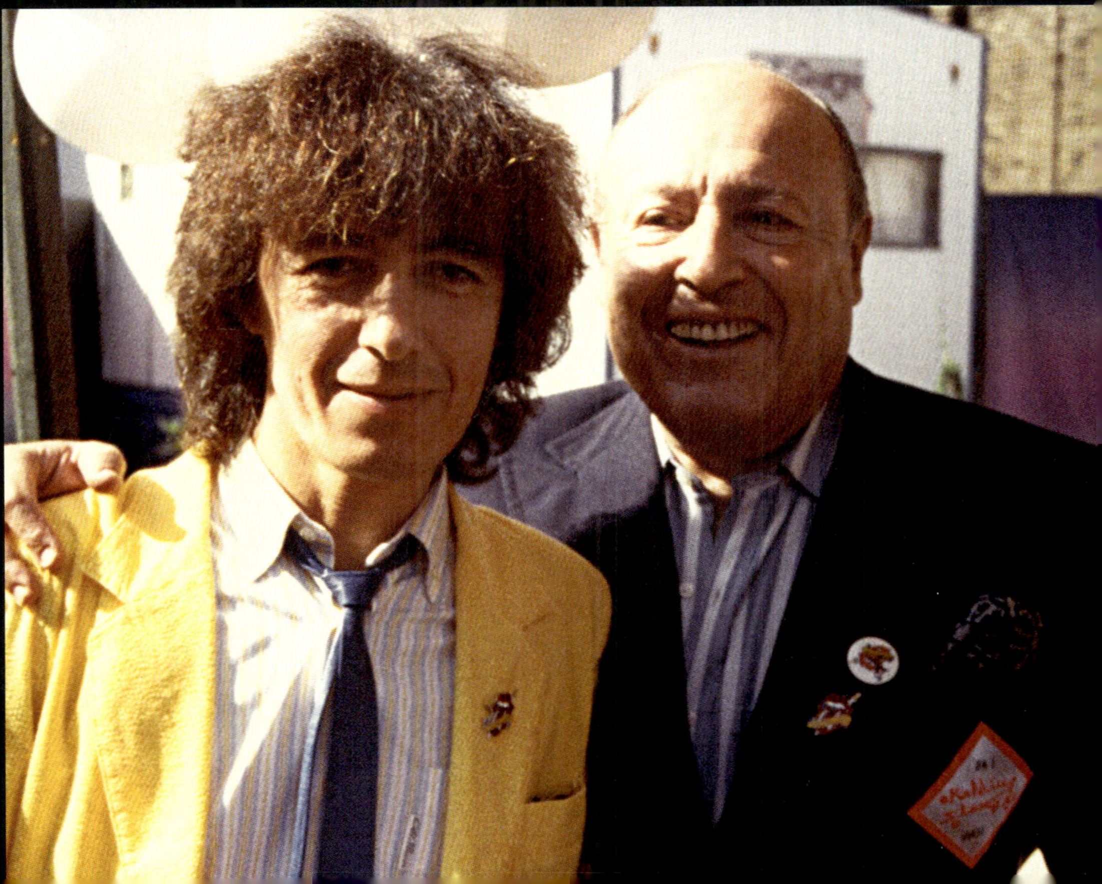

Three shots of me enjoying my birthday celebrations, seen with Charlie and Truman Capote backstage at The Tangerine Bowl in Orlando, Florida – 24 October 1981

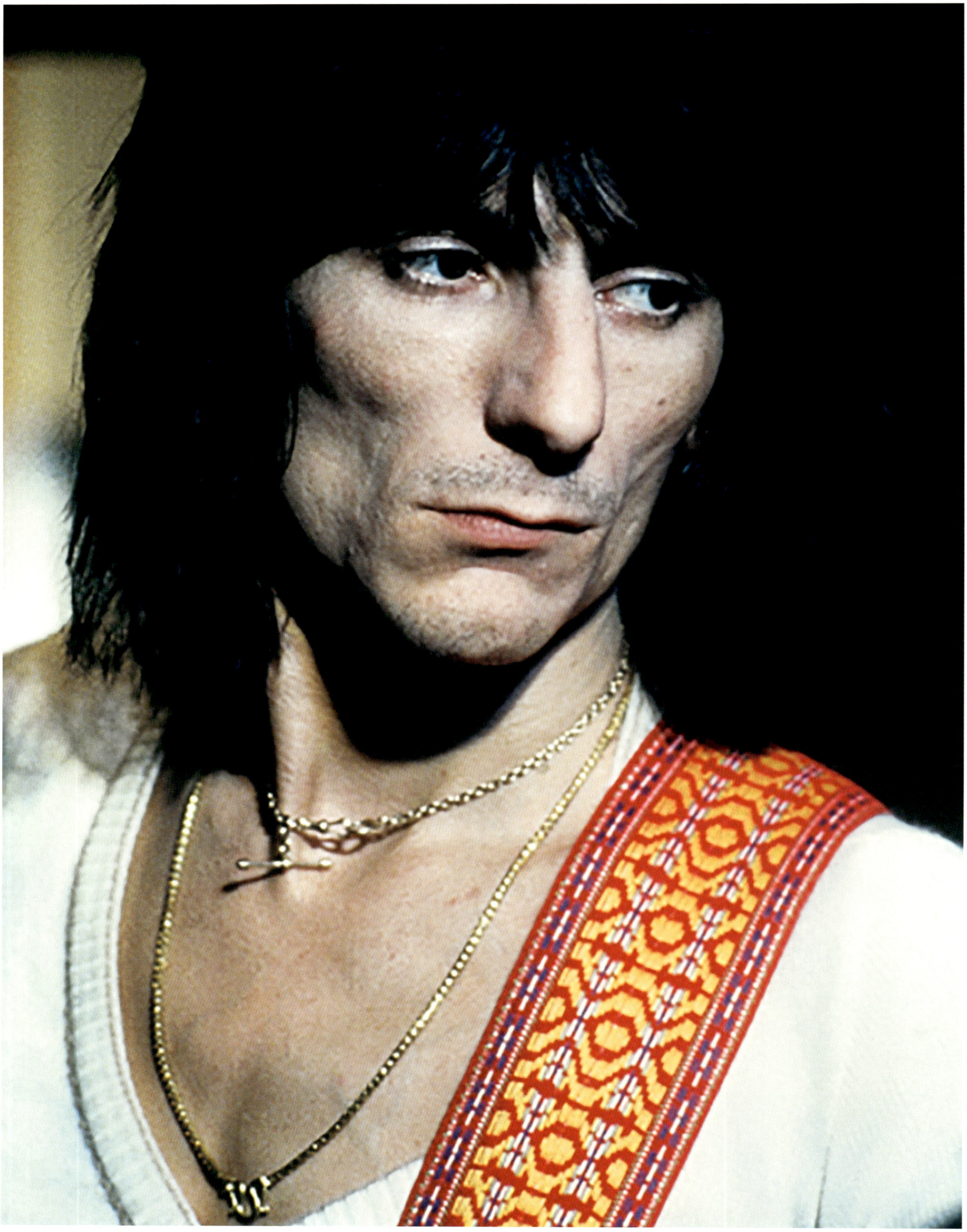

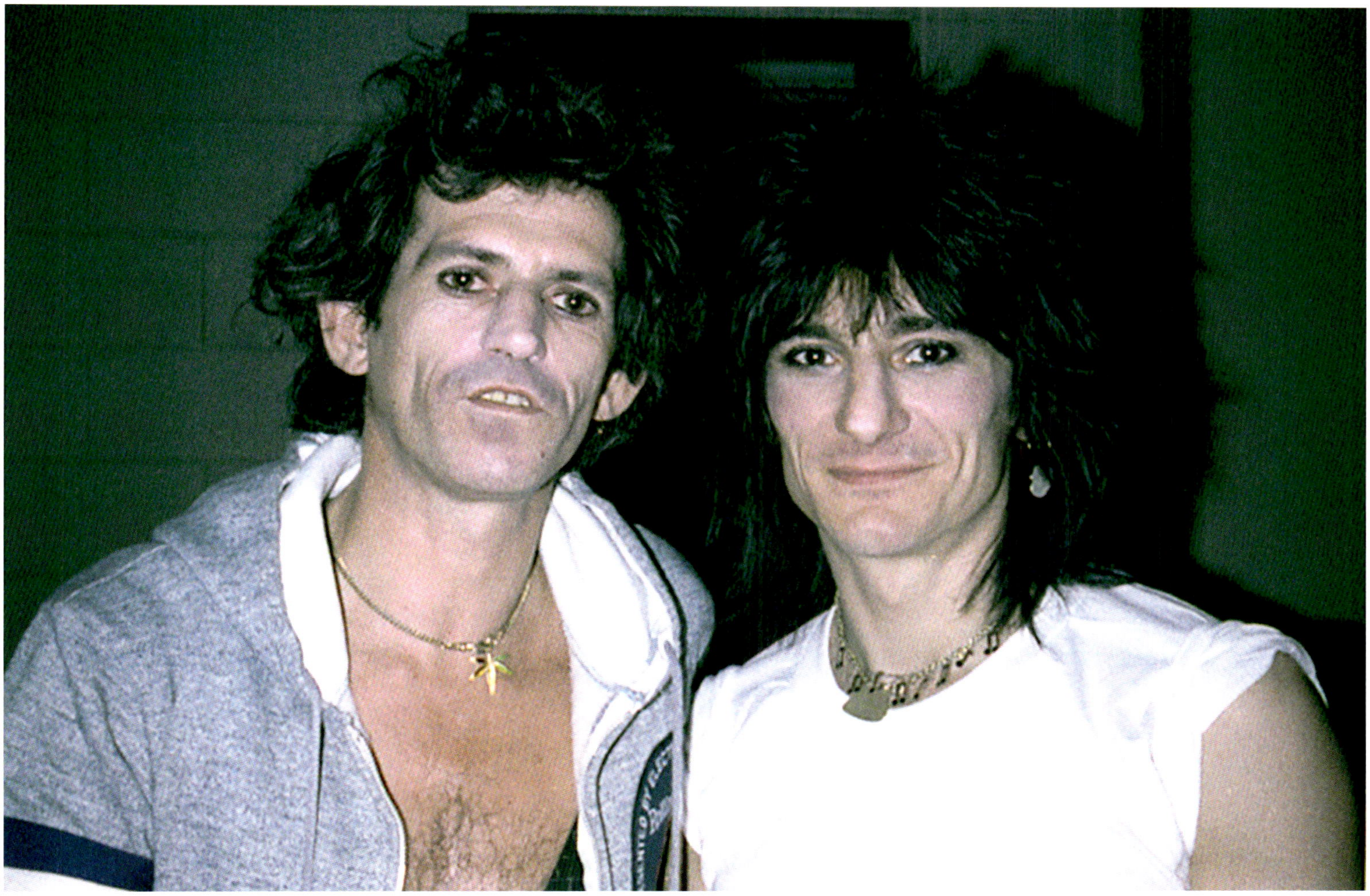

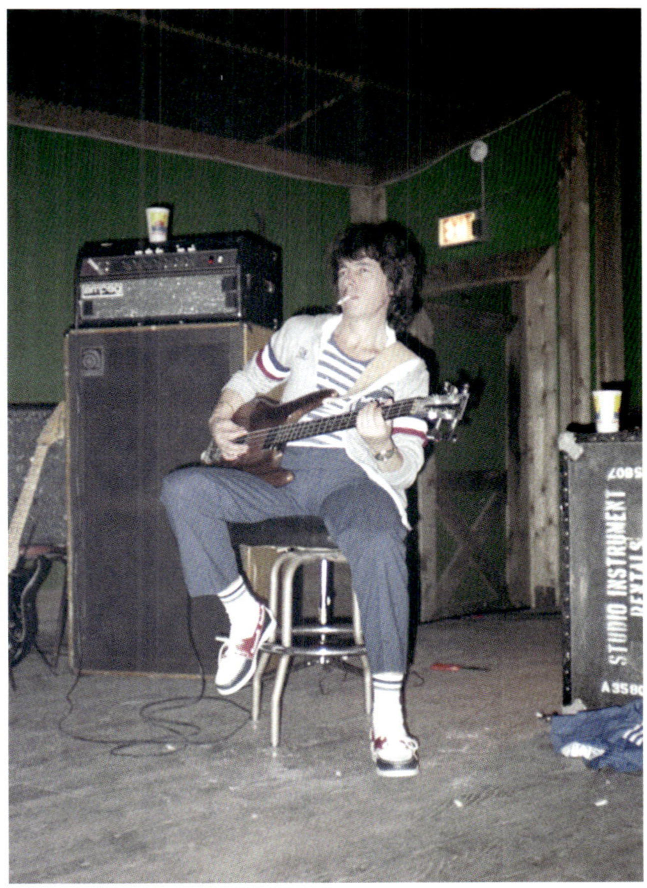

Keith and Ronnie posing for me backstage at the MetroCentre in Rockford, Michigan – 1 October 1981.
Left: A serious Ronnie backstage before the show – October 1981.
Right: Me at the Stones' rehearsal at the SIR Studio in Chicago, Illinois – 28 September 1981.

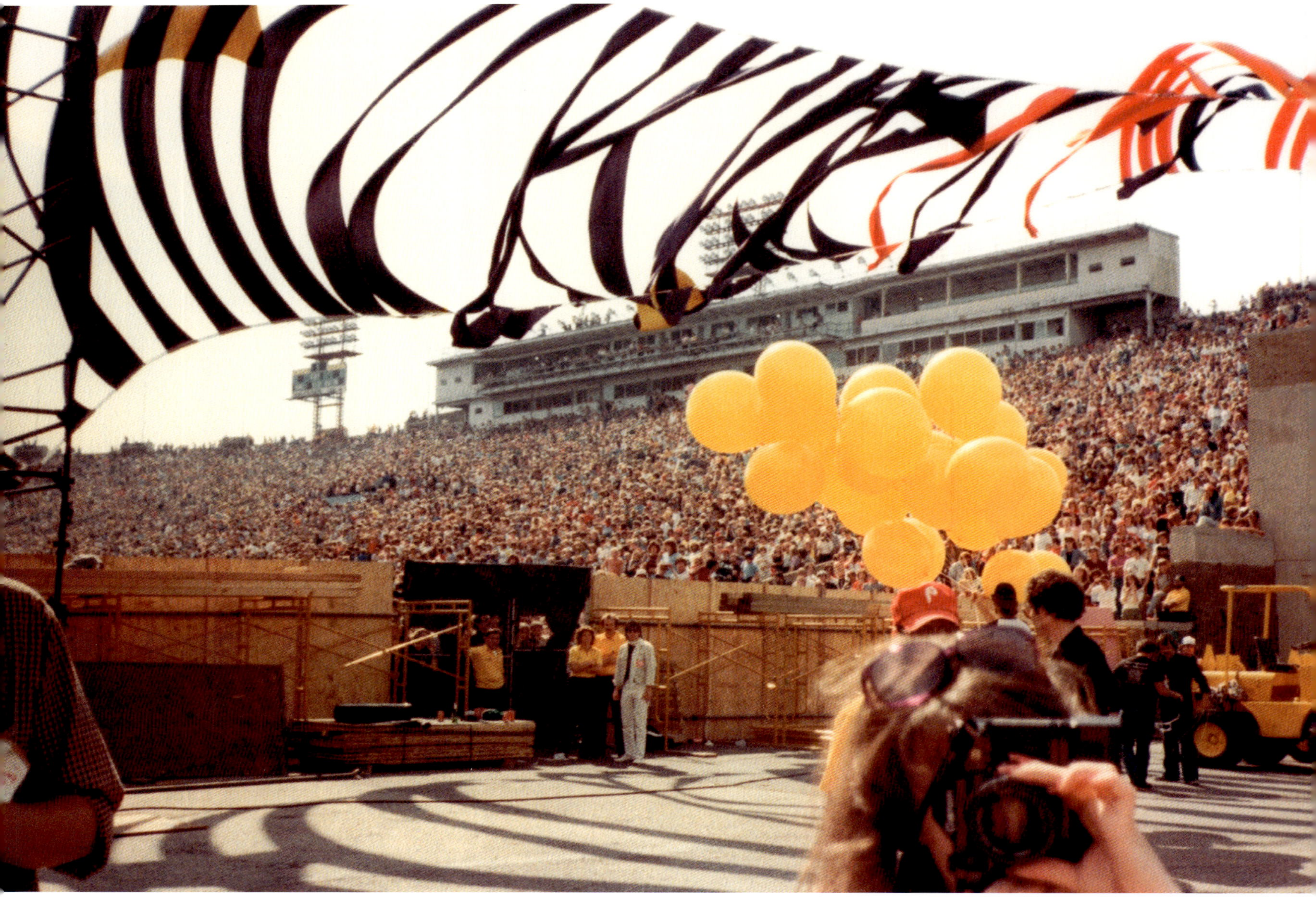

Shot of part of the 90,000-strong audience from backstage at The JFK Stadium in Philadelphia, Pennsylvania – 26 September 1981.

Right: Shot from backstage of part of the 70,000-strong audience at the Jack Murphy Stadium in San Diego, California – 7 October 1981.

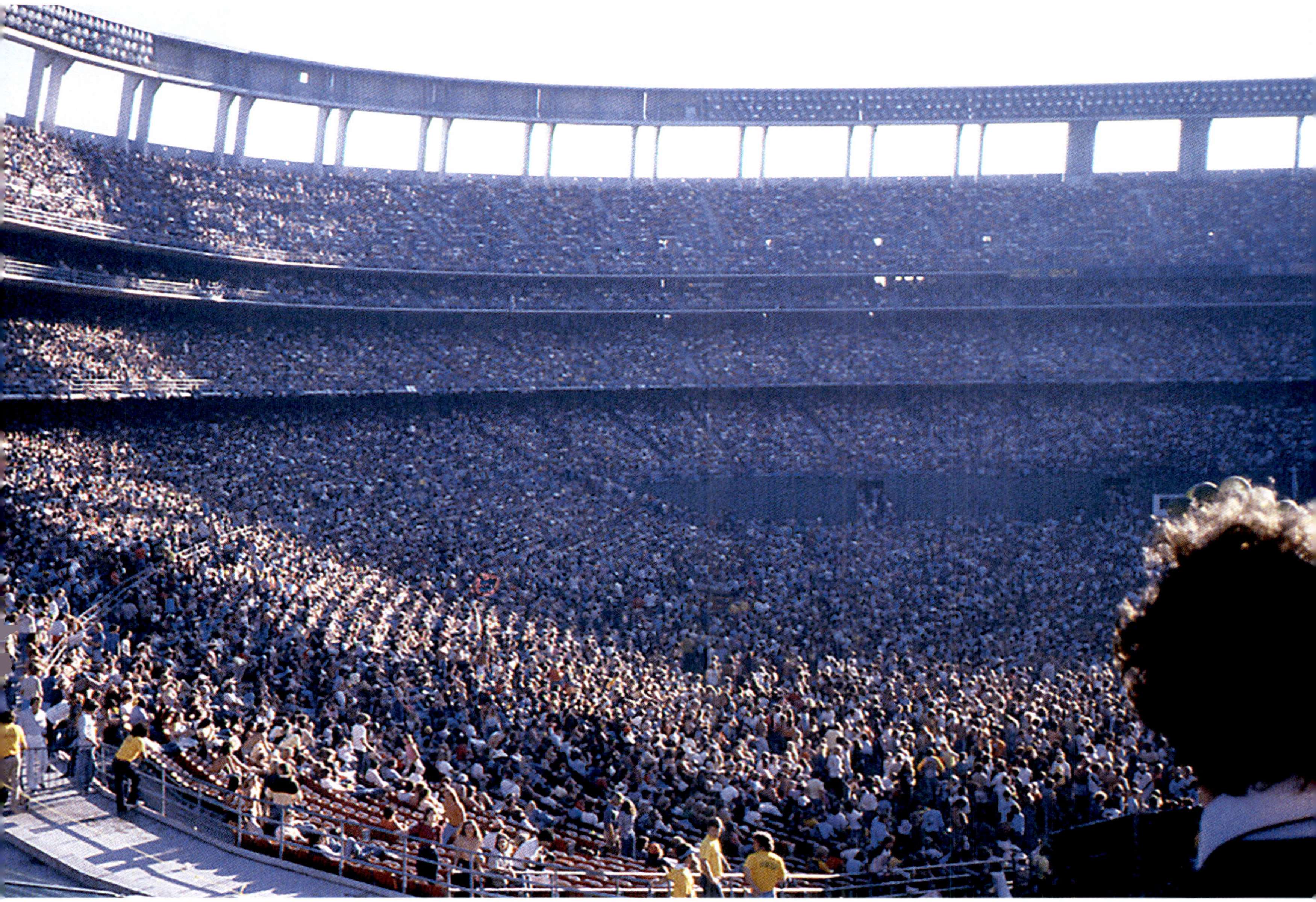

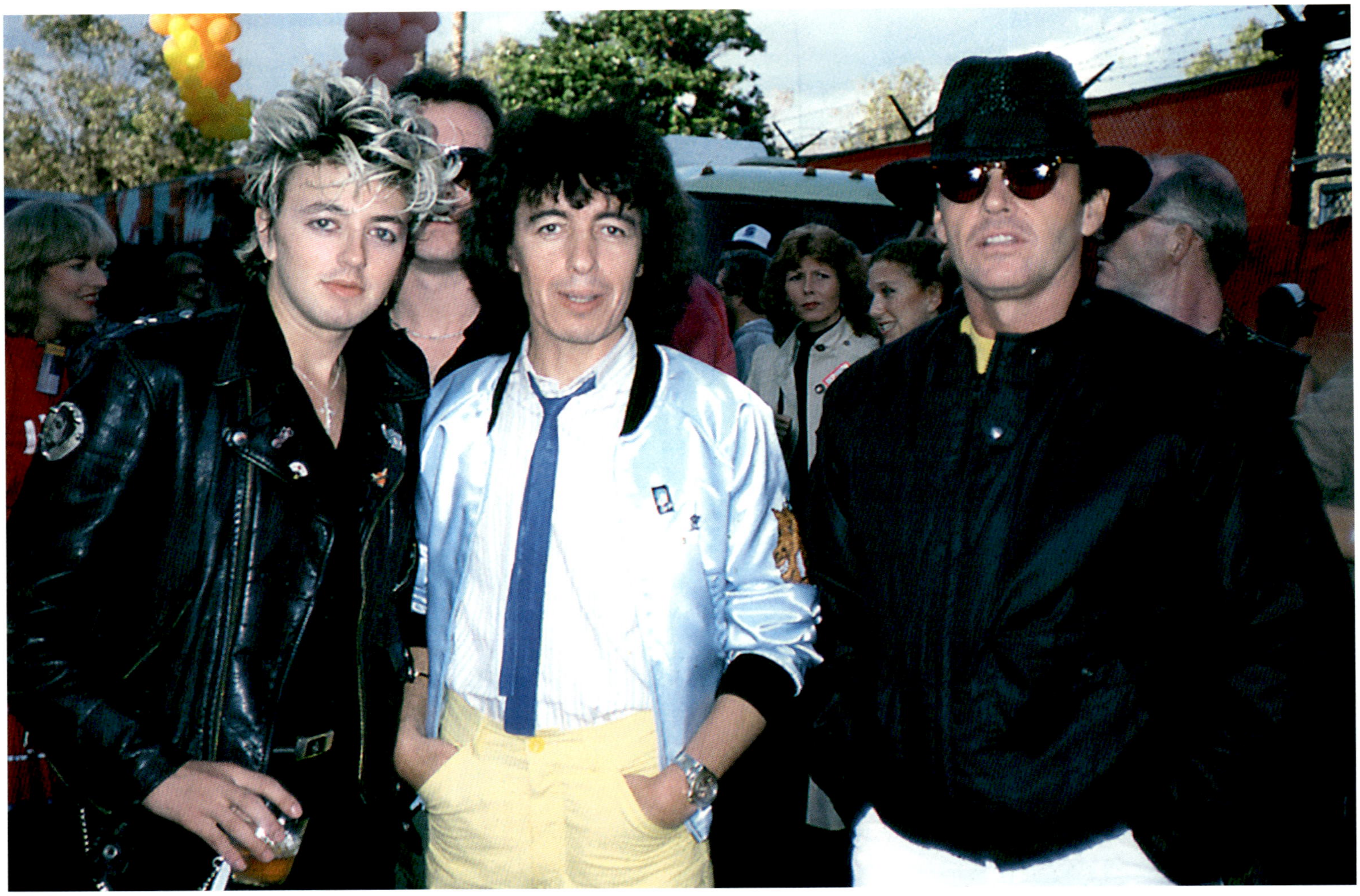

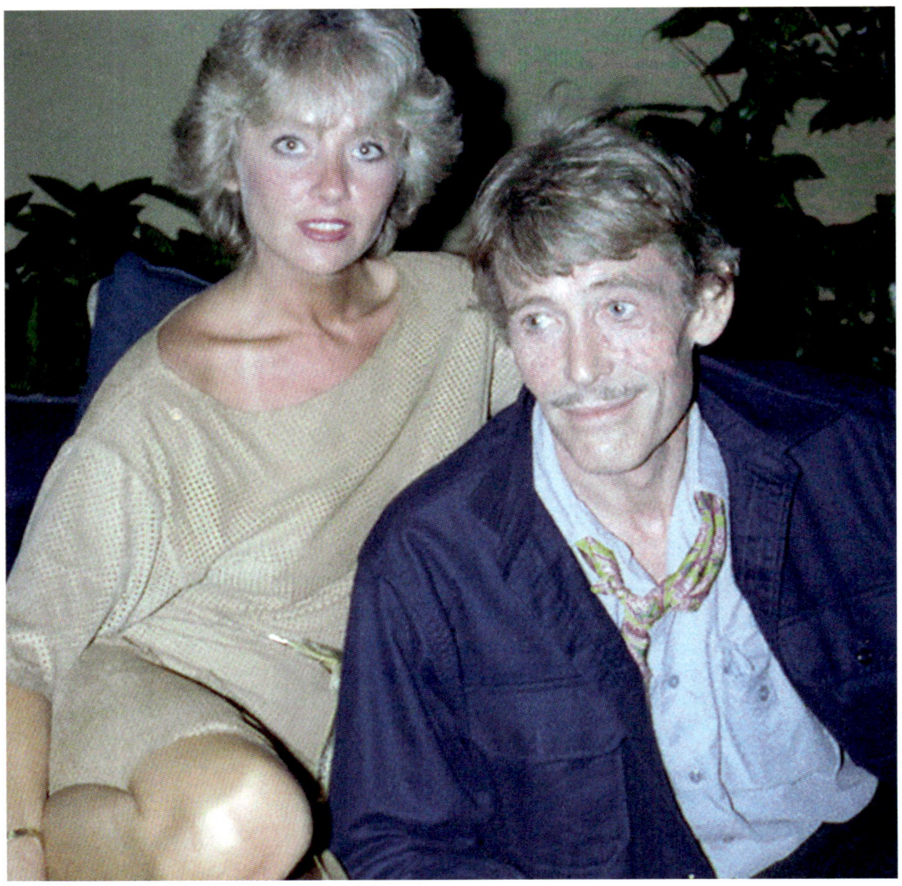

Me with Stray Cat friend Brian Setzer and Jack Nicholson backstage at The Coliseum in Los Angeles – 11 October 1981.

Right: Having a big laugh with Tina Turner at The Coliseum.

Left: My girlfriend Astrid Lundstrom with Peter O'Toole, who I brought to The Coliseum – 9 October 1981.

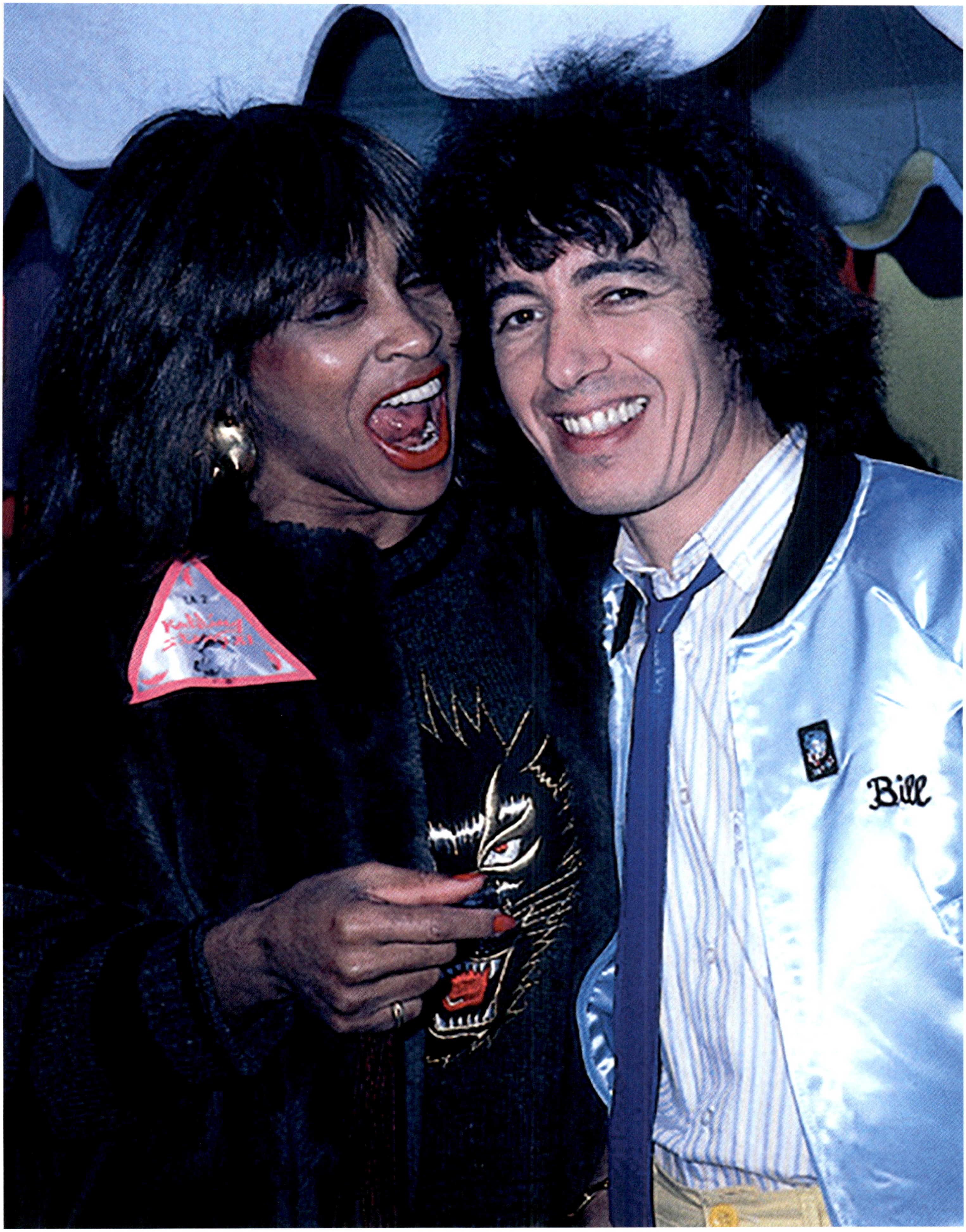
Bill

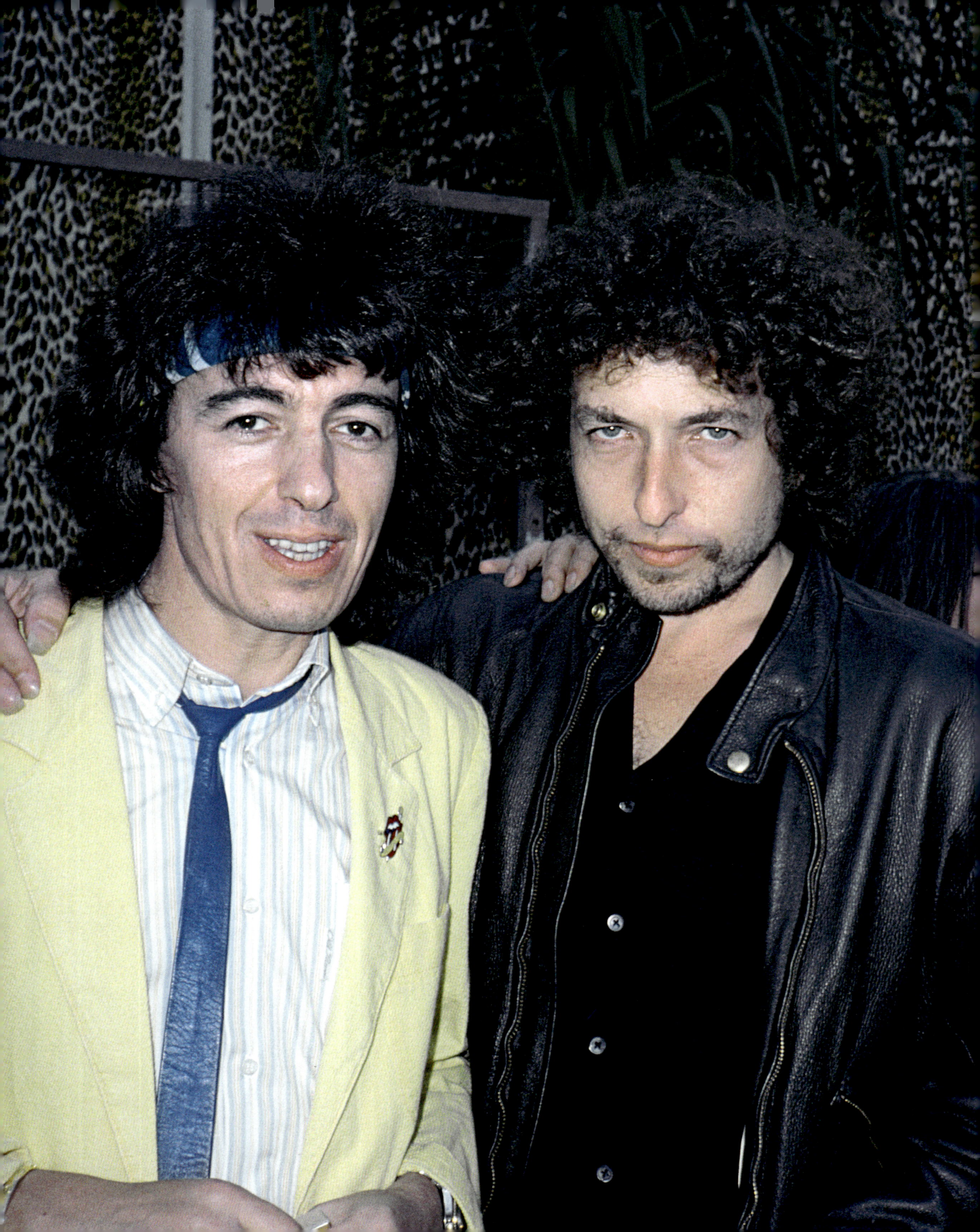

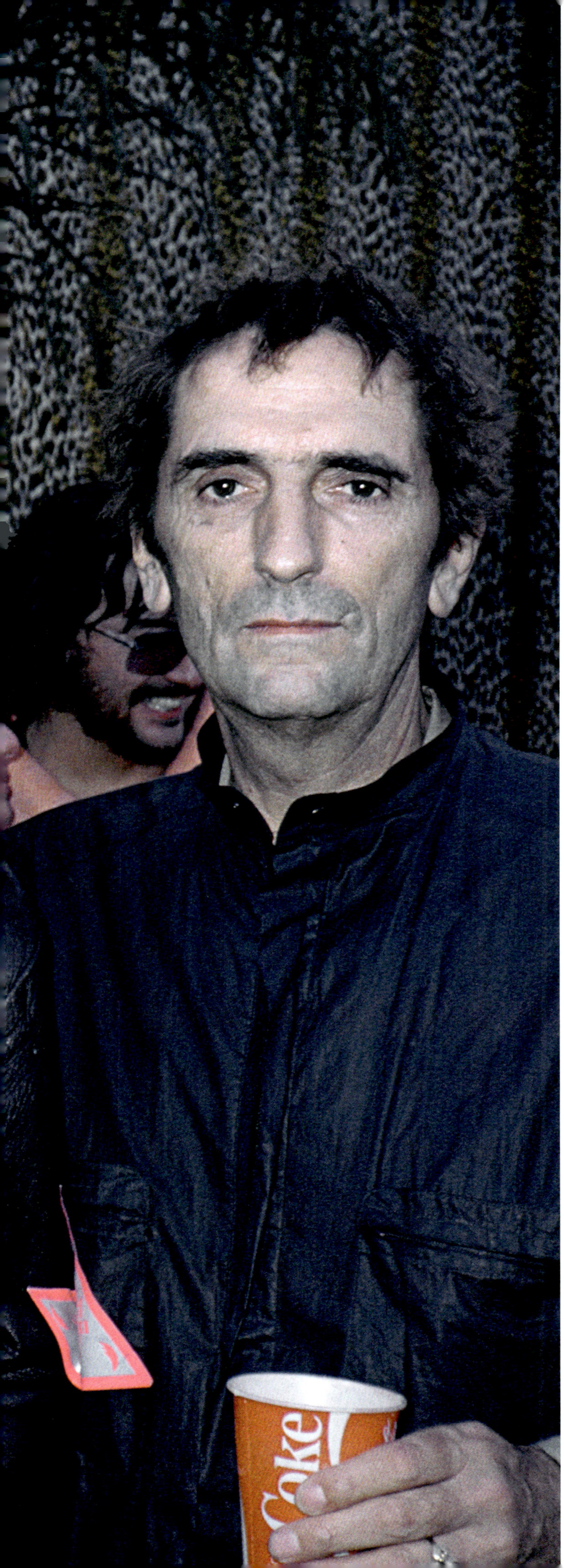

Me with Bob Dylan and actor Harry Dean Stanton backstage at The Coliseum – 11 October 1981.

Below: Me with the talented blues artist Bonnie Raitt backstage at the Jack Murphy Stadium in San Diego – 7 October 1981.

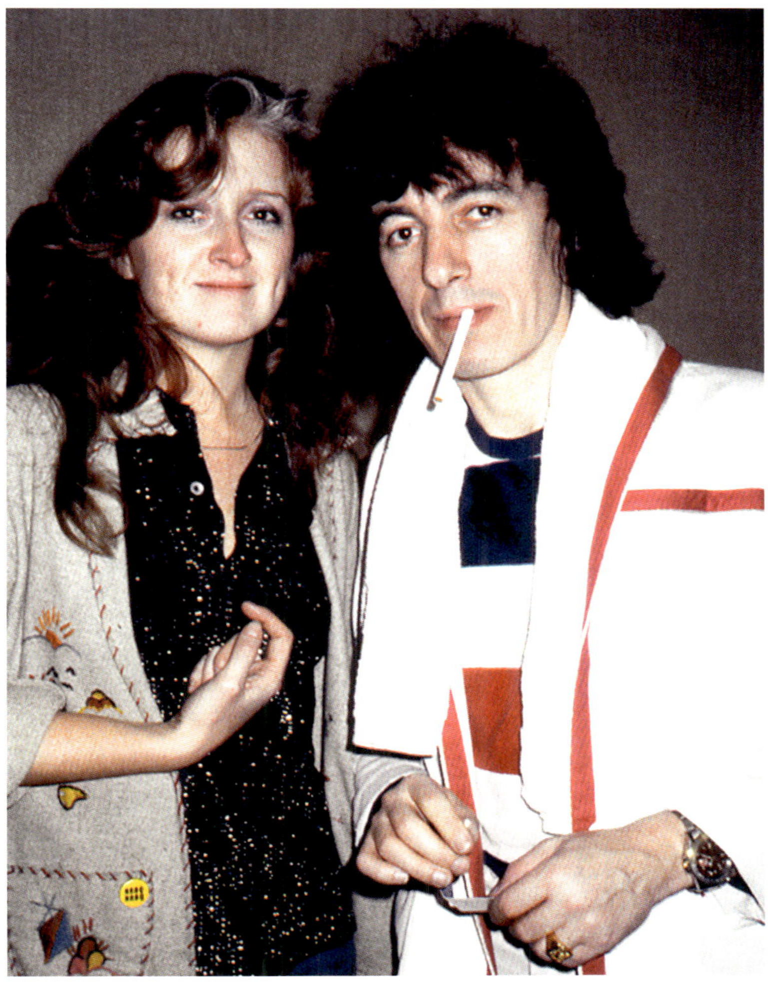

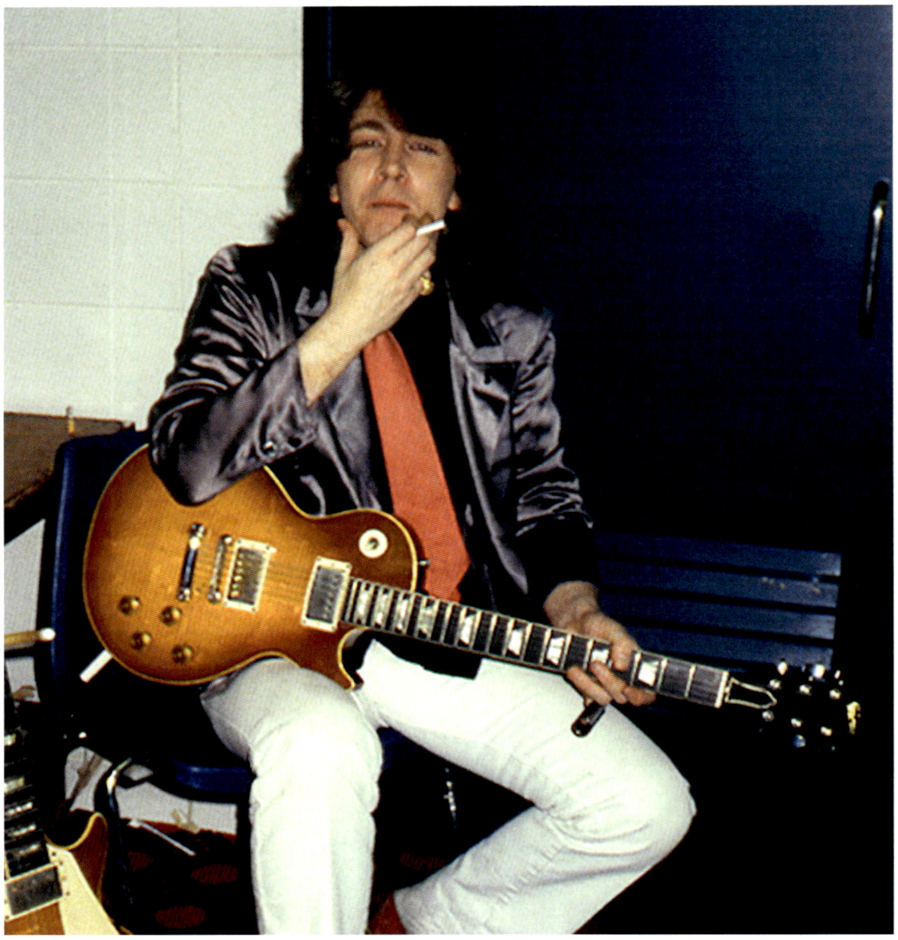

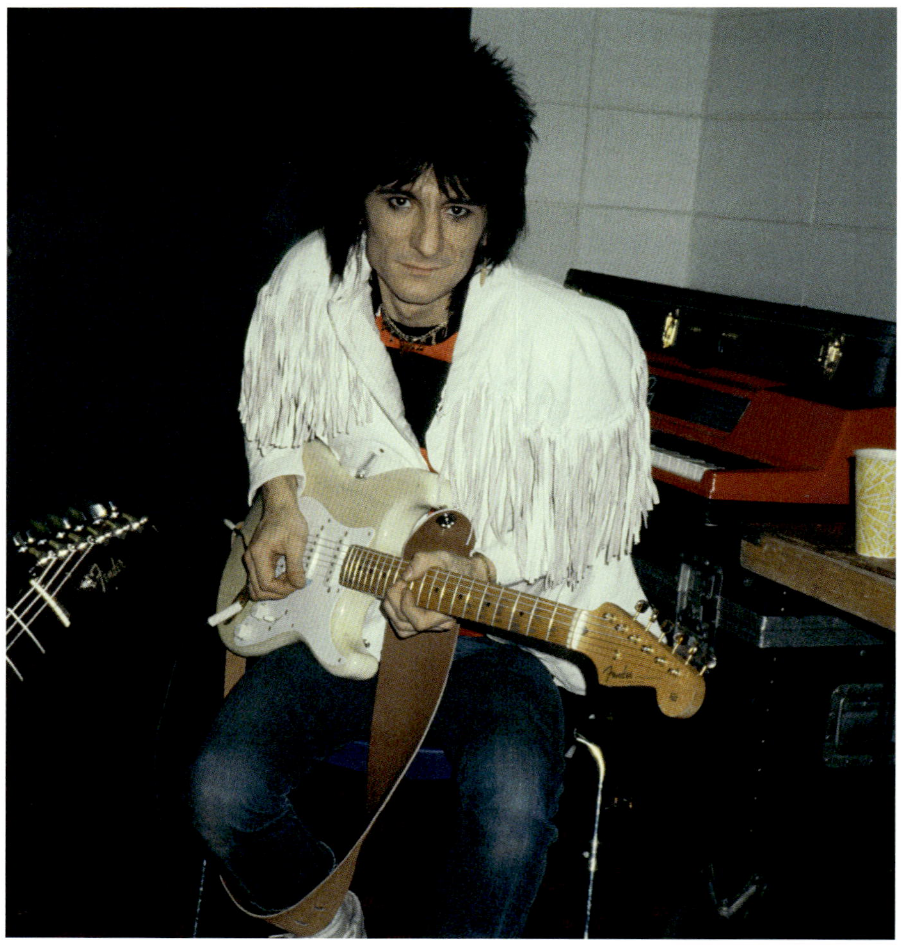

Mick Taylor rehearsing with Ronnie and Keith backstage before joining the Stones onstage at their concert at the Kemper Arena in Kansas City – 14 December 1981.

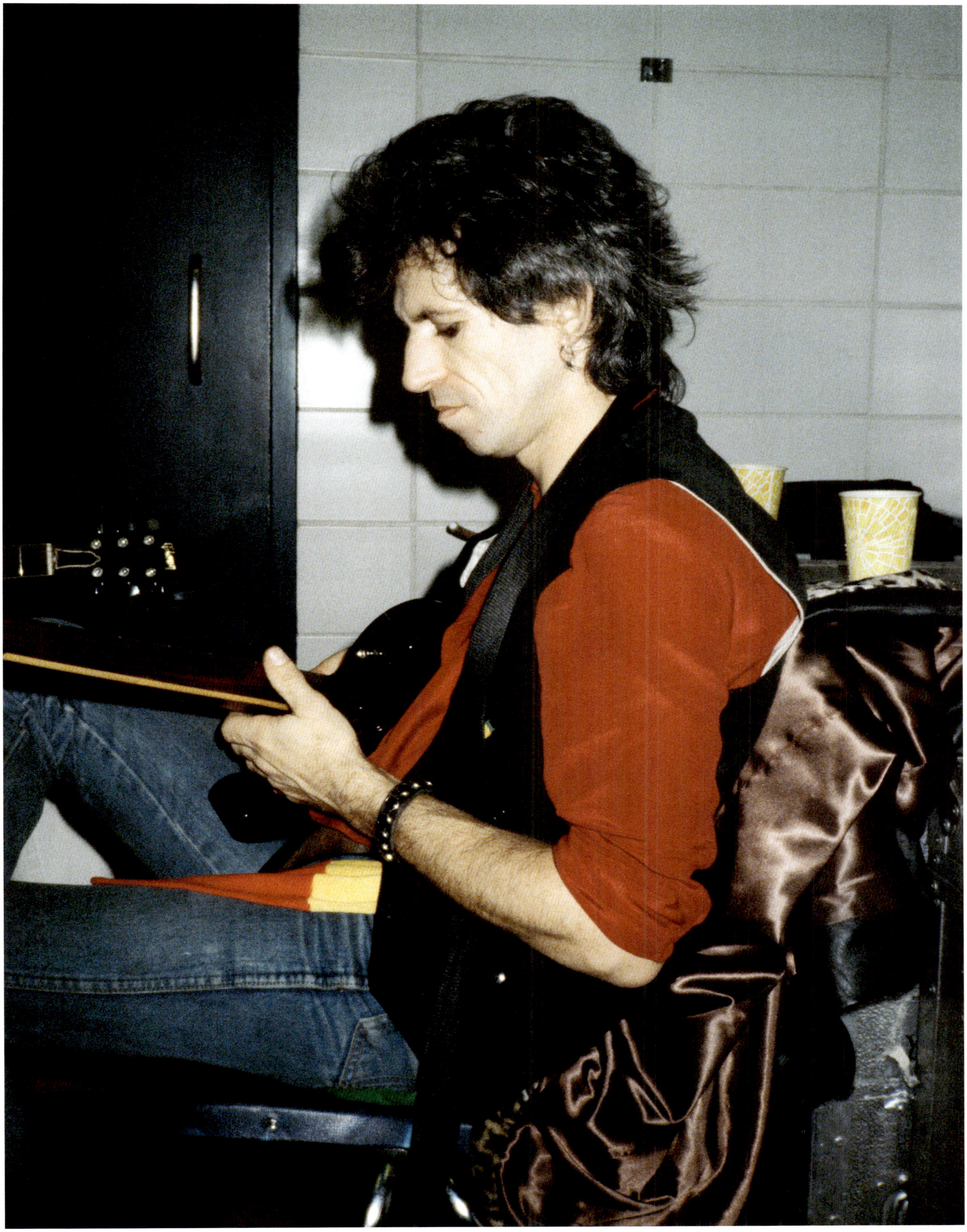

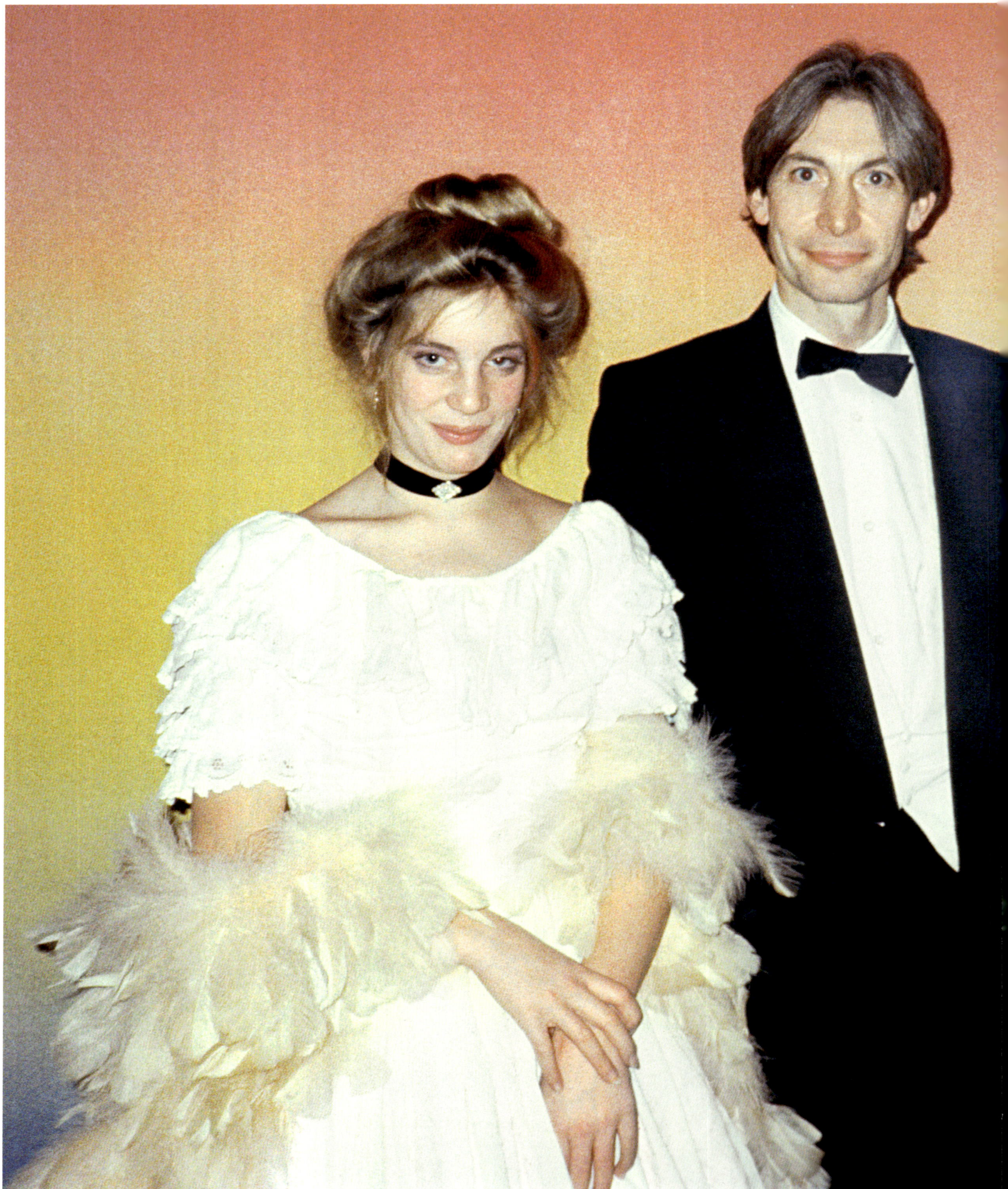

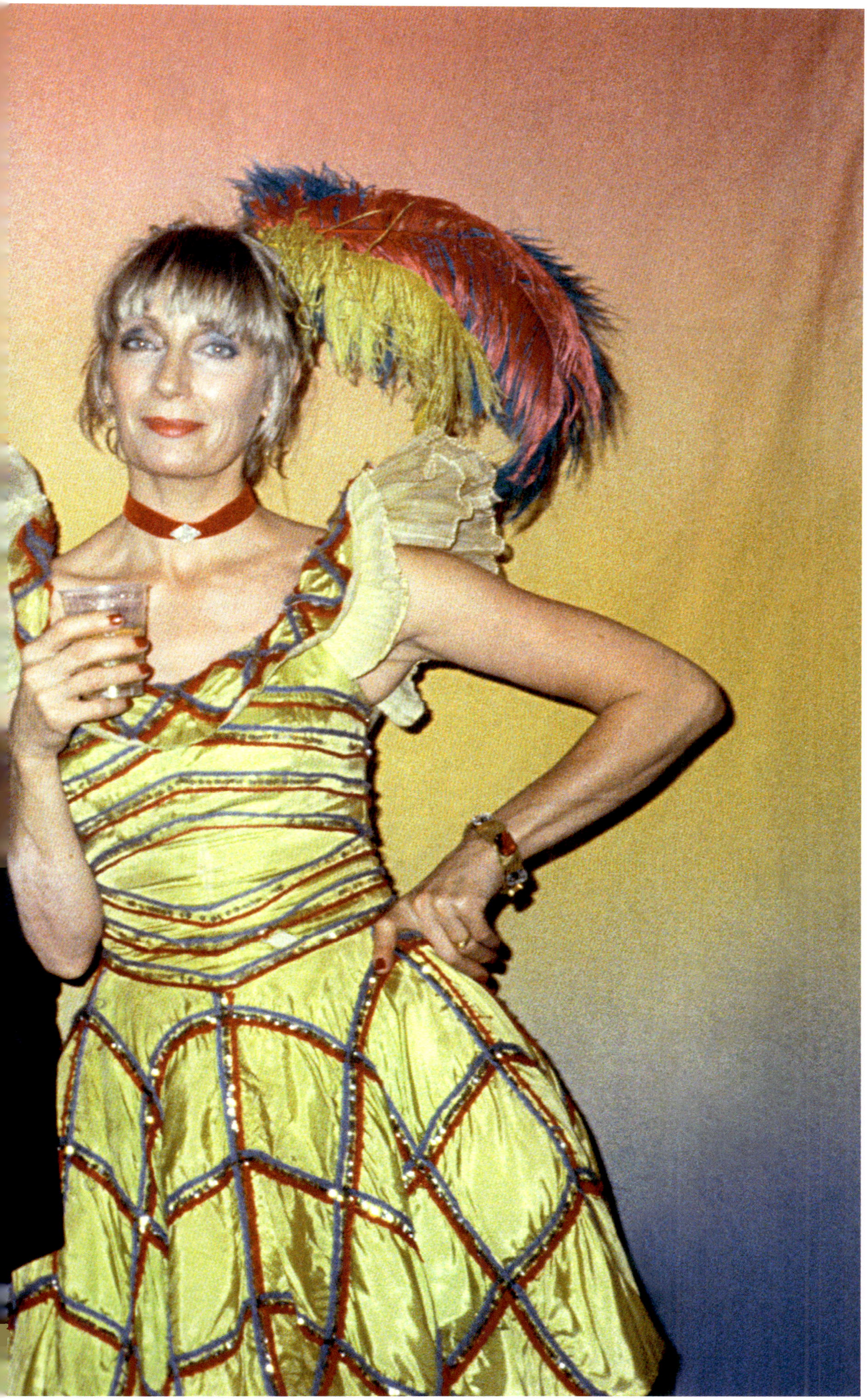

Charlie with wife Shirley and daughter Seraphina, all dressed up for the New Orleans riverboat party – 3 December 1981.

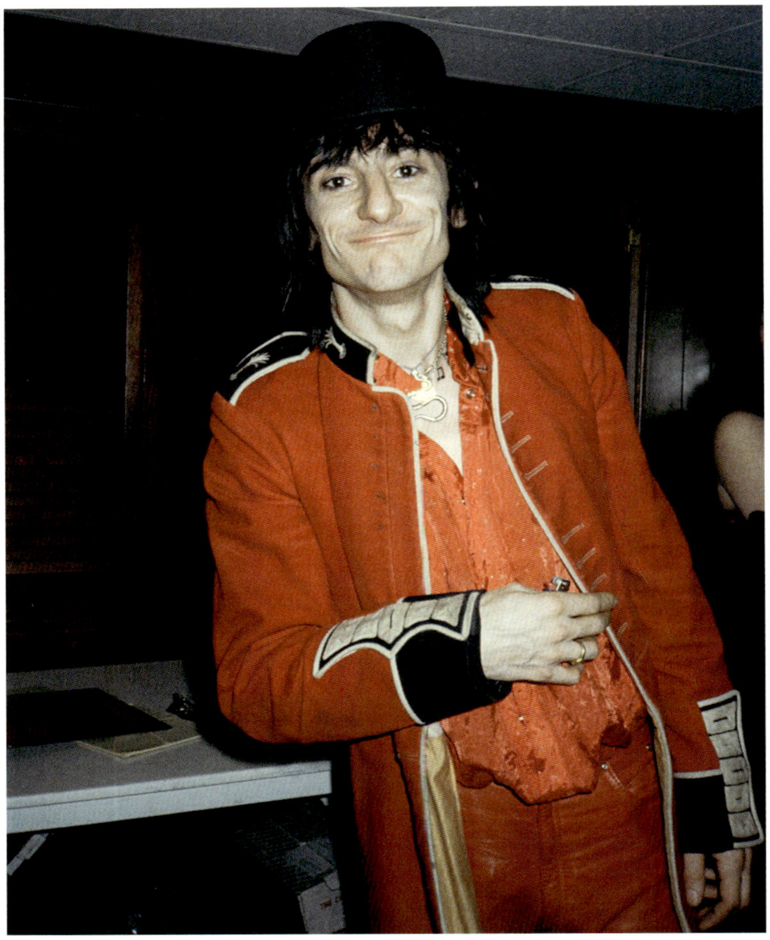

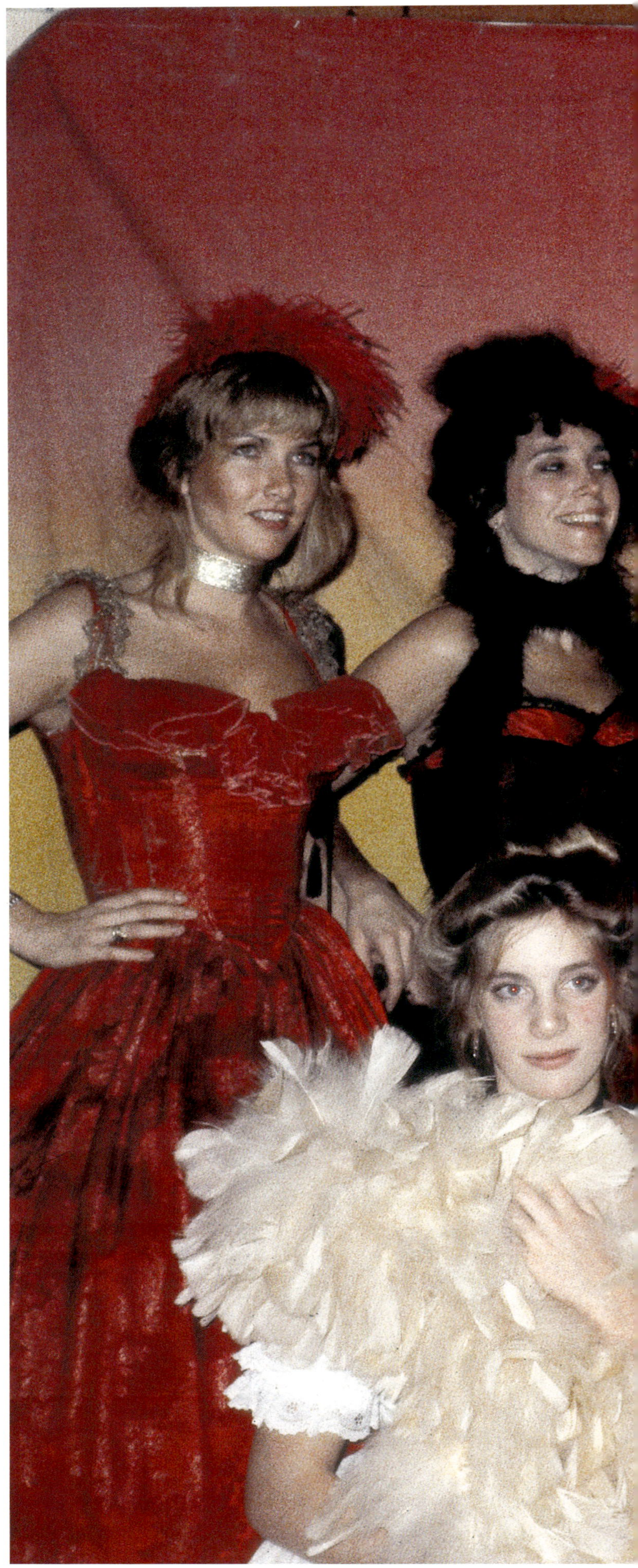

Mick amongst the ladies on the New Orleans riverboat party – 3 December 1981.
Above: Ronnie all dressed up for the Stones' New Orleans riverboat party – as above.

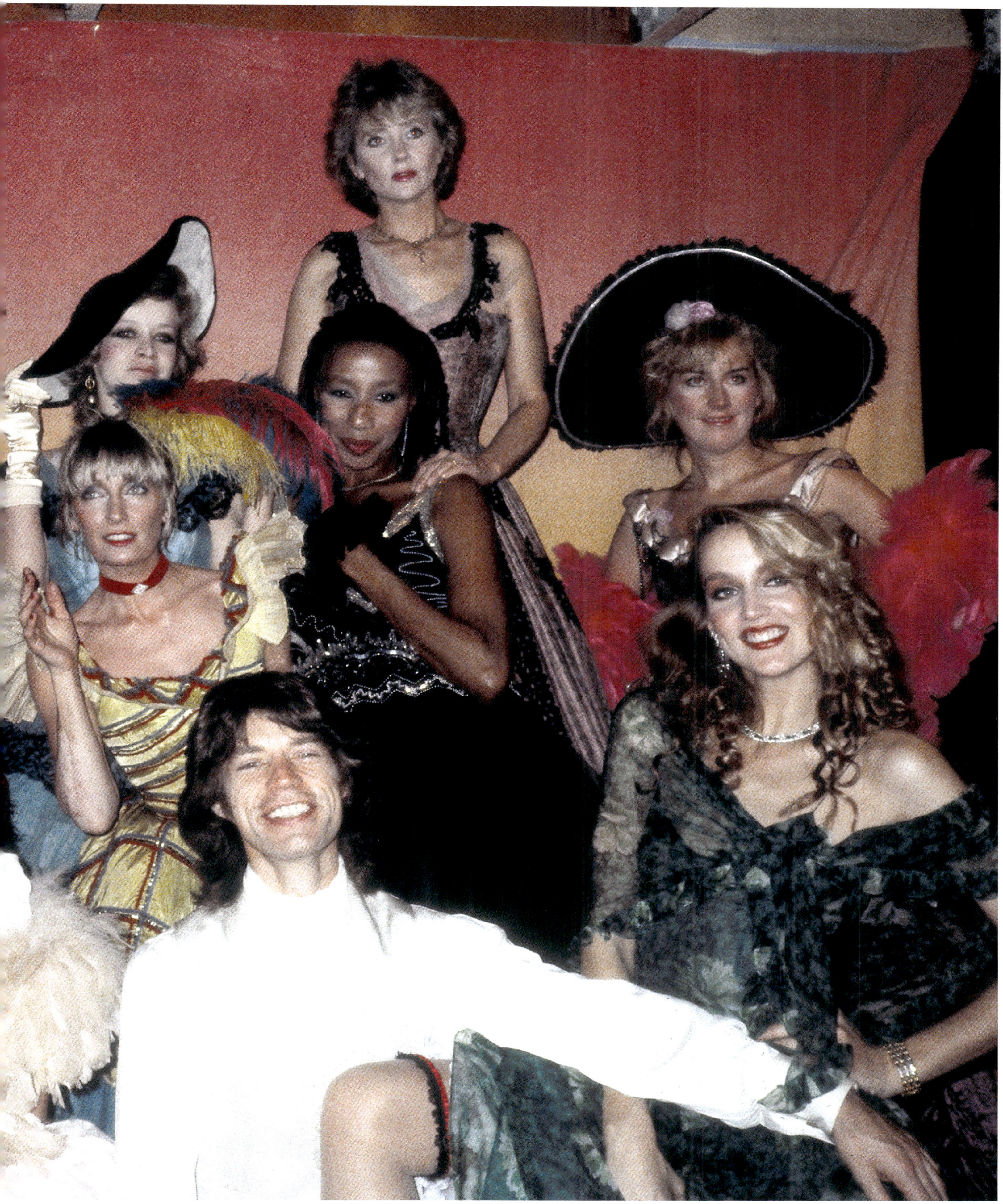

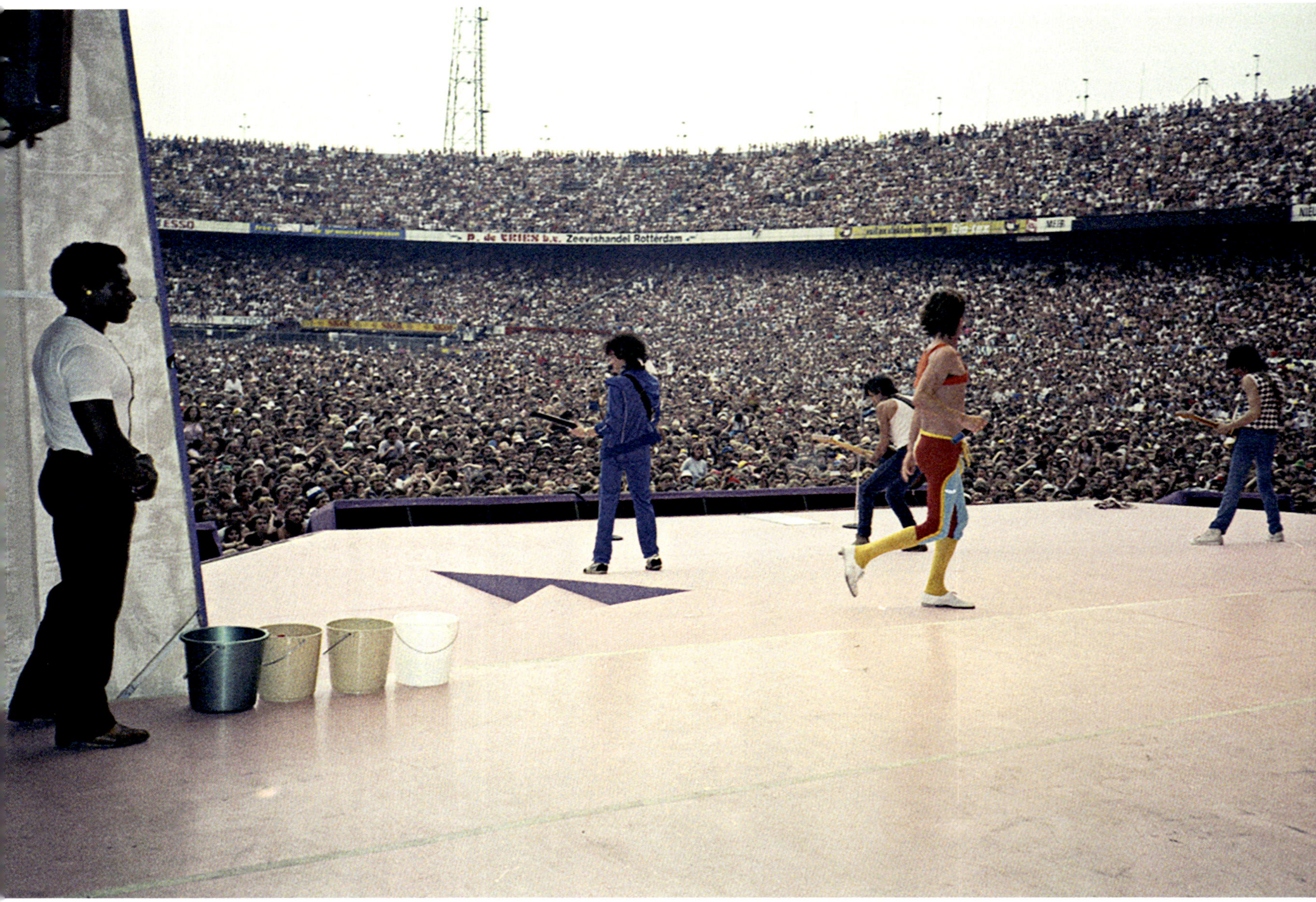

Shot from behind of the Stones onstage at The Ullevi in Gothenburg, Sweden – 19 June 1982.
Right: The Stones' audience at the Slane Castle concert in County Meath, in Dublin, Eire – 24 July 1982

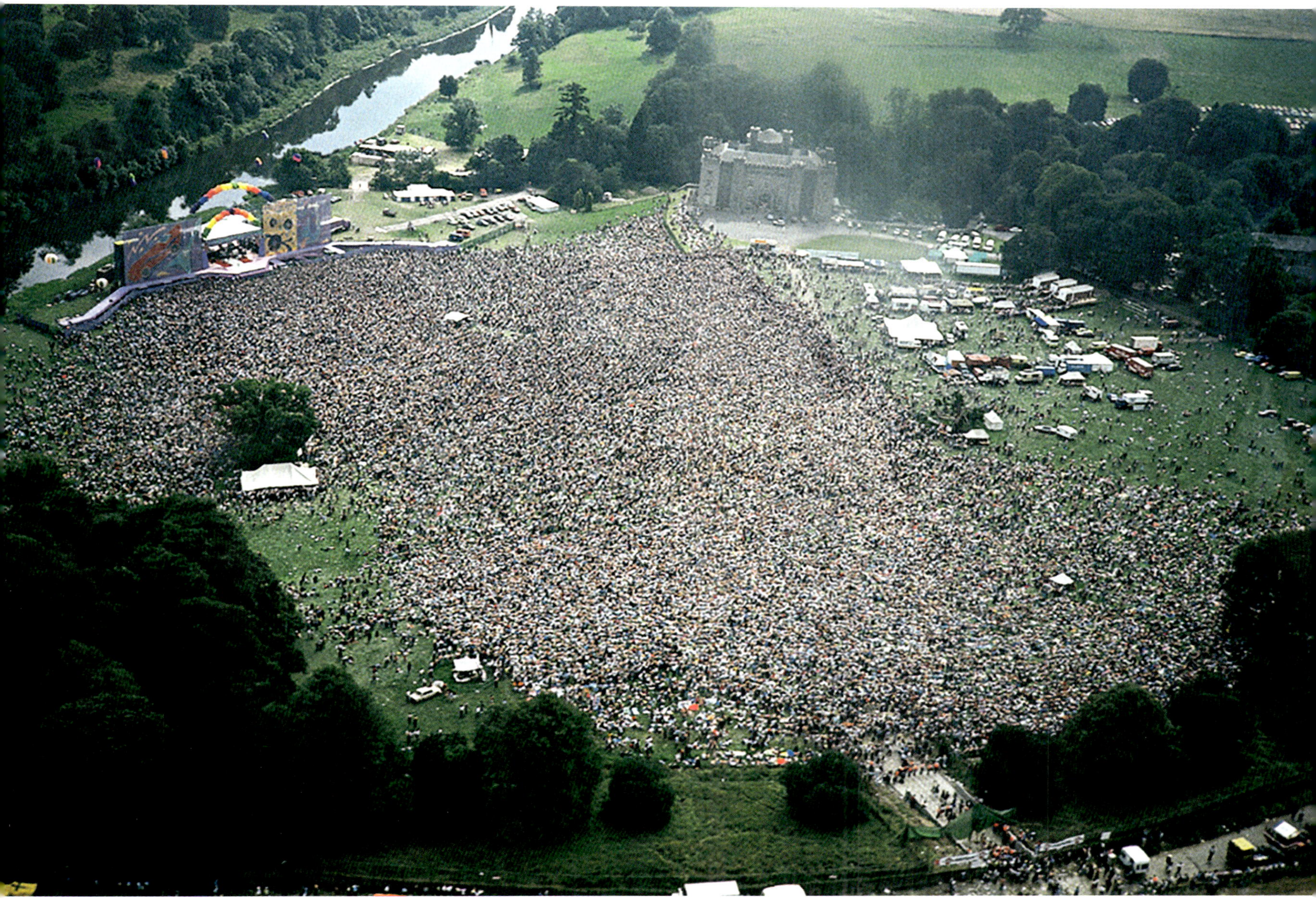

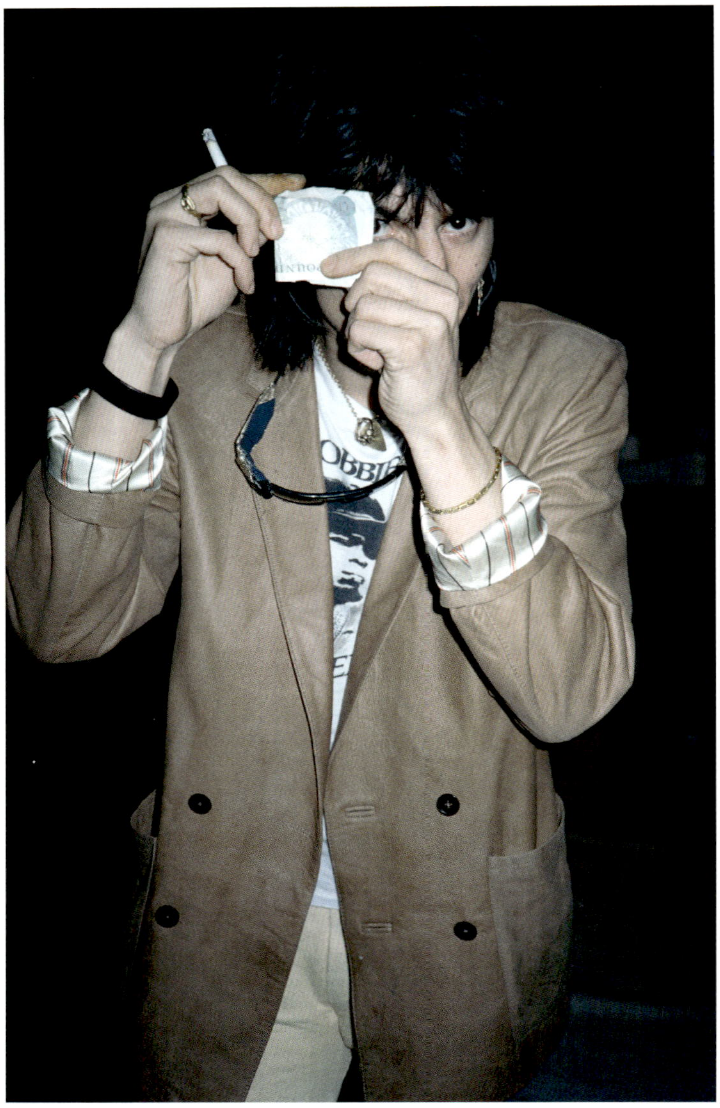

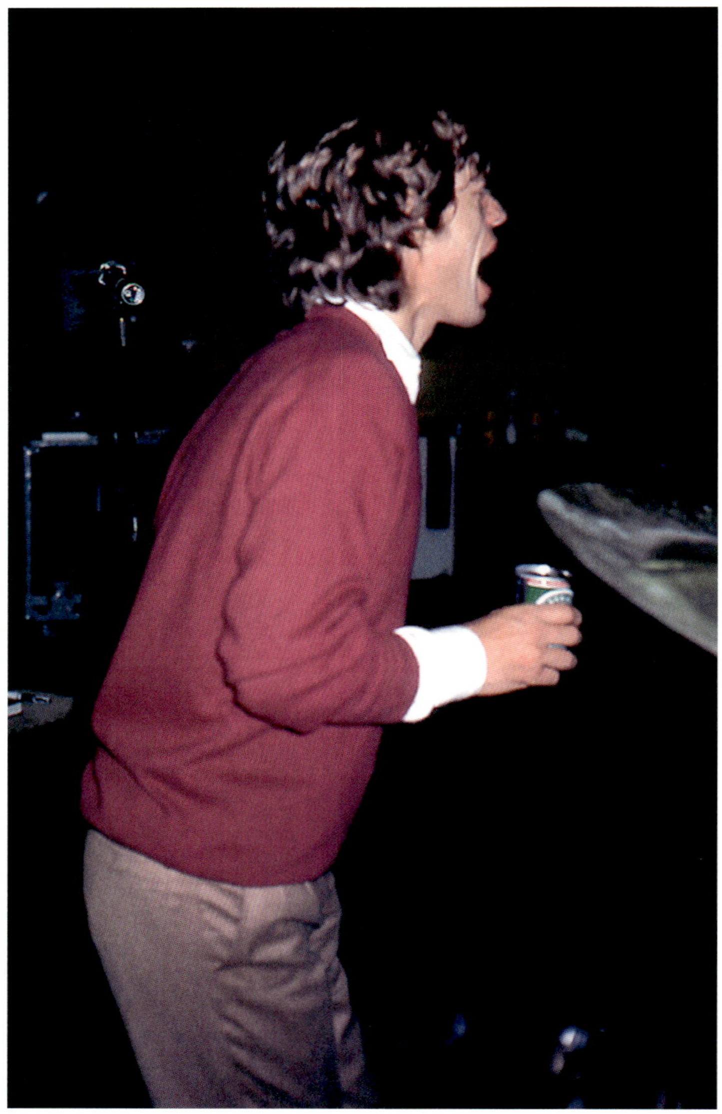

Ronnie flashing his Scottish paper money at The Capitol Theatre, Aberdeen, Scotland – 26 May 1982.
Right: Mick highly amused at the Stones' rehearsals at Shepperton Studios, Surrey, England – 7 May 1982.
Far right: Keith flashing his new suggestive t-shirt at the Stones' rehearsals at Shepperton Studios – 17 May 1982.

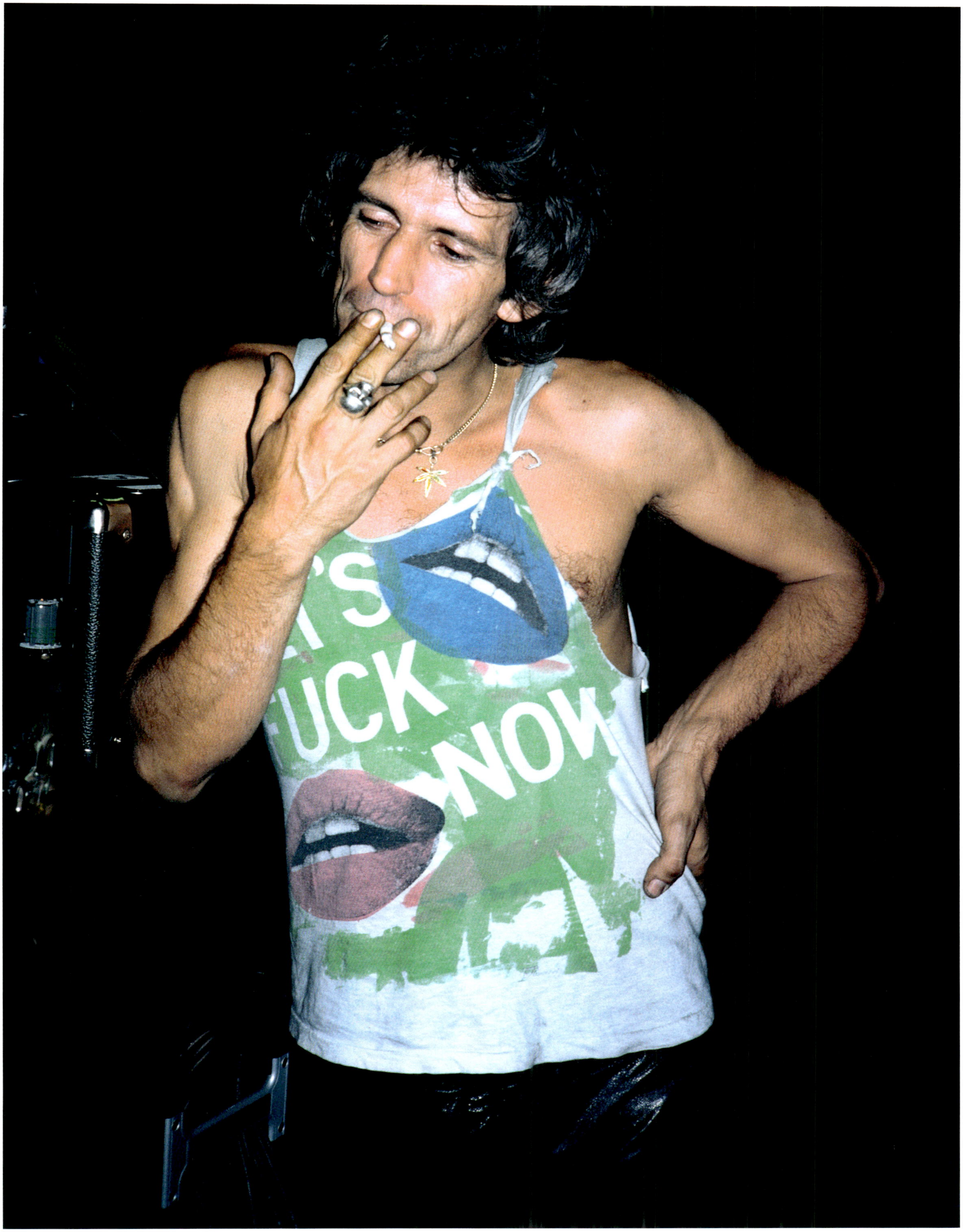
NOW

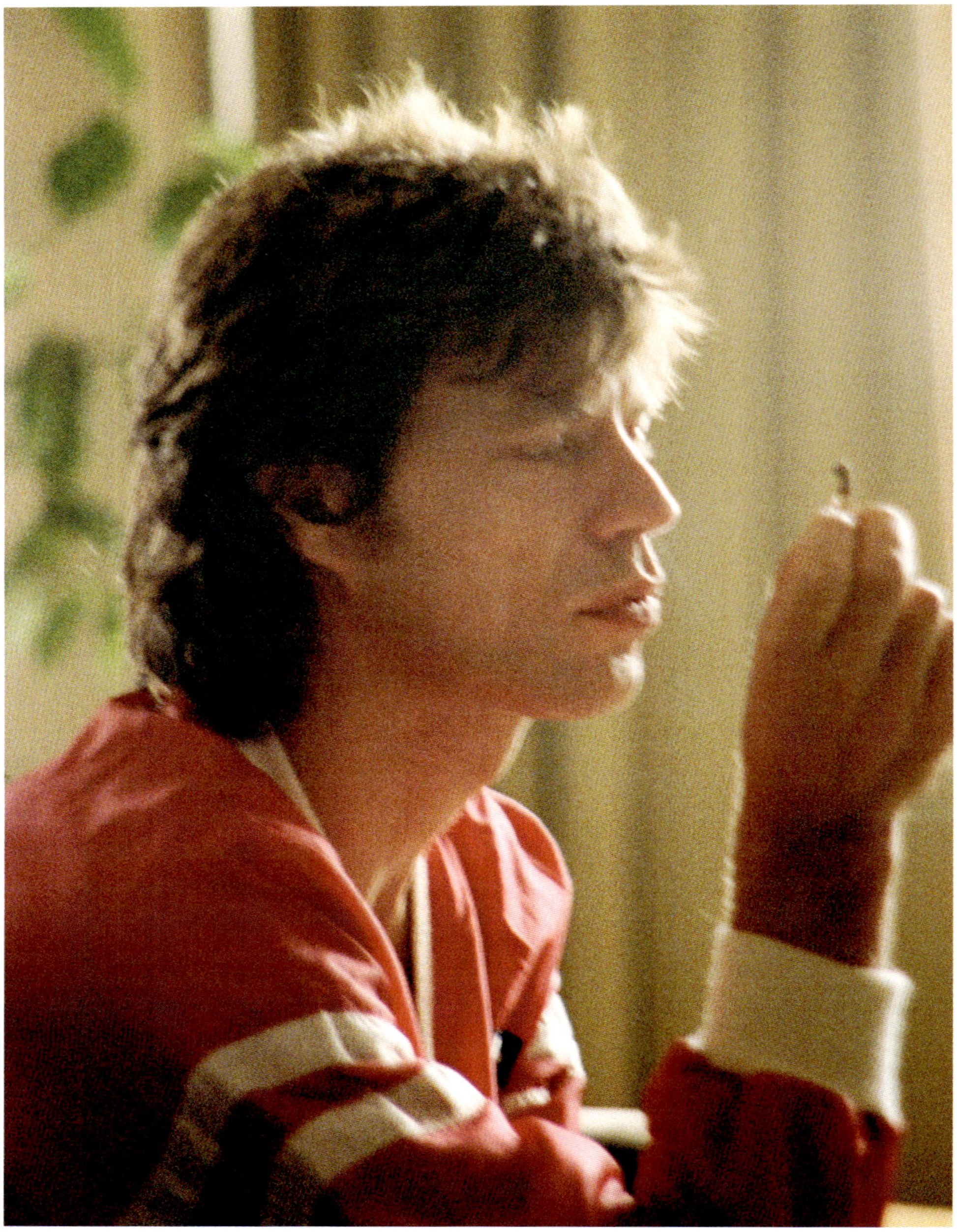

Mick and Jerry arrived and relaxed in my suite in Frankfurt, West Germany, where I shot Mick smoking and thinking, while Jerry was enjoying a dreamy moment, having matched the room's colours perfectly – 1 July 1982.

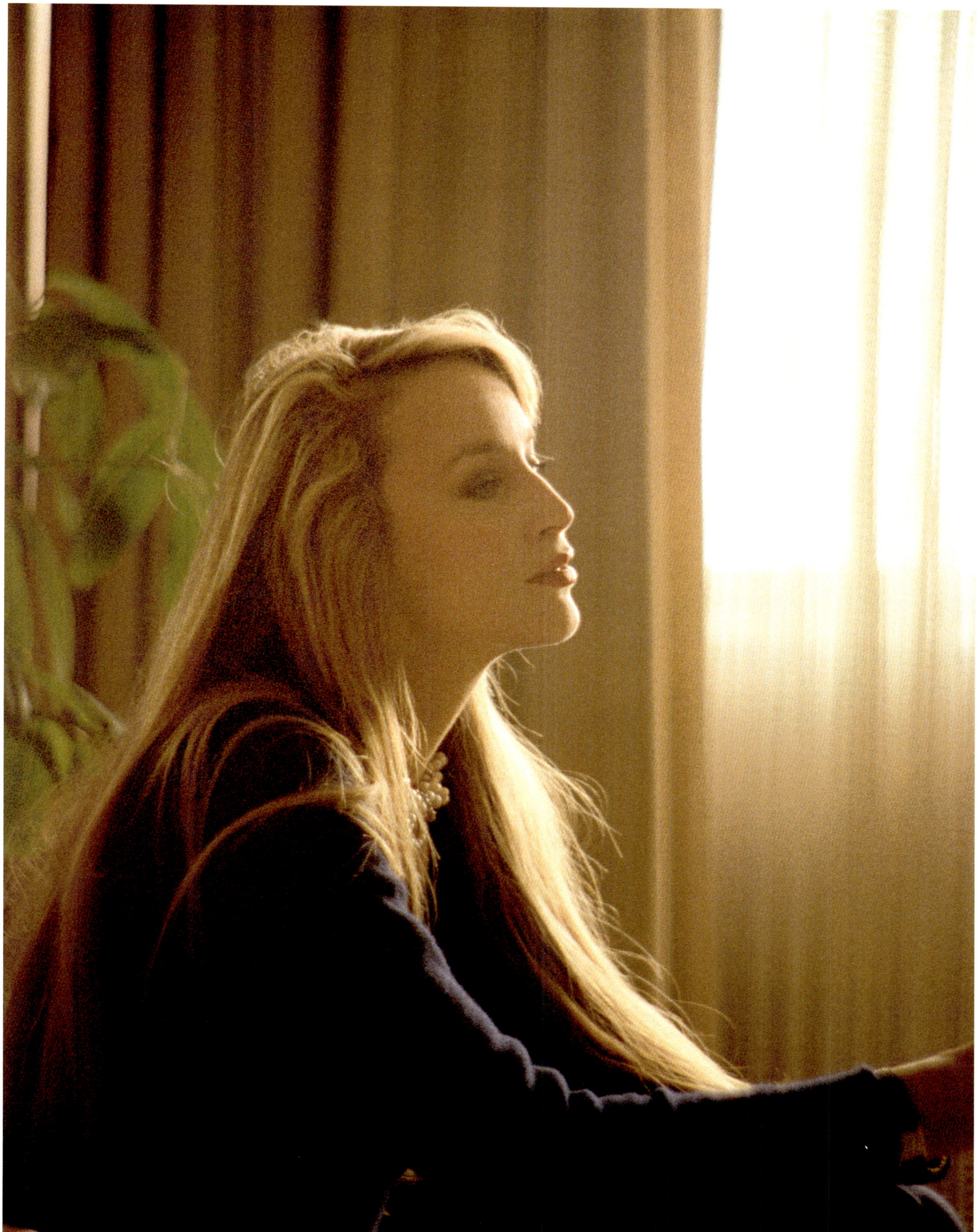

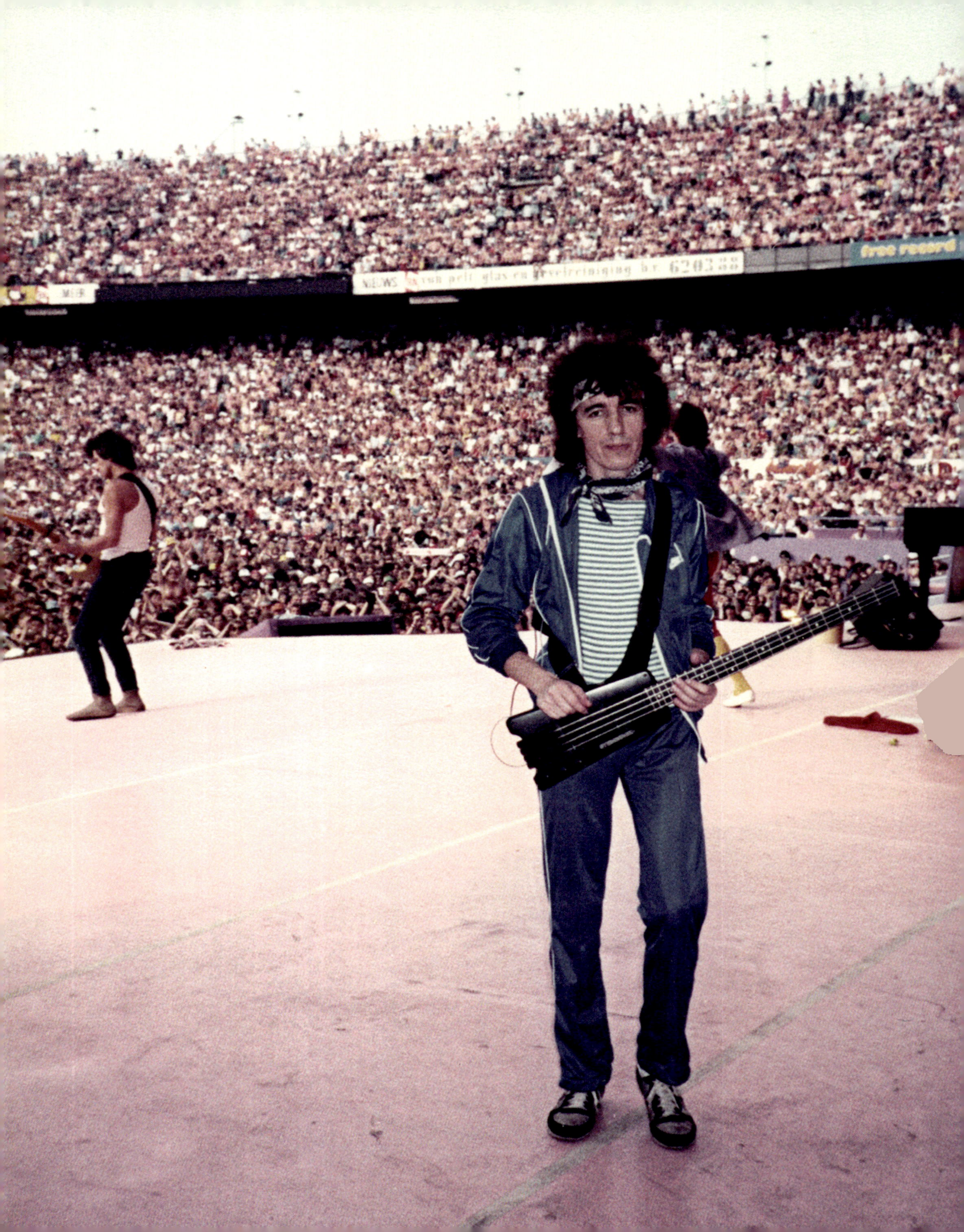
MEER
NIEUWS
free record

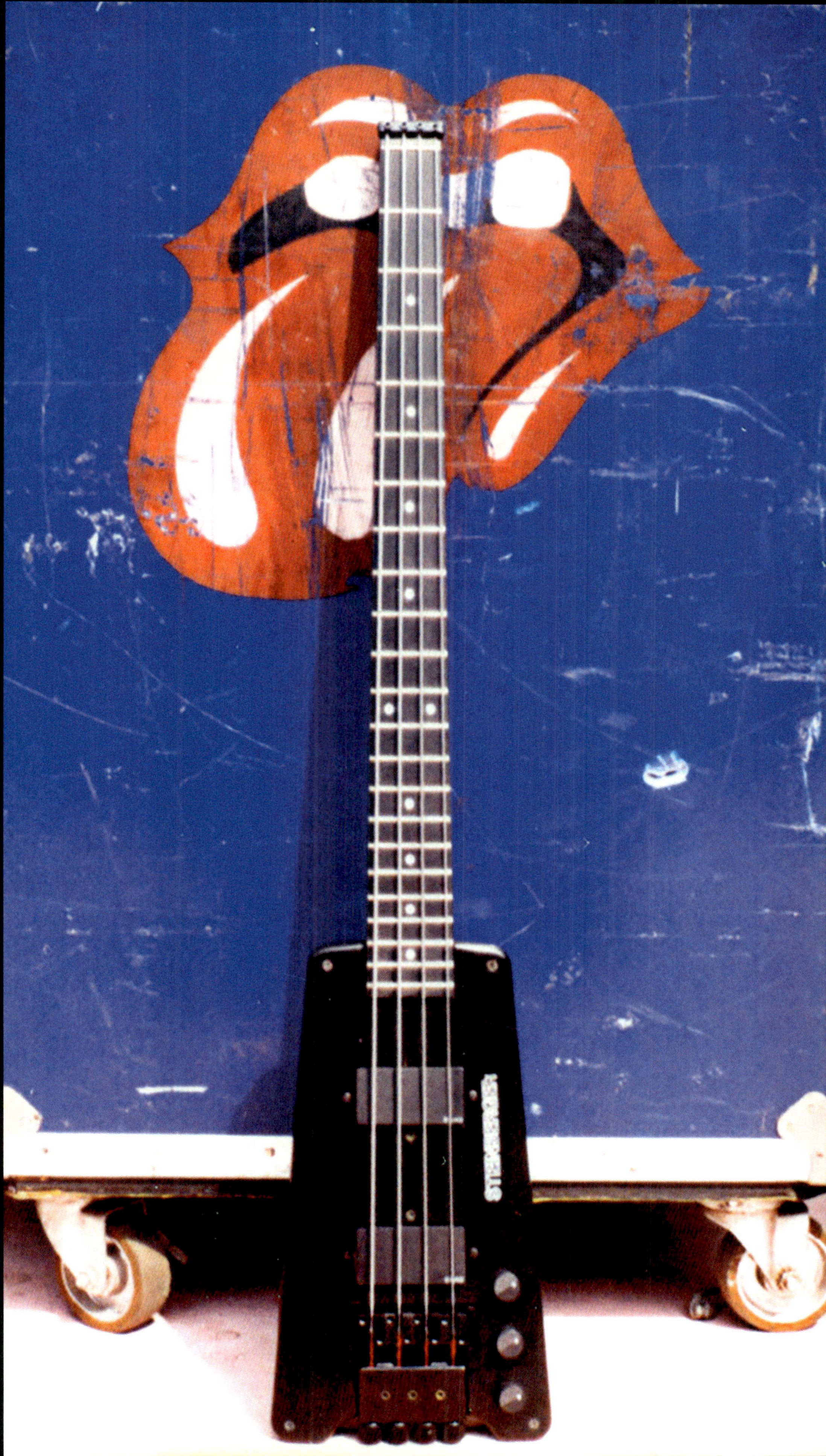

My bass guitar leaning against the flight case while the Stones were recording at the Olympic Studios, Barnes – 27 August 1982.

Left: Stones onstage from behind with a partial view of the audience at the Feyenoord Football Stadium in Rotterdam, Holland – 5 June 1982.

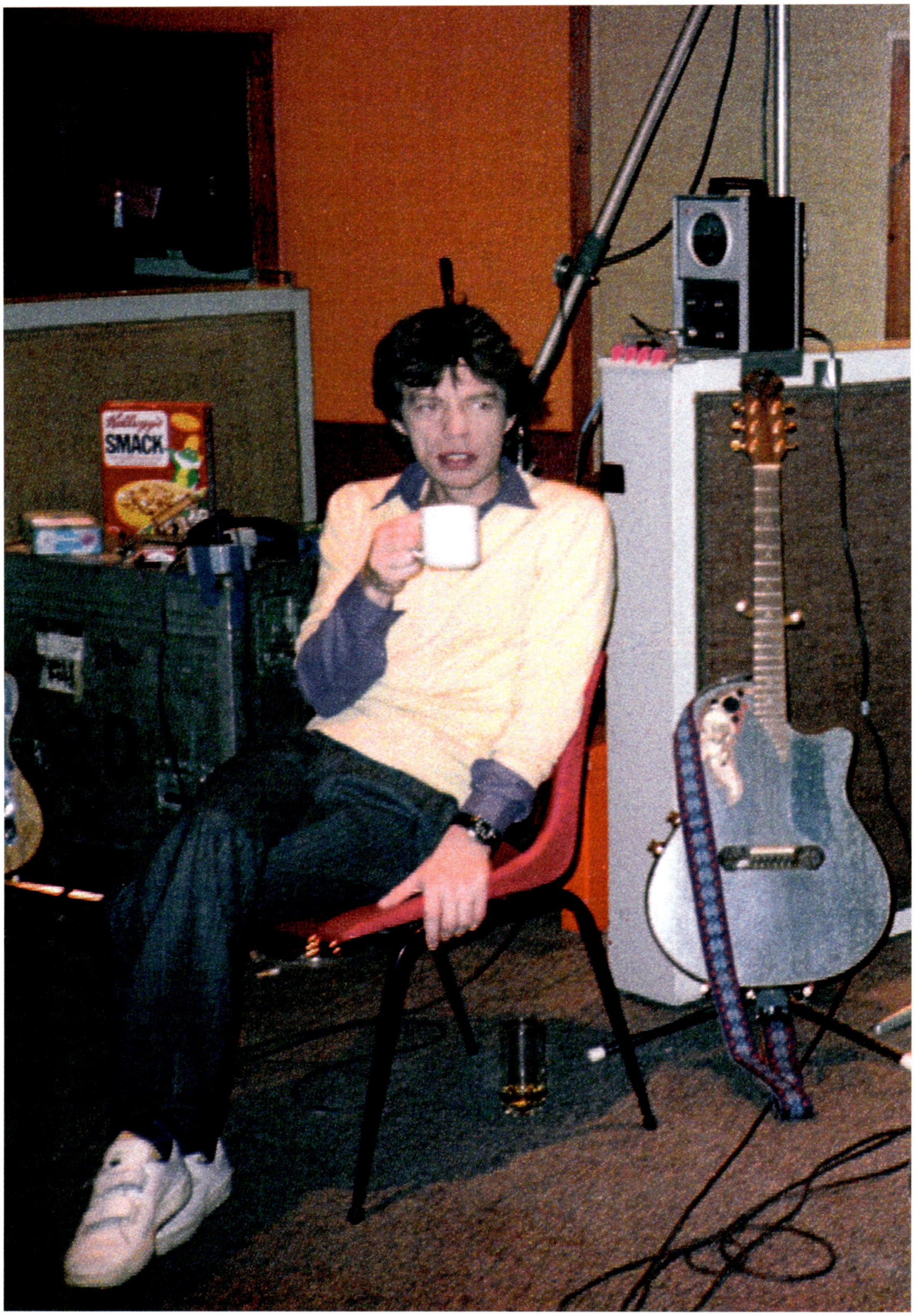

Mick enjoying 'a cuppa' at the Pathé Marconi recording studio, in Paris, while Keith laid down a riff to work on – 3 December 1982.

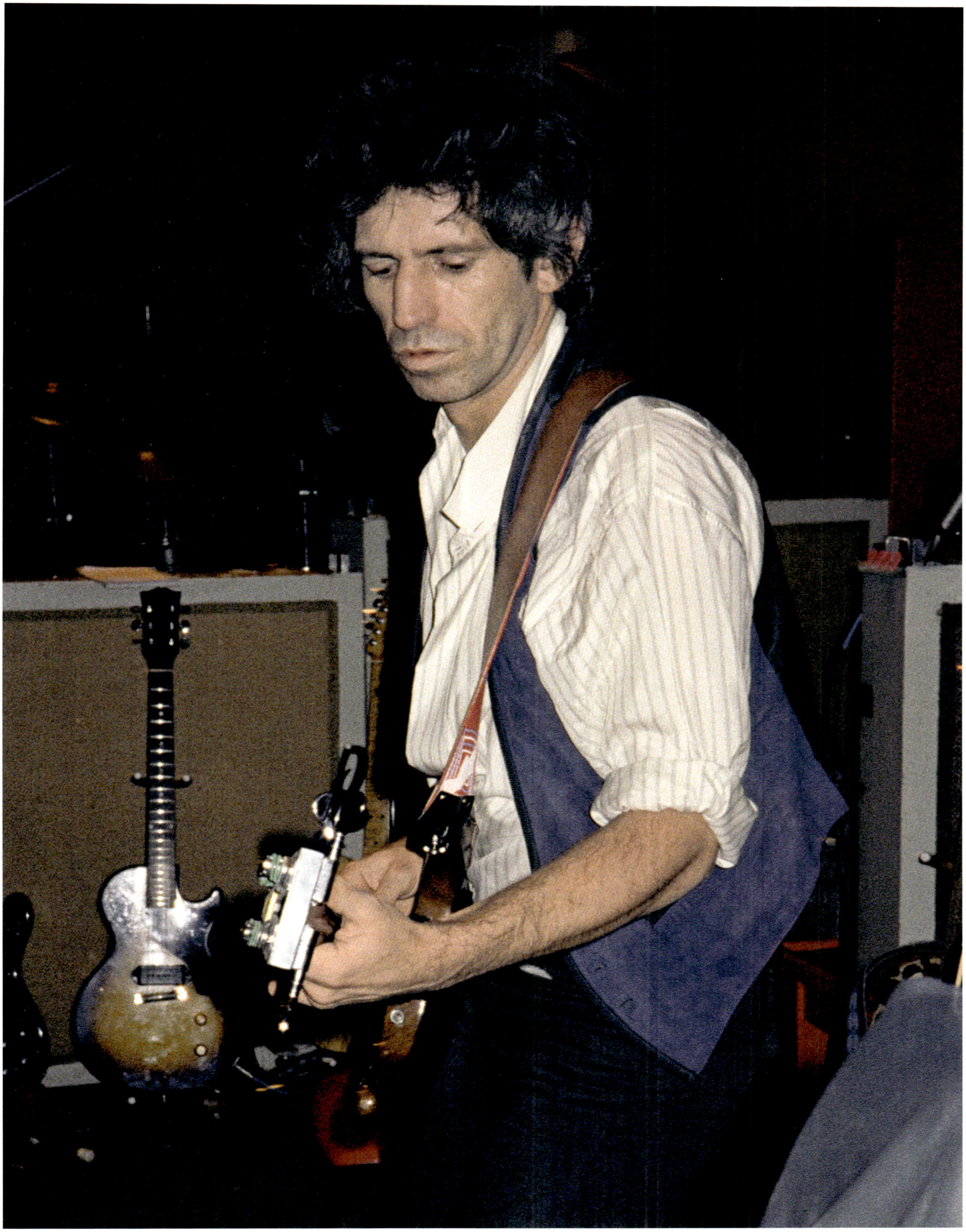

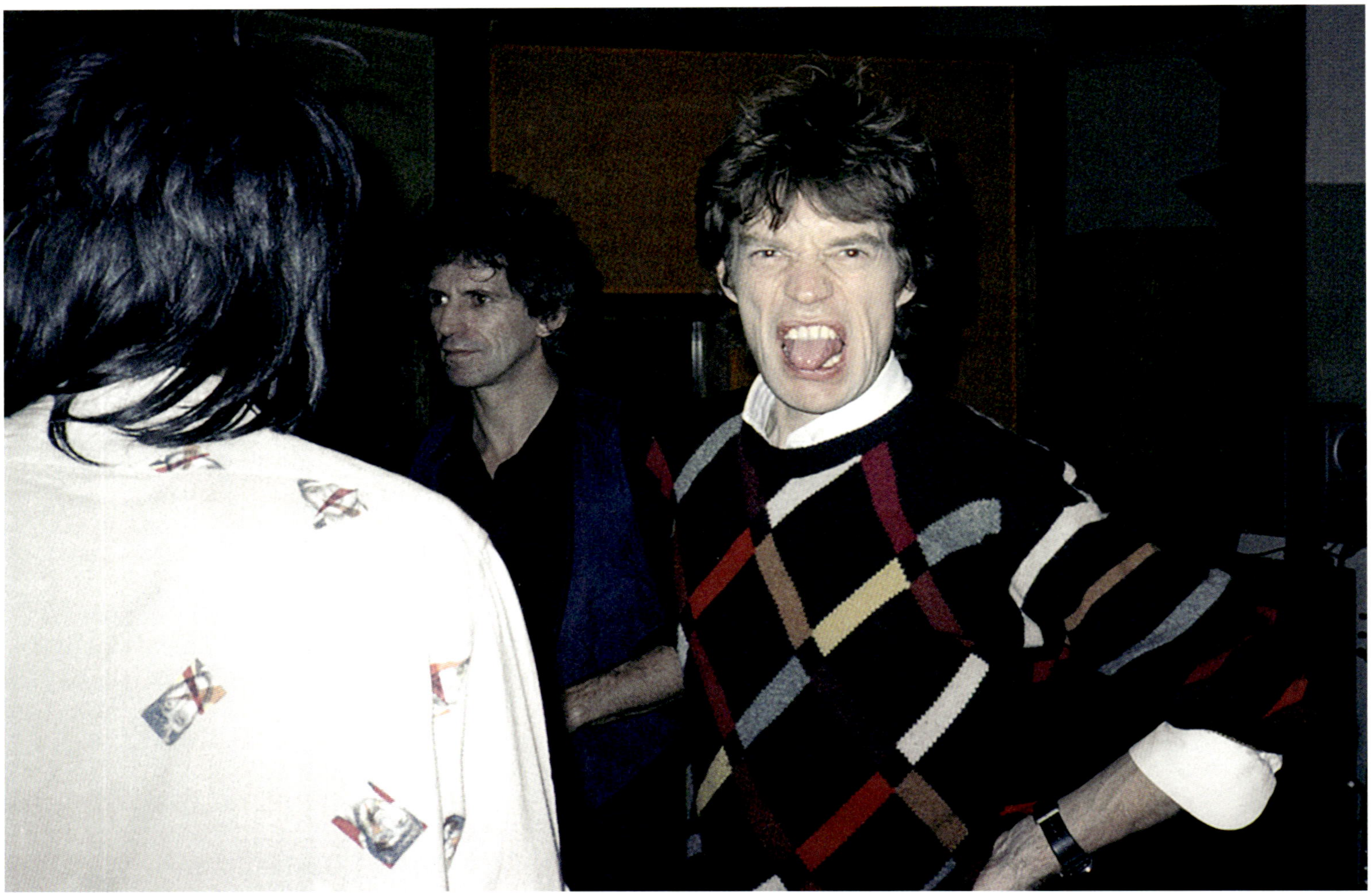

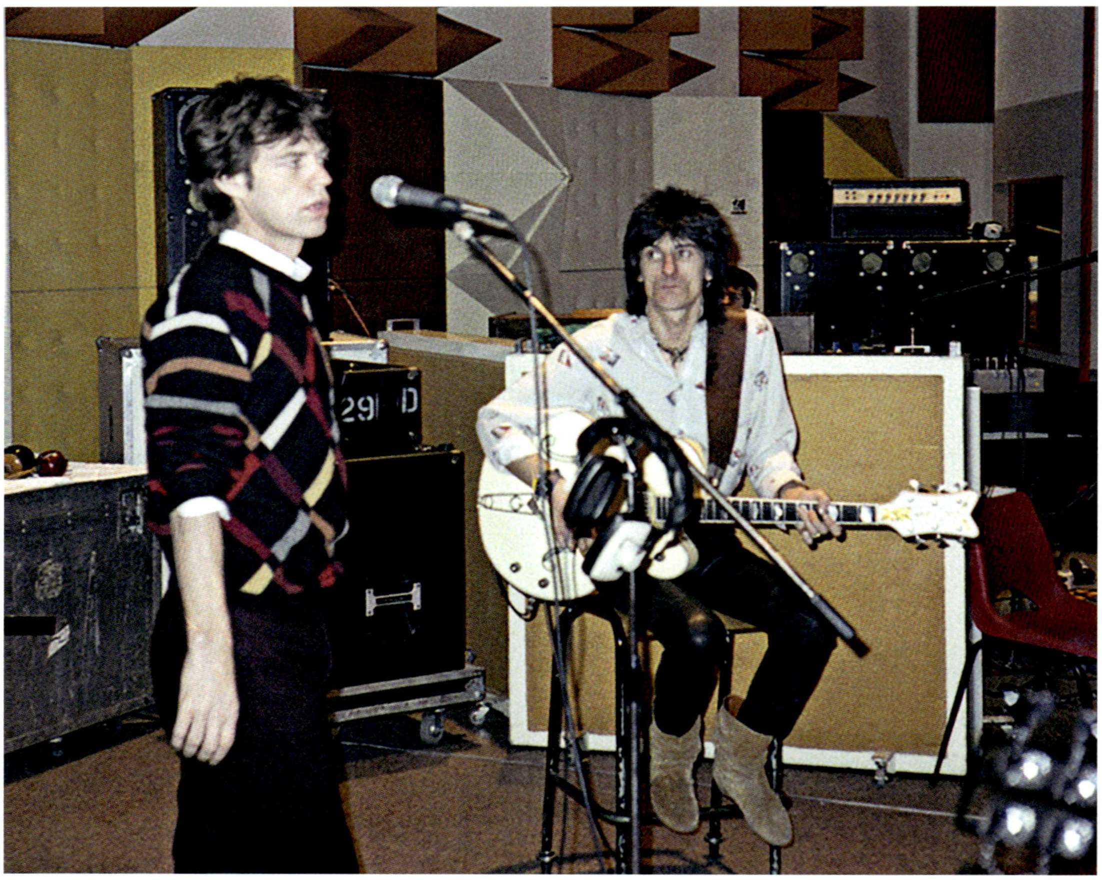

Three shots of Mick, Keith and Ronnie at the Pathé Marconi recording studio – 13 December 1982.
Following pages: Keith remonstrating in the Pathé Marconi recording studio – 15 December 1982.
Iggy Pop using the studio's door frame for support – 13 December 1982.

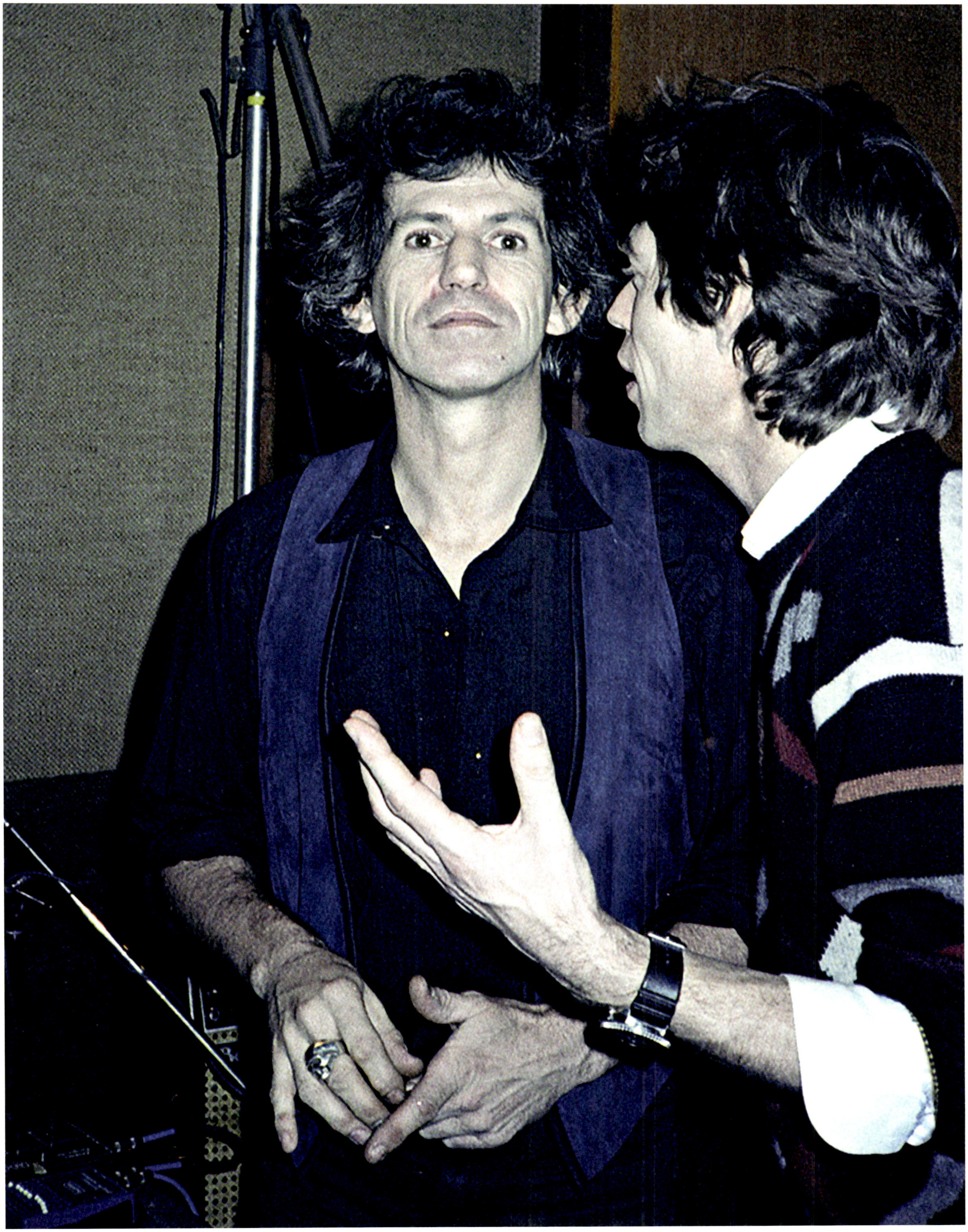

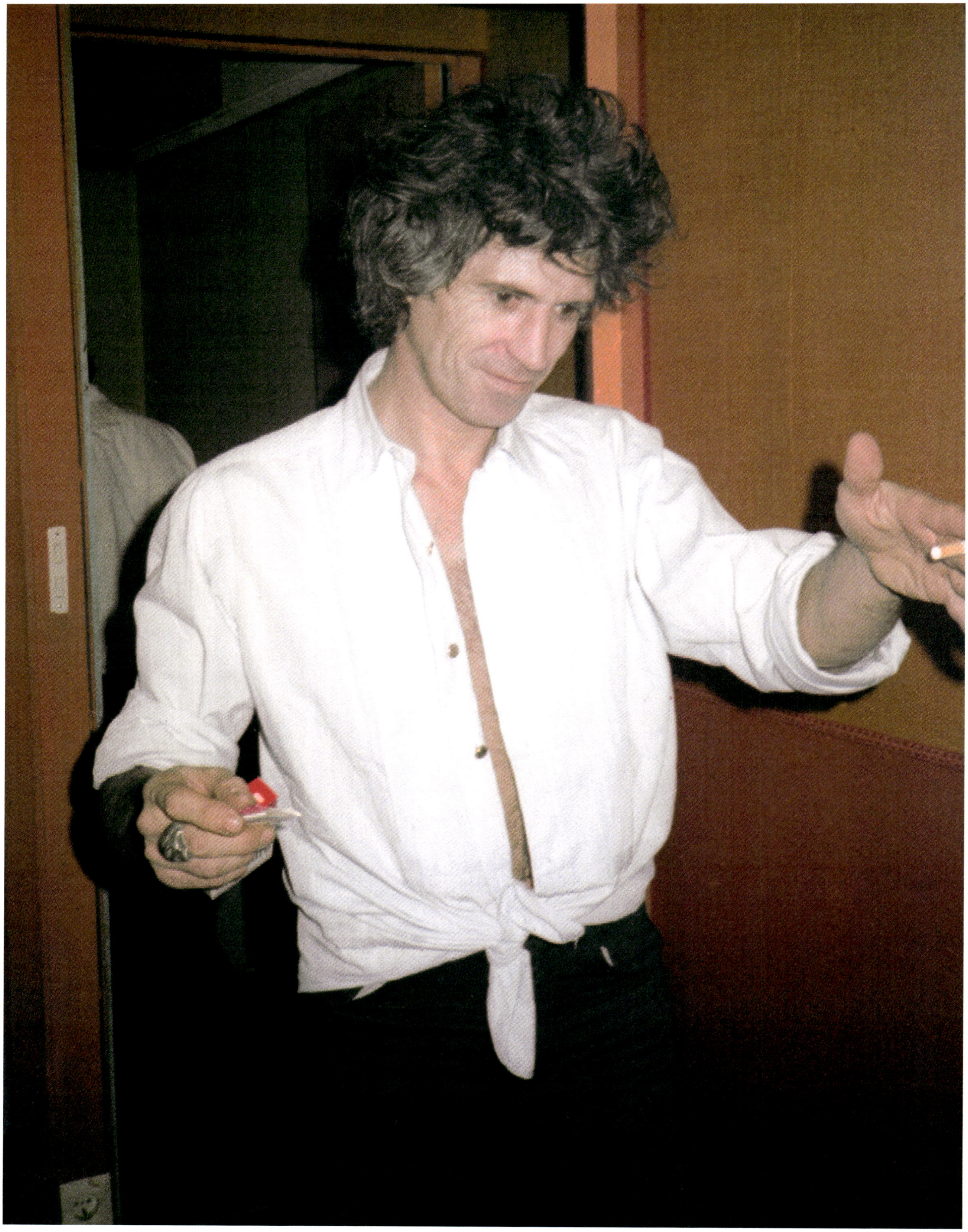

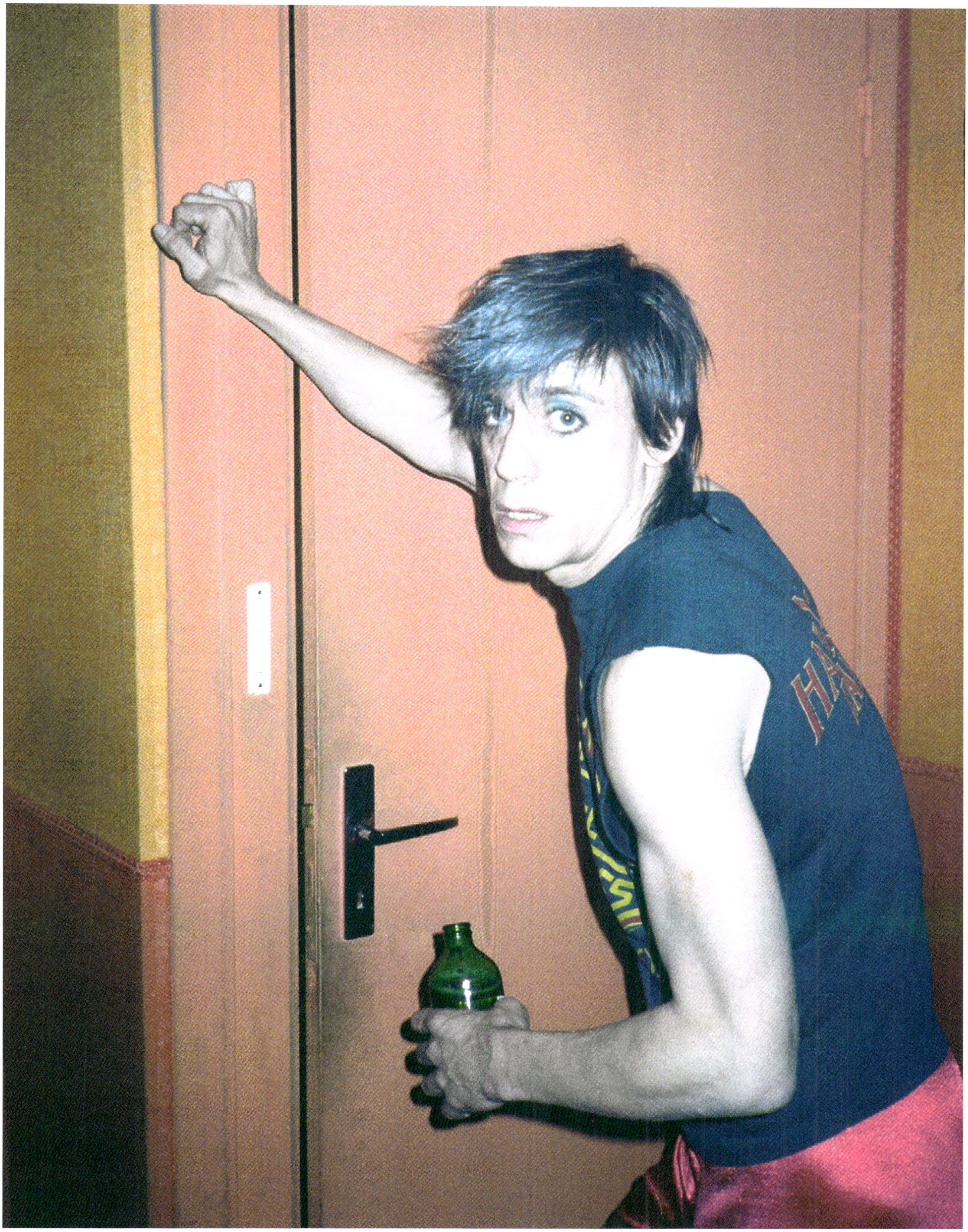

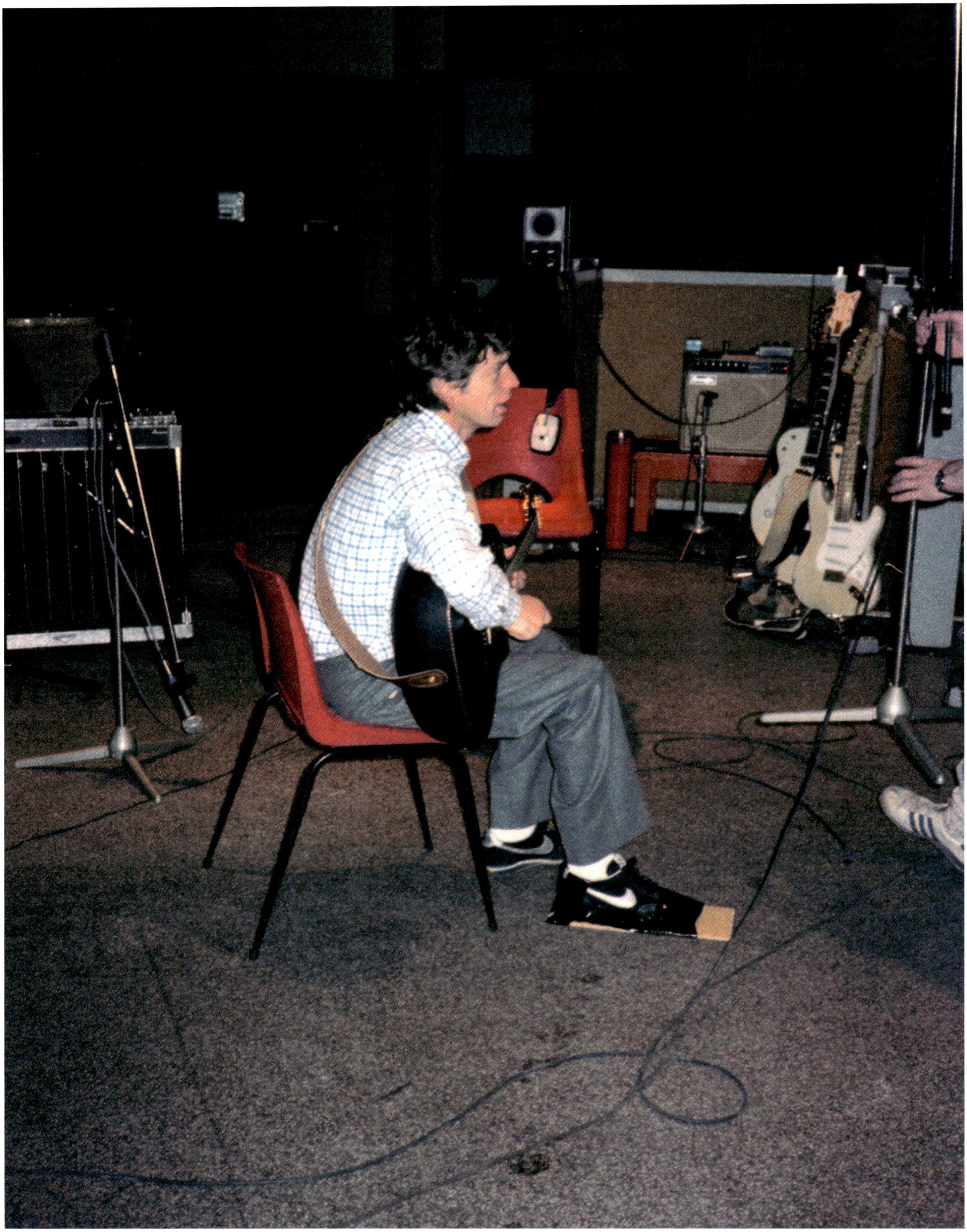

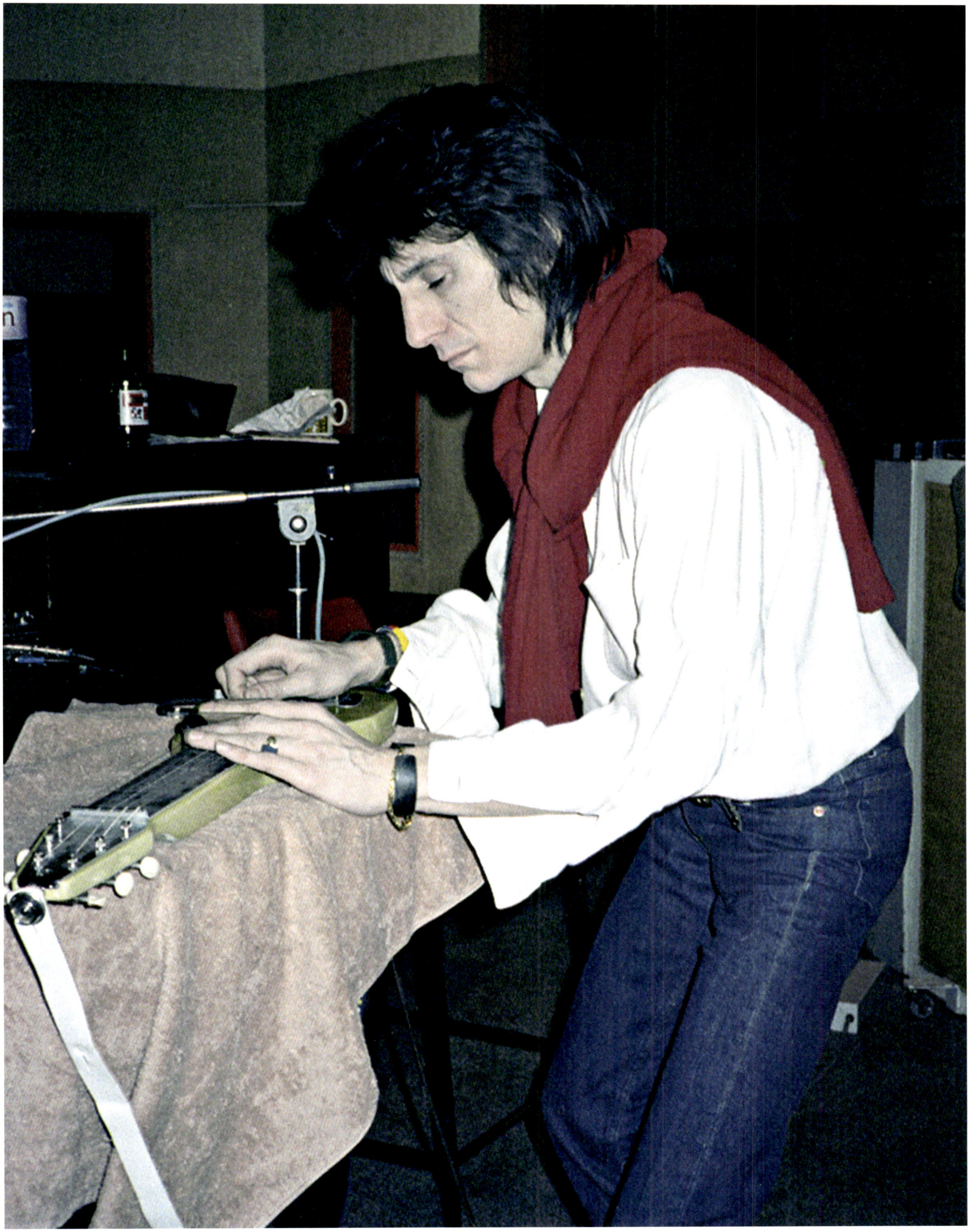

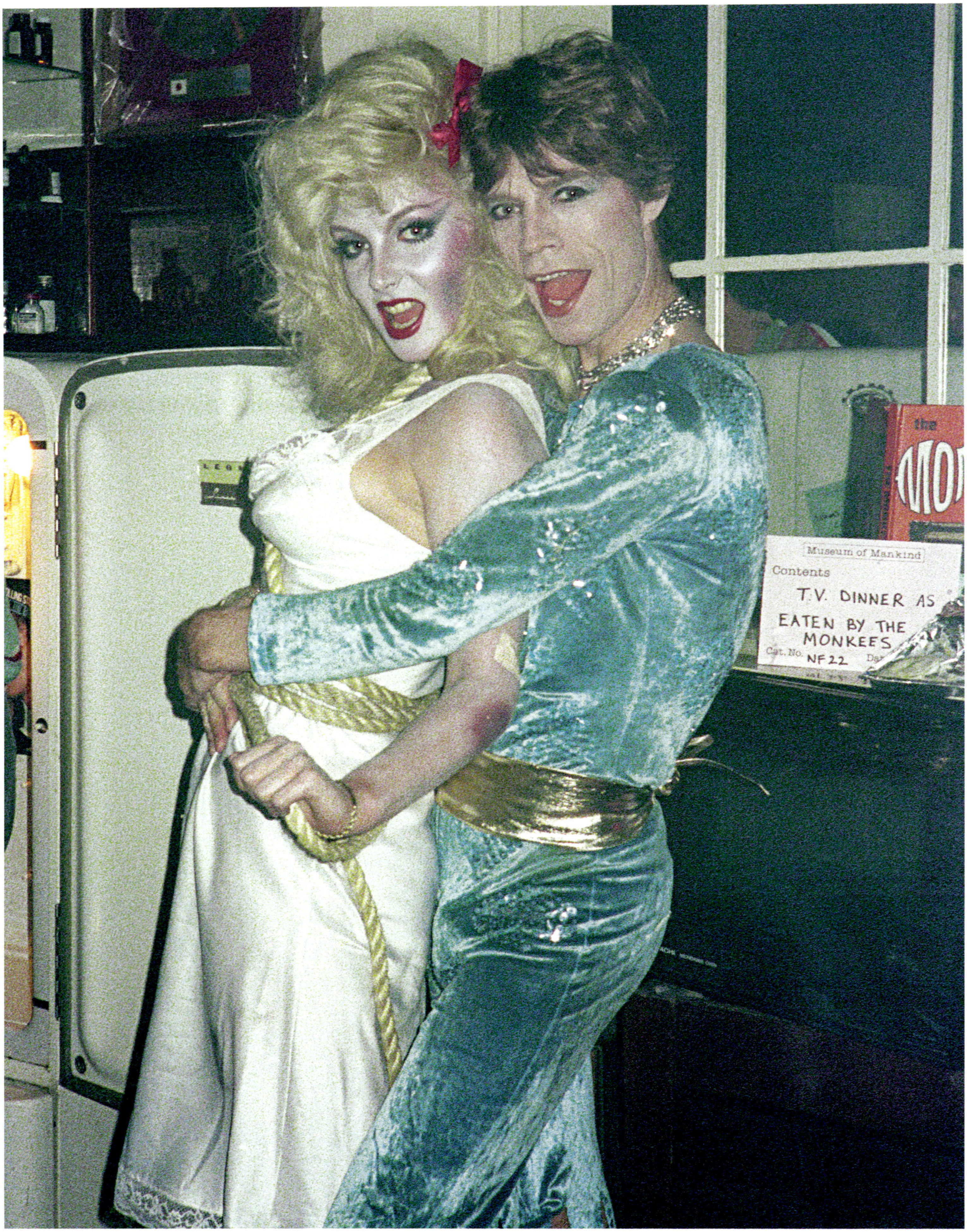
Museum of Mankind
Contents
T.V. DINNER AS
EATEN BY THE
MONKEES
Cat. No. NF22

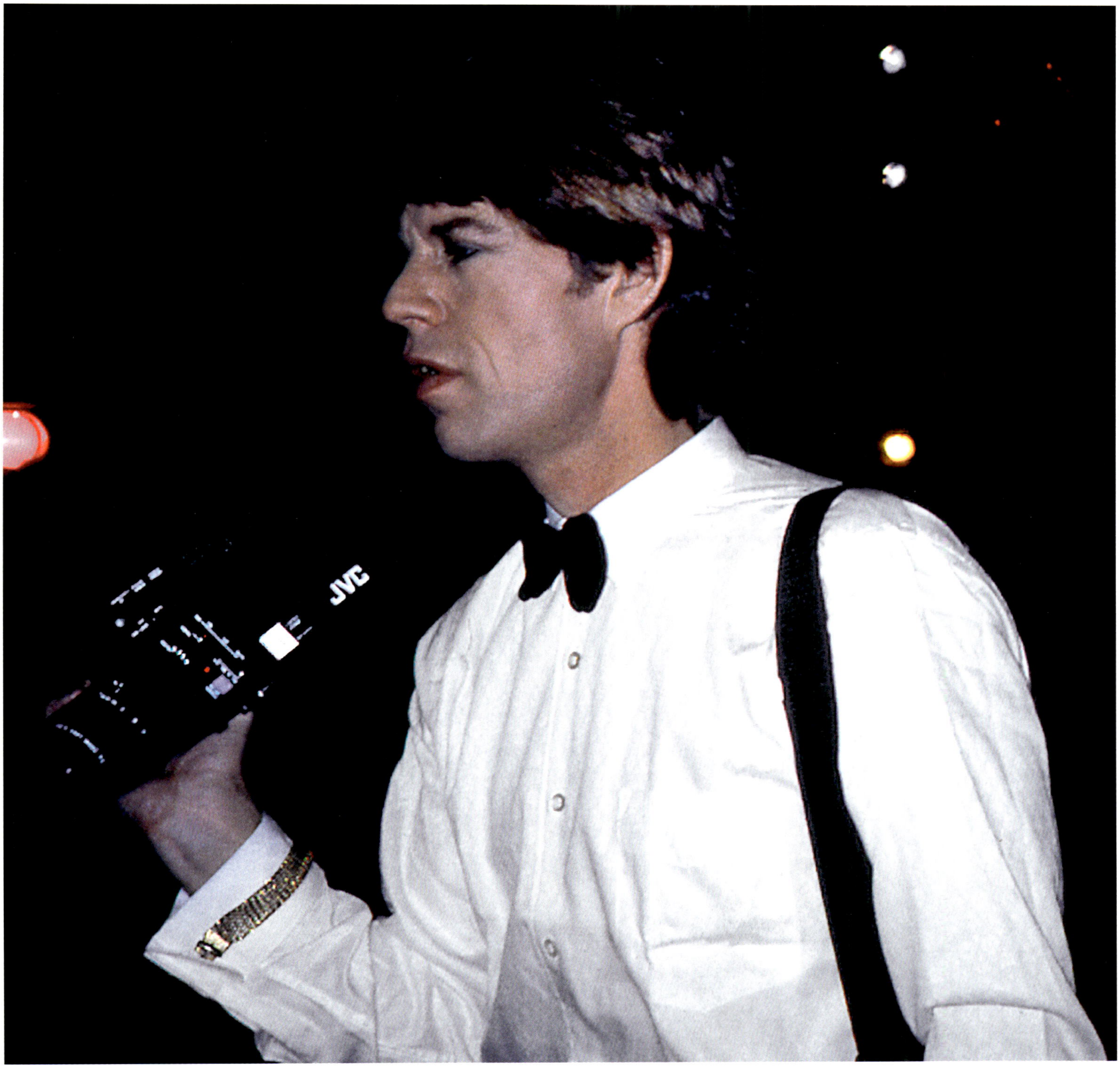

Mick filming with a 16mm movie camera at the Stones' video filming in Mexico City – 20 January 1984.

Left: Mick posing with the video model at the Stones' *Rewind* video shoot at the Museum of Mankind in London – 25 June 1984.

Previous pages: Mick trying out a guitar, while Ronnie tries slide guitar on top of the piano, at the Pathé Marconi recording studio, in Paris – 21 February 1983.

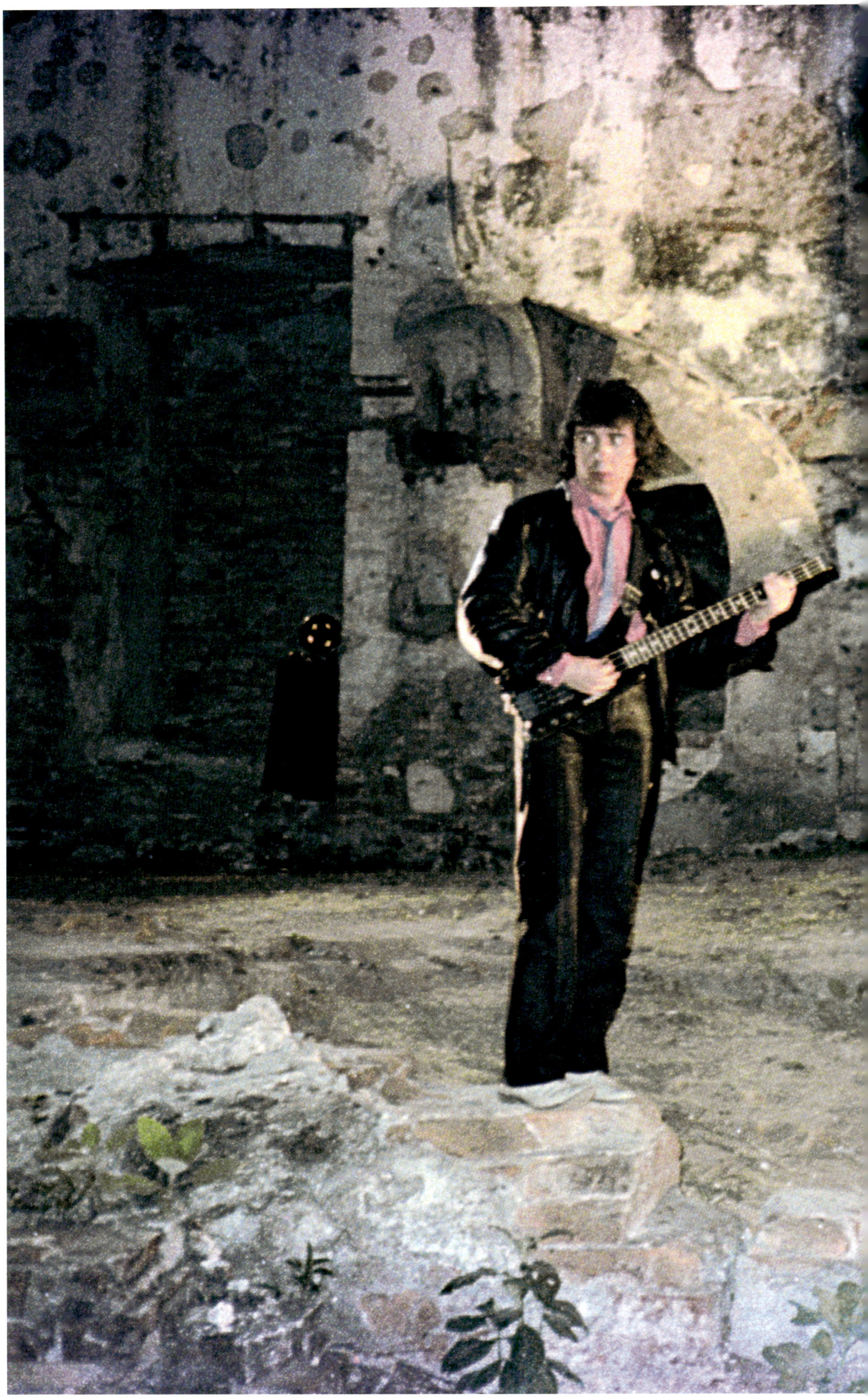

Bill and Charlie being filmed at the Stones' video shoot in the ruins outside Mexico City – 24 January 1984.

Following pages: Two shots of Keith with guitar and chainsaw, that same day and venue.

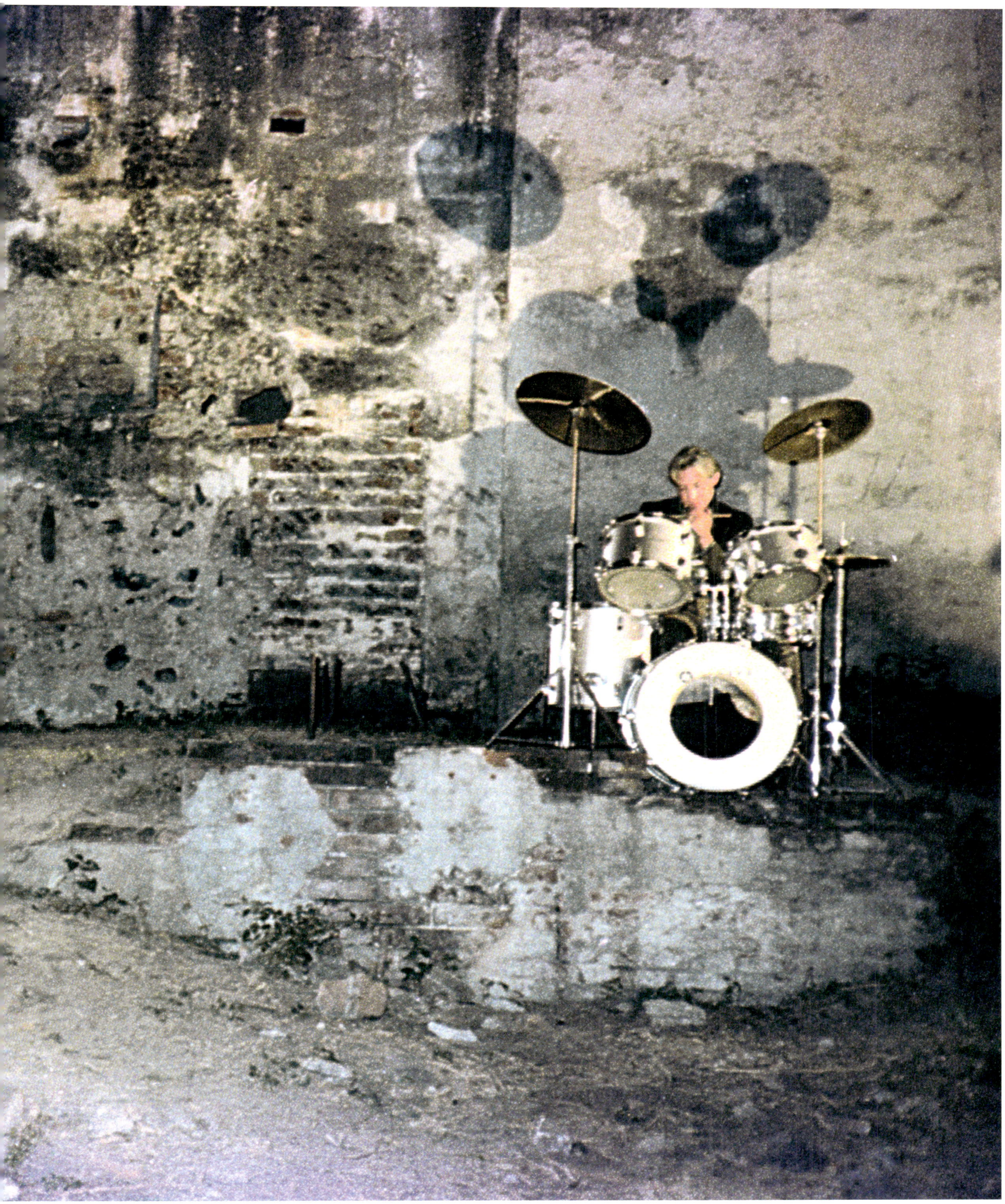

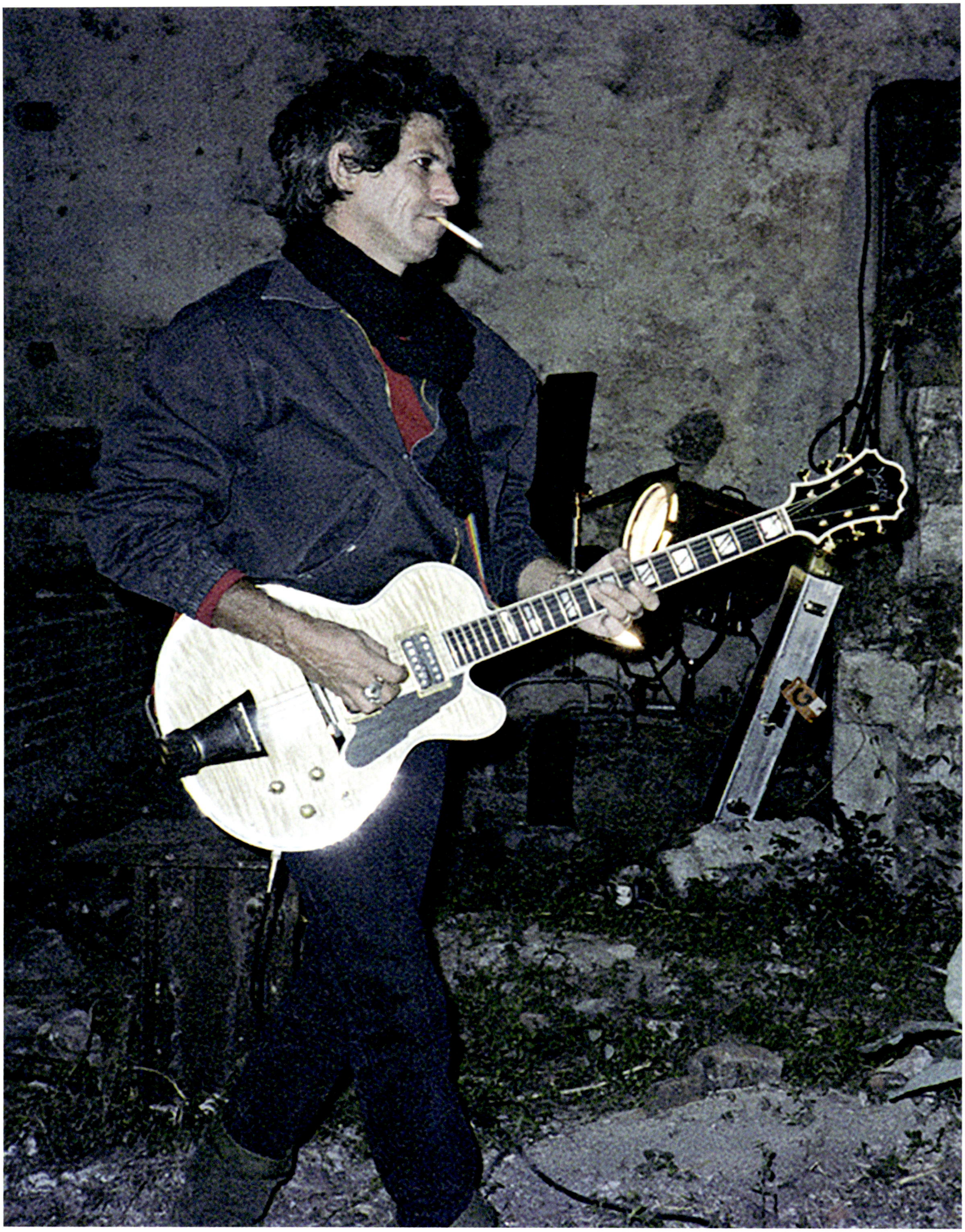

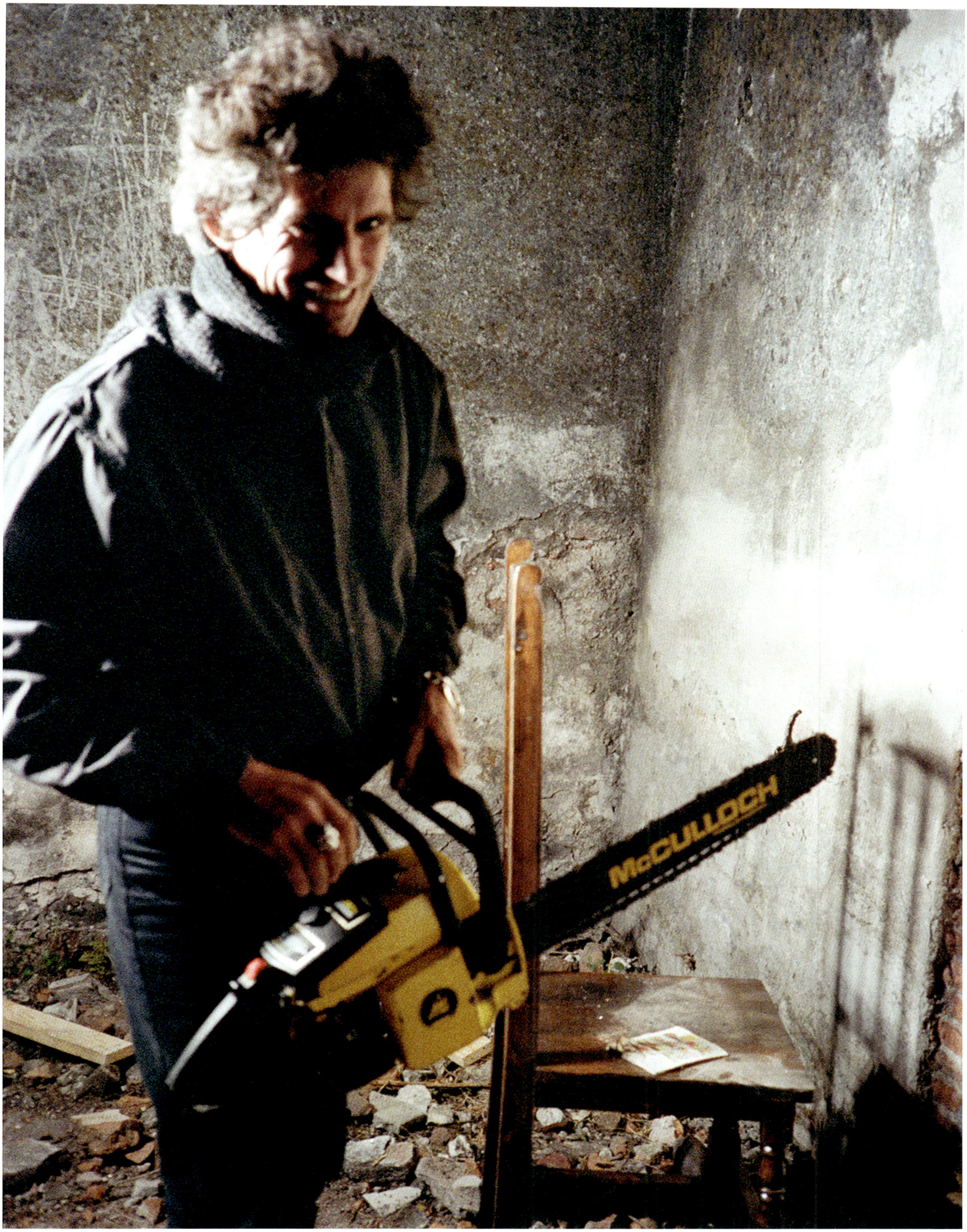
McCULLOCH

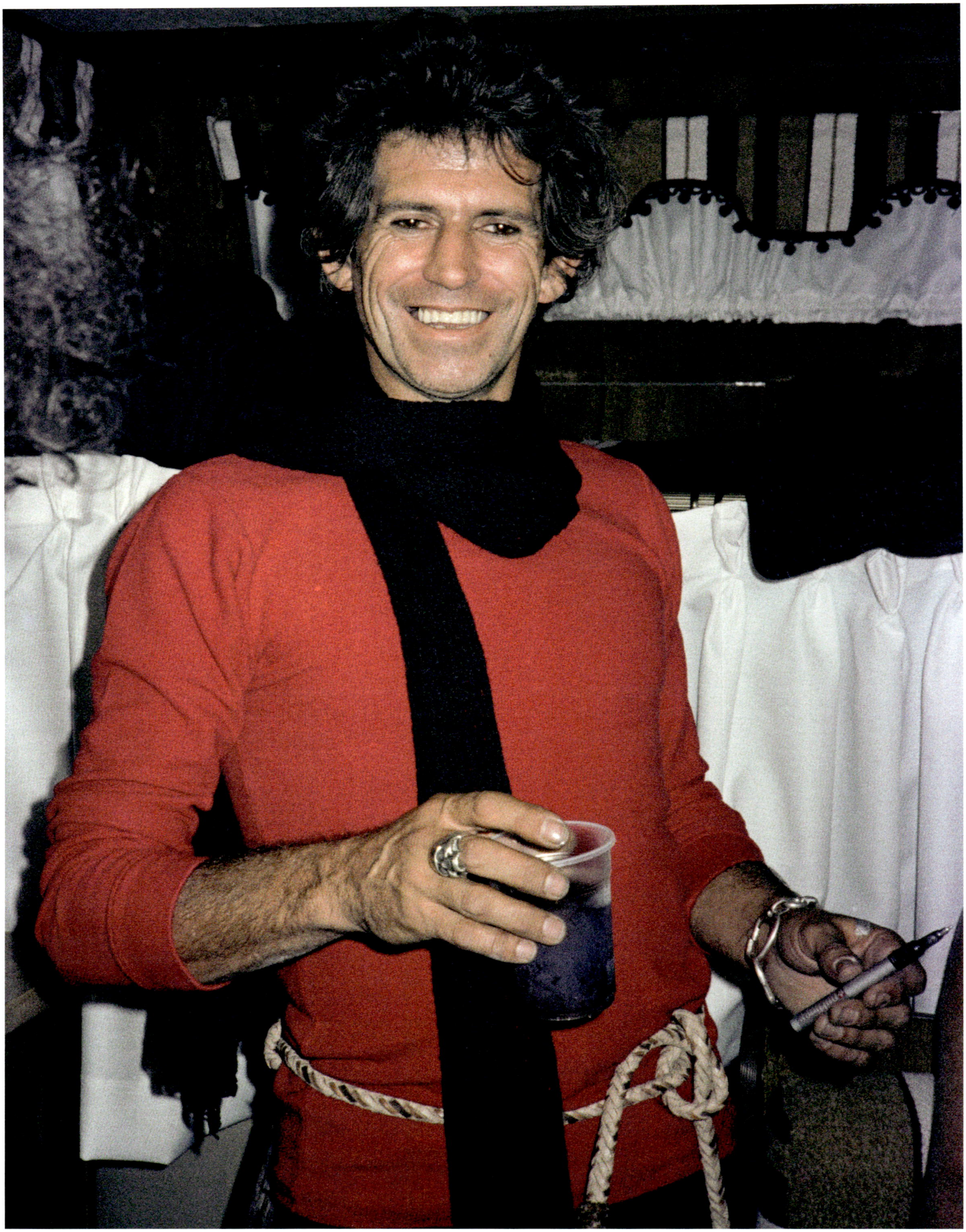

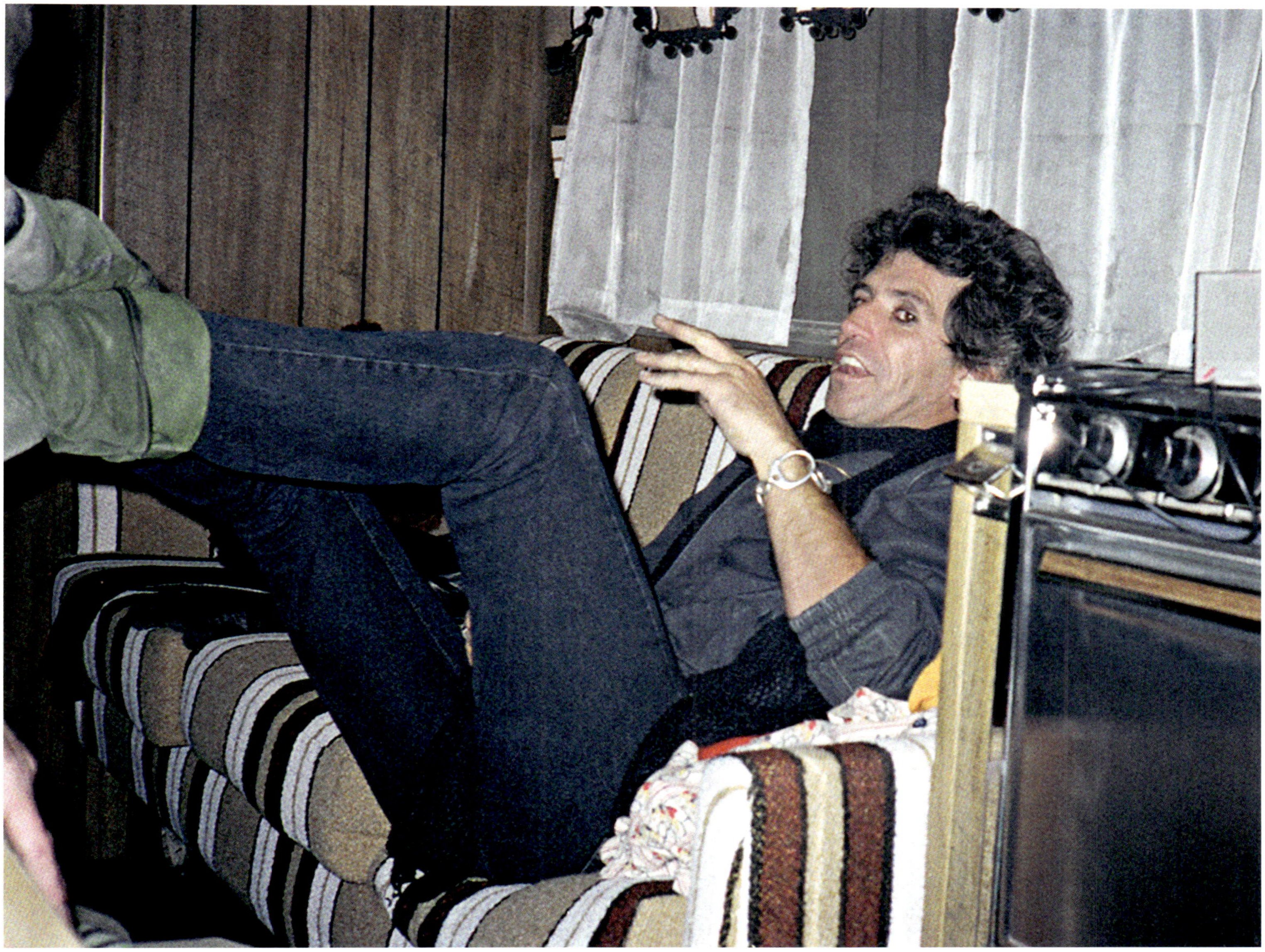

Shots of Keith relaxing with a drink and fooling about on a sofa, after the video filming in Mexico.

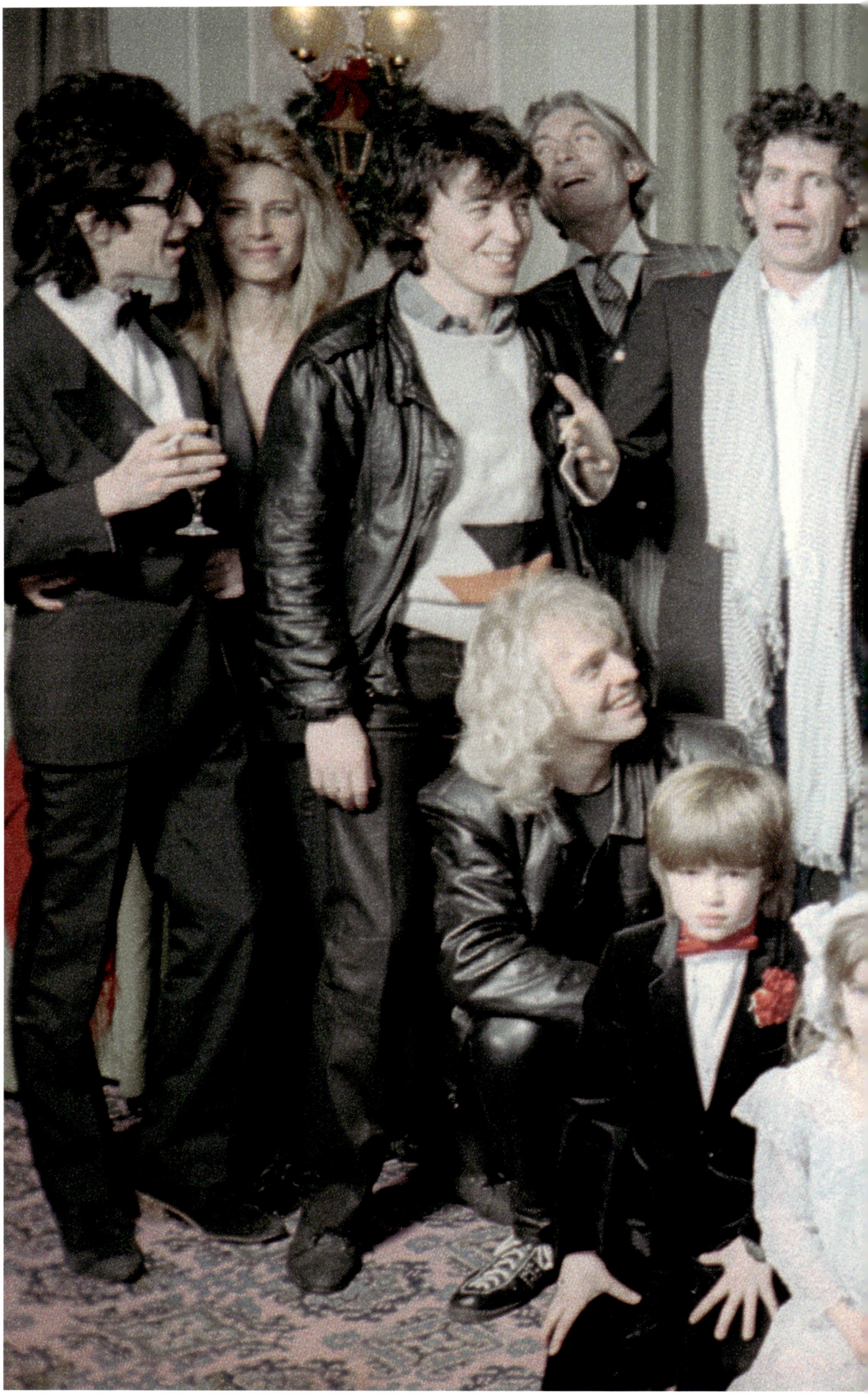

Ronnie's wedding to Jo Howard, with a host of celebrities, at The Bull at Gerrards Cross, just outside London – 2 January 1985.

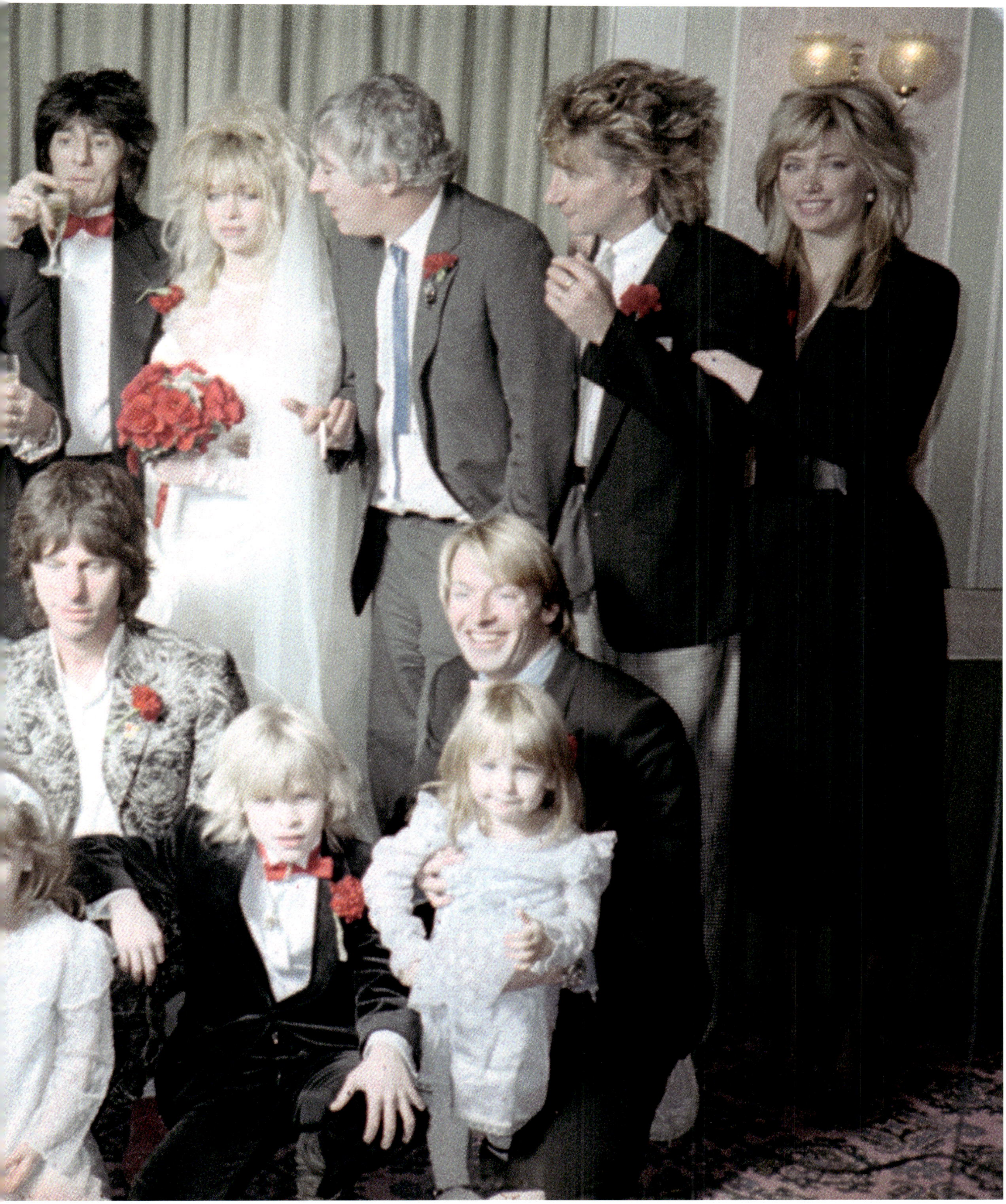

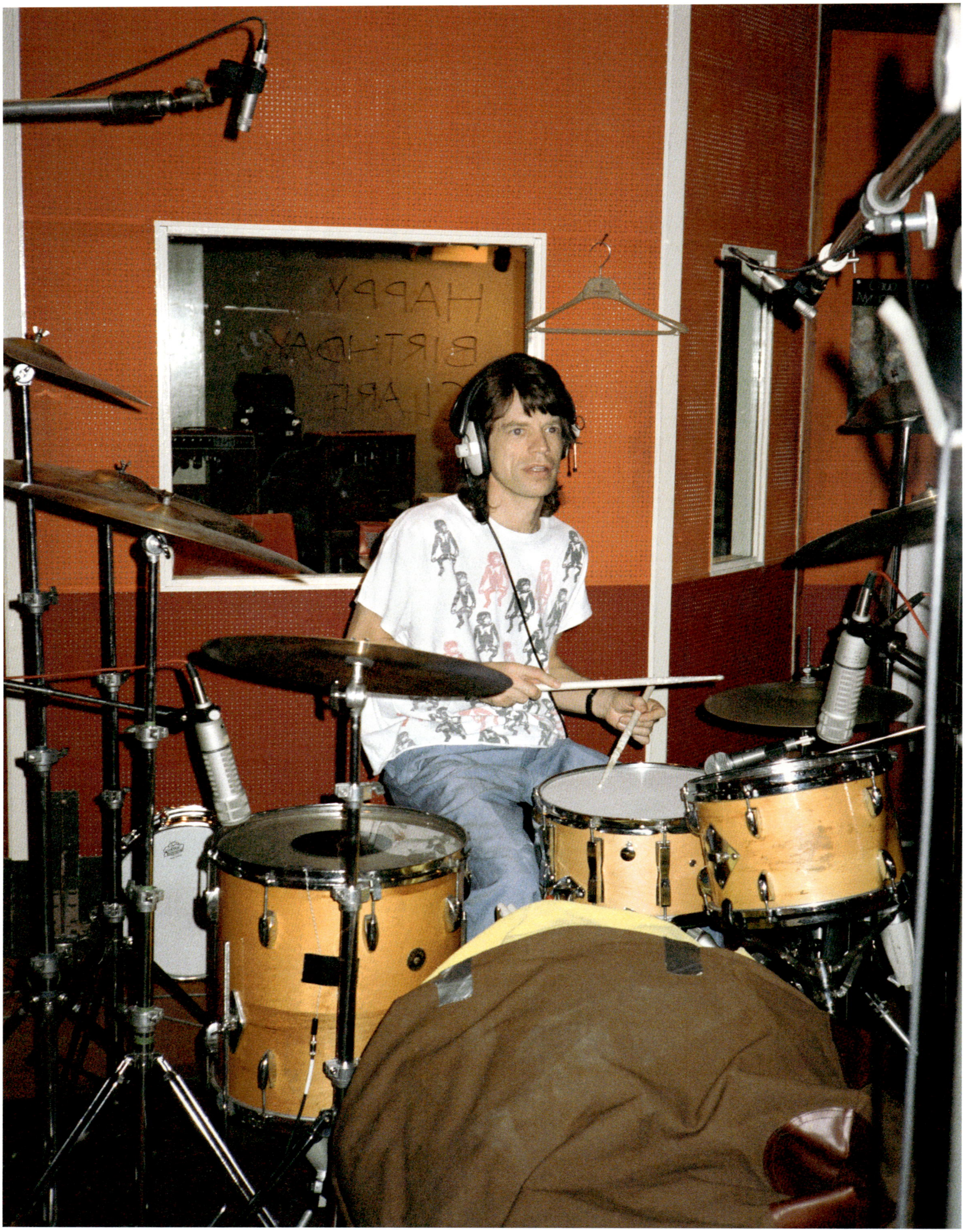
HAPPY
BIRTHDAY

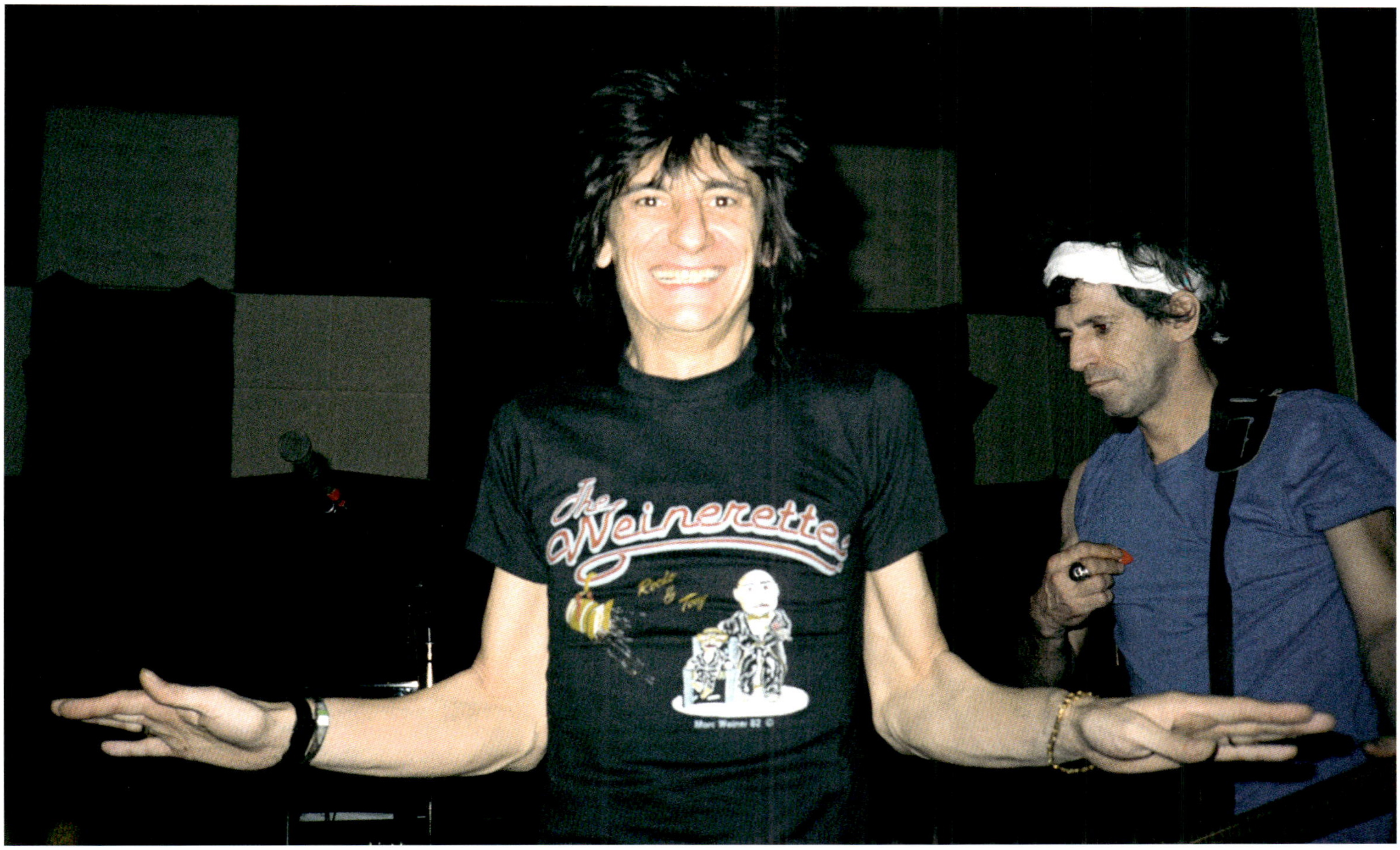

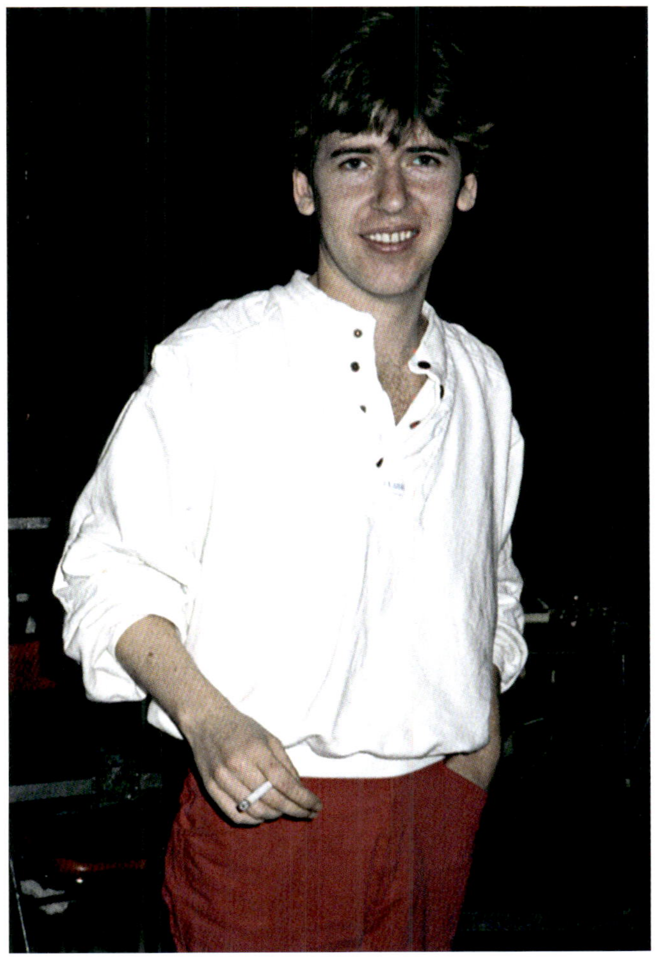

Ronnie and Keith working in the studio – June 1985 .
Left: Mick playing drums at the Pathé Marconi Studios in Paris – June 1985.
Right: Record producer Steve Lillywhite in the studio – June 1985.

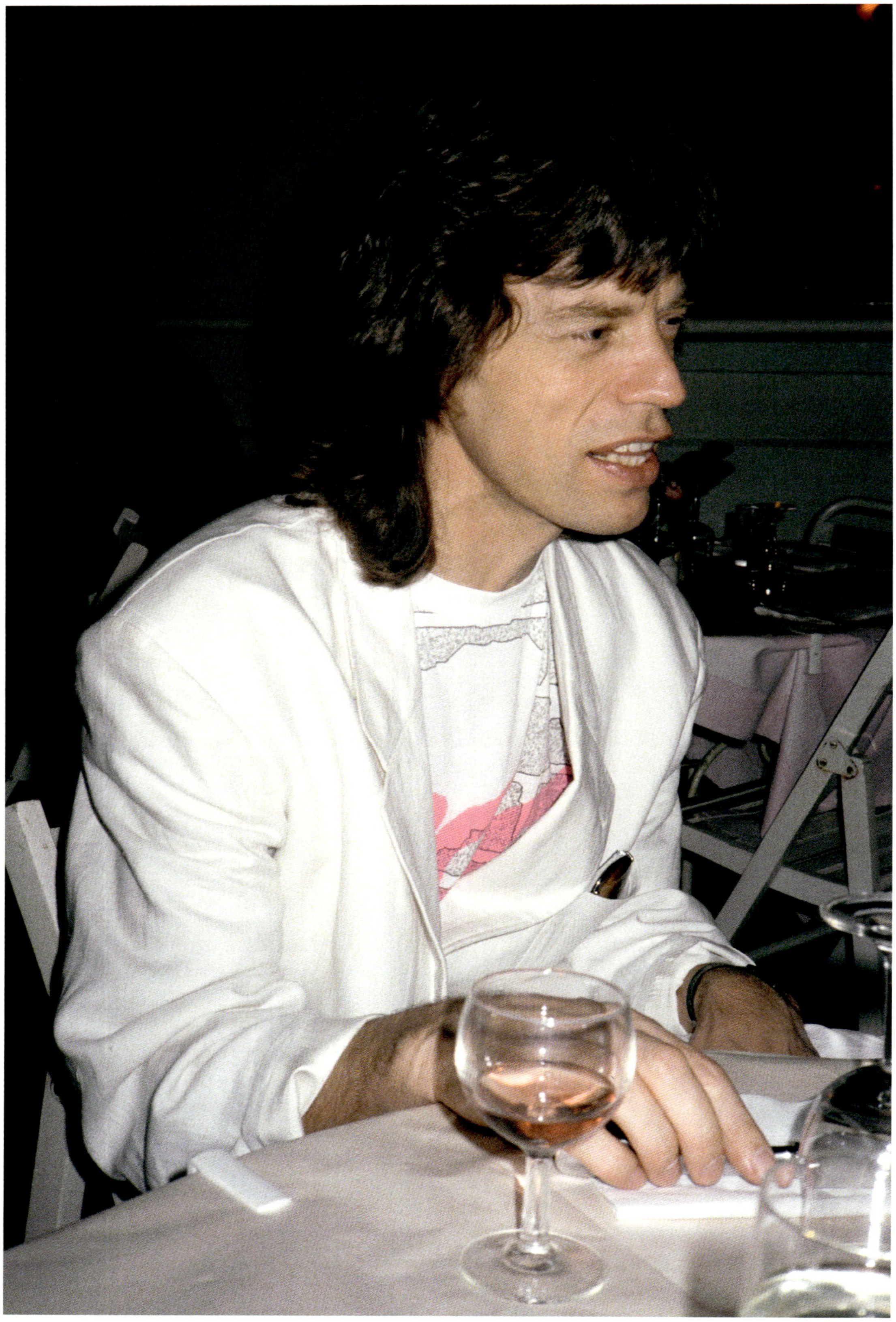

Two shots of Mick at Ronnie's birthday celebrations in a boat restaurant on the River Seine, Paris – 1 June 1985.

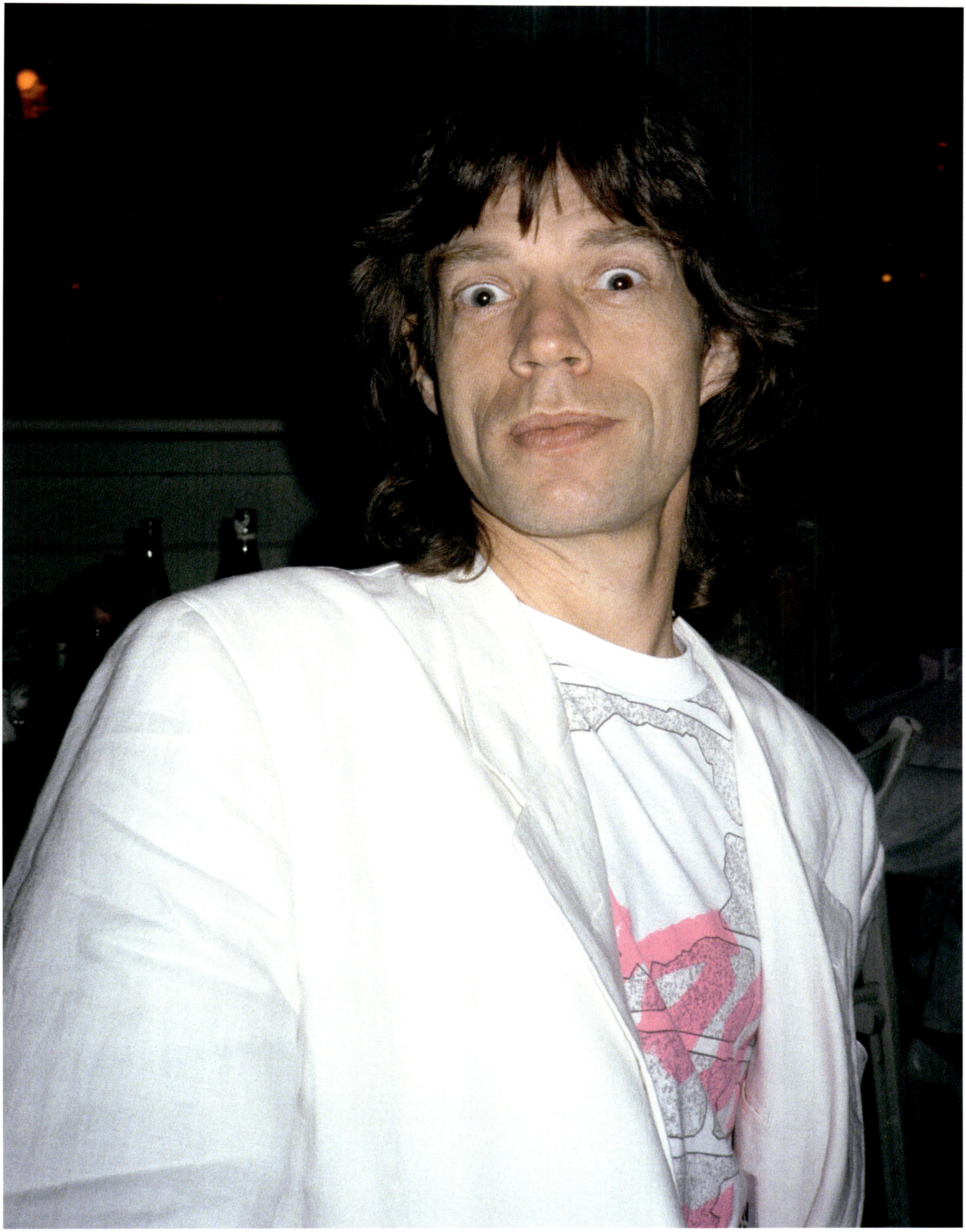

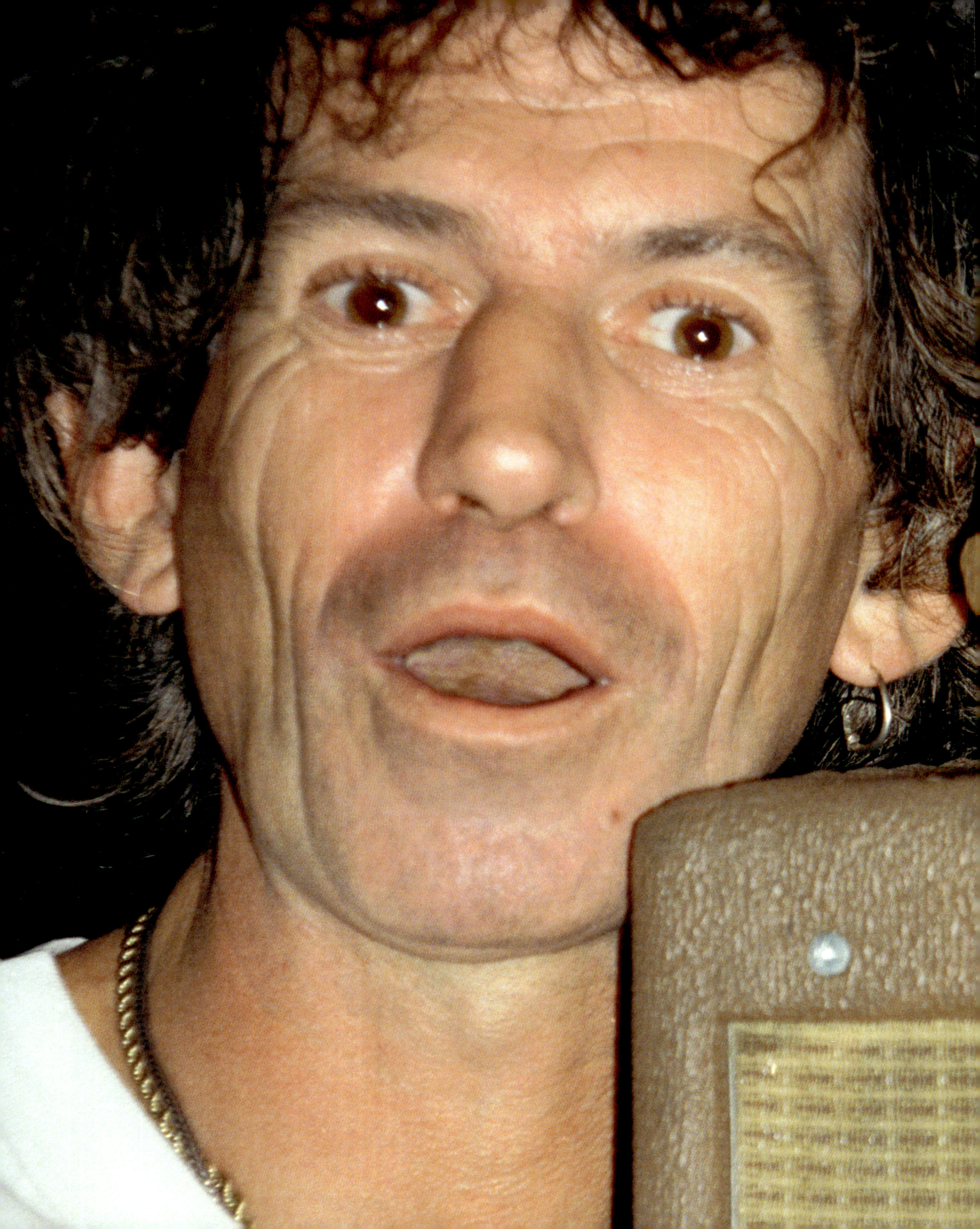

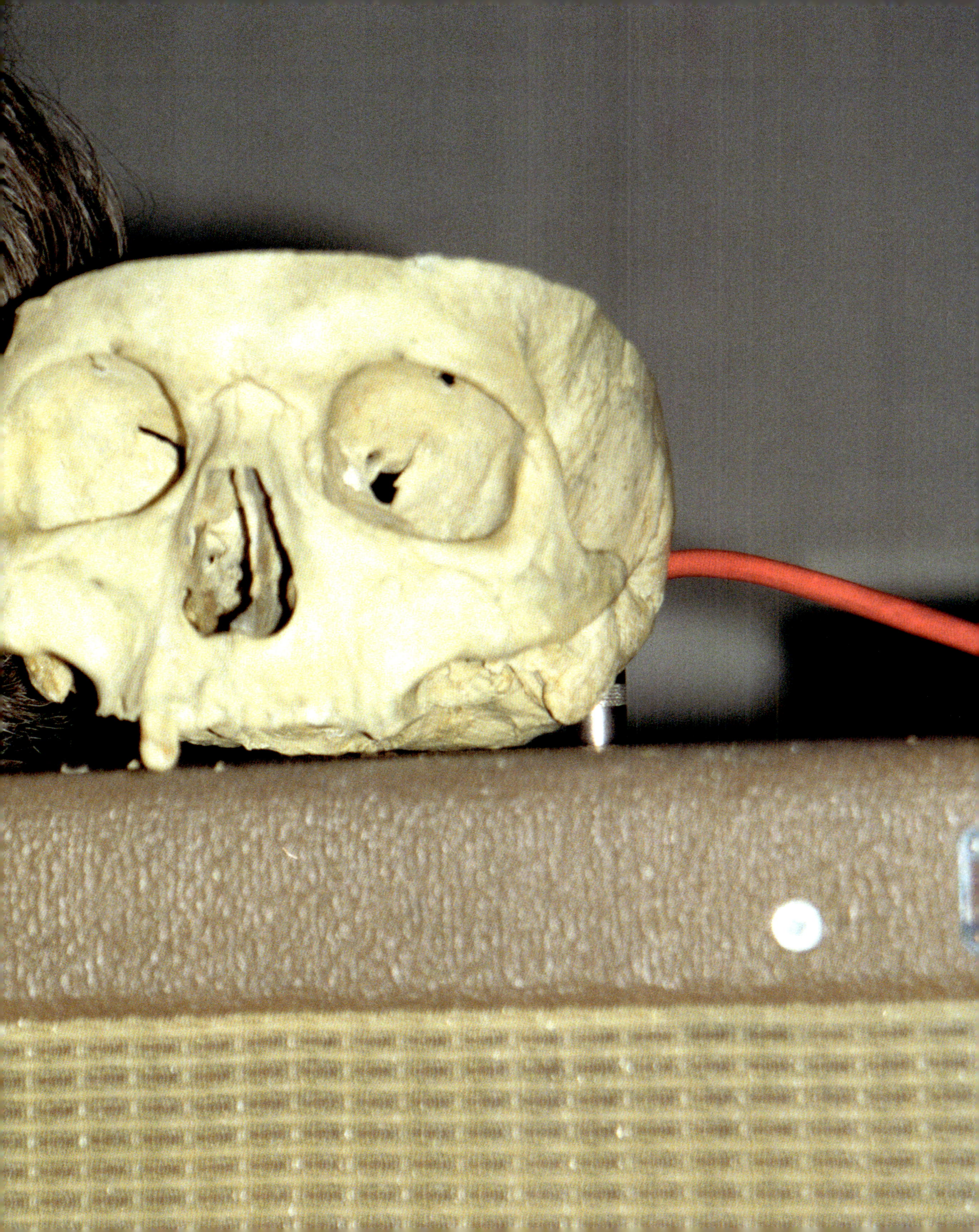

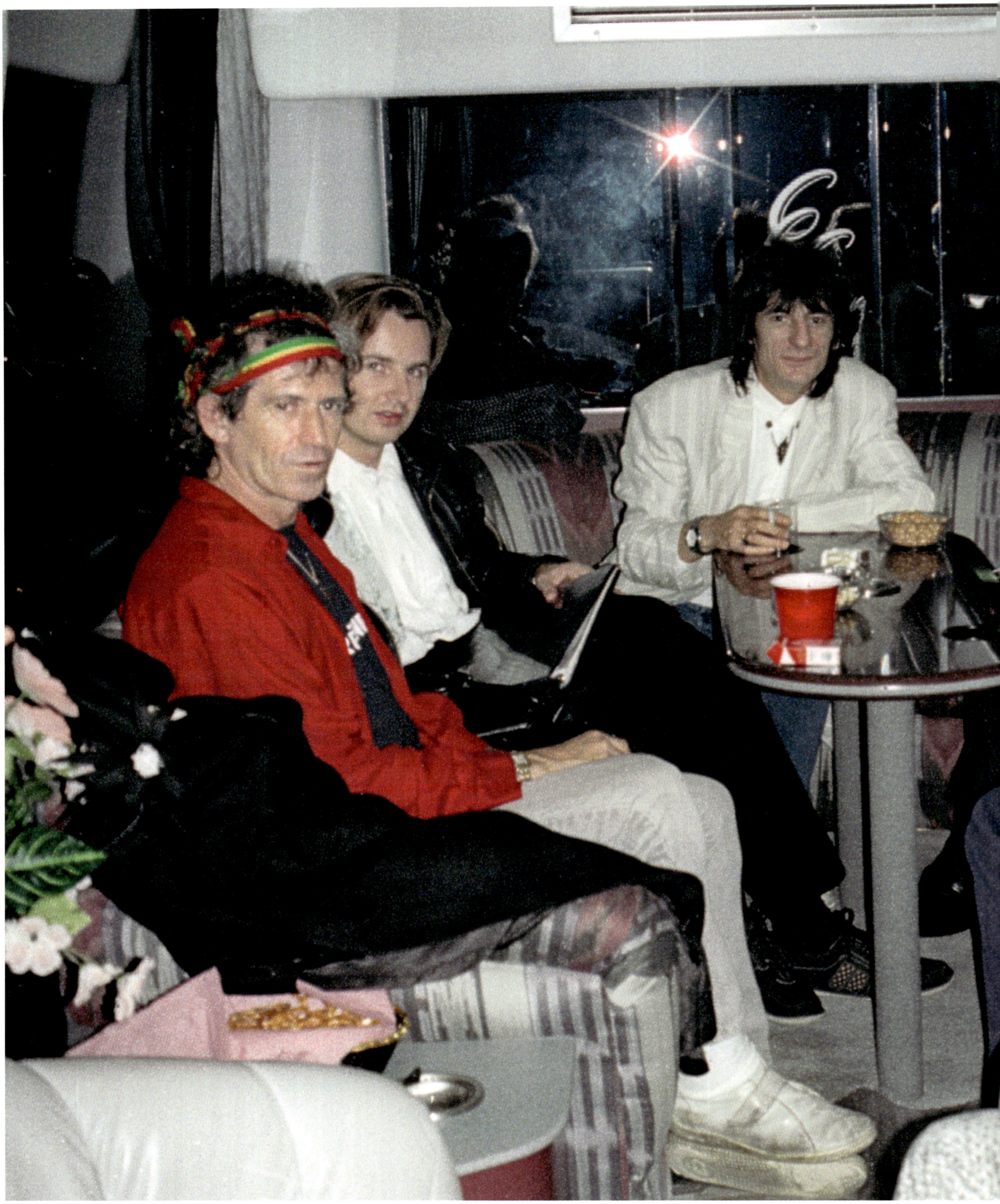

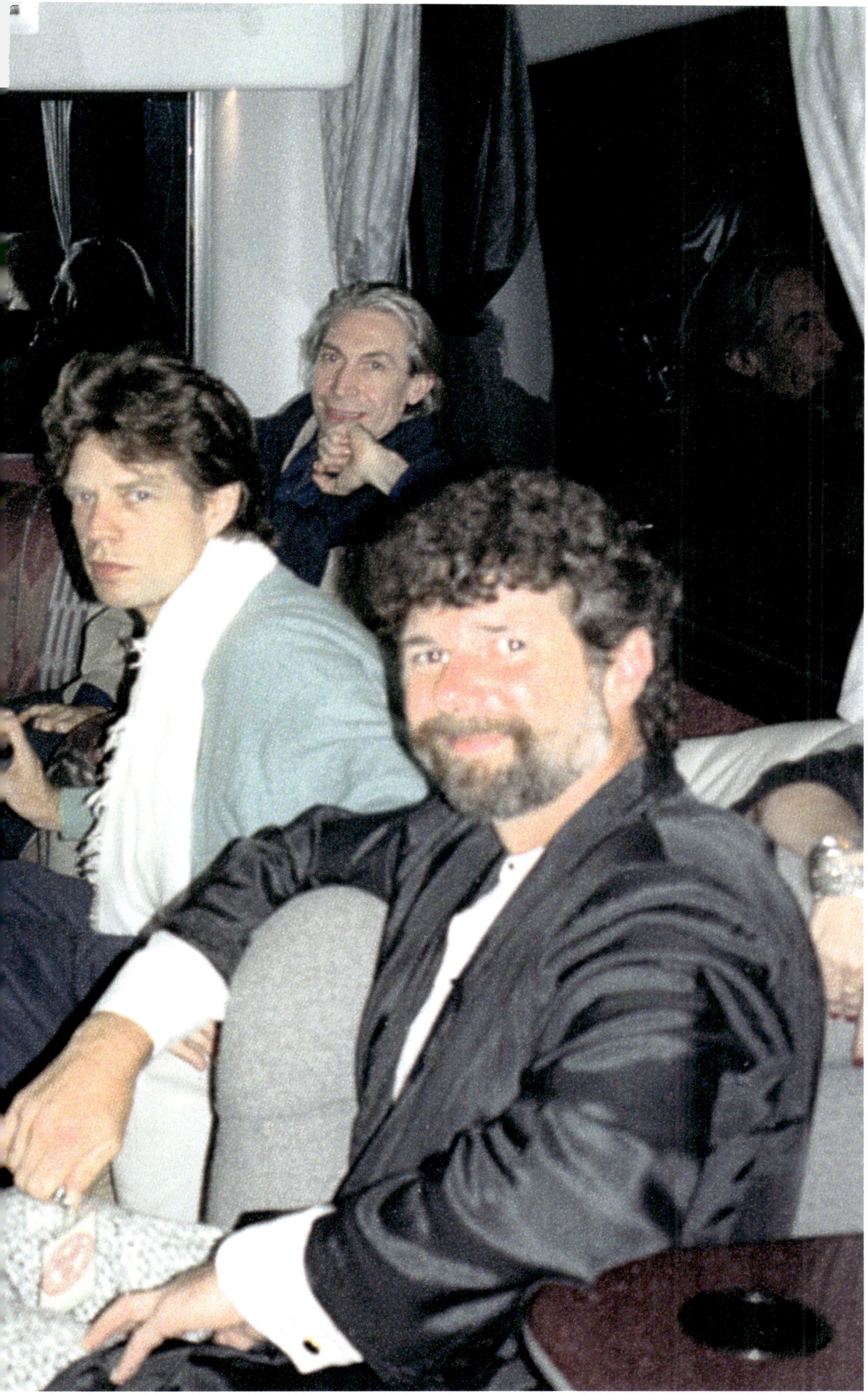

The Stones and support musicians in the van on their way to the rehearsal and a photo session at the Wykeham Rise girl's school in Southbury, Connecticut – 1 August 1989.
Previous pages: Keith beside a skull he liked in the rehearsal room at the same school – 13 July 1989.

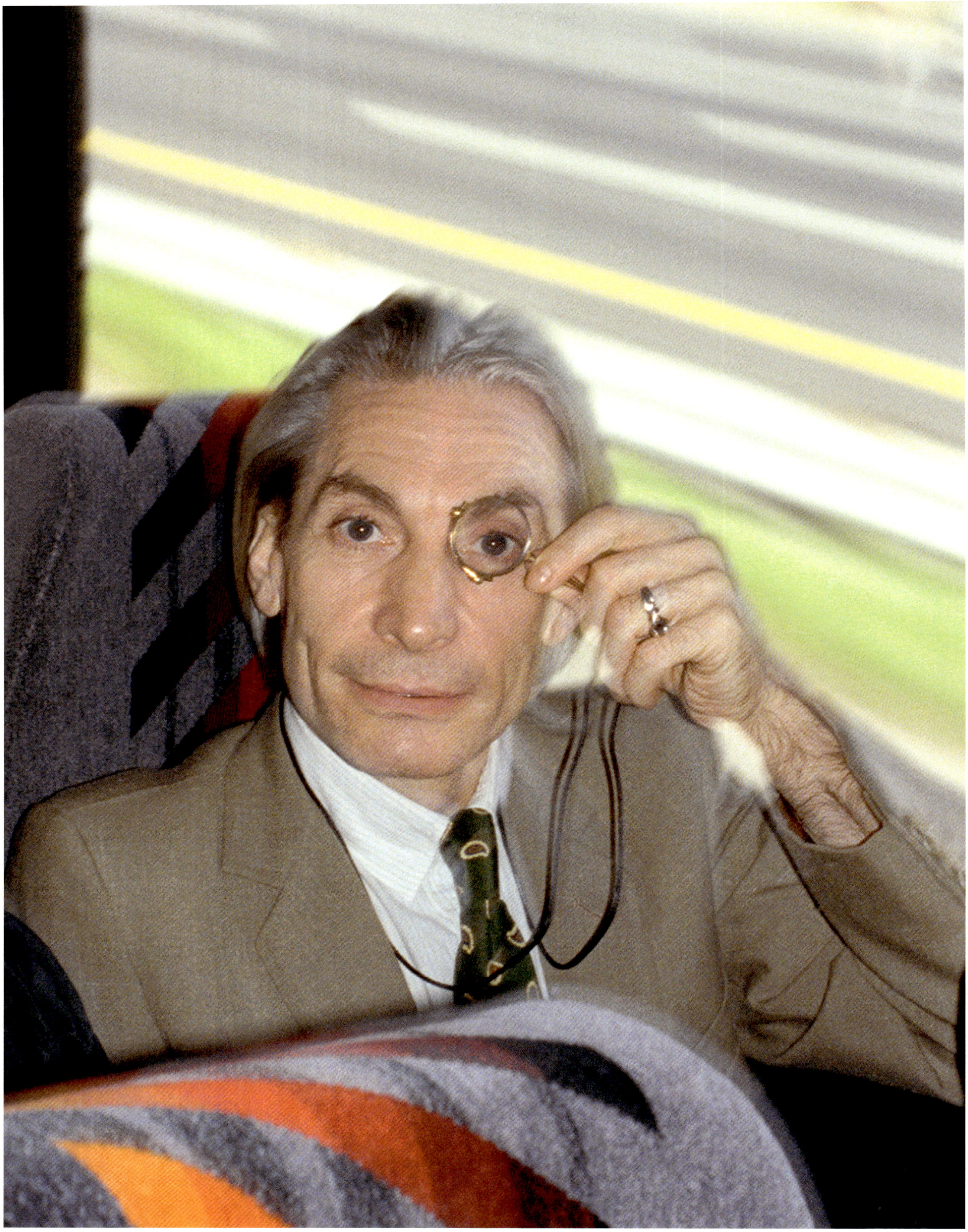

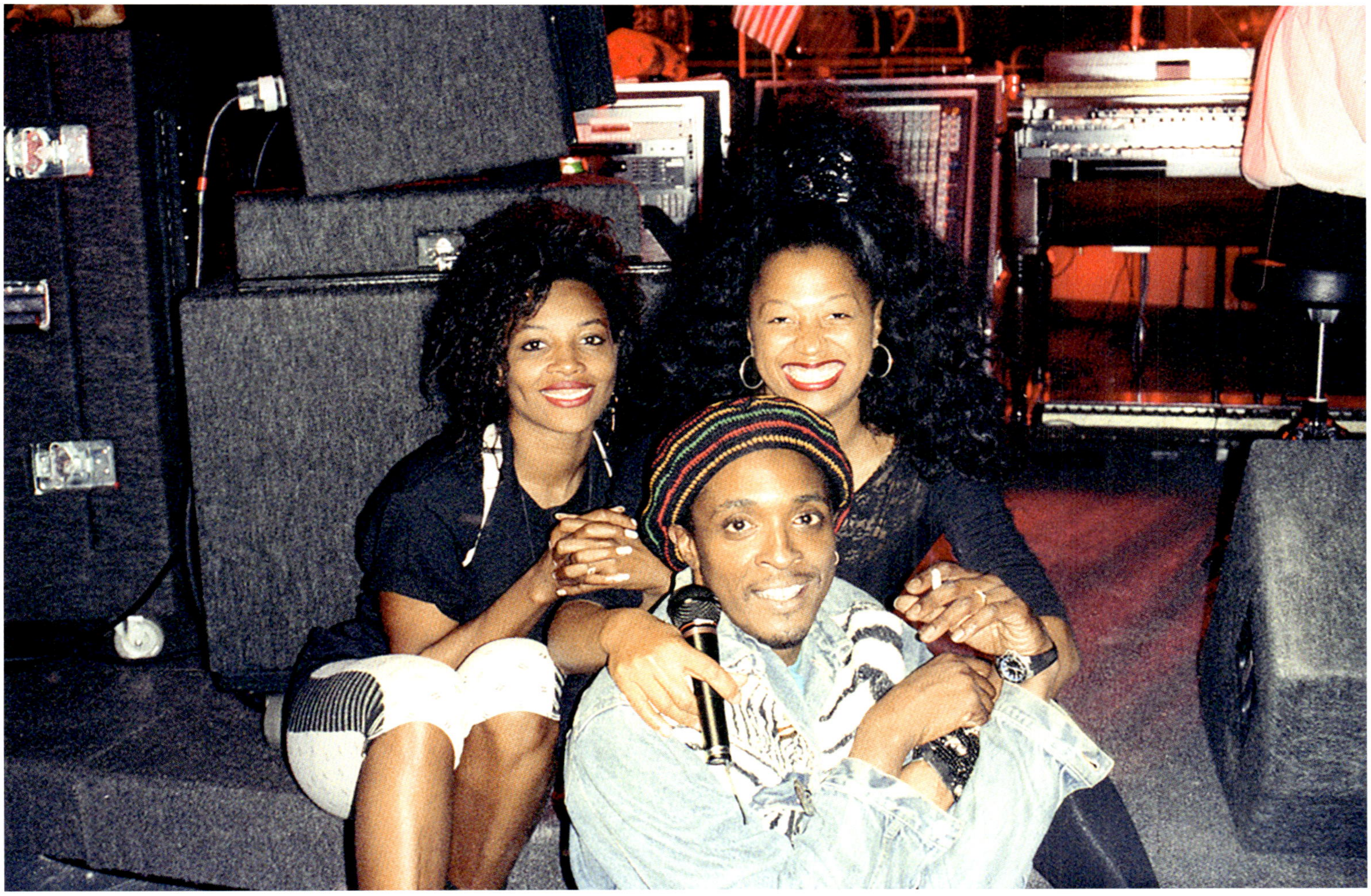

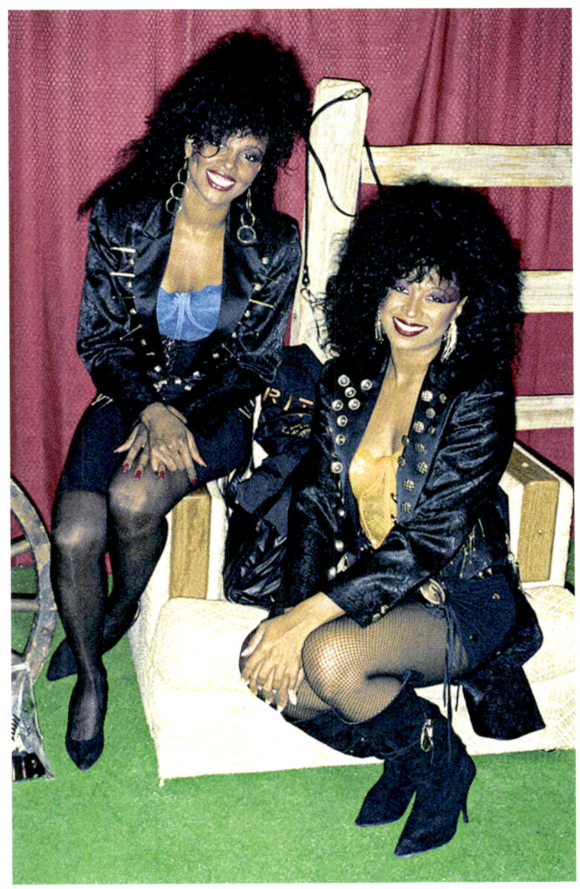

Backing singers Bernard Fowler, Cindy Mizelle and Lisa Fischer backstage in the Nassau Coliseum in Garden City, New York – 14 August 1989.
Right: Cindy and Lisa backstage at the Busch Stadium, in St. Louis, Missouri – 17 September 1989.
Left: Charlie in the bus from Garden City to Philadelphia, Pennsylvania, with his monocle – 26 August 1989.

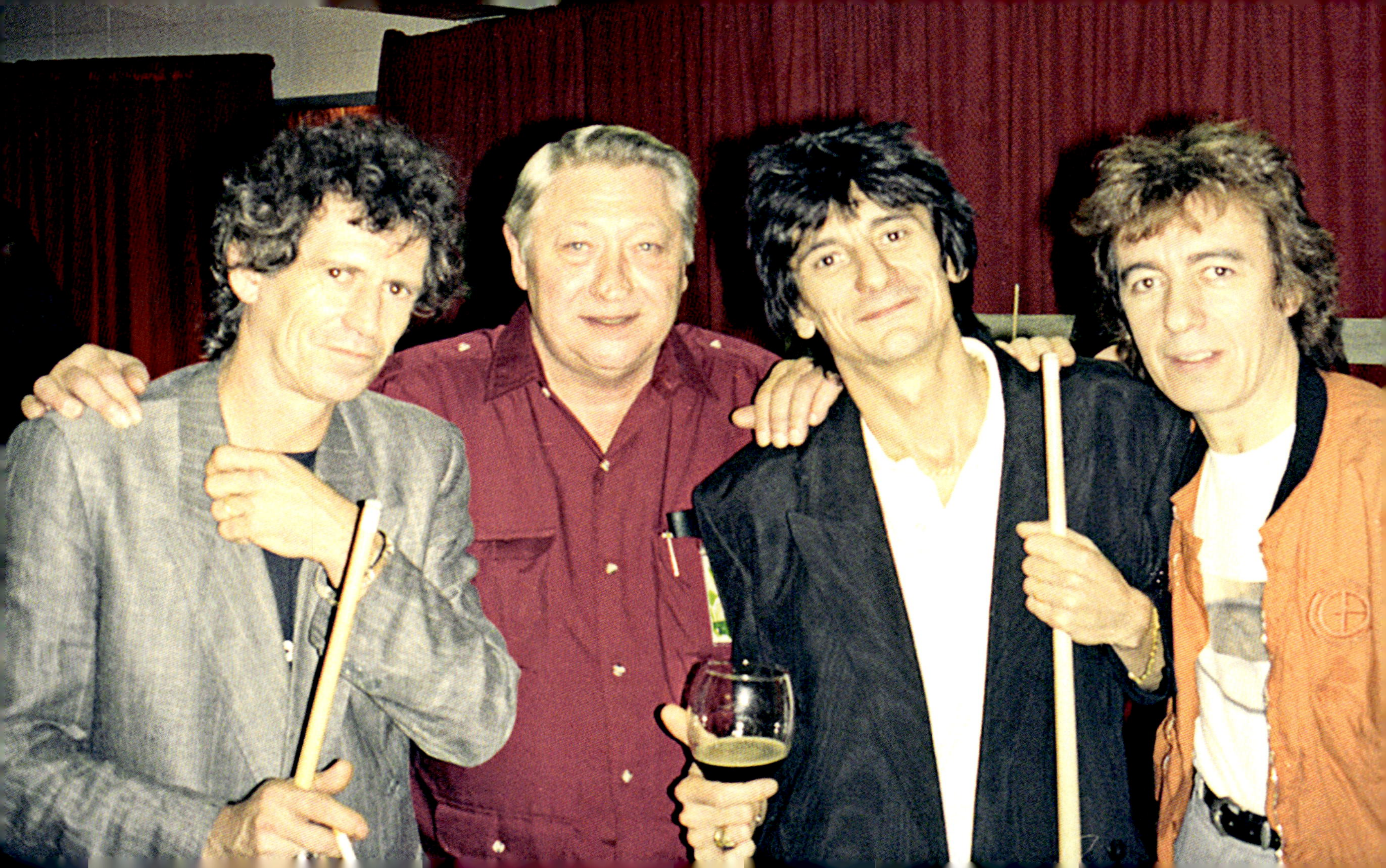

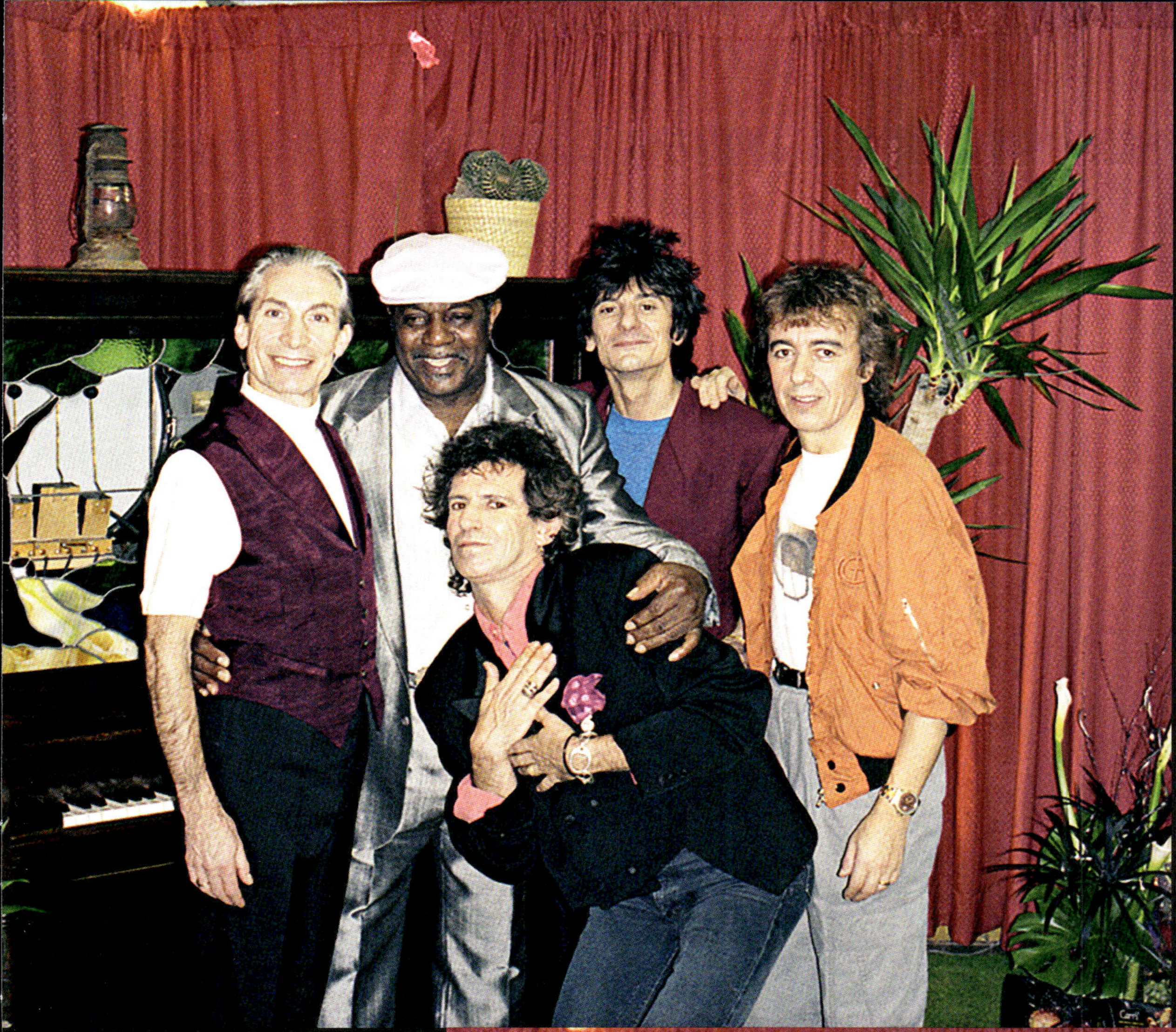

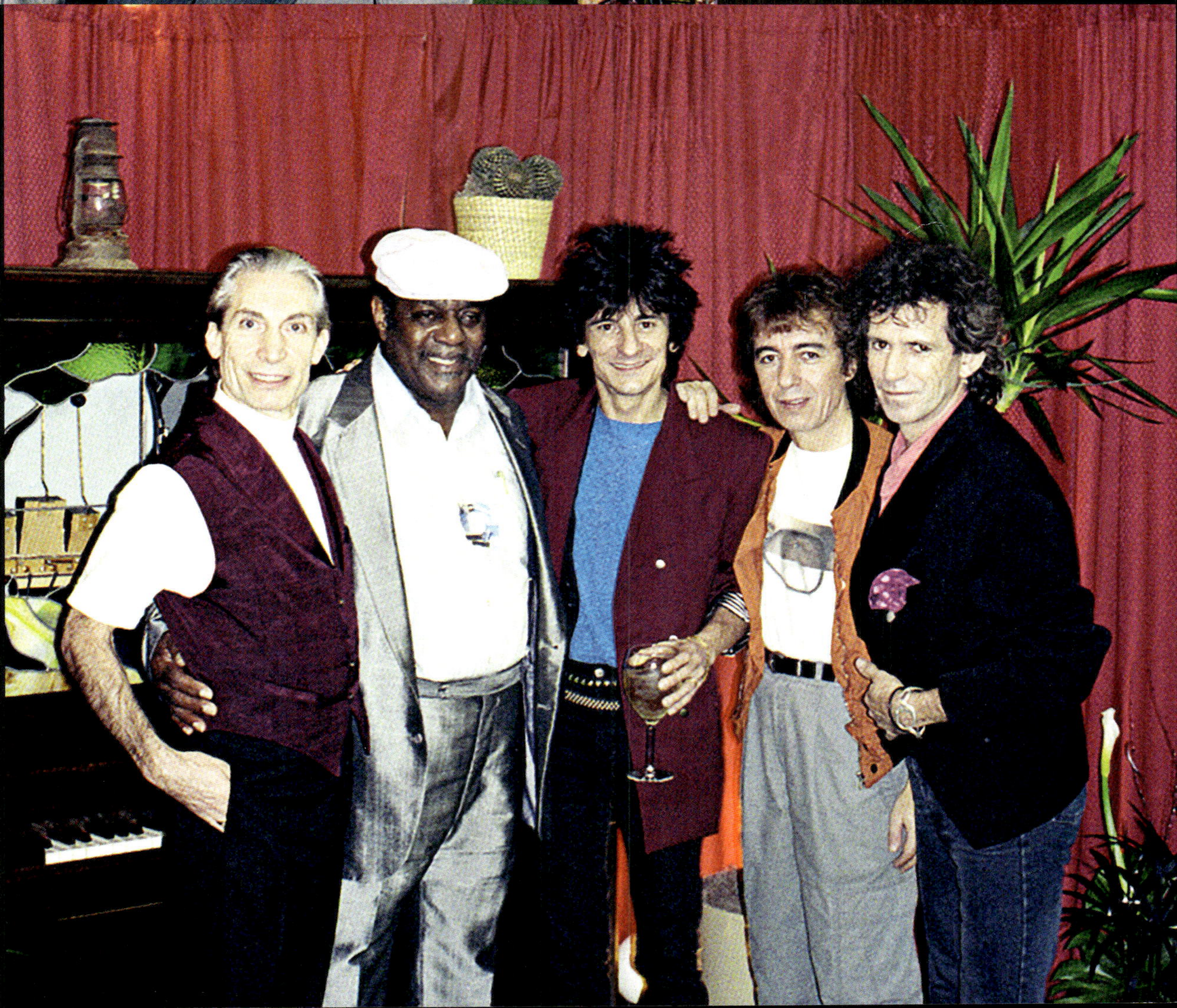

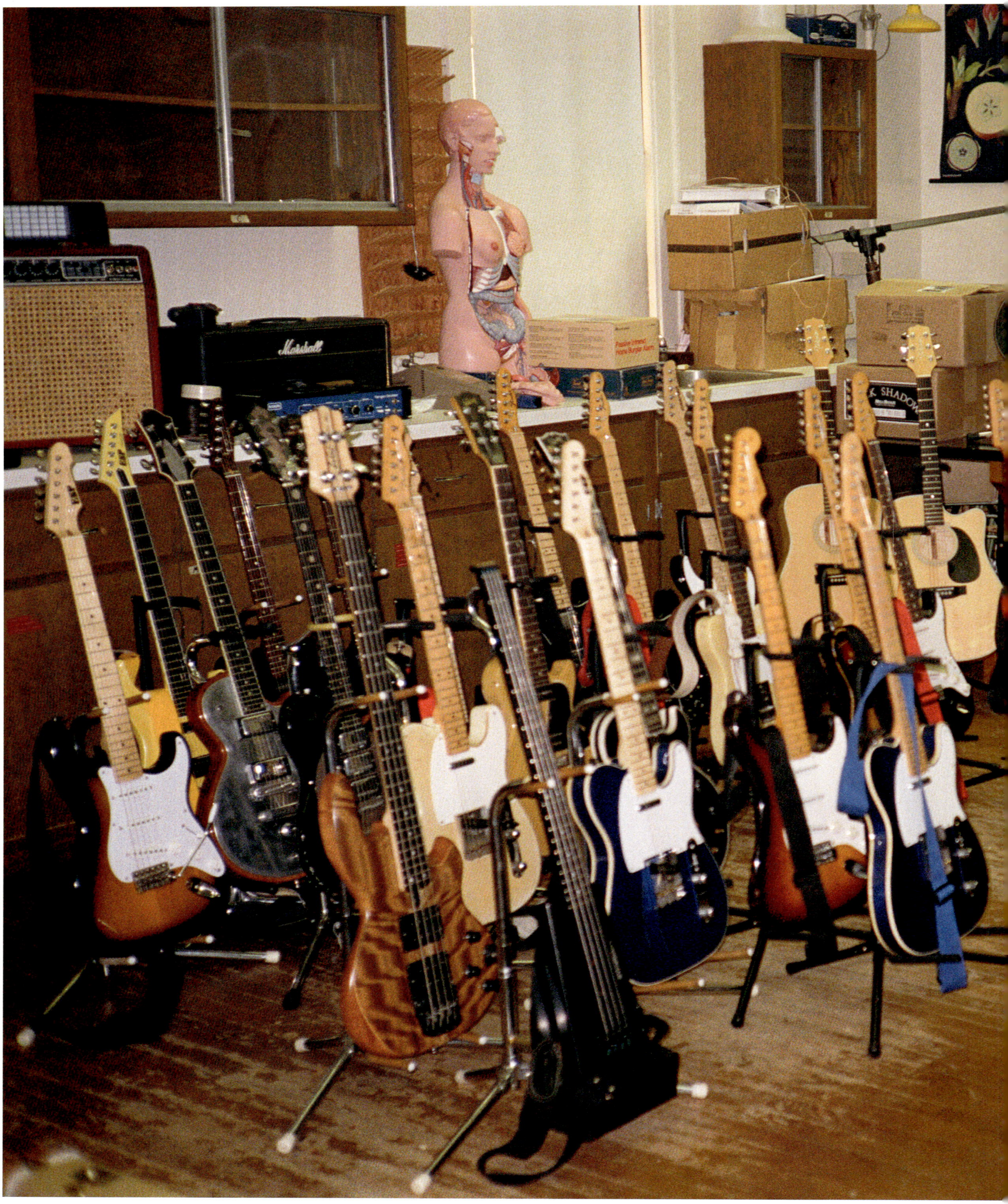
Marshall

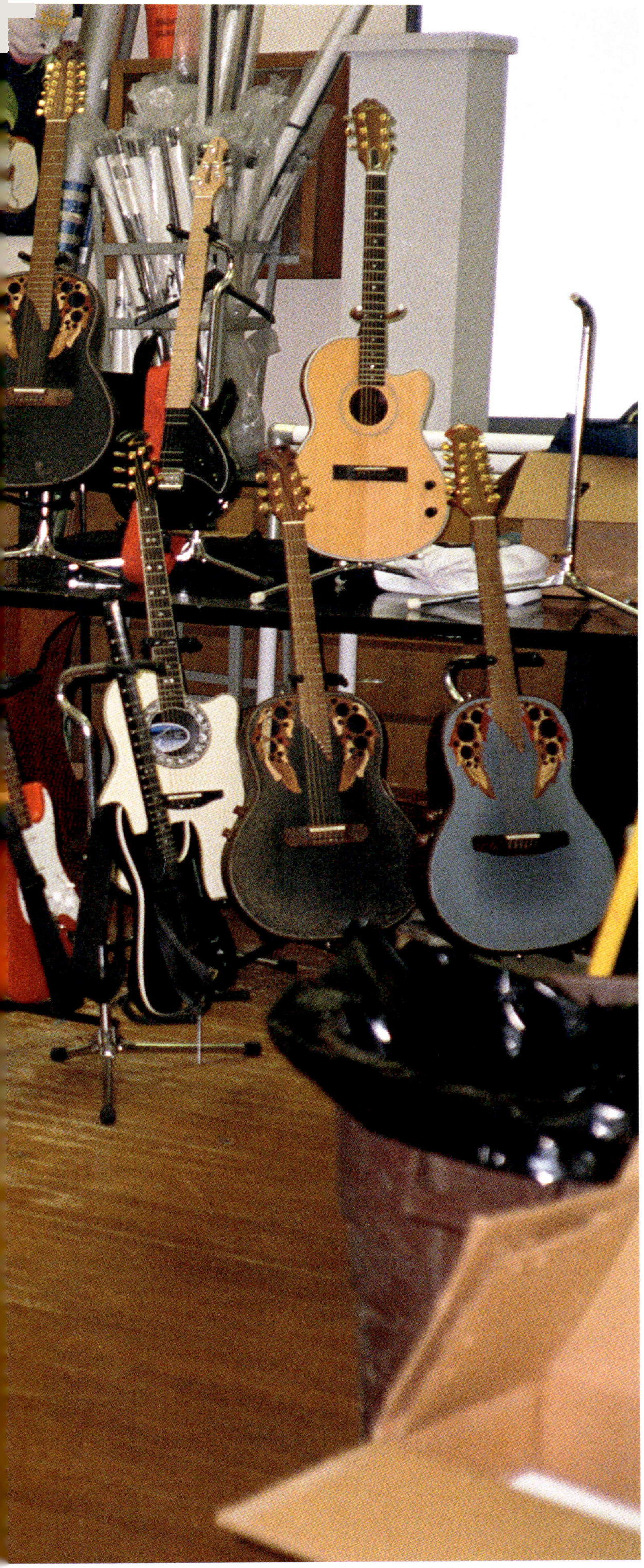

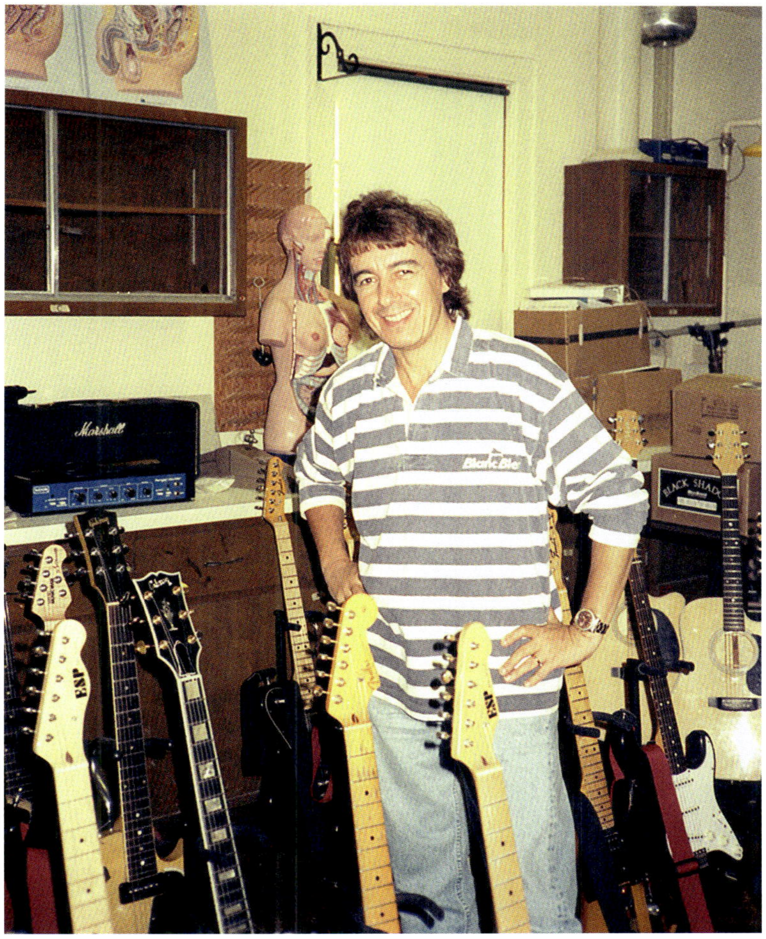

Me and the mass of Keith and Ronnie's guitars plus my one bass at the rehearsal room in the school in Southbury, Connecticut – 2 August 1989.
Following pages: Stones audience shot from side-stage at the Valle Hovin Stadion, in Oslo, Norway – 6 August 1990.

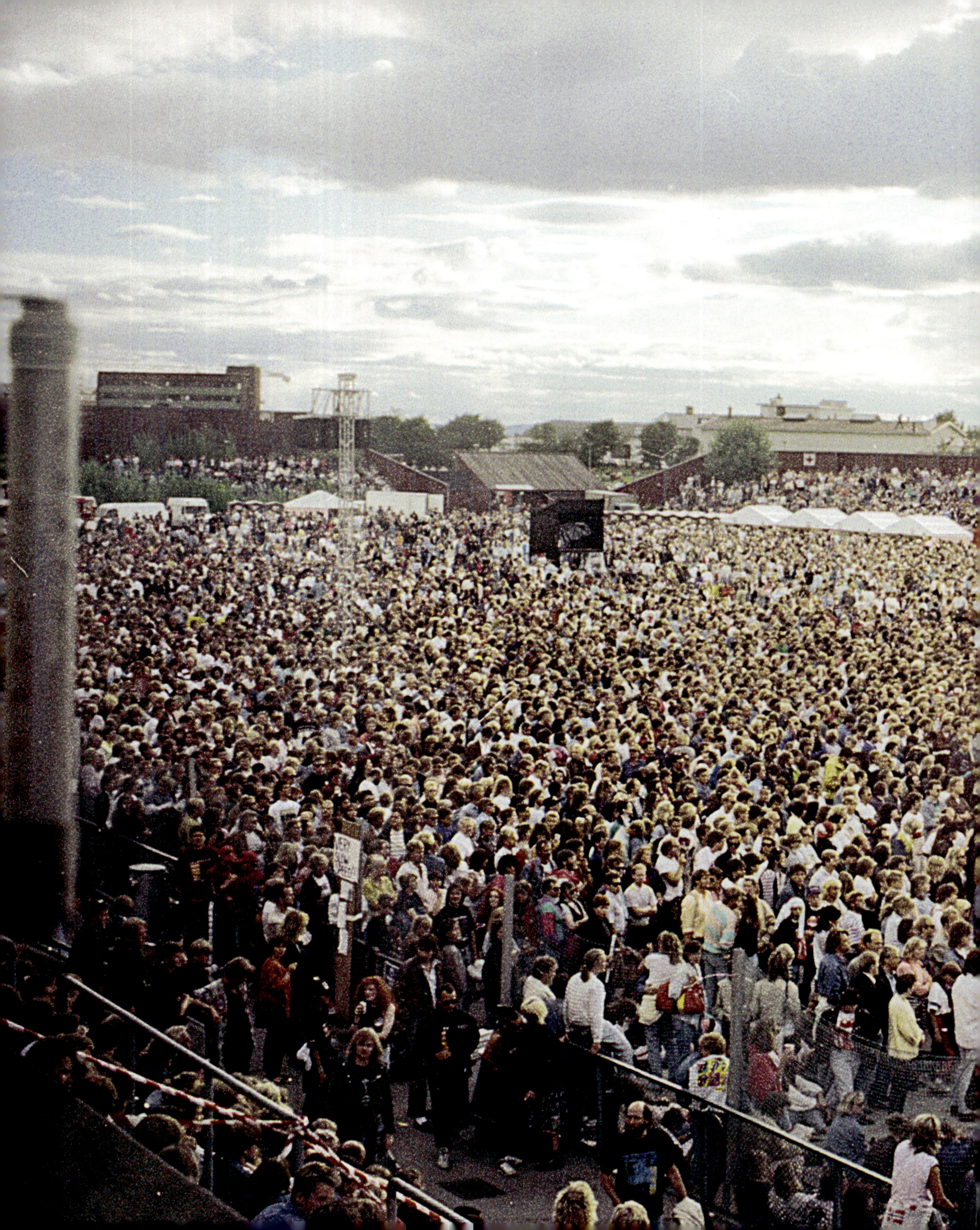

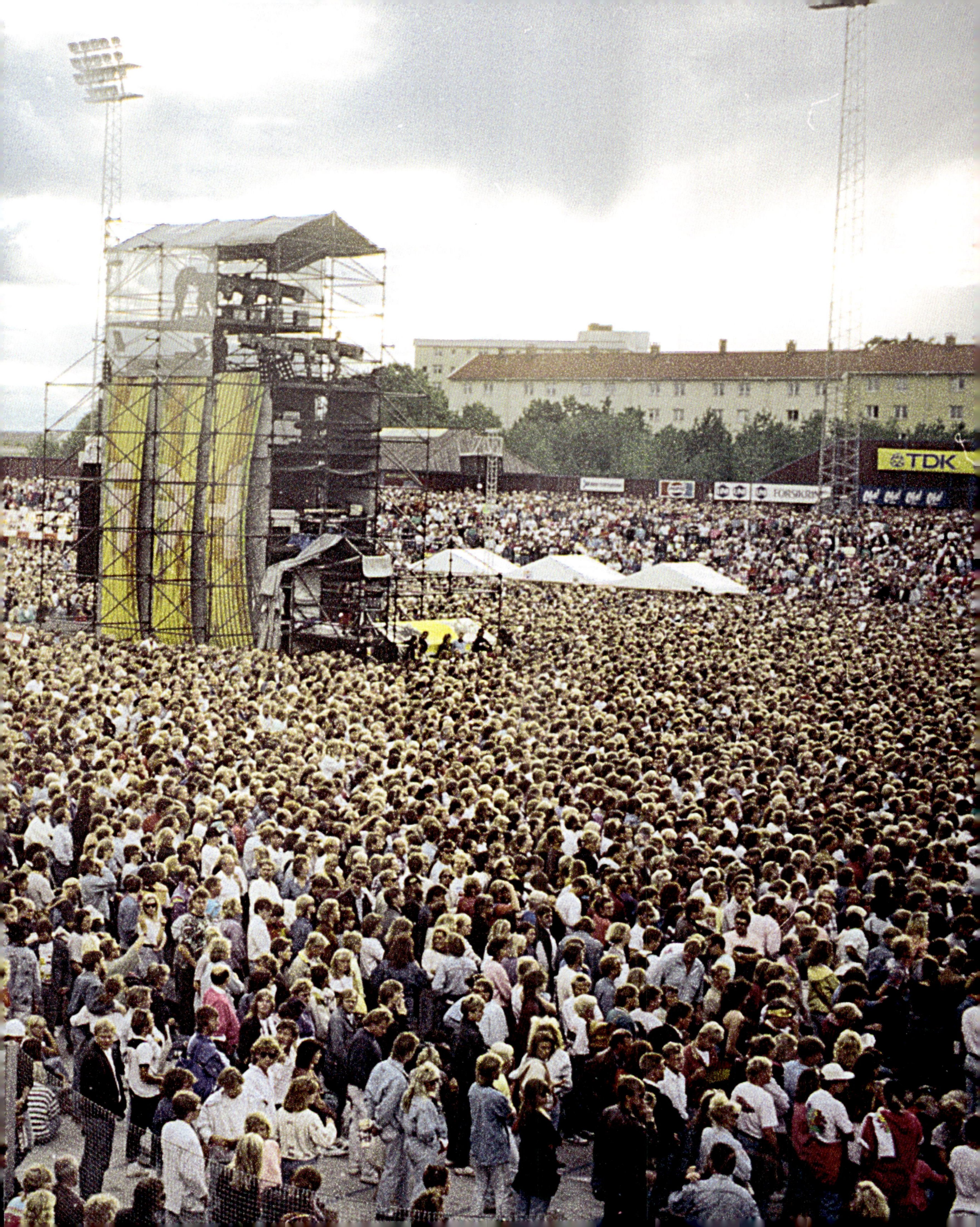
TDK

"THIS HAS BEEN A CRAZY LIFE I'VE HAD, AND I HOPE THAT YOU HAVE ENJOYED SOME OF THE MOMENTS OF MY LIFE'S JOURNEY, CAPTURED THROUGH MY PHOTOGRAPHS"

BILL WYMAN

Right: My self-portrait, taken in a shop window in Kyoto, Japan – 2 April 1982.

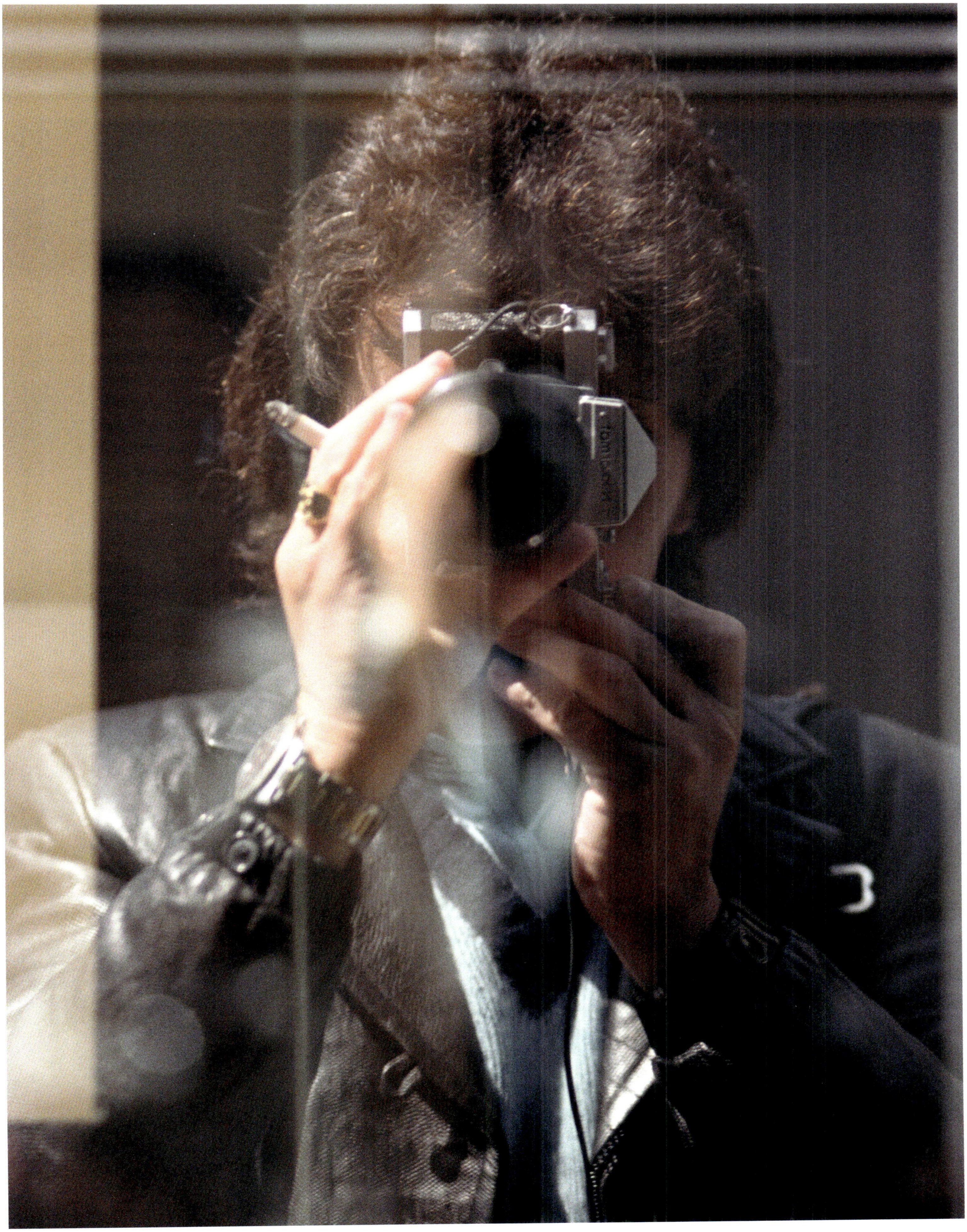

First published 2020 (February)
Reprinted 2020 (March)

ISBN: 9781788840699

British Library Cataloguing-in-Publication Data
A catalogue record for this book is available from the British Library

MIX
From responsible sources
FSC® C014767

Printed in Belgium
for ACC Art Books Ltd., Woodbridge, Suffolk, England

www.accartbooks.com

ACC ART BOOKS

STONES
FROM THE INSIDE
RARE AND UNSEEN IMAGES

BILL WYMAN